ELEMENTS OF DIRECT MARKETING

ELEMENTS OF DIRECT MARKETING

Martin Baier

Senior Vice President—Marketing Group
Old American Insurance Company
Kansas City, Missouri

Adjunct Professor of Marketing
University of Missouri—Kansas City

McGRAW-HILL, INC.

New York St. Louis San Francisco Auckland Bogotá Hamburg
Johannesburg London Madrid Mexico Montreal New Delhi
Panama Paris São Paulo Singapore Sydney Tokyo Toronto

This book was set in Times Roman by
Monotype Composition Company, Inc.
The publisher is Howard E. Flood,
McGraw-Hill Publications Company.
The project consultant was Robert L. Davidson, MacDhai, Inc.
Project supervision was done by Annette Bodzin, The Total Book.
The book was designed by Robin Hessel.
Kingsport Press, Inc. was printer and binder.

ELEMENTS OF DIRECT MARKETING

1 2 3 4 5 6 7 8 9 0   KPKP   8 9 8 7 6 5 4 3

ISBN 0-07-002986-5

Library of Congress Cataloging in Publication Data

Baier, Martin.
    Elements of direct marketing.

    Includes index.
    1. Direct marketing.   I. Title.
HF5415.122.B34   1983   658.8′4   83-7928
ISBN 0-07-002986-5

To my wife, Dorothy,
who has shared with me
the emergence of direct marketing,
which this book records;
and
To my daughter, Donna,
who—together with the other
young people of direct marketing—
nurtures it with creativity and enthusiasm.

CONTENTS

FOREWORD

In my opinion, *Elements of Direct Marketing* is destined to become *the* definitive college text. It is a book whose time has come.

There are those in the direct marketing fraternity, myself included, who feel strongly that the major deterrent to the continued explosive growth of direct marketing is a dearth of trained talent, starting at the college level. This book has come along not a year too soon.

The utilization of direct marketing methods has shown spectacular growth over the past decade. No longer a discipline relegated only to mail-order sales of goods and services or to be used principally by small business firms, direct marketing has become integrated into the total marketing programs of major corporations such as AT&T, IBM, Xerox, Ford, Chrysler, and General Motors.

Nor is direct marketing any longer dominated by direct mail as an advertising medium. Multimedia—newspapers, magazines, telephone, radio, TV, cable, and new electronic media—lend themselves likewise to the measurement and accountability of direct marketing.

It is small wonder then that the direct marketing fraternity is thirsting for young minds who can learn the fundamentals of their discipline in the classroom in preparation for application in the world of commerce. For those who succeed, there is a bright, exciting, and challenging world on the horizon.

There is no one better qualified to have written this text than its author—Martin Baier. As a practicing professor at the University of Missouri—Kansas City and as a direct marketing practitioner at Old American Insurance Company he brings the worlds of academia and commerce together. I have little doubt that this book will prove to be the catalyst for establishing direct marketing as a major for B.B.A.s and M.B.A.s in leading universities across the land.

The author puts direct marketing into proper perspective by establishing the discipline as an aspect of total marketing. He schools the reader in the decision-making process, explains the roles of research and experimentation and provides the analytical techniques essential to direct marketing success.

It's all here in one comprehensive text with emphasis on the aspects which distinguish direct marketing from general marketing. Ability to buy versus proneness to buy. Buying patterns. Models of customer behavior. The chapters on market segmentation and mailing lists get to the heart of the differences.

The knowledge that can come only from the experienced practitioner shows through in Martin Baier's concluding chapters on promotion alternatives and strategies. His instruction reflects the real world of direct marketing.

Bob Stone, Chairman
Stone & Adler, Inc.

INTRODUCTION

As a discipline, direct marketing has finally come of age on the college campus. Slow in arriving, it has now reached the point where hundreds of schools across the country are offering full or partial courses in direct marketing. In fact, at the Direct Marketing Educational Foundation (DMEF), we are in touch with more than 2300 professors who include direct marketing, in one way or another, in their classes.

Of course, this wasn't always the case. In its early years, the Foundation had to struggle to make direct marketing a legitimate subject for study in colleges and universities. But that time has passed. Now we can't keep up with the requests we get for materials, information, speakers, and other teaching assistance. And the instructors who contact us teach all kinds of courses: Advertising, Marketing, English, Journalism, and Mass Communications. Direct marketing seems to find a place in all of these areas. It's surely a sign of the times.

All of this activity in the classroom closely parallels what's happening in the business community. The use of direct marketing is growing and expanding rapidly, and colleges and universities are now faced with the challenge of providing appropriate instruction for developing talent in this "new" discipline.

Over the past several years, one of the most frequent and urgent requests we have received is for a textbook on direct marketing. The urgency stems from the fact that more and more schools are either offering or plan to offer full courses in direct marketing and a good textbook is essential.

Here at DMEF, where our mission is to improve the teaching of direct marketing at the college level, a "good textbook" meant finding the best qualified person in the country to write it, and an outstanding publisher to bring it to the campus. We found both. The author is Professor Martin Baier of the School of Business and Public Administration at the University of Missouri—Kansas City. And the publisher, thanks to Howard E. Flood, is McGraw-Hill.

Martin Baier, who is Senior Vice President—Marketing Group at Old American Insurance Company, is both a theorist and a practitioner. He has written a book which is a rich blend of both the "why" and the "how" of direct marketing. Without question, it is one of the best books written on the subject, and a veritable blueprint for college instructors.

Elements of Direct Marketing combines the best of theory and the best of practice for both the college instructor and the experienced direct marketer. However, it was written with the classroom instructor specifically in mind. To that end, it contains all of the elements normally associated with first-rate teaching materials. There are review questions and discussion items at the end of each chapter.

There are valuable case histories. There are tables and illustrations to enhance understanding and comprehension. And all of the material in the book has been classroom tested.

We have always regarded the textbook as the quintessential teaching tool, and *Elements of Direct Marketing* is the most useful tool we've seen on the subject of direct marketing. It's a substantial book, a relevant book, and a *necessary book*. It has our full approval and endorsement as *the* textbook of direct marketing.

Richard L. Montesi, President
Direct Marketing
Educational Foundation, Inc.

PREFACE

Elements of Direct Marketing was conceived as a college textbook for use by both graduate and undergraduate students in a core course in direct marketing. It was developed, however, so as to have practical relevance for those interested in, about to enter, or already involved in direct marketing. Richard L. Montesi, president of the Direct Marketing Association's Educational Foundation, provided the original impetus for the undertaking. Howard E. Flood and Robert L. Davidson at McGraw-Hill saw fit to turn desire into reality. I was "picked" to be the author—to combine theory and practice for the college classroom as well as for the experienced professional.

My assignment was to identify and organize the proven principles and correct concepts of direct marketing. Although that occurred during early-1981, what appears in this text had been evolving long before then, in my learning, in my teaching, and in my own experience coupled with that of dozens of others. While direct marketing was emerging as a discipline in its own right, its roots lay in the basic philosophy of the total marketing concept. It interacted with the two other major functions of organizations—finance and production—as well as many related academic disciplines including computer science, quantitative analysis, economics, and the behavioral sciences. These related disciplines are viewed and sometimes even repeated in this text, but always in the context of direct marketing.

Key attributes of direct marketing, distinguishing it from general marketing, are *measurement* and *accountability* along with reliance on *lists* and a *database*. As costs have soared, business firms as well as nonprofit organizations of every size have recognized that the efficient use of the elements of direct marketing can be one of the best ways to produce positive results. Most direct marketers are practical, pragmatic people. They do enough things right, but they can improve by measuring what they do against proven theory. Theory guides practice. Understanding "why" is as important as knowing "what" or "how."

Virtually everyone uses direct marketing.

Today, mounting numbers of both commercial firms and nonprofit organizations are initiating or expanding direct marketing in their operations. These actions can be observed in a broad range that includes big corporations, small companies, organizations, associations, educational and health institutions, theater and arts groups, services, financial firms, in fact, all types of enterprises. The effective use of the elements of direct marketing has become one sure means of improving objectives to increase profits, fund-raising contributions, attendance, memberships, or political actions.

The explosive growth of direct marketing has made it difficult to find enough people with the skills demanded in the discipline. By gaining the knowledge needed to guide firms and organizations to direct marketing success, trained professionals also boost the chances for their own career advancement. Burgeoning education in direct marketing includes the establishment of the nation's first Direct Marketing Center at the University of Missouri—Kansas City. Here college level concentrations in the discipline are being offered to both graduate and undergraduate students, coupled with applied research and continuing education for professionals.

Organization and Pedagogy

The total marketing concept serves as a basic philosophy in developing a systems approach to the elements—concepts and theories—of direct marketing. Tools and techniques relative to these elements are presented as appropriate. Many principles derived from other course work are repeated, but all in the context of direct marketing so as to provide completeness and continuity.

Four major sections of the book deal with (1) *Perspective*: an overview of direct marketing; (2) *Place*: markets and understanding them; (3) *Product and Price*: offer planning; (4) *Promotion*: alternatives and strategies. Individual chapters within these four major sections deal with such subjects as decision making, research and experimentation, forms of analysis, models of customer behavior, market segmentation, product research and development, pricing theory and strategy, promotion formats, and media.

As pedagogical aids to learning, all chapters are summarized at their conclusion. Additionally, review questions and discussion points appear at the end of each chapter. And, for each chapter there is a case specifically structured to the content of that chapter. These are *real world* cases, with real names, facts, and figures. They were developed with the cooperation of the organizations themselves. Figures, tables, and illustrations are visual aids to comprehending and are used liberally throughout the text.

All of the material in this book has been classroom-tested; most has been field-tested. Much of the theory espoused herein has been put into practice by the author. As the manuscript was evolving, however, early reviewers expressed some concern over what they felt to be difficult and technical chapters placed at the beginning of the book, rather than at the end, as such material usually is. Although the individual instructor using this text may see fit to rearrange his own teaching order, the real world fact is that decision making in direct marketing must be at the beginning, not the end of the process. Unlike a language or mathematics text, *Elements of Direct Marketing* does not progress from the "easy" to the "difficult." Neither does the real world!

Acknowledgments

Although I am the author and personally responsible for this first comprehensive textbook in direct marketing, I hasten to acknowledge lots of input and lots of help from lots of others. Much has been derived from my direct marketing career experiences: from the firms that provided me with the opportunities and field laboratories, from my work colleagues at these firms as well as from literally hundreds of other direct marketers who have shared their own successes and failures with me. In college classrooms many seeds were planted by those who taught me. And, during the 29 semesters I myself have taught a variety of marketing courses at UMKC, my own presentations of concept and theory have been considerably enriched by challenging and perceptive interaction with hundreds of students.

The corporate dedication to career enrichment and education of its people by Old American Insurance Company is especially evident in the opportunity provided me to write this book. Joseph J. McGee, Jr., Old American's president and himself a past president of the Direct Marketing Association, has given me special encouragement and understanding. Stephen D. McDaniel provided considerable technical and statistical assistance; his perceptions and words are found herein. Faith E. Wylie's art and graphic expertise are evident in many of the illustrations. The manuscript itself, a dozen pounds of it, which project supervisor Annette Bodzin described as "beautifully prepared," was typed time and time again (originally from tape) by Betty J. Whitaker. Her translation of my scribbled handwriting, her organization of material, and her fantastic speed typing, to say nothing of her extreme patience, deserve special acknowledgment. I want to express appreciation, too, for the diligent copy editing by Sally S. Fields and the thorough proofreading by Marcy Stamper; for the expressive artwork done by Fine Line, Inc., Illustrators; and for the distinctive cover design rendered by Robin Hessel. Sincere thanks for "putting it all together," so to speak, go to Annette Bodzin, who was such a delight to work with and whose own company, The Total Book, is so aptly named.

Professors Charles D. Schewe (University of Massachusetts) and William J. Stanton (University of Colorado) provided encouraging academic reviews of the initial chapters and proposed content of this textbook as did David M. Edwards. Later, Professors Dik Warren Twedt (University of Missouri–St. Louis) and Richard A. Hamilton (University of Missouri–Kansas City) meticulously read the entire manuscript and their perceptive, sometimes argumentative, inputs were extremely helpful. My long-time friend and former work colleague, Bob Stone (chairman, Stone & Adler) counseled me and stimulated my thinking throughout the book's preparation. Henry R. Hoke, Jr. (publisher, *Direct Marketing*) often challenged me, complimented me, and provided (via his "Monday morning" telephone calls) much input for many of the case studies. The organizations featured in most of the case studies not only read and approved of them, but were anxious to provide even more input. To all of these, I express my thanks.

Martin Baier

PART ONE

PERSPECTIVE: AN OVERVIEW OF DIRECT MARKETING

THE BREADTH AND DEPTH
OF DIRECT MARKETING

Direct marketing, with its historical roots in direct mail (an advertising medium) and mail order (a selling method), has evolved as an aspect of the total marketing concept. It is characterized by *measurability* and *accountability* as well as reliance on *lists* and *data*.

Those who adopt the marketing concept and use the elements of direct marketing deliberately seek responses to their promotion efforts as they interact with the marketplace to offer, through a variety of media, their tangible products and intangible services. Businesses and nonprofit organizations as well as governments seek out their target market segments whether the desired response be a sales transaction, a fund-raising contribution, or a political action. All of these, in part or in total, are encompassed in this definition:

> Direct Marketing is an interactive system of marketing which uses one or more advertising media to effect a measurable response and/or transaction at any location.

THE MARKETING CONCEPT: CUSTOMER-ORIENTED, PROFIT-MOTIVATED, ORGANIZATIONALLY INTEGRATED

Peter F. Drucker observed that "there is only one valid definition of business purpose—to create a customer."[1] Companies are not in business to make *things,* he said, but to make *customers.* The marketing concept is customer-oriented. It is not product-oriented.

The importance of customer orientation was also emphasized by Theodore Levitt, when he blamed the trouble of the railroads and their loss of passenger revenues not on competition (airplanes, buses, cars, and trucks) but rather on their mistaken assumption that they were in the *railroad* business rather than in the *transportation* business. "The reason they defined their industry incorrectly," Levitt wrote, "was because they were railroad-oriented instead of transportation-oriented; they were product-oriented instead of customer-oriented."[2] The railroads had not adopted the total marketing concept.

The marketing concept is a *philosophy,* an attitude, really, in the sense that all of an organization's planning, policies, and operations should put the wants of the marketplace above the simple desire to create and sell a particular product or to use a particular distribution system or a particular promotion strategy. Further, the most important goal in the marketing process should be *profitable* sales volume; not just growth. Finally, the philosophy of the marketing concept dictates that organization and management should be integrated toward common marketing objectives; that is, all of the specialized functions of marketing should be under a central management. The marketing concept is, thus, *customer-oriented, profit-motivated,* and *organizationally integrated.*

Although the marketing concept is a philosophy, marketing itself has been defined as "a total system of business activities designed to plan, price, promote, and distribute want-satisfying goods and services to present and potential customers."[3] Marketing is, in other words, the bringing together of markets (customers) and products or services through promotion techniques along with a properly administered organizational structure and procedure. It embraces all of the demand-creating activities of a business firm, a nonprofit organization, or a political entity. Marketing's primary focus on demand contrasts with the cost emphasis of other functional areas of an enterprise.

---

[1] Peter F. Drucker, *The Practice of Management,* Harper, New York, 1959, p. 37.

[2] Theodore J. Levitt, *Innovation in Marketing,* McGraw-Hill Book Company, New York, 1962, pp. 39–41.

[3] William J. Stanton, *Fundamentals of Marketing,* 5th ed., McGraw-Hill Book Company, New York, 1978.

PRODUCTION ORIENTATION	ATTITUDE	MARKETING ORIENTATION
Internal forces dominate; emphasis on efficiency and technology in the short run.	**OBJECTIVES**	Consumer forces dominate; emphasis on long-range planning.
Decisions are imposed on the consumer.	**PLACE OF THE CONSUMER**	Decision-making starts with the consideration of the consumer.
Company sells what it can make.	**PRODUCT MIX**	Company makes what it can sell.
Used to determine consumer reaction, if used at all.	**ROLE OF MARKETING RESEARCH**	Used to determine customer needs and test how product satisfies these needs.
Satisfy existing markets.	**MARKETING STRATEGY**	Create new markets as well as serve present markets.
Focus on technology.	**INNOVATION**	Focus on market opportunities.
Always follow, react; defensive posture.	**COMPETITION**	Sometimes lead, sometimes follow; offensive posture.
A residual, what's left over after all costs are paid.	**PROFIT**	An objective.
Focus on manufacturing and finance problems.	**OTHER CORPORATE FUNCTIONS**	Focus on marketing problems.

Figure 1-1 Model of the marketing concept: *attitude.* (*Robert F. Vizza, Thomas F. Chambers, and Edward J. Cook,* Adoption of the Marketing Concept—Fact or Fiction, *Sales Executives Club, New York, 1967.*)

Marketing Orientation vs. Production Orientation

In contrast with today's customer orientation, it was not many years ago that most enterprises were product/service-oriented, their chief objective being to "make it better and cheaper," often without regard to whether or not it was salable. The typical organization plan consisted of three major functions: production, sales, and finance. The production department was responsible for the product line, the sales department sold what was produced, and the finance department determined whether or not the venture was worthwhile. Each of these major departments created staff specialists speaking a language no one else understood with the emphasis placed on volume of production and volume of sales.

The vivid differences between production orientation and marketing orientation were made clear in a 1967 study of organizations conducted by the Sales Executives Club of New York.[4] Figures 1-1, 1-2, and 1-3 summarize the findings of this study with regard to the attitude, structure, and procedure reported by the respondents to that survey. The survey noted that, although most firms touted the marketing concept, only a few had really adopted it organizationally.

[4] Robert F. Vizza, Thomas F. Chambers, and Edward J. Cook, *Adoption of the Marketing Concept—Fact or Fiction*, Sales Executives Club, New York, 1967.

PRODUCTION-ORIENTATION	STRUCTURE	MARKETING-ORIENTATION
Production or finance personnel in top job.	**TOP MANAGEMENT**	Marketing personnel.
On lower level.	**PLACE OF MARKETING EXECUTIVE**	On same level as heads of production, finance and personnel.
On same level, or higher, than the top Marketing Executive; sometimes not a separate department.	**SALES EXECUTIVE, ADVERTISING DEPARTMENT, MARKETING RESEARCH**	Reports to top Marketing Executive.
Reports to engineering, production, top executive; sometimes not a separate function.	**PRODUCT PLANNING**	Reports to top Marketing Executive.
In the controller's department; seen as necessary evil.	**CUSTOMER CREDIT**	In the marketing group; seen as customer service.
Reports to production department.	**INVENTORY FUNCTION, TRANSPORTATION**	Reports to marketing department.

Figure 1-2 Model of the marketing concept: *structure.*

Adoption of the total marketing concept by management is based on a philosophy that commits management to find out what products and services customers need and want and to direct the economic factors of production accordingly. Unless there is a need for a product/service, unless the product/service fulfills that need, and unless customers buy what has been produced, the process has failed. The system devised to prevent such failures is called *marketing.*

Product planning, in which product differentiation is associated with market segmentation, is essential to such a marketing system. Product planning starts with a customer. Who is he? What does he need and want? Where is he located? When is he ready to buy? How much will he buy? Why does he buy? The product or service that results is a complex of tangible and intangible attributes directed to-ward the satisfaction of customer needs and wants. These attributes are frequently psychological as well as functional.

Creating customers doesn't end with developing the right product or service, however. That's still just the beginning. Promotion is vital in marketing strategy. Generally defined, promotion consists of personal selling, advertising, publicity, and an array of techniques commonly called support sales promotion. Marketing embraces the professional coordination of these various elements. It is also finding the most efficient channels for distribution of products and services to various markets.

Marketing Viewed as a System

Integrated organization is an absolute requirement to create customers through a marketing system. It is the framework that holds the system together, maintains it, inspects it for weaknesses, and builds in refinements and improvements. And organization management designs frameworks for systems of the future. Total marketing must be a total organized effort. To create customers, every function of a marketing system must be operating smoothly. Marketing management is a marketing system in action.

Figure 1-4 visualizes a marketing system. Such a marketing system calls for:

1 A clear understanding of the markets to be served and the wants to be satisfied (obtained through marketing research)

2 An attitude favorable to innovation (as a result of creative and imaginative thinking)

3 A scientific approach to decision making (through quantitative methods, operations research, and computer science)

4 Sound administration (embracing both objective planning and evaluation of results)

It is within the context of the marketing concept and within the framework of a marketing system that the elements of direct marketing will be viewed.

	PROCEDURE	
PRODUCTION ORIENTATION		**MARKETING ORIENTATION**
Begins with consideration of production and technological capacities; looks to utilize excess capacity and waste material.	**PRODUCT PLANNING**	Begins with determination of customer needs; seeks to identify a market opportunity.
Costs determine price.	**PRICE**	Customer determines prices; price determines costs.
Individual efforts by each department, often resulting in conflict and wasted effort. No integration of marketing and other functions.	**MARKETING CAMPAIGN**	A co-ordinated approach including all aspects of the Marketing Mix. Marketing integrated into all functions of the business.
Seen as protection and a container for the product.	**PACKAGING**	Designed for customer convenience; seen as sales tool.
Emphasizes product features, quality and ego of the producer. Producer motives paramount.	**ADVERTISING**	Communicates need-satisfying benefits of the product; consumer motivations paramount.
Levels set with production requirements in mind.	**INVENTORY**	Level set with customer requirements in mind.
Seen as extension of production and storage functions.	**TRANSPORTATION**	Seen as customer service.
Seeks to "sell" to the buyer; often unaware of advertising, promotion research and distribution activities.	**SALES**	Helps the buyer to buy; seeks to match product to customer needs; co-ordinates with advertising, promotion, distribution; determines unfilled customer needs.

Figure 1-3 Model of the marketing concept: *procedure.*

PRODUCER ──────▶ DISTRIBUTION ──────▶ CUSTOMER

Offer:	Channel:	Markets:
Product/Service	Negotiation	Consumer
Price	Logistics (physical)	Industrial
	Promotion:	
	Selling	
	Advertising	
	Publicity	
	Support Promotion	

Figure 1-4 A marketing system logistically.

THE EMERGENCE OF DIRECT MARKETING[5]

There's nothing "new" about direct mail as an advertising medium; it is as old as communications itself. The term "circular letter" was, albeit facetiously, once attributed to the round clay tablets used in biblical times. History books show that the fires of liberty were stoked before the American Revolution by the Committee of Correspondence, through which such patriots as John Hancock and Samuel Adams, who were dispersed in colonial America, kept one another informed. Not unlike the methods of today, a "circular letter" was printed and mailed (circulated) to members in Boston, Philadelphia, New York, and wherever else patriotic groups existed.

The first *trade* catalogs are said to be those of the midfifteenth century, which appeared soon after Gutenburg's invention of movable type. There is record of a gardening catalog, the predecessor of today's colorful seed and nursery catalogs, issued by William Lucas, an English gardener, as early as 1667. By the end of the eighteenth century, there was a proliferation of such catalogs in England and a broadside catalog was published in 1771 in colonial America by William Prince. It is reported that George Washington visited Prince's Gardens in 1791 and that Thomas Jefferson was a mail-order buyer, in both

[5] Many of the early historical references contained in this section are based on documentation by Nat Ross for the *1982 Fact Book* of the Direct Marketing Association, 6 East 43rd St., New York, New York 10017.

America and England. Benjamin Franklin, America's first important printer, published a catalog of "near 600 volumes in most faculties and sciences" in 1744. That catalog is especially notable, in a direct marketing sense, in that it contained a guarantee of customer satisfaction along with this statement on its cover:

> Those persons who live remote, by sending their orders and money to said B. Franklin, may depend on the same justice as if present.

Although not mail order in today's terms, a Connecticut custom clockmaker, Eli Terry (whose neighbor and sometime adviser was the inventor Eli Whitney), deserves mention in the evolution of direct marketing in that he is credited as being the creator of the free trial offer. A Yankee peddler, a direct seller, Terry would pack his custom-made clocks in his saddle bags and would leave them, on trial, with the farmers on his route, collecting for them, even in installments, during ensuing trips along the route. In 3 years Terry reportedly sold 5,000 clocks and had reduced their price from $25 to $5.

Birth of Mail-Order Catalogs

From these early beginnings, there followed a proliferation of mail-order catalogs during the post-Civil War period when agrarian unrest, through the National Grange, fueled the popular slogan "eliminate the middleman." Then, as now, mail-order catalogs reflected social and economic change. Beginning as books featuring seed and nursery products, mail-order catalogs of the late nineteenth century included sewing machines, dry goods, medicines, and musical instruments. Most firms were product specialists and mail order was an alternative mode of distribution.

It was during this period in 1872 that Aaron Montgomery Ward produced, on a single unillustrated sheet of paper, a mere price list offering the rural farmer savings of 40 percent. Just 12 years later in 1884 Ward's single sheet of prices had been expanded to a 240-page catalog containing 10,000 items. He, too, featured a "guarantee of satisfaction or your money back."

Two years later came the forerunner of what was to become by 1893 Sears Roebuck & Company. Young Richard Warren Sears, a telegraph operator in the remote location of North Redwood, Minnesota, acquired a shipment of undeliverable gold-filled watches. He reasoned that the best prospects for the purchase of these watches would be other railroad agents, like himself, and he had a mailing list of 20,000 railroad agents. By 1897 his original offer of a fine watch to a specific market segment had expanded to a catalog of more than 750 pages with 6,000 items. (See Figure 1-5.) By 1902 the sales of Sears Roebuck & Company exceeded $50 million annually.

Ward and Sears were followed in 1905 by Joseph Spiegel, who introduced credit terms with catalog copy reading "We are willing to trust you indefinitely . . . and to receive our pay by the month, so that no purchase is a burden." The Henry Field Seed & Nursery Company was established in 1892 and the roots of today's L. L. Bean, Inc. go back to 1912.

Mail Order Diversifies

While mail-order merchandise catalogs were becoming more and more accepted, especially in rural America, the new cultural, social, and economic phenomena of the times were breeding another form of mail order. New magazines reflecting these changes, *Time, The New Yorker,* and *Saturday Review of Literature,* appeared during the early 1920s, with subscriber-prospects solicited by direct mail. In 1926 a particular milestone was reached with the founding of the Book-of-the-Month Club by Harry Sherman and Maxwell Sackheim. Both of these pioneers were already veteran direct

marketers, having earlier noted how few bookstores there were relative to the large number of post offices capable of delivering direct mail and books economically and expeditiously. Sherman and Sackheim created another innovation in mail order, the "negative option," through which a book was sent to subscribers on a regular basis, each month, unless a subscriber advised the publisher not to send a particular selection. Doubleday Company launched a similar operation, the Literary Guild, in 1927. Today, more than one-half of all hardcover books are sold by mail-order methods.

On the industrial scene, too, direct marketing has played an important role in the evolution of business-to-business distribution. John H. Patterson, who founded the National Cash Register Company, was probably the first to use direct mail to get qualified leads for follow-up by salespeople. Today, this basic method of sales prospect qualification, augmented by direct response advertising media other than direct mail, plays an important role in the total scheme of industrial direct marketing.

Credit Cards, Computers, and Media

Since the advent of credit cards during the 1950s, there has been enormous growth of mail order as a selling method. The "T & E" (travel and entertainment) credit cards came first, with Diners Club, followed by American Express. The "bank" credit cards, notably MasterCard and VISA, came along almost simultaneously. Credit cards greatly enhanced and expedited mail-order transactions, which up to that time had been mainly cash with order.

The 1950s, too, witnessed the growing proliferation of computers. These greatly enhanced the emergence of direct marketing through their tremendous capabilities for storing and retrieving immense amounts of data (including mailing lists) together with their lightning-fast calculation capabilities.

1897 SEARS ROEBUCK CATALOGUE 1897

Figure 1-5 An introductory page from the 1897 catalog of Sears, Roebuck & Co.

Further enhancing the growth of direct marketing, during the 1960s and to this day, has been the increasing availability of advertising media other than direct mail suitable for direct response advertising, especially those geared to highly defined market segments. The readers of selective publications, such as the magazines *Psychology Today* and *Organic Gardening* and *The Wall Street Journal* newspaper, are not only mailing lists in and of themselves but also provide an audience for direct response print advertising geared to specialized market segments. The same evolution has been occurring in the broadcast media, television and radio, through special programming geared to market segments and with, most recently, the advent of cable and satellite transmissions in interactive modes of electronic transmission.

American Telephone & Telegraph (AT&T) first introduced in-WATS, "800" service, in 1961, thus providing respondents to direct marketing promotion the convenience of toll-free long-distance telephone calling. This convenience has been a tremendous stimulus to response. The Bell System itself is today not only a sizable user of the elements of direct marketing, including "800" service, but it is also a major medium for other direct marketers.

Changing Life-Styles and Psychographics

Vast social and economic changes that have occurred since the middle of the twentieth century, including changes in the nature of the marketplace itself, have been vital contributors to the evolution of direct marketing as an aspect of the marketing concept. More than one-half of all women are in the labor force. More than two-thirds of new household formations are described as two-income households. These observations mean that there is less time for shopping, in the traditional sense, in stores. For many, too, in-store shopping itself is no longer the pleasant experience that it used to be. Transportation costs have further

contributed to a decline in the utilization of shopping malls. Although the growing ranks of working women, rising energy costs, and the increasing frustrations of the shopping experience itself are all socioeconomic realities contributing to the emergence of direct marketing, the availabilities of new credit techniques, computer technology, and the broad spectrum of available goods have also played a role.

New and emerging life-styles and value systems of consumers are also major contributors to the growth of direct marketing. Psychographic measurements reflect the changing habits, attitudes, and behavior patterns of a variety of modern life-styles. Direct marketers realize that there is not one single, homogeneous marketplace, but rather that the total market consists of a great many heterogeneous market segments reflecting a variety of contemporary life-styles. Direct marketing provides opportunities for not only recognizing these socioeconomic changes but also identifying, measuring, and reaching the new life-styles as market segments. The characteristics of direct marketing make this so.

THE CHARACTERISTICS OF DIRECT MARKETING

Direct marketing is an aspect of total marketing that is characterized by *measurability* and *accountability,* with heavy reliance on *lists* and *data*. Whereas all marketing cuts across a variety of academic disciplines and needs to be viewed and analyzed in a scientific and objective manner, this is especially true of direct marketing. Every direct marketing effort has a cost that must be related to an expected or actual result.

Measurability and Accountability

Every promotion expenditure, for example, must be justified. A retail department store may not always be able to measure the specific results from a newspaper or television advertising expenditure except, possibly, through measurement of total sales of a particular offering as advertised. On the other hand, this same retail store might issue a periodic or seasonal catalog inviting orders by mail or telephone. Through proper "keying" of the response device, a preprinted code on the mailed order form or a request for a specific department or individual in the telephoned response, the sales transactions resulting from a particular promotional effort can be measured and the total catalog expenditure can be accounted for. Not so easily measured or accounted for, however, is the store traffic that this same catalog generates. Our definition of direct marketing, as presented on page 4, includes the response to the catalog advertising that is measurable in that it generates sales transactions by mail or by telephone. It also includes response in the form of store traffic, buyers coming to the seller's location, but the specific medium (catalog) generating that visit is not always ascertainable.

Another example of the quandary of measurement involves a manufacturer of office equipment, who uses direct mail or other appropriate direct response advertising media to get inquiries for salespeople to follow up by a personal visit to the buyer's location. The inquiry response to advertising is fairly easily measurable through coded reply forms. The sales transaction, involving as it does human intervention, may not always be accounted for. A similar instance would occur when an insurance company, on the one hand, obtains inquiry leads for its agents to follow up, and, on the other hand, generates direct sales (that is, no agent is involved) through either mail or print advertising. The latter is totally measurable; the former is only partially so. Both involve the elements of direct marketing, in part or in total.

A fund-raising organization solicits charitable contributions just as a political candidate solicits campaign contributions. Both use the elements of direct marketing in a measurable and accountable sense; that is, the total dollar contributions resulting in both cases can be directly related to the cost of soliciting those contributions through direct mail or other direct response media. That same political candidate, mailing a letter to you or circulating a handbill to your front door, both of which are methods intended to encourage you to vote for him or her, is further using the elements of direct marketing. Measurement of response at the voting polls relative to these particular expenditures is possible only insofar as to whether or not the candidate is elected. Even then it is impossible to ascertain how many of the total votes were stimulated by the candidate's direct marketing efforts.

Lists and Data

Other important characteristics of direct marketing, besides measurability and accountability, are lists and data. Lists can be looked at as market segments to which promotion efforts are directed and from which other lists are generated. Lists most commonly are thought of as mailing lists. They also might be thought of as readers of a particular publication or as viewers of a particular television program. The readers of *Fortune,* for example, represent a very different market segment (demographically and psychographically) than do the readers of *National Enquirer;* the viewers of a Shakespeare production on television have life-styles different, probably, from those viewers of a televised wrestling match. These segments of readers or viewers may have different purchase preferences and will probably respond to different promotional strategies.

Such mailing lists or lists of publication readers or television viewers or radio listeners compose target market segments, which direct marketers describe based on their own prior experience or on the experience of others. Promotional efforts are *directed toward* certain lists in a manner that can be quantified and

---

DEFINITIONS

Direct marketing is an interactive system of marketing that uses one or more advertising media to effect a measurable response and/or transaction at any location.

Direct response advertising in any medium, including direct mail, is that which effects a measurable response and/or transaction at any location.

Mail order is a method òf selling that relies on direct response advertising to effect a measurable response and/or transaction by mail, telephone, or other interactive medium.

Alternative methods of selling, encompassed in the definition of direct marketing, are those in which, as a result of direct response advertising

• the buyer personally visits the *seller's location* (store, market, exhibit, etc.) to effect a transaction.
• the seller calls at the *buyer's location* (home, business, organization, etc.), in person or by telephone, to effect a transaction.

---

measured. Other mailing lists *result from* these promotional efforts. These are the lists of inquirers or buyers. These inquirers or buyers or contributors or action takers later have distinct value as future direct marketing transactions are generated.[6]

Lists are made even more important when selective data accompany them. Such data record the nature of the response, whether an inquiry for further follow-up or an actual transaction, as well as such vital information as the product/service involved, the monetary amount of the transaction, and the recency and the frequency of purchase. Individual characteristics of the respondent, such as age or sex, might also be known and included in the database about that individual. Geographic location of the respondent, especially within an identifying ZIP Code area, can further enhance the database.

Direct Mail Advertising vs. Mail-Order Selling

Direct marketing, as an aspect of total marketing, evolved from the use of direct mail as

an advertising medium and also from the use of mail order as a selling method. The terms "direct marketing," "direct mail," "direct response," and "mail order" are *not,* however, synonymous, and this section will clarify why they are not.

Direct mail, as an advertising medium, along with newspapers, television, magazines, radio, and other lesser-used media, has consistently ranked in third place, behind newspapers and television, in dollar expenditures. The expenditure for direct mail advertising during 1982, which included postage, paper, and production only and no creative or other costs, was approximately $10.5 billion.

As detailed in Figure 1-6, there are other media besides direct mail used for direct response advertising. The total expenditure for direct response advertising in all media is estimated at $25 billion.[7] In reviewing these published figures, however, it should be borne in mind that not all direct mail involves direct response. Additionally, other media components might be understated, affecting only

---

[6] See Chapter 2, pages 35–46, for extended discussion of "The Value of a Customer."

[7] *1983 Fact Book,* Direct Marketing Association, New York, p. 1.

	(in millions)
Coupons	$ 94.6
Direct Mail (postage, paper & production)	10,566.7
Magazines (mail order merchandise only)	150.0
Business Magazines (industrial products only)	59.0
Newspapers	73.0
Newspaper Reprints	2,288.5
Telephone	11,467.0
Television	295.0
Radio	29.0
Total	$25,022.8

Note: Creative costs not included in these figures.

Figure 1-6 Total estimated direct response advertising expenditures, 1982. (*Source:* 1983 Fact Book, *Direct Marketing Association, New York, p. 1.*)

mail-order response and not visits to buyer or seller locations.

Mail order usually means the sale of products or services to consumers or industrial users by means of a catalog or a direct response advertisement. In many cases the medium used to reach the customer is direct mail and fulfillment is also by mail. (It can also be by United Parcel Service or other carriers or can even involve pickup by the customer at a store.) As distinguished from direct mail, which is but one of several advertising media used by direct marketers, mail order is a selling (or transaction) method. Counterpart methods of selling include the intervention of salespeople at either the seller's or buyer's location.

At present, only that portion of direct marketing activities resulting in mail-order (by mail *or* telephone) transactions is readily measurable. Those transactions involving advertising media alone, out to the buyer and back to the seller without intervention of a salesperson, are defined as mail order. Consumer mail-order sales totaled $30.9 billion in 1981, approximately 8% of retail general merchandise sales. Total mail order (consumer, industrial, and fund raising) was estimated to be $72.1 billion during 1981.[8]

[8] Arnold Fishman, "Guide to Mail Order Sales, 1981," *Direct Marketing*, July 1982, p. 36.

The DMA has estimated that more than one million people are employed in consumer mail-order selling. There are an estimated 6,500 mail-order firms and some 7,000 retail catalogs are published each year! The United States Postal Service has reported handling annually as many as 6 billion catalogs, industrial as well as consumer.

Among the variety of mail-order catalogs is a product array for left handers and one for women's survival. There are even catalogs of catalogs! From today's mail-order catalogs, you can buy, at your discretion, such diverse items as lobsters, toasters, beehives, sharks' teeth, wedding bands, steam baths, and butterflies.

By product category, the major components of mail-order sales to consumers include general merchandise, insurance, magazine subscriptions, records and tapes, sporting goods, collectibles, food items, crafts, educational services, and photo finishing.[9] According to research conducted by the Maxwell Sroge Company, mail-order sales by retailers grew considerably faster than total retailing in the United States and by early 1981 accounted for $1 of every $2 spent on hardcover books, close to 15 percent of gardening products, 70 percent of magazine subscriptions, and nearly 20 percent of all film processing. Further, the Sroge firm noted that the after-tax profit of publicly owned mail-order companies was 2.5 times higher than that of all retail companies.

Mail-order sales by industrial firms, businesses selling to businesses, by product category, included general office supplies and equipment, educational services, trade publications, and general catalogs of business services. Catalog and direct mail expenditures by publicly owned industrial firms represented approximately 30 percent of total industrial marketing budgets.[10]

[9] *Mail Order Industry Estimates, 1980,* Maxwell Sroge Publishing, Inc., Chicago, p. 6.
[10] *Non-Store Marketing Report,* October 20, 1980, Maxwell Sroge Publishing, Inc., Chicago, vol. 3, no. 25, p. 1.

Fund raising by direct mail accounts for approximately 40 percent of all philanthropic giving, including religion, health and hospital, education, social welfare, arts and humanities, civic, and public contributions. It has been estimated that, during 1981, approximately $21.4 billion was contributed by direct marketing methods, of total philanthropic giving in that year of $53 billion.[11]

Who Uses Direct Marketing and How?

A direct response advertisement, regardless of the medium, can be readily identified by noting if the reader or listener or viewer is requested to take an immediate action: mail an order form, call a telephone number, come to a store or an event, fill in a coupon, ask for a salesperson to call, send a contribution, vote for a particular candidate, attend a meeting.

At some time or another, virtually every business and every organization, civic, charitable, political, educational, cultural, and even every individual, uses direct response advertising and, indeed, has a database for so doing.

As individuals, we use direct mail whenever we send greeting cards, wedding invitations, birth or graduation announcements. Job hunters find the mail is an excellent way to get their résumés to prospective employers.

Businesses, and especially small businesses, use a variety of media for direct response advertising and also employ many of the other elements of direct marketing. This is true of giant corporations as well as small retailers and industrial service organizations. The leading enterprises using many of the elements of direct marketing include:

Periodical publishers
Food stores and distributors
Mail-order houses
Department stores
Book and record publishers
Automotive manufacturers
Drug manufacturers

[11] Fishman, loc. cit.

Book and stationery stores
Newspaper publishers
Home furnishing stores
Insurance companies
Credit card companies
Financial institutions

Among nonprofit organizations, civic, charitable, political, educational, and cultural, the list of users of the elements of direct marketing is virtually endless. PTAs, religious organizations, colleges and universities, as well as charities, use direct marketing techniques to keep members informed, to solicit funds, and to promote understanding. Political organizations, officeholders, and candidates alike use direct response advertising to change public opinion, to inform constituents, and to raise campaign funds.

The range of representative businesses/organizations that have embraced direct marketing is diverse. It includes superb examples, such as those organizations listed in the box on the following page, many of which have included mail order to augment their traditional distribution.

The range of users of direct marketing is indeed diverse. The exploits of Eli Terry and Aaron Montgomery Ward now range from the sophisticated and expensive products of Neiman-Marcus and Horchow's to the fine sporting goods of L. L. Bean and Eddie Bauer to the art products of the Metropolitan Museum of Art and Lincoln Center to the specialty products of Fingerhut and JS&A. Even the American Telephone & Telegraph Company uses direct mail to market a variety of products of the Bell System. A direct marketing experiment in San Diego during May 1981 resulted in a 67 percent voter turnout when an election was conducted entirely by direct mail!

Attitudes toward Direct Mail Advertising

How much direct mail advertising do people receive each day and why do some people receive more than others?

Businesses:

Allstate Insurance Company
American Airlines
American Express
American Heritage Publish-
  ing Co.
American Oil Co.
American Telephone & Tele-
  graph Co.
Brooks Brothers
CBS/Columbia House
Citibank
Colgate Palmolive Company
E. I. duPont de Nemours &
  Co.
Encyclopedia Britannica
Exxon Travel Club
Fingerhut Corporation
Ford Motor Company
Funk & Wagnalls, Inc.
Harvard Business Review
Highlights For Children

J. C. Penney Insurance
  Companies
L. L. Bean, Inc.
McGraw-Hill, Inc.
Merrill Lynch, Pierce, Fenner
  & Smith
Mobil Oil Company
Montgomery Ward
The Mother Earth News
Ms. Magazine
National Cash Register Co.
Newsweek Magazine
Old American Insurance Co.
Pepperidge Farm Mail Order
  Co.
Pitney Bowes, Inc.
The Readers Digest Associ-
  ation, Inc.
Sakowitz
Saks Fifth Avenue
Swiss Colony

Time, Inc.
United Airlines
Wall Street Journal
Xerox Corporation

Nonprofit Organizations:

AFL-CIO
American Bar Association
American Civil Liberties
  Union
Billy Graham Evangelistic
  Association
CARE, Inc.
Common Cause
Fordham University
National Geographic Society
National Trust for Historic
  Preservation
Salvation Army
Smithsonian Institution

Businesses and organizations using direct-marketing methods.

According to a study commissioned by the United States Postal Service (USPS), and conducted by the Survey Research Center of the University of Michigan, the average number of advertising and promotional pieces of mail received per week per household was 2.6 at the time of the study.[12] Of the sample surveyed, 30 percent of the households received no advertising direct mail during the week of the study, whereas 15 percent of the households received six or more pieces.

The study further revealed that 65 percent of all advertising and promotional material was opened and read by a member of the house-hold. Additionally, 13 percent of the promotional material was set aside for later reading, making a total of 78 percent of all advertising mail being read either immediately or on a delayed basis. A total of 43 percent of the people surveyed described their direct mail as "the kind of useful information I like to receive." Only 9 percent of the households reported that they discarded direct mail advertising without opening it. Of those opening and reading, 23 percent found it "interesting or enjoyable, but not especially useful to me." Thirty-six percent of the households surveyed regarded direct mail advertising as "favorable" whereas 14 percent regarded it as "unfavorable."

Although direct mail advertising has often been characterized as "junk mail," that is,

[12] U.S. Postal Service Studies, *The Household Advertising Mailstream,* U.S. Postal Service, Washington, D.C., 1974.

unsolicited mail not wanted by recipients, the USPS study belies that. The accusation that direct mail advertising (mainly categorized as third class mail, which is handled on a non-preferential basis with considerable presorting done by the mailer) creates a taxpayer-subsidized loss to the Postal Service is denied by the following May 1978 statement by then Postmaster General William F. Bolger:

Direct mail advertising is valuable business for the Postal Service. The revenue from this class of mail makes a large contribution towards the fixed costs of a delivery network that serves more than 70 million homes, farms and businesses. Without this volume, we would be forced to increase rates for letters and other classes of mail.

At a December 11, 1975, hearing conducted by the Privacy Protection Study Commission, Robert F. Jordan, then director of the Office of Product Management for USPS, testified:

. . . 16¢ out of every dollar earned by the Postal Service in the 1973 base year is traceable to the direct marketing industry. Overall, the Postal Service earned $1.287 billion from services used by the industry that year. Of this amount, $793 million was used to pay 100% of the attributable cost of the services we provided. The remaining $494 million helped defray the institutional costs of maintaining the postal system. Advertising mail not only pays its own way, but helps support the postal system for the use of other mailers.

In a separate survey of consumer attitudes toward direct mail advertising conducted during 1979 it was concluded that "in most cases, a clear majority of the respondents indicated they enjoyed receiving direct mail and that they read and use the contents of such mailing." With the majority of households surveyed reporting the receipt of less than five pieces of direct mail per week, only 1 percent of those surveyed said they threw away these advertisements without reading them first. The results of cross classification of responses to the questions within selected demographic variables produced a number of generalizations. Among those generalizations were these:[13]

1 Younger respondents tended to have a more favorable attitude toward the receipt of direct mail advertising.

2 A number of respondents blamed direct mail advertising for the problems of the post office.

3 The most frequently written responses to the open-end questions regarding direct mail advertising were of a positive nature.

4 Respondents used the term "junk mail" to describe unwanted or undesirable direct mail they received but not all of the direct mail they received.

In still another survey of consumer attitudes toward direct mail advertising, conducted during 1978 and 1979 by Goldring & Co., Inc.,[14] it was found that consumers do not consider the term "junk mail" derogatory and most were not offended by being on mailing lists. The survey also found that people who enjoy mail-order shopping say it is convenient, provides merchandise not available in stores, is fun, offers good value, and gives the buyer control of the purchase situation. By contrast, consumers surveyed in the Goldring study who disliked shopping by mail said they cannot inspect the item before purchasing, dislike waiting for delivery, feel it is harder to make returns or adjustments, feel retail values are better, and are concerned about "rip-offs" by unscrupulous firms.

As to what they are most likely to buy by mail, the Goldring study participants cited products not readily available at retail stores,

[13] Robert A. Hansen, "National Survey of Consumers' Attitudes Toward Direct Mail Advertising," The University of Minnesota, Graduate School of Business Administration, Minneapolis, Minnesota, 1979.
[14] Goldring & Co., "Direct Mail in Focus," Direct Marketing Association, New York, 1979.

ones easily shipped with little risk of damage, things not needed immediately, items not involving size or color choices, and ones that are not expensive "big ticket" items. The research concluded that consumers can be categorized into general groups based on their opinions about mail order and their use of it as a way to shop. These groups range from what the Goldring study calls "readers," who study catalogs intently but seldom ever buy, to "shut-ins," who enjoy reading direct mail advertising and frequently depend on it as their primary way to shop. Goldring cautions that this study, involving focus group interviews, was qualitative in nature and, therefore, limited in scope.

DIRECT MARKETING VIEWED AS AN ASPECT OF TOTAL MARKETING

A total marketing system is often presented in terms of "Ps": product, price, place, and promotion, along with perspective, plans, and profit.

Direct marketing can be viewed in these terms, too. The "product" can be a book, a record, a magazine, an insurance policy, an item of clothing, a box of grapefruit.

"Place" can be thought of in terms of lists or market segments to which direct response advertisements together with products and services are distributed. Such list segments include mailing lists (if the advertising medium is direct mail) or lists of readers, listeners, or viewers. When market segmentation is thought of as lists, the various media of direct marketing become targeted, extremely selective like a rifle shot as opposed to a shotgun scatter. Such market segments can describe "senior citizens" or "collectors" or "outdoorsmen" or specific industrial classifications.

When thinking in terms of the "P" designating "promotion," we are concerned with the direct mail package or the printed maga-

zine/newspaper advertisement or the broadcast television/radio commercial. The offering can be presented in a large variety of formats. Direct mail formats are abundant: letters, bulletins, self-mailers, postcards, booklets, brochures, folders, broadsides, catalogs, house magazines, newsletters, with specialties including calendars, memo pads, phonograph records, charts, manuals. With all these options, however, the basic format for direct mail advertising is the *classic* format: (1) an outside envelope, (2) a letter, (3) a circular (if needed), (4) an order form, and (5) a return envelope.

When all of its elements and characteristics are put together, in terms of the definition presented on page 4, we view direct marketing as an *aspect* of total marketing. Direct marketing is distinguished from general marketing in that it is *measurable* and *accountable* and it relies heavily on *lists* and a base of *data* about these lists. It can be viewed as a total system in the manner presented in Figure 1-7.[15]

It is generally recognized among businesses and organizations, profit and nonprofit alike, that marketing, along with production and finance, embrace the key activities of an enterprise. Direct marketing, as we have presented it thus far, is an aspect of marketing that emphasizes measurement and accountability as well as the collection of lists and a database. Marketing research is an essential part of the system in that it implies information gathering and a scientific approach to objective decision making. Direct response advertising is created for use in a variety of media directed to specific consumer or industrial market segments. Direct response/transaction methods culminate in either mail or telephone orders, a personal visit to the seller's location, or a

---

[15] This visualization was conceived and developed by Henry R. Hoke, Jr., Martin Baier, and Bob Stone. It appeared originally in *Direct Marketing*, Garden City, New York 11530. It is reproduced with permission.

Definition: Direct Marketing is an interactive system of marketing which uses one or more advertising media to effect a measurable response and/or transaction at any location.

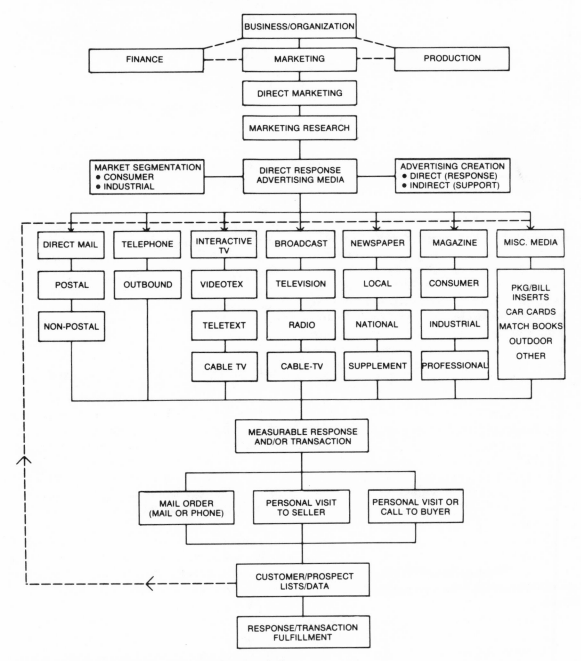

Figure 1-7 Direct marketing: an aspect of total marketing.

personal call to the buyer's location. The cycle may end when the response or transaction has been fulfilled, but only after measuring results in relation to costs and only after capturing the resulting lists and updating the cumulative database. Because of the value of the customer list in subsequent transactions, however, the cycle usually becomes a loop and starts all over again.

What has been presented thus far is summarized in Figure 1-7. This system comprises the elements of direct marketing. Each of these elements will be dealt with in detail in following chapters.

Related Elements of Direct Marketing

The overall management of direct marketing embraces a variety of related academic disciplines. These include finance, production, operations and control, organizational development, accounting, computer science, and quantitative analysis. Knowledge in depth of all these areas is a prerequisite to the management of direct marketing. To understand markets, knowledge in a variety of the behavioral sciences is also desirable: psychology, sociology, cultural anthropology, and human ecology are especially relevant. At the core of direct marketing are the disciplines of economics and statistics.

The direct marketing manager must be versatile and possess at least an overview of these and other academic disciplines. The jobs and functions of direct marketing are widespread and diverse. All of the jobs in a marketing system come into play. The scientific mind is a prerequisite, and the objective thinker is a necessity. Job functions range from the creativity of the arts to the discipline of the sciences.

Bob Stone, in *Successful Direct Marketing Methods,* lists and details eight major responsibilities of the direct marketing executive.

These include:[16]

1 Product selection and development
2 Markets and media selection
3 Creative development and scheduling
4 Testing procedures
5 Fulfillment
6 Budget and accounting
7 Customer service
8 Personnel and supplier relations

Many of the communications and advertising techniques of direct marketing are being taught, even though to a limited degree, in college advertising courses, especially in schools of journalism. Direct marketing as a concept and an aspect of total marketing, however, is more appropriate to the curriculum of schools of business and/or public administration. Direct marketing has relevance to both private and public (including nonprofit) institutions and, as we have seen, goes considerably beyond being used simply as an advertising medium (direct mail) or as a selling method (mail order).

INNOVATIONS, TRENDS, AND CHALLENGES IN DIRECT MARKETING

The social and economic changes that have given impetus to the burgeoning rise of direct marketing since the midtwentieth century have been coupled with equally impressive advances in the technology used in various elements of direct marketing. Certain of these technological advances warrant mention.

Computers In little more than a quarter century, computers have revolutionized direct marketing, making possible the record keeping, work-operation, and model building that are so much a part of the art and science of direct marketing. The complex maintenance

[16] Bob Stone, *Successful Direct Marketing Methods,* Crain Books, Chicago, 1979, p. 27.

of lists and the retrieval of data associated with them are but two examples of the computer's contribution. The processing of orders and the maintenance of inventories are others. And, of course, the use of highly sophisticated analysis can mean the difference between direct marketing success and failure. Although there have been spectacular examples of individual foul-ups by computer-related errors, on balance, the computer's contribution of great speed, lower-than-human error, and reasonable cost have made it indispensable to users of direct marketing.

Electronic Media The proliferation of telephone usage has been augmented by commensurate advances in other electronic communication, including cable, satellite, and interactive television.

Printing Technology The versatility of laser printing, personalization possibilities of ink-jet printing, advances in press technology, and computerized typesetting are examples of how the printing process is becoming more and more conducive to the "demassification" of the printed word.[17]

Credit Systems The ready availability of worldwide credit systems, together with rapid electronic funds transfer, has contributed to the feasibility and viability of direct marketing by simultaneously offering convenience and security.

Segmented Markets Special interest magazines, newspaper sections, and specifically directed television programs, along with the technology of computerized mailing lists, have all been conducive to the growth of direct

marketing through the availability of segmented markets for differentiated products.

These and other technological advances have contributed to the growth of direct marketing. They are coming at a time when many retailers engaged in the post-World War II phenomenon of distribution through shopping centers, discount stores, and supermarkets may, as a result of demographic shifts and transportation costs not favorable to this form of shopping, be changing to direct marketing methods and even using mail order in the interest of efficiency. There is already evidence that the sprawling suburban shopping centers are giving way to compact, multilevel urban malls from which much shopping may one day take place through home computers. Even those who live or work in close proximity to urban malls may choose to shop electronically from their homes or businesses.

As travel becomes more expensive and communications becomes less expensive, there is further impetus to the use of the mail and the telephone. Mailed catalogs and toll-free telephone numbers for ordering are increasing as time-saving shopping at home becomes more popular. Further, as more women enter the work force, families are placing a greater emphasis on time utilization. Once a leisurely pastime, shopping has become more of a chore, especially for 50 percent of the households in which both spouses work. The advent of mail order makes anytime day-or-night shopping even more convenient for these working spouses.

As retail stores become more complex, as discount stores and supermarkets use less personal selling, shoppers rely more and more on their own purchasing judgment. Shopping, to be sure, is still an enjoyable experience for many individuals, including the 50 percent of spouses who are not regularly employed outside the home. They want to see, touch, and

[17] For more on the demassification of the media, see Alvin Toffler, *The Third Wave,* William Morrow & Company, Inc., New York, 1981, pp. 155ff.

feel the items they buy, even though the many advantages of remote shopping may be superseding these personal inspections.

In *The Third Wave,* a book that describes the period that many of the world societies are entering following the agricultural society and the industrial society, Alvin Toffler sees not only the demassification of society but also the advent of "electronic cottages" in which each of us will live and work, as well as negotiate and shop.[18] He predicts a distinct trend away from these features of the second (industrial) wave: standardization, specialization, synchronization, concentration, maximization, and centralization. In *The Third Wave,* Toffler presents an important perspective for direct marketing.

Adjusting to a Changing Environment

Many forces, demographic, economic, technological, and legal/political, have influenced the way in which distribution channels are established and maintained.[19] At the beginning of the twentieth century, the majority of the United States population lived on farms and in small towns; today, only 5 percent of the population is classified as full-time farmers. In the past decade, there has been a shift back to center-city living. The composition of households is very different, too. In the majority of families, both spouses work, and there has been a proliferation of one parent, childless, and single households. These pronounced demographic shifts have had a distinct impact on distribution channels and especially on forms of retailing.

Economic forces that have affected distribution channels include rises in disposable personal income and changes in land and home values, as well as the proliferation of new product needs for homes, automobiles, and persons.

Among technological forces, the automobile has been a leader in changing life-styles, modes of living, and shopping. So has the increasing availability of refrigeration, and the adoption of Universal Product Codes (UPC) with front-end automation of food stores. Technological product innovation has created distribution change, such as the pin-lever watch, which replaced the jewel-movement watch at substantially lower selling prices, only to be replaced by the electronic circuit, battery-operated watch at an even lower price.

Most notable, however, have been increasing legal and public policy constraints. Regulation and compliance have become, increasingly, a way of life for all marketers and particularly for those direct marketers using mail-order methods.

SUMMARY

Direct marketing is an aspect of total marketing, which evolved from direct mail (an advertising medium) and mail order (a selling method). It is characterized by measurability and accountability together with reliance on lists and data. And, like the marketing concept itself, direct marketing is customer-oriented, profit-motivated, and organizationally integrated.

Since its historical beginnings by persons such as Aaron Montgomery Ward and Richard Warren Sears, the mail-order distribution system has reflected social and economic change. Even today, the new and emerging life-styles and value systems of consumers are major contributors to the growth of mail order and the adoption of elements of direct marketing. Computers, credit cards, electronic media, printing technology, and specialized advertising media directed to market segments have all accelerated this growth. Changing demographics, working women, for example, to-

[18] Alvin Toffler, *The Third Wave,* William Morrow & Company, Inc., New York, 1981.

[19] Much of the discussion in this section is based on J. Taylor Sims, J. Robert Foster, and Arch G. Woodside, *Marketing Channel Systems and Strategies,* Harper & Row, New York, 1977, pp. 325–347.

gether with the increased transportation costs and the growing inconvenience of in-store shopping have further enhanced the process and popularized mail order as a method of selling.

Although the definition of direct marketing embraces mail order, in which media alone are used, without intervention by salespeople, it also signifies the use of nonpersonal media to bring potential buyers to the seller's location, where the sale is consummated by a salesperson. Or, it can bring a member of the seller's staff to the buyer, at the buyer's location. The terms "buyer" and "seller" are used broadly because the elements of direct marketing are equally applicable to nonprofit organizations, including governments, in instances such as fund raising and political action. The entire transaction may not be consummated by mail or by telephone but the very process of bringing about a response, such as procuring a lead for a salesperson to follow up or getting out the vote in an election or building store traffic from mailed catalogs, benefits from the direct marketing philosophy.

At the core of this philosophy are lists and data about them. The term "lists" is used broadly to include mailing lists, lists of readers, or listeners, or viewers. Collecting data about lists, both prospects and action takers, is imperative and might include individual characteristics of the transaction or respondent as well as vital information about the product or service involved together with the recency, frequency, and size of purchase.

Direct marketing is, to some extent, used by virtually every individual, every business, every organization: civic, charitable, political, educational, cultural. Direct marketing includes sales consummated by salespeople, at any location, as a result of use of nonpersonal media, to elicit responses in the form of leads for salespeople, to create store traffic, or to obtain involvement in an event.

Direct marketing, as an aspect of total mar-keting, can be viewed in terms of product, price, place, and promotion, along with perspective, plans, and profit. The direct marketing process is visualized in Figure 1-7 on page 19. Direct marketing reflects the social and economic environment, together with the lifestyles, of a society.

CASE: ADOPTING THE MARKETING CONCEPT
Learning Objective

The purpose of this case study is to apply the theoretical principles described as elements of the marketing concept, place/product/price/promotion plus perspective/plans/profit, to actual practice so as to demonstrate these bases of the marketing concept:

1 Customer orientation
2 Profit motivation
3 Organizational integration

Overview

In most organizations conflicting goals are found among the major components of production, finance, and marketing. Although "profit" is the *dominant* goal of such organizations, the component departments frequently have differing philosophies, structures, and procedures for reaching the profit goal. Possibly the first step in resolving such differences is recognizing their existence. This case provides an objective means of recognizing the elements and bases of the marketing concept, thus leading to its adoption.

Procedure

Read the learning objective, the overview, and the case that follows. Be prepared to choose a position on how this organization can (or did) adopt the marketing concept. Consider specifically and individually how the organization should think about: (1) place; (2) product; (3) price; and (4) promotion. How should it plan in order to maximize long-range profits?

In the process, think about your own organization and the relevance to it of your chosen position.

Case

The Peruvian Connection began when Annie Hurlbut, age 19, packed a duffel bag and headed for South America. It was the summer of her sophomore year at Yale and, drawn by an interest in archaeology, she volunteered to help an American archaeologist working at the pre-Inca site of Pachacamac outside Lima. She arrived in Peru knowing not a word of Spanish, and unsure if anyone would meet her. Often asked how she survived those 3 months in South America, Annie grins and says, "blind luck, I guess." But what started as a whimsy has evolved into a fascinating retail business.

Midway through graduate school in anthropology, much of which was spent doing research on women who sell in markets in the Andes, Annie learned about the extraordinary properties of alpaca. The wool from the alpaca is light enough for year-round wear, but warm due to an unusually high lanolin content, and few fibers in the world equal its softness. Annie began to export alpaca sweaters, and within a few months the new company was christened The Peruvian Connection. Her mother, Biddy, a partner in the business, got the first orders while Annie was doing field work for her thesis in Peru. Since its beginning, the business has been run from the family's farm in Tonganoxie, Kansas.

Annie, who had virtually no background in clothes designing, began by working with beautiful and unusual sweaters of local artisans. A sense of style enabled her to adapt the sweaters to North American tastes. Now Annie does her own designing, but the same artisans knit for her on the same antique looms.

Most of the designs are creations of soft alpaca fur and finespun alpaca wool. Despite heavy price increases in alpaca over the last few years, Annie insists on using the finest. She keeps prices low by selecting and buying raw materials directly from the producers, and maintains control over quality by checking each product before it is exported from Peru. Her hope was that quality would be recognized.

The Peruvian Connection is a growing company, no longer exclusively a wholesaler, and uses mail order as its only distribution system. Its luxury fiber clothing, blankets, rugs, and hangings are available only from it. Customers range from enthusiasts of "cheap chic" to collectors of colonial (from Pizarro's conquest to the Republican era, 1825) native crosses. Contemporary clothing is complemented by wearing art from Peru's rich past. Authenticity and complete satisfaction are guaranteed.

The Peruvian Connection's original coterie of custom-order buyers has been augmented manyfold by word of mouth and advertisements such as those in Figure 1-8.

In the process of building her retail mail-order business, Annie learned the value of a customer. After a first sale, her promotional strategy involves periodic mailings to these customers. She seeks new customers via market segmentation techniques matching the profile of her present customers and calculates a "present value" of these new acquisitions to justify their cost.

The New York Times lauded her "Alpaca Styles From Peru" on June 25, 1979; see Figure 1-9.

DISCUSSION QUESTIONS

1 Elaborate on the definition of direct marketing presented in this chapter. In your own words, state its meaning.

2 Exactly what is meant by the marketing concept? Describe in detail these attributes of the concept: **a** customer orientation; **b** profit motivation; **c** organizational integration.

3 Distinguish between an organization that is pro-

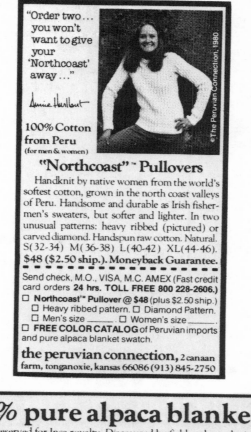

Figure 1-8   Direct response advertisements of The Peruvian Connection.

Alpaca Styles From Peru

By ANGELA TAYLOR

Annie Hurlbut is an anthropologist who spent her sophomore summer when she was at Yale working at an archeological dig in Peru. There she encountered the alpaca, a cameloid animal related to the vicuña and the llama. Although the alpaca has an unpleasant disposition — it spits at people, she says — it is the mainstay of the economy of the Andes, serving as food and, along with the llama, as beast of burden. That is, it will carry a 50-pound load. "Put 51 pounds on it and it balks," Miss Hurlbut explains.

But the alpaca is raised mainly for its extraordinary wool, which is very lightweight and warm. And since the wool grows naturally in a variety of colors — from white to beige, brown and gray — it is not dyed. Miss Hurlbut returned to Peru again when she was a graduate student in anthropology to do research on a thesis about women who sell in primitive markets. Among their wares were handloomed alpaca garments, which were warm and practical, but not exactly stylish.

So Miss Hurlbut turned designer. She worked with the Peruvians to give the sweaters more flair, so they would be acceptable to women in North American cities. With her first stock, she returned to the Hurlbut farm in Tonganoxie, Kan., and started a business called The Peruvian Connection, with her mother as partner. They produced a catalogue, and Annie Hurlbut brought the sweaters to New York to show them to store buyers. Bendel's bought them, and so did Sermonetta, the Madison Avenue boutique.

The most popular styles (they will be in stores in late August or September) are a flight-jacket sweater knitted of alpaca, with a tuxedo collar of alpaca fur ($130), and a boot-top version that also has the fur around the hem ($175). Miss Hurlbut also imports the Andean padre hat, made of waterproof felt, which she says is the best rain hat in the world. Sermonetta will have it at $35.

What took Miss Hurlbut from a working Kansas farm to Yale? She laughs and explains that her father's journey had been the other way around. He was a Yalie who met her mother at a New Haven party when she was a student a Finch College, where her Kansas family had sent her to be "finished."

"My mother had happily settled into the Junior League in Connecticut," Miss Hurlbut related, "and then my father decided he really wanted to be a farmer, so they went back to my grandfather's farm, and there we are, raising corn unprofitably."

The Peruvian collection also includes ponchos, shawls, scarves, other sweaters and alpaca fur hats. A catalogue and price list is available from The Peruvian Connection, Canaan Farm, Tonganoxie, Kan., 66086.

Annie Hurlbut in a boot-top sweater rimmed in alpaca fur and an Andean padre hat.

The New York Times / Gene Maggio

Figure 1-9 News story about The Peruvian Connection. (The New York Times, *June 25, 1979.*)

duction-oriented and one that is marketing-oriented.

4 What do we call the process that brings producer and user together, and what does it involve?

5 Discuss the historical roots of direct marketing; specifically, how has it been influenced by technological, economic, and social change?

6 "Direct marketing is an aspect of total marketing which is characterized by *measurability* and *accountability* with heavy reliance on *lists* and *data*." Consider that statement and explain briefly what it means.

7 Can the principles of direct marketing be applied to nonprofit organizations as well as to businesses?

8 Define "lists" as used in this chapter.

9 Distinguish between "direct marketing," "direct mail," and "mail order."

10 What is "direct response advertising" and how does it relate to "direct mail"?

11 It is a common notion that direct marketing cuts costs by eliminating middlemen and salespeople. Is that true?

12 Name, from your own personal experience, six mail-order firms. Then, name six more direct marketers that are not mail order.

13 What are the "Ps" of marketing and how do they relate to direct marketing?

14 As presented by Bob Stone, what are the major responsibilities of a direct marketing executive?

15 Explain how these innovations and trends have hastened the emergence of direct marketing as an aspect of total marketing: **a** computers; **b** electronic media; **c** laser, ink-jet, and other printing technology; **d** credit systems; **e** segmented markets; **f** changing life-styles.

16 Describe the use of direct marketing by a nonbusiness organization with which you are familiar.

DECISION MAKING IN DIRECT MARKETING

Key attributes of direct marketing are measurability and accountability. Scientific decision making is at the heart of the marketing concept but is especially apparent in direct marketing. Interestingly enough, direct marketers, or, actually, their predecessors using "mail order" and "direct mail," were applying scientific techniques for research and analysis even before there *was* a marketing concept!

Typically, as an adjunct to scientific decision making, one of the first questions asked about direct marketing is: "What should my response be?" Put another way, if the direct marketer approaches a thousand qualified prospects with a direct mail offer, a catalog, or a direct response advertisement in a magazine or on television, how many of these thousand recipients of a communication will be motivated to action?

This chapter will be concerned with answering that question, and others, in terms of scientific decision making. In order to accomplish this, every action must be demonstrably *measurable* and *accountable*. Results must always be related to costs, risks related to rewards, in the long run. Although anything worth doing is worth doing well, as we shall see, some things may not be worth doing!

VIEWING DIRECT MARKETING AS A SYSTEM

Perhaps the most important single factor in launching a successful direct marketing program is the understanding and support of its concepts and goals throughout the organization. This is true in profit-making business enterprises as well as in the multitude of nonprofit organizations, charities, educational institutions, political parties, and even governments, that engage in direct marketing activities. An important step toward understanding and support is organizational integration.

Marketing is an "umbrella"! It covers a great many related activities that were once considered separate and independent entities within the structure of organizations. To provide the necessary coordination and to assure that all of these marketing activities are functioning, it is essential that the ultimate responsibility rests with one individual, strategically located in the organizational hierarchy. The marketing umbrella covers not just sales and advertising but other functions as well, such as product development, price determination, distribution planning, product servicing, and marketing personnel development.

As is already well known, one of the most important considerations in direct marketing, along with organizational integration and profit motivation, is an orientation toward the customer.

Scientific decision making, whether used for problem solving, explanation, or prediction, is much more difficult to practice in direct marketing than in many other disciplines. Much of what is being measured in direct marketing involves human nature and thus calls for a degree of subjective analysis as well as abstract reasoning.

Furthermore, direct marketing strategies, tactics, and policies are formulated within a framework of forces, some of which are controllable but many of which are not. Political and legal forces (including intervention and regulation), for example, are most often uncontrollable, as are social and ethical influences. Market demand—environmental influences on and the behavior of consumers themselves—is not easily subject to control nor is the environmental influence of other firms; that is, competition.

On the other hand, forces at work which *are* controllable lie within the marketing mix itself: product, price, place, and promotion, together with nonmarketing resources, finance, personnel, production, research/development, image, location.[1]

---

[1] For additional discussion of these forces, see William J. Stanton, *Fundamentals of Marketing,* 6th ed., McGraw-Hill Book Company, New York, 1981, pp. 21–32.

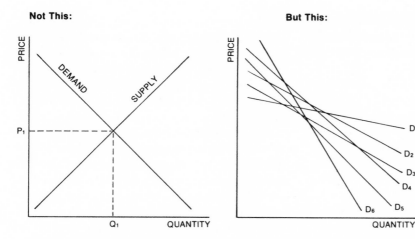

Not This:

But This:

"The lower the price, the higher the demand." P_1Q_1 = Equilibrium Price, where demand inevitably equals supply.

There are many demand curves based on such things as product life cycle, promotional strategies, brand preferences, etc.

Figure 2-1 Economic theory vs. the real world of direct marketers.

Operations Research

It has been said that "economics is to marketing as physics is to engineering or as biology is to the practice of medicine."[2] However, direct marketing is not just the theoretical world of the rational "economic person." There is no well-ordered scheme of the inevitable intersect of the supply and demand curves at a point of "equilibrium," which determines price (see Figure 2-1). Rather, it is the complex interacting of many specialized fields, with economics at its core.

Psychology helps the direct marketer understand human personality through interviewing and projective testing. Sociology helps in understanding the social system and the impact of social-class participation. Anthropology helps the direct marketer appreciate the heritage of various cultures and become sensitive to their taboos. A knowledge of political science helps in understanding foreign competition. And, of course, the need for long-range planning and forecasting, as well as scientific and objective decision making, brings into play statistical and mathematical techniques. There is a blending of many specializations in order to direct market efficiently and effectively. It is not conventional economic theory alone.

Technology preceded adoption of the marketing concept, and many scientific techniques, in the behaviorial as well as in the physical sciences, are now available. Direct marketers are concerned with a variety of management science procedures: simulation, model building, testing, and statistical analysis are among them.

Operations Research Defined Operations research (OR) has been defined as "the systematic, method-oriented study of the basic structure, characteristics, functions and relationships of an organization—in order to provide a sound, scientific and quantitative basis for decision-making."[3] Operations researchers

[2] Walter B. Wentz and Gerald I. Eyrich, *Marketing Theory and Application,* Harcourt, Brace & World, Inc., New York, 1970, p. 3.

[3] An excellent reference is Russell L. Ackoff and Patrick Rivett, *A Manager's Guide to Operations Research,* John Wiley & Sons, New York, 1963.

are concerned with a variety of problems involving inventory, allocation, queuing, sequencing, routing, replacement, competition, and search.

It is only in recent years, mainly since World War II, that there has been much attention given to the decision-making process. The effort has met with considerable success, especially in the development of methods, techniques, and tools of OR along with the advent of high-speed electronic computers. Operations research is based on the fact that, in economic systems, just as in the physical world, there is a great deal of orderliness, even if it is not readily apparent. Operations research is devoted to providing a scientific basis for making decisions that involve the interaction of functional units of any organization in terms of the best interests of the total organization.

Although initially used by the military to solve logistical problems and later used to solve industrial production problems, OR has more recently been applied to direct marketing decision making. The inherent concern in such otherwise objective analysis, however, is that some things are not readily measurable—consumer behavior and consumer environment, for instance—except in relative terms. The statistical techniques of OR, therefore, must be coupled with subjective judgment.

The ultimate goal of OR is *optimization,* identifying the most efficient of available alternative courses of action. The operations researcher systematically seeks to determine the very best of the available possibilities.

An Example of Operations Research   A classic OR problem, in a marketing context, concerns the training of flight attendants for airlines. It considers the conversion of a person (the raw material) into a flight attendant (the finished product) through extensive training classes (the production process). It considers, too, the cost of an excess inventory of flight attendants versus the opportunity cost of flights

canceled due to a shortage of flight attendants, both in relation to the initial cost of setting up a training class. There are constraints, too, related to "hours in the air," "deadheading," etc. This is but one example of a highly complex problem, especially when time lag is considered.

Similar OR problems and solutions abound in direct marketing and include inventory requirements for seasonal catalogs (an OR "inventory" problem); the qualified segments of a total mailing list to which particular versions of this seasonal catalog should be directed (an OR "search" problem); and the number of telephone communicators to be on hand when the orders begin arriving (an OR "queuing" problem). Furthermore, the analyst may need to determine how much of a direct marketing promotion budget should be used in direct mail, how much in print advertising, and how much in broadcast (an OR "allocation" problem) or what might be a competitor's response to price cuts (an OR "competition" problem).

Direct Marketing Research

A systems approach to direct marketing calls for research, analysis, evaluation. Direct marketing research enables scientific decision making. Richard D. Crisp defined marketing research as "the systematic, objective and exhaustive search for and study of the facts relevant to any problem in the field of marketing."[4] As will be made clearer in Chapter 3, *marketing* research covers a much broader scope than does *market* research.

Direct marketing research attempts to reduce *uncertainty* to a manageable risk and to eliminate the undesirable alternatives from all the alternatives being considered. It is an aid to sound executive judgment but not a substitute for it. It takes three primary forms:

• *Exploratory:* This is a "pilot project" approach that is designed to develop a hy-

[4] Richard D. Crisp, *Marketing Research,* McGraw-Hill Book Company, New York, 1957, p. 3.

pothesis of some sort. Such research can take the form of test mailings, surveys, depth interviews, or focus-group interviews.

• *Descriptive:* Here the researcher takes a "logical reasoning" approach and draws conclusions from observed facts such as census data, surveys, and polls.

• *Causation:* In this type of research, the researcher uses a "cause and effect" approach. Relying heavily, as it does, on an abundance of historical data and statistical techniques, it is at once most difficult, least understood, and generally most costly.

Recently, there has been a trend away from *quantitative* research toward *qualitative* research. Quantitative research is concerned with "how much," whereas qualitative asks "why." This latter form, especially, calls for experienced judgment and the use of many of the behavioral science methods.

Conducting research to obtain information for decision making costs money, and thus it must provide benefits. Expected results must be related to expected costs. Potential risk must be related to potential reward. Bertram Schoner and Kenneth P. Uhl identify three basic elements that ultimately determine the value of research information to a business decision:[5]

1 The degree of uncertainty regarding the outcome of the various possible courses of action
2 The economic consequences of making an incorrect decision
3 The amount by which the information, if obtained, is expected to reduce the initial uncertainty

BASIC DECISION-MAKING PROCESS

There has been much development and there is abundant literature relative to the decision-making process. Utilization has been greatly aided by the outstanding capabilities of modern-day computers, which can deal with staggering amounts of information together with highly complex calculations. Much of what transpires in the contemporary environment of direct marketing would not have been possible 20, or even 10, years ago. Information is at the crux of scientific decision making together with sophisticated analytical techniques.

Although described in the literature in a variety of ways, the basic decision-making process consists of four stages:

1 *Determine objectives* Is the objective increased sales volume, increased response to advertising, greater return on investment, or accelerated cash flow?
2 *Array alternatives* What are the possible courses of action and how can these best be evaluated, including (but not limited to) such statistical techniques as decision trees, payoff matrices, and mathematical models?
3 *Deal with uncertainty* How can one assign probabilities, based on judgments, simulation, statistical techniques, to arrive at a proper choice?
4 *Perform evaluation* How does one determine the alternative, from all those available, that best suits the objective under conditions of uncertainty; then implement it, monitor it, and provide for feedback?

It must be emphasized that the proper role of information, as well as calculation, is to enable the direct marketing researcher to make a proper decision. Information and calculation, therefore, are *means* not *ends*. The objective of research is not simply to gather information and perform calculations. The objective is to aid in making decisions. In this context, the following exchange between a researcher and a product manager, as reported in a *Harvard Business Review* article, is worthy of note:[6]

---

[5] Bertram Schoner and Kenneth P. Uhl, *Marketing Research: Information Systems and Decision-Making,* 2d ed., John Wiley & Sons, Inc., New York, 1975, p. 14.

[6] Stewart A. Smith, "Research and Pseudo-Research in Marketing," *Harvard Business Review,* March–April 1979, p. 76.

Researcher: "What if the test results are favorable?"

Product Manager: "Why, we'll launch the product nationally, of course."

Researcher: "And if the results are unfavorable?"

Product Manager: "They won't be. I'm sure of that."

Researcher: "But just suppose they are."

Product Manager: "I don't think we should throw out a good product just because of one little market test."

Researcher: "Then why test?"

Product Manager: "Listen, Smith, this is a major product introduction. It's got to have some research behind it!"

CASE: THE ENTREPRENEURIAL RAINCOAT VENDOR

Here is a simple illustration of a decision-making process. It involves "the entrepreneurial raincoat vendor," who, as a middleman, purchases raincoats from a manufacturer at $10 each and resells them at $35 each to individual customers who get a general clothing catalog. For a particular seasonal mail-order catalog promotion, the decision, under a condition of uncertainty (whether or not it will be a rainy spring season), must be made: how many raincoats to purchase from the manufacturer in order to maximize profit. Thus:

• *Objective:* Maximize profits through a proper determination of how many raincoats to buy for resale in a seasonal mail-order catalog.

• *Alternatives:* (1) Buy 100 raincoats at $10 each; sell them all at $35 each; gross profit is $2,500. (2) Buy 200 at $10 each; sell them all at $35 each; gross profit is $5,000. (3) Buy none, leave the item out of the catalog, and avoid the uncertainty entirely.

• *Uncertainty:* It might *not* be a rainy season. If the mail-order merchant sells only 50, gross profit would be $750 on the purchase of 100. The loss would be $250 on the purchase of 200! (Example assumes no later salvage value.) The *chance* that it will *not* be a rainy season is 40 percent.

• *Evaluation:* The three alternatives provided, along with the associated probabilities of rain, are arrayed in the form of the decision tree and payoff matrix in Figure 2-2. This example is simplified to facilitate understanding. In reality, there could be an infinite number of purchase alternatives and a great many other uncertainties, such as timely delivery of the catalog, economic conditions, and competition. And, of course, the promotion cost of the catalog itself needs to be considered.[7]

In the foregoing Bayesian approach to decision making, which subjectively injects the researcher's own judgment in establishing the probability of rain, there is no pat answer as to *what* to do. Still, such analysis *does* provide the basis on which to make a decision. Whatever the attitude of the individual decision maker, one at least knows what one is doing. And, individual judgment beyond the choice of probability of rain does enter into the analysis.

The figures contained in the column headed "expected value," in Figure 2-2, are derived by multiplying the percentages shown in the "probability" column of the payoff matrix by the corresponding amounts shown in the "profit" column. From this calculation is derived the profit under each condition of uncertainty for each alternative given. The column headed "risk," in one instance, displays the potential $250 "out-of-pocket" loss in the event the mail-order merchant purchases 200 raincoats for inventory and there is, in fact, a lack of rain.

[7] For a more technical discussion of this form of decision making, see William A. Chance, *Statistical Methods for Decision Making,* Richard D. Irwin, Inc., Homewood, Illinois, 1969, chap. 10. Also, Paul E. Green and Donald S. Tull, *Research for Marketing Decisions,* 2d ed., Prentice-Hall, Inc., Englewood Cliffs, N.J., 1970, chap. 2. Also, Gerald Zaltman and Philip C. Burger, *Marketing Research: Fundamentals and Dynamics,* The Dryden Press, Hinsdale, Illinois, 1975, pp. 572–574.

DECISION TREE

NO RAIN	Sell 50	Profit $ 750	40% probability
BUY 100 **RAIN**	Sell 100	Profit $2500	60% probability
BUY 200 **NO RAIN**	Sell 50	Loss $ 250	40% probability
RAIN	Sell 200	Profit $5000	60% probability
BUY 0 **NO RAIN**	Sell 0	0	40% probability
RAIN	Sell 0	0	60% probability

PAY-OFF MATRIX:

Alternative	Probability	Profit	Expected Value	Risk	Attitude
Buy 100:	40%-No Rain 60%-Rain	$ 750 $2500	$ 300 $1500 $1800	$ 0	Play it safe—earn a modest profit
Buy 200:	40%-No Rain 60%-Rain	($ 250) $5000	($ 100) $3000 $2900	$250	Take the risk—earn a higher profit
Buy None:	40%-No Rain 60%-Rain	$ 0 $ 0	$ 0 $ 0	$ 0	Do nothing—lose/gain nothing

Figure 2-2 A simplified example of decision making: The Entrepreneurial Raincoat Vendor.

Although, as already indicated, there is no pat answer here as to what to do, the column headed "attitude" displays how an individual's own intuition, or conservative bent, might influence what action would be taken. Again, bear in mind that this case is very much oversimplified and that there would, in reality, be many more conditions of uncertainty beyond just the probability of a rainy season.

MODEL BUILDING

A model, when used by direct marketers in a research sense, may be thought of as a "representation," but it is not in and of itself a "copy." Zaltman and Burger define a model as "a simplified but organized and meaningful representation of selected attributes of an actual system or process."[8] Further, when

[8] Zaltman and Burger, *Marketing Research: Fundamentals and Dynamics*, p. 60.

used in marketing, models are often thought of in terms of theory. The purpose of the model is a major determinant of the form of the model itself.

Perhaps the concept of models can be more clearly understood if we look at their forms (characteristics) and their purposes. There are three basic purposes for which models might be developed:

1 *Explanation* (or description): When used for this purpose, models provide frameworks and aids to systematic thinking, discussion, or hypothesis testing.

2 *Prediction:* Whereas some models explain, others predict. In this category are forecast models, including the impact that the injection of simulated variables might have on end results. A variation of prediction models would be those that validate descriptive models.

3 *Problem solving:* Models are often used in the decision process to provide solutions to problems. For example, how many telephone operators and 800-service telephone lines are required to avoid queuing of incoming calls during high traffic periods of response to seasonal mail-order catalogs?

Models take many forms and display a variety of characteristics, among which are these:

1 *Iconic models:* These are basically images such as road maps, photographs, or architectural mock-ups.

2 *Analog models:* These are representations in the form of, as examples, flow charts or graphs that represent differences of sales resulting from different flights of a test comparison.

3 *Symbolic models:* Such models are concerned with mathematical and/or logical symbols and include definitional equations (example: *P*rofit = *R*evenue − *C*ost) or more complex technical equations (example: Commission = $1,000 + 0.05 times sales).

4 *Behavioral models:* These models look at happenings over time, such as time series or trend analysis, or establish functional relationships (example: D = f(P), read "*D*emand is a function of *P*rice").

Oftentimes, and especially in direct marketing, models can be constructed to predict response, from particular categories of mailing lists or from particular promotional strategies, which we are unable to explain. In other words, we generally know *what* happens but not *why* it happens. These are sometimes referred to as "black box" models.[9]

All models, whether used for explanation, prediction, or problem solving, rely heavily on the concept of causation. A broad-based compiled mailing list of prospects might, in its entirety, be unsuitable for a particular direct marketing offer. However, when direct response is analyzed in terms of certain demographic characteristics of *segments* of the list, age and marital status as examples, we might determine that the response rate from those persons on the list identified as "older age" is somewhat higher than that from those identified as "younger age." Further, we note, the response rate is increased even more when we look at only those "older age" persons who are also "widowed." This difference is shown in Figure 2-3. From an analysis of Figure 2-3, we can infer that "older age" and/or "widowed" marital status might be the *cause* of higher response or, conversely, higher response might be the *effect* of mailing to older-aged persons who are widowed.

Computer Support in Model Building

"If the computer did not exist today, it would have to be invented," predicted *Fortune* two decades ago. The computer's impact on direct marketing management has indeed been dramatic during recent years. But, because the computer is ineffective unless it is given all the relevant information about a problem, guesses and hunches as inputs are of no value. New clarity and precision are required.

Today's direct marketers frequently use computers for order processing, shipping, and billing as well as inventory and distribution control. They frequently use computers, too, for sales performance analysis as well as for customer/market (mailing lists) identification.

Less frequently, however, do direct marketers use the capabilites of today's computers for market penetration analysis and for allocation of promotion efforts. Even less frequently do they use computers in the application of decision theory, return-on-investment (ROI) evaluation and market simulation. With the emerging capabilities of interactive television, direct marketers are now using the computer to completely control a transaction.

Computers are used by direct marketers in

[9] Schoner and Uhl, *Marketing Research: Information and Decision-Making,* p. 54.

EXAMPLE OF A MODEL

Age/Marital Status	Single	Married	Widowed	Divorced
Under Age 30	.53%	.64%	.87%	.56%
Ages 30-39	.75%	1.40%	1.50%	.85%
Ages 40-49	1.03%	1.75%	1.95%	1.09%
Ages 50-59	1.10%	1.80%	2.05%	1.15%
Ages 60-69	1.30%	1.92%	2.23%	1.32%
Ages 70-79	1.36%	2.03%	2.38%	1.40%
Over 79	1.42%	2.56%	2.72%	1.50%

Figure 2-3 Hypothetical response rates illustrative of differences in age and marital status within a broad-based compiled mailing list.

two ways: (1) centralized data gathering, storage and retrieval, such as order entering and processing, inventory and distribution control and resultant sales analysis; and (2) upgrading the decision-making process. Examples of the latter include simulation of alternative decisions and measuring impact of changes in promotional strategies through testing. In the second type of computer use, the tremendous capacity and retrieval capabilites of modern-day computers are of singular value. Direct marketers are in a particularly good position, because of the very nature of direct marketing, to use computer support—and model building—for record keeping as well as decision making.

THE VALUE OF A CUSTOMER

As was suggested at the beginning of this chapter, possibly the most frequently asked question in direct marketing is that related to response expectations; that is, "What should my response be?" This question is asked as though there is a "norm" or, at least, an expectation. Usually, the question is phrased

in relation to a specific expenditure such as "responses per thousand pieces mailed" or "responses from a thousand newspaper readers" or "responses from a thousand radio listeners."

In reality, there is no universally "normal" expectation. It should be apparent that response will vary relative to such important considerations as the product itself as well as the demand for it, price competition, market preference, and the nature of the promotional offer. Furthermore, response will vary widely according to prequalification of the mailing list used or to the narrowness and appropriateness of market segments that may be exposed by the delivery of the advertisement through some other direct response medium. Typically, all other factors being equal, present customers will respond at a much higher level to an offer for a new product than will nonqualified prospects. A preprinted circular inserted in a Sunday newspaper will generate more response to the advertiser if there are no directly competitive offers in the same issue. A product in the early stages of its life cycle will create more attention and more interest than one that is generally available and displays little if any product differentiation.

Breaking Even in the Long Run

More importantly, and probably more realistically, the question should be rephrased to ask: "What responses do I *need?*" or, "What is the value of a customer?" What would it take to just break even on a particular offering? Or, what lesser level of response would be required in order to break even over an extended period of time during which a new customer demonstrates his worth through repurchases?

As we have already established, a cornerstone of the marketing concept is *customer orientation*. Organizations are concerned with creating, caring for, and keeping customers. This implies that customers have value over time way beyond the first sale. Thus, a realistic answer to the classic question "What should my response be?" will more likely be found in the answer to another question, "What is the value of a customer?"

Some years ago, Edward C. Bursk titled an article in the *Harvard Business Review* "View Your Customers as Investments."[10] Bursk observed that "a company's investment in customers can be just as real as its investment in plant and equipment, inventory, working capital, and so forth. And it can be even more valuable in dollars and cents."

He went on to point out, however, that although some companies used the "investment" approach to new product planning and brand promotion, almost none applied it in an area in which, if anything, it is more needed and more likely to sharpen decision making. Whereas companies almost always capitalize plant, equipment, and inventory, they almost never capitalize what could be their most important asset, their customers.

[10] Edward C. Bursk, "View Your Customers as Investments," *Harvard Business Review,* May–June 1966, pp. 91–99.

Direct marketers spend a major part of their time, effort, and money in developing mailing lists of customers and qualified prospects. In fact, it is felt by many in direct marketing that such mailing lists, along with descriptive databases, are, in fact, the key ingredients that differentiate *direct* marketing. Therefore, direct marketers *especially* should view their customers as investments. These are the lifeblood of a direct marketing organization from which future sales accrue at a cost that is generally significantly lower than that attributable to the first sale.

It follows from this thesis that if a marketing action (expenditure) can result in the acquisition of *new* customers, who will generate value over time and in the long run, then that action is desirable even though the initial "response per thousand" is not adequate to recapture the initial expenditure. Some might call this negative return on investment or simply the cost of "goodwill." Professional direct marketers call it "the value of a customer."

Establishing the Break-Even Point

The microeconomist describes profit maximization as occurring at the point at which marginal revenue is equal to marginal cost. That is, the revenue derived from the sale of one *additional* unit is equal to the cost of producing *that* unit. At that point, with the cost of producing each additional unit continuing to rise, it follows that the average cost (of all units produced) will also rise so that average profit, being the residual between average revenue and average cost, will decrease.

Total cost, in this context and in a production sense, generally consists of a combination of *fixed* and *variable* costs. *Fixed* costs are those costs, such as plant and equipment depreciation and maintenance, that remain fairly constant regardless of the volume of production (up to a point), and *variable* costs are those costs such as raw materials that generally increase proportionate to the production level. Keep in mind that here the microeconomist is concerned only with production, and not promotion, total cost.

To the direct marketer, promotion costs also have fixed and variable elements. Relatively fixed, for example, are the costs of creating a direct mail package or direct response advertisements in other media: copy, art, photography, recording, typesetting, plate making, etc. These costs generally remain the same no matter how many thousand promotion pieces are ultimately printed and distributed. Other costs, such as paper, printing, postage, and mailing list rental, typically increase in proportion to the volume of pieces; some (such as printing) increase at a decreasing rate, whereas others (such as postage) increase at a flat rate. Similarly, other costs in other direct response media, such as those for space or time, vary with expected circulation or expected number of exposures.

It is also conceivable that promotion costs in direct marketing, once the expenditure has occurred, might all be considered as fixed. The expenditure, once made, is the same, regardless if just one or 100 or 1,000 orders result. This contrasts with a salesperson's commission, which is a variable cost since it is paid only if and when a sale is consummated.

Figure 2-4 presents graphically a typical situation of "production" break even (B/E) (without direct marketing promotion) occurring when total revenue (TR) is exactly equal to total production costs (TPC). Total production costs, in turn, consist of the combination of fixed production costs (FPC) and variable production costs (VPC). It should be noted that although, in this example, FPC remain level, these would probably scale up as plant capacity was reached. For example, there could be a need for a new machine or a new factory or warehouse building.

Variable production costs, as shown, typically increase less rapidly as higher production volume is achieved, ultimately reaching an optimum level of increase, and then begin to accelerate once more as plant capacity is approached. As shown in Figure 2-4, to the left of the TR line and underneath the TPC line lies an area in which there is a total production loss (TPL) at which level the increasing returns of scale have not yet been realized.

In this illustration, the TPC divided by the quantity of units produced is equal to the FPC divided by the quantity produced plus the VPC divided by the quantity produced, thus:

$$TPC/Q = FPC/Q + VPC/Q$$

Also, as shown in this illustration, TR divided by the quantity sold minus TPC divided by the quantity sold is equal to unit profit (UP), which is break even at point (A) *without promotion,* thus:

$$TR/Q - TPC/Q = UP$$

Until now we have been concerned with production costs and potential break even relative only to fixed plus variable costs. The direct marketer must also be concerned with promotion costs. These are the costs of selling and advertising as well as other support activities necessary to communicate information about products or services in order to achieve distribution.

For the purpose of illustration, let's assume that our promotion consists of a direct mail offer sent to 500M prospects. The cost of the mailing averages $250/M pieces mailed, and totals $125,000 for the 500M pieces. Superimposing this assumed total promotion cost (TPRC) of $125,000 on TPC, which varies according to the total volume of production, it becomes apparent that we must increase sales by 1,500 units, from the production break even of 6,500 units to the production *plus*

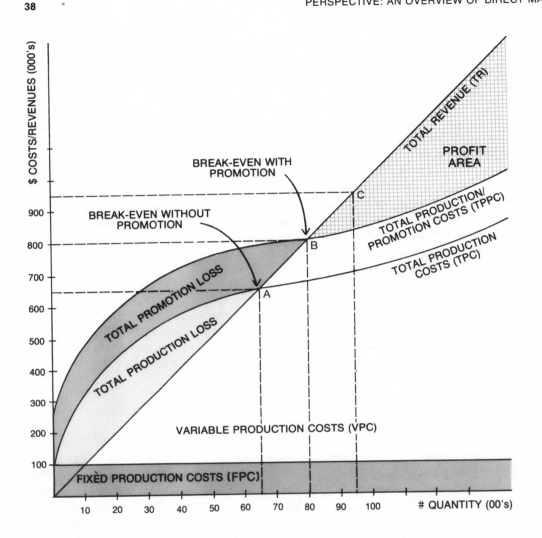

promotion break even of 8,000 units, in order to absorb FPC and VPC *in addition to* fixed and variable promotion costs, which average $250/M pieces mailed.

In this example, therefore, average promotion costs per thousand pieces mailed (APRC/M) divided by UP becomes break even at point (B) *with promotion,* or:

$$\text{APRC/M} \div \text{UP} = \text{B/E}$$

We further note that total sales in units per thousand pieces mailed (TS/M) less break-even sales per thousand pieces mailed (B/E sales/M) multipled by the UP becomes equal to net profit per thousand pieces mailed or, at point (C) on the chart:

$$\text{TS/M} - \text{B/E sales/M} \times \text{UP} = \text{net profit/M}$$

For further illustration, let's use some actual numbers in this example, with reference to points (A), (B), and (C) in Figure 2-4, as follows:

Point (A):

$$TPC/Q = FPC/Q + VPC/Q$$

$$\frac{\$650,000}{6,500} = \frac{\$100,000}{6,500} + \frac{\$500,000}{6,500}$$

$$\$100 = \$15.38 + \$84.62$$

Point (B):

$$TR/Q - TPC/Q = UP$$

$$\frac{\$800,000}{8,000} - \frac{\$675,000}{8,000} = \frac{\$125,000}{8,000}$$

$$\$100 - \$84.38 = \$15.62$$

$$APRC/UP = B/E\ sales/M$$

$$\frac{\$250}{\$15.62} = 16\ sales/M\ (1.6\%)$$

Point (C):

$$TS/M - B/E\ sales/M \times UP = net\ profit/M$$

$$19 - 16 \times \$15.62 = \$46.86$$

An Example of Break-Even Calculation

Figure 2-5a demonstrates the use of a profit work sheet, which direct marketers find useful when calculating a break-even point and, beyond break even, net profit at various levels of net sales per thousand pieces mailed. A variation can be used for print or broadcast advertising. A most important consideration, of course, is that promotion is a *cost,* whether direct mail, space, or broadcast, and that cost, like FPC and VPC, must be considered in determining net profitability.

With reference to Figure 2-5a, lines 3 ~~~~ h 8 represent the cost of ~~~~ $12.44/copy, of ~~~~ ics. C~~~~

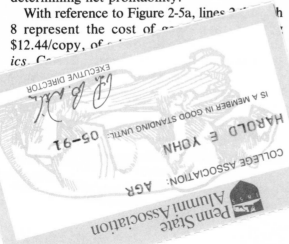

Having arrived at a cost of goods sold per book sold, unit profit (line 10) is calculated by subtracting $12.44 from an assumed selling price of $30/unit.

Unit profit in this example is, thus, $17.56. In the manner demonstrated in the preceding illustration, from Figure 2-4, this unit profit (line 10) is then divided into promotion cost per thousand pieces of direct mail (line 25) in order to arrive at break-even net sales per thousand (line 26), which, in this example, is 14 units. Total promotion cost per thousand pieces of direct mail is tabulated, for illustrative purposes only, in lines 11 through 22 to total $242.83. To this amount is added an assumed overhead cost of $3.00 to arrive at the total promotion cost in line 25, $245.83/M pieces mailed.

Keep in mind that the form in Figures 2-5a and 2-5b is simply a guide and must be modified to cover each situation. Promotion costs can be calculated in a similar way for space advertising in magazines and newspapers or time on television and radio. Or, space cost within a printed catalog can be similarly allocated. In any event, the formula for calculating break-even net sales is the same:

$$\frac{average\ promotion\ cost}{unit\ profit} = break\text{-}even\ sales$$

Having calculated a break-even point of 14 unit sales, the remainder of Figure 2-5a (lines 27 through 33) illustrates calculation of total profit at various levels of net sales beyond the break-even point. When projected net sales are 17/M (line 27), for example, the net profit (line 31) is $52.68/M. Similarly, net sales of 20/M would result in a net profit of $105.36/M and a projected net sale of 25/M would result in a net profit of $193.16/M.

Although the form for calculation shown in Figures 2-5a and 2-5b is different, the formula itself is the same as in Figure 2-4.

OFFER: _Practical Mathematics_ Date: ___2/8/83___

LINE

1. Selling Price $ 30.00
2. Merchandise Cost $ 5.00
3. Shipping Cost   .75
4. Delivery Cost   1.20
5. Processing & Collection Cost   2.50
6. Cost of Returns   .27
7. Bad Debt Cost   2.50
8. Premium Gift Cost   .22
9. Total Cost   12.44

10. UNIT PROFIT $ 17.56 ___ (UP)

PROMOTION COSTS PER M

11. Circulars $ 19.34
12. Inserts   8.53
13. Letters   14.45
14. Order Forms   9.52
15. Coin Envelopes   1.94
16. Envelopes-Mailing   13.84
17. Envelopes-Business Reply   11.21
18. List Rental   40.00
19. Inserting & Mailing   10.00
20. Addressing (or Labelling)   3.00
21. Postage (Third-class bulk rate)   109.00
22. Miscellaneous-Author Royalty   2.00
23. Total Promotion Cost $ 242.83
24. Fixed Overhead Costs Per M   3.00
25. Total Promotion & Overhead Costs $ 245.83 (PRC)
26. Break-even Net Sales Per M (PRC ÷ UP)   14

TOTAL PROFIT AT VARIOUS LEVELS OF NET SALES

27. Projected Net Sales (Units) Per M	17	20	25
28. Less: Break-even Net Sales (Units) (Line 26)	14	14	14
29. Unit Sales Earning Full Profit (Line 27 - Line 28)	3	6	11
30. Unit Profit (Line 10)	× 17.56	× 17.56	× 17.56
31. Net Profit Per M (Line 29 x Line 30)	$ 52.68	$ 105.36	$ 193.16
32. M Pieces Mailed	× 9,508	× 9,508	9,508
33. Total Net Profit (Line 31 x Line 32)	$ 500.88	$ 1001.76	$ 1836.57

Figure 2-5a Direct marketing profit worksheet (a).

PROMOTION *Practical Mathematics*

ASSUMPTIONS:

No. Pieces Mailed	*9,508*	M
Gross Orders Rejected as Result of Credit Check	*0*	%
Gross Shipments Returned	*10*	%
Net Sales Uncollectable	*8.33*	%
Terms	*Net – 30 Days*	

ORDER PROCESSING AND COLLECTION COSTS

Gross Orders		*100*	x $ *N/A*	= $ *N/A*
Less: Credit Rejects		*0*		
Gross Sales		*100*	x $ *1.80*	= $ *180.00*
Less: Returns		*10*		
Net Sales	(A)	*90*	x $ *.50*	= $ *45.00*
Total				$ *225.00* (B)
Cost Per Net Sale (B ÷ A)				$ *2.50*

COST OF RETURNS

Return Service	$ *0.50*
Shipping Cost	*0.75*
Delivery Cost	*1.20*
Missing Items	*N/A*
TOTAL	$ *2.45* (A)
% Returns Projected	*10%* (B)
Return Cost Per Net Sale (A x B)	$ *.27*
$\overline{\text{(100 -B)}}$	

BAD DEBTS

Total Selling Price	$ *30.00* (A)
% Reserve For Bad Debts	*8.33%* (B)
Bad Debt Cost Per Net Sale (A x B)	$ *2.50*

Figure 2-5b Direct marketing profit worksheet (b).

Such a calculation, however, assumes the offering of only a single item and anticipates a desirable net profit at various levels of response beyond the break-even point. In contrast to such a *single item* break-even calculation, however, the more likely and realistic calculation for direct marketers will involve continuity, and is applicable to long-term recovery such as that experienced by magazine and book publishers, insurance companies, fund raisers, and catalog merchandisers who expect repeat orders from new customers. In such cases the value of a customer is figured similarly to single item break even with two critical adjustments. *First,* an attrition rate must be calculated and accounted for month to month, year to year, or even catalog to catalog. *Second,* a periodic contribution to cover acquisition cost must be determined and discounted to its present value to provide an acceptable return on investment. This is explained in the following section.

Calculating Continuity Break Even over Time: The Concept of "PAR"

Determining the value of a continuity customer over time, a value we will call PAR, can be an extensive, involved, and sometimes complex calculation. In its simplest form, however, this procedure is followed:

1 Develop a stream of *total revenues,* chronologically over a period of time or, possibly, the life of a catalog, taking into account ordering frequency as well as average order size. Provide, too, for *attrition,* the assumed (historic) drop off in active customers from one time period to the next.

2 From this total revenue stream, deduct for each time period the cost of goods sold together with general/administration expenses. The residuals derived from total revenues, in each period, represent a series of annual contributions available for two purposes: (a) defraying promotion cost expenditures associated with acquiring new customers together with ultimately (b) producing a profit.

3 This stream of contributions to acquisition needs to be discounted, at some rate appropriate to the risk of investing in new customers. The sum of these discounted values represents the *present value of a customer* and provides a measure of how much could or should be spent to acquire this customer at the yield rate assumed when discounting.

The process of PAR calculation calls forth several qualifications. Preferably, the calculation should be done by product and, if feasible, even by source of new business if certain fulfillment costs (such as credit loss) are expected to vary by source. In certain cases, insurance sales, for example, PAR measures only the ongoing value of a single insurance policy. Some other way must be found to measure the value of corollary sales (a second insurance coverage, for example) to the same individual or household. In view of these qualifications, an organization might willingly spend *more* than a customer appears to be worth, for reasons to be brought out shortly; or, it might spend *less* as a result of its own marketing effectiveness.

An Example of Continuity Break Even

An example of calculating the continuity value of a customer over time is shown in Figure 2-6. Projected over a 5-year period, an initial base of 100 new customers is assumed together with an attrition of 35 percent during the first year; 20 percent of the remainder during the second year; 15 percent of the remainder during the third year; and 10 percent of the remainder during the fourth year. We further expect costs of goods sold plus general/administration expenses to average 65 percent of revenue during the first year, increasing to 75 percent of revenue during the fifth year. The contribution to acquisition is then discounted by an interest factor of 10 percent to arrive at present value. Assuming a mailing cost of $250/M and an initial fulfillment (order entry and processing) cost of $5/customer, we calculate, as shown in Figure 2-6, a continuity break-even point of 18.08 sales/M.

So far, we have considered the value of a customer as an investment, in terms of the sale of a single item, and, beyond that, we have calculated the value of a continuity sale over time, arriving at a break-even level for the long run called *PAR*. We next need to look at a situation in which the true value of a customer would be *greater* even than the PAR value calculated in Figure 2-6. This might occur, as an example, when related products are developed for and subsequently offered to a specific customer base. These incremental sales to present customers quite likely will cost less to produce than their PAR value

because, typically, less promotional effort (cost) is required to resell to an existing customer than to acquire a new one.

The amount by which we might thus exceed PAR can be expressed as a ratio: cost/PAR. In certain instances of marketing effectiveness, such a *PAR ratio* could even be *less* than PAR, that is, value exceeds cost.

Calculating PAR Ratio: The Ultimate Value of a Customer

PAR ratio is defined as the ratio of cost to PAR value, thus:

$$\text{PAR ratio} = \frac{\text{cost}}{\text{PAR value}}$$

If the PAR ratio is 1.00, new business is being acquired at exactly what it is worth (over

Time Period	Customers Active	% Retention	Total Revenue (@ $25/Customer)	Cost/ Revenue	Total Cost	Contribution To Acquisition	Discounted Contribution
1	100		$2,500	65%	$1,625	$875	$ 795
2	65	(65%)	$1,625	68%	$1,105	$520	$ 430
3	52	(80%)	$1,300	70%	$ 910	$390	$ 293
4	44	(85%)	$1,100	72%	$ 792	$308	$ 210
5	40	(90%)	$1,000	75%	$ 750	$250	$ 155

Total Present Value of 100 Initial Customers $1,883
Total Present Value of one Customer $18.83

Assume: Mailing Cost: $250/M
               Fulfillment Cost: $ 5 per customer
               Customer Value: $18.83 (present value @ 10% discount)
               B/E Sales/M =   A (to be determined)

Continuity Break-even Calculation:

(Mailing Cost) + [(Fulfillment Cost) x A] = (Customer Value) x A
$250 + [$5.00 (A)] = $18.83 (A)
or . . . $250 = $18.83 (A) - $5.00 (A) = $13.83 (A)
A = $250/$13.83 = 18.08
thus . . . B/E Sales/M = 18.08/M

Figure 2-6 Continuity value of a customer calculated over time.

time) and yields an assumed rate of return on investment, discounted to a present value. If the PAR ratio is less than 1.00 (0.85, for example), new business is being acquired at a cost somewhat less than its value, that is, its ultimate value over time. Discounted to a present value, it yields *more* than the assumed rate of return. If the PAR ratio exceeds 1.00 (1.40, for example), more is being paid for the acquisition of a customer than that customer is seemingly worth unless there is another source of revenue, such as related or increased sales to that customer base.

If the direct marketer is, in fact, to view the cost of acquiring new customers as a *value received,* to be amortized over time in terms of present and future profits from the initial as well as subsequent and related sales, it behooves him to array every marketing effort, calculating for each a ratio of total cost to total value. From such an array, shown in Figure 2-7, individual marketing efforts can be ranked from best to worst, in ascending PAR ratio order, until one of three criteria stops the process. First, all available alternatives for promotion have been exhausted, a possible but unlikely occurrence. Second, all available new customer acquisition funds have been committed, certainly possible and also likely at times. Third, all of the present alternatives, when relative (cost) weights are given to each PAR ratio, represent a strategy that yields a *cumulative* PAR ratio of 1.00. That is, the selection process continues, beginning with the best alternative, until the weighted average PAR ratio of all chosen alternatives equals 1.00. In Figure 2-7 that would be at the conclusion of marketing effort "I."

Such a process represents the ultimate value of a customer, a procedure by which direct marketers can systematically select the best from among a rank ordering of alternative marketing efforts with some calculable measure of yield resulting from progressive investment in each new customer acquisition opportunity. If budget constraint is a consideration, for example, there is a desired limited expenditure of $1 million, the direct marketer will conceivably stop after having processed marketing effort "G."

An Example of the Use of PAR Ratio

All that has been presented thus far is summarized in Figure 2-8. This is described as a product and source mix forecast wherein customer acquisition is viewed as an investment.

Effort	$ Cost (000)	Par Ratio	Accum. $ Cost (000)	Accum. Par Ratio
A	75	.40	75	.4000
B	125	.71	200	.5500
C	235	.98	435	.7196
D	120	1.00	555	.7658
E	115	1.12	670	.8097
F	145	1.19	815	.8589
G	125	1.20	940	.8928
H	75	1.23	1015	.9112
I	245	1.24	1260	.9611
J	240	1.30	1500	1.0027
K	185	1.40	1685	1.0349
L	145	1.70	1830	1.0681
M	220	2.00	2050	1.1243

Figure 2-7 Using PAR ratio in accumulative selection of direct marketing efforts.

Product	Source	Promotion Cost	Inquiry Fulfillment Cost	Product and Fulfillment Cost	Total Cost	Mailing Volume (or Circulation)	Inquiries #	Inquiries Per M	Sales #	Sales Per M	Sales Volume	Value (Par) Per Cust	Total Value	Par Ratio	Cum. Par. Ratio
A	1 Customers	$ 17,500		$20,000	$ 37,500	100,000			4000	40	$100,000	$12.19	$ 48,750	.77	
	2 Direct Mail	$ 40,000		$12,500	$ 52,500	250,000	5000	10	2500	10	$ 62,500	$12.19	$ 30,475	1.72	
	3 Space	$ 15,000	$10,000	$10,000	$ 35,000	(500,000)			2000	4	$ 50,000	$12.19	$ 24,380	1.44	
	Subtotal	$ 72,500	$10,000	$42,500	$125,000	---			8500		$212,500	$12.19	$103,605	1.21	1.21
B	1 Customers	$ 17,500		$ 7,200	$ 24,700	100,000			3600	36	$ 54,000	$ 7.55	$ 27,183	.91	
	2 Direct Mail	$ 39,000		$12,600	$ 51,600	300,000			6300	21	$ 94,500	$ 7.55	$ 47,565	1.08	
	3 Space	$ 2,700	$ 6,480	$ 8,100	$ 17,280	(270,000)	3240	12	1620	6	$ 24,300	$ 7.55	$ 12,231	1.41	
	Subtotal	$ 59,200	$ 6,480	$27,900	$ 93,580	---			11520		$172,800	$ 7.55	$ 86,979	1.03	1.15
C	1 Customers	$ 50,000		$ 8,000	$ 58,000	200,000			2000	10	$120,000	$28.35	$ 56,700	1.02	1.12
D	1 Customers	$ 35,000		$ 8,400	$ 43,400	200,000			4200	21	$147,000	$14.94	$ 62,748	.69	1.03
E	1 Customers	$ 2,000 (Stuffer)		$ 1,200	$ 3,200	200,000			1200	6	$216,000	$11.12	$ 13,344	.24	1.00
	TOTAL	$218,700	$16,480	$88,000	$323,180	---			27420		$673,900	$11.79	$323,376		1.00

Figure 2-8 Product and source mix forecast, viewing customer acquisition as an investment.

Products are designated A, B, C, D, and E. Three sources of business are shown: present customers, prospective customers reached through direct mail promotion, and prospective customers reached through space advertising promotion. PAR ratio is demonstrated to vary by product as well as by source. The bottom line objective, all product lines and all sources of business combined, should not exceed a cumulative PAR ratio of 1.00, when cost exactly equals PAR value.

As has been demonstrated, the direct marketer should always relate results to costs, reward to risk. Further, he should view customer acquisition as an investment, just as is the acquisition of plant, equipment, and inventory, and he recaptures this investment over time through continuity sales as well as corollary sales.

Ultimately, a favorable PAR ratio (less than 1.00) enables him to invest in still more new customers at an accelerating rate. Ultimate profit becomes an objective. Customer orientation remains a cornerstone.

In our consideration of the broad subject of decision making in direct marketing, which relies so heavily on *measurability* and *accountability,* we should develop an understanding of planning relative to forecasting and its further relationship to evaluating.

PLANNING, FORECASTING, AND EVALUATING

Profit, in an industrial or capitalistic economy, is generally viewed as a return on capital. Beyond that, in a marketing sense, profit can also be a measurement of productivity in that it describes the difference between revenue and cost. Professor Yevsei G. Liberman, a Soviet economist, during the mid-1960s described "profit" in the Soviet Union, a noncapitalistic economy, as "the major overall indicator of the efficient operation of our enterprise . . . (and) generalizes all aspects of operation, including quality of output."[11]

When profit is viewed in this manner as a measurement of efficiency, it can accrue in one of two ways: (1) more revenue or (2) less cost. To achieve either objective calls for planning and evaluating together with scientific forecasting.

Direct marketers are concerned with proper "mixes" of products, prices, places, and promotional strategies. As was demonstrated in the calculation of the value of a customer on the preceding pages, such value is determined in the long run. Profit, too, is a long-run objective, including the social implications of economic actions. Traditional accounting methods cannot always serve as a proper measurement. Functional accounting, including allocations by product, price, customer category, and promotional strategy, becomes a first step in future planning.

Planning for Profit

Direct marketers, through measurement and accountability and the ultimate capturing of a mailing list and database about their customers, plan for profit. Planning is the essence of the marketing concept from which evolves a system based on scientific decision making. Planning looks at means vs. ends, inputs vs. outputs. Planning minimizes risks. Forward-looking organizations adopting such a systematic approach, aided by computer technology, are formalizing planning rather than relying on haphazard, informal ways based on their own "seat-of-the-pants" hunches and personal biases. Theory provides the tools for planning; organizations provide the laboratories.

More and more organizations are engaging in long-range planning for periods of 2, 3, 5, and even 10 or more years. There is a definite

---

[11] Yevsei G. Liberman, "Are We Flirting with Capitalism? Profits and 'Profits'," *Soviet Life,* July 1965.

need for updating these plans periodically to adjust to a changing environment, and highly sophisticated computer models have been developed and are being used on an ongoing basis.[12] In contrast to such long-range planning, planning in the short run, often called *forecasting* and/or *budgeting,* usually covers periods of 3 months, 6 months, or 1 year.

Properly administered planning in a direct marketing system should encompass all phases of the system: market, product, price, distribution, and promotion. Although direct marketing planning frequently begins with market planning reduced to quantitative measurements, all phases of the system must ultimately be integrated. Planning forces a thought process and often a reduction to writing of the plan. If the objective itself can't be defined, its achievement is highly doubtful. A planning model, whether mathematical or verbal, is essentially a simulation procedure. It is possible to array alternatives for decision making through use of sophisticated computer technology and advanced statistical techniques.

J. W. Tukey and W. B. Wilk pointed to four major influences that were acting on systematic data analysis. These are: "(1) the formal theories of statistics; (2) accelerating developments in computers and display devices; (3) the challenge, in many fields, of more and even larger bodies of data; (4) the emphasis on qualifications and an even wider variety of disciplines." They see, too, the highly important interaction between statistics and the flexibility of the informed mind. Such analysis cannot make knowledge grow out of numbers, "it can only bring to our attention a combination of the content of the data with the knowledge and insight about its background which we must apply. Accordingly, validity and objectivity of data analysis is a dangerous myth."[13]

At this juncture, certain definitions should be considered insofar as they relate to an organization's planning objectives:

- *Market potential:* The expected combined sales volume for all sellers of a product during a stated time in a stated market: a geographic area, a demographic market segment, an industry, etc.
- *Market penetration:* The organization's objective (or achieved) market share. In a monopoly situation, market share would equal market potential
- *Market factors:* Items, elements, or indicators that can be quantitatively measured, such as income or educational level
- *Market index:* Market factors reduced to percentages

Market factors are frequently used to determine the market potential of a firm. Market penetration is measured against this potential. Such measurement hinges on, first, determination of single or multiple relevant market factors, and, then, as one alternative, using correlation analysis to relate these factors to the penetration of potential. Alternatives to such planning measurement might be surveying buying intentions, measuring test markets, relating the characteristics of present customers to the potential market, trend analyzing past sales, or simply making an executive judgment.

Whatever direct marketing planning technique is used, however, it must be objective, achieved through predetermined goals, and often calls for using a wide array of theoretical tools.

---

[12] One such model is described by Philip Kotler, "Corporate Models: Better Marketing," *Harvard Business Review,* July–August 1970, pp. 135–149.

[13] J. W. Tukey and M. B. Wilk, "Data Analysis and Statistics: An Expository Overview." (Paper presented at the Fall 1966 Joint Computer Conference, San Francisco, California, November 7–10, 1966.)

Forecasting and Budgeting

Forecasting is the cornerstone of successful direct marketing planning. Budgeting involves the process of activating a direct marketing plan.

In *Statistical Forecasting for Inventory Control* (McGraw-Hill, 1969) Robert Goodell Brown presents two conflicting quotations:

> You can never plan the future by the past.
> —Edmund Burke

> I know of no way of judging the future but by the past.
> —Patrick Henry

Brown observes that Edmund Burke, in reincarnation, would probably be a sales manager and that Patrick Henry would probably be making statistical forecasts.

Forecasts are, in effect, mathematical models formulated in terms of statistical probabilities, calculated to be correct a high percentage of the time and, on the average, reasonably close to the actual occurrences.

Although it is possible and entirely feasible to perform these statistical manipulations manually, the advent of the electronic computer, with its vast capabilities for immense data retrieval and lightning-speed calculations, has made the use of mathematical forecasting techniques feasible and even commonplace. This, coupled with long-range simulation planning, incorporating alternative courses of action, is largely replacing ''seat-of-the-pants'' judgment by the *entrepreneur* with scientific decision making by the *manager*.

Objective, computerized forecasting is becoming a routine matter in direct marketing, enabling the decision maker to concentrate on the evaluations about the forecast and to predict and act accordingly. Although such forecasts are objective in the sense that they are unemotional and thus dependable, it is well to remember that they necessarily incorporate given assumptions. Such assumptions change over time and so the input data for any math-

ematical model used in forecasting may also change over time.

There are two major categories of forecasting methodology in common use today. The ''build-up'' techniques derive total estimates from various components of the forecast, such as an accumulation of estimates by sales territories into a total sales forecast. The second major category consists of the ''relationship'' techniques in which potential results are estimates derived from correlations with market factors.

Planning vs. Forecasting It is important, at this juncture, to more carefully distinguish between *planning* and *forecasting*. Whereas a direct marketer can engage in long-range planning, the use of long-range forecasting is primarily a supplement and check on the feasibility of a firm's plans. Not the least of the factors that can influence the ''best laid'' plan, and thus upset even scientifically accurate forecasts, are those that are environmental or exogenous in nature, over which no control can be exercised. An organization plans for the long run based on short-run forecasts but updates these plans as the underlying assumptions change. It is in this area that experience comes into play, when mechanical methods do not in themselves provide wholly adequate forecasts.

Forecasting should be viewed not as an alternative to planning but rather as a check on planning. During the recent past, growth has come to be a necessary feature of many forecast models. Such growth patterns may not always be wholly consistent with profit motivations, another cornerstone (along with customer orientation and organizational integration) of the philosophy called the marketing concept.

Forecasting Activities Basically, forecasting involves certain key activities that are set forth below:

1 Collection of reliable and pertinent data (information).

2 Selection of the proper forecasting methodology (model) and the relevant assumptions. It should be noted that the selection process is dependent on the general availability of data, events to be forecast, the decision-making activities needing forecasts, and alternative procedures for constructing forecasts.

3 Estimating values in the methodology selected through use of appropriate statistical techniques.

4 Doing the necessary calculations, including the injection of alternative courses of action through the use of simulation procedures.

5 Arriving at confidence limits and tests of statistical significance.

6 Judging the results and predicting the future.

7 Updating the prediction based on new and relevant data.

Forecasting Methodologies[14]   There are a variety of forecasting methodologies, including highly sophisticated models, in use today. Classified according to the techniques employed, they include the following:

Judgment forecasts   These are largely "seat of the pants," based mainly on prior experience and insight. They are sometimes data free and are used most often when there are many variables (which are hard to quantify), simple situations, and/or when the cost of more sophisticated procedures cannot be absorbed. Such forecasts are not readily susceptible to post-facto analysis. Still, judgment forecasts are possibly the most widely used.

Surveys of expectations   This methodology goes beyond the preceding one in that it involves a process of asking knowledgeable people about future events. For example, salespeople might be asked to generate their individual expectations as a basis for developing a composite of the expectations of the entire sales force, but such expectations are more often based on personal motivations than market realities. Such procedures as "polling" call for a high degree of judgment, are expensive, are dependent on the availability of knowledgeable people, and become more suitable when there is a historic point of reference.

Time series or mechanical extrapolation models   Such procedures attempt to identify movements or trends that existed over past time periods. The dependent variable is the event to be predicted. The determinants, rather than being considered as independent variables, appear collectively under the heading "time." Important considerations in mechanical extrapolation are which data are relevant and how best to fit an "explanatory" curve to the selected data. Too long a history, for example, or a pattern reversal, creates a need for caution. Naive models of time series range from predictions based on "no change" to "equal percent change" to "some percent proportion of past change." In all such cases, the rationale employed is simple but not always valid: "the future mirrors the past."

Moving averages   The injection of a series of averages that more nearly approximate a trend tends to cancel out the high and low values of the average over the time period and more nearly approximates realistic prediction. Injection of "exponential smoothing" helps even further to cancel out highs and lows or reversal trends through placing more weight on the more recent observations.

Analytical forecasts   Whereas all the preceding methodologies, including the extrapolation procedures, assume to some extent that the future will mirror the past, truly analytical

[14] An excellent presentation of forecasting methodology is made by John C. Chambers, Satinjer K. Mullick, and Donald D. Smith, "How to Choose the Right Forecasting Technique," *Harvard Business Review*, July–August 1971, pp. 45–74.

forecasts predict on the basis of information obtained from *other* economic variables rather than simply the past history of the variable being projected.

An example of a causal method of analytical forecasting is that using correlation and regression analysis. Such a model functionally relates sales (or another dependent variable) to one or more independent economic or social variables in order to estimate an equation of the form $Y = a + bX$, using the "least squares" technique. A more thorough discussion of this analytical technique may be found in Chapter 4.

Some regression forecasts include only one predicting variable, such as the sale of automobiles predicting the need for automobile servicing. A more common need, however, is for the injection of *several* independent variables, such as the sale of snow blowers being dependent on a variety of factors including the amount of snowfall, seasonal temperature fluctuation, discretionary income, and even related variables such as the sale of snow tires or the sale of snow shovels.

Like meteorologists and economic forecasters, direct marketing planners and forecasters oftentimes, after the fact, *explain* rather than *predict*. The late Professor Marcus Nadler is credited with providing this caution: "If you have to forecast, do it frequently."

Planning vs. Evaluating

Planning sets forth what is to be done. *Evaluating* reviews what was actually accomplished.

A *budget,* whether open-ended or constrained by financial resources or profit requirements, necessarily follows a *forecast*. The budget, too, is a fundamental tool for direct marketing planning, against which ultimate results are to be evaluated.

Budgets can be most effective when they are departmentalized or related to *cost centers* or *profit centers*. It is important to recognize

that a budget is intended to be a tool of efficient management, not an obstacle or a challenge. Thus, the statement "it's not in my budget" is not a valid excuse for nonperformance as much as it is a forecasting oversight if, in fact, the expenditure is a desirable one.

Budgets are of three basic types:

1 *New business acquisition* The cost of promoting, acquiring, and processing new customers. To the direct marketer, these are primarily advertising expenditures together with sales promotion and fulfillment expenses in connection with acquiring new business.

2 *Production* The fixed and variable costs of providing products and/or sevices. Production budgets can be directly related to new business acquisition budgets in that more effective promotion, through the increasing returns to scale, can make possible more efficient production.

3 *General/administration* The largely fixed overhead costs involved in running an organization. Some of these costs can be allocated to product lines or market segments, in that they are directly related to them, whereas other costs in this category must either be allocated in a different manner or else cannot be allocated at all.

The evaluation process by direct marketing management must consider actual results in relation to forecasted results and budgeted costs. It must look, too, at the factors responsible for these results, good *or* bad. Plans, policies, and procedures for improvement must be developed and implemented. Or, put another way, management must find out *what* happened, *why* it happened, and *what* to do about it!

A major objective of the evaluation is to identify misdirected direct marketing efforts. *What* profit comes from *where?* What responses to direct marketing efforts are *ultimately* profitable? What should be the investment in *future* sales?

Because of the measurable and accountable

attributes of direct marketing, it is often possible to project results from promotional efforts at a suitable time after appearance of the effort itself, 4 weeks after direct mailing of a magazine subscription offer, for example. Such a projection is shown in Figure 2-9. In this example, representing a particular offering to nine mailing list segments, it is assumed that the response at the end of 4 weeks is 70 percent complete and, from this projection, the presumed final figure can be related to forecast at an early stage in time. As a check, actual results are looked at, in this example, 13 weeks after mailing when, historically, results are virtually final. This presentation of actual results vs. forecast results, when compared with the earlier 4-week comparison of projected results to forecast results, can be used as a check on the "percent complete" assumption used.

It is important to repeat that results must always be related to costs. The objective in the direct marketing system is not simply

volume as much as it is *profitable* volume. The benefits to be derived from such an evaluation are obvious: better market decisions, better product decisions, better price decisions, better promotional decisions, and better decisions regarding such factors as the marginal costs of customer groups, order size, and continuity experience.

Scientific decision making is a necessary element of direct marketing. From this premise, we will move into the areas of research and experimentation in direct marketing. These provide the information base for decision making.

SUMMARY

In this chapter we have presented the premise that *measurability* and *accountability* are key attributes of direct marketing and that scientific decision making is a necessary element. Like the philosophy of the total marketing concept, direct marketing must be viewed as a system

Effort (List)	Quantity Mailed	Actual #Sales	4 Weeks %	Projected %Complete	Projected to Final #Sales	%	Quota #Sales	%	Proj./ Quota	Actual Final #Sales	%	% Actual/Quota
A	23,658	240	1.01	70.00	343	1.45	300	1.27	114.53	356	1.50	118.67
B	15,416	120	0.78	70.00	171	1.11	196	1.27	87.24	162	1.05	82.65
C	23,930	230	0.96	70.00	329	1.37	304	1.27	109.66	318	1.33	104.60
D	15,416	190	1.23	70.00	271	1.76	196	1.27	138.26	234	1.52	119.39
E	50,436	340	0.67	70.00	486	0.96	639	1.27	76.06	402	0.80	62.91
F	17,549	120	0.68	70.00	171	0.98	223	1.27	76.68	177	1.01	79.37
G	50,116	350	0.70	70.00	500	1.00	636	1.27	78.62	593	1.18	93.24
H	17,549	140	0.80	70.00	200	1.14	223	1.27	89.69	218	1.24	97.76
I	11,928	430	3.60	70.00	614	5.15	151	1.27	406.62	572	4.80	378.80
TOTAL	225,998	2,160	0.96	----	3,085	1.37	2,868	1.27	107.56	3,032	1.34	108.72

Figure 2-9 Relating interim results (projected to final) to forecasted results and actual final results to forecasted results.

with economics at its core and a variety of the behavioral sciences providing input. Direct marketers, fortunately, are not totally reliant on surveys but rather, through tests of direct mail or other advertising media, can readily determine whether or not a particular promotional strategy, product, price, or market is desirable, and to what extent it will be profitable.

The basic decision-making process is a four-step one: determine objectives, array alternatives, deal with uncertainty, and, finally, perform evaluation. Decision making in this way is aided and abetted by mathematical and other forms of model building, which often are augmented by sophisticated computer support.

Uppermost in the mind of direct marketers is the *value of a customer* and it is important to determine that value as a first step in any direct marketing strategy. That value may need to be calculated *over time,* and examples are provided for calculating break even for a single sale as well as a continuity relationship. The concept of PAR ratio relates to various aspects of the marketing mix: product, price, place, and promotion.

DISCUSSION QUESTIONS

1 What is the meaning of the statement that marketing is an "umbrella"?

2 Name and describe the eight kinds of problems with which operations researchers are concerned. Relate each of these, by example, to direct marketing.
3 What form of research can be viewed as a "pilot project" and how is it used by direct marketers?
4 Why has there been a trend from quantitative to qualitative research?
5 What are the four basic stages of the decision-making process?
6 What are models in research, and for what purposes are they used?
7 Distinguish between these four types of models and give examples of each: iconic, analog, symbolic, behavioral.
8 What is a "normal" response from direct response advertising?
9 Compare the value of a customer list to an organization's other assets such as plant, equipment, inventory, and working capital.
10 Distinguish between the calculation of break even on the sale of a single item and that for a series of continuity sales.
11 Discuss the concepts of PAR and PAR ratio, as presented in this chapter.
12 What is the difference between planning and forecasting?
13 Briefly describe each of these forecasting methodologies: judgment forecasts, surveys of expectations, time series, moving averages, and analytical forecasts.

CHAPTER 3

DIRECT MARKETING RESEARCH AND EXPERIMENTATION

Direct marketing research is concerned with fact finding and information gathering but not these alone. It is also concerned with problem solving and action recommending. The nature of direct marketing makes it conducive to scientific research as well as field and laboratory experimentation or "testing," as this is often called by practitioners.

The complexity and scope of direct marketing activity, the great amount of information available, and the shortening of the time span allotted for decision making have all played a part in the increasing acceptance of basic tools as well as advanced techniques for direct marketing research, surveys, and experiments. This and the following chapter will be devoted to some of these tools and techniques.

THE NATURE OF RESEARCH

The result of research is often quantitative, that is, it is concerned with numbers: population sizes, income levels, housing values, and the like. Recently, however, there has been a shift away from pure numbers to qualitative matters. Research has become more concerned with consumer behavior and reasons why people buy, rather than just who or how many buy.

In collecting primary data, as with surveys, what respondents *say* and what they *do* are frequently quite dissimilar. The most valid research is that which measures *results* and not *opinions*. In one study by a direct marketing insurance company, for example, in which the company itself remained anonymous during interviewing, the majority of the respondents replied negatively to the question "Would you purchase insurance by mail?" Yet, it was already known that every one of these respondents *had* purchased insurance by mail from the company conducting the survey! A better alternative available to those who use direct marketing is to offer the product or service for sale and measure those who actually buy, not simply those who say they would if given the opportunity. This is an option direct marketers have which is not always available to traditional marketers.

Surveys vs. Experiments

It may be helpful, at this juncture, to distinguish between *surveys* and *experiments*. A survey looks at things the way they are; that is, a mailed questionnaire tries to profile respondents to an offer or to measure product preferences or to determine future buying intentions. An experiment is designed to measure the effect of change. What happens, for example, when a price level is raised or lowered? What is the result of selective promotion to specific market segments? What is the influence on response of one particular promotional strategy vs. another? Direct marketers, like traditional marketers, have the ability to conduct surveys. When it comes to experimentation, however, they can be particularly adept with the tools and techniques of *testing*.

Aside from the knowledge of the processes of surveys and experiments, direct marketers also need to know how to define people, things, and events in quantitative as well as qualitative terms. How do they design research and how do they structure problems? Where do they obtain what kinds of information and what do they do with it? How do they conduct valid experiments, through proper sampling and estimation techniques? How do they present findings, evaluate them, and ultimately use them?

Direct marketing researchers need to know how information is gathered, synthesized, and analyzed. They need to know when direct marketing research is needed, and how problems are formulated. Importantly, they need to know how to relate risks to rewards, costs to benefits, the impact of wrong decisions. The tools and techniques of direct marketing research help them do all of these things.

Problem Structure

How do direct marketing researchers define and structure problems? First, we should consider typical problem areas, such as:

- *Amount of advertising effort:* How is this to be determined, in dollars and cents? Is it a result (based on past sales) or is it a cause (based on future sales)? Do expected results warrant estimated costs? Do anticipated rewards outweigh potential risks?
- *Direct marketing mix:* Once determined, how will the budget be allocated? What products will be offered and at what prices? What market segments will be selected? And, certainly a major area for testing, what is the best promotional strategy: offer, copy, graphics, and the variations thereof?
- *Special allocations:* Is geographical concentration desirable, relative to such considerations as climate and the logistics of distribution? Should emphasis be placed on allocations over time when there are potential seasonal or cyclical variations or, as with many goods, what is the stage of the product's life cycle?

William Stanton provides a helpful procedure to be followed in marketing research investigation:[1]

1 Define the objectives of the project; identify and define the problem.

2 Conduct a situation analysis; formulate the problem into a hypothesis for further testing. (A hypothesis is a tentative presumption or a possible solution to a problem, assumed or conceded for purposes of argument or action.)

3 Conduct an informal investigation; obtain more background from exploration or discussion.

4 Plan and conduct a formal investigation. Is the research to be designed as a survey or an experiment? At this stage, there is need to:

a Determine the sources of data.

b Determine the methods for gathering data, whether this be a survey method or an experimental method.

c Prepare the data-gathering forms.

d Pretest the questionnaire or other forms.

e Plan the sample.[2]

f Collect the data.

5 Tabulate and analyze the data; prepare a written report.[3]

6 Follow up the study; validate the findings.

Problem definition may seem somewhat artistic in its nature, but its importance cannot be overemphasized. Not all solutions derive from problems, of course. Many are definitions of objectives. Research is simply the way in which direct marketing managers either seek solutions to problems or become knowledgeable about objectives so that solutions may be found or new opportunities may be presented.

It is well to note (and to caution) that the actual problem solution or objective definition can be influenced by researcher/experimenter bias, especially when there is a tendency to "put your best foot forward." The findings are also subject to sampling errors when the respondents are nonrepresentative; there is error either in the randomness of the sample or in the sampling process itself. And, of

---

[1] William J. Stanton, *Fundamentals of Marketing,* 6th ed., McGraw-Hill Book Company, New York, 1981, pp. 41–50.

[2] See pp. 61–65 for discussion of sampling methods and techniques.

[3] For a presentation of a variety of analytical techniques, see Joseph F. Dash and Conrad Berenson, "Techniques in Marketing Research," *Harvard Business Review,* September–October 1969, pp. 14–29. "Mature Techniques" described are these: Regression and Correlation Analysis, Discounted Cash Flow, Incremental Analysis, Multiple Regression/Multiple Correlation, Random Sampling, and Sampling Theory. "Modern Techniques" described are these: Bayesian Approach, Cost-Benefit Analysis, Critical Path Method (CPM), Decision Trees, Dynamic Programming, Exponential Smoothing, Industrial Dynamics, Input-Output Analysis, Linear Programming, Markov Processes, Monte Carlo Simulation, Nonlinear Programming, Numerical Taxonomy, Program Evaluation Review Technique (PERT), Queuing Models, Risk Analysis, Sensitivity Analysis, and Technological Forecasting.

course, it is well to remember that "people are human" and their behavior as consumers cannot be measured precisely.

DATA: TYPES, SOURCES, AND COLLECTION

The keys to research are data (information). It is important to know, after a problem is structured or an objective is defined, how to arrive at the solution or derive the plan of action. After determining what information is needed, the direct marketer must determine where and how to obtain it and what to do with it. Information is all around us, if we would but recognize it, collect it, catalog it, refer to it.

Data are usually categorized into two broad groups: *primary* and *secondary*. Secondary data are those that were collected originally for another purpose but that have relevance to, and are available for, the research needs of others. Primary data, on the other hand, are those collected specifically for the research need. Collection of primary data involves survey research as well as experimental research. Surveys are usually conducted by personal interview by mail or telephone, or by on site observation. Experiments, very often used by direct marketers in testing, can be conducted in either a field or a laboratory environment. Primary data should be collected only when secondary data are not readily available from outside sources or even from the organization's own internal records including its own prior experimentation.

Secondary Data

Figure 3-1 lists a variety of sources of secondary data. Digging for and obtaining information that is already available, as contrasted to either survey research or experimental testing, doesn't appear to be a very exciting activity. Still, one of the most costly mistakes researchers make

is literally "reinventing the wheel." It is quite likely that someone has already traveled your road, including yourself. The use of secondary data, when available, can save valuable time and is usually less costly. (Secondary data might well have been primary data for the organization originally gathering them.)

The volume of secondary data is virtually limitless. The problem, actually, is how to manage the information. Where is it? How do you find it? How do you get it? What do you do with it? How do you analyze and evaluate it? Most importantly, how reliable and relevant is it?

The first source to consider for secondary data, although not always thought of as such, should be the internal records of the business or organization itself. For example, there is no need for an insurance company to conduct survey research to determine the average age of its policyholders; a quicker and easier way is to look at its own records already on file.

A. The Business or Organization's Own Internal Records.
B. Government Sources: Federal, State, Local.
   1. U. S. Department of Commerce
       — Bureau of The Census
   2. U.S. Department of Labor
       — Bureau of Labor Statistics
   3. U.S. Department of Agriculture
   4. Other U.S. Government Sources
       — President's Office
       — Congress
       — Treasury Department
       — Interior Department
       — Health & Human Services Department
   5. State and Local Government
       — Economic Surveys
       — License Registrations
       — Tax Records
C. Trade, Technical, Professional and Business Associations
D. Private Research Organizations
E. Foundations, Universities and Other Nonprofit Research Organizations
F. Libraries, Public and Private
G. Advertising Media
H. Financial Institutions, Utilities and Other Public Service Organizations

Figure 3-1 Some sources of secondary data.

Traditionally, business firms have collected and used relatively little internal marketing information. Although media costs of advertising, for example, are duly recorded on a typical accounting statement, there is little or even no allocation of advertising costs on that statement. Similarly, comprehensive distribution cost programs are virtually nonexistent. Traditional accounting approaches and the resultant operating statements, typically, are not adequate nor have they been designed in the past to provide the information needed by direct marketing decision makers. It is interesting to note that these decision makers go to great lengths to measure and predict direct marketing *results,* but they expend only a fraction of their effort on the matter of *costs.* Typically, such costs are listed on accounting statements by the objective of the expenditure; that is, advertising, printing, postage, mailing list rental. More appropriately, these should be looked at by products, by price level, by type and/or size of customer, by market segment, and/or by promotion effort.

As can be seen in Figure 3-1, there is a great variety of potential sources of secondary data outside the organization's own records. In addition to the government and other public sources listed, there are many private organizations, including research firms, as well as communications media, that provide syndicated or custom-designed data on a periodic or one time basis. The A. C. Nielsen Company, for example, provides ongoing information about food and drug purchasing and the automobile aftermarket. Daniel Starch and his staff monitor magazine readership and advertising recall. Other organizations, the Yankelovich Group, George Gallup, the Harris Poll, and the Roper Poll, monitor social, economic, and political changes.

Other types of commercial information include consumer panels, diary groups, store audits, and field enumerations.

Primary Data

As contrasted with secondary data, primary data are those gathered specifically for current needs through surveys and experiments. These types of information are usually sought from respondents:[4]

- *Behavior:* what respondents have done or are doing
- *Intentions:* anticipated or expected future behavior
- *Knowledge:* how respondents perceive specific offerings
- *Socioeconomic trends:* age, income, education, occupation, sex, etc.
- *Attitudes and opinions:* respondents' views or feelings
- *Motivations:* reasons for respondents' behavior
- *Psychological traits:* respondents' state of mind; that is, personality

There are four major survey methods:

Personal Interview This is the most costly method of survey but it has several advantages: it provides the opportunity for a more complete and accurate sample; it provides the opportunity for more complete information; it offers greater flexibility in structuring questions to the situation; and high response is assured. Its major disadvantage, besides cost, is the possibility of bias created by the interviewer along with the need for extensive interviewer supervision and control in order to standardize handling and avoid cheating.

Telephone Interview The advantages here are economy, speed, representative sampling, minimal nonresponse, simple call-backs, the ability to coincide with other activities (such

---

[4] Bertram Schoner and Kenneth P. Uhl, *Marketing Research: Information Systems and Decision-Making,* 2d ed., John Wiley & Sons, Inc., New York, 1975, pp. 217–222.

as television viewing), and the ease of getting the respondent's participation. The disadvantages include limited availability of information at the time of contact, the inability to use certain types of questions, and the fact that non–telephone subscribers are not included. Those with unlisted numbers can only be reached through random-digit dialing.

Mail Questionnaire   This method provides great versatility at low cost. There is no interviewer bias and no field staff is needed. Certain people are more easily approachable this way. The respondent may remain anonymous and replies are kept confidential; he or she can reply at leisure and without interruption. Disadvantages include the relatively high rate of nonresponse; the need for follow-up; response bias induced by those with strong feeling (either way) tending to respond; the time required in development; the lack of assurance that respondents clearly understand questions.

Observation   The key advantage of this technique is that it removes respondent bias. As an example, the Johnson Wax people found that respondents' reported usage of their wax products differed as much as 50 percent from reality when compared with the actual brand that the consumer had at home. The major observation methods include in-store and in-home audits, recording devices (such as the A. C. Nielsen audimeter), and direct observations at the point of purchase, such as a shopping center. An automobile dealer wanting to know what radio stations are listened to by prospects for service work didn't ask them; the dial settings on radios in cars brought in by present customers were observed.

Experiments are probably more widely used by direct marketers, in testing, than are surveys. This method of gathering data involves careful control and an avid adherence to statistical techniques to assure validity. Because of the heavy reliance by direct marketing researchers on experimentation, certain relevant tools and techniques of statistics will be dealt with in somewhat more detail in the next section.

EXPERIMENTATION AND EXPERIMENTAL DESIGN

Many people equate marketing research with survey research. This is not so. Survey research attempts to observe and record various activities as they naturally arise in the environment. Experimentation, on the other hand, involves the manipulation of one or more controllable factors (called independent variables) to determine their influence on various events or outcomes (called dependent variables). Experimentation is a common practice among individuals as well as among organizations. It is especially prevalent and useful in direct marketing, where it is called "testing." Experimentation is a process in which results are measured in an environment that the experimenter creates and in which controls serve to pinpoint the causes of behavior differences among respondents.

Experimentation as Testing

Some examples of direct marketing questions that might call for experimentation are these:

• How does the frequency of mailing to a particular list affect total response?
• Is it possible to increase profits by servicing small industrial accounts totally by mail rather than using personal salespeople?
• How productive are various segments of a total market?
• Is a given newspaper advertisement more effective in color than in black and white?
• What is the best season to mail; that is, when is the best time to offer for sale spring-blooming bulbs, which are planted in the fall?
• What is the most profitable pricing strategy?

In an experiment, the factor manipulated is termed the *independent* variable. This could be the product or service offered, its price structure, or some attribute of the promotional strategy used in the offer. Independent variables are often used to describe the demography or geography of a market. It is axiomatic in direct marketing testing that only one independent variable should be measured at a time. Certain advanced statistical techniques, however, such as multivariate regression analysis, offer opportunities to measure the interaction of many independent variables simultaneously.

Typically, in the environment of direct marketing the *dependent* variable most frequently used in measurement is resultant responses and/or transactions. In other research situations the dependent variable could be favorable or unfavorable reactions to a product or overall rating of a brand preference.

In determining the independent variables to be used it is important that they be representative of the real world. At least three levels of observation are needed for measurement. Although it is possible to use several independent variables, the dependent variable is usually the measured responses of subjects that are attributable to either a single or a combination of independent variables. The groups to be measured, both test and control groups, must be randomly assigned and must be of a sufficient size to provide acceptable statistical validity.

Experiments are usually conducted in a field setting, as is the case with most direct marketing tests, but may also be conducted under laboratory conditions. When conducted in a laboratory setting, however, it is important that the setting be realistic and that the subjects be typical of the real world. It would not be appropriate to use, for example, college students in a laboratory setting involving a product geared to the senior citizen market. Laboratory experiments are often used, also, to measure the impact of particular advertisements through such devices as eye motion cameras and mechanical devices that gauge emotional reactions through measurement of dilation of eye pupils.

Experimental Designs

There has evolved in the literature of marketing research a series of notations used to describe the design of experiments. That used here was originally presented by D. T. Campbell and J. C. Stanley.[5]

Valid experiments are characterized by (1) random assignment of subjects to groups so that differences between groups occur by chance alone, and (2) the presence of a control group on which the experiment is not conducted but that is otherwise identical. The term "preexperiment" was assigned by Campbell and Stanley to designs in which there was no randomly assigned control group and measurement did not go beyond that observed after the experiment or that derived from premeasurement vs. postmeasurement observations, but without a valid comparison.

Shown in Figure 3-2 are the basic experimental designs together with a key to the notation used to describe them. The first three designs listed—one shot study case, premeasurement/postmeasurement, and static group comparison—are designated as preexperiments because they have neither control nor randomization to allow comparative measurement.

Control

The importance of control in experimentation is illustrated by the case of the mathematician Blaise Pascal, who hypothesized in 1648 that atmospheric pressure declined with increasing altitude.[6] Pascal first took a barometric reading

[5] This notation was initially developed by D. T. Campbell and J. C. Stanley, "Experimental and Quasi-Experimental Designs for Research on Teaching," in N. L. Gage (ed.), *Handbook of Research on Teaching,* Rand McNally, Chicago, 1963.

[6] Excerpted from an article by E. G. Boring, in R. Rosenthal and R. L. Rosnow, *Artifacts in Behavioral Research,* Academic Press, New York, 1969, p. 1.

(KEY: X = an experimental treatment, manipulation of an independent variable;
O = an observation of a dependent variable; b = before manipulation;
a = after manipulation; R = random assignment to group; P = pairings;
S = matched pairings)

Name of Design	Form of Design	Experiment/Control
1. One-Shot Study Case	X Oa	No control
2. Pre-Measurement/Post-Measurement	Ob X Oa	No control
3. Static Group Comparison	X Oa 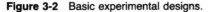 - Oa	No Control-groups not equated randomly
4. Simple Randomization	R X Oa R - Oa	Experimental Group Control Group
5. Randomized Matched Subjects (Predetermined after Ob)	Ob P X Oa Ob P - Oa	Experimental Group Control Group
6. Single Group Control (Successive treatments)	S X₁ Oa S X₂ Oa	Same Individual— usually impossible

7. Single Group Control (Simultaneous treatments)	R {S₁ X₁ O₁a
	   {S₁ - X₂ O₂a
	R {S₂ X₂ O₃a
	   {S₂ - X₁ O₄a
		Experimental #1
		Experimental #2
		Experimental #3
		Control

8. Randomized Pre-test/Post-Test	R Ob X Oa R Ob - Oa	Experimental Group Control Group
9. Solomon Four-Group	R O₁b X O₁a R O₂b - O₂a R - X O₃a R - - O₄a	Experimental Group Control Group #1 Control Group #2 Control Group #3

Figure 3-2 Basic experimental designs.

in his village. An hour later, after he had climbed to the top of a 3,000-foot mountain, he took another measurement and this second observation did indeed show significantly lower atmospheric pressure. What Pascal did not know, however, was whether the atmospheric pressure had become lower at the bottom as well as the top of the mountain during the hour that it took him to climb to the higher elevation.

Pascal wisely changed his experimental design. He calibrated two barometers to each other and read them simultaneously before he began his trek up the mountain with one of them. At the precise time he read the barometer in his hand at the top of the mountain, another villager read the control barometer at the bottom of the mountain. His subsequent comparison, with control, showed that although both barometers had lower readings at the end of the hour it took him to climb the mountain, the barometer he carried with him to the top had a significantly lower reading than the one left in the village.

Design 3 in Figure 3-2 injects a control but it is naive in that the two groups are not randomly equated. An example of this naivete is the oft-repeated statement, in comparing those who receive a college education against those who do not, that the former earn more in their lifetimes than do the latter. Obviously, the two groups are not comparable and thus it would be foolish to draw the conclusion that a college education in and of itself causes higher lifetime income. It is conceivable that the "drive" that caused the student to enter college in the first place is also a cause.

Randomization   Design 4 in Figure 3-2 injects simple randomization as well as control. The effect of the experiment is the difference between the observation of the dependent variable after the experiment and the observation of the dependent variable of the control group which did not receive the treatment. Design 4 is probably the most frequently used form of experimental design in direct marketing testing. It is important to note, however, that this form of experiment, with control, even after randomization, still does not guarantee that the two groups are identical. The differences arising by chance alone may be substantial.

Comparative Measurement   One method of obtaining better matching groups involves selecting subjects in pairs in a pretest, after observation. This is Design 5, randomized matched subjects. This design helps minimize potential differences between the chosen groups.

Even the pairing of randomized matched subjects does not guarantee that the two resultant groups will be identical. If each subject served as its control during successive treatments, as shown in Design 6, single group

control, that would be ideal. Of course, this is usually impossible inasmuch as the first treatment results in a residual influence on the subsequent treatment. An improvement is Design 7, which involves simultaneous, rather than successive, treatments on randomized matched pairs. Even single group control with simultaneous treatments is virtually impossible.

Some of the advantages of matched pairs without actual matching are shown in Design 8 in which there is observation of the randomized groups both before and after the experiment. The Solomon four group Design 9 combines elements of Designs 4 and 8, although it is doubtful that this design is as useful as the simple two group, randomized Design 4.

SAMPLES AND ESTIMATIONS

Implicit in any discussion of experimentation or testing in direct marketing is an understanding of the methods for obtaining valid samples and for determining proper sample sizes. Sampling is a method of choosing observations from which estimations can be predicted. Without adequate samples, the resultant estimations and predictions will be invalid. Direct marketers must know the major means of selecting samples of potential respondents from a population, and they need insight into sampling problems and opportunities.

Note that statistical methods, no matter how sophisticated, are not useful for inferring any traits of a larger population if the sample itself is bad. The direct marketing researcher should be able, at least, to obtain adequate samples from a population, to compute sample sizes and confidence intervals, and to know what is there and why. It is also necessary to understand the key terms that are used, as presented in summary form in Figure 3-3.

Random Sample Designs

To assure that experimental and control groups are as nearly alike in makeup as possible, any

Population or Universe or Sampling Frame — total domain or group of items being considered.

Parameter — characteristic of a population.

Sample — subsets of the population for which data are available.

Statistic — characteristic of a sample.

Sampling Unit — i.e., marketing unit.

Sampling Method — the means of obtaining the sample from the population.

Mean — arithmetic average . . . a measure of central tendency.

Mode — an average, a value that occurs most frequently . . . also a measure of central tendency.

Median — an average, the mid-point of values . . . also a measure of central tendency.

Variance — a measure of dispersion about the mean.

Standard Deviation — also a measure of dispersion . . . square root of the variance.

Simple Random Sample — every possible sample of equal size has an even probability of selection.

Sampling Error — the difference between sample results and the population parameter (which is often unknown). Sampling error declines as the size of the sample increases, assuming an unbiased sampling procedure.

Bias — a methodical error that occurs in selection of respondents or measurement, i. e., the difference between the expected value of a statistic and the population parameter estimated by the statistic.

Accuracy — difference between the sample statistic and the actual population parameter.

Valid — a statistic without bias.

Reliability — the standard error of a statistic (its precision).

Random Event — an occurrence which has several possible values and occurs with some definable frequency if many repetitions are undertaken.

Figure 3-3   Definitions.

differences between the two groups should be those attributable to chance. There are a variety of ways to obtain samples that can be so described. The major ones are explained below:

• *Simple random samples:* Using preprinted tables or computer-generated random numbers assures the equality of probability of sample selection. Ideally, each consecutive selection is made randomly from a population from which the immediately preceding selection has been removed.

• *Systematic random samples:* This is technically not a pure random sample but, since it requires only one pass through a large mailing list, it is most frequently used by direct marketers. Starting with a random number, every *n*th name is selected in the proportion that the desired sample represents of the entire population.

• *Stratified random samples:* In this selection the names are drawn in proportion to a particular parameter of a population; that is, the distribution of the sample by age is proportioned to the known age distribution of the population.

• *Cluster samples:* Rather than ordered lists, area clusters are picked at random and the entire cluster is selected; that is, the entire ZIP Code in an *n*th selection of all ZIP Codes.

• *Replicated samples:* Several independent random samples are taken, such as first choosing a stratum from among all 50 of the United States, then choosing a stratum of counties within these selected states, then choosing a stratum of census tracts within the selected counties. The variation would be selections over periods of time.

• *Sequential samples:* Using this method, projection is based on progressive data; that is, selection based on prior predictions such as the manner in which election outcomes are predicted by television networks.

It is possible that the arrangement of a list from which a sample is drawn could itself bias the selection. Alphabetic arrangement of a list, for example, could result in ethnic concentrations within certain letters rather than having these equally divided throughout the file. A similar problem could occur when a list is geographically arranged so that location differences are concentrated. Most large lists today are arranged in ZIP Code sequence, numerically from East Coast to West Coast, and this form of arrangement is probably as conducive as any to *n*th name selection without bias.

Sampling error can arise when not everyone in the population of interest is included, such as selection from a telephone directory, which includes neither households without telephones nor those with unlisted numbers. Another instance of sampling error would be the inclusion of nonprospects; that is, obtaining a sample from a list that includes apartment dwellers to test an offering of lawn furniture. Another form of error, nonresponse error, occurs when an individual is included in the sample but, for one reason or another, is not reached or else refuses to respond.

Determination of Sample Size

The determination of a proper sample size is influenced by two major considerations: (1) the cost involved in reaching the sample and (2) the need for adequate information to make an efficient decision; that is, having enough responses to a test to be able to predict future response within a comfortable limit of certainty. Samples can be determined by a judgment call, "test 5,000" or "test 10 percent of the list," or they can be determined by some calculated method.

The basis for sample-size determination is found in probability theory. The law of large numbers assures us that, as sample size increases, the distribution of sample means (responses) concentrates closer to the true mean (response) of the total population. Further, the central limit theorem assures us that, in a number of random samples taken from a population, the sample means (responses) tend to be normally distributed. This concept is presented graphically in Figure 3-4, which shows a normal distribution. Such a normal curve is completely determined by its two parameters: mean and standard deviations.

Statistics, the tool of probability theory, helps the direct marketing researcher arrive at conclusions that are reassuring. Having determined a confidence level that is satisfactory, as well as an acceptable limit of error, it is necessary to estimate the response to determine an appropriate sample size. Or, after the fact, knowing the actual response, the limit of error can be calculated. All four elements, *confidence level, limit of error, expected (or actual) response,* and *sample size,* enter into this calculation. We should define these terms:

• *Confidence Level:* The number of times in 100 attempts that the resultant predictions must be correct. This degree of confidence is expressed in terms of number of standard deviations. The number of standard deviations refers to the area covered under a normal curve, as represented in Figure 3-4.

• *Limit of Error:* The number of percentage points by which the researcher is allowed to miscalculate the actual percent of response. In other words, if we expect a 1 percent response, by how much can we miscalculate and still be in an acceptable, or at least a safe, position? A 20 percent limit of error, for example, assuming a 1 percent response, could result in a range of actual response as low as $\frac{8}{10}$th of 1 percent to as high as 1.2 percent; that is, 1 percent ± 20 percent of 1 percent.

• *Expected (Actual) Percent of Response:* The number of times, in percentage, that our response will be positive. In terms of the toss of a coin, how often will "heads" appear? In terms of a direct mailing, how many positive responses will be received? The difference between this positive response and the total quantity mailed describes the percentage of nonresponse or negative response. If there was 1 percent response, then R (for "response") would equal 0.01 (expressed as a decimal) and 1 minus R would equal 0.99.

• *Sample Size:* The number of observations in our experiment. This is the number of individual pieces of direct mail sent out in a test from which we will determine, ultimately, both the percentage of response and the percentage of nonresponse. The formula for determining sample size is:

$$N = \frac{(R)(1-R)(C)^2}{E^2}$$

where (R) is the frequency of response, a percentage expressed as a decimal; (1 − R) is the frequency of nonresponse, also a percentage expressed as a decimal; (C) is the confidence level, expressed as a number of standard deviations; (E) is the limit of error expressed

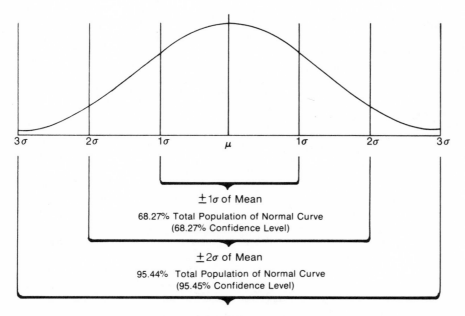

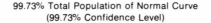

NOTE 1: σ is standard deviation

NOTE 2:   Tables usually use: 90% Level   1.65 Std. Dev.
                                    95% Level   1.96 Std. Dev.
                                    99% Level   2.58 Std. Dev.

Confidence Level: Is the number of times out of 100 attempts that the resultant predictions must be correct. This degree of confidence is expressed in terms of number of standard deviations. The number of standard deviations refers to the area covered under a normal curve.

Limit of Error: Is the number of percentage points by which the researcher is allowed to miscalculate the actual percent of response. In other words, if we expect a one percent response, by how much can we miscalculate and still be in an acceptable, or at least a safe, position. A 20% limit of error, for example, assuming a 1% response, could result in a range of actual response as low as 8/10th of 1% to as high as 1.2%; i.e., 1% $\pm$ 20% of 1%.

Expected (Actual) Percent of Response: Is the number of times, in percentage, that our response will be positive. In terms of the toss of a coin, how often will "heads" be turned up? In terms of a direct mailing, how many responses will be positive? The difference between this positive response and the total quantity mailed describes the percentage of non-response or negative response. If there were 1% response, 99% non-response, then R (for "Response") would equal .01 (expressed as a decimal) and 1 minus R would equal .99.

Sample Size: Is the number of observations in our experiment. This is the number of individual pieces of direct mail sent out in a test from which we will determine, ultimately, both the percentage of response and the percentage of non-response.

Figure 3-4   A normal distribution.

as a decimal; and (N) is the sample size, the number of pieces to be mailed.

To illustrate the use of the above formula, we determine the sample size required in terms of mailing pieces when the expected response is 1 percent and the desired limit of error is ±0.2 percent at a confidence level of 95 percent. Thus:

R = 1% . . . or 0.01, expressed as a decimal
1 − R = 99% . . . or 0.99, expressed as a decimal
C = 1.96 standard deviations, assuming a 95% confidence level
E = 0.2% . . . or 0.002, expressed as a decimal
N = to be determined

Substituting the above values into our formula, we have:

$$N = \frac{(0.01)\,(0.99)\,(1.96)^2}{(0.002)^2}$$

$$= \frac{(0.01)\,(0.99)\,(3.8416)}{0.000004}$$

$$= \frac{0.03803184}{0.000004}$$

$$N = 9{,}508 \text{ pieces to be mailed}$$

Suppose that, in the above experiment, we had mailed 9,508 pieces, and the actual response turned out to be 1.5 percent, rather than 1 percent. Still at a 95 percent confidence level, what would be the limit of error of continuation mailings projected from this experiment? The formula for determining limit of error follows:

$$E = \sqrt{\frac{(R)\,(1 - R)}{N}} \times C$$

Substituting the new values (with the same notation as before) into this formula, and solving for limit of error, we have:

$$E = \sqrt{\frac{(0.015)\,(0.985)}{9{,}508}} \times 1.96$$

$$= \sqrt{\frac{0.014775}{9{,}508}} \times 1.96$$

$$= \sqrt{0.000001554} \times 1.96$$

$$= 0.00124 \times 1.96$$

$$E = 0.00243 \text{ or } 0.243\% \text{ limit of error}$$

These two examples illustrate, first, the statistical importance of setting up direct mail experiments in such a manner as to assure a sample size adequate for meaningful projection of response within acceptable tolerances. Second, they demonstrate the need for accurate determination of the limit of error, the variation that could occur by chance alone and not as a result of significant differences in particular direct marketing efforts. When comparing the response from two diverse market segments, for example, we must recognize such "error by chance" difference during the evaluation process. In the example above, in which actual response was 1.5 percent and the error limit was calculated to be 0.243 percent, any response from continuation mailings or comparative tests within the range of 1.257 and 1.743 percent would be statistically "the same as" 1.5 percent, and such variation could have occurred sheerly by statistical chance alone, at a 95 percent level of confidence.

Fortunately, it is not necessary to perform this calculation in every instance inasmuch as probability tables have already been calculated that provide, within desired confidence levels, the sample-size requirements at various levels of response and within acceptable limits of error. Such tables for confidence levels of 95 and 99 percent are given in Appendixes A-1 and A-2 to this chapter.

MEASUREMENTS OF DIFFERENCES

Assuming that a sample has been properly selected and is of an adequate size and that the experiment itself is designed and conducted in a valid manner, it remains for the direct marketing researcher to be able to recognize and express *differences* with some degree of confidence and within an acceptable limit of error. Although knowledge of means and variances is important, there must also be comprehension of the methods used for *validating* differences between the means of two or more groups. Only through such understanding can direct marketers decide whether to change from one promotional strategy to another or from one market segment to another or to adopt a new product in place of an old one.

Typically, in direct marketing experimentation, the mean response to a direct mail solicitation is the average number of responses for each 1,000 pieces of mail sent out, and attributable to one effort (the test) in relation to another (the control) in which a single variable has been injected. That variable could be the mailing list used. Or, it could be a pricing variance or a product difference. Mean response from a control mailing is compared with mean response from one or more test mailings, each differing from the control in only a single variable. In such a comparison, the researcher must determine if, in fact, the differences are *real,* in a statistical sense, or if these differences might have occurred through chance alone. These differences in results, when they are significant, must be further related to differences in cost, if there are any. In effect, one tests the hypothesis that there is no difference between the test and the control.

Hypothesis Testing

The phrase "hypothesis testing" means that the researcher decides, on the basis of observed facts that have been collected, from observation of relative response to tests of variation of direct mail copy, for example, whether or not an assumption seems to be valid. The assumption is called the "null hypothesis" and must be stated in such a way that it can be tested. So stated, on the assumption that the null hypothesis is in fact true, one can determine the probabilities to assign to the *alternative* hypothesis. Hypotheses are typically stated in negative terms; that is, a null hypothesis (H_o) versus an alternative hypothesis (H_a) in a form such as the following:

H_o: Direct mail response from the test promotion is at or below direct mail response from the control promotion.
H_a: Direct mail response from the test promotion is above direct mail response from the control promotion.

The null hypothesis, then, states that direct mail response will *not* be better than the control. Our measurement sets out to *disprove* this null hypothesis. The probability of this happening might be very small, especially considering that the experiment involves a new and untried test designed to outperform the control, which presumably is the best we have available at this time.

In the event that we decide to *reject* the *null* hypothesis, we reject it in favor of the alternative. In this instance, if we reject the null hypothesis that test response is at or below control response, we do so in favor of the alternative that test response is significantly better than control response.

Whether or not the result in a test is significant is a matter to be decided by the direct marketer making the test. Some results, as one would suspect, are more "significant" than others. Because of this, a statistician puts a special interpretation on the word "significant"; the term "significant" is associated with a specific probability, often denoted by the Greek letter alpha (α), which is decided on prior to testing the hypothesis. The researcher might state that the hypothesis (of equality) will be rejected only if the result is significant at a level of, say, 0.05 (5 percent). That is, the test result must diverge far enough from the control result, in the manner stated in the hypothesis, so that such a result would occur with the probability of 0.05 or less if the hypothesis was true. The statement of a level of significance should be made *prior* to testing the hypothesis in order to avoid vacillation on the part of the decision maker when the actual response is observed.

"A Priori" vs. "A Posteriori" Analysis

At this juncture, a differentiation should be made between the statistical analysis used in setting up a test, particularly the choice of sample size, *before the fact* ("a priori"), and the statistical analysis used in evaluating a test for significant differences *after the fact* ("a posteriori").

As noted earlier in discussing sampling, a priori analysis assumes (1) a response level, (2) a confidence level, and (3) an acceptable variation for limit of error to be deemed significant, if attained. Based on these three assumptions, sample size can be determined by formula (see page 63).

A posteriori analysis, performed *after* the test vs. control experiment has been conducted, uses the *known* sample size and *known* response level as inputs to a calculation of confidence intervals; that is, the degree of variation or limit of error associated with varying levels of significance. For an $\alpha = 0.05$, there is one set of very broad limits; for an $\alpha = 0.10$, there is a set of different, more narrowly defined limits; for an $\alpha = 0.25$, there is a set of different and even more narrowly defined limits.

In a priori analysis the direct marketing decision maker is asked to use his or her best judgment in arriving at three assumptions:

expected response, confidence level, and acceptable limits of error. In a posteriori analysis, having already established a confidence level in the a priori setting (and having the willingness to live with the choice after the fact) together with known sample size and response level, the variation (limit of error) around the known response level becomes a simple mechanical calculation as shown on page 65.

Note that a posteriori analysis is possible regardless of the level of response; the analysis can be made even if the actual level achieved differs widely from the level assumed in the a priori analysis. The important point is: test results must be read and calculations must be made in relation to what actually occurred, irrespective of what was assumed would occur at the time the test was initiated.

An Illustrative Example

To illustrate the application of the statistical procedures developed thus far in this chapter, let's assume that we have a control promotional strategy that we want to "test" in the form of an experiment against a new promotional strategy. Past experience indicates we can expect a 2 percent response rate from the control promotion.

Here is the framework within which the testing activity will proceed:

1 State the hypothesis
2 Develop, by a priori analysis, the assumptions required and compute the appropriate sample size
3 Structure and perform the test experiment
4 Develop, by a posteriori analysis, statistics for judging hypothesis validity
5 Make the decision

This procedure sounds simple and appears to be reasonable. Let's follow it through, step-by-step.

1. State the Hypothesis The null hypothesis should be structured as H_o: Direct mail response from the test promotion is at or below direct mail response from the control promotion.

Although it is not necessary to state an alternative hypothesis at this stage, so doing could imply that we are hoping to reject the null hypothesis in favor of the alternative; that is, the tested promotion would be better than the control, so that H_a: Direct mail response from the test promotion is above direct mail response from the control promotion.

2. A Priori Analysis   The response level of 2 percent is the first of three assumptions. The second assumption is the significance level, which, when $\alpha = 0.05$, describes a confidence level of 95 percent. (The confidence level is equal to 1.0 minus α, thus $1.0 - 0.05 = 0.95$, or 95 percent.) The final assumption relates to "limit of error" or "variation around the mean" or more descriptively, the error limits we wish to maintain around the assumed level of response. In this example, we will assume 15 percent.

Having established figures for our three assumptions, 2 percent response, 95 percent confidence level, and 15 percent limit of error, we can either access the tables or use the formula on page 63 to establish the sample size. The three assumptions and resultant sample size are summarized in Figure 3-5. Figure 3-5 shows the effect of the 15 percent error limit. At a 95 percent confidence level, any response below 2.3 percent would not be better than a control response (as assumed) of 2.0 percent.

3. Structure of the Test   Having determined (from Appendix Table A-1, page 79) an objective sample size of 8,365 pieces to be mailed for the control and a comparable volume for the test promotion and having obtained the sample in a valid manner, we conduct the

Expected (Assumed) Response: 20/M Pieces Mailed (2%)

Significance Level (α): .05

Confidence Level $(1.0 - \alpha) = 95\%$

Limits of Error:

%	Response/M Pieces Mailed
+15%	20/M + 3/M = 23/M (2.3%)
−15%	20/M − 3/M = 17/M (1.7%)

Sample Size: 8,365 Pieces To Be Mailed

Figure 3-5   A priori analysis of illustrative example.

experiment through release of the test mailing vs. the control mailing.

4. A Posteriori Analysis   When all results are in, we examine the response level of both the test and the control promotions. One evaluation procedure for determining if an observed difference is (or is not) *statistically significant* is the chi-square (χ^2) test, as described on pages 70–71.

5. Make the Decision   Our decision in accepting or rejecting the promotion test in our experiment should be clear-cut, based on the a posteriori analysis.

Types of Errors in Hypothesis Testing

There are two types of error that can occur in tests of hypotheses. A Type I error results when the decision maker rejects the null hypothesis even though it is, in fact, true. In this instance the "wrong" decision involves taking an action when one shouldn't. The probability of doing this is fixed and equal to α. Note that α determines the critical rareness of a result, so rare that we prefer to reject the null hypothesis rather than believe that an event that rare actually occurred. Thus, α measures the probability of committing a Type I error.

The other type of error is Type II error. A Type II error occurs when the decision maker accepts the null hypothesis when it is, in fact, *not* true. In this instance the "wrong" decision is to not do something when one should. The probability associated with a Type II error is called beta (β) which, as contrasted with α, is somewhat more difficult to measure, particularly in a priori analysis. It requires a fixed value, other than the one assumed within the null hypothesis, around which confidence intervals associated with an alternative hypothesis can be based. Although we are chiefly concerned with Type II errors in a posteriori analysis, they can, in opportunity costs, be every bit as expensive as Type I errors. We usually think of "wrong" decisions in terms of doing something when we should not, but there is a lost "opportunity" cost (or a revenue foregone) associated with *not* doing something when we should!

These error types can be further described by referring to the table shown in Figure 3-6. Note that, before a decision is reached, both risks of error exist. After the decision, the decision maker may or may not have made an error. Only validation testing (that is, a second test "in reverse") will tell and even that test will be subject to all the same uncertainty associated with the first test.

The graph shown in Figure 3-7 further displays the risk of error. Some explanation of this graph is in order. The "actual response/ M" portion of the graph for the control represents the result generated from the control section of the test. The shape of the graph is determined both by response level and by sample size. The same is true for the test result and its graph. The dotted line represents the value above which, for the test portion of the experiment, one would reject the null hypothesis (of equality of response) in favor of an alternative that the test promotion is better. Note how α and β relate to decisions to reject or accept the null hypothesis.

A very important point can be made from the graph and from the knowledge that the larger the sample size, the less dispersed (spread out) will be the graph. Raising the sample size *decreases* the probability associated with *both* types of errors *simultaneously. Thus we become less likely to make wrong decisions as the sample size increases.* Also, we would be able to judge smaller differences as significant, by using larger samples.

This examination of risks should have even the die-hard nonbeliever convinced that probability theory is a way of *measuring risk* and *assessing uncertainty,* not a way of *eliminating either*! To make an adequate decision, the direct marketing researcher must sample a population, measure relevant variables (one at a time), compute statistics using these variables, infer something about the probability distributions that exist in the population, and, finally, make a decision based on the chance of incurring either a Type I or Type II error.

Statistical Evaluation of Differences

Frequently, when evaluating the results of an experiment and comparing the response from a test with the response from a control, one needs to know if a difference is (or is not) *statistically significant*. The chi-square (χ^2) test is commonly used for determining such a difference.[7] The null hypothesis offered in

Course of Action	Null Hypothesis Is	
	True	False
Accept Null Hypothesis	No Error	Type II Error P (Type II) = β
Reject Null Hypothesis	Type I Error P (Type I) = α	No Error

Figure 3-6 Error types and associated actions.

[7] Other statistical techniques used for measuring significant differences include ANOVA (analysis of variance, the F-test), the T-test (for sample sizes through 30), and the Z-test (for sample sizes larger than 30).

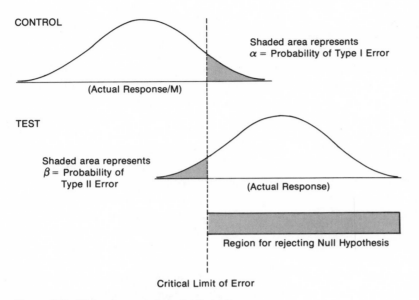

Figure 3-7 Risks of error in hypothesis testing.

making the determination is that there is, in fact, no difference between the response from the test and the response from the control. A statistic χ^2 is computed from the observed samples and compared with a table (see Appendix B, on page 81) that lists probabilities for a theoretical sampling distribution.

The shape of a χ^2 distribution varies according to the number of degrees of freedom, defined as the number of observations that are allowed to vary. The number of degrees of freedom is determined by multiplying the number of observations in a row (minus 1) times the number of observations in a column (minus 1) thus: $(r - 1)(c - 1)$, where r is the number of rows and c is the number of columns. For example, the contingency table below, expressed as "2 × 2" (and read "2 by 2") would involve just one degree of freedom, $(2 - 1)(2 - 1) = 1$. A table of this form can be used for evaluating the significance of the difference between a test and its control in an experiment:

	Test	Control	Totals
Response	A	C	A + C
Nonresponse	B	D	B + D
Total mailed	A + B	C + D	A + B + C + D = N

The statistic χ^2 is computed as follows:

$$\chi^2 = \frac{N[|(A \times D) - (C \times B)| - N/2]^2}{(A + B) \times (C + D) \times (A + C) \times (B + D)}$$

This statistic has one "degree of freedom" and is compared to the table on page 81.

Here is an example:

	Test	Control	Totals
Response	200	100	300
Nonresponse	800	900	1,700
Totals	1,000	1,000	2,000

$$\chi^2 = \frac{2,000 \times [|180,000 - 80,000| - 1,000]^2}{1,000 \times 1,000 \times 300 \times 1,700}$$

= 38.4, which is significant at the 99 + percent level since it exceeds the value in the χ^2 table for one degree of freedom for a significance level of 0.001, given as 10.83.

CONTROL OF EXPERIMENTATION

Direct marketing is susceptible to experimentation by its very nature. One reason this is so is that the direct marketer has complete control over not only what is tested but also the manner in which the experiment is to be conducted. One area that cannot be controlled, of course, is the marketplace itself, including conditions of the environment at any particular time as well as the inconsistency of human behavior.

Direct marketing experimentation is usually performed under the most rigidly controlled circumstances, with but one purpose in mind: to assure that only the test factor is allowed to vary. Thereafter, the results of an experiment are projected to a population as similar to the test sample as is feasible, by virtue of the methodology associated with selecting that sample in the first place.

Direct marketers do not, however, enjoy a completely pure laboratory environment; rather, it is a marketplace environment. These two environments differ significantly in the degree of control that can be exercised over the exogenous factors that affect the realities of the marketplace environment. A few examples will accentuate this point.

• Does seasonality affect results?

• Is the list used in the continuation mailing to the total population derived from the same group as the test sample?
• How does the environment in which the experiment was conducted compare with that of the continuation; that is, current economic conditions, consumer optimism, and world events? All can be significantly different.
• At what stage is the product in its life cycle; that is, have new models been developed and is there increasing competition?

Put simply, the actual level of response of even a meticulously controlled experiment may not always be projectable into the future. Conditions might be different. Thus, whereas the *relationship* between a test and its control may be the same, that is, one is still better than the other, the entire level of response for both might be either higher or lower than that originally experienced.

Extent of Experimentation

Under rigidly controlled conditions, direct marketing offers a great deal of opportunity for experimentation. It is this opportunity that provides an environment susceptible to measurement and accountability. It is the availability of lists and data about these lists, too, which provide populations from which scientifically determined samples can be drawn in order to properly conduct experiments. Experimentation can be conducted within lists or segments of them. Additionally, the profiling of these lists makes it possible to further describe market segments for prospecting whether the medium be direct mail, magazines and newspapers, or television and radio.

Within such list refinements, described as market segments, product and price variations can be tested. So can the multitude of variables that compose promotional strategies: copy, art, graphics, color, format, and the offer itself. Individual components of advertising can be tested or the effort itself, such as a completely new direct mail package, can be tested in its entirety. With this limitless array of possibilities, however, it is exceedingly important to test only the *important* things and to test them *adequately*. "Adequately" refers to not only the size of the sample but also the nature of the sample. "Important" refers to the *big* things such as product/services, media, offers, formats, timing.

Direct marketers of an earlier era, once they had discovered the applicability of experimentation to what they did, tested a host of relatively insignificant things, which, even if they worked, caused little difference. A few of these insignificant factors, which the cost of today's experimentation makes even less susceptible to testing, include the manner of addressing (typing vs. handwriting vs. computer labels), the manner of paying postage (stamps vs. meter vs. printed indicia), the covering of the window in a mailing envelope (glassine vs. cellophane vs. open window), the color of ink used for the signature on a letter. Today's direct marketers test the big things, the important things. And, they test in a manner that will provide statistically valid results that are projectable. To assure control, they test one variable at a time or everything, such as a complete package or a new product. Even though the tools are there, they try not to become "test happy." As we have seen,

the less the potential difference in an experiment, the higher the cost of the test.

A priori planning of experiments includes proper structuring. Not only must samples be obtained that are representative and of adequate size, but also experiments must be structured so that every test segment is related to a control, even if this control, as in the case of a brand-new product, is a historical reference or a break-even calculation. In experimenting with direct mail, nth name selections can provide random samples. In other print media, including newspapers and magazines, A/B splits are often possible so that every other issue, as printed, contains either the test or the control advertisement.

Proper scheduling, including timely release and adequate key coding, is of great importance. Figure 3-8 visualizes the form of a "mailing schedule" that could be used to describe not only the purpose of the test but also its various components, costs, and expected results, for the test segment as well as the control.

A posteriori evaluation is essential in that it faces the rigors of statistics or the tests of significance. Do we observe, as a result of our experimentation, any significant differences between tests and controls? Obviously, we cannot measure these differences unless we have a record of results for all segments of the experiment. Figure 3-9 visualizes a form that can be used to record response on either a day-to-day or a week-to-week basis. Not only must the experiment be adequately described, a separate sheet for each test segment as well as the control, but also the nature of the results must be tabulated and identified. Recording is facilitated by the use of a *key code* on each response device. In the case of direct mail, this can be a unique number or other identifying feature placed on the order form coming back to the direct marketer. When the telephone is used for response, the key

MAILING SCHEDULE

☐ STANDARD—OR ☐ TEST OF —-- ☐ PRODUCT ☐ MARKET ☐ PRESENTATION

REPORT DATE---

LIST		STATE OR SEGMENT	JOB NO.	TYPE	MAILING DATE	ORIGINATED BY	DATE ORIGINATED

GENERAL DESCRIPTION

PRODUCT AND OFFER

STANDARD COSTS   SALES EXPECTED

per M per M

TEST COSTS

PURPOSE

SALES REQUIRED ON TEST

PRIOR TESTS

☐ NO ☐ YES—EXPLAIN

☐ STANDARD ANALYSIS

☐ OTHER—EXPLAIN

DETAIL INSTRUCTIONS

☐ APPROVED   SIGNATURE

☐ DISAPPROVED

TEST NO.	DESCRIPTION OF TEST	KEY NO	QUANTITY	O. S. ENV.	NOTICE OR APP.	LETTER	RETURN ENVELOPE	SAFETY ENVELOPE	OTHER	OTHER

MAILING COMPONENTS

SUPPLIES	FORM NUMBER										
	QUANTITY ORDERED										
	DATE AVAILABLE										

Figure 3-8 An example of a mailing schedule for an experiment.

73

DATE RELEASED			STATE			KEY					

TEST #	KIND OF TEST					REMARKS					

MAKE UP OF OFFER	O. S. ENV	LETTER	ORDER FORM	RET. ENV.	INSERT			COPY #			

WEEK ENDING			# MAILINGS		VOLUME			# SALES			#UNITS			# CONVERSIONS		
#	MO.	DAY	CURRENT	TO DATE	CURRENT	TO DATE	P/M	CURRENT	TO DATE	P/M	#	MO.	CUM	CURRENT	TO DATE	P/M
1											1					
2											2					
3											3					
4											4					
5											5					
6											6					
7											7					
8											8					
9											9					
10											10					
11											11					
12											12					
13											13					
14											14					
15											15					
16											16					
17											17					
18											18					
19											19					
20											20					
21											21					
22											22					
23											23					
24											24					
25											25					
26											26					

Figure 3-9 An example of a key record.

code can be a unique telephone number, a departmental number, or an individual's name. Many direct marketers using the telephone extensively for response ask respondents for the advertisement or catalog that motivated their actions.

Advanced statistical techniques for measuring and evaluating experimentation, multivariate regression analysis, discriminant analysis, factor analysis, and cluster analysis, are discussed in Chapter 4. They, too, play a vital role in a posteriori evaluation of experimentation as well as profiling market segments and observing differences between respondents and nonrespondents.

Survey Alternatives to Experimentation

It is apparent that direct marketers, as opposed to general marketers, favor experimentation over survey research because many of the techniques used to ask prospects if they *intend to buy* can be translated to direct marketing offers wherein the prospect is actually *asked to buy*.

One happy compromise of survey research with experimental research, often used when a new product is being contemplated but is not yet actually available in the marketplace, is called *dry testing*. This technique involves sending out promotion for a proposed magazine, for example, even though the magazine does not yet exist. If the response is adequate, the magazine is published. Those who use the dry-testing technique must be meticulously careful not to misrepresent; the promotional effort itself could explain the objective. Remittances, if received, should be returned promptly and those who respond should receive first priority if and when the product ordered becomes a reality.

Another survey research tool frequently used by direct marketers is the *focus group interview,* wherein unstructured small groups, representative of appropriate market segments, under skilled leadership, converse in a relaxed environment relative to the subject of the research, which is often not specifically identified. Although such groups can be used for creative stimulation or evaluation, they cannot be scientifically controlled. Scientific projections are really not possible.

Motivation research, involving *in-depth interviews,* has been used in survey research, also, by direct marketers. In the environment of an unstructured conversation between an interviewer and a subject, attempts are made to ascertain attitudes and motivations. Like focus group interviews, in-depth interviews are not statistically quantifiable and are used mainly to obtain specific background information. Projections involve a high degree of subjectivity.

SUMMARY

Direct marketing is research-oriented and is especially susceptible to the tools and techniques of experimentation. Such experimentation is most often called "testing" by practitioners and usually measures the impact of changing a variable within product, price, place, or promotion.

Although research is concerned with fact-finding and information gathering, it has as its objective problem solving or action recommending. The keys to research are data. Data are categorized as *secondary* (collected originally for another purpose) and *primary* (collected specifically for the research need). Collection of primary data involves either survey research or experimental research, the latter most often utilized in testing by direct marketers.

Survey research observes various activities as they naturally arise in the environment whereas experimentation involves the manipulation of one or more independent variables to determine their influence on an outcome, which is the dependent variable. Valid experiments require controls and randomized samples. In designing experiments it is important to understand the methods for obtaining samples and determining sample sizes. Otherwise, resultant estimations and predictions will not be helpful. Samples may be obtained in many ways. Determination of sample size is concerned with confidence level, error limit, and expected percent of response. Sample size and error limit can be calculated statistically, with tables readily available for such determination.

Direct marketers must evaluate statistically significant differences in observed responses between test and control. The chi-square distribution describes a statistical tool for analyzing the significance of such differences.

Experiments must be controlled in ways that are measurable and accountable. It is important to schedule experiments carefully and to record results for accurate evaluation.

CASE: STRUCTURING AN EXPERIMENT

Learning Objective

The purpose of this case study is to stimulate consideration of key elements that determine the adequacy and validity of a direct marketing experiment: sample design, sample size, conduct of the experiment, and measurement of difference. The need for experimentation and the importance of control should also be considered.

Overview

Experimentation, or testing, as it is more often called, is second nature to direct marketers. All too often, however, such experimentation is conducted under the guise of scientific procedure, but the sample selected is not representative, the structure of the test itself is often faulty, and the sample size is inadequate. The resultant measurement of differences between the segments of the test reveals differences that are not statistically significant.

True experimentation, if such is to be ac-

complished properly, should be structured in a valid manner. The results, when measured statistically, should be at an acceptable level of significance so as to provide a prediction with which the researcher can be comfortable. This case provides a means for evaluating a typical direct marketing test structure, one intended to measure the response differences among five advertisements run in a national newspaper.

Procedure

Read the learning objective, the overview, and the case that follows. Be prepared to discuss the validity of the following elements of this experiment: (1) objective of the test; (2) design of the test and the determination of the sample; (3) adequacy of sample size; (4) measurement and significance of differences; (5) adequacy of the resultant prediction; (6) explanation of why the response differences occurred.

Case[8]

Omaha Steaks International has offered six 6-ounce filet mignons, 1¼ inch thick, for $29.95 (plus $2.00 shipping/handling) through space advertising in print media. In the October 2, 1979, issue of *The Wall Street Journal,* the direct marketer scheduled an experiment of a control advertisement (A) against four test advertisements (B), (C), (D), (E), all of which are illustrated in Figure 3-10.

In testing the existing control advertisement against the four alternatives, each of which had a particular promotional theme, it was desired to find out if the existing control or any of the four new advertisements would produce better response and more sales. After experimentation, it was determined that the existing control advertisement did, in fact, produce orders at a lower cost per sale than

---

[8] This case was developed from data provided by Fred Simon, Omaha Steaks International, Omaha, Neb. 68127.

Figure 3-10 Alternative space advertisements (control plus four experiments) tested by Omaha Steaks International.

did any of the alternatives tested. This determination was based on the following results:

Advertising copy	Circulation	Adv. cost	Results index
(A) "Try A Little Tenderness" (Control)	367,000	$ 578	100%
(B) "Perfect Steaks" (Experiment 1)	634,000	$ 824	28%
(C) "Journal" (Experiment 2)	652,000	$ 863	29%
(D) "Love At First Bite" (Experiment 3)	458,000	$ 721	74%
(E) "Attention Steak Lovers" (Experiment 4)	652,000	$1,027	76%

Although the product offer is itself identical in each of the five direct response advertisements, there is considerable difference in the benefits featured in each of the headlines as well as the body copy and illustrations. It was presumed that, if any of the four experimental advertisements resulted in more sales than did the control, that sales differential could be attributed to the differences in the advertisements themselves, provided that the sample is properly drawn, that the sample size is adequate for statistical validity, and that there is, in fact, a significant difference when the results are measured.

DISCUSSION QUESTIONS

1 For what reasons might a survey of buying expectations not be a valid indication of actual behavior in the marketplace?
2 Distinguish the difference between surveys and experiments. Which is more used by direct marketers and why?
3 Where might a direct marketing researcher obtain secondary data about:
  a age distribution of a population?
  b number of corrugated carton manufacturers in an MSA (Metropolitan Statistical Area)?
  c number of households with automatic dishwashers in a ZIP Code area?
  d retail sales of shopping goods in a county?

4 What are the advantages and disadvantages of seeking primary data by each of these survey methods:
  a personal interview?
  b telephone interview?
  c mail questionnaire?
  d observation?
5 To what questions besides those specifically prescribed in this chapter might a direct marketer seek answers through experimentation (testing)?
6 What is the ideal way for a direct marketer to structure an experiment (test)?
7 Why is the determination of a proper sample size important in an experiment (test)? What must be considered?
8 In testing a hypothesis, is a Type I or Type II error more serious? That is, are there greater consequences in (I) "doing something when you shouldn't," or (II) "not doing something when you should?"
9 Why is it important in measuring an experiment (test) that the researcher determine the statistical significance level of observed differences?
10 Does the direct marketing researcher have absolute and complete control over an experiment? Discuss possible situations in which the researcher may not.
11 Why should direct marketing researchers confine experimentation to only those tests that have high consequences?

LIMITS OF ERROR (EXPRESSED AS PERCENTAGE POINTS)

R (Response)	.02	.04	.06	.08	.10	.12	.14	.16	.18	.20	.30	.40	.50	.60	.70
.1	95,929	23,982	10,659	5,995	3,837	2,665	1,957	1,499	1,184	959	426	240	153	106	78
.2	191,666	47,916	21,296	11,979	7,667	5,324	3,911	2,994	2,366	1,917	852	479	307	213	156
.3	287,211	71,803	31,912	17,951	11,488	7,978	5,861	4,487	3,546	2,872	1,276	718	459	319	234
.4	382,564	95,641	42,507	23,910	15,303	10,627	7,807	5,977	4,723	3,826	1,700	956	612	425	312
.5	477,724	119,431	53,080	29,858	19,109	13,270	9,749	7,464	5,987	4,777	2,123	1,194	764	530	390
.6	572,693	143,173	63,632	35,793	22,908	15,908	11,687	8,948	7,070	5,727	2,545	1,432	916	636	467
.7	667,470	166,867	74,163	41,717	26,699	18,541	13,622	10,429	8,240	6,675	2,966	1,669	1,068	741	545
.8	762,054	190,514	84,673	47,628	30,482	21,168	15,552	11,907	9,408	7,621	3,387	1,905	1,219	847	622
.9	856,447	214,112	95,160	53,528	34,258	23,790	17,478	13,382	10,573	8,564	3,806	2,141	1,370	951	699
1.0	950,648	237,662	105,628	59,415	38,026	26,407	19,401	14,854	11,736	9,506	4,225	2,376	1,521	1,056	776
1.1	1,044,656	261,164	116,072	65,291	41,786	29,018	21,319	16,322	12,897	10,446	4,643	2,611	1,671	1,160	853
1.2	1,138,472	284,618	126,496	71,155	45,539	31,624	23,234	17,788	14,055	11,385	5,060	2,846	1,821	1,265	929
1.3	1,232,097	308,024	136,899	77,006	49,284	34,225	25,145	19,251	15,211	12,321	5,476	3,080	1,971	1,369	1,006
1.4	1,325,529	331,382	147,280	82,845	53,021	36,820	27,051	20,711	16,364	13,255	5,891	3,314	2,121	1,473	1,082
1.5	1,418,769	354,692	157,640	88,673	56,751	39,410	28,954	22,168	17,515	14,188	6,305	3,547	2,270	1,576	1,158
1.6	1,511,818	377,954	167,980	94,489	60,473	41,995	30,853	23,622	18,664	15,118	6,719	3,780	2,419	1,680	1,234
1.7	1,604,674	401,168	178,297	100,292	64,187	44,574	32,748	25,073	19,811	16,047	7,132	4,012	2,567	1,783	1,310
1.8	1,697,338	424,334	188,592	106,083	67,894	47,148	34,639	26,521	20,955	16,973	7,543	4,243	2,716	1,886	1,385
1.9	1,789,810	447,452	198,868	111,863	71,592	49,717	36,526	27,966	22,096	17,898	7,955	4,474	2,863	1,988	1,461
2.0	1,882,090	470,523	209,121	117,631	75,284	52,280	38,410	29,407	23,235	18,821	8,365	4,705	3,011	2,091	1,536
2.1	1,974,178	493,544	219,352	123,386	78,967	54,838	40,289	30,846	24,372	19,742	8,774	4,935	3,158	2,193	1,611
2.2	2,066,074	516,518	229,564	129,129	82,643	57,391	42,165	32,282	25,507	20,661	9,182	5,165	3,306	2,295	1,686
2.3	2,157,778	539,444	239,753	134,861	86,311	59,938	44,036	33,715	26,638	21,578	9,590	5,394	3,452	2,397	1,761
2.4	2,249,290	562,322	249,920	140,581	89,972	62,480	45,903	35,145	27,769	22,493	9,997	5,623	3,599	2,499	1,836
2.5	2,340,609	585,152	260,068	146,288	93,624	65,017	47,767	36,572	28,896	23,406	10,403	5,851	3,745	2,600	1,911
2.6	2,431,737	607,934	270,192	151,983	97,269	67,547	49,627	37,996	30,021	24,317	10,807	6,079	3,891	2,702	1,985
2.7	2,522,673	630,668	280,296	157,667	100,907	70,074	51,483	39,416	31,144	25,227	11,211	6,307	4,036	2,803	2,059
2.8	2,613,416	653,354	290,380	163,339	104,537	72,595	53,335	40,834	32,264	26,134	11,615	6,534	4,181	2,904	2,133
2.9	2,703,968	675,992	300,440	168,998	108,159	75,110	55,183	42,249	33,382	27,039	12,017	6,760	4,326	3,004	2,207
3.0	2,794,328	698,582	310,480	174,645	111,773	77,620	57,026	43,661	34,497	27,943	12,419	6,986	4,471	3,105	2,281
3.1	2,884,495	721,124	320,499	180,281	115,380	80,125	58,867	45,070	35,611	28,845	12,820	7,211	4,615	3,205	2,355
3.2	2,974,470	743,618	330,496	185,904	118,979	82,623	60,702	46,476	36,721	29,745	13,220	7,436	4,759	3,305	2,428
3.3	3,064,254	766,063	340,471	191,516	122,570	85,118	62,535	47,878	37,830	30,642	13,619	7,660	4,903	3,404	2,501
3.4	3,153,845	788,461	350,427	197,115	126,154	87,607	64,364	49,278	38,936	31,538	14,017	7,884	5,046	3,504	2,574
3.5	3,243,244	810,811	360,360	202,703	129,730	90,089	66,188	50,675	40,040	32,432	14,414	8,108	5,189	3,603	2,647
3.6	3,332,452	833,113	370,271	208,278	133,298	92,568	68,009	52,069	41,141	33,325	14,811	8,331	5,332	3,702	2,720
3.7	3,421,467	855,367	380,163	213,842	136,859	95,041	69,825	53,460	42,240	34,214	15,207	8,554	5,474	3,801	2,793
3.8	3,510,290	877,572	390,031	219,393	140,412	97,507	71,638	54,848	43,336	35,103	15,601	8,776	5,616	3,900	2,865
3.9	3,598,921	899,730	399,878	224,932	143,957	99,969	73,446	56,233	44,430	35,989	15,995	8,997	5,758	3,998	2,938
4.0	3,687,360	921,840	409,706	230,460	147,494	102,426	75,252	57,615	45,522	36,874	16,388	9,218	5,900	4,097	3,010

Appendix A-1 Sample sizes for responses between 0.1% and 4.0%. Confidence level 95%.
(Source: John E. McNichols, Alan Drey Company, Inc., 333 N. Michigan Avenue, Chicago, IL 60601.)

R (Response)	LIMITS OF ERROR (EXPRESSED AS PERCENTAGE POINTS)			.08	.10	.12	.14	.16	.18	.20	.30	.40	.50	.60	.70
	.02	.04	.06												
.1	165,709	41,427	18,412	10,357	6,628	4,603	3,381	2,589	2,046	1,657	736	414	265	184	135
.2	331,087	82,772	36,787	20,693	13,243	9,197	6,756	5,173	4,087	3,311	1,471	827	529	368	270
.3	496,132	124,033	55,126	31,008	19,845	13,781	10,125	7,752	6,125	4,961	2,205	1,240	794	551	405
.4	660,846	165,212	73,427	41,303	26,434	18,356	13,486	10,325	8,158	6,608	2,937	1,652	1,057	734	539
.5	825,228	206,307	91,692	51,577	33,009	22,923	16,841	12,894	10,187	8,252	3,667	2,063	1,320	916	673
.6	989,279	247,320	109,919	61,830	39,571	27,480	20,189	15,457	12,213	9,893	4,396	2,473	1,582	1,099	807
.7	1,152,997	288,249	128,111	72,062	46,120	32,027	23,530	18,015	14,234	11,530	5,124	2,282	1,845	1,281	941
.8	1,316,384	329,096	146,265	82,274	52,655	36,565	26,864	20,569	16,251	13,164	5,850	3,291	2,106	1,462	1,074
.9	1,479,439	369,859	164,381	92,465	59,178	41,095	30,192	23,116	18,264	14,794	6,575	3,698	2,367	1,643	1,208
1.0	1,642,163	410,541	182,463	102,635	65,687	45,616	33,513	25,658	20,273	16,422	7,299	4,105	2,627	1,825	1,340
1.1	1,804,554	451,138	200,505	112,784	72,182	50,126	36,827	28,195	22,278	18,045	8,020	4,511	2,887	2,004	1,473
1.2	1,966,614	491,654	218,512	122,913	78,665	54,628	40,134	30,728	24,279	19,666	8,740	4,917	3,146	2,185	1,605
1.3	2,128,342	532,085	236,482	133,021	85,134	59,121	43,435	33,255	26,275	21,283	9,459	5,321	3,405	2,365	1,737
1.4	2,289,739	572,435	254,414	143,108	91,590	63,603	46,729	35,777	28,268	22,897	10,176	5,724	3,663	2,544	1,869
1.5	2,450,803	612,700	272,310	153,175	98,032	68,077	50,016	38,293	30,256	24,508	10,892	6,127	3,921	2,723	2,000
1.6	2,611,536	652,884	290,170	163,221	104,461	72,542	53,296	40,805	32,241	26,115	11,607	6,529	4,178	2,901	2,132
1.7	2,771,937	692,984	307,992	173,246	110,877	76,997	56,569	43,311	34,221	27,719	12,319	6,930	4,435	3,079	2,263
1.8	2,932,007	733,002	325,777	183,250	117,280	81,444	59,836	45,812	36,197	29,320	13,030	7,330	4,691	3,257	2,393
1.9	3,091,744	772,936	343,527	193,234	123,670	85,881	63,096	48,308	38,169	30,917	13,741	7,729	4,946	3,435	2,523
2.0	3,251,150	812,788	361,238	203,197	130,046	90,309	66,350	50,799	40,137	32,512	14,449	8,128	5,202	3,612	2,654
2.1	3,410,224	852,556	378,912	213,139	136,409	94,728	69,596	53,284	42,100	34,102	15,156	8,525	5,456	3,789	2,783
2.2	3,568,967	892,242	396,551	223,060	142,759	99,138	72,836	55,765	44,061	35,690	15,862	8,922	5,710	3,965	2,913
2.3	3,727,377	931,844	414,152	232,961	149,095	103,537	76,068	58,239	46,016	37,273	16,566	9,318	5,964	4,141	3,042
2.4	3,885,456	971,364	431,716	242,841	155,418	107,929	79,294	60,710	47,968	38,855	17,268	9,714	6,216	4,317	3,172
2.5	4,043,203	1,010,800	449,245	252,700	161,728	112,311	82,513	63,174	49,915	40,432	17,970	10,108	6,469	4,492	3,300
2.6	4,200,619	1,050,155	466,734	262,538	168,025	116,682	85,726	65,634	51,859	42,006	18,669	10,501	6,721	4,667	3,429
2.7	4,357,702	1,089,425	484,187	272,356	174,308	121,046	88,932	68,088	53,798	43,577	19,367	10,894	6,972	4,842	3,557
2.8	4,514,454	1,128,614	501,606	282,153	180,578	125,402	92,131	70,538	55,734	45,145	20,064	11,286	7,223	5,016	3,685
2.9	4,670,874	1,167,718	518,984	291,929	186,835	129,745	95,324	72,982	57,664	46,708	20,759	11,677	7,473	5,189	3,812
3.0	4,826,963	1,206,741	536,327	301,685	193,079	134,081	98,508	75,421	59,591	48,270	21,453	12,067	7,723	5,363	3,940
3.1	4,982,719	1,245,679	553,635	311,420	199,309	138,409	101,687	77,854	61,514	49,827	22,145	12,457	7,972	5,536	4,067
3.2	5,138,144	1,284,536	570,903	321,134	205,526	142,725	104,858	80,284	63,433	51,381	22,836	12,845	8,221	5,709	4,194
3.3	5,293,237	1,323,309	588,135	330,827	211,729	147,034	108,024	82,706	65,348	52,932	23,525	13,233	8,469	5,881	4,321
3.4	5,447,999	1,362,000	605,333	340,500	217,920	151,333	111,183	85,124	67,258	54,480	24,213	13,620	8,716	6,053	4,447
3.5	5,602,428	1,400,607	622,490	350,152	224,097	155,621	114,334	87,537	69,165	56,024	24,899	14,006	8,964	6,224	4,573
3.6	5,756,526	1,439,132	639,611	359,783	230,261	159,903	117,479	89,945	71,067	57,565	25,584	14,391	9,210	6,395	4,699
3.7	5,910,292	1,477,573	656,699	369,393	236,412	164,174	120,616	92,347	72,966	59,103	26,268	14,775	9,456	6,567	4,824
3.8	6,063,727	1,515,932	673,746	378,983	242,549	168,435	123,749	94,745	74,860	60,637	26,949	15,159	9,702	6,737	4,949
3.9	6,216,829	1,554,207	690,756	388,552	248,673	172,688	126,872	97,137	76,750	62,168	27,629	15,542	9,947	6,907	5,074
4.0	6,369,600	1,592,400	707,733	398,100	254,784	176,933	129,991	99,525	78,636	63,696	28,309	15,924	10,191	7,077	5,199

Appendix A-2 Sample sizes for responses between 0.1% and 4.0%. Confidence level 99%.
(Source: John E. McNichols, Alan Drey Company, Inc., 333 N. Michigan Avenue, Chicago, IL 60601.)

df	.99	.98	.95	.90	.80	.70	.50	.30	.20	.10	.05	.02	.01	.001
					Probability under H_o that $\chi^2 \geq$ Chi-Square									
1	.00016	.00063	.0039	.016	.064	.15	.46	1.07	1.64	2.71	3.84	5.41	6.64	10.83
2	.02	.04	.10	.21	.45	.71	1.39	2.41	3.22	4.60	5.99	7.82	9.21	13.82
3	.12	.18	.35	.58	1.00	1.42	2.37	3.66	4.64	6.25	7.82	9.84	11.34	16.27
4	.30	.43	.71	1.06	1.65	2.20	3.36	4.88	5.99	7.78	9.49	11.67	13.28	18.46
5	.55	.75	1.14	1.61	2.34	3.00	4.35	6.06	7.29	9.24	11.07	13.39	15.09	20.52
6	.87	1.13	1.64	2.20	3.07	3.83	5.35	7.23	8.56	10.64	12.59	15.03	16.81	22.46
7	1.24	1.56	2.17	2.83	3.82	4.67	6.35	8.38	9.80	12.02	14.07	16.62	18.48	24.32
8	1.65	2.03	2.73	3.49	4.59	5.53	7.34	9.52	11.03	13.36	15.51	18.17	20.09	26.12
9	2.09	2.53	3.32	4.17	5.38	6.39	8.34	10.66	12.24	14.68	16.92	19.68	21.67	27.88
10	2.56	3.06	3.94	4.86	6.18	7.27	9.34	11.78	13.44	15.99	18.31	21.16	23.21	29.59
11	3.05	3.61	4.58	5.58	6.99	8.15	10.34	12.90	14.63	17.28	19.68	22.62	24.72	31.26
12	3.57	4.18	5.23	6.30	7.81	9.03	11.34	14.01	15.81	18.55	21.03	24.05	26.22	32.91
13	4.11	4.76	5.89	7.04	8.63	9.93	12.34	15.12	16.98	19.81	22.36	25.47	27.69	34.53
14	4.66	5.37	6.57	7.79	9.47	10.82	13.34	16.22	18.15	21.06	23.68	26.87	29.14	36.12
15	5.23	5.98	7.26	8.55	10.31	11.72	14.34	17.32	19.31	22.31	25.00	28.26	30.58	37.70
16	5.81	6.61	7.96	9.31	11.15	12.62	15.34	18.42	20.46	23.54	26.30	29.63	32.00	39.29
17	6.41	7.26	8.67	10.08	12.00	13.53	16.34	19.51	21.62	24.77	27.59	31.00	33.41	40.75
18	7.02	7.91	9.39	10.86	12.86	14.44	17.34	20.60	22.76	25.99	28.87	32.35	34.80	42.31
19	7.63	8.57	10.12	11.65	13.72	15.35	18.34	21.69	23.90	27.20	30.14	33.69	36.19	43.82
20	8.26	9.24	10.85	12.44	14.58	16.27	19.34	22.78	25.04	28.41	31.41	35.02	37.57	45.32
21	8.90	9.92	11.59	13.24	15.44	17.18	20.34	23.86	26.17	29.62	32.67	36.34	38.93	46.80
22	9.54	10.60	12.34	14.04	16.31	18.10	21.24	24.94	27.30	30.81	33.92	37.66	40.29	48.27
23	10.20	11.29	13.09	14.85	17.19	19.02	22.34	26.02	28.43	32.01	35.17	38.97	41.64	49.73
24	10.86	11.99	13.85	15.66	18.06	19.94	23.34	27.10	29.55	33.20	36.42	40.27	42.98	51.18
25	11.52	12.70	14.61	16.47	18.94	20.87	24.34	28.17	30.68	34.38	37.65	41.57	44.31	52.62
26	12.20	13.41	15.38	17.29	19.82	21.79	25.34	29.25	31.80	35.56	38.88	42.86	45.64	54.05
27	12.88	14.12	16.15	18.11	20.70	22.72	26.34	30.32	32.91	36.74	40.11	44.14	46.96	55.48
28	13.56	14.85	16.93	18.94	21.59	23.65	27.34	31.39	34.03	37.92	41.34	45.42	48.28	56.89
29	14.26	15.57	17.71	19.77	22.48	24.58	28.34	32.46	35.14	39.09	42.56	46.69	49.59	58.30
30	14.95	16.31	18.49	20.60	23.36	25.51	29.34	33.53	36.25	40.26	43.77	47.96	50.89	59.70

Appendix B   Critical Values of Chi-Square (χ^2). (*Source: George Kress,* Marketing Research, *1979, p. 36. Reprinted with permission of Reston Publishing Co., a Prentice-Hall Co., Reston, VA 22090.*)

MULTIVARIATE ANALYSIS IN DIRECT MARKETING

There are a variety of advanced statistical techniques used for measurement and evaluation of research and experimentation. This chapter will be concerned with those multivariate analytical techniques that have particular relevance to direct marketing: regression and correlation analysis, discriminant analysis, factor analysis, and cluster analysis. An awareness of these techniques can be of help to the direct marketing decision maker in evaluating the results of tests as well as profiling market segments and observing differences between respondents and nonrespondents in order to calculate a probability of response to a particular direct marketing effort.

MULTIVARIATE ANALYTICAL TECHNIQUES

Since most results, especially those involving human behavior, have many causes, a working knowledge of multivariate analytical techniques is essential to the direct marketing researcher. Direct marketers are conditioned to test only one independent variable at a time, but dependent variables are most often influenced by *many* independent variables, some of which can be controlled, some of which cannot.

The intent of *regression and correlation analysis* is to bring data about one or more independent variables together in order to predict the value of a dependent variable. Correlation analysis, in general, quantifies the relationship (if any) between the independent variable(s) and the dependent variable. For instance, through correlation analysis one can attempt to develop the relationship (if any) between response per thousand pieces of direct mail (the dependent variable) and the length of the letter contained within that direct mail package (the independent variable).[1] If the

values of both the independent variable(s) and the dependent variable move upward together, the correlation is positive. If one increases when the other decreases (an inverse relationship), then the correlation is negative. Highly correlated variables (positive *or* negative) are then entered into regression.

Discriminant analysis is not intended to predict the value of a dependent variable, as in regression analysis, but rather it is concerned with whether or not an event will occur and endeavors to predict the probability of the event's occurrence. Given the demographic makeup of a mailing list, for example, discriminant analysis enables the researcher to predict the likelihood of positive response to a promotion directed to that list. Note that only the *likelihood* of response is predicted in this form of analysis, and not the *level* of response.

Regression analysis was originally developed by statistically oriented economists (econometricians) to describe economic activity in terms of, for example, Gross National Product or national income. More recently, businesses and organizations have used the tools of regression analysis to predict marketing effectiveness (sales).

Discriminant analysis, on the other hand, has its roots in anthropology and in medicine. Through measurement of a patient's level of cholesterol, blood pressure, smoking habits, and other attributes, a physician is able to predict the probability that a person will have a heart attack. Similarly, the anthropologist can, through measurement, calculate the probability that a particular bone might have come from a particular type of human. Likewise, the direct marketer is able to predict potential readership of a particular magazine through analysis of the life-style characteristics of its present subscribers. A catalog merchandiser can do the same.

---

[1] Correlation between independent and dependent variables is measured by a coefficient expressed in a decimal form ranging from 0 to 1 (for positive correlation) and 0 to -1 (for negative correlation). In both instances, 1

(positive or negative) indicates a perfect correlation and 0 indicates no correlation.

Regression and Correlation Analysis[2]

In general, regression analysis is a technique for finding and describing a functional (mathematical) relationship between a dependent variable (such as sales results) and one or more independent variables (such as demographic characteristics of buyers). This is done by fitting a line to observed points (depicting relationships) in such a way as to minimize the sum of the squares of the differences between these observed points (actual response) and the estimated points (predicted response) as determined by the regression line.

When only one independent variable is used, the technique is termed simple regression. When more than one independent variable is used, it is termed multivariate regression. (In reality, the relationship is not always linear; more than likely, in direct marketing analysis, the relationship is curvilinear; that is, sales might increase at an accelerating rate relative to the rate of change of the causal variable.)

The general form of a linear regression equation is

$$Y = a + bX_1 + cX_2 + dX_3 \ldots + nX_n$$

where X = some independent variable (age of respondent, price level, promotion, offer)

a = some constant that brings the scale of X into the same scale as Y

b = some slope of a straight line or degree of relationship of X and Y

Y = the dependent variable (such as response to a mailing)

There is a degree of uncertainty or randomness associated with the equation in that every prediction involves some error. The larger the

uncertainty, the more potential for error in prediction.

The mechanics of regression and correlation analysis are shown in Figure 4-1. In this illustration, response to a direct marketing effort (Y) is evaluated according to the known educational level of respondents (X_1). The various dots on the chart (termed a scatter diagram) are the actual measured responses; that is, the response from those with less than 6 years of schooling is 1/M pieces mailed; the response from those with 8 years is 3/M; the response from those with 12 years is 5/M; and the response from those with 16 years of schooling is 14/M. The regression line is mathematically fitted among the points so that the sum of the distances between the observed points and the prediction regression line, when squared (so as to eliminate negative numbers or those below the line), is as small as possible. Thus, the definitional term often applied to regression analysis is "least squares."

In terms of the regression formula, the intercept "a" represents the amount of response that would occur under any conditions, regardless of educational level; the coefficient "b" represents the slope of the regression line measured as rise/run (vertical movement divided by horizontal movement of the regression line). The dependent variable "Y," measured on the vertical axis, is response per thousand pieces of direct marketing effort mailed whereas the horizontal axis measures the independent variable "X_1," which, in this instance, is educational level of respondent.

This example involves just one independent variable and is termed simple regression analysis. When two or more variables are involved, the process is termed multivariate and each variable enters the regression calculation in rank order of correlation (with the dependent variable), in a manner termed stepwise. Figure 4-1 could thus be extended, in stepwise fashion, to include a *second* independent variable, age of respondent, for example, as a third

[2] For a more extensive discussion of regression analysis, see George G. C. Parker and Edilberto Segura, "How to Get a Better Forecast," *Harvard Business Review,* March–April 1971, pp. 99–109.

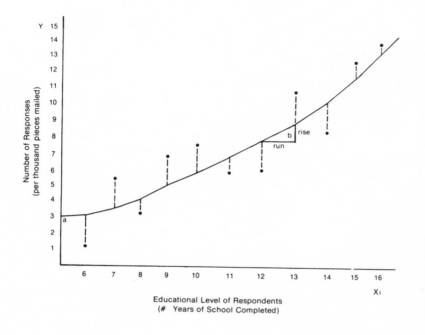

Figure 4-1 Regression and correlation analysis—"fitting a line" to the observed relationship between response to a promotional effort (Y, the dependent variable) and educational level of respondents (X_1, the independent variable).

dimension. Beyond two independent variables, the process is not easily visualized graphically, but it is not uncommon for 25 or more independent variables to interact with each other in a process of stepwise multivariate linear regression analysis.

Although Figure 4-1 visualizes a positive correlation, in which response increases as educational level increases, correlation can also be negative wherein response would increase as educational level decreases. In multivariate regression analysis, it is not uncommon to find both positive and negative correlations among the variables used. In a stepwise procedure involving a large number of independent variables, it sometimes happens that a variable will enter the regression and later be removed as the calculation proceeds. Only the absolutely smallest number of variables will result when the process is completed. This involves the principle of *parsimony,* which simply means that the regression evaluation will seek the *minimum* number of variables required for optimum explanation,

without regard to the nature of the variables. (Rarely does the addition of independent variables beyond, say, five, significantly improve the accuracy of the regression evaluation.)

In seeking, through regression analysis, a summary of relationships of independent variables to a dependent variable, the researcher must be concerned with how valid the prediction will be. As with other statistical procedures, there is an element of error involved, which mainly identifies the distance from the actual observed points to the prediction line. This error is reflected by the coefficient of correlation and is described by the statistic R. Squaring this value (R^2) gives the coefficient of determination. An R value of 0.70 (which some consider to be a minimum acceptable statistic in the use of regression analysis in direct marketing) gives an R^2 value of 0.49. This means that 49 percent of the observed difference in response is associated with (or explained by) the independent variables observed.

The b constant is the regression coefficient

and measures the slope of the regression line. It can be positive or negative, depending on whether the line slopes upward or downward. It shows the amount of change in the dependent variable, Y, which is associated with change in one (or more) independent variable(s), X.

Discriminant Analysis

Discriminant analysis is increasingly popular among direct marketers. In typical marketing situations, it has been used to note differences in such factors as promotional efforts, credit risks, and brand preferences. It has also been used to predict response to direct marketing promotional efforts through development of profiles of customer groups and relating these to the profiles of mailing lists.

An example of the use of discriminant analysis in direct marketing is reported by Zaltman and Burger.[3] The technique was used to determine variables that would discriminate between readers and nonreaders of *Reader's Digest*. Nineteen independent variables were applied to a sample of known readers and known nonreaders. The variables related to age and sex of children, family income, family mobility, husband's age group, education of husband, husband's occupation, family religious denomination, and personality scale readings.

In summary, analysis of the 19 independent variables effectively discriminated between readers and nonreaders. Families considered more likely readers included those with older husbands, fewer female children under 6 years of age, husbands who were blue-collar workers, those who had lived in fewer houses, and cases where the respondent was perceived as being "friendly." Discriminant analysis uncovered distinctions between readers and nonreaders of *Reader's Digest* and thus facilitated

search for market segments that were described by reader characteristics.

Factor Analysis

Most direct marketing organizations have accumulated a great deal of information that is stored in large databanks. To be truly useful, however, there must be an integrated approach toward the retrieval and use of this information. The electronic computer, which made possible the accumulation and storage of such data, can also be used to retrieve and analyze relevant parts of these data.

One analytical technique for coping with large numbers of independent variables is termed factor analysis. This statistical technique serves as a data-reduction method. A large number of data variables, through identification of communality, are combined into factors that convey statistically all the essential information of the original set of variables, but result in fewer, more recognizable factors than there were original variables. It does this through recognition of the fact that if there is a systematic interdependence among these *manifest* variables, this must be due to some *latent* fundamental relationship creating the communality. Thus, factor analysis makes possible not only the reduction of large bodies of data, but it can also point out relationships among the variables. Without factor analysis, these relationships are often not easy to see. Ultimately, the technique can be used to group life-styles, media, emotional stimuli, price levels, or products.

The notion of *taxonomy,* the grouping of individuals or objects, is quite straightforward. If a researcher tests a model using a sample, all people in the sample are assumed to behave according to the model and its parameters. When there is strong a priori reason to believe nonconforming individuals are present, these individuals should be grouped and either removed or analyzed separately. An example of

[3] Gerald Zaltman and Philip C. Burger, *Marketing Research: Fundamentals and Dynamics,* The Dryden Press, Hinsdale, Ill., 1975, pp. 468–472.

taxonomy, or grouping, would be in the definition of certain animals such as birds, amphibians, mammals, and rodents. Certain species fit quite easily. But how would you classify a bat? Is it a rodent or a bird?

Factor analysis and cluster analysis are both techniques for grouping variables or characteristics or persons or objects into natural aggregations. They are techniques allowing the researcher to examine the properties of the data as well as of the population studied. Factor analysis is designed to group variables, characteristics, or question responses into common elements called *factors*. Cluster analysis is designed to group persons or objects having the same underlying traits into common elements called *clusters*.

In the Life-Style Market Segmentation model to be described later in this chapter, factor analysis is used to group up to 103 independent variables into a manageable number of factor definitions. Cluster analysis is used to group more than 40,000 ZIP Code areas into clusters that display a communality when measured simultaneously on 22 of these variables.

The process of factor analysis involves the reading of a correlation matrix by the computer, which looks for patterns of high intercorrelations and then proceeds to take linear combinations of the variables so that the information and the correlation is reduced to a smaller number of variables. After principal components are extracted, these are rotated (analytically) from their beginning position in order to simplify interpretation of the factors. These variables are then regressed against each *factor loading* and the resultant regression coefficients are used to generate *factor scores*.

An example of the results of a factor analysis is shown in Figure 4-2. In this instance, certain population and household characteristics were grouped into a factor called "location" because it simultaneously described certain *area, occupation,* and *household characteristics of geographical units* (ZIP Code areas) from

VARIANCE	FACTOR LOADING
Rural Non-Farm Area	.75622
Rural Farm Area	.73567
Occupation: Farm Manager	.71982
Occupation: Farm Laborer	.65893
Household Equipped with Freezer	.63383
Household Equipped with Public Water	.63363
Household Equipped with Public Sewer	.57970
Household Lacking Kitchen Facilities	.43027

Figure 4-2 A factor grouping of demographic characteristics of location of respondents after rotation, ranked by factor loading.

which a direct marketer received highest response rates.

As with any analytical technique, factor analysis poses problems of reliability and validity. Therefore, it is incumbent on the user of factor analysis to show that the resultant factors are more than artifacts of the sample. In addition, the factors should "make sense" and relate in some way to actual, observable behavior. The results shown in Figure 4-2 might be questioned if the product offered were of primary interest to urban dwellers in high-rise apartment buildings.

Cluster Analysis

Cluster analysis is a statistical technique designed to measure similarity among a number of entities (persons, objects) when these are simultaneously compared on several different dimensions. The objective is to classify these entities into homogeneous groups using available variable information. Such grouping implies that subgroups behave differently in response to stimuli such as product differentiation or promotional strategy.

Cluster analysis is of two types: "teardown" and "buildup." An example of the "teardown" variety is so-called TREE analysis, which breaks a total population into subgroups. One of the best known of TREE techniques is the computer program AID (automatic interaction detector), developed by John A. Sonquist and James N. Morgan at the University of Michigan.[4] Direct marketers have used the AID procedure, which requires discrete input of independent variables, to identify an infinite number of subgroups of a total mailing list according to response rates.

The second type of cluster analysis, the "buildup" variety, constructs groupings depending on how similar a person or object is to another person or object. From a total population, groups of individuals are constructed through the addition of one individual at a time to each group, based on how similar that individual is to another individual. This form of cluster analysis is sometimes referred to as Q factor analysis in that it examines similarities in the characteristics of persons and can be used to create clusters of individuals (or objects) depending on how similar each individual is to another individual. The cluster analysis used in the Life-Style Market Segmentation model, later in this chapter, is of the "buildup" variety.

A Word about Complexity

This chapter, together with the preceding two chapters relative to decision making, research, and experimentation, has touched on a variety of statistical techniques, some simple and others highly complex and requiring knowledge in depth about sophisticated analytical systems. Of necessity, these have been approached in a cursory fashion with the premise that it is important for direct marketers to know *of* these systems and methods even though they do not have a grasp of everything *about* them. It is beyond the purview of this book to describe these techniques in detail. For those wanting to know more about the

underlying mathematics and methodology, reading a contemporary statistics or marketing research text is suggested. Although such a reference will enable the reader to better understand the statistical basis for these evaluation techniques, calculations are most often performed through highly complex computer programs, rather than manually.

This observation about complexity is especially relevant to the four forms of multivariate analysis, regression, discriminant, factor, and cluster, discussed thus far in this chapter. Direct marketers, in their quest for measurability and accountability, collect vast amounts of information. The key need for these marketers is to extract more use from their data. How, given certain data, do they derive future marketing strategies? How do they make intuitive judgments and draw conclusions from data? The evaluation techniques described thus far can help them. An awareness of these tools, even without an exact knowledge of their conceptual bases and the actual calculations will, in itself, go a long way toward supporting proper decision making.

With this understanding about how deeply the direct marketing researcher should delve into the complexities of statistical analysis, the balance of this chapter will be devoted to a presentation, first of background and then of a model, for measuring direct marketing effectiveness. The model utilizes regression and correlation analysis together with factor analysis and cluster analysis. It describes the potential of a total market; calculates penetration of specific subgroups, called market segments; mathematically describes those market segments; then, it seeks to retrieve key prospects among the market segments; and, finally, the model is concerned with validating the total process. The model is called Life-Style Market Segmentation, and it is an example of using direct marketing information through a variety of advanced multivariate statistical techniques.

[4] John A. Sonquist and James N. Morgan, *The Detection of Interaction Effects,* University of Michigan, Ann Arbor, Michigan, Monograph No. 35, 1969.

BACKGROUND FOR A MODEL: LIFE-STYLE MARKET SEGMENTATION

There are many ways to segment a market. A market can be grouped according to geography, sex, age, occupation, income, recency/frequency/monetary, product/brand preference, life-style, in dozens of ways. Many mailing lists are detailed enough to permit a variety of types of segmentation. However, if a direct marketer is selling a women's product, all women may not be prime prospects. If it is a lawn item, all home owners may not be prime prospects. If it is a product for cars, all car owners may not be prime prospects.

In market segmentation[5] the entire idea is to zero in on a specific homogeneous group, people likely to show an interest in your product or service, and to buy it. At the same time, it is important to eliminate those people who are not likely to buy a particular product. Otherwise, the marketer is spending more money in marketing than necessary and is reducing the chances of success.

Nature of ZIP Code Areas

ZIP Code areas have been viewed, by many direct marketers, as ideal units for describing market segments, in geographic as well as psychographic (life-style) terms. ZIP Code areas are fairly small, relatively homogeneous geographic units. The population totals for ZIP Codes in the same type of metropolitan area (that is, central city, urban fringe, rural) are usually similar. The very nature of ZIP Codes, as part of the U.S. Postal Service delivery system, makes them readily identifiable through a location number assigned to each consumer and business address.

The structure of ZIP Code areas also makes them economically similar. Their homogeneity, coupled with accepted concepts of the interdependence of consumer behavior, causes

them to be environmentally measurable. If, through analysis of actual marketing experience, a direct marketer can select the best types of ZIP Code areas. chances for direct marketing success can be dramatically improved.

Life-Style Market Segmentation is a model, oriented to ZIP Code areas, which identifies and measures the characteristics of the people who live in these areas.[6]

Beginnings of the Model

Earliest findings (1966) from research into the use of ZIP Code areas for definition of market segments were significant and encouraging, although limited by time and experience with empirical observations. The initial approach to evaluation of direct mail sales of an insurance product, as a first example, was to measure market penetration vs. potential within 19 sectional center segments of a mailing list in a single state. (Sectional centers, of which there are more than 600 in use, are geographic confines of postal delivery described by the first three digits of the five-digit ZIP Code number.) Whereas, over a good many years of recording and reporting, it had been observed that certain states were consistently twice as productive of direct mail sales as were others, it was found that there was as much as a 300 percent difference in buying activity for the insurance product *within a state,* between the best and the worst of the 19 sectional centers considered as marketing units.[7]

Data collected during the second stage of research (1967) were considerably more extensive than those which formed the basis for the earlier findings. Response data for two direct marketed insurance products, which

[5] Market segmentation in direct marketing is discussed in some detail in Chapter 7.

[6] See Chapter 7 for a comprehensive discussion of the identity and nature of ZIP Code areas.

[7] Martin Baier, "ZIP Code . . . New Tool for Marketers," *Harvard Business Review,* January–February 1967, p. 133.

were offered by mail to a total of more than 3 million prospective buyers residing within a geographic cross section of 19 states, were collected and analyzed. The mailing list used was a carefully developed and controlled compilation of economically qualified persons, ages 60 and over. One of the two product offers (an accident policy for older persons) was sent only to 60- to 64-year-old prospects. The second product offer (a policy with hospitalization benefits supplemental to Medicare) was sent to prospects aged 65 and over.

The accumulated response data were reported by number of sales that resulted from each 1,000 persons exposed to each offer within each ZIP Code sectional center. A record of the number of mailing pieces sent to prospects in each sectional center had been accumulated at the time of mailing. An average of sales per thousand pieces mailed was established for each of the 19 states, as well as an average for each sectional center. Results from the two product offers, sent to two demographic age groupings, were recorded separately. An index was developed for each product within each state, with "100" representing the average response of sales per thousand pieces mailed for each individual product within each state. The preliminary (1966) observation was confirmed by the more extensive (1967) analysis. There was a *consistent* variation of 300 percent between the most productive and the least productive sectional centers within each state, for both products. The demographic grouping by age was identical in all. The compilation of each mailing list was otherwise identical. Only the geography (ZIP Code areas) and the environment of that geography varied.

A Related Research Experiment

To further test the usefulness of ZIP Code area characteristics for determining buying potential by area, an index of current automobile value was developed, by ZIP Code

area. Referencing each of approximately 55 million private passenger automobiles registered in 1968, a current dollar value was assigned to each according to its year, make, model, and major optional features, such as automatic transmission and air conditioning. These individual records were accumulated within each of approximately 37,000 five-digit ZIP Code areas then in use. When total households were divided by the number of known automobile-owning households within each area, a mean valuation for automobile-owning households was established as an index. This technique provided for the inclusion of values for households with more than one automobile as well as the exclusion of nonautomobile households in areas that have a low penetration of automobiles (such as New York City). The results of this analysis are shown in Figure 4-3 wherein we conclude that, the

CURRENT AUTOMOBILE VALUATION INDEX	AUTO-OWNING HOUSEHOLDS*	ALL HOUSEHOLDS**	PERCENT (%) PENETRATION
0600	60,729	120,620	50.347
0700	269,517	415,036	64.938
0800	254,156	397,194	63.987
0850	357,274	565,865	63.137
0900	553,713	877,004	63.136
0950	656,071	994,374	65.978
1000	909,067	1,415,376	64.227
1050	1,071,733	1,728,778	61.993
1100	1,107,139	1,711,440	64.690
1150	1,191,913	1,861,284	64.037
1200	1,235,820	1,682,365	73.457
1250	1,219,108	1,779,794	68.497
1300	1,105,192	1,507,434	73.316
1350	1,012,256	1,362,063	74.317
1400	1,882,474	2,482,318	75.835
1500	1,228,598	1,550,098	79.259
1600	741,136	904,886	81.903
1700	1,366,892	1,598,919	85.488
Unknown	0	209,880	0.000
Total	16,222,788	23,164,708	70.032

*Source: R. L. Polk & Co., Detroit, Michigan (from auto registrations).
**Source: Mail Advertising Corporation of America, Lincoln, Nebraska (from Bureau of Census data).

Figure 4-3 Penetration by current automobile valuation index of automobile-owning households vs. all households within central city ZIP Codes.

higher the automobile valuation within ZIP Code areas, the greater the percent penetration of automobile ownership within those areas.

The Need for Explanation

Our concern to this point had been primarily in the measurement of a firm's *penetration* of its *potential* market, as defined in terms of ZIP Code areas. When significant differences of penetration were observed, the need for explanation became apparent. The independent (explanatory) variables, such as the current automobile valuation index in Figure 4-3, could be used either alone or in combination with other independent variables. Once the individual firm's most productive ZIP Code areas had been identified (in terms of percentage penetration of the potential market) and classified (even in so simple a form as by central city/ urban fringe/rural types of ZIP Code areas), the need for qualification and explanatory measurement in terms of the chosen independent variables became apparent.

The validity of such measurement is directly related to the homogeneity of the marketing unit, in this instance ZIP Code areas. Not the least of the needs for measurement is making possible the transfer of marketing results, within units which have been productive, to other units, in which prior experience is lacking but similar characteristics (independent variables) were observed. The statistical technique used to accomplish this was regression analysis, which established coefficients of correlation between independent variables and a dependent variable, described as percentage penetration of the potential market.

Examples of Explanation

A simple two-variable example will serve as a first illustration. This is a correlation of the new car "buy rate" of a state with a direct sales response to the insurance product offer described earlier, as well as median household

ZIP Code Areas:	19 Sectional Centers		29 Sectional Centers	
Variables	Correlation Coefficient	Confidence Level*	Correlation Coefficient	Confidence Level*
Direct sales vs. "buy-rate"	−.45878	95.0%	.01528	None
Income vs. "buy-rate"	.86798	99.9%	.24486	80.0%

*Confidence levels shown represent the degree of statistical significance which can be attached to the observed correlation between the variables in each instance. The null hypothesis tested and rejected took the form of "H_0: The correlation coefficient of the population = 0."

Figure 4-4 Correlation coefficients* derived from univariate analysis of the new car "buy rate" with direct marketing response and with median household income within 19 rural and within 29 rural, urban fringe, and central city sectional centers of a state.

income. As displayed in Figure 4-4, an inverse correlation coefficient of −0.45878 was established for 19 nonmetropolitan (rural) ZIP Code sectional centers of the state. However, no correlation could be established within all 29 of the state sectional centers—that included central city and urban fringe ZIP Code areas as well as the 19 rural ZIP Code areas. These findings served to point up the need for finer five-digit ZIP Code area analysis within the more heterogeneous metropolitan (central city and urban fringe) areas. As expected, the "buy rate" was highly correlated with household income: a correlation of 0.86798 was observed within the 19 rural sectional centers.

A second illustration will serve to demonstrate just how versatile such an evaluation procedure can be, dependent on the marketing needs of the individual firm. In this example, which is summarized in Figure 4-5, the measurement of penetration of the firm's potential market has been accomplished at the five-digit ZIP Code area level, as opposed to the three-digit sectional center area level measurement used in the preceding illustration. The analysis involved numbers that were large and significant. Nearly 500,000 customers of the firm were related to 59 million households within

LENGTH OF TIME CUSTOMER ACTIVE	PRODUCT LINE A		PRODUCT LINE B		PRODUCT LINE C		PRODUCT LINE D	
	EDUCATION	INCOME	EDUCATION	INCOME	EDUCATION	INCOME	EDUCATION	INCOME
Less than 6 mos.	.4424	.4940	.6854	.8203	N.A.	N.A.	.8018	.7020
6 mos. to 1 yr.	.6942	.7299	.7657	.6652	N.A.	N.A.	.7426	.5875
1 yr. to 3 yrs.	.9336	.8448	.9549	.7744	.7793	.8304	.6822	.7802
3 yrs. to 5 yrs.	.9667	.9029	N.A.	N.A.	.9200	.9748	.8770	.9450
5 yrs. or more	N.A.	N.A.	N.A.	N.A.	.8891	.9603	.9653	.9062

*The null hypothesis (H_0: The correlation coefficient of the population = 0) was used to measure the level of significance for the coefficients. This null hypothesis could be rejected at a statistically significant level in all cases. The confidence level at which the null hypothesis was rejected ranged from a low of 80.0 percent for the smallest correlation coefficient (.4424) to 99.9 percent for the largest correlation coefficient (.9967).

**The relationship estimated for each product line and each time interval is in the form of this equation: $Y = a + bX_1 + cX_2$, where Y = penetration of potential market and X = the independent variable.

Figure 4-5 Correlation coefficients* derived from univariate analysis of potential market within central city ZIP Code areas and each of two independent variables by product lines and according to length of time customers have been active**.

37,000 five-digit ZIP Code areas throughout the United States.

Both the listing of the firm's customers and the potential market were grouped and sorted along a scale for each of two independent variables against which penetration (the dependent variable) was to be measured: education level and income level. Penetration against each of the two independent variables was measured within each of four major product lines (identified here simply as A, B, C, and D) and according to length of time the customer had been active (less than 6 months, up to 1 year, up to 3 years, up to 5 years, and more than 5 years). The estimated relationship for each product line and each time interval was shown by the regression equation, $Y = a + bX_1 + cX_2$, where Y = penetration of the potential market and X = the independent variables, education and income, against which penetration is being measured.

As will be seen in Figure 4-5, there was an increase in correlation established with the length of time during which the customer had been active. This was true in all four product lines. There was generally a close correspondence, as shown in Figure 4-5, between the correlations established for education and those

established for income. It should be noted, however, that this correspondence occurred only when income was indexed to the larger environment of a state, the median income of each individual state. The buildup of correlation over time is of particular importance, since it demonstrates the long-range *value of a customer*. Thus, although a sale might be made more easily in low median income ZIP Code areas, an investment in new customers in high income areas paid dividends in the long run.

The technique for evaluation and measurement of penetration of market potential, described here in terms of one independent variable at a time, is not changed in a multivariate regression analysis. Such analysis, when practical, would be desirable, especially if the relationship is curvilinear, between income and education in relation to current automobile valuation, as an example. For instance, relatively high income coupled with moderate educational level and moderate car value could help identify areas of certain occupational and/or social-class behavior.

One more case is worthy of being cited as background for the description of the Life-Style Market Segmentation model to follow.

This analysis involves a consumer financial service operating throughout the United States in its owned and franchised offices. A measurement of the penetration of its multimillion customer list against its potential market, divided among central city, urban fringe, and rural ZIP Code areas, resulted in the correlations shown in Figure 4-6, using univariate regression analysis.

Apparent from Figure 4-6 is a relatively close correspondence of the correlations for educational level and those for the state median income index within central city and rural ZIP Code areas although there is a somewhat lower relationship of either with the U.S. median income index. The latter measures absolute dollars, rather than income indexed to the localized environment of an individual state. Disregarding the U.S. index, therefore, it becomes apparent that this firm's penetration of its potential market is correlated positively with relative (indexed) income and education in both central city and rural markets. Whereas the correlation within education and both income indices is negative in urban fringe areas, it should be noted that, in this instance, the U.S. median income index is a more appropriate measure.

With this information, the consumer financial service, which already had several thousand offices nationally, could locate its *new* offices in ZIP Code areas comparable to those in which it had the greatest penetration in the past.

AN ILLUSTRATIVE MODEL: LIFE-STYLE MARKET SEGMENTATION

Life-Style Market Segmentation is a computerized system that uses three of the multivariate analytical techniques described earlier in order to enable a direct marketer to measure and identify market segments having most (or least) relevance to the organization's particular

TYPE OF ZIP CODE AREA	EDUCATIONAL LEVEL	STATE MEDIAN INCOME INDEX	U.S. MEDIAN INCOME INDEX
Central City	.7217 (99.0%)	.6797 (99.9%)	.3789 (90.0%)
Urban Fringe	−.7080 (99.0%)	−.3647 (90.0%)	−.6617 (99.9%)
Rural	.7508 (99.0%)	.6156 (99.0%)	.0193 (None)

* Confidence levels are shown in parentheses and represent the degree of statistical significance which can be attached to the observed correlation coefficients. The null hypothesis tested and rejected took the form of "H_0: The correlation coefficient of the population = 0."

Figure 4-6 Correlation coefficients* derived from univariate analysis between penetration of potential market and each of three independent variables within central city, urban fringe, and rural ZIP Code areas.

offering. A system such as this must be designed so as to satisfy two objectives. First, it should have the capability to reliably *predict* direct marketing effectiveness. Second, the system should be able to *explain* variations in direct marketing effectiveness. The methodology of Life-Style Market Segmentation is described here to illustrate the multivariate analytical techniques that have been presented thus far.

Conceptual Bases

In viewing the model in this form, certain conceptual bases for it should be kept in mind. These include the nature of market segmentation itself as well as the suitability of the U.S. Postal Service's ZIP Code areas as units of observation. Anticipating a more thorough discussion of the conceptual background of these units in Chapter 7, the reader, for now, should keep in mind, when reviewing the model, these assumptions:

• ZIP Code areas have become well established as marketing units that are readily identifiable and in which a relative homogeneity of consumer behavior makes possible measurement of the characteristics of an *area,* as opposed to those of an *individual.*
• The *ability* to buy is not the same thing as the *proneness* to buy, a fact well established by the marketing literature.
• So-called *environmental* measurement is more valid than absolute measurement in the instances of certain independent variables; that is, an absolute amount of income earned in a rural area of Arkansas would provide relatively more spending power than would that same absolute amount of income in New York City.
• Life-style can often be described through the measurement of the *interaction* of a variety of independent variables, educational level interacting with occupation, for example.

Modeling Requirements

The principal presumption behind the major objectives of Life-Style Market Segmentation, prediction and explanation, is that direct marketing effectiveness is somehow related to a degree of presence or absence of certain demographic variables, individually or in combinations. If penetration of a potential market can be related to these variables, the system can attain its specified objectives. In order to promote these objectives, the system requires:

• that the marketing unit (clusters of ZIP Code areas) be large enough to make measurement statistically reliable
• that the clusters be homogeneous enough to make detection of distinct demographic profiles possible
• that the clusters be readily identifiable with a customer's location, as are ZIP Code areas

It is important, too, that vast amounts of data be used in a manageable form. If a computer were to compare every single bit of data (up to 103 independent variables) about all ZIP Code areas (more than 40,000 currently, at the five-digit level) to see how a particular type of area measures up against the data for a "good" ZIP Code area, the time and cost would be prohibitive. Even a simple multiplication (40,000 ZIP Code areas times 103 data variables in each) results in 4.12 million individual comparisons! Instead, certain multivariate analytical techniques described thus far are used:

• Factor analysis is used to combine independent variables that appear together in a good ZIP Code area; that is, an area recording high penetration of potential (marketing effectiveness).
• Cluster analysis is used to combine individual ZIP Code areas with similar characteristics, so as to assure measurement of statistically valid numbers of observations.
• Regression and correlation analysis provides a customer profile and prediction of results.

Profiling Market Segments by Life-Style

Based on this resultant profile and prediction, the direct marketer seeks to locate other ZIP Code areas in which people are likely to respond in a similar way to a particular product or offer. Life-Style Market Segmentation first mathematically analyzes customer penetration (using either an existing customer list or test mailing results) to determine in which potential ZIP Code areas a product or service sells best. Then, by referencing an extensive databank and using multivariate statistical techniques, the life-styles prevalent in those ZIP Code areas are determined and a customer profile is developed. In this way the system can identify for retrieval additional ZIP Code areas that should also be likely to produce a satisfactory level of response.

This method is superior to analyzing ZIP Code areas by demographics alone. The Life-Style Market Segmentation system enables direct marketers to define their best prospects, seek them out, establish sales potentials, predict consumer behavior, and look at penetration in a manner that can be statistically evaluated. It is based on the fact that people with similar life-styles tend to cluster and are prone to purchase similar types of products or prefer particular brands.

The model has identified, statistically, a number of life-styles. Here are a few of them:

- *Affluent buyers:* With a relatively high income, the spender usually has a home value, or pays rent, in the upper brackets. Occupation is most likely to be in professional, managerial, or technical areas, and the buyer is probably a college graduate.
- *Singles:* Many are in the 19-to-24 age bracket, have never been married, and are mobile, changing residence approximately every 2 years. Men 22 to 24 years of age often have had military service.
- *Loners:* Typically, a loner has never been married or is divorced, owns one automobile, and rents an apartment (usually a small one) in a multidwelling unit.
- *Senior citizens:* The typical senior citizen is age 55 or older, often has outlived a spouse, and has lived for 20 years or more in the same building, which was probably built 30 or more years ago. He or she is often native born, but of foreign-born parents.

- *Rural residents:* The typical rural resident lives in a farming area (a small community) and probably works on a farm, in many cases self owned. Households usually are equipped with freezers but lack city water and sewers.
- *Poverty people:* These are characterized by low individual and/or family incomes, low home value or rent, and a general absence of telephone services. Kitchen facilities more likely are lacking. He or she rarely has completed more than 8 years of education.[8]

The Model

A procedural flow chart for the Life-Style Market Segmentation system is shown in Figure 4-7. There are five stages:

Stage 1: Potential of the market
Stage 2: Penetration of the market
Stage 3: Market segmentation
Stage 4: Retrieval of market segments
Stage 5: Validation of retrieval

Stage 1: Potential of the Market Each ZIP Code area is characterized as a metropolitan type (metro) described as either central city (I), urban fringe (II), or rural (III). All available data (those in the model as well as those in the firm's file) are segregated into and are analyzed within these three metropolitan types. Firm data from nongeographic, nonresidential ZIP Code areas (such as businesses, post office boxes, libraries, military bases, foreign areas) are characterized as "metro IX" and new ZIP Code areas, for which census data is not available, are identified as "metro X." Metro IX and metro X ZIP Code areas, since no demographic data exist for them, are dropped from the analysis.

The ZIP Code areas relevant to a particular direct marketer are combined, through cluster

---

[8] The Census Bureau reported that in 1981 approximately 31.8 million people were living below the poverty level, approximately 14 percent of the population. In 1980 the poverty threshold was defined by the government as one person earning $4,284; two persons in a household earning $5,514; three persons, including a child, with an income of $6,628; four persons, including two children, with an income of $8,351.

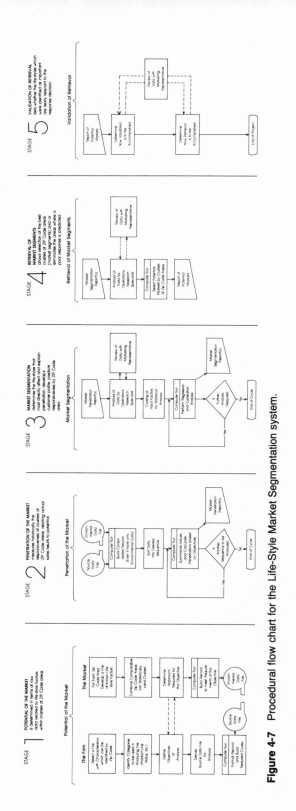

Figure 4-7 Procedural flow chart for the Life-Style Market Segmentation system.

analysis, into homogeneous groupings to perform subsequent measurement with adequate numbers of observations so as to assure that the results will provide statistically valid predictions. Cluster analysis, as described earlier in this chapter, is a multivariate statistical technique designed to assure similarity among a number of persons or objects, in this instance, ZIP Code areas, when these are simultaneously compared on several dimensions. The model uses 22 such dimensions, including urban/rural metropolitan type, race, nativity, ethnicity, age, marital status, education, income, mobility, occupation, family size, and various housing characteristics, such as home/rent value, structure age and tenure of residence, type of dwelling, and household or structure equipment. The process of clustering can be visualized by thinking of each ZIP Code area as a centroid with 22 rays, the length of which describes the presence (or absence) of a particular independent variable. Cluster analysis involves the *simultaneous* comparison of the length of each of these 22 rays, pairwise, as between each of 40,000 five-digit ZIP Code areas, and brings together, as the clustering proceeds, those areas that are *most alike on all 22 dimensions.*

Certain of these data for five-digit ZIP Code areas are indexed to some larger geographical area such as a three-digit ZIP Code sectional center or a complete state, in a manner that makes possible environmental (as opposed to absolute) measurement of that area's characteristics. Although ZIP Code areas are the marketing units used in this presentation, cluster analysis is equally applicable to other small geographic area marketing units, such as census tracts or block groups, provided that there is accurate identification of these within the file being analyzed.

In addition to clustering several ZIP Code areas, many with relatively small mailing and/or response quantities, into more useful marketing groupings, we need information about many independent (explanatory) variables, including interaction between and among these independent variables. The size of clusters is a function of "base count" (the universe of all potential observations, such as the number of mailing pieces or the number of households). Using these base counts as weights, the 103 independent variables contained in the system's database are transformed from individual ZIP Code areas to the larger clusters.

The 103 independent variables contained within the database, in total involving 27 individual characteristics of a ZIP Code area, are summarized in Figure 4-8. Up to 25 of these variables can be available to regression and correlation analysis for use in *prediction.* Factor analysis is used for *explanation,* to group those variables that occur in the same relative degree (are highly intercorrelated) over all of the ZIP Code areas of interest. These groupings of *manifest* variables, called "factors," are then analyzed subjectively to determine what *latent* dimensions they seem to have in common. These latent dimensions can describe life-styles.

Such life-style factors (demographic profiles) may or may not influence penetration. The degree to which they do has an important bearing on the practical value of the system's results. If the factors not only exist but also influence penetration, the system will satisfy its second analytical objective: *explanation.* Such factors convey most of the essential information of the original set of variables, but result in fewer, more recognizable life-style factors than there were original variables.

An array of typical life-style factors with associated independent variables is shown in Figure 4-9. Although these factors are derived statistically, the reader should note especially the logical clustering of variables within factors. Because each factor so defined appears to some greater or lesser degree within each ZIP Code area cluster of interest, these can then be considered as independent variables

CHARACTERISTIC	VARIABLE DESCRIPTION	CHARACTERISTIC	VARIABLE DESCRIPTION
Metro	% Urban	Industry of	% Construction
	% Rural Non-Farm	Work Force	% Manufacturing
	% Rural Farm		% Transportation
Race	% White		% Communications
	% Black		% Wholesale/Retail
	% Indian		% Finance
	% Japanese		% Professional
	% Chinese		% Educational
	% Filipino		% Public Administration
	% Spanish American		% Other
	% Other	Family Size	Average Family Size
Nativity	% Native of Native Parents	Poverty	% Individuals Below Poverty
	% Native of Foreign Parents		% Families Below Poverty
	% Foreign Born	Owner-Occupied	% Owner-Occupied
Origin of Foreign	% United Kingdom	Home/Rent Value	Median Owner-Occupied Value
Born	% Ireland		Median Renter-Occupied Value
	% Sweden	Structure	Median Structure Age
	% Germany	Tenure	Median Tenure of Residence
	% Poland	Income	Median Family Income
	% Czechoslovakia		Median Individual Income
	% Austria	Conspicuous Consumption	Mean Auto Value
	% Hungary	Dwelling Size	Median Owner-Occupied
	% USSR		Median Renter-Occupied
	% Italy	Dwelling Type	% Single Family Dwellings
	% Canada		% 2-Unit Structures
	% Mexico		% 3–4 Unit Structures
	% Cuba		% 5–49 Unit Structures
	% Other		% 50+ Unit Structures
Mother Tongue	% English		% Mobile Homes and Trailers
	% German	Household Equipment	% With Washer
	% Polish		% With Dryer
	% Yiddish		% With Dishwasher
	% Italian		% With Freezer
	% Spanish		% With Television
	% All Others		% With UHF–TV
	% Not Reported		% With Battery Operated Radio
Age	Median Age	Structure Equipment	% With Air Conditioning
Marital Status	% Married		% With Multi-Bath
	% Widowed		% With Central Heat
	% Divorced		% With Public Water
	% Separated		% With Public Sewer
	% Single (Never Married)	Kitchen	% Lacking Kitchen
Education	Median Education Level	Direct Access	% Lacking Direct Access
Mobility	% Moved Past 2 Years	Telephone	% Having Telephone
Occupation of	% Professional, Technical	Auto Registration	% With One Auto
Work Force	% Farm Manager		% With Two Autos
	% Managerial		% With Three+ Autos
	% Clerical		
	% Sales		
	% Craftsman		
	% Operatives		
	% Service		
	% Farm Laborer		
	% Other Laborer		
	% Armed Services		
	% Unemployed		

Figure 4-8   A list of 103 independent variables describing ZIP Code areas.

to be correlated with penetration, the dependent variable. Penetration is defined as a measure of marketing effectiveness in terms of either customers or responses/transactions. It is especially important to observe interactions of various factors within each cluster.

Stage 2: Penetration of the Market Now we are ready to look at actual response in relation to the potential of a direct marketing effort or possibly a customer list in relation to some larger universe of households. To optimize the number of observations, and thus help assure statistical validity of our subsequent measurement and prediction, individual five-digit ZIP Code areas have been clustered into larger marketing units that have common characteristics. Ultimately, these units will be further described as market segments.

Penetration is the ratio of items of interest (responses, customers) to the base count (the universe of all potential observations such as number of mailing pieces or the number of available households), expressed as a percentage. In statistical terms, penetration is the dependent variable whose variation over all the ZIP Code area clusters is to be explained by one or more selected independent variables.

The direct marketer, in measuring penetration of the potential market (the dependent variable) and searching for correlation with factors defined by environmental characteristics (the independent variables), might do well to first categorize the customers or measure the responses within certain broad groupings. Such groupings might be according to product line or by various characteristics of customers or their degree of transaction activity. Within each of these groupings, the direct marketer should look at penetration (in terms of customers or responses) as a percentage of the total potential (in terms of households or mailing pieces). Through regression analysis, it is possible to establish correlation between the varying degrees of penetration and the mea-

FACTOR 1: AFFLUENCE

Education	13–15 years of school completed
	16+ years of school completed
Occupation	Mgr., official, proprietor, professional, technical, sales
Industry	Finance
Value/Owner-Occupied	$50,000+
Value/Renter-Occupied	$300+
Structure Equipment	Multibath
Household Equipment	Dishwasher
Average Auto Value	High
Family Income	$25,000+
Individual Income	$15,000+

FACTOR 2: SETTLED – SINGLES

Household relationship – primary individual or non-relative of head

Divorced

Renter-Occupied Housing

Multiple Family Dwelling Unit

1 – 2 Room Owner-Occupied

1 – 2 Room Renter-Occupied

1 Auto per Household

FACTOR 3: POVERTY

Education	1–8 years of school completed

Lacking Kitchen Facilities
Lacking Telephone

Value/Owner-Occupied	$0–$4,999
Value/Renter-Occupied	$0–$59

Families below Poverty Level
Individuals below Poverty Level

Family Income	$0–$6,999
Individual Income	$0–$999

FACTOR 4: SENIOR CITIZEN

Native Born of Foreign Parents

Country of Origin – Eastern Europe
                                  Italy

Ages	55–64
	65+

Widowed

Structure Age 30+ years

Tenure of Residence 20+ years

FACTOR 5: RURAL

Rural, Farm

Occupation – Farmer, Farm Manager, Farm Laborer

Industry – Other

Figure 4-9 Typical life-style factors with associated variables.

surement of the characteristics of the clusters of ZIP Code areas of the present and future market. Emphasis, again, in Life-Style Market Segmentation, is on the *interaction* among the independent variables selected from the potential of 103. At this stage of the system both the *environmental* (or indexed) measurement and the *interaction* among these indices are important.

Calculation of penetration is a relatively simple arithmetic process. Within each cluster of ZIP Code areas, responses (or customer counts) are related to mailings (or household counts) in the following manner:

ZIP Code cluster	Total mailed	Total responses	% Responses/ mailed
A	5,793	60	1.04
B	2,735	33	1.21
C	6,731	138	2.05
D	4,341	119	2.74

Our concern to this point has been the measurement of a firm's *penetration* of its *potential* market, which market is defined in tems of the characteristics of clusters of ZIP Code areas as described by one or more independent variables. If significant differences of penetration are observed betweeen clusters, the need for *explanation* becomes apparent, as does the need for *prediction* of future results. Explanatory variables (or factors), it has been suggested, can be used either alone or in combination. Measurements (prediction) and identification (explanation) are accomplished in Stage 3 of the model, through the use of multivariate regression and correlation analysis.

Stage 3: Market Segmentation Observing a variation of penetration between clusters of similar ZIP Code areas, we next set out to explain these differences in a manner that can

lead to useful predictions of future responses. One reason such measurement is needed is that it makes possible the transfer of direct marketing results within those clusters that have been particularly productive to other clusters in which prior experience is lacking but similar environmental characteristics are observed.

The statistical technique used at this stage is stepwise multivariate correlation and regression analysis. Correlation analysis identifies the strength of the relationship between penetration (the dependent variable) and each of the 103 selected demographic characteristics (independent variables) present in the previously established ZIP Code area clusters. The strength of this relationship predicates the system's capability to predict a future penetration estimate reliably. This capability is measured by a multiple correlation coefficient (R) which is expressed in decimal form ranging from 0 to $+1.00$ (for positive correlation) and 0 to -1.00 (for negative correlation). In both instances, 1.00 (positive *or* negative) indicates perfect correlation and 0 indicates no correlation.

If, in fact, there is an acceptable degree of correlation observed in the analysis to this point, the ensuing analysis mathematically identifies a formula (a linear combination of independent variables and constant) for predicting penetration. It uses the input data (penetration percentage) plus the correlations to produce the "best" statistical predictions for penetration. In proceeding stepwise through the regression analysis, we allow the selected independent variables (up to 103), acting as surrogates of factors defining life-styles, to enter the regression in the order in which they most explain the prediction variations observed; that is, the most predictive enters first and so on.

The resultant linear equation (of the form $Y = a + bX$) becomes a formula for predicting estimated penetration by cluster and serves as a basis for rankordering clusters from the highest to the lowest estimated penetration. The regression process simultaneously generates statistics for gauging the reliability of the prediction penetrations. Success at this stage satisfies the first of the system's objectives: *prediction*.

If the process isn't always clearly understood, the results can be: a rank ordering of predicted penetration (responses vs. direct marketing efforts) attributable to each five-digit ZIP Code area contained within statistically measurable clusters of ZIP Code areas. The manner of doing this is visualized in Figure 4-10, which shows the highest to the lowest (as well as accumulative) predicted penetration, along with individual and accumulated mailing (or household) availabilities within each ZIP Code area contained within each cluster. (Note that prediction for the cluster applies for each ZIP Code area within the cluster.) The direct marketing researcher decides how big a market segment is needed, and determines what the overall penetration would be. Or, the minimum marketing requirement (either average or marginal) is set and how big the resultant market segment would be is determined.

Reference to Figure 4-10 reveals that, from a total mailing quantity of 1,277,262 direct marketing efforts, the overall average response is predicted to be 1.95 percent, with the response from the best cluster being 4.49 percent and that from the worst being 0.76 percent. The response from the best cluster (No. 39 at the top of the list) is $2\frac{1}{2}$ times the average. The response from the worst cluster (No. 30 at the bottom of the list) is less than 40 percent of the average. The range from worst cluster to best cluster is more than five to one. To attain an average response of 2.55 percent (an overall 30 percent improvement above the average), it would be necessary to stop at cluster No. 10, which averages 2.06 percent, and the resultant mailing quantity would be 511,276 pieces.

Or, if the mailing quantity was limited to 242,935 pieces, approximately 20 percent of the availability, the average response would be 2.87 percent, an improvement of 47 percent over the average of 1.95 percent.

Figure 4-11 reproduces a condensed printout of an actual stepwise multivariate regression analysis. In this example, from an availability of 25 independent variables demonstrating some degree of correlation with the dependent variable, 10 steps were taken and eight variables remained. (One variable, No. 5, entered in Step 1 and was removed in Step 7, since it contributed nothing to the explanation at that point.) The resultant R^2 value was 0.803748 (the multiple coefficient of determination), thus indicating that 80 percent of the variance in the prediction was "explained" by the eight independent variables remaining after the stepwise regression analysis.

Stage 4: Retrieval of Market Segments When the statistical profile has been developed (as in Stages 1 and 2 of the model) and the measurement has been evaluated (as in Stage 3 of the model), there follows selection of the best clusters of ZIP Code areas (market segments) and/or the elimination of those areas in which a poor response is predicted. Unless the findings from the measurement (prediction) and identification (explanation) procedures described thus far can be practically applied to retrieve the most desirable market segments for the individual direct marketer, the wisdom of the process thus far can and should be questioned.

For a firm or organization that offers its products or services through direct marketing, the mailing list of its customers and prospects, together with collected data about these, can be used to selectively identify particular ZIP Code areas of interest. It is a relatively simple matter to select and mail to only those ZIP Code areas that have the characteristics desired.

CLUSTER #	ZIP #	PENETRATION ACTUAL	PERCENTAGES ** PRED	CUM PRED	*****BASE COUNTS**** ZIP ONLY	CUMULATIVE
39	32009	.00	.0449	.0449	89	89
	32265	.00	.0449	.0449	4	93
	32560	.1070	.0449	.0449	93	186
	32563	.00	.0449	.0449	6	192
	32710	.00	.0449	.0449	37	229
	32732	.00	.0449	.0449	200	429
	32740	.00	.0449	.0449	42	471
	32766	.1500	.0449	.0449	200	671
	33070	.0460	.0449	.0449	651	1322
	33470	.00	.0449	.0449	132	1454
	33527	.00	.0449	.0449	716	2170
	33534	.0590	.0449	.0449	505	2675
	33550	.00	.0449	.0449	194	2869
	33556	.0750	.0449	.0449	528	3397
	33569	.0480	.0449	.0449	1637	5034
	33584	.0390	.0449	.0449	1001	6035
	33586	.00	.0449	.0449	62	6097
	33592	.0770	.0449	.0449	518	6615
	33600	.0750	.0449	.0449	398	7013
	33943	.00	.0449	.0449	139	7152
3	32600	.0420	.0342	.0363	28855	36007
11	32301	.0560	.0327	.0360	3533	39540
	32304	.0230	.0327	.0358	2532	42072
	32500	.0360	.0327	.0355	4873	46945
	32570	.0120	.0327	.0354	2312	49257
	32601	.0330	.0327	.0350	7826	57083
	33030	.0120	.0327	.0348	5564	62647
13	32211	.0240	.0246	.0291	6134	222185
	32303	.0160	.0246	.0290	4243	226428
	32561	.0330	.0246	.0289	1203	227631
	32701	.0140	.0246	.0289	2038	229669
	32751	.0140	.0246	.0288	3379	233048
	32786	.00	.0246	.0288	229	233277
	32789	.0170	.0246	.0287	7543	240820
	33511	.0370	.0246	.0287	2115	242935
10	33900	.0210	.0206	.0255	53503	511276
37	33062	.0170	.0111	.0198	6834	1234153
	33140	.00	.0111	.0198	56	1234209
	33154	.0060	.0111	.0198	3120	1237329
	33160	.0130	.0111	.0197	16354	1253683
	33306	.0100	.0111	.0197	986	1254669
30	33064	.0210	.0076	.0196	8201	1262870
	33516	.00	.0076	.0195	11202	1274072
	33570	.0090	.0076	.0195	3190	1277262

Figure 4-10 Rank ordering of ZIP Code area clusters according to predicted penetration.

Life-Style Market Segmentation is not limited to direct response applications. A knowledge of market segments affording the individual firm its greatest potential for penetration is a prerequisite for any marketer. Such knowledge enables optimal location of dealer outlets, franchises, and salespeople as well as pinpoint distribution of direct mail advertising or other promotional efforts.

A market segment, in the sense illustrated here, is a cluster, or a combination of clusters, of ZIP Code areas with life-style factor definitions relevant for the individual direct marketer. Having identified these explanatory life-style factors in the manner described, it remains to retrieve that segment in terms of individual ZIP Code areas to achieve the predicted result. Of course, the system cuts across any other known characteristics of the list. The process is additive and designed to improve direct marketing direction, especially that which is already marginal.

Stage 5: Validation of Retrieval   After using a complex market measurement/identification model such as Life-Style Market Segmentation, there must be validation: follow-up direct marketing to confirm whether the life-styles that were identified as important in the evaluation are really relevant to the response decision.

One of many such validations of the model's prediction/explanation that has been documented was a follow-up to the analysis shown

```
STEP #  1
   VARIABLE  ENTERING              X- 5
R =0.583959      R SQ. =0.341008
   F LEVEL =      23.8036
   STANDARD  ERROR OF Y =     0.06341
   CONSTANT  TERM =     0.27470726

   VARIABLE  NO.         COEFFICIENT          STD ERR OF COEFF
      X-  5               -0.28683022E-01              0.00594

STEP #  2
   VARIABLE  ENTERING              X- 2
R =0.717396      R SQ. =0.514658
   F LEVEL =      16.1004
   STANDARD  ERROR OF Y =     0.05504
   CONSTANT  TERM =     0.25037676

   VARIABLE  NO.         COEFFICIENT          STD ERR OF COEFF
      X-  2                0.11710477                  0.02951
      X-  5               -0.25006641E-01              0.00524

STEP #  3
   VARIABLE  ENTERING              X- 16
R =0.814453      R SQ. =0.663334
   F LEVEL =      19.4310
   STANDARD  ERROR OF Y =     0.04637
   CONSTANT  TERM =     0.17120540

   VARIABLE  NO.         COEFFICIENT          STD ERR OF COEFF
      X-  2                0.12946498                  0.02503
      X-  5               -0.21160301E-01              0.00450
      X- 16                0.10500204E-01              0.00241

STEP #  4
   VARIABLE  ENTERING              X- 14
R =0.831825      R SQ. =0.691934
   F LEVEL =       3.9919
   STANDARD  ERROR OF Y =     0.04488
   CONSTANT  TERM =     0.11676645

   VARIABLE  NO.         COEFFICIENT          STD ERR OF COEFF
      X-  2                0.12659431                  0.02427
      X-  5               -0.18140811E-01              0.00462
      X- 14                0.27103789E-01              0.01373
      X- 16                0.99606328E-02              0.00235

STEP # 10
   VARIABLE  ENTERING              X- 22
R =0.896520      R SQ. =0.803748
   F LEVEL =       2.8542
   STANDARD  ERROR OF Y =     0.03766
   CONSTANT  TERM =     0.39812356

   VARIABLE  NO.         COEFFICIENT          STD ERR OF COEFF
      X-  2                0.13928533                  0.02095
      X-  9               -0.20301903E-02              0.00064
      X- 10               -0.87198131E-02              0.00257
      X- 14                0.69082797E-01              0.01875
      X- 15                0.13623666E-01              0.00421
      X- 16                0.22368859E-01              0.00380
      X- 22               -0.15226589E-02              0.00091
      X- 23               -0.21373443E-02              0.00081
```

Figure 4-11 Stepwise multivariate regression analysis.

in Figures 4-10 and 4-11. The original analysis was performed on a mailing of 1,277,262 pieces and resulted in a response rate of 1.95 percent. The best cluster of ZIP Code areas produced a response rate more than 500 percent higher than that of the worst and 2½ times the average.

After dropping down in the rank ordering through clusters composing 511,276 pieces, 40 percent of the total mailing volume, average response was increased better than 25 percent. This is shown in Figure 4-10. The relevant variables are shown in Figure 4-11.

In this particular evaluation, factor analysis explained that results were largely attributable to *locality* (rural location characteristics, farm-related occupations, strong European ancestry); *social class* (laborers and service employees, nonwhite population, low mobility, older living structure); and *Hispanic ancestry* (immigration from Spanish cultures, high use of Spanish language).

To validate the findings, the entire list was remailed, rankordering in quintiles of predicted response, 6 months after the original direct marketing effort. As expected, the overall response rate dropped to approximately 50 percent of the first effort, but what is important is that the relationship (response indices) of the quintiles was virtually the same in both efforts, as shown in this comparison:

Quintile	No. of pieces mailed	No. 1 effort response %	No. 1 effort response index	No. 2 effort response %	No. 2 effort response index
1	242,935	2.87	147%	1.36	143%
2	268,341	2.26	116%	1.08	111%
3	230,592	1.94	99%	0.96	99%
4	290,001	1.54	79%	0.81	84%
5	245,393	1.19	61%	0.67	67%

The Bottom Line

How does Life-Style Market Segmentation, and other models using multivariate analytical techniques, help improve direct marketing results? There are at least nine ways such segmentation helps:

1 *Isolation of best customers:* Who are they? Where are they? Once the direct marketer finds that certain areas are most responsive, offerings can be sent to the most profitable areas.

2 *Remailing of best respondents:* By knowing in which ZIP Code areas respondents live, it's relatively easy to retrieve that portion of a mailing list for more frequent use and/or follow-up efforts.

3 *Increasing penetration in profitable areas:* By identifying the most responsive areas, penetration can be increased in those areas. For example, if a home study school discovers that men in urban fringe areas are the most likely prospects, direct marketing efforts can be concentrated in those areas.

4 *Making marginal or unprofitable lists pay off:* Mailing to everyone on a certain list may be marginally profitable or even unprofitable. But, by selecting only those on the list who reside in ZIP Code areas proven to be responsive, results can be improved.

5 *Making mass compiled lists work:* Unlike mail-responsive customer lists, compiled lists contain an unknown percentage of mail-order buyers. By selecting only those people in a compiled list who live in a particular area, a compiled list can be made to pay off, even those mammoth lists with no distinct customer profiles.

6 *Selectively mailing large mail-responsive lists:* As with compiled lists, it may be unprofitable to mail to an entire list of mail respondents. But only those buyers in good areas can be selected to increase the number of transactions or responses or to reduce the cost per response.

7 *Qualifying credit:* In the final analysis, it's the bottom line figure that counts. And, if analysis shows that buyers in certain areas pay slowly or not at all, these areas can be eliminated in future solicitations.

8 *Selecting optimum retail store locations:* The described analysis is useful not only in direct marketing, but also in finding the best locations for retail stores, service centers, regional warehouses, etc.

9 *Developing new products or services likely to gain acceptance:* A study of what sells best in certain areas can lead to the development of other products or services likely to appeal to the same types of customers.

SUMMARY

Four multivariate analytical techniques which have particular relevance in direct marketing are presented and briefly described in this chapter: regression and correlation analysis, discriminant analysis, factor analysis, and cluster analysis. These techniques help the direct marketer to evaluate the results of experiments. An understanding of them is particularly important inasmuch as an effect (dependent variable) can have many causes (independent variables).

Regression analysis is designed to describe relationships between cause and effect to predict future happenings under conditions of minimal uncertainty. Not only the happening but also the level of response is capable of measurement through regression and correlation techniques.

Discriminant analysis, on the other hand,

develops profiles of groups and relates such profiles to other groups of prospects. The *Reader's Digest,* for example, was able to predict the likelihood of response to a mailed subscription offer after deriving a profile of its present subscribers. The technique of discriminant analysis, unlike regression analysis, does not predict the *level* of response.

Factor analysis enables the direct marketing researcher to deal with vast amounts of data through identification of communality of variables in such a way as to combine statistically all the essential information of the original set of variables into fewer, more recognizable factors.

Whereas factor analysis groups common characteristics (such as independent variables), cluster analysis is designed to measure the similarity among entities (such as ZIP Code areas) that have characteristics in common. Cluster analysis is of two types: "teardown" and "buildup."

The four multivariate analytical techniques presented in this chapter are necessarily complex, generally requiring the use of computers to perform adequately, but they are powerful. Direct marketers in their quest for measurability and accountability collect vast amounts of information and the described techniques not only provide a means of data reduction but also provide useful ways to obtain accurate information for decision making.

An illustrative example, described in detail in the chapter, is an analytical model called Life-Style Market Segmentation. This model incorporates three forms of analysis discussed in the chapter: regression, factor, and cluster. The model is concerned with shaping a profile in terms of the characteristics of ZIP Code areas in which customers live to improve the efficiency and effectiveness of direct marketing efforts. The model is able to describe the potential of a market, calculate a firm's penetration of that market, derive a segmentation of the total market, retrieve the desired market segment(s), and validate the research findings.

CASE: STIMULATING DEMAND THROUGH A MAILING LIST

Learning Objective

This case demonstrates the use of an appropriate and valid mailing list in direct marketing. It is intended to stimulate thinking about direct marketing as an aspect of total marketing and not simply mail order. Direct marketing is always measurable and accountable, even when there is personal intervention. The mailing list is the medium. As a database, it is also the market.

Overview

Direct response advertising, by definition, requires some kind of transaction, very often an actual direct purchase. Because such responses in the form of direct purchases can be traced, the effectiveness of individual direct marketing promotion programs can be proven. Those who sell or get inquiries for salespeople through direct marketing find their promotions relatively easy to evaluate. Those who use direct response advertising to persuade readers to buy through retail outlets find this more difficult to evaluate because such results are harder to track. It appears almost impossible to determine if direct response advertising is effective under these circumstances unless somehow the direct marketer could implement a program in a "vacuum" with everything that might affect response, other than the test promotion, filtered out. The potential for measurability is always a challenge to direct marketers as is the optimum use of a mailing list.

Procedure

Read the learning objective, the overview, and the case that follows. Suggest the type and source of mailing list that should be used: house list, response list, or compiled list. How could the reliability and validity of such a list be determined? In terms of the list, discuss the relationship of the sender of direct mail to the receiver. In this instance, how does the receiver become an influencer of a third party, who ultimately purchases from a fourth party?

Case[9]

Dow Pharmaceuticals (now Merrell-Dow) consulted with their direct mail agency, Yeck Brothers Company, to devise an accurate way to measure direct mail's effectiveness. They decided to make direct mail the *only* promotional and sales effort for one of their prescription products throughout an entire selling season. They chose a well-established product that had reached a plateau in sales and had even begun to slip slightly. With this situation, they felt, if they suspended all other efforts to promote the product, any positive effect of the direct mail could be accurately measured.

The product, Singlet, is well known by professionals for treatment of cough and colds. For over 20 years, it has provided symptomatic relief of colds and allergies. However, for more than a year, it hadn't been doing well against competitive products. If sales in the cold relief category dropped, Singlet went down even further; if category sales rose, Singlet sales were also up but not as far up. The result was a steady erosion of market share.

In conducting its experiment, Dow used a single unsolicited sample mailing. The package consisted of a letter/folder; two product disclosure notes; a brochure entitled "The Three Faces of URI"; and 10 boxes of single samples of Singlet. The mailing was released during August 1979 to 27,742 physicians. Since physicians receive approximately 4,000 pieces of mail a year, it is reasonable to wonder whether busy doctors open the mail and read it, and,

---

[9] Material for this case was provided by John D. Yeck, Yeck Brothers Group, Dayton, Ohio, the direct mail agency for Dow Pharmaceuticals.

more important, act on it. Dow Pharmaceuticals had decided to find out.

Finding out can be difficult. This type of direct mail doesn't "sell" anything directly to doctors. In fact, doctors don't actually purchase a prescription medicine themselves; they *prescribe* it to a third person, who buys it from a fourth (a pharmacist). It appears almost impossible to determine exactly to what degree direct mail affects sales under these circumstances.

The direct mail letter used by Dow was a simple, clear, understated reminder of the proven value of a product (Singlet) that had been available for 20 years. The required product disclosure notes were designed so they would fold and fit into the standard medical reference file, as would the more visible brochure entitled "The Three Faces of URI."

With all other advertising for Singlet suspended for the test period, there remained one more possibility that might have a positive effect on sales. Dow's "detail" people, the sales force calling on doctors to encourage the use of Dow products, might distribute product information and samples, which would affect Singlet sales during the period of experimentation. Since this was a 20-year-old product, detail people hadn't been treating its existence as "news," but, to be on the safe side, Dow's sales manager specifically instructed the detailers not to mention Singlet on their calls. "We want to test this direct mail in a vacuum," he said, "we'll let the mail do all the 'detailing'." And that's the way the experiment was conducted. No other promotion. No advertising. No sales effort. Just *one* persuasive direct mail "call" on the doctors at the beginning of the season. Nothing else.

What happened? By April, at the end of the winter season, sales figures proved that the direct mailing had reversed Singlet's long record of low product performance compared to others in its product category. During the fourth quarter, sales of all prescription medi-

cation similar to Singlet were lower than for the previous year. Sales of Singlet were up. During the first quarter, the category gained, but Singlet gained even more. Over the entire winter season, Singlet gained more than four times as much as all other brands.

Although the results of this experiment cannot be tied to responses from specific individuals, it was apparent that a 20-year-old product with a steadily dropping share of the market had reversed itself dramatically and had increased its sales over four times as fast as those of its competition. This happened immediately following an isolated direct mailing, with no other change in promotion.

Dow Pharmaceuticals concluded that doctors read some mail, at least, and that such direct response advertising *can* and *does* affect the action these doctors take in referring an appropriate medication to their patients. Dow concluded: "Mail works."

The results of the Dow Pharmaceuticals experiment are recapped below:

Increase in New Prescriptions Written during 6-Month Period Following Direct Mailing

Quarter results	Category % Increase	Singlet % Increase
4th	− 3.0	+12.0
1st	+11.0	+15.0
6 Mos.	+ 7.7	+28.8

DISCUSSION QUESTIONS

1 Distinguish between these forms of multivariate analysis as presented in this chapter:
   a correlation and regression analysis
   b discriminant analysis
   c factor analysis
   d cluster analysis
2 To predict whether a defined market segment is likely to purchase season tickets for a ballet, what form of multivariate analysis might be used? What form might be used to predict the impact

of demographic characteristics in defining a market segment that would be receptive to such an offer?

3 Discuss the notion of *taxonomy*, the grouping of individuals or objects, and its relevance to direct marketing.

4 How can an individual's life-style (habits, attitudes, behavior patterns) influence his or her purchase behavior?

5 Can life-style be "measured"? How would such measurements help predict purchase behavior?

6 Explain why certain demographic characteristics of buyers, income or wealth, as examples, have a variable impact on purchase behavior, dependent on the location of the buyer. How can the income of a household in rural Arkansas be equated to that of a household in urban New York?

7 Explain what is meant by the interaction of independent variables shaping buyer behavior.

8 Why is the *ability* to buy not the same as the *proneness* to buy?

9 Distinguish between measurement of the characteristics of an *area* and those of an *individual* in predicting buyer behavior.

PART TWO

PLACE: MARKETS AND UNDERSTANDING THEM

ECONOMIC AND SOCIAL INFLUENCES ON DIRECT MARKETING

Effective direct marketing, to be customer-oriented, must begin with at least a basic appreciation of the marketplace and how it operates. It also requires an understanding of buyer behavior and how such behavior is influenced by a variety of social, economic, and environmental conditions. This is because the direct marketing of a product or service necessarily starts with both quantitative and qualitative analysis of the potential market demand. And, although demand in the perspective of economics is most often viewed as being a function of money (income *or* wealth), it becomes apparent that money is not the *only* determinant of demand and, in fact, might not even be a major one. This chapter will be concerned with economic and social influences on direct marketing. A subsequent chapter will be concerned with buyer behavior and especially environmental influences on such behavior.

HISTORICAL PERSPECTIVE OF MARKET ECONOMY

The total marketing concept implies that "the consumer is king." Economists of the past 200 years have had differing views, however, and until the 1920s their attention was devoted almost entirely to production, rather than consumption. To better understand today's marketplace, it will be helpful to highlight those 200 years insofar as attitudes toward production and/or consumption are concerned.[1]

Although the history of economics can be traced in varying ways, the late eighteenth century marks the real beginning of an economic system, as contrasted to isolated expressions of political thought. Strangely enough, the system of "natural liberty" followed closely after the period of the mercantilists, when

intervention by the state was considered a necessity for proper economic management of society.

Perfect Competition and "Natural" Behavior

Our quick trip through the history of economic thought starts with the emergence of a market economy in Great Britain, a situation characterized by the offering of commodities and services of the factors of production (labor, capital, and natural resources) in a perfectly competitive manner, with profit the accepted objective.

The foundation work of this period was Adam Smith's *An Inquiry into the Nature and Causes of the Wealth of Nations,* published in 1776. Smith's doctrine is frequently referred to as laissez faire, literally "let it happen." It is characterized by perfect competition among sellers, rational behavior among buyers, and an observance of "natural laws." The behavior of Adam Smith's classical buyer was assured to be in his or her own best interest as well as that of the economy. He was, postulated Adam Smith, "led by an invisible hand to promote an end which was no part of his intention."[2] To this Smith added: "I have never known much good done by those who have affected to trade for the public good." Buyer behavior was thus seen to be a "natural" phenomenon. There was no incentive to study buyer behavior as apparently nothing could be done about such behavior, even if it were understood.

Marginal Utility and Diminishing Returns

The paradox of value, why diamonds cost more than water, even though water is a necessity of life itself, was never explained by Adam Smith and the classical economists who came after him. It was not until the late

---

[1] Much of this historical discussion is based on Richard T. Gill, *Evolution of Modern Economics,* in Otto Eckstein (ed.), *Foundations of Modern Economics Series,* Prentice-Hall, Inc., Englewood Cliffs, 1937.

[2] Adam Smith, *An Inquiry into the Nature and Causes of the Wealth of Nations,* Canaan ed., Random House, New York, 1937, p. 423.

nineteenth century that the principle of marginal utility was applied in economic theory to explain the actions of buyers.

Scarcity became the cause of value whereas abundance created a diminishing return, or decreasing utility, for the buyer. Central to an understanding of consumer behavior under this theoretical approach is the fact that marginal utility represents the addition to total utility (or satisfaction) that one more unit of a commodity provides the buyer. It's as simple as the first piece of cherry pie tasting better than the second, much better than the third, far better than the fourth.

This law of diminishing marginal utility assumes that buyers seek to maximize their satisfactions. They do this in such a manner that the marginal utility received from a dollar spent on any one commodity is equated to that received from a similar expenditure on an alternative commodity. The buyer is presumed to act with complete rationality and with the ultimate ability to rank order the respective satisfactions.

Those theorists who classify themselves as ordinalists dispute the ability of a buyer subjectively to value utility on an objective scale, and present another analytical tool. Using indifference curves, with alternative collections of commodities shown on the horizontal and vertical axes of a map, buyer preferences are described in terms of ranking of two collections of goods. As between points on a given curve, the buyer is "indifferent" to substitutions of commodities. Any collection of commodities along the curve affords the buyer equal satisfaction and thus has equal value to him.

Preference patterns of the real buyer in the real world, of course, are neither as constant nor as rational as economic utility analysis would have us believe. Largely absent from such economic theory is psychological analysis. This is evident from such mechanistic human behavior predictions as "the lower the price, the higher the demand."[3] Nor does a preference for product A over product B and B over C necessarily imply a preference of A over C. Neither is a buyer all knowing, discriminating, and rational in his actions. Most important to our discussion about environmental influences, which follows in Chapter 6, is the questioning of another general assumption of economic theory, that the consumer is not influenced by other consumers.

Imperfections in Competition

By the early twentieth century, economic theory viewed the buyer as the innocent victim of monopolistic or imperfect competition among firms. It had become apparent in the real world that perfect competition, which is characterized by an economy based on a large number of small firms, each of which is powerless to regulate the marketplace, did not in fact exist. Neither was there, in reality, pure monopoly in which industries were controlled by a single large firm since most products have substitutes, at least at the generic level of benefits being purchased.

It was clear that even corner grocery stores, of which there were literally thousands in the 1920s, varied their prices for identical products by small amounts, with no particular loss of business or revolt by consumers who, for the sake of convenience, were at the mercy of these stores. At the same time, although Ford was the major automobile producer in the 1920s, it certainly was not free of major competition and thus not a monopoly in the true sense. In fact, by 1931, General Motors held the position of leader in the industry, with Chrysler (formed in 1925) taking second place from Ford by 1937.[4]

Contrary to the economic theory that assumes either *pure competition* or *monopoly*

[3] George Katona, *Psychological Analysis of Human Behavior*, McGraw-Hill Book Company, New York, 1951, pp. 6–7.

[4] Gill, *Evolution of Modern Economics*, p. 77.

(rule by one), often industries are controlled and markets are regulated by a few large firms, a condition termed *oligopoly* (rule by a few). Buyer behavior in the marketplace of oligopoly is influenced not only by price, as economic theory assumes, but also by such factors as product differentiation, brand preference, planned obsolescence, and appeal to a market segment. Although these practices are considered by some to be the epitome of waste, many economists (and most antitrusters) are more concerned with price regulations and undue profits that may result from oligopolistic practices.

The Keynesian Revolution

While economic theory moved slowly toward economic reality, the publication of a relatively small volume in 1936 had an extraordinary impact on economic thought and took economics a gigantic step toward the real world. The book was titled *The General Theory of Employment, Interest and Money*. Its architect was John Maynard Keynes, later Lord Keynes, Baron of Tilton. This work has deeply influenced the course of economic events by shifting the emphasis of economic thought from supply (production) to demand (marketing). As Keynesian thought developed, it became apparent that it was the buyer's consumption and industry's resultant investment that determined economic activity.

Keynes' departure from traditional economic thought was extensive, and included a "fundamental psychological law" that related consumption to income, the so-called *consumption function*. Although this law was given only in rough and general terms by Keynes, it is of special significance to those who study buyer behavior:

Now since these facts of experience do not follow of logical necessity, one must suppose the environment and the psychological propensities of the modern world must be of such a character as to produce these results. It is, therefore, useful to consider what hypothetical psychological propensities would lead to a stable system; and then, whether these propensities can be plausibly ascribed, on our general knowledge of contemporary human nature, to the world in which we live.[5]

Whereas Keynes treated consumption solely as a function of income, the so-called Pigou effect (propounded by a distinguished British economist, A.C. Pigou, whose work is treated critically by Keynes) suggests that accumulations of wealth, and not current income alone, has a profound effect on consumer decisions. More recently, an American economist, Milton Friedman, presented a theory that relates consumption to permanent income as contrasted with windfall gains and losses, which he describes as transitory income.[6]

Of related significance, as it concerns the buyer in modern economic theory, is a characteristic of consumer behavior that another American economist, James Duesenberry, developed. Instead of the absolute income hypothesized by Keynes, this analysis looks at relative income. That is, it recognizes that consumer preferences are *interdependent* rather than independent of one another. Consumer behavior becomes emulative, the desire to purchase goods being positively affected by the purchases of other consumers.

Duesenberry argues further that, as a consumer's income rises, so will his consumption. Should his income revert back to its former lower level, however, his consumption will fall, although not to its former level. A consumer, once attaining a level of consumption, is resistant to downward adjustments even if

[5] John Maynard Keynes, *The General Theory of Employment, Interest and Money,* Harcourt, Brace & World, Inc., New York, 1936, p. 250.
[6] Milton Friedman, *A Theory of the Consumption Function,* Princeton University Press, Princeton, 1957.

his income is falling. Duesenberry terms this a "ratchet effect."[7]

Veblen's Conspicuous Consumption

An economist as well as a social critic of consumer behavior, one whose influence is evident and relevant to this day, was Thorstein Veblen. It was his contention that the proper scope of economic analysis was to be found in real life motives and institutions and their evolution over time. His concept of *conspicuous consumption,* with its emphasis on the social character of consumption decisions and the interdependence of consumer choices, has proved important and durable. As Veblen put it, three-quarters of a century ago, "The accepted standard of expenditure in the community or in the class to which a person belongs largely determines what his standard of living will be."[8]

Perhaps the most striking feature of consumer behavior was the desire to prove superior reputability to others, as Veblen observed in these words:

> That is to say, in concrete terms, in any community where conspicuous consumption is an element of the scheme of life, an increase in an individual's ability to pay is likely to take the form of an expenditure for some accredited line of conspicuous consumption.[9]

Such behavior, Veblen theorized, "is at its best in those portions of the community where the human contact of the individual is widest and the mobility of the population is greatest."[10] Further, as wealth accumulates beyond the consumer's own individual needs, he extends conspicuous consumption "by resorting to the giving of valuable presents and expensive feasts and entertainment."[11] Although Thorstein Veblen has been termed both a skeptic and a satirist, his observation of the buyer in economic theory in terms of conspicuous consumption was a valid one, as the passage of the years has verified. More recently, the idea has been expressed in such terms as "keeping up with the Joneses."

Economist Paul Samuelson has put it this way: "Because man is a social animal, what he regards as necessary comforts of life depends on what he sees others consuming." Samuelson also points out that, because "one man's consumption depends on the income and consumption of others," one cannot expect the national consumption pattern to be the aggregated total of observed individual patterns. Further, from this it follows that a continual rising standard of living is to be expected.[12]

Galbraith's Materialism

Another economist and discerning critic of the contemporary consumer has been John Kenneth Galbraith. Galbraith contended that the modern consumer minimizes certain social values such as art galleries, parks, schools, highways, clean air and water in favor of a materialism that puts greater value on new automobiles, stylish clothing, convenience foods, and ostentatious housing.[13]

Galbraith's concern with such behavior by consumers is expressed in what he terms the "dependence effect." As affluence increases within a society, increases in consumption "act by suggestion or emulation to create wants." This process is expedited through "advertising and salesmanship." Since consumption is the counterpart of production, the

[7] James S. Duesenberry, *Income, Saving and the Theory of Consumer Behavior,* Harvard University Press, Cambridge, 1947, pp. 17–46.

[8] Thorstein Veblen, *The Theory of the Leisure Class,* The Macmillan Co., London, 1917, p. 111.

[9] Ibid., p. 110.

[10] Ibid., p. 87.

[11] Ibid., p. 75.

[12] Paul A. Samuelson, *Economics,* 6th ed., McGraw-Hill Book Company, New York, 1964, p. 218.

[13] John Kenneth Galbraith, *The Affluent Society,* College ed., Houghton Mifflin Co., Boston, 1960.

fulfillment of increasing consumer wants is dependent on increasing production. Higher production is, in turn, dependent on the stimulation of wants. Thus, "wants are increasingly created by the process by which they are satisfied."[14]

ECONOMIC THEORY AND BEHAVIORAL ECONOMICS

From the preceding brief overview of the buyer as he has evolved through two centuries of economic theory, it should be apparent that his behavior cannot be taken as "given" or "assumed" as many economic theorists would have us believe. In the real world of managerial economics, such assumptions are oversimplifications. The need for bridging the gap between economic theory and managerial economics has become more and more recognized by the theorist as well as the manager. Economists, who have long been smug about the empirical state of their art in relation to the other social sciences, concede that a shakeup leading toward behavioral economics has already begun.

Although the economist juggled with the factors of production—labor, capital, and natural resources—it was most expeditious to assume away and consider as given and static such important variables as the nature of competition, the state of technology, and the expectations of buyers. These factors cannot be so neatly quantified as are land, labor, and capital. There are complex human variables involved in the innovative and creative behavior of the real world in which the direct marketer functions.

Consumer behavior in today's industrial society is interacting and is dependent not so much on income as on the buyer's perception of his or her place in the environment. This concept of consumer behavior is generally accepted in the marketing literature, and should be clearly understood by direct marketers.

Taking a psychological overview of economic behavior, George Katona demonstrated that attitudes and expectations along with hopes and fears of tens of millions of individuals are what largely determine the progress of an economy. The *ability* to buy is dependent on income, assets, and credit. The *willingness* to buy, however, results from individual motives, attitudes, expectations, felt needs and wants.[15] Drawing on this observation, and in terms of the four "P's" of marketing, direct marketers appropriately use price and place to increase the buyer's *ability* to buy whereas they use product and promotion to increase *willingness* to buy.

This approach to economics has tremendous implications for direct marketers. It is not only a matter of combining labor, capital, and natural resources in the most efficient way, as pure economic theory led us to believe. Although economics is at the core of direct marketing, it is really a new and unconventional kind of economics, a behavioral science that draws heavily on other social sciences.

Application of Behavioral Economics to Direct Marketing

It is individual consumers within societies and not just entrepreneurs who undertake economic activity. Because in industrial societies the producers have become physically separated from the consumers, it has become the function of marketing to bring buyer and seller together. How well this is done depends to a great extent on an understanding of human behavior. Marketing is not a simple matter of the inevitable intersect of supply and demand curves, in the manner shown in Figure 2-1 on page 29. Rather it is the complex interacting

[14] Ibid., p. 158.

[15] George J. Katona, *The Powerful Consumer*, McGraw-Hill Book Company, New York, 1966, p. 27.

of many specialized disciplines, especially economics.

Psychology helps the marketer understand human personality through analysis of buying motives. Sociology explains the social system and the impact of social class participation. Anthropology gives appreciation of the heritage and taboos of various cultures. A knowledge of political science is helpful in understanding foreign competition.

The need for long-range planning and forecasting, as well as scientific and objective decision making, brings into play statistical and mathematical techniques. There is a blending of the many specializations involved to market efficiently and effectively. It is not conventional economic theory alone.

PEOPLE, PRODUCTS, MONEY IN AN INDUSTRIAL SOCIETY

A market has been defined by William J. Stanton as "people with needs to satisfy, money to spend and the willingness to spend it."[16] Within this broad definition, however, we must distinguish between consumer markets and industrial markets, and, ultimately, further identify smaller and more homogeneous direct marketing units described as market segments.

There is a distinction to be made, too, between consumer goods and industrial goods as well as products differentiated for specific market segments. Further, we need to understand the difference between consumers and *customers*. The latter term embraces industrial buyers as well as individual buyers.

Consumer Markets

The total consumer market in the United States, of which each of us as an individual or household is a part, numbered just under

210 million in 1970 and increased to nearly 230 million by 1980, an average annual increase of approximately 1 percent. It is anticipated that the total consumer market will increase, at about the same annual growth rate, to some 240 million in 1985 and 250 million in 1990.[17]

As a total market, however, we are certainly not all alike in demographic, geographic, or psychographic terms. More than one-half of us are females, with that proportion increasing. Less than one-half of us are married, and indications are that that's going down. Nearly two-thirds of us are old enough to vote and our total population is becoming older. Nearly two-thirds of us are city or suburban dwellers.

After the birth rate slumped to an all-time low during the mid-1970s, there is evidence that it is beginning to rise again. The age-adjusted death rate, by 1980, stood at an all-time low of 600 per 100,000 population, a rate one-half that recorded 40 years earlier.[18] The net effect of a declining birth rate and a declining death rate is shown graphically in Figure 5-1, which visualizes the changing population distribution by sex and age between 1970 and 2000.

Male/female and age differences are but two of many demographic variables that occur within the total consumer market and ultimately become the basis for market segmentation and product differentiation. More young people have been putting off marriage or are not getting married at all. Whereas the marriage rate has been declining, the divorce rate has been increasing. The net effect of this change in marital status is that, of approximately 80 million households in the United States, only approximately 75 percent of these are *family* relationships compared with approximately 90 percent a quarter century ago.

---

[16] William J. Stanton, *Fundamentals of Marketing*, 6th ed., McGraw-Hill Book Company, New York, 1981, p. 65.

[17] U.S. Census Bureau, *Current Population Reports*, Series No. 721, p. 25, 1980.
[18] National Center for Health Statistics, *Monthly Vital Statistics Report*, vol. 29, no. 6, supplement and vol. 28, no. 13, 1980.

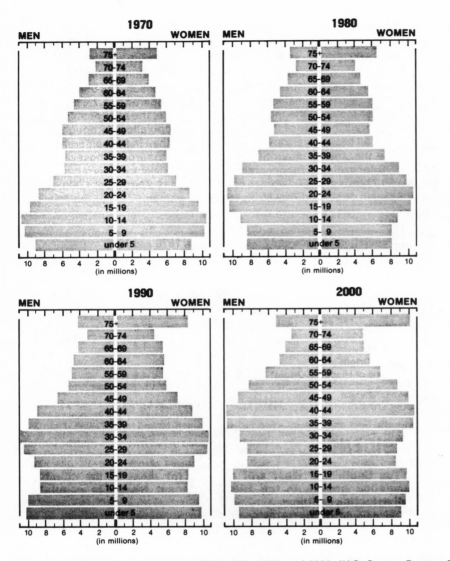

Figure 5-1 Population pyramids for 1970, 1980, 1990, and 2000. (*U.S. Census Bureau,* Current Population Reports, *Series P-25, No. 870 and unpublished data; American Council of Life Insurance, Washington, D.C.,* DataTrack 8, *"A Population Profile: The 1980s and Beyond,"* 1981.)

Another distinguishing feature of consumer markets is the fact that two of three of us live in metropolitan areas, approximately one-half in the suburbs and the other one-half within central cities. There is a so-called megalopolis (several contiguous metropolitan areas) run-ning from Boston down the eastern seaboard to Washington. Approximately 20 percent of the total United States population lives in the "Bo-Wash" megalopolis.

We move around frequently, too, approxi-mately 20 percent (mostly young people) move within a 12-month period. A relatively small number of these, approximately 1 of 7, move as far as a different state, however. This mobility impacts on consumer demand, too.

The median income of United States households continues its rise upward as visualized in Figure 5-2. Approximately 16 percent of American households reported incomes of $25,000 or more per year (in constant 1977 dollars) in 1970 but that proportion could grow to nearly 44 percent by 1995.

The Census Bureau reports, too, that 90 percent of our houses are *not* dilapidated and contain all essential plumbing features. Virtually all have television and there are many more radios in the United States than there are people. In contrast to the rest of the world, nearly all U.S. households have telephones (a vital communication link for direct marketers) and 80 percent have one or more automobiles. Such facts not only describe markets but also indicate their potential.

Although ours is still predominantly a blue-collar nation, the number of white-collar workers (including professional, technical, and managerial categories) has increased, mainly because of increases at the technology and educational level. There are more women working than ever before, with nearly one-half in the work force.

Industrial Markets

Contrasted with consumer markets, industrial markets are much smaller in numbers but certainly not in sales volume.

Industrial markets are commonly categorized according to a United States government coding system termed Standard Industrial Classification (SIC). This system is used to designate industry groups by function and product and, in a way, parallels the demographic characteristics of consumer markets in that these codes are commonly used for segmenting and analyzing demand. Four-digit

Figure 5-2   Median income of all households, 1970 to 1978 with projections to 1995, in constant 1977 dollars. (*U.S. Census Bureau,* Current Population Reports, *Series P-60, No. 122 and American Council of Life Insurance, Washington, D.C.,* DataTrack 8, *"A Population Profile: The 1980s and Beyond," 1981.*)

Median Income (thousands of dollars)

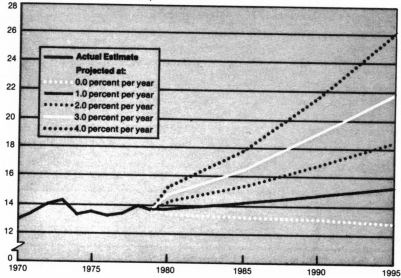

codes are assigned by the federal government in connection with the taking of the census of business.

The first two digits of the four-digit code indicate a major classification of industry, of which there are 10:

01 through 09	Agriculture, Forestry, and Fisheries
10 through 14	Mining
15 through 19	Contract Construction
20 through 39	Manufacturing
40 through 49	Transportation, Communication, and Public Utilities
50 through 51	Wholesale Trade
52 through 59	Retail Trade
60 through 69	Finance, Insurance, and Real Estate
70 through 89	Services (including medical, legal, schools, churches, social services, and nonprofit organizations)
90 through 99	Public Administration

Industrial markets are often categorized, in addition to SIC, by financial strength or size in terms of number of employees or sales volume. Geographic selectivity is often used, too, including city size and location as well as whether or not the particular enterprise is a headquarters or branch office. Sometimes there is selection by form of ownership: individual, partnership, corporation.

The final two digits of the SIC code classify individual organizations by subgroup and further detail within industry. For example, SIC No. 2300 identifies manufacturers of wearing apparel. Within this classification, SIC No. 2310 categorizes manufacturers of men's clothing and SIC No. 2311 specifically identifies men's suits and coats manufacturers. See Figure 7-18 on page 176.

Within firms and other organizations, industrial markets are often thought of in terms of job functions. Demand within industrial firms is not generated by purchasing agents alone,

but, more likely, by engineers, chemists, architects, and a host of other specialists. Direct marketers must appeal not only to organizations but also to relevant individuals within organizations.

There are public sector organizations, too, that can be described in the sense of industrial markets. These include medical and health services, legal services, schools, libraries, social services, cultural organizations, and churches.

Buying Power

Stanton's definition of a market given earlier implies that it is not people alone who make up markets. They must have the money to spend, either income or accumulated wealth, and, equally important, they must possess a willingness to spend it.

The United States government in its own accounting system looks on the one hand at *national income,* individual wages and salaries as well as corporate profits, and further describes, after appropriate adjustments, that portion of national income that is personal as well as that which is disposable. National income is related to *Gross National Product,* both consumption and investment expenditures, with appropriate adjustment for import and export and government purchases of goods and services.

From the perspective of the individual consumer or organization, *money income* is described as the cash or equivalent payment received in the form of wages, salaries, rents, interest, dividends, and other earnings. This money income can be further translated into *real income* in terms of purchasing power; that is, what that money will buy in goods and services. There is also *psychic income,* an intangible, that relates expenditures to satisfactions. And, as has already been noted, income can be derived from current activity or from accumulations of wealth.

Disposable income is usually described as

that which is available for consumption after taxes are deducted. *Discretionary income* is that which is left after the purchase of necessities in the categories of food, clothing, and shelter. Reductions in discretionary income hurt retailers of shopping goods and specialty goods, especially those involved in mail order.

Buying Patterns

Whereas income and wealth are determinants of the *ability* to buy, the *proneness* (or *willingness*) to buy is dependent on a variety of other factors. A 1972–1973 study by the Bureau of Labor Statistics[19] demonstrated conclusively that blue-collar workers spent differently than did professionals and managers, even at the same income level. The study showed a higher-than-average percentage expenditure of money income among lower income families for such things as food, tobacco, personal care items, and medical care. At the other end of the spectrum, higher income families spent a lesser proportion of income on automobiles, matters connected with housing, and on such items of current consumption as eating out, alcoholic beverages, clothing, recreation, education, and travel.

Of special interest to direct marketers, regardless of the way in which their sales are consummated (mail order, in store, personal selling), the study showed that particular product markets are not, as might commonly be expected, confined to households with high income. Such products are generally looked on as symbolic of class status by moderate as well as high income households. Specific examples are Scotch whisky, sterling silver, furs, pianos and organs, tickets to concerts and plays, private school tuition, car rentals, and expenditures connected with recreational boating. The Bureau of Labor Statistics study demonstrates, too, that there is not necessarily

a correlation between the purchase of luxury food products and the income level of the people who buy these. Lower income groups often purchase more expensive, luxury brands.

Geography, as well as demography, is an important determinant of the proneness to buy. Direct marketers would do well to understand, as an example, that rural buyers, even at comparable income levels and demographic characteristics, purchase different products in different ways than do their counterpart city or suburban dwellers. Ethnic groups, which often concentrate geographically, also purchase differently. Obviously, climate relative to geography often plays an important part in determining whether snowblowers or swimsuits are purchased with discretionary income.

Direct marketers ultimately must look at aggregates in macroeconomic terms. They must segment the total heterogeneous market into smaller submarkets or market segments. They think of individuals but rarely sell to just one individual in direct marketing promotion. Such market segmentation, as will be discussed more extensively in Chapter 7, can be demographic or geographic or even psychographic, dependent on the habits, attitudes, and lifestyles of individuals or clusters of buyers.

ECONOMIC VALUES VS. SOCIAL VALUES

In economic terms under conditions of perfect competition, price is the prime determinant of resource allocation. Considering our contemporary economic system and the realities of imperfections in competition, however, certain value judgments must be made as scarce resources are allocated. For example, is the freedom of choice worth the embarrassment of riches from which to choose? The answer to that query is obviously a value judgment by the respondent.

Another dilemma lies in valuation of *benefits*. Some benefits can be identified, divided, and quantified; others cannot, since the crea-

[19] U.S. Dept. of Labor, Bureau of Labor Statistics, *Consumer Expenditure Survey Series*, 1972–1973, Report 455.

tion of certain benefits can have negative impact, on the ecology, for example. Consider a purchase of a one-quarter-inch drill bit (a product) in order to produce a one-quarter-inch round hole (a benefit). Somewhere during the production process, there may have been air or water pollution (a negative social value). In today's direct marketing environment, economic values cannot be viewed apart from social values.

The Purpose of Promotion

Marketing costs and especially those related to promotion, that is, advertising and selling, should be looked on as "value added" just as intangible benefits received by consumers are also values. Organizations work continually to improve the efficiency of direct marketing, to measure its costs accurately. The statement is trite, but it is true: "If it weren't for advertising, you would pay more for most things you buy." The *informational* value of promotional activities makes this so. Mass marketing, through promotional activities, makes possible mass production, which ultimately lowers costs and prices and increases demand at these lower prices. Direct marketing is especially attuned to such promotional and informational activities. The ultimate objective is to derive benefits, without inefficiencies. Direct marketing thrives on innovation.

Goal of the Marketing Concept

A goal of the marketing concept is to develop a customer orientation on the part of an organization's management. In line with this philosophy it seems reasonable to establish as an objective the satisfaction of customer wants and needs, as expressed by customers. Thus, direct marketing should be evaluated in terms of satisfied customer wants as these customers themselves express or value them. At the same time, the direct marketer needs to be aware of whether or not the provision of such benefits

to customers might have detrimental social impact on others.

To what extent does marketing succeed?

Whereas a quantitative price measures what customers are *willing* to pay, such a price cannot really measure satisfaction or benefit. Certainly, price alone cannot measure what customer satisfaction *should* be, particularly if we accept the contention that consumers themselves are not capable of optimizing social values through their individual economic actions. As a result, much of the evaluation of marketing and the efficiency with which it allocates economic resources and satisfies consumer wants must be subjective.

Marketing is *not,* as Theodore Levitt wrote, "the devious art of separating the unwary consumer from his loose change."[20] Although there have been criticisms of the marketing concept, these have been directed more toward individual components of the system rather than the process itself. Promotional activities have been singled out as often being raucous with overemphasis on materialism at the expense of cultural, spiritual, ethical, and moral values, even creating demand at the expense of more important values. Attitudes of retail sales personnel are said to be deteriorating in quality. Advertising has been criticized on economic as well as social grounds for adding relatively too much to the price of products and creating an imbalance of expenditures between the private and public sectors.

Distribution systems are criticized as being unnecessarily complex with too many middlemen and too much "nonprice" competition. Products and services are said to be of poor quality with exaggerated features and built-in obsolescence along with excessive selections and confusing alternative arrays.

As students of direct marketing become

[20] Theodore Levitt, *The Marketing Mode,* McGraw-Hill Book Company, New York, 1969, p. 1.

aware of the increasing economic and social importance of marketing, and as they recognize the opportunities in the field, greater numbers of qualified personnel will be attracted to a career in direct marketing.

These direct marketing professionals, in return for the privilege of existing and operating in our economic system, must conduct themselves and their affairs in an efficient, ethical and socially desirable manner. It is becoming increasingly apparent that whatever direct marketing executives do to develop a socially desirable operation, this will also help to strengthen and perpetuate the economic structure in which they work. For individual business firms and nonprofit organizations alike, within the total socioeconomic system, modern direct marketing can be a key to successful expansion.

There hardly seems to be a limit to the potential for scientific direct marketers to make detailed analyses of responses, customers, industries, and promotional performances; to make sales forecasts; to do short-range and long-range planning; to determine product mix; to select media and physical distribution programs; and to participate in the myriad of other direct marketing activities.

Regulations vs. Regulators

These observations about the role of government in the regulation of marketing are worth noting:

- Some government intervention is *voluntary* in an effort to foster and preserve competition and to increase business efficiency.
- Other government intervention is *regulatory,* often in an effort to preserve free competition, but, ironically, frequently brought on by marketers themselves when they seek to achieve regulation of that which hampers them.

Can inadequacies in a marketing system be best rectified by governments (through regulation) or by consumers (through marketplace actions) or by direct marketers themselves (through their own ethical standards)? Certainly consumers can call the shots by their actions in the marketplace. Whether these actions are adequate to maximize social value, in deference to economic value, is a point for argument.

ETHICS OF DIRECT MARKETING

Ethics is a branch of philosophy, a system of human behavior concerned with morality: the rightness and wrongness of individual actions and needs. In a sense, it is a system of *self-regulation.*

The Direct Marketing Association in its efforts to provide direct marketers with principles of conduct that are generally accepted has published the following Guidelines for Ethical Business Practices to achieve an atmosphere of self-regulation.[21]

The Direct Marketing Association Guidelines for Ethical Business Practices

THE TERMS OF THE OFFER

Honesty

Article No. 1 All offers should be clear, honest and complete so that the consumer may know the exact nature of what is being offered, the price, the terms of payment (including all extra charges), and the commitment involved in the placing of an order. Before publication of an offer, direct marketers should be prepared to substantiate any claims or offers made. Advertisements or specific claims which are untrue, misleading, deceptive, fraudulent or unjustly disparaging of competitors should not be used.

[21] Direct Marketing Association, Inc., 6 East 43rd St., New York, N.Y. 10017, revised March 10, 1981.

Clarity

Article No. 2   A simple statement of all the essential points of the offer should be clearly displayed in the promotional material. When an offer illustrates goods which are not included or cost extra, these facts should be made clear.

Print Size

Article No. 3   Print which by its small size, placement or other visual characteristics is likely to substantially affect the legibility of the offer, or exceptions to it, should not be used.

Actual Conditions

Article No. 4   All descriptions and promises should be in accordance with actual conditions, situations and circumstances existing at the time of the promotion. Claims regarding any limitations (such as time or quantity) should be legitimate.

Disparagement

Article No. 5   Disparagement of any person or group on grounds of race, color, religion, national origin, sex, marital status or age is unacceptable.

Standards

Article No. 6   Solicitations should not contain vulgar, immoral, profane, or offensive matter nor promote the sale of pornographic material or other matter not acceptable for advertising on moral grounds.

Advertising to Children

Article No. 7   Offers suitable for adults only should not be made to children.

Photographs and Art Work

Article No. 8   Photographs, illustrations, artwork, and the situations they represent should be accurate portrayals and current reproductions of the product, service, or other subject in all particulars.

Sponsor and Intent

Article No. 9   All direct marketing contacts should disclose the name of the sponsor and each purpose of the contact. No one should make offers or solicitations in the guise of research or a survey when the real intent is to sell products or services or to raise funds.

Identity of Seller

Article No. 10   Every offer and shipment should sufficiently identify the full name and street address of the direct marketer so that the consumer may contact the individual or company by mail or phone.

Solicitation in the Guise of an Invoice

Article No. 11   Offers that are likely to be mistaken for bills or invoices should not be used.

Postage and Handling Charges

Article No. 12   Postage or shipping charges and handling charges, if any, should reflect as accurately as practicable actual costs incurred.

SPECIAL OFFERS

Use of the Word "Free" and Other Similar Representations

Article No. 13   A product or service which is offered without cost or obligation to the recipient may be unqualifiedly described as "free."

If a product or service is offered as "free," for a nominal cost or at a greatly reduced price and the offer requires the recipient to purchase some other product or service, all terms and conditions should be clearly and conspicuously disclosed and in close conjunction with the use of the term "free" or other similar phrase.

When the term "free" or other similar representations are made (for example, 2-for-1, half price or 1-cent offers), the product or service required to be purchased should not be increased in price or decreased in quality or quantity.

Negative Option Selling

Article No. 14 All direct marketers should comply with the FTC regulation governing Negative Option Plans. Some of the major requirements of this regulation are listed below:

Offers which require the consumer to return a notice sent by the seller before each periodic shipment to avoid receiving merchandise should contain all important conditions of the plan including:

a A full description of the obligation to purchase a minimum number of items and all the charges involved and,

b the procedures by which the consumer receives the announcements of selections and a statement of their frequency; how the consumer rejects unwanted items and how to cancel after completing the obligation.

The consumer should be given advance notice of the periodic selection so that the consumer may have a minimum of ten days to exercise a timely choice.

Because of the nature of this kind of offer, special attention should be given to the clarity, completeness and prominent placement of the terms in the initial offering.

Sweepstakes

Article No. 15 All direct marketers should abide by the DMA Guidelines for Self-Regulation of Sweepstakes Promotions. Articles Nos. 16 through 18 (below) contain the basic precepts of these guidelines.

Clear and Conspicuous Disclosure of Rules

Article No. 16 All terms and conditions of the sweepstakes, including entry procedures, the number and types of prizes, the closing dates, eligibility requirements, and the fact that no purchase is required should be disclosed in a clear and conspicuous manner in the promotion.

Devices, check boxes, reply envelopes and the like used for entering the sweepstakes only should be as conspicuous as those utilized for ordering the product or service and entering the sweepstakes.

Prizes

Article No. 17 All prizes advertised should be awarded. Winners should be selected in a manner that ensures fair application of the laws of chance.

Chances of Winning

Article No. 18 No sweepstakes promotion, or any of its parts, should state or imply that a recipient has won a prize or overstate the chances of winning.

Price Comparisons

Article No. 19 Price comparisons may be made in two ways:

a between one's price and a former, future or suggested price or

b between one's price and the price of a competitor's comparable product.

In all price comparisons, the compared price against which the comparison is made must be fair and accurate.

In each case of comparison to a former, suggested or competitor's comparable product price, substantial sales should have been made at that price in the recent past.

For comparisons with a future price, there should be a reasonable expectation that the future price will be charged in the foreseeable future.

Guarantees

Article No. 20 If a product or service is offered with a "guarantee" or a "warranty," the terms and conditions should either be set forth in full in the promotion, or the promotion should state how the consumer may obtain a copy. The guarantee should clearly state the name and address of the guarantor and the duration of the guarantee.

Any requests for repair, replacement or refund under the terms of a "guarantee" or "warranty" should be honored promptly. In an unqualified offer of refund, repair or replacement, the customer's preference shall prevail.

SPECIAL CLAIMS

Use of Test or Survey Data

Article No. 21 All test or survey data referred to in advertising should be competent and reliable as to source and methodology, and should support the specific claim for which it is cited. Advertising claims should not distort the test or survey results nor take them out of context.

Testimonials and Endorsements

Article No. 22 Testimonials and endorsements should be used only if they are:

a Authorized by the person quoted,
b Genuine and related to the experience of the person giving them and
c Not taken out of context so as to distort the endorser's opinion or experience with the product.

THE PRODUCT

Product Safety

Article No. 23 Products should be safe in normal use and be free of defects likely to cause injury. To that end, they should meet or exceed current, recognized health and safety norms and be adequately tested, where applicable. Information provided with the product should include proper directions for use and full instructions covering assembly and safety warnings, whenever necessary.

Product Distribution Safety

Article No. 24 Products should be distributed only in a manner that will provide reasonable safeguards against possibilities of injury.

Product Availability

Article No. 25 Direct marketers should only offer merchandise when it is on hand or when there is a reasonable expectation of its receipt.

Direct marketers should not engage in dry testing unless the special nature of that offer is disclosed in the promotion.

FULFILLMENT

Unordered Merchandise

Article No. 26 Merchandise should not be shipped without having first received a customer's permission. The exceptions are samples or gifts clearly marked as such, and merchandise mailed by a charitable organization soliciting contributions, as long as all items are sent with a clear and conspicuous statement informing the recipient of an unqualified right to treat the product as a gift and to do with it as the recipient sees fit, at no cost or obligation to the recipient.

Shipments

Article No. 27 Direct marketers are reminded that they should abide by the FTC regulation regarding the prompt shipment of prepaid merchandise, the Mail Order Merchandise (30 Day) Rule.

Beyond this regulation, direct marketers are urged to ship all orders as soon as possible.

CREDIT AND DEBT COLLECTION

Equal Credit Opportunity

Article No. 28 A creditor should not discriminate on the basis of race, color, religion, national origin, sex, marital status or age. If the individual is rejected for credit, the creditor should be prepared to give reasons why.

Debt Collection

Article No. 29 Unfair, misleading, deceptive or abusive methods should not be used for collecting money. The direct marketer should take reasonable steps to assure that those collecting on the direct marketer's behalf comply with this guideline.

USE OF MAILING LISTS

List Rental Practices

Article No. 30 Every list owner who sells, exchanges, or rents lists should see to it that

each individual on the list is informed of those practices, and should offer an option to have the individual's name deleted when rentals or purchases are made. The list owner should remove names from the owner's customer or donor lists when requested directly by the individual, and by use of the DMA Mail Preference Service name removal list.

List brokers and compilers should take reasonable steps to assure that the list owners follow these list practices.

Personal Information

Article No. 31 All list owners, brokers and compilers should be protective of the consumer's right to privacy and sensitive to the information collected on lists and subsequently considered for transfer.

Information supplied by consumers such as, but not limited to, medical, financial, insurance or court data should not be included on lists that are rented or exchanged when there is a reasonable expectation by the consumer that the information would be kept confidential.

List Usage Agreements

Article No. 32 List owners, brokers, compilers and users should make every attempt to establish the exact nature of the list's intended usage prior to the sale or rental of the list. Owners, brokers and compilers should not permit the sale or rental of their lists for an offer that is in violation of any of the Ethical Guidelines of DMA. Promotions should be directed to those segments of the public most likely to be interested in their causes or to have a use for their products or services.

List Abuse

Article No. 33 No list or list data should be used in violation of the lawful rights of the list owner or of the agreement between the parties;

any such misuse should be brought to the attention of the lawful owner.

TELEPHONE MARKETING
(See Articles Nos. 9 and 27)

Reasonable Hours

Article No. 34   All telephone contacts should be made during reasonable hours.

Disclosure and Tactics

Article No. 35   All telephone solicitations should disclose to the buyer during the conversation the cost of the merchandise, all terms, conditions, and the payment plan and whether there will be postage and handling charges. At no time should "high pressure" tactics be utilized.

Use of Automatic Electronic Equipment

Article No. 36   No telephone marketer should solicit sales using automatic electronic dialing equipment unless the telephone immediately disconnects when the called person hangs up.

Taping of Conversation

Article No. 37   Taping of telephone conversations should not be conducted without notice to the person called and that person's consent, as well as the use of a beeping device.

Telephone Name Removal/
Restricted Contacts

Article No. 38   Telephone marketers should remove the name of any contact from their telephone lists when requested to do so.

Telephone marketers should not call telephone subscribers who have unlisted or unpublished telephone numbers unless a prior relationship exists.

FUND RAISING
(See Article No. 26)

Commission Prohibition/Authenticity of
Organization

Article No. 39   Fund raisers should make no percentage or commission arrangements whereby any person or firm assisting or participating in a fund raising activity is paid a fee proportionate to the funds raised, nor should they solicit for nonfunctioning organizations.

LAWS, CODES, AND REGULATIONS

Article No. 40   Direct marketers should operate in accordance with the Better Business Bureau's Code of Advertising and be cognizant of and adhere to laws and regulations of the United States Postal Service, the Federal Trade Commission, the Federal Reserve Board, and other applicable Federal, state and local laws governing advertising, marketing practices, and the transaction of business by mail, telephone, and the print and broadcast media.

SUMMARY

Effective direct marketing requires a basic understanding of the marketplace and how it operates as well as an understanding of buyer behavior as it is determined by a variety of social, economic, and environmental conditions. Contrary to what economic theory would have us believe, market demand is not simply a function of price or of income or wealth.

In tracing the history of the modern market economy during the past 200 years, one sees that the buyer evolved from a passive to an active position, from being a responder to supply to being a stimulator of demand. Buyer behavior in modern industrial society is interacting and is dependent not so much on income or wealth as on the buyer's perception of his or her place in the environment. Direct marketers must understand buyer behavior to develop product, price, and promotion strategies.

A distinction should be made between markets that serve consumers and those that serve industrial buyers, and these broad categories must be further divided into smaller, more homogeneous direct marketing units described as market segments. Although the distinction is not always clear since many products and services are used in both consumer and industrial markets, differentiation may also be made between consumer goods and industrial goods.

Whereas consumer markets total larger numbers, ultimately most consumer goods go through an industrial process and thus industrial markets, in terms of sales volume, can be as large or even larger than consumer markets.

Market segments can be described in *geographic, demographic,* and *psychographic* terms according to location, characteristics, and attitudes. Research data are amply available for both markets, and the descriptions for segmentation are also readily available.

Economic values in terms of costs and benefits should be related to social values as well as related costs, such as environmental impact of air and water pollution. Since a goal of the marketing concept is to develop a customer orientation on the part of management, and thus be more apt to satisfy real customer wants and needs, the marketer should be aware of potential detrimental social impact on others in the production and marketing process.

There has been a trend toward government regulation to rectify the inadequacies of our marketing system, yet it is conceivable that marketers themselves, through their own high ethical standards, can ideally develop a system of self-regulation. The Direct Marketing Association, in its effort to provide direct marketers with principles of conduct that are generally accepted, has established the above *Guidelines for Ethical Business Practices*.

CASE: BOOSTING A DECLINING MARKET DEMAND

Learning Objective

This case study presents a situation in which social change (a declining birthrate) and resultant economic change (a declining market demand) stimulated development of a direct marketing strategy that would influence buyer behavior toward a particular product line. It shows an example of how the elements of direct marketing can enable an organization to cope with social and economic change.

Overview

It is incumbent on the direct marketer to have at least a basic understanding of the marketplace and how it operates. A variety of social and economic conditions over which little influence can be exerted can affect the sales and profitability of an organizaton. Knowing how involves both quantitative and qualitative analysis of the factors that can affect market demand.

Procedure

Read the learning objective, the overview, and the case that follows. Be prepared to discuss how a declining birthrate affects the market demand for particular products. What alternatives are available to an organization experiencing such a decline in the demand for its products?

Case[22]

England's largest shoe manufacturer, C&J Clarks, Ltd., faced a difficult sales problem in 1977. The declining birthrate in the United Kingdom caused a 13.1 percent decline in market demand for children's shoes. It became obvious to the firm's executives that this declining market needed special attention. They knew that the initial purchases made by indi-

[22] Adapted from ''British Shoe Manufacturer Builds Traffic for Retail Outlets,'' *Direct Marketing,* December 1978, pp. 38–40.

vidual parents for each new child had become increasingly more important in forming their purchasing patterns during the child's first 10 years.

The declining market for infants' shoes was affecting retailers severely. They were carrying less stock and thus restricting choice. Salespeople for C&J Clarks, Ltd., who called on some 2,000 retailers every 6 to 8 weeks, found it increasingly difficult to maintain retailer interest in a full range of styles and colors, in spite of a full schedule of magazine advertising that the firm was running in specialized media.

As an alternative to this general magazine advertising, executives of the firm decided to contact new mothers in another way and to measure specific results from that contact. The new promotional strategy that they decided to try involved use of The Bounty Box, a gift pack containing advertising and product samples, given to a new mother while she was still in the hospital. Approximately 280,000 new mothers were reached through this medium every year, making up 80 percent of the potential market.

A mailing piece with a special offer was designed. The package contained a letter, a four-color brochure, and a reply card, low-key in nature and designed to position Clarks as a company that knows about babies. The letter offered a handsome color poster, 16 by 20 inches, which could be hung in the new infant's room at home. The poster depicted toy blocks, each containing copy describing ''stepping stones'' the infant would pass: crawling, sitting, speaking, standing, teething, including, of course, the first pair of shoes from Clarks.

This offer from Clarks, distributed within The Bounty Box, resulted in a 15 percent response requesting the poster. Clarks thus generated its own mailing list of new mothers, approximately 42,000 annually, to whom follow-up mailing would be sent several months later, when it was time for the baby's first shoes. The following letter, sent at that time, had enclosed a leaflet providing the mother with the names of two Clarks retailers close to her:

Dear Mrs. Jones:

During the next nine months or so your baby's going to start to walk. And although one of the healthiest things in the world is for him to run around in bare feet, sooner or later he's going to need shoes.

Obviously, you're going to want good looking shoes. But there are more serious considerations that should affect your choice. That's why we've sent you this leaflet explaining what you should be looking for in a child's first shoes and, more importantly, why you should take so much trouble over them.

When you've read the facts in the leaflet, we believe you'll decide to buy Clarks First Shoes. So at the bottom of this letter, we've listed your nearest First Shoes stockists.

Everyone of them has a trained fitter on the staff who'll be able to give you all the help you need in choosing the most important shoes you'll ever buy.

Yours Sincerely,

Not to leave a stone unturned, Clarks' salespeople presented to each retailer an outline of the program and a sample of The Bounty Box. They also left a 5-by-7-inch spiral-bound presentation, printed on heavy paper stock. Each page described a typical fitting situation. It was suggested that the fitter ask for the name of the family to contact them when the baby should be ready for another pair, another size. Salespeople also left a window decal, a die-cut illustrating the baby's block idea, and, as an in store display, a building block box stand on which to display shoes.

What were the results? Against a declining market of 13.1 percent, Clarks First Shoes volume increased 4 percent. Retailers upped their stock orders 8 percent. After testing, the program became a continuing one.

DISCUSSION QUESTIONS

1 If money is not the only determinant of demand, what else is?
2 Explain the economic principles of marginal utility and diminishing returns.
3 Distinguish between "perfect" and "imperfect" competition in a marketplace. What forms might the latter take?
4 What is the meaning of "conspicuous consumption"? What is its relevance to direct marketers?
5 Elaborate on this statement: Consumer behavior in today's industrial society is interacting and is dependent not so much on income as on the buyer's perception of his or her place in the environment.
6 Discuss the relevance of the social sciences in direct marketing.
7 Distinguish between consumer markets and industrial markets. How can each be described and measured?
8 Define discretionary income.
9 Name some products that might be considered as symbolic of social status.
10 How is the cost of promotion justified in our economic system striving for optimum allocation of resources?

DIRECT MARKETING CUSTOMER BEHAVIOR

Within the context of the definition of direct marketing presented on page 4, those who effect a measurable response and/or transaction may be viewed as present or potential *customers*. (These responses could involve other than products or services, such as voting for a political candidate or contributing to a civic or charitable cause.) These customers, in turn, could be *consumers* (acting on behalf of their own personal consumption or other interest) or they could be industrial buyers (acting for an organization or enterprise). In either event, it would be an oversimplification to state that variations in their purchasing behavior can be explained in demographic, geographic, or economic terms alone.

Ability to buy is not the same as *proneness* to buy. Quantitative analysis of markets in terms of demographic, geographic, and economic factors alone is not enough. We need to know more about the qualitative aspects of buyer behavior. The sensitive direct marketer wants to know *why* customers react. Why do buyers behave in the manner they do?

One of the most interesting areas of marketing theory development is that of *human ecology*. Although ecology was initially a concept of the biological sciences, concerned with the adaptation of living organisms to their environments, it has been borrowed by the social sciences to explain the interaction and interdependency of individuals and social groups in relation to their cultural environments.

Direct marketers must look at customer behavior in terms of the individual as well as the environment. Even though mass production depends on mass marketing, any study of customer behavior must necessarily start with the *individual* and his or her psychological (psychogenic) and physiological (biogenic) needs. One should consider the "rational" economic person, as presented in the preceding chapter, in terms of marginal utility, indifference curves, and the price mechanism and compare this to the *real world* of direct marketers.

PHYSIOLOGICAL AND PSYCHOLOGICAL NEEDS AND MOTIVATIONS

It is *inherent* that a newborn baby cries when it is hungry. Later, however, it *learns* to cry to demonstrate that it is hungry. Direct marketing promotion techniques endeavor to affect the *learned* behavior of people. Learned needs evolve from the individual and the environment and are relatively slow to change.

Learning Theories

A variety of learning theories have been presented in the literature of psychology. Possibly one of the best known is that labeled "stimulus-response" and best remembered through Pavlov's experiments with animals in which their current behavior patterns, influenced by rewards and punishments, ultimately became established habits. Seeing a perspiring athlete gulp down a soft drink in a television commercial, for example, might cause the observer to crave a similar drink.

Another area of learning experiences that has particular relevance for direct marketers is that of Gestalt or field theory. Such theory is concerned with the "whole" observation: the total scene including the individual's participation in it. William Stanton presents an interesting example of Gestalt psychology; most people looking at the configuration below will see railroad tracks, trees, telephone poles, or even four pairs of lines but rarely will they "see" simply eight vertical lines:[1]

[1] William J. Stanton, *Fundamentals of Marketing*, 5th ed., McGraw-Hill Book Company, New York, 1978, p. 126.

In terms of Gestalt theory, individuals tend to blend into their environment of which, in effect, they themselves are a part. Their life-styles tend to be influenced by peer groups and they tend to associate advertising messages with the credibility of the deliverer of those messages. Thus, a model in an advertisement wearing a white hospital smock implies medical authority.

Psychoanalytic Theories

Psychoanalytic theories including those of Sigmund Freud, are concerned with the id, ego, and superego, and postulate that real buying motives may be hidden. Motivation researchers, notably Ernest Dichter, have thrived providing explanations of "hidden emotions." As an innovator and leader in the so-called qualitative school of motivational research, Dichter expressed the belief that the real reason people buy one product over another is often based on a deep-seated emotion and only deep probing of the consumer's psyche will reveal that emotion. This is accomplished through the "depth interview."[2] Dichter's theories of psychoanalytic motivators of consumers, arriving at what ultimately came to be known as "hidden persuaders," have often been controversial. In one motivation study done for the Forest Lawn Cemetery in Los Angeles, Dichter determined that the bereaved "prefer large plots so that the deceased will have room to move about." Additionally, he found, research revealed a strong preference for caskets with locks since "many people fear that the dead will get out."[3]

Abraham Maslow's Hierarchy of Needs, visualized in Figure 6-1, developed a theory of motivation that ranked physical needs first, social needs next, and actualization of self last. In that order, he described a five-step ladder labeled: physiological needs, safety needs, belongingness, esteem, and self-actualization.[4]

PSYCHOGRAPHICS AND LIFE-STYLES

Psychographics emerged recently as the study of life-styles, habits, attitudes, beliefs, and value systems of individuals. Such study has merged psychological theory with demographics to make possible more effective promotional plans. Although not yet an organized scientific discipline, psychographics and the measurement of life-styles have been of particular interest to direct marketers because of their ability to crossbreed mailing lists demonstrating particular purchase patterns with the demographic characteristics of the areas in which buyers live or of the other lists on which they appear.

It has been suggested by Emmanuel H. Demby, William D. Wells, Daniel Yankelovich, and others that supplementing demographic profiles with life-style characteristics can provide useful information not only about *who* an organization's customers are, but, more importantly, *why* they buy.[5]

The marketing research organization of Yankelovich, Skelly, and White has, since 1970, tracked some 50 life-style trends. Through a service called *Monitor,* subscribers have been kept aware of dominant themes in social change affecting life-styles. These trends carry names such as: New Naturalism, Search for Community, Full Rich Life Phenomenon, Fitness and Figure Kick, Personalization, and Concern about Environment. A general conclusion from the *Monitor* research is that consumer values,

---

[2] Ernest Dichter, *Handbook of Consumer Motivation,* McGraw-Hill Book Company, New York, 1964.

[3] Roger Ricklefs, "Ernest Dichter Thrives Selling Firms Research on 'Hidden Emotions'," *Wall Street Journal,* November 20, 1972, p. 1.

[4] Abraham H. Maslow, *Motivations and Personality,* Harper & Row, New York, 1954.

[5] An illuminating book of readings on the subject is William D. Wells, ed., *Psychographics and Life-Styles,* American Marketing Association, Chicago, 1979.

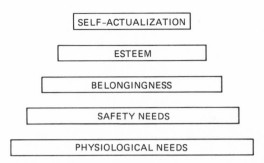

Figure 6-1 Maslow's Hierarchy of Needs.

more than demographics alone, determine buyer behavior.

Emmanuel H. Demby, who has been credited with coining the word "psychographics," defined it as "the measurement of consumers' propensity to purchase under a variety of conditions, needs and stimuli." He would use the techniques of psychographic research not to replace demographics but to augment them. The resultant buyer profile, contends Demby and others, can be highly useful in development of advertising messages that can be pinpointed to segments of mass audiences.

A variety of psychographic dimensions, such as "adventurous," "introvert/extrovert," "cynical," and "brand-innovative" (see Figure 6-2), have been used to describe life-styles (see Figure 6-3) and thus help devise advertising messages appealing to these particular characteristics. A 1977 bibliography published by the American Marketing Association[6] synopsized 195 studies on personality research in marketing, including psychographic and life-style research. The study suggested that a heuristic value of such research might lie in the insight it provided as "mood music for advertising copywriters." Beyond that justification, however, the report concluded that

of the studies reviewed, "only a few have found the significant relationships between measures of consumer behavior and personality research that were anticipated."

The direct marketer, on the other hand, is most interested in describing mailing lists, TV and radio stations and programs, magazine and newspaper editorial content, that pinpoint people with certain life-style characteristics rather than simply segmenting mass audiences with direct response advertising messages (see Figure 6-4). The balance of this chapter will be devoted primarily to providing the groundwork for such consumer and industrial market identification in terms of demographics, geographics, and psychographics. Chapter 7 will be concerned with how direct marketers segment markets.

THE ENVIRONMENT OF PSYCHOGRAPHICS

People with like interests tend to cluster; and their behavior, including buying habits and attitudes, tends to be influenced by their environment, of which, in effect, they themselves are a part. So the need is to be able (a) to identify areas in which such groupings occur; (b) to classify these in terms of economic potential; and, (c) to measure their cultural patterns—all the effects of environments on buying behavior—or, to sum it up with one term, to measure them *culturologically*. Once the direct marketer has determined the common denominator, or tone, of one or more of these units, in terms of mailing lists and in relation to product, price, and promotion, it is possible to apply this qualification to other mailing lists and thus locate those clusters with similar characteristics, expecting the same kind of reactions to future direct marketing moves.[7] The foundation for *environmental* influences

[6] Dik Warren Twedt, Lyndon E. Dawson, Jr., Hugh G. Wales, and Gary H. Bronner, *Personality Research in Marketing: A Bibliography,* American Marketing Association, Chicago, 1977.

[7] Martin Baier, "ZIP Code—New Tool for Marketers," *Harvard Business Review,* January–February 1967, p. 136.

Psychographic Dimensions
Profiles of respondents: bottom quartile would disagree, top quartile would agree

Positive Self-concept	I am self-confident; a leader; influential; have greatest achievements still ahead
Stress	I dread the future; can't relax; have trouble sleeping; have headaches and indigestion under a great deal of pressure
Adventurous	I like to take chances; changes in routine; the adventurous life; challenges
Travel-Oriented	I would like to spend a year in London or Paris; take a trip around the world; visit places and foreign cultures
Introvert/Extrovert	I am a swinger, enjoy parties; going out evenings; visiting friends; anything for fun
Liberal/Conservative	Communism is the greatest peril in the world today; there should be a gun in every home; police should use whatever force necessary for law and order
Cynical	Most big companies are out for themselves, the energy shortage is a hoax created by government and corporations; an honest man can't get elected
Women's Attitudes	A woman's place is in the home; the father should be the boss; the working world is no place for a woman; Women's Lib is not good
Family-Oriented	Children are the most important thing in a marriage; when making decisions children come first; I don't like to be away from my family
Style-Conscious	I have more stylish clothes than my friends; enjoy fashion magazines, enjoy being noticed; dressing well, feeling attractive
Advertising Attitudes	Advertising insults my intelligence; is condescending to women; not to be aimed at children; places too much emphasis on sex
Television Attitudes	There is too much sex and violence on TV; magazines are more interesting than TV; TV is not my primary form of entertainment
Economy-Minded	I shop for specials; check prices even on small items; can't get ahead; am pessimistic about economic future
Brand-Innovative	I like to buy new and different things; usually first to try new products; do not stick to well known brands

Figure 6-2 Psychographic dimensions. (*Edward J. Forrest, David S. Anderson, Barry J. Solomon, and Jaren M. Bruce, "Psychographic Flesh, Demographic Bones,"* American Demographics, *September 1981, pp. 25–27. Study based on data provided by Needham, Harper & Steers Advertising, Inc., Chicago, Ill.*)

on behavior has long been firmly established in the literature of marketing.

The Influence of Environment on Behavior

The cycle of change in marketing, which progresses from product innovation and early adoption through obsolescence and consumption by laggards, ranges from rugged individualism to peer group conformity. Emerging life-styles and their resultant consumption pat-terns have become symbols of class membership. Class membership, in turn, has been seen by many, although with limited empirical evidence, as being a more significant determinant of economic behavior than current income or accumulated wealth.

Economists and marketers have long relied on income as the primary, if not the only, determinant of buying behavior. This assumption is not wholly valid. Modern marketing theory has developed a relationship between consumer behavior and the cultural, as well as the economic, environment. Neither consumer behavior nor the cultural environment can be accepted as "given." Marketing practices must be related to the environment in which they are conducted. These practices must recognize that the marketing pattern and the consumer behavior pattern are constantly changing, just as the life-styles of consumers themselves are constantly changing.

In Chapter 5 we looked at the rational buyer in economic theory, who had been assumed to act in his or her own best interest as well as that of the community. The buyer in economic theory has also been viewed as a seeker of maximum satisfaction, which in turn has been seen to result from scarcity, whereas

Figure 6-3 The study of psychographics reveals life-style types. (*Peter W. Bernstein, "Psychographics is still an issue on Madison Avenue,"* Fortune, *January 16, 1978, pp. 78–84. Based on a study by Needham, Harper & Steers Advertising, Inc., Chicago, Ill.*)

Ben, the Self-made Businessman

Scott, the Successful Professional

Cathy, the Contented Housewife

Candice, the Chic Suburbanite

Herman, the Retiring Homebody

Dale, the Devoted Family Man

Mildred, the Militant Mother

Thelma, the Old-Fashioned Traditionalist

Eleanor, the Elegant Socialite

Fred, the Frustrated Factory Worker

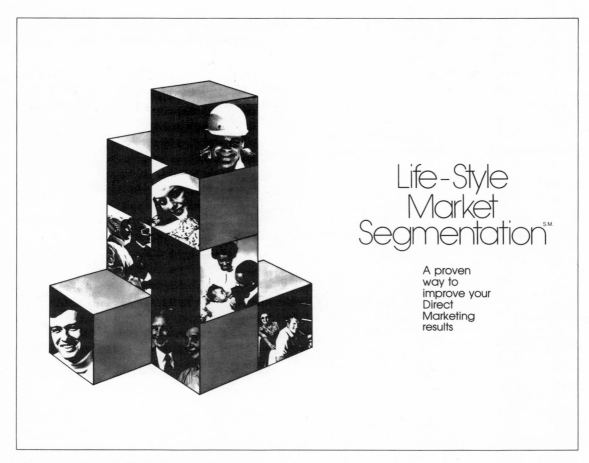

Figure 6-4 Life-Style Market Segmentation.

diminishing utility has been caused by abundance. The ability of the buyer to measure satisfaction has been assumed, whether in absolute terms or as between alternative selections of goods to which the buyer is "indifferent." Some economists have seen the buyer as acting impulsively, at the whim of fashion, fad, and style. Many behavioral scientists, although relatively few economists, have seen the buyer in ecological terms, responding to cultural as well as economic environment. Consumers are classified not by their economic resources alone but also by their culturological attitudes and expectations.

Cultural behavior is influenced by the folklore and mores of various ethnic groups as well as their taboos. Although it is difficult to visualize or quantify such intangible differences in attitudes as these, they do exist. These varying patterns must be recognized by the direct marketer who would truly understand consumer behavior and thus segment markets in terms of mailing lists. Substantial differences in consumer patterns occur between economic and cultural segments and frequently these parallel geographic differences.

From their analysis of subcultural market

segmentation, social class, and geography, Wasson, Sturdivant, and McConaughy have summarized these conclusions about consumer behavior:[8]

- The cultural patterns that set most of our standards of conduct have two major dimensions: *social class* and *geography*.

- Social class is a subcultural phenomenon, not a purely economic one. The major determinants are *education* and type of *occupation*, and there is a heavy overlap in income, even between the upper classes and those in the lower classes.

- Each class has a clearly discernible set of standards of behavior, producing significantly differing patterns of expenditure.

- Lower classes tend to emphasize food and material possessions; middle and upper classes tend to spend more for quality of neighborhood and education and reading.

- Social class operates within the broader patterns of the regional culture. Every region in the world has its own clearly discernible set of priorities of conduct and consumption and these standards determine not only what items are normally bought but also what kinds of innovations will be accepted and which will be rejected.

- Within each larger region are smaller subregions, each with its own culture patterns and expenditure patterns.

- The differences in total expenditures reflect even deeper differences in tastes and social conduct.

- Markets are segmented further by other cultural factors, such as ethnic and religious preferences, and by personality factors. As a result, demographic measures help only in identifying the market for broad product classifications but not for individual brands and models.

Aside from geographic definition and environmental influences, groups that affect consumer behavior (see Figure 6-5) may be broadly classified as the family and other small reference groups on the one hand with the larger environs of social class and culture on the other. We will look at each of these broad influences on life-styles separately.

Family and Household Reference Groups

Family and household groups of individuals living together frequently influence buying decisions. Most often, the decision is shared by husband and wife, but, in a number of situations, children are the ultimate determinants. Nelson Foote has asked, "Is it not possible that some of our frustrations in research in consumer behavior have been due to our conceiving of the individual as the unit of observation, rather than using the household as the unit of observation?"[9] Foote, along with others, viewed the decision-making process between family members as being the major variable in household consumption.

John Scanzoni, in looking toward the future of consumption patterns, predicted more than a decade ago that a major revolution in family consumption patterns "will emerge from rising levels in education and occupations of women." He concluded that "we may expect the traditional 'husband-centered' pattern of family consumption to decline considerably." Aspirations and expectations of the conjugal family unit are seen to be a major determinant of consumer behavior. Scanzoni saw conspicuous consumption as an important dimension of these family aspirations and expectations.[10]

Other "Face-to-Face" Small Reference Groups

Not just the family and household, but other face-to-face small reference groups have strong influences on consumer decisions. Such groups include work associates, social acquaintances, religious affiliations, and, of course, neighbors.

[8] Chester B. Wasson, Frederick D. Sturdivant, and David H. McConaughy, *Competition and Human Behavior,* Appleton-Century-Crofts, New York, 1968, pp. 114–143.

[9] Nelson Foote, *Consumer Behavior: Models of Household Decision-Making,* New York University Press, New York, 1961.

[10] John Scanzoni, *The Conjugal Family and Consumption Behavior,* McCahan Foundation, Bryn Mawr, 1968.

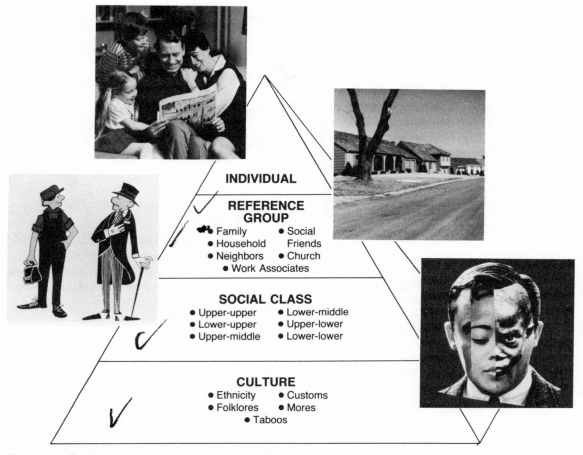

Figure 6-5 Environmental influences on consumer behavior.

"Keeping up with the Joneses" helps to explain the direct marketing success that the prestigious *National Geographic* magazine experienced when it mailed an invitation to the next-door neighbors of its present subscribers. The invitation read: "Your next-door neighbor reads the *National Geographic*. Shouldn't you?" Another similar direct marketing success was a letter from American Motors that started out with "Have you noticed that new Rambler in your neighbor's driveway?"

So-called referral selling, the use of a third party to directly or indirectly recommend a product or service, is a notable example of reference group influence which has special applications for direct marketers. A consumer is inclined to respect the judgments of associates. On the other hand, the person doing the recommending is often reselling himself or herself as well. Urging a friend, associate, or neighbor to duplicate the purchase serves to reinforce the decision as well as the desire to conform and be accepted in the environment. As much as 20 percent or more of the new business acquired by many direct marketing organizations is attributable to such referral-recommendation from present customers.

George Katona, for many years associated

with the University of Michigan's Institute for Social Research, saw group belonging and group influences as major determinants of consumer behavior. "In many instances, group influences take the form of similar stimuli affecting all group members and similar needs arising in them."[11] Such similarities may even extend beyond face-to-face groups to income groups, age groups, and life cycle groups. One interesting observation of the impact of neighborhood group influences was a photographic study, reported by Katona, that showed clusterings of window air conditioners in certain neighborhood blocks, with none at all in nearby blocks. "What our friends own we own, too—or shall soon own," contended Katona.

It was also reported by Katona in a study of new car buying, automobiles being a prime example of conspicuous consumption, that most Americans expressed fondness for their cars and many looked on frequent repurchases not as planned obsolescence but rather as improvements in operation. Although only relatively few of our associates and friends visit our homes, the mobility of automobiles helps to place them in front of a much wider array of neighbors and work associates. Thus, the automobile has come to be looked on as a status symbol. As a result, tabulations of new car buyers, with appropriate segmentation of these by such factors as make and model of automobile as well as household demographics, have become prime mailing lists for direct marketers. There is, relatively, a much broader range of automobile purchase prices within an income range than there is in income itself.

An excellent summary of the importance of reference groups in shaping consumer behavior is that of Pierre Martineau:[12]

Each human is motivated by various compulsive forces within him—certain biological urges and

certain wants—to realize numerous goals. But the yardsticks for evaluating the worth of these goals are supplied by group pressures. Other people have to validate our choices. The things we buy and do that offer the most satisfaction are those which are also valued by our friends, our group, our class. Very rarely do our actions, our attitudes or our purchases run counter to the approved tastes of those around us. The penalty for non-conformity is literally ostracism. An imposing list of studies points out that those who do not accept group standards have few friends, little influence and much anxiety. After all what is the essence of society's punishment through imprisonment? It means solitary confinement—separation from other people.

The friends we choose, the neighborhoods we live in, the way we spend and save our money, the educational plans we have for our children are determined in large degrees along social class lines. A rich man is not just a poor man with more money. Every class in America today indulges in conspicuous consumption.

Social Class Influences

Social class does exist and frequently it clusters in neighborhoods, such as ZIP Code areas, that can be geographically defined through mailing lists. A buyer is strongly influenced by his or her social class, or that to which the buyer aspires, rather than by income alone. Culture, too, exerts a strong influence on buying decisions. Through the years, cultural exchange has taken place from people to people, just as mail and other economic exchange goes from people to people, and with regard to transportation patterns. Such flow patterns are also the basis for defining ZIP Code areas.

Social class has been seen by some market researchers as a meaningful manner of market segmentation. Noting that income level alone does not determine social class, these researchers have pointed to housing, educational level, and occupation as being more important variables that determine class membership. The beginning plumber and the new lawyer, for instance, possibly have comparable in-

[11] George Katona, *The Powerful Consumer*, McGraw-Hill Book Company, New York, 1966, pp. 155–169.

[12] Pierre D. Martineau, *Motivation and Advertising*, McGraw-Hill Book Company, New York, 1957, p. 166.

comes although they do not command the same status or social-class membership.

On the basis of a 3-year study of the social structure of metropolitan Chicago, W. Lloyd Warner, Marchia Meeker, and Kenneth Wells developed a social classification scheme that included occupation, source (but not amount) of income, type of housing, and residential area. The findings of this study group are summarized in Figure 6-6.[13]

Using Warner's classification system, the so-called "mass" market (comprising the lower-middle and upper-lower social classes) in total contains approximately three-fourths of the United States population. And, although we have long been referred to as a middle-class society, the upper-middle and lower-middle categories comprise less than one-half of the population. The upper-upper class contains approximately 1 percent and the lower-lower class approximately 15 percent of the population. Such a breakdown of social classes, considering absolute numbers of population, offers a particularly meaningful manner of market segmentation and product differentiation. It suggests, too, variations in promotion techniques. The direct marketing strategies used, of course, need to be relevant to the social class, especially within the so-called "quality" and "mass" markets.

Extensive research into social-class membership and the consequent behavior has been conducted by Pierre Martineau. This market researcher contended that "in a very real sense, everyone of us, in his consumption patterns and style of life, shows an awareness that there is some kind of superiority-inferiority system operating, and that we must observe the symbolic patterns of our own class."[14] The kinds of things a person will or

SOCIAL CLASS	MEMBERSHIP
Upper–Upper	Old families and the traditional leaders.
Lower–Upper	Socially-prominent new rich.
Upper-Middle	Professional and managerial successes. (Combined with the class above, this is commonly referred to as the "quality" market.)
Lower-Middle	White-collar workers.
Upper-Lower	Blue-collar workers. (Combined with the class above, this is sometimes called the "mass" market.)
Lower-Lower	Unskilled laborers, transients, non-respectable occupations.

Figure 6-6 Social-class membership.

will not buy are strongly related to his perception of his social class, as are his spend/save aspirations.

Using Warner's classification scheme, originally developed for sociological studies, Martineau with Warner applied this scheme to a market research study in the Chicago area. They used a rating classification that was based on type of income (rather than amount), occupation, house type, and place of residence, with significant findings. Where and what the consumer buys will differ not only by economic values but according to symbolic values.

Further, the study revealed, Thorstein Veblen's conspicuous consumption, which Veblen had applied only to the aristocracy of the upper-upper class in his own research, was found to run all the way through the social-class system, from top to bottom. Although Martineau reported a rough correlation between income and social class, the latter displayed a much richer dimension of meaning in analyzing consumer behavior and specific purchases. Among the lower-lower class, for instance, there was evidence of a much more ostentatious spending on clothing and automobiles than on housing. Martineau's major conclusions from this study of social class in Chicago were these:[15]

[13] W. Lloyd Warner, Marchia Meeker, and Kenneth Wells, *Social Class in America,* Harper & Row, New York, 1960. See also Richard P. Coleman and Bernice C. Newgarten, *Social Status in the City,* Jossey-Bass, Inc., San Francisco, 1971.

[14] Pierre D. Martineau, "Social Class and Spending Behavior," *Journal of Marketing,* vol. 23, 1958, p. 122.

[15] Ibid., p. 130.

• There is a social class system operating in metropolitan markets that can be isolated and described.

• There are far-reaching psychological differences between the various classes.

• Consumption patterns operate as prestige symbols to define social-class membership, which is a more comprehensive explanation of behavior than mere income.

Research for the *Workingman's Wife* by Rainwater, Coleman, and Handel afforded further insights into the relations of social class, symbolic behavior, and human motivation. This study examined the inherent values of blue-collar families in sociological terms rather than with the use of the usual demographics such as income, home value, and rent paid. The study found five basic goals that activate the consumer behavior of the working-class homemaker. They are: "(1) the search for social, economic and physical security; (2) the drive for a 'common man' level of recognition and respectability; (3) the desire for support and affection from the people important to her; (4) the effort to escape a heavy burden of household labor; and (5) the urge to decorate, to 'pretty up' her world."[16]

Importance of Culture

Each of us, even as a consumer, is a product of the culture (see Figure 6-7). We behave against the background of the culture from which we emerged, in which we grew up, and in which we live. Whereas the human race has undergone relatively little change biologically during the past thousands of years, there is an immense difference culturologically, not only in historical perspective but also geographically. The person who expresses relief at not being born in China "because I cannot speak a word of Chinese" should know that, by being born into the culture of China, the

Figure 6-7 As consumers, each of us is a product of the culture.

language would have been inherently "learned," along with traditions, folklore, mores, customs, and taboos that are a part of Chinese heritage. Unwittingly, we all respond to our cultural environment.

What exactly is culture? Omar K. Moore and Donald J. Lewis have defined culture in terms of seven functional assumptions that they believe are inherent to it.[17] Culture, they contend, is *learned;* it is not instinctive or innate or transmitted biologically. Culture is *inculcated.* Through repeated admonition, it becomes ingrained in the individual. Culture is *social.* It is not just the action of an individual but rather the aggregated habits of groups and societies. Culture is *ideational.* It is learned linguistic and symbolic behavior. Culture is *gratifying.* It always and necessarily satisfies biological needs and secondary needs derived from them. Culture is *adaptive.* It is an ongoing process that is cumulative and changing in a manner comparable to biological evolution. Culture is *integrative.* Because of its ability to

[16] Lee Rainwater, Richard P. Coleman, and Gerald Handel, *Workingman's Wife,* Oceana Publications, Inc., New York, 1959, p. 205.

[17] Omar K. Moore and Donald J. Lewis, "Learning Theory and Culture," *Psychological Review,* vol. 59, 1952, pp. 308–388.

perpetually adapt, it tends to shape itself into an integrated whole form.

Many aspects of culture, such as courtship and status, have been found by anthropologists to be universal to all known cultures. Some symbols, such as a young man's purchase of life insurance to signal to his relatives and friends that he is on his own, have telling influence on consumer behavior.[18]

Cultural anthropologists have been concerned in marketing with establishing themes of a culture as well as determining the sensitivity toward taboos within various cultures. The anthropologist is trained, too, to understand the differences created by national origins. Among the things looked for within a culture are the technological level, the procedures for the inheritance of property, how kinship was reckoned and described, how the spouses were brought together. The anthropologist is interested, too, in the family's food and housing, the language level and dialect.

Anthropologists want to know about the influence of age on individual family members as well as the trends in illnesses. Most important, they look at how culture has rubbed off on family members. They have a sensitivity to certain facets of social life that are not generally within the scope of either psychology or sociology. Anthropologists are aware of the larger values of a culture, the customs that are taken for granted and the violation of which represents a taboo. Certain colors, phrases, or symbols are frequently taboo within specific cultures although these are looked on favorably in others.[19]

Environmental Influences on Consumer Behavior

On a Sunday evening in October 1938, thousands of people on the East Coast of the United States fled their homes in panic. The word had spread rapidly that invaders from Mars were landing on Earth. The source of this misinformation had been a strangely realistic radio drama produced by Orson Welles. The effect was comparable to that of one person looking skyward while hundreds of others curiously follow the gaze. What causes people to panic or look skyward? Why do people smoke cigarettes in spite of the fact that every package has a clear warning that the contents are dangerous to health? Why do individuals respond to peer pressure? Why do they adopt life-styles of others? Is the influence environmental?

Leslie A. White in *The Science of Culture* traces the history of the infant science of culturology and demonstrates that, although humans cannot control their culture, they can predict its course. Culturology, contends White, repudiates and rejects free will, and, at the same time, is deterministic.[20]

Since it is culture ("an extra-somatic tradition . . . a specific kind of symbolic behavior") and not society ("the social process, social interaction") that is the distinctive feature of humans, the scientific study of this feature should be known as culturology rather than sociology. Dr. White found that culturology was first classified as a biological science (along with physiology and psychology) by a distinguished German chemist and Nobel laureate, Wilhelm Ostwald, who wrote that a "sure mastery of at least the fundamental principles of all the sciences . . . is therefore a necessary pre-supposition of the scientific mastery of culturological problems."[21]

In a chapter entitled "Culturological vs. Psychological Determinants of Mind,"[22] White observes that "human behavior is made up of two separate and distinct elements, the one biological and the other cultural" (p. 122).

[18] Ernest Dichter, *Handbook of Consumer Motivations*, McGraw-Hill Book Company, New York, 1964, p. 458.

[19] Charles Winick, "Anthropology's Contributions to Marketing," *Journal of Marketing*, vol. 26, 1961, pp. 53–60.

[20] Leslie A. White, *The Science of Culture*, Grove Press, Inc., New York, 1949.

[21] Wilhelm Ostwald, *The System of Sciences*, English translation, Rice Institute Pamphlet, no. 11, 1915, p. 169.

[22] White, *The Science of Culture*. (Specific page references to quotations are given in parentheses in the text.)

Culture consists of "languages, beliefs, customs, tools, dwellings, works of art, etc. . . . [and] from the standpoint of subsequent behavior, everything depends on the type of culture into which a baby is introduced at birth" (p. 122). "Man is a constant, culture is a variable. Cultures . . . possess the people who have been born into them . . . [their] attitudes, sentiments and behavior" (p. 126). "Human behavior is the response of the organism man to a class of external, extra-somatic, symbolic stimuli which we call culture" (p. 139). "The culturologist explains the behavior of a people by pointing out that it is merely the response of a particular type of primate organism to a particular set of stimuli" (p. 144). Culture, not man, is a determinant. "Differences of mind among different ethnic groups of human beings are due to differences of cultural tradition" (p. 148). Thus, what is termed "human nature" is not so much natural as it is cultural. "Cultures may change . . . but human nature, biologically defined . . . has undergone no change in the past 30 thousand years at least" (p. 152). "It is the individual who is explained in terms of his culture, not the other way around" (p. 168). What is considered proper in one cultural environment may be taboo in another.

Thus it is that the direct marketer should look at consumers in a manner that measures all of the effects of their environments (reference groups, social class, culture) on their lifestyles as well as their buying behavior. As will be demonstrated in Chapter 7, ZIP Code areas can provide direct marketers with the means to identify clusters of consumers with like interests. Their buying habits and attitudes are very much influenced by their cultural environments as well as their perceived social class and their reference groups.

ABILITY TO BUY VS. PRONENESS TO BUY

The *ability* to buy is most frequently evaluated by such demographic indicators as income, wealth, age, sex, and marital status. The practice of using demographic indicators as measurements of the ability to buy is, of course, well understood by direct marketers. However, consumer behavior is as much or more influenced by environmental factors, psychographic as well as other indicators of lifestyles, that are not so readily identifiable or so easily measurable. It is desirable for direct marketers to be able to measure these environmental factors to determine the *proneness* to buy. Such measurements as income in relation to what others are earning in a particular environment, purchase actions of record as well as the educational level, the social class, and, as Veblen observed, the conspicuous consumption of an area can all be important media selection qualifications.

The basic concept of human ecology that behavior is a response to environmental influences tells us that a household with a $12,000 annual income located in a ZIP Code area in which the median household income is $20,000 is likely to emulate that median level. The reverse is also true, with a $25,000 household tending to behave like its $20,000 ZIP Code area neighbors. It is this tendency that contributes to the homogeneity of the behavior within such clusters, even though there is a great variance of characteristics among and between individual households.

Discretionary purchases by households under such circumstances are dependent not just on the *ability* to buy but also on the *proneness* to buy. Because this is such a potentially powerful economic force, direct marketers would be well advised to understand it as they study the qualifications available within mailing lists, the readership of magazines and newspapers, or the characteristics of viewers and listeners of television and radio.

FAMILY LIFE CYCLE

Direct marketers often find it useful to segment markets by age and develop offers for specific family or household characteristics. An awareness of the concept of the *family life cycle* can be useful. Direct marketers of educational materials, for example, often need to relate to the age of children in the various "Full Nest" stages whereas a catalog of maternity clothing might have greatest receptivity among "Full Nest I" or "Young Married Couples." Likewise, needs for such direct marketed products as books, magazines, records, and insurance are often related to the family life cycle. This concept has evolved in the marketing literature in the form of nine distinguishable periods:[23]

Bachelor Stage: Young and single individuals, not living at home
Newly Married Couple: Young and without children
Full Nest I: Younger married couples, youngest child under 6
Full Nest II: Younger married couples, youngest child 6 or older.
Full Nest III: Older married couples, with dependent children
Empty Nest I: Older married couples, no children living with them, in labor force
Empty Nest II: Older married couples, no children living with them, retired
Solitary Survivor I: Older single people, in labor force
Solitary Survivor II: Older single people, retired

THE BUYING DECISION

There are several models of the buying process. A common purchase decision model, illustrating the procedure that consumers, consciously or not, go through in deciding to respond to an offer, is visualized in Figure 6-8. There are five stages in this particular process.

Awareness: Through one or more of a

---

[23] Adapted from William D. Wells and George Gubar, "Life Cycle Concept in Marketing Research," *Journal of Marketing Research,* August 1968, p. 267.

variety of stimuli, the buyer becomes aware of a need or of a product to fulfill an existing need. This stimulus could be a direct marketing promotional offer received by mail, the recommendation of a friend, or even a news story.
Interest: Through the study of received information (promotion), alternatives for fulfillment of the need are identified.
Evaluation: Information about the alternatives is studied in relation to their potential satisfaction of the need.
Decision: The buyer decides to buy, possibly on a trial basis.
Repurchase: Postpurchase evaluation leads to potential repurchase.

BUYING PATTERNS

In addition to knowing *why* people buy, it is also important to know *where, when,* and *how* people buy as well as *who* influences the buying decision. Obviously, this is most important for the mail-order marketer, who has developed not only product, distribution, and promotional strategies mindful of these variables but must also be able to anticipate objections and overcome them without face-to-face contact.

Mail-order marketers need to know *where* people buy, not just where the purchase takes place but where the buying decision is made. They need to target their promotions not just to buyers but to influencers and, in many cases, even to third party decision makers. Their visual displays of products must be every bit as compelling and descriptive as the physical displays that appear in traditional sales outlets.

A determination of *when* people buy involves not only the day of the week and the time of the day but also the season, including holidays and major events, as well as climatic influences. *How* people buy is of special concern to the mail-order marketer who provides the convenience of mail and electronic ordering. But, at the same time, the customer

Figure 6-8 A common purchase decision model.

necessarily faces time lags involved in shipment and delivery and foregoes the opportunity to actually touch, feel, and demonstrate the purchase immediately.

Packaging, although tremendously important for display purposes in the retail store, may be more concerned with shipping considerations in mail-order marketing since most products are delivered to the purchaser via the United States Postal Service (USPS) or an alternative private delivery system such as United Parcel Service (UPS). Such shipment is necessary regardless of which direct response advertising medium was used and regardless of whether the mail order was placed by mail or telephone.

Credit terms and pricing policy, important in traditional distribution, are equally important factors in mail-order marketing. So are variety, assortment, and the principle of "one-stop" shopping.

Recent Trends in Shopping

Changing population demographics and especially the accelerating role of women in the labor force have had impact on buying patterns that are favorable to mail-order marketing. So have the trends toward impulse buying and toward conformity.

Shopping today is not so much a leisure-time experience as it once was, and time itself has become an increasingly important consideration: that allocated to work, that allocated to leisure, as well as that allocated to shopping. Even though retailers have lengthened their shopping hours considerably in recent years to include evening, weekend, and holiday hours, many are augmenting traditional distribution with mail-order marketing to provide

"24-hours-a-day, 7-days-a-week, no-holidays-excepted" shopping opportunities.

The desire for convenience, in form, quantity of units, time, and place, also favors mail-order marketing. So does the high cost of transportation to and from shopping centers.

Types of Goods

There are traditionally three types of goods with which shoppers are concerned as consumers. These are:

Convenience goods: Examples are products that we typically buy spontaneously such as bread, coffee, soap, toothpaste, and hair preparations. The particular product and even its brand or a possible substitute are well known to the customer who also tends to know exactly what to get before going out to buy it. The purchase of convenience goods is usually made with a minimum of effort and virtually no involvement of sales personnel. They are usually nondurable and inexpensive relative to other types of goods.

Shopping goods: Examples include major purchases such as automobiles, home appliances, furniture, and clothing. As these examples indicate, shopping goods are generally products that invite price and quality comparison, and may involve a visit to various stores and conversations with several salespeople before a purchase is made. They are typically more durable and are higher priced than are convenience goods. The nature of shopping goods and the process of comparing these helps to explain why certain retailers—automobile dealers are a good example—cluster together.

Specialty goods: Examples include such distinctive products as designer fashions, brand name cosmetics, unique gift items, and imports. As with shopping goods, these involve sought for characteristics and/or brand preferences that in turn call for a special purchasing effort. A significant number of buyers are willing to go out of their way to acquire such goods. Specialty goods have been particularly well promoted in mail-order marketing.

A MODEL OF CONSUMER BUYER BEHAVIOR

To this point consumer behavior has been examined in terms of physiological and psychological motivations. We have seen, too, that there are economic, social, and environmental influences on the buying decision. It would help to understand the process, however, if all these elements could be viewed in terms of a comprehensive theory of consumer behavior.

Several such theories have evolved in marketing literature. Unfortunately, most of these have not been tested extensively and, for the most part, the models are difficult to understand and to relate to real world situations.

One of the earliest of such theories to be presented is that developed by John A. Howard and Jagdish N. Sheth and originally published in 1969.[24] The Howard-Sheth model in simplified form is shown in Figure 6-9. The input (stimuli) for the model are described as *significative* (such as quality, price, distinctiveness, service, availability); *symbolic* (the same attributes as seen through advertising media); and *social* (influences of family and other reference groups together with social class).

The outputs of the model consist of *attention* (buyer's response); *comprehension* (store of knowledge); *attitude* (buyer's evaluation); *intention* (buyer's predisposition); and *purchase behavior* (actual buyer behavior).

[24] John A. Howard and Jagdish N. Sheth, *The Theory of Buyer Behavior,* John Wiley & Sons, Inc., New York, 1969.

Between these inputs and outputs there lies an explanatory process that assumes complete rationality, as well as systematic analysis by consumers. Elements included in the learning process are *motives, choice, criteria,* and *brand comprehension.* These lead to *attitude, confidence,* and *intention.*

THE NATURE OF INDUSTRIAL MARKETS

Industrial direct marketing involves the process of providing industrial goods and services to industrial users. Although the distinction is not always easy to make, industrial goods are differentiated from consumer goods based on their ultimate use. Such goods are generally used as raw materials or in the fabrication of other products. Whereas iron ore is almost always an industrial good, a typewriter can be either an industrial good or a consumer good, depending on its ultimate use.

Approximately 50 percent of all manufactured goods are sold to the industrial market and approximately 80 percent of all farm products are considered industrial goods. As a farm product, for example, wheat is considered an industrial good when it is sold for the manufacture of flour; flour is considered a manufactured industrial good when it is sold to a bakery for the production of bread; bread is considered an industrial good when it is sold to a restaurant; but it is a consumer good when sold to a household.

Types of Industrial Goods

Like the classification of consumer goods into three categories, convenience, shopping, and specialty, industrial products have similar distinctions:

Raw materials: These are products destined to become part of another product, subject to further processing.
Fabricating materials and parts: In contrast to raw materials, these have already been

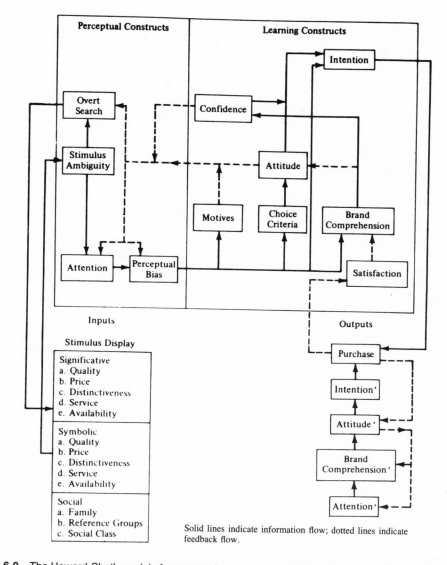

Figure 6-9 The Howard-Sheth model of consumer buyer behavior. (*John A. Howard and Jagdish N. Sheth,* The Theory of Buyer Behavior, *John Wiley & Sons, Inc., New York, 1969. Simplified version as presented in Gerald Zaltman and Philip C. Burger,* Marketing Research: Fundamentals and Dynamics, *The Dryden Press, Hinsdale, Ill., 1975, p. 147.*)

processed to some extent; that is, flour (from wheat) or pig iron (from ore).

Installations: These consist of major equipment with long lives such as buildings, power generators, and locomotives.

Accessory equipment: Such equipment is used to aid and implement production and includes office machines as well as machine tools.

Operating supplies: In the industrial market, operating supplies might be compared to convenience goods in that they are consumable. Examples include lubricating oil, ball-point pens, and floor wax.

Characteristics of Industrial Demand

Industrial market demand has four characteristics that often distinguish it from consumer market demand and these characteristics are worth noting and understanding.

Derived demand: Demand for industrial goods is usually *derived* from some ultimate use demand. For example, the industrial demand for automobile tires or glass is ultimately dependent on the consumer demand for automobiles.

Inelastic demand: Because a variety of industrial goods go into the processing of a single product, and thus each represents only a fraction of the product's total cost, there is not as much price sensitivity in industrial goods. The cost of tires for an automobile, for example, might double, but this increase would represent a relatively small part of the total cost of an automobile.

Widely fluctuating demand: The demand for industrial goods is subject to wide fluctuations, ultimately dependent on consumer demand but also dependent on rises and falls in inventories as well as rises and falls in the optimism of entrepreneurs.

Knowledgeable demand: Industrial buyers are usually much better informed, have more specialized interests, and benefit from the process of joint decision making.

Although the number of industrial organizations is but a fraction of the number of consumers among us, the volume of purchasing is as great in the industrial market as it is in the consumer market. Buying power of industrial organizations is highly concentrated and there are also heavy concentrations regionally and geographically. Such buying power is often measured by various forms of activity such as manufacturing, mining, agriculture, and construction.

Industrial Direct Marketing

Business and industry use the tools and techniques of direct marketing to:

- Develop sales leads
- Achieve direct sales
- Reinforce sales efforts
- Introduce new products
- Develop new markets and applications
- Build goodwill
- Market research

According to the Direct Marketing Association, business/industrial mail-order marketing expenditures for 1981 were estimated at $2.32 billion. Sales volume resulting from this expenditure is estimated at $23.24 billion.[25]

A major factor contributing to the increasing use of direct marketing by business and industry is the rising cost of the average sales call. According to McGraw-Hill Research, the average industrial sales call, which was $49.30 in 1969, had risen to more than $200 by 1982, a fourfold increase.[26] It should be noted that this cost is per *call*, not per *sale*.

A comparison of mailing list demographics, as between consumer markets and industrial markets, is shown in Figure 6-10. These characteristics are not all inclusive, of course. They are, however, indicative of the differences and, at the same time, the similarities

[25] Direct Marketing Association, *1983 Fact Book*, p. 11.
[26] Ibid., p. 10.

CONSUMER	INDUSTRIAL
Age	Year Business Started
Income	Sales Volume/Net Worth
Family Size	Number of Employees
Occupation	Line of Business (SIC)
Credit Rating	Credit Rating
Education	Company Status, i.e., Headquarters, Branch, Subsidiary
Life Cycle Stage	Sales Trend or Number of Employees
Own or Rent Home	Private or Public Ownership
Ethnic Group	Minority or Non-Minority Ownership
Sex	Sex of Key Decision-Makers
Interests	Interests of the Decision-Maker
Mail-Respondent	Mail-Respondent

Figure 6-10 A demographic comparison of consumer and industrial mailing lists (1982 Fact Book, *Direct Marketing Association, 6 East 43rd Street, New York, N.Y. 10017, p. 14.*)

between consumer lists and industrial lists. The subject of mailing lists will be discussed more thoroughly in Chapter 8.

A Model of Industrial Buyer Behavior

Related to the Howard-Sheth model of consumer buyer behavior is the model of industrial buyer behavior developed by Jagdish N. Sheth and first published in the October 1973 issue of the *Journal of Marketing*.[27] The Sheth industrial buyer model is an attempt to reconcile and integrate existing knowledge into a realistic and comprehensive presentation of buyer behavior within organizations. The major difference of the industrial buyer model compared with the consumer buyer model, other than its applicability to organizational rather than individual buying, is a provision for the joint decision-making process occurring within organizations.

As visualized in Figure 6-11, organizational buying behavior consists of three distinct aspects: the psychological world of individuals involved in organizational buying decisions;

[27] Jagdish N. Sheth, "A Model of Industrial Buyer Behavior," *Journal of Marketing*, vol. 37, 1973, pp. 50–65.

conditions precipitating joint decision making among individuals; and the process of joint decision making itself with its inevitable conflicts.

SUMMARY

Those who effect a measurable response and/or transaction in the context of direct marketing may be viewed as present or prospective *customers* (*consumer* or *industrial* buyers) broadly defined to go beyond just product/service transactions such as voting for a political candidate or contributing to a charitable cause. Behavior of these customers should be looked at in terms of the individual as well as the environment. Learning theories, such as stimulus-response and Gestalt, have certain relevance for direct marketers as do the psychoanalytic theories, especially those of Sigmund Freud, Ernest Dichter, and Abraham Maslow.

Of special relevance to direct marketers, however, is the emerging study of psychographics and life-styles as pioneered by Emmanuel Demby, William Wells, and Daniel Yankelovich. Such studies have been used mainly in helping to devise advertising messages appealing to particular life-styles. The direct marketer, however, is more interested in describing *mailing lists* or *direct response media* that pinpoint people with relevant life-style characteristics.

There are environmental influences on buyer behavior and these, in turn, mold life-styles. Key influences are those exerted by family, household, and other small reference groups on the one hand, as well as the larger environs of social class and culture on the other.

The *ability* to buy, most frequently evaluated by such demographic indicators as income, wealth, age, sex, and marital status, must be related to the *proneness* to buy. This distinction can often be evaluated in terms of environmental influences and measurement of life-

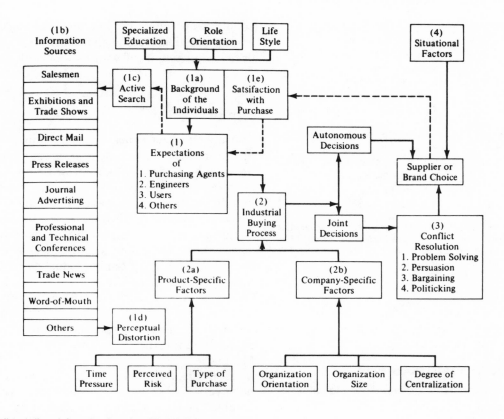

Solid lines indicate information flow; dotted lines indicate
feedback flow.

Figure 6-11 The Sheth model of industrial buyer behavior. (*Jagdish N. Sheth, "A Model of Industrial Buyer Behavior," Journal of Marketing, vol. 37, 1973, pp. 50–65. Published by the American Marketing Association, Chicago, Ill.*)

styles, using a model such as that for Life-Style Market Segmentation.

Buying decisions, too, may be looked at in terms of the stages of the family life cycle: Bachelor Stage, Newly Married Couples, Full Nest I, Full Nest II, Full Nest III, Empty Nest I, Empty Nest II, Solitary Survivor I, and Solitary Survivor II. A common buying process consists of : awareness, interest, evaluation, decision, and repurchase.

Buying patterns should be looked at in terms of who, what, when, where, and how, as well as why. Consumer goods are distinguished from industrial goods according to their ultimate use and are categorized as convenience, shopping, or specialty goods. Industrial goods are categorized as raw materials, fabricating materials and parts, installations, accessory equipment, and operating supplies.

The Howard-Sheth model of consumer buyer behavior is presented as is the Sheth model of industrial buyer behavior. Direct marketing is just as applicable to industrial markets as it is to consumer markets.

CASE: BUSINESS-TO-BUSINESS UTILIZATION OF DIRECT MARKETING

Learning Objective

This case study demonstrates a variety of ways, as suggested in this chapter, in which the tools and techniques of direct marketing can be used by business and industry.

Overview

Industrial direct marketing, business-to-business transactions, involves recognition of four characteristics of industrial demand that distinguish it from consumer demand: (1) industrial demand is typically derived from consumer demand; (2) industrial demand is relatively inelastic to price changes; (3) industrial demand is generally more widely fluctuating than is consumer demand; (4) industrial purchase decisions within an organization are usually made jointly by knowledgeable buyers. These characteristics of industrial demand need to be considered and understood in evaluating industrial direct marketing and this case discussion should help that understanding.

Procedure

Read the learning objective, the overview, and the case that follows. Be prepared to discuss which of these main uses of industrial direct marketing are identifiable: developing sales leads, achieving direct sales, reinforcing sales efforts, introducing new products, developing new markets and applications, conducting market research, and building goodwill.

Case[28]

Federal Express is a nationwide air express delivery service with headquarters in Memphis. It uses its own fleet of airplanes and trucks to transport letters and packages for delivery overnight. Every night Federal Ex-

---

[28] Adapted from John Yeck, "Federal Express Mail Program Successful in Many Areas," *Direct Marketing,* July 1982, pp. 60–66.

press planes leave 85 key cities throughout the country, loaded with packages from those originating airports. They converge on Memphis, where their valuable cargo is sorted, reloaded, and flown out for delivery door to door by noon the next day to any one of more than 14,500 destination cities.

Federal Express markets and prices this delivery service in a number of categories, depending on type and weight of what is being delivered. One of its most profitable categories is Priority 1. This includes the delivery of nearly any shape or size package weighing between 5 and 70 pounds. Because Priority 1 has become a popular and profitable product, competitors of Federal Express have increased their promotion for similar services.

To expand its market, increase its penetration, and hold its present customers, Federal Express decided to step up its own promotion, too. A month-long concentrated direct mail effort was prepared by Yeck Brothers Company, direct mail agency for Federal Express, to promote Priority 1 and announce a new discount schedule in connection with it.

Based strictly on its potential value in the immediate future, the market for the direct mail promotion program was divided into three categories:

1 Frequent users of Priority 1: 29,126 individuals
2 Infrequent users of Priority 1: 121,705 individuals
3 Other Federal Express customers who had never used Priority 1: 63,431 individuals

The symbol to be used for dramatizing the 5-to-70-pound Priority 1 service was the same for all three market segments: a 5-pound reproduction of a 1913 exercise weight. Frequent users of Priority 1 received the exercise weight immediately as a goodwill gift; infrequent users had to request it; nonusers received it as a premium with the purchase of Priority 1 service for the first time.

Frequent users were asked to identify other prospects and decision makers within their own organizations. A total of 7,044 (24.1 percent) of the 29,126 frequent user recipients of the promotion did just that.

Of the 121,705 infrequent users contacted, a total of 25,985 (24.0 percent) responded by requesting the gift, and, in the process, they also supplied 14,723 names of new prospects within their own organizations.

Of the 63,431 nonusers of Priority 1 among Federal Express customers, a total of 9,300 (15 percent) actually purchased the service and submitted a copy of the Federal Express air bill as proof of purchase to receive the exercise weight.

In summary, the following total results were tabulated:

21,767 new prospects
40,000 responses from *old* customers
25,985 "market research" forms returned
9,300 proven direct sales to *new* customers
$500,000 in immediate traceable sales to these *new* customers alone

Since each user of Priority 1 service is known to average $4,000 in sales per year for an undetermined number of future years, the potential value of these new customers is most impressive.

DISCUSSION QUESTIONS

1 Distinguish between learning theories and psychoanalytic theories.
2 How do direct marketers use the concept of psychographics in their measurement of lifestyles? How does this differ from the approach taken by general marketers?
3 How do "face-to-face" reference groups, including family and household groups of individuals living together, influence buying decisions?
4 Which do you view as a more important influence on buyer behavior: social class or cultural heritage? Why?
5 What is meant by the statement that "culture is adaptive?"
6 Why is a knowledge of the family life cycle important to direct marketers? How does this concept influence the purchase of household goods, educational materials, and insurance?
7 What are the five stages of a typical buying decision?
8 Distinguish between convenience, shopping, and specialty goods.
9 What are the classifications of industrial goods?
10 Explain these characteristics of industrial demand: derived, inelastic, widely fluctuating, and knowledgeable.

MARKET SEGMENTATION IN DIRECT MARKETING

Market segmentation is a natural outgrowth of the marketing concept. Customers can be served best by organizations that know the characteristics of their buyers. Since all buyers are not alike, they are placed into groups or market segments, according to geographic, demographic, and psychographic factors. These market segments become the focal points of product differentiation and positioning.

Even before there was a marketing concept, direct marketers were segmenting markets and positioning products to them. The young telegraph operator who in 1886 acquired a shipment of undeliverable gold watches, Richard Warren Sears, reasoned that the best prospects for their sale would be other railroad agents, like himself. Thus, employing the principle of market segmentation, he took the first step toward what was to become Sears Roebuck & Company.

The concept and theory of market segmentation and its special relevance in both consumer and industrial direct marketing are the subject of this chapter. We will also be concerned with product differentiation and product positioning. A particularly appropriate marketing tool for direct marketers, the United States Postal Service ZIP Code area, will be reviewed.

THE NATURE OF MARKET SEGMENTATION

The increasing complexity of marketing activities within an industrial society brought with it an increasing need for segmentation of the heterogeneous total market into smaller and more homogeneous subgroups. These subgroups can be thought of as marketing units or *market segments*.

Unless a product or service is unique and appeals equally to everyone, it is vitally important to think in terms of such marketing units. Many times it is necessary to *differentiate* products for particular market segments and to *position* these products so that they will have special appeal to the units to which promotion is to be directed.

There are several ways to segment markets. Frequently, market segmentation has been *geographic*, urban vs. rural or by region, state, county, or metropolitan area. Sometimes market segmentation has been according to *demographic* grouping, such as by age, sex, marital status, occupation, or education. Many recent market segmentation efforts have been based on *psychographic* characteristics: habits, attitudes, life-styles, and behavior patterns of buyers.

Because the total market for most types of products and services is so diverse, geographically as well as demographically, market segmentation has become increasingly important. Ideally, a market segment should not only comprise a marketing unit whose definition is readily identifiable but also be one whose homogeneity makes it capable of being measured in economic and cultural as well as demographic terms.

Market Segmentation vs. Product Differentiation

Market segmentation divides the total heterogeneous market into smaller, more homogeneous segments. Although the total market may be viewed in terms of a single demand curve, each market segment has its own demand curve, and the total market at best represents a composite of such curves. This is visualized in Figure 7-1, wherein examples of geographic, demographic, and psychographic segmentation have been employed to illustrate increasing quantities of demand as price level decreases.

Product differentiation, like market segmentation, is an alternative to price competition. The difference might be real or simply an advertised difference between a firm's product and that of its competition. A toothpaste that contains fluoride is intrinsically different from one that does not. An airline designating its

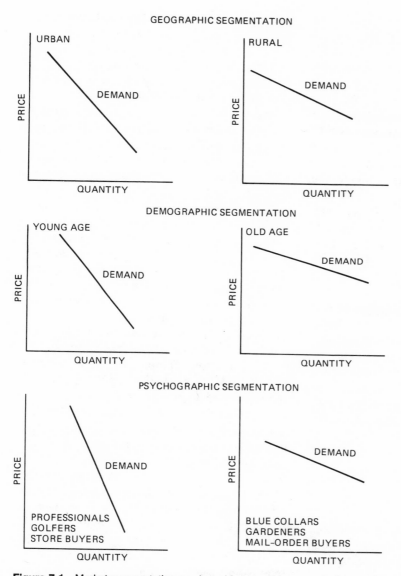

Figure 7-1 Market segmentation as viewed in terms of economic theory.

Boeing 727 aircraft as a "Star-Stream Jet" may have planes identical to its competitors. Product differentiation can distinguish its product from its competition, but market segmentation and appropriate product positioning can make it appear different, even if it is not actually different.

Product Positioning The image projected by a product in relation to a particular use or market segment is termed *positioning*. In effect, positioning combines the principles of both product differentiation and market segmentation. Examples of positioning abound: "7-Up, The Uncola"; "Avis is No. 2." These are more than simply advertising slogans. The "Marlboro Man" is more than just an art treatment. Comparing the traditional Ford automobile with a Mustang involves more than just two brand names. Irish Spring is not just any soap. All of these product references are examples of *positioning,* employing product differentiation to appeal to specific market segmentation. Most "big ticket" direct marketers (such as Neiman-Marcus, Horchow, Sakowitz) thrive on positioning. So do the mail-order sellers of specialty foods (Harry & David, Omaha Steaks, Swiss Colony) and nursery products (Jackson & Perkins, Wayside Gardens, Breck's).

ALTERNATIVE MARKETING UNITS

There are many subgroups offering potential as marketing units or market segments. These subgroups or clusters of buyers or prospective buyers can be geographic, demographic, or psychographic. Or, markets can be segmented on the basis of brand preferences, characteristics related to products, potential purchase volume, or recency and frequency of purchase. We will be concerned here, however, with only these segmentation bases: geographic, demographic, and psychographic.

Geographic Segmentation

Potential geographic subdivisions range in size from the country as a whole down through census divisions and Federal Reserve districts to states, counties, trading areas, cities, towns, census tracts, and even individual city blocks. In addition, there are numerical codes such as ZIP Codes, telephone area codes, computer "match" codes, territory and route numbers.

Dik Warren Twedt, in mid-1965, urged the formation of and then served as chairman of a joint American Marketing Association/American Standards Association Task Group on Standard Geographic Units. The group's

objective was "to evaluate and recommend a single system of standard geographic units—to be used for purposes of both communication and analysis." After a thorough study of alternative systems, the Task Group concluded that the postal ZIP Code area system for delivery of mail probably had the greatest investment (by both business and government) and the widest acceptance. Reservations were expressed, because of the system's incompatibility with existing units (mainly counties) and existing data.[1]

The major geographic units then in use, as identified by the American Marketing Association Task Group headed by Twedt, are shown in Figure 7-2.[2] From the perspective of the direct marketer, none of these geographic divisions (with the single exception of ZIP Code areas) is both readily identifiable with a buyer or adequately homogeneous in the sense that it is in-and-of-itself economically meaningful and environmentally measurable.

Consider, for example, the 3,134 counties in the United States: the county is probably the most used and possibly the least justifiable of all available geographic units used for marketing control and analysis. These political divisions are the product of a surveyor's sextant, 50 or 100 or more years ago, and are of little use in marketing. The boundaries of counties are most often either straight lines or natural barriers such as rivers. Many counties predate railroads, most are older than the automobile, and almost all were formed prior to the airplane and modern telephone and television. Hence, they pay little heed to either transportation or communication patterns through which economic and cultural exchange take place.

[1] American Marketing Association, *Progress Reports of Task Group on Standard Geographic Units,* New York, August 10, 1965–October 7, 1966.

[2] Dik Warren Twedt, "Urgently Needed: A Standard Geographic Unit," *Journal of Marketing,* vol. 20, 1969, pp. 61–62.

Census Regions
Census Divisions
Federal Reserve Districts
States
Telephone Area Codes
Metropolitan Statistical Areas
Media Communications Areas
Congressional Districts
State Economic Areas
ABC City or Retail Trading Zones
Counties
ZIP Code Areas
Census Tracts
Block Groups

Figure 7-2 Major geographic market segments.

It is indeed puzzling why the county has been and still remains the basic building block in the distribution superstructure. The Census Bureau's units of measurement, metropolitan statistical areas (MSAs), use counties as the basic unit although certain other metropolitan or trading area definitions split counties in some cases. Possibly by default as much as any other reason, the day-to-day activities of business, industry, and government have been largely patterned along county lines.

An important form of geographic market segmentation is that which recognizes inherent differences among those buyers who reside in central cities, suburban, urban fringe, and rural areas. The last may be further divided between farm and nonfarm households.

Demographic Segmentation

Demographic statistics, although compiled for a geographic area, are frequently related to some social or economic characteristic or even to a time comparison. The primary unit of observation in demography is the individual, with the family unit and household being secondary.

There are three main sources for such data: (1) by population enumeration as in a census;

(2) by registration on the occurrence of some event, such as births, marriages, and deaths; and (3) by sample surveys or tabulation of special groups.[3] The various data obtained in these ways are generally available for marketing and other uses from government sources, especially the Census Bureau.

To indicate the wealth of demographic data available, that from the 1980 Census of Population and Housing is shown in Figure 7-3. As a practical expedient, it is often desirable to tabulate the effect of interaction of many demographic variables simultaneously, even with geographic variables, to measure lifestyles. An example of performing such measurement is contained beginning on page 93 of Chapter 4. It utilizes a model for Life-Style Market Segmentation.

Often, *change* in demography is significant. For example, if a single person marries or if a baby is born, these events have marketing significance. So does decreasing population of a geographic area or high mobility of the population in an area. Direct marketers are able to capture such major happenings in mailing lists to offer differentiated products to geographic or demographic market segments.

Psychographic Segmentation

As was presented in Chapter 6, psychographics is the study of life-styles, habits, attitudes, beliefs, and value systems of individuals. Even though buyers have common geographic or demographic characteristics, they often have different buying characteristics. The interaction of many demographic characteristics, along with geographic patterns, can be used to describe psychographic behavior patterns. Individual buyer behavior is influenced not only by demographics and geographics but also by such not so easily defined variables as environment, self-perception, and life-styles. When

[3] Mortimer Spiegelman, *Introduction to Demography,* rev. ed., Harvard University Press, Cambridge, 1968, p. 1.

100-Percent Items

POPULATION	HOUSING
Household relationship	Number of units at address
Sex	Access to unit
Race	Complete plumbing facilities
Age	Number of rooms
Marital status	Tenure (whether unit is owned
Spanish/Hispanic origin or	or rented)
descent	Condominium identification
	Value of home (owner-
	occupied units and
	condominiums)
	Contract rent (renter-occupied
	units)
	Vacant for rent, for sale, etc.;
	and duration of vacancy

Sample Items*

POPULATION	HOUSING
School enrollment	Type of unit and units in
Educational attainment	structure
State or foreign country of	Stories in building and
birth	presence of elevator
Citizenship and year of	Year built
immigration	Year moved into this house
Current language and English	Acreage and crop sales
proficiency	Source of water
Ancestry	Sewage disposal
Place of residence five years ago	Heating equipment
Activity five years ago	Fuels used for house heating,
Veteran status and period of	water heating, and cooking
service	Costs of utilities and fuels
Presence of disability or	Complete kitchen facilities
handicap	Number of bedrooms
Children ever born	Number of bathrooms
Marital history	Telephone
Employment status last week	Air conditioning
Hours worked last week	Number of automobiles
Place of work	Number of light trucks and
Travel time to work	vans
Means of transportation to work	Homeowner shelter costs for
Number of persons in carpool	mortgage, real estate taxes,
Year last worked	and hazard insurance
Industry	
Occupation	
Type of employment	
Number of weeks worked in	
1979	
Usual hours worked per week	
in 1979	
Number of weeks looking for	
work in 1979	
Amount of income in 1979	
by source	

*For most areas of the country in 1980, one out of every six housing units or households received the sample form. Areas estimated to contain 2,500 or fewer persons in 1980 had a 3-out-of-every-6 sampling rate, which is required in order to obtain reliable statistics needed for participation in certain Federal programs.

Figure 7-3 Subject items included in the 1980 census. (1980 Census of Population and Housing, *August 1979, U.S. Department of Commerce, Census Bureau.*)

such influences can be identified and measured, they can be used by a direct marketer in segmenting mailing lists in the manner described and demonstrated in the model for Life-Style Market Segmentation that was presented in Chapter 4.

In addition to measuring environmental influences as independent variables, direct marketers have the ability to measure life-styles (and thus predict response, the dependent variable) through noting the simultaneous appearance of a prospect's name on a variety of merged lists. For example, a registered owner of a particular type of automobile might also appear on the subscriber lists of *Wall Street Journal* and *Better Homes & Gardens* as well as the customer lists of up-scale catalogs such as Neiman-Marcus and Gump's. This same prospect might even be a contributor to Planned Parenthood and a member of the Cousteau Society. When merged, such multiple list identifiers can describe activities, interests, and opinions (the psychographic researcher's "A-I-O's") more specifically than do surveys that have the heuristic value of providing "mood music for advertising copywriters."

Another means of psychographic identification of specific prospects is a comprehensive data file developed by National Demographics, Ltd., under the trade name, The Life-Style Selector. The database is developed from consumer questionnaires packaged in a wide variety of hard goods products, with permission for mailing list use granted by the respondent. Included for each of several million consumer names and addresses are eight demographic characteristics: sex, age range, income range, occupation, marital status, housing tenure, credit cards held, and number of children at home. Also recorded are participation by the respondent in any of 48 activities or hobbies. It is possible for a consumer direct marketer to develop a profile of the organization's house lists, in terms of psychographics and demographics, through matching with The Life-Style Selector, and to extend the prospect base through use of similar names within the data file.

Thus, measurement of environmental influences within geographic units combined with demographic and psychographic indicators derived from list cross-referencing and other expressions of activities, interests, and opinions can all interact to enable the direct marketer to reach individual consumers within market segments. Such list selection is obviously more efficient and can be more effective than directing pinpointed messages to the total marketplace.

ZIP CODE AREAS AS MARKET SEGMENTS

Geographic units that have been used in segmenting markets have lacked *homogeneity* as well as ready *identity* with a consumer. The need has been for a marketing unit in which physical boundaries could be defined in terms that are *economically meaningful* and *environmentally measurable*.

ZIP Code areas, although originally conceived and developed by the Post Office Department (now the United States Postal Service) for the sorting and distribution of mail, have become a convenient as well as a logical method of geographic market segmentation, especially in direct marketing. Mail goes from people to people in the same manner in which trade is conducted and in the same manner in which cultural exchange takes place. This people-to-people relationship explains why the ZIP Code system was established with regard to transportation patterns. This same relationship explains why, in effect, ZIP Code areas define marketing units that can be measured with regard to environmental influences. Counties and other politically defined geographic areas have no meaning in mail handling or in other economic or social activities.

Rationale

Because people with like interests tend to cluster and because their purchase decisions are frequently influenced by their desire to emulate their friends, neighbors, and community innovators, ZIP Code areas provide the means to *identify* clusters of households that have a high degree of *homogeneity*. This homogeneity is inherent in the manner in which ZIP Code areas have been constructed and relies on accepted principles of reference group theory as well as the concept of environmental influences on buyer behavior.

The *identity* results from the ready availability of a five-digit number that has become a standard part of the address of virtually every individual and organization.

The *homogeneity* of ZIP Code areas makes it possible to classify and qualify them in such a manner as to measure the effects of economic and social environment and demography and geography on buying behavior within these marketing units. Such units can then be conveniently clustered to form larger and more accessible segments. Determining predictability of buyer behavior in this manner is not the same thing as manipulation and exploitation of behavior. Rather, such analysis enables advertising to be more effectively created and efficiently directed.

Applications and Uses

Although the use of ZIP Code areas as geographic market segments is a recent innovation, their value as a readily identifiable and relatively homogeneous marketing unit has already been demonstrated in a variety of practical applications. Small area data, including those for census tracts as well as ZIP Code areas, are relevant for business and plant locations, commercial and industrial development, market and sales analyses, along with long-range corporate and financial planning.

In addition, there are many social and economic problems facing communities today and the data for these local areas are of significance as well for education, health, housing, economic forecasting, workforce planning, poverty programs, transportation planning, plus a host of other public concerns. Although major emphasis to date has been placed on market applications and notably those for direct marketing, the importance of government and other public applications of ZIP Code areas as planning units is also worthy of noting.

The cornerstone of measurement of the effect of environmental influences on customer behavior is, of course, the interdependence of buyer behavior. As is generally accepted in the marketing literature, purchase decisions are not so much dependent on income per se as on the buyer's perception of his or her relative position, or that aspired to, in the environment. Thorstein Veblen called it "conspicuous consumption." John Kenneth Galbraith refers to "materialism" and the "dependence effect." The less scholarly sum it up by the phrase "keeping up with the Joneses." Such recognition of environmental influences within ZIP Code areas enables direct marketers to more readily define their best prospects, seek them out, establish sales potentials, predict buyer behavior, and look at penetration in relation to potential in a manner that can be mathematically measured and statistically evaluated.

Geographic Structure

Although devised originally and basically for the purpose of sorting and distributing an ever-increasing volume of mail to a growing number of delivery stops, in spite of a sharp reduction in railroad service, ZIP Code areas have become a key basis for market segmentation in direct marketing, combining, in effect, the characteristics of geographics, demographics, and psychographics. The socioeconomic usefulness of these units, especially from a direct marketing perspective, results from the three criteria used in establishing them:

1 A hub city for each clustering of ZIP Code areas (termed a sectional center) that is the natural center of local transportation

2 An average of 40 to 75 individual post offices within each sectional center, resulting

in fairly consistent equating of population within the units

3 An optimum of 2 to 3 hours' normal driving time from each natural transportation hub to the farthest post office in the sectional center

An obvious convenience of these geographic units, setting them apart from commonly used divisions such as counties, is that each household and business within the unit is readily identifiable by a five-digit number assigned to it as a part of its street address.

The first digit of the five-digit code identifies one of 10 (0 through 9) geographic areas of the nation, with the digit ascending from east to west. These regions are identified in Figure 7-4.

The next two digits of the five-digit number identify a major city or major distribution point (sectional center) within a state as visualized in the map for the state of Missouri shown in Figure 7-5.

The last two digits of the five-digit ZIP Code fall into two geographic categories: (1) key post offices in each area, which normally have stations and branches in the city's neighborhoods; and (2) a series of associate small town or rural post offices served by the sectional center. Thus, the five-digit number can represent either an individual post office in a rural area served out of the sectional center transportation hub (as shown graphically in Figure 7-6) or a specific neighborhood or delivery unit within a city (as visualized in Figure 7-7).

Five-Digit vs. Nine-Digit ZIP Codes What the five-digit ZIP Code designations represent is summarized in Figure 7-8. The United States Postal Service is developing extension of the present five-digit ZIP Code to nine digits, with four additional digits separated by a hyphen from the first five. The first two additional digits denote a *sector* and the last two denote a *segment* within a sector. A four-digit add-on sector/segment combination would be unique within each five-digit ZIP Code area. The

Figure 7-4 ZIP Code national area designations. (*United States Postal Service, Washington, D.C.*)

additional four digits would permit mail to be sorted to carrier delivery routes.

Examples of the two types of five-digit numbers designating ZIP Code areas, that is, sectional centers and large cities, are shown in Figure 7-9 for the state of Nebraska and for the city of Omaha. Within 10 U.S. regions (the first digit of the five-digit number), sectional centers (the next two digits) are designated within states and these in turn serve major cities as well as associated rural post offices (the last two digits). The entire system is based on local transportation and trade, the hubs of social and economic activity.

Validity of Areas

Sectional centers have a geographic boundary definition almost totally dependent in size and shape on the area's transportation pattern, which in turn represents the local economic pattern and, ultimately, the social and cultural pattern. Up to 1,000 sectional centers are potentially identifiable within the system, with more than 600 of those assigned at present.

Similarly, the boundaries of large cities, with their local neighborhood delivery units, tend to reflect the economic city and not the political city. Like school districts, these boundaries do not follow existing political boundaries. Very large cities, such as Los Angeles and New York, have necessarily been assigned more than one three-digit sectional center coding. It should be noted, too, that many three-digit numbers have been assigned to military installations, federal government, and other noncensus units. These specially assigned numbers are not usually relevant for direct marketing since census data are not available for them. For the same reason, neither are those five-digit numbers assigned to

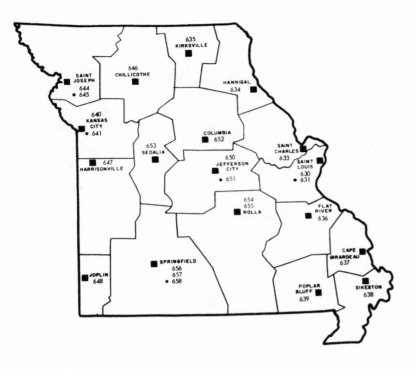

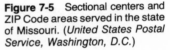

Figure 7-5 Sectional centers and ZIP Code areas served in the state of Missouri. (*United States Postal Service, Washington, D.C.*)

post office boxes and major businesses and organizations that receive large volumes of mail.

There are as many as 100,000 five-digit numbers possible, with more than 40,000 currently in use, including those assigned to post office boxes, military bases, and businesses that receive large volumes of mail.

Some direct marketers have confined analysis to the three-digit sectional center whereas others, to gather adequate statistical data, find it feasible to cluster five-digit areas that are not necessarily geographically contiguous but have similar characteristics.

Even major users who send out large volumes of direct mail find it difficult to gather adequate statistics from individual five-digit ZIP Code areas. This need for large numbers is why the forthcoming addition of four digits to create a nine-digit ZIP Code number will have little analytical relevance for direct marketers. Smaller units, such as census tracts,

have to be clustered, just as do five-digit ZIP Code areas in most cases. A further drawback to the use of census tracts as an alternative is the fact that these units are not readily identifiable with names on mailing lists.

The need for the smaller five-digit ZIP Code area (or clusters of these) is probably greater, too, within the confines of large city areas, where there is more heterogeneity among the population concentrated in a neighborhood.

Note that a five-digit number assigned to an outlying post office, within a sectional center area, represents nothing more than an individual post office. These are numerically arranged generally in alphabetic order by the post office or town name within the sectional center. Clustering of these would most likely be by geography, rather than according to demographic characteristics.

There is, obviously, considerable spread among households within and between five-digit ZIP Code areas just as there is among households within and between cities, towns, and counties. The direct marketer should be aware of this in weighing the relative need for three-digit vs. five-digit units or clusterings of such units. The opportunities for measurement are desirable in either instance, due, it bears repeating, to the ready *identity* and *homogeneity* of ZIP Code areas, coupled with a convenience heretofore lacking in the definition of geographic areas.

It is well to keep in mind, too, that although we recognize the basic *homogeneity* of households within a ZIP Code area, this does not mean that all households have the same characteristics. Rather, it is a basic concept of human ecology that clusters of households, even though each household has different demographics, tend to emulate each other. It is the *environment* that is being measured, not the *individual household*.

Clustering Areas to Segments

A key advantage of ZIP Code areas is that they can be combined, like building blocks, to suit the individual need of the direct marketer relative to product differentiation or promo-

Figure 7-6 Detail of the ZIP Code areas served by the Springfield, Missouri sectional center. (*State of Missouri, Division of Highways and Roads, Jefferson City, Mo.*)

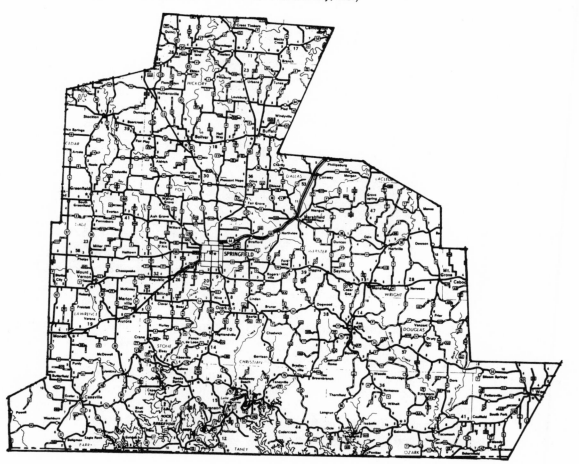

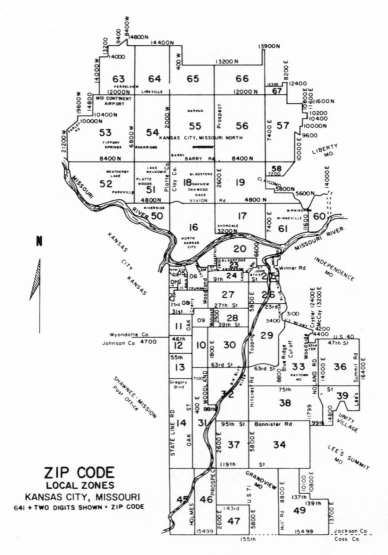

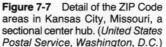

Figure 7-7 Detail of the ZIP Code areas in Kansas City, Missouri, a sectional center hub. (*United States Postal Service, Washington, D.C.*)

tional strategy. Examples of clustering ZIP Code areas are given in Figure 7-10. These similar areas do not necessarily have to be geographically contiguous, as in traditional retailing, when direct marketing promotional strategies are used.

A ZIP Code–based marketing information system enables direct marketers to know more about their markets and, additionally, to have them organized according to local transportation patterns. Further, territories can be assigned and identified more effectively, and salespeople can cover territories more efficiently, at less cost. Of course, promotion effort can be more economically coordinated, advertising with selling.

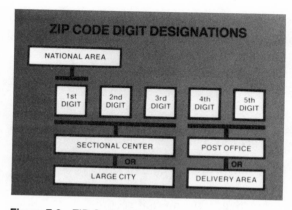

Figure 7-8 ZIP Code digit designations. (*United States Postal Service, Washington, D.C.*)

AVAILABILITY OF STATISTICAL DATA

A key reason for the adherence to traditional geographic units by both business and government has been the fact that most statistical data have historically been set up and published on a county basis. Within metropolitan statistical areas (MSAs) which have been generally composed of groupings of counties, there has been a finer breakdown by census tracts and minor civil divisions. Correlation of existing data to the boundaries of a more useful marketing unit, such as ZIP Code areas, re-

quires specialized and often highly sophisticated mathematical allocation techniques not usually available to the smaller user of published data.

During the past decade, however, as marketers have become increasingly aware of the validity of ZIP Code areas as market segments, increasing amounts of data have become available for these units. There has been extensive use of the allocations by ZIP Code provided for the first time by the Census Bureau within MSAs as part of the 1970 census. The 1980 census has been tabulated for *all* five-digit ZIP Code areas, even those in rural areas beyond MSAs.

Rand McNally ZIP Code Atlas This privately published volume, first available in 1969 and updated periodically since then, contains a map of each of the 50 states printed in two colors, with the boundaries of ZIP Code sectional center areas in red ink overlaid onto the boundaries of counties, which are printed in blue ink. Individual maps are included for several large cities as well, together with a variety of statistical data. These data include:

Sectional center number
Sectional center name

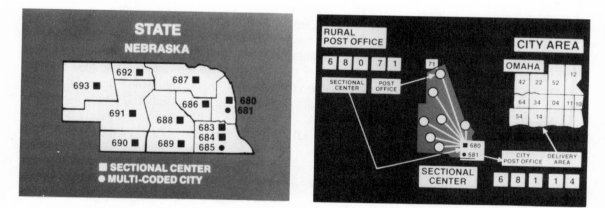

Figure 7-9 Examples of ZIP Code area identification. (*United States Postal Service, Washington, D.C.*)

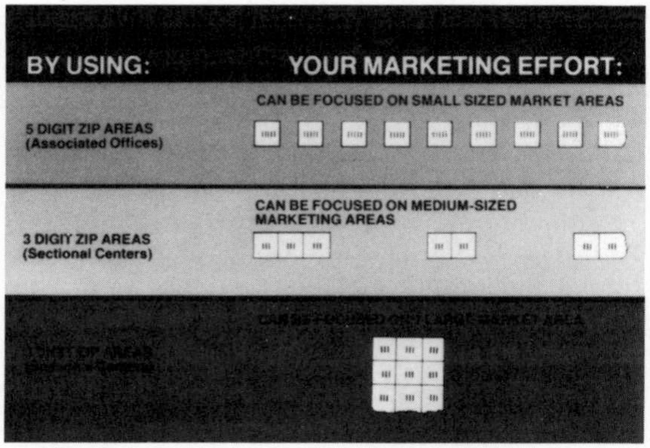

Figure 7-10   Examples of clustering ZIP Code areas.

Classification as a Rand McNally trading area

Sectional center population as a percent of the state population

Number of households

Total retail trade

Shopping goods sales

Passenger car registrations

Zip-O-Data   Updated annually, this privately published service is the work of Yuan

Liang and the Metromail Corporation. To subscribers, it is available on magnetic tape or in hard copy, updated each year, and includes these data for each five-digit ZIP Code area (with sectional center totals) as shown in Figure 7-11. The boxed list below clarifies headings abbreviated on the Zip-O-Data form.

A variety of other privately published data are also available in addition to those mentioned. Still, the most important information to be accumulated by ZIP Code is that which firms and organizations themselves tabulate from their own internal records. Tabulations of responses to direct response promotion efforts or tabulation of customers in relation to households, by five-digit ZIP Code area, is an essential requirement for any direct marketer who would benefit from knowledge of house mailing lists.

SPECIFIC USES OF ZIP CODE AREAS

There are many specific ways in which ZIP Code areas can be used by individual direct marketing organizations:

Clarification of abbreviated headings in Figure 7-11.

ZIP Code five-digit number	Percent dwelling units that are owner-occupied	Mean number of children per household
Post office name	Percent population nonwhite	Percent individuals in labor force who are professional or managerial
County name	Persons per household	
County code	Percent households that are single-family dwelling units	
MSAs (market) code		Percent households headed by person aged 65+
Area of Dominant Influence (ADI) code	Median home value	
County size	Percent length of residence 5+ years	Median household income indices:
Household count	Index of social position for small areas	Percent sectional center
Median income of households		Percent state
Median educational level of individuals age 25+	Percent labor force that is female with children	Percent United States
Median age of individuals age 25+		

STATE- MISSOURI ZIP-O-DATA PAGE 399

ZIP CODE	POST OFFICE	COUNTY	CTY CDE	MKT CDE	ADI CDE	CTY SZE	HH COUNT	INCOME	ED	MED AGE 25+	PCT OO	PCT NW	PER /HH	PCT SFDU	MED HV	PCT LOR 5+ YRS	ISPSA	PCT FEM L/F CH	CH/ HH	PCT PRO MGR	PCT POP 65+	SEC CTR	INC INDICES ST	US
64057	INDEPENDENCE	JACKSON	095	136	027	A	2,088	$24,900	12.6	40	83	0	3.1	95	51.6	44	3100	31	1.0	23	6	117	132	125
64058	INDEPENDENCE	JACKSON	095	136	027	A	1,034	$23,700	12.4	38	86	0	3.4	98	38.4	45	3542	36	1.3	12	3	111	126	119
64061	KEARNEY	CLAY	047	136	027	A	362	$21,200	12.4	43	69	0	2.8	86	47.4	46	3335	28	.8	21	10	100	113	106
64062	KINGSVILLE	JOHNSON	101		027	D	592	$16,600	12.3	44	85	0	3.0	82	21.5	70	3810	21	.9	10	13	78	88	83
64063	LAWSON	RAY	177	136	027	A	1,459	$19,700	12.4	40	86	0	3.0	94	36.2	58	3478	29	1.0	17	9	92	105	99
64064	LEES SUMMIT	JACKSON	095	136	027	A	13,731	$23,800	12.9	49	61	1	2.5	71	56.7	43	3048	22	.7	25	22	112	127	119
64066	LEVASY	JACKSON	095	136	027	A	70	$23,500	12.2	49	85	0	2.9	90	31.0	70	3973	17	.7	10	13	110	125	118
64067	LEXINGTON	LAFAYTTE	107		027	D	2,570	$17,600	12.1	51	69	8	2.4	81	28.0	59	3630	21	.6	20	19	83	94	88
64068	LIBERTY	CLAY	047	136	027	A	7,433	$24,200	12.8	44	69	0	2.7	78	51.0	48	3078	24	.8	25	8	114	129	121
64070	LONE JACK	JACKSON	095	136	027	A	460	$20,300	12.8	41	81	0	3.0	84	34.0	60	3529	22	1.1	12	8	95	108	102
64071	MAYVIEW	LAFAYTTE	107		027	D	276	$14,700	9.7	44	85	14	3.0	91	16.3	72	4262	16	.8	6	15	69	78	74
64072	MISSOURI CITY	CLAY	047	136	027	A	117	$17,800	11.8	46	85	0	3.1	87	20.8	73	3645	16	.7	15	9	84	95	89
64073	MOSBY	CLAY	047	136	027	A	81	$14,200	10.2	42	80	0	3.0	93	18.5	75	4222	11	.8	2	10	67	76	71
64074	NAPOLEON	LAFAYTTE	107		027	D	219	$18,000	12.2	44	81	0	2.9	93	24.3	77	3704	14	.7	19	15	85	96	90
64075	OAK GROVE	JACKSON	095	136	027	A	2,275	$18,800	12.3	41	76	0	3.0	87	37.5	46	3537	26	1.1	15	10	88	100	94
64076	ODESSA	LAFAYTTE	107		027	D	2,065	$19,100	12.2	49	79	2	2.6	83	34.3	57	3518	22	.7	17	17	104	118	111
64077	ORRICK	RAY	177	136	027	A	709	$21,000	12.4	47	84	0	2.7	85	23.3	69	3591	17	.8	14	14	90	102	96
64078	PECULIAR	CASS	037	136	027	A	1,424	$21,000	12.4	41	67	0	3.0	80	51.3	55	3223	27	1.0	26	8	99	112	105
64079	PLATTE CITY	PLATTE	165	136	027	A	1,876	$22,200	12.5	42	68	1	2.6	77	48.8	54	3173	28	.9	19	11	104	118	111
64080	PLEASANT HILL	CASS	037	136	027	A	2,404	$19,200	12.2	46	73	1	2.5	85	31.3	62	3576	21	.7	15	14	90	102	96
64083	RAYMORE	CASS	037	136	027	A	1,841	$26,700	12.7	42	90	1	3.1	93	65.3	30	2971	31	1.0	25	12	125	142	134
64084	RAYVILLE	RAY	177	136	027	A	506	$15,400	9.9	53	88	0	2.7	93	12.1	67	4189	16	.8	3	18	72	82	77
64085	RICHMOND	RAY	177	136	027	A	3,337	$17,800	12.1	50	74	4	2.4	88	29.7	63	3572	21	.6	19	18	84	95	89
64088	SIBLEY	JACKSON	095	136	027	A	375	$17,300	13.2	43	86	0	2.3	94	33.6	64	3844	32	.9	11	8	80	90	85
64089	SMITHVILLE	CLAY	047	136	027	A	1,411	$20,000	12.4	49	66	0	2.5	83	40.7	55	3449	17	.6	19	19	94	106	100
64090	STRASBURG	CASS	037	136	027	A	74	$15,500	10.7	48	86	2	2.7	94	15.0	77	3761	15	.7	7	15	73	82	7.
64092	WALDRON	PLATTE	165	136	027	A	65	$25,200	12.7	42	70	1	2.8	81	57.7	64	3109	25	.8	24	7	118	134	126
64093	WARRENSBURG	JOHNSON	101		027	D	6,452	$15,700	13.4	44	50	5	2.3	62	38.4	35	3091	16	.6	26	14	74	84	79
64096	WAVERLY	LAFAYTTE	107		027	D	483	$14,800	12.2	53	77	0	2.5	84	24.3	68	3797	13	.6	16	25	69	79	74
64097	WELLINGTON	LAFAYTTE	107		027	D	676	$19,200	12.2	51	82	1	2.6	88	25.3	72	3637	21	.7	18	17	90	102	96
64098	WESTON	PLATTE	165	136	027	A	1,138	$19,300	12.3	48	69	0	2.5	87	36.9	59	3394	24	.7	20	18	91	103	97
	SEC CENTER 640 KANSAS CITY						145,544	$21,300	12.5	45	70	2	2.7	81	41.1	51	3298	23	.8	20	12		113	107
64105	KANSAS CITY	JACKSON	095	136	027	A	1,336	$12,600	13.2	51	80	10	2.5	12	14.6	29	3436	0	.0	19	30	61	67	63
64106	KANSAS CITY	JACKSON	095	136	027	A	3,945	$12,300	11.3	51	10	31	1.9	25	18.0	39	3656	9	.5	14	27	60	65	62
64108	KANSAS CITY	JACKSON	095	136	027	A	3,554	$15,900	10.5	48	36	38	2.4	55	13.1	50	3737	13	.6	18	16	78	85	80
64109	KANSAS CITY	JACKSON	095	136	027	A	8,246	$12,300	10.1	45	33	62	2.3	49	21.8	43	3676	17	.5	18	15	60	65	62
64110	KANSAS CITY	JACKSON	095	136	027	A	9,184	$16,900	13.3	38	52	37	2.5	67	30.9	39	3073	19	.6	26	12	82	90	85
64111	KANSAS CITY	JACKSON	095	136	027	A	13,099	$17,200	13.2	38	23	6	1.7	31	35.3	32	2974	8	.1	29	34	84	91	86
64112	KANSAS CITY	JACKSON	095	136	027	A	7,276	$22,500	14.0	43	23	1	1.5	32	73.6	43	2429	4	.1	44	34	110	120	113
64113	KANSAS CITY	JACKSON	095	136	027	A	4,753	$35,700	16.1	46	91	0	2.6	95	81.9	62	2129	16	.7	52	17	174	190	179
64114	KANSAS CITY	JACKSON	095	136	027	A	11,468	$25,200	13.2	53	91	1	2.3	87	52.1	62	2718	13	.4	34	23	123	134	126
64116	KANSAS CITY	CLAY	047	136	027	A	6,210	$21,500	12.9	46	50	0	2.2	78	46.0	47	2986	17	.4	25	14	105	114	108
64117	KANSAS CITY	CLAY	047	136	027	A	5,453	$21,900	12.5	44	69	0	2.8	91	40.4	54	3320	24	.8	17	7	107	116	110
64118	KANSAS CITY	CLAY	047	136	027	A	13,161	$24,700	12.7	43	69	1	2.6	79	51.6	50	3042	25	.7	23	6	120	131	124

Figure 7-11 Zip-O-Data example for typical five-digit ZIP Code area. (Zip-O-Data, 1982, 16th ed., published by Metromail Corporation, Lincoln, Neb.)

• Establish and define market segments, including sales potentials based on environmental data about the unit

• Evaluate direct marketing results performance, based on a measurement of actual penetration against the projected potential, and realign market segments as such analysis warrants

• Process inquiries and orders more efficiently and effectively, without need for reference to a map, since the address immediately identifies the sales territory

• Forecast more accurately, based on objective analysis of the marketplace rather than on a collection of individual opinions about it

• Pinpoint market segments in relation to profits

• Increase regional and national advertising effectiveness when direct mail, magazines, or newspapers are used

• Determine optimum distribution centers

• Set up a territorial rating system for credit evaluation and perform continuing analysis of accounts receivable

• Conduct market research, especially if demographic cross sections or probability sampling is called for

• Develop differentiated products that have special interest to specific market segments that can be defined by ZIP Code areas, certain educational levels or target occupation groups, for example

• Analyze penetration of present customers according to specific ZIP Code area characteristics to more effectively direct and control marketing efforts

• Identify growth areas, with updated demographics

• Direct new product sampling more effectively

• Control inventories according to historical territorial patterns

• Coordinate data processing and information systems through use of the ZIP Code as part of the computerized ''match code''

• Distribute seasonal and climate-oriented products and information on a chronological schedule by ZIP Code area

Identify, Classify, and Qualify

An article in the January–February 1967 *Harvard Business Review* concluded:[4]

> The ZIP Code five-digit number represents a ''built-in'' and universal means of geographic identification (particularly now that its use has become mandatory for certain types of mail), and the Sectional Center boundaries provide meaningful units for marketing research in relation to economic and environmental data.
>
> We predict that the identification of area characteristics by Sectional Centers, when combined with other demographic qualifications, will provide marketers with a valuable new marketing tool. There is one important proviso: *that the significance of such qualifications must be determined through research and then applied in the case of each marketer.* This involves the accumulation and then application of pertinent environmental knowledge about a market as it relates to a product, as well as the promotion techniques for merging the two.

The research accomplished since that time has taken direct marketers considerably further toward verification of the logic of ZIP Code areas as marketing units that are both meaningful and measurable. Sophisticated computer technology enables direct marketers to develop techniques for establishing market potential, measuring penetration, locating the most profitable market segments, and evaluating the statistical validity of the findings.

AN ILLUSTRATIVE CONSUMER MARKET SEGMENT: SENIOR CITIZENS

Market segmentation can be more clearly understood by examining one such market segment: senior citizens. Direct marketing is

[4] Martin Baier, ''ZIP Code . . . New Tool for Marketers,'' *Harvard Business Review,* January–February 1967, p. 140.

especially suited for reaching and serving senior citizens as a market segment (see Figure 7-12) in terms of demographics. However, in terms of psychographics and life-styles, not all senior citizens are alike. Some prefer to spend their mature years in a continuation of the life-style of their middle years. Others prefer to move to new neighborhoods offering the more convenient life-style of condominiums and high-rise apartments. Still others leave family and friends in old neighborhoods to establish entirely new life-styles in sun belt locations.

The *total* senior citizen market is substantial in numbers but it is heterogeneous in its attitudes and life-styles. Considering such differences, a variety of homogeneous market segments can be readily identified, and the targeted advertising medium of direct mail is particularly suited for reaching these segments. Further, the ease and convenience of shopping in this way is especially appreciated by older people.

Frequently not as mobile as when younger, the older person often views mailed literature as information about products and services to which he or she may not otherwise be exposed. And, free to read and study this information at leisure, the senior citizen can make a decision in an individual way, without outside pressures.

A likely hypothesis that has grown out of research in the senior citizen market concerns the apparent need of the older person for stimulation from the surrounding world, coupled with an increased need for contact with other people. As the physical vitality and the intellectual vigor of the older person diminish, greater need for vicarious satisfactions and stimulations is experienced. Reading materials (including direct mail), along with television and radio, provide contact with others, particularly those materials that report news of some type.

Figure 7-12 Direct marketing can be targeted to senior citizens—a market segment.

Senior Citizens as a Market Segment

An obvious demographic variable used to describe the senior citizen market is age. Often the market is considered to be composed of those people age 55 or older. Another common age segmentation is age 65-plus, due, quite probably, to consideration of "normal" retirement from work jobs.

This 65-plus age group is increasing at an accelerating rate. Fifty years ago, when the population of the United States was one-half what it is now, approximately 6 percent was over age 65. Today, with double the population, approximately 12 percent of the U.S. population is in that age group.

Old age is becoming as certain as are death and taxes. The average American (and European, too), with a life expectancy at birth of 71 years, is living 20 years longer than did his grandfather 75 years ago (see Figure 7-13). This, coupled with a birth rate that has been hovering around "zero" population growth in recent years, makes senior citizens an increasingly important market segment in absolute numbers as well as percentage distribution.

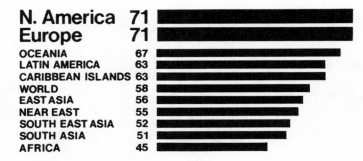

N. America	71
Europe	71
OCEANIA	67
LATIN AMERICA	63
CARIBBEAN ISLANDS	63
WORLD	58
EAST ASIA	56
NEAR EAST	55
SOUTH EAST ASIA	52
SOUTH ASIA	51
AFRICA	45

Figure 7-13 Expectation of life at birth by world regions as of 1972, in years. (*Estimates from Bureau of the Census,* "World Population: 1973, Recent Demographic Estimates for the Countries and Regions of the World," *May 1974, pp. 5–11.*)

Scope of the Senior Citizen Market Segment

Although the total population of the United States has been increasing at a relatively constant rate, the percentage distribution of people over 65 years of age has been and is expected to continue rising at an increasing rate. This phenomenon of the changing population age mix and particularly the constant increase in the number of people in the 65-plus age group is shown in Figure 7-14 for the period 1920–1985.

Man/Woman Ratio   One characteristic of the senior citizen market worth noting is the ratio of men to women and the trend in that ratio. In a reversal of what was true prior to 1900, there were, in 1950, approximately 90 men to every 100 women 65-plus years of age in the United States. Twenty-five years later, for a variety of reasons, such as wars and health stresses, there were only 70 men to every 100 women in the older age groups.

Marital Status   The man/woman ratio is further dramatized when one looks at the marital status of people 65-plus, man vs. woman. There is a much greater population of widowed and divorced women compared with men age 65-plus, as Figure 7-15 illustrates.

Figure 7-14   The changing population age mix. (*Department of Commerce and Conference Board.*)

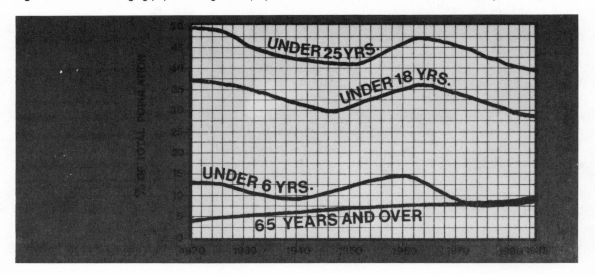

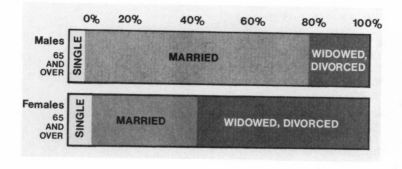

Figure 7-15 Marital status by age and sex. (*Department of Commerce and Conference Board.*)

Educational Level   As one indicator of life-styles, educational level has proven itself to be an important determinant of direct marketing effectiveness. As will be observed from Figure 7-16, however, the number of years of school completed is greater among younger people than in the older age groups.

Mobility   Another important consideration for direct marketers, who must rely on the accuracy of mailing lists, is the lessened mobility of the population as people get older. During a recent 12-month period, within the "Over 50 Index" (a mailing list of 24 million older Americans), for example, only 8.7 percent of people ages 65-plus changed addresses, compared with 9.1 percent for ages 45–64; 13.6 percent for ages 35–44; 27.5 percent for ages 25–34; and 41.2 percent for ages 20–24.

Product Planning

Senior citizens are capable of giving a considerable boost to the marketing of many products and services such as dietary foods, small housing units, hobbies, books, home study courses, and travel.

In a study of consumer expenditures and income conducted by the United States Department of Labor, Bureau of Labor Statis-

tics,[5] it was observed that the senior citizen, with lower average family size and lower money income, spent relatively *more* of that income for food, housing and house operations, medical care, reading, and transportation (other than by automobile). Relatively *less* was spent for clothing, recreation, and automobiles. Food, the study found, was the most important expenditure for the senior citizen. Most of this expenditure went for standard items, but a good share went for special dietary needs, with a strong emphasis on softer and blander foods.

Product Differentiation   An estimated 20 percent of all baby food sold in the United States is consumed by older people. There is also a high usage incidence among senior citizens of packaged proprietary medicines: laxatives, pain relievers, tonics, vitamins, denture cleansers and fixatives, mouthwash, and cold remedies.

Special features in housing for the older person include nonskid floors, wide doors and hallways (for wheelchair travel), strategically located grab-bars (for safety in bathrooms),

[5] U.S. Department of Labor, Bureau of Labor Statistics, *Consumer Expenditure Survey Series,* 1972–1973, Report 455.

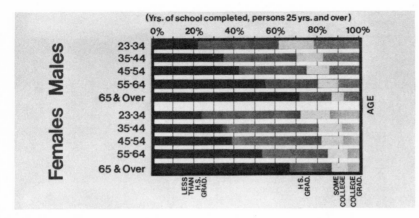

Figure 7-16 Educational profile by age. (*Department of Commerce and Conference Board.*)

lowered cabinets and sinks in kitchens (to permit sit-down working), perimeter heat (for warm floors), and hobby-workshop areas.

Product differentiation presents some distinctive way of treating a product for specific appeal or use by a market segment. It is thus very much related to market segmentation. Toothpaste, for example, would not appeal so much to older people as a market since many no longer have all of their natural teeth. A likely product differentiation would be a denture cleanser.

Product Array The variety of products that might have appeal to senior citizens could include: retirement housing, nursing homes, hearing aids, bibles, real estate, insurance, travel tours, banking services, fund raising, health services, books, magazines, political campaigns, financial management, encyclopedias, annuities, home appliances, vitamins, proprietary medicines, prescription drugs, senior citizen clubs, clothing, cereals and other specialty foods, home study courses, collector items, whirlpool baths and other therapeutic devices, cameras, trees and plants, cosmetics, eyeglasses.

Product Categories One study of the product needs of senior citizens revealed that those categories having the greatest appeal involved reading, television, health, travel, writing, listening, recalling the past, cooking, and religion.

Promotional Strategies

The life-style of senior citizens is, obviously, different from their younger age counterparts, yet, as direct marketers have found, they do not like to be singled out as "being old" nor do they like to be treated differently in promotional efforts.

In support of this idea, the Swiss Society for Market Research reported the experience of two Swiss convenience foods firms. The advertising of one of the firms featured a series on single-portion canned meals being enjoyed in solitary fashion by persons of all ages living alone. These eat-alone-and-like-it products became quite popular in Switzerland. The other firm, a baby food manufacturer, directed its advertising specifically to what it felt to be the needs of senior citizens, who were singled out from other ages. These products were a total failure.

Although this and similar studies have demonstrated that it is not wise to single out senior citizens as being "different," that is not the same as differentiating products for senior citizens. An example of such a promotional strategy is shown in Figure 7-17, which visu-alizes the letter and application form sent by a direct marketing insurance firm offering specific accident coverage for persons ages 50–85.

INDUSTRIAL MARKET SEGMENTATION

Like consumer markets, with which this chapter has been chiefly concerned, industrial markets may also be considered in terms of smaller,

Figure 7-17 Direct marketed insurance offer to senior citizens.

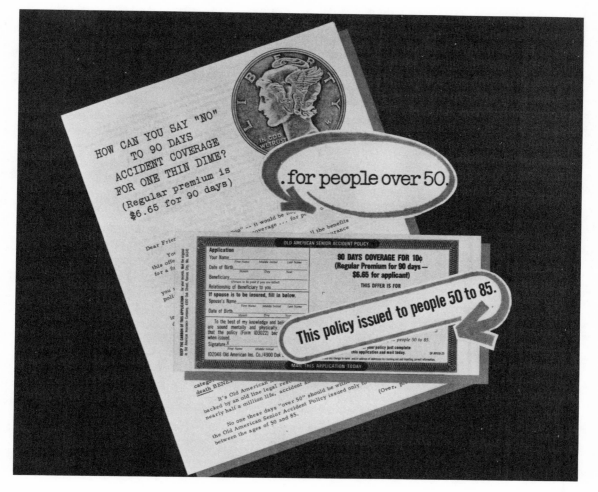

more homogeneous segments of the hetero-geneous total industrial market. Market seg-mentation may be even more important in industrial applications because of the diversity of activities involved.

Standard Industrial Classifications

A common means of industrial market seg-mentation is through the Standard Industrial Classification (SIC) coding system developed by the federal government. These SIC codes, serving as a basis for statistical data, are in broad use by government, trade associations, and business enterprises. An example of the primary four-digit coding system applied to manufacturers of apparel and other textile products is shown in Figure 7-18. This example breaks down the 2300-series SIC codes, as-signed to such manufacturers, into subgroups, such as men's and women's categories, and further divides these categories into specific types of apparel manufacturing concerns.

Within the broad SIC classification system, it is well to understand these terms:

Industry: A grouping of establishments en-gaged in a common economic activity is iden-tified by the four-digit primary SIC code. Approximately 950 industries make up the U.S. economy. These produce approximately 75,000 products and services that are further divided by five- and seven-digit SIC codes.

Establishment: Within four-digit SIC codes describing their primary lines of business, these are economic units producing at a single physical location, such as a manufacturing plant, a farm warehouse, or a retail store.

Company: An entity that owns one or more establishments. It is important to remember that SIC codes are assigned to establishments (economic units) rather than to companies (legal entities). These, in turn, may be further designated as *headquarters* or *branch offices.* They also can be identified by *form of own-ership:* individual, partnership, corporation.

Within SIC codes, which designate the pri-mary and secondary lines of business, estab-

SIC #	DESCRIPTION
2300	Apparel and other textile product manufacturers
2310/2320	Men's, youth's and boy's clothing
2311	Suits and Coats
2321	Shirts and Nightwear
2322	Underwear
2323	Neckwear
2327	Trousers
2328	Work clothing
2329	Clothing not elsewhere classified
2330	Women's, Misses and Junior's outerwear
2331	Blouses and Waists
2335	Dresses
2337	Suits and Coats
2339	Outerwear, not elsewhere classified
2340	Women's, Misses and Children's undergarments
2341	Underwear and Nightwear
2342	Brassiere and Allied Garments
2350	Hats, Caps and Millinery
2351	Millinery
2352	Hats and Caps
2360	Girls', Children's and Infant's Outerwear
2361	Dresses and Blouses
2363	Coats and Suits
2369	Outerwear Manufacturers, not elsewhere classified

Figure 7-18　Standard Industrial Classification (SIC) System.

lishments can also be segmented on other bases: sales volume, credit rating, age of busi-ness, number of employees, net financial worth, subsidiary, and geographic location.

Industrial Markets by ZIP Code

As with consumer markets, industrial markets have become defined by ZIP Code as well as by county, which has historically been the basic geographic marketing unit. Zip Code areas better reflect economic reality and they are also better definitions of sales territories.

ZIP Code Business Patterns　This service, published by Economic Information Systems, Inc.,[6] identifies the top 10,000 five-digit ZIP

[6] Economic Information Systems, Inc., 310 Madison Avenue, New York, N.Y. 10017.

Code areas in terms of business activity according to number of employees. Each ZIP Code area is broken down by the number of business establishments within 10 major economic sectors (major SIC categories as identified by the first digit of the SIC code). For each ZIP Code area and for each SIC category, the following information is provided:

- Number of employees
- Number of business establishments (by employment class)
- Identification of the city and state in which located
- Total payroll levels in the ZIP Code

INPUT-OUTPUT ANALYSIS OF INDUSTRIAL MARKETS

Input-output matrices, derived basically from Census Bureau data, trace the distribution of goods from their origin to their destination. In such a matrix, each industry (SIC) appears as both seller and buyer in row and column headings. At the point at which the rows and columns of any two industries intersect, the matrix records the transaction between those two industries.

Input-output analysis, in its broader form, thus determines the impact that specific industries have on the total economy, not just in what they sell but in what they buy. A decrease in sales of new automobiles, for example, would result in reduced purchases from the steel industry. This, in turn, would result in reduced sales by the steel industry and would ultimately reduce the steel industry's purchases from the mining industry.

Input-Output Data Banks

Input-output tables have become particularly useful to organizations producing industrial goods for further processing by other organizations. Such a table can systematically record how much of the organization's product is consumed by every other industry in the economy and thus describe market segments utilizing that product.

Economic Information Systems, Inc., pioneered the application of input-output economics to industrial market segmentation problems through merging of input-output government data with specific mailing lists of industrial organizations.

An example (see Figure 7-19) provided by Economic Information Systems, Inc., relates to the demand for corrugated boxes (SIC No. 2653), which are used by at least 75 percent of all SIC manufacturing industries. A box manufacturer seeking a description of the national market for corrugated boxes can compile consumption data for each plant in each county (or ZIP Code) in each state in the nation. The total number of plants that are included in the compilation is determined by the number of consuming industries for the product (corrugated boxes) as well as the number of plants in each industry using corrugated boxes.

SUMMARY

Direct marketers must know the characteristics of their buyers and prospective buyers. These buyers and prospects can then be clustered into groups or market segments according to geographic, demographic, and psychographic factors. This process of market segmentation breaks the heterogeneous total market into smaller and more homogeneous subgroups. Tied to market segmentation is product differentiation, distinguishing a product from its competition. Positioning projects an image of a product in relation to its particular use within a market segment.

Market segmentation can be performed in a variety of ways, including product characteristics and brand preferences. Geographic segmentation considers units such as states, counties, trading areas, and census tracts. Demographic segmentation is concerned with such factors as age, sex, marital status, edu-

STATE AND COUNTY NAME	SIC #	# OF PLANTS	ANNUAL PURCHASE OF CORRUGATED BOXES
ALABAMA			
Autauga County			
Botany Inds., Inc.	2256	1	$10.9M
Nappies, Inc.	2631	1	25.8M
Continental Gin Co.	3559	1	15.0M
County Total		3	$51.7M
Baldwin County			
Woodhaven Dairy	2024	1	$22.4M
Hale Mfg. Co.	2221	1	8.0M
Bay Slacks, Inc.	2253	1	20.4M
Std. Furn., Mfg. Co.	2511	1	82.0M
Kaiser Alumn. Co.	3643	1	31.9M
County Total		5	$164.7M
Barbour County			
Cowikee Mills	2211	1	$13.3M
Dixie Shoe Corp.	3141	1	9.2M
County Total		2	$22.5M

Figure 7-19 Example of a mailing list of users of corrugated boxes (SIC No. 2653) derived from input-output analysis and showing user's name and SIC arranged within county (or ZIP Code) within state. (*Economic Information Systems, Inc., 310 Madison Avenue, New York, N.Y. 10017.*)

cation, and occupation. Psychographic segmentation involves the study of life-styles, habits, attitudes, beliefs, and value systems.

ZIP Code areas have emerged as a strong basis of segmentation for direct marketers in that their geographic structure, combined with demographic characteristics of the area, results in a psychographic or life-style definition of *clusters* of consumers. These units, based as they are on transportation patterns, have been demonstrated to be not only economically meaningful but also environmentally measurable. Their value to direct marketers lies in their *homogeneity* as well as their ready *identity* with a consumer.

Because people with like interests tend to cluster and because their purchase decisions are frequently influenced by their desire to emulate their friends, neighbors, and community innovators, ZIP Code areas can provide the means to identify clusters of households that have a high degree of homogeneity. And, as is generally accepted in the marketing literature, purchase decisions are not so much dependent on income per se as on the buyer's

perception of his or her relative position, or that to which he or she aspires, in the environment.

A key reason for adherence to traditional geographic market segments, such as counties, has been the fact that most statistical data have historically been set up and published this way. Allocation of existing data to the boundaries of more meaningful marketing units, such as ZIP Code areas, has required specialized and often highly sophisticated mathematical techniques. Since the advent of ZIP Code areas, however, more and more data have been published for these units, including most importantly, the data that direct marketers themselves collect about their own customers.

In much the same way that consumer markets are described in terms of geographics, demographics, and psychographics, industrial markets can be segmented through a system of Standard Industrial Classification (SIC) numbers derived from government sources. Data for these can be collected for establishments within industries.

Through coupling of input-output economic

analysis with mailing lists of industrial organizations as described by SIC numbers, direct marketers selling in the industrial market can closely identify the buyers of their own products and services.

CASE: IDENTIFYING AND REACHING A MARKET SEGMENT

Learning Objective

This case study puts into perspective the relationship of market segmentation to product differentiation and the resultant concept of positioning. The student is encouraged to think about identifying potential market segments and consider which product features would have particular appeal to specific submarkets. And, he or she should look ahead to the promotional strategy that might best position the defined product to the chosen market.

Overview

The total consumer market is much too heterogeneous to be thought about as a totality. Rather, the direct marketer must think in terms of market segments and even submarkets within these segments. Geographic and demographic segmentation, for example, might be further refined according to the psychographics and life-styles of particular subgroups.

Once a market segment is identified, it remains for the direct marketer to differentiate the product so as to appeal to that segment that offers greatest potential. This is the process of positioning a product to a market. The direct marketer then reaches the prospects through lists of readers, viewers, and listeners about which there are data.

Procedure

Read the learning objective, the overview, and the case that follows. See how many potential market segments you can identify and determine which should be the prime target and which might be logical submarkets that can be reached without alienating other submarkets. Think especially about the profitability potential of each market segment, how each might be reached, and the underlying psychographic factors that could be important in developing positioning and promotional strategy.

Case[7]

Park Manor was a condominium apartment community located 25 minutes from downtown Milwaukee, Wisconsin. (A condominium is a building in which individuals own separate apartments but share the ownership and maintenance of common facilities such as halls, roofs, heating systems, and outdoor areas.) Park Manor was developed especially for individuals who have passed their 48th birthday. In the first 5 years, the 200-acre development sold nearly 400 apartments priced from $35,000 to $65,000, with an aggregate value of some $16 million.

Park Manor differed from the retirement communities that have been so successful on the West Coast and in Florida in that it tried to attract both retired and working individuals. It had succeeded in this attempt, and more than two-thirds of the residents were regularly employed. Further, Park Manor was designed to serve and draw from a local, rather than a national market. It also differed from the "family" condominiums that have sprouted in most large cities and that abound with children. No one with children under 16 was permitted to live at Park Manor. In other respects, however, Park Manor was similar to the other types of condominium communities. Numerous recreational and personal achievement activity opportunities were available. The chief rationale for Park Manor was that it provided

[7] The case of "Park Manor Condominium" was written by Prof. John M. Hess, University of Colorado, and appears in William Stanton, *Fundamentals of Marketing*, 6th ed., McGraw-Hill Book Company, New York, 1981, pp. 155–157.

"elegant but economical living in a maintenance-free, parklike atmosphere."

Troubled by a significant decline in sales in recent months, the developers debated whether their age and no-children barriers had curtailed the market too severely. One of the developers believed they had already exhausted the "over 48" market and should lower the minimum age. Most present residents, however, viewed the peaceful, childless atmosphere as a major advantage and would fight such a change. Another of the developers contended that the market was hardly touched. He felt that they had drawn too heavily on retired individuals. They had not spent enough of their energies attracting working people whose children have left home and who no longer desire a large house with its attendant maintenance problems. The third developer thought that they had taken the wrong tack entirely in terms of their geographic market. He suggested that Park Manor should attempt to draw retirees from a regional, or even a national market. He pointed out that the Chicago area alone had some 200,000 eligible retirees, with an additional 20,000 persons retiring each year: "Just give me one percent of the Chicago retirement market, and I'll be happy."

A recent market study conducted for Park Manor had revealed some public misconceptions and prejudices. There had been a tendency to shift promotional emphasis entirely each time one of the three partners perceived a new market segment that might be approached. This, in turn, had contributed to the public's confusion. A summary statement from the market study report read as follows:

In review, the chief objections to Park Manor are:

1 *Age*. Most respondents view Park Manor as an old-people's home. It is clearly identified with the retirement, perhaps even the nursing-home, market. Most people, regardless of their age, just do not think they are old enough to move there yet.

2 *Income*. The majority of the respondents identify Park Manor as an expensive, high-income, high-cost place to live. They frequently parroted words from Park Manor's advertising such as "exclusive," "luxurious," and "country club atmosphere." Another group has taken the economy advertising seriously and sees Park Manor as low-cost housing.

3 *Institutionalization*. People feel that they would lose their freedom if they moved to Park Manor. They associate the many activities and facilities with regimentation and institutionalism.

4 *Not quite respectable*. Many respondents perceive Park Manor as being not quite respectable. They suggested that the residents were probably rather shiftless and hedonistic. Words such as "playground," "leisure-living," "pleasure," and "fun" were apparently drawn entirely from advertising copy by such respondents.

5 *Apartment living*. Homeowners do not like the idea of living in an apartment, and apartment dwellers do not wish to invest or tie-up funds in their residence.

It appeared that each segment of the market read or heard only that portion of the advertising that confirmed their feeling that Park Manor was for someone else.

The development company had learned that buying a home and moving were emotion laden activities, and that each segment of the market had substantially different motives for changing residences. Unfortunately, it also appeared that the motives of various segments were often at cross-purposes, so appeals to one segment may well have alienated other segments. Park Manor, however, could no longer prosper by appealing to one segment of the market, so it had to identify and select those market elements that are most compatible.

DISCUSSION QUESTIONS

1 Why is it necessary to view the total marketplace in terms of market segments?

2 Briefly describe these three ways of segmenting

markets: geographic, demographic, psychographic.

3 How is product differentiation related to market segmentation? What is positioning? Give examples.

4 What is the basis for the use of ZIP Code areas to describe marketing units? Why are these geographic areas useful for evaluating buyer behavior?

5 Discuss the advantages and disadvantages of alternative geographic marketing units, especially the county, which is probably still the most widely used.

6 List several specific direct marketing uses of ZIP Code areas.

7 Using the senior citizen market segment described in this chapter as a model, describe another demographic market segment, pointing out potential psychographic differences among the individuals composing the chosen segment.

8 What is the most common means of industrial market segmentation? What are alternatives?

9 Describe input-output analysis and how it can be useful to industrial direct marketers.

DIRECT MARKETING LISTS AND DATA

Lists and data are at the very core of direct marketing. Lists identify prospects as well as customers who have effected a response and/or transaction in behalf of the direct marketer. Lists are not just *mailing* lists, since those on them are often reached through media *other* than direct mail: telephone, magazines and newspapers, television and radio.

If lists are to be viewed as market segments, it follows that the direct marketer needs to accumulate data about these lists. For customers as well as prospects one must identify relevant geographic, demographic, and psychographic information, transferring information known about customers to identify prospects with similar characteristics. In the case of customer lists, the direct marketer needs to record activity in terms of responses and/or transactions. What direct response medium triggered the activity? Did the person buy, inquire, or take some other action? What product was involved? Was there a credit experience? Direct marketers want to know, too, how recently the activity occurred, how frequently it occurred, and the dollar amount of the transaction.

LISTS VIEWED AS MARKET SEGMENTS

Lists, whether the names are recipients of mailed, telephoned, broadcast, or print messages, can be viewed as market segments. They are the "place" (marketplace) of the 4 P's of direct marketing: place, product, price, and promotion. Typically, the individual names on lists should be collectively profiled through recording and evaluation of data.

The direct marketer promotes to prospect lists for which there are established profiles from the results of prior promotion experience. From such ongoing promotion, customer lists are acquired. Newly acquired customers become established and repeat buyers, and thus, over time, reflect added value. Resultant activity may be regular or sporadic. It may be frequent or, at some point, not at all. Data about the activity are acquired along with data about the lists themselves.

A Perishable Commodity

Lists are a perishable commodity. Not only does the degree of activity (or inactivity) fluctuate, but also the people and organizations on lists are far from static. They move. They marry. They die. Their attitudes change. In 12 months, for example, an average customer list could change as much as 25 percent in terms of address revisions.

Such volatility demonstrates the importance of adequate list maintenance. It demonstrates, too, that lists that are mailed to and maintained regularly have greater deliverability value to the direct marketer than do lists from rosters or directories, especially as these sources age.

The direct marketer must not only be aware of the condition of lists acquired from others but also be assured that the maintenance of the house list is current and adequate. Otherwise, part of the communication with an out-of-date list will be undeliverable and result in cost without potential benefit.

Data about a list are also perishable. Any advertiser, and especially the scientific direct marketer, does not want to distribute messages indiscriminately. He or she wants to make sure not only that the message is delivered but also that it is delivered to the right prospect. The direct marketer is especially sensitive to the issue of mass communication if it results in not only waste but also antagonism among nonprospects. In terms of front-end cost, a 30-second commercial message televised during the Super Bowl, with an audience of as many as 100 million viewers, could cost as little as $4.00 per thousand viewers. A direct mail message, on the other hand, sent to an audience of only 100,000 might cost as much as $250 per thousand prospects. The direct marketer who advocates market segmentation and has the proper lists, along with data about these lists, might be better off with the latter *selective* distribution than with the former *mass* communication.

When properly directed, direct mail can be very cost efficient. This form of advertising distribution involves list maintenance as well as adequate data for market segmentation.

TYPES OF LISTS

There are three basic types of lists. In order of importance to the direct marketer, these are:

1 House lists
2 Response lists
3 Compiled lists

House Lists

The lists of an organization's own customers (active as well as inactive) are, in effect, the most productive mailing lists available in terms of future response. This is because of the very special relationship that an organization enjoys with its own customers, sometimes called "goodwill." Of lesser potential (in terms of future response) but probably still more productive than lists from sources outside the organization would be the names of those former buyers who have become inactive, those who have inquired but not purchased, and those who have been "referred" or recommended by present customers of the firm.

Indeed, such house lists—active customers, inactive customers, inquirers, and referrals—may collectively be among an organization's most valuable assets, inasmuch as they generate future business at a cost much less than that of acquiring responses from outside lists.[1]

The value of house lists or their potential for future sales can be predetermined, often from historical experience. It is not uncommon

[1] For a complete discussion of the value of a customer (respondent), see Chapter 2.

for a house list to be four times, or even ten times, as productive as an outside list with which there is no existing customer relationship.

Of relevance, too, is the kind and degree of customer activity, in terms of products purchased as well as the recency, the frequency, and the dollar value of such purchases. With inquiries, there is only an expression of interest rather than an actual purchase. With referrals, the recommendation by a customer of the organization could offer an advantage, especially when the name of the present customer can be used in the promotional effort sent to the referred prospect.

The source of the customer as well as the promotional strategy used to acquire that customer initially can also be a determinant of future response. The original list source and whether this source was direct mail, space advertising, broadcast media, or even a salesperson have bearing on future productivity.

House lists can be made more productive, just as can prospect lists, if these are looked at as specific market segments in terms of geographic, demographic, and psychographic segmentation. What is known about these customers as individuals (such as age or marital status) can have a bearing on future response. So can geographic location affect the future sale of, for example, nursery plants or snowblowers.

Response Lists

Right behind house lists in terms of future productivity are lists of those who have responded to another direct marketer by mail or by telephone or even by personal visit. As a result, they appear on the house list of that direct marketer. Obviously, the more allied the activity of that direct marketer, the more potential for response to a similar, or even directly competitive offer. A customer who has subscribed to a news magazine by mail, for example, could be an ideal prospect for a competitive news magazine, just as one who has purchased hospitalization insurance by mail could be an ideal prospect for a competitive insurer.

The first important qualification is that the name on a list from an outside source have a history of response to direct marketed offers. The second, and possibly equally as important, characteristic would be an indication of response to a similar direct marketed offer. Beyond this could be a history of purchase of related items. Those who have purchased gourmet meat products, for example, might be good prospects for gourmet fruit products. They might even be good prospects for classical records or a book on interior decorating.

From this discussion, it should be apparent that relationships do exist and these can be identified through experimentation (testing). There are many response lists available for such testing.

Lists of directly competitive firms, if available, are obvious choices. On the other hand, one of the real challenges to direct marketers is to determine *why* the purchaser of a home study course by mail, as an example, might be a particularly good prospect for a book club.

Like an organization's house lists, other response lists should be looked at in terms of geographics, demographics, and psychographics. They should also be segmented by type of response and/or ultimate transaction or purchase. And, they should be considered in terms of source as well as the promotional strategy that caused them to be responsive in the first place.

Compiled Lists

Falling behind both house lists and response lists in expectations, usually, are compiled lists. Examples of such lists include: telephone directory listings; automobile and driver's license registrations; the newly married and the newly born; high school and college student rosters; public records, such as property tax rolls and voter lists; rating services, such as Dun & Bradstreet; and a multitude of "rosters," such as those for service and civic organizations. Other potential sources of compiled lists include manufacturer warranty cards and coupon redemptions.

Although compiled lists typically do not have a response qualification built into them, market segmentation techniques coupled with sophisticated computer systems for duplication identification make possible selection of the best prospects (those most likely to effect a response and/or transaction) from very large compiled lists. Modern computers can also cross identify characteristics of compiled lists, such as telephone or automobile registration lists, with known response and thus even further improve response potential. Combining a response list with an automobile registration list and further identifying those on the response list who own a station wagon, for example, is a way of identifying responsive households with children. Compiled lists used in such ways thus offer considerable promise in market segmentation and in even further qualifying response and house lists.

DEVELOPMENT OF HOUSE LISTS

The discussion of house lists earlier anticipates that they need to be compiled and developed along with relevant data through some appropriate mechanical means. Although a variety of record keeping and addressing systems are available, the trend in recent years has been toward computerized systems that offer a great deal of flexibility as well as long-range economy. Our discussion will, therefore, be confined to computerized systems.

Aside from the obvious requirements of a list to make it usable, such as accurate name and mailing address, it is necessary to determine just what other useful data, in terms of qualification of individual names on the list, must be collected and recorded and in what form. Consider, too, just what will be done with the data in the future. (Keep in mind that collection of information costs money and must therefore produce benefits commensurate with its cost.) How will the data be used and can they be analyzed and evaluated properly?

It is highly important to consider maintenance of the mailing list. Such maintenance concerns not only name and address correction but also continual updating of the data carried within the customer's record.

Record Layout

An example of a layout for a mailing list record is shown in Figure 8-1. It shows the customer name and mailing address as well as the initial and latest order dates. Also shown are order and payment characteristics. Demographics of

the customer, that is, sex and age, could also be shown.

Recency/Frequency/Monetary Formula

Direct marketers usually capture within their house list records of customers certain key data about activity, such as transactions and responses. Such data might be concerned with product preferences or with credit experience, if relevant.

They often also provide the mechanics for recording purchasing history. Usually this is accomplished through some variation of the recency/frequency/monetary (R/F/M) formula. By carrying in the master list record the date and volume of purchases, over a period of time, it is possible to determine periodically the performance record of each customer, which helps determine the future potential of that customer. The giant catalog houses, such

Figure 8-1 Data/record format of a customer's history file. (Direct Marketing Manual, *Direct Marketing Association, 6 East 43rd Street, New York, NY 10017.*)

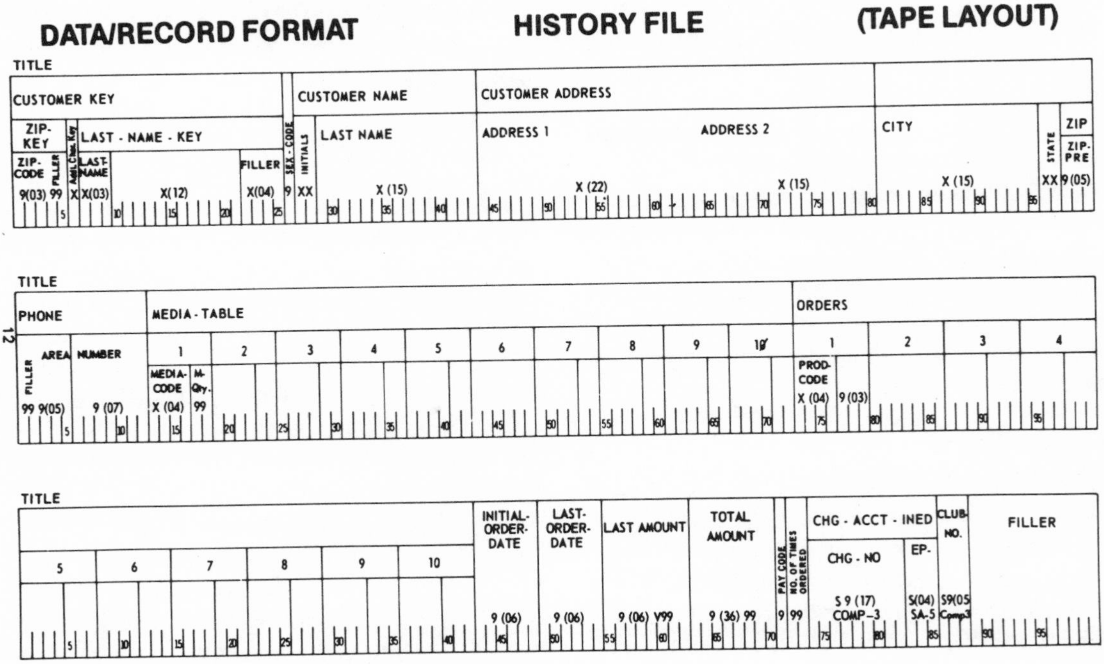

ASSUMPTIONS:

Recency of Transaction:	20 Points If within Past 3 Months
	10 Points If within Past 6 Months
	5 Points If within Past 9 Months
	3 Points If within Past 12 Months
	1 Point If within Past 24 Months
Frequency of Transaction:	Number of Purchases within 24 Months Times 4 Points Each (Maximum: 20 Points)
Monetary Value of Transaction:	Gross Dollar Volume of Purchases within 24 Months Times 10% (Maximum: 20 Points)
Weighting Assumption:	Recency = 5
	Frequency = 3
	Monetary = 2

EXAMPLE:

Cust.	Purchase #	Recency	Assigned Points	(x5) Wght. Points	Frequency	Assigned Points	(x3) Wght. Points	Monetary	Assigned Points	(x2) Wght. Points	Total Wght. Points	Cum. Points
A	#1	3 Mths.	20	100	1	4	12	$ 30	3	6	118	118
A	#2	9 Mths.	5	25	1	4	12	$100	10	20	57	175
A	#3	24 Mths.	1	5	1	4	12	$ 50	5	10	27	202
B	#1	12 Mths.	3	15	2	8	24	$500	20	40	79	79
C	#1	3 Mths.	20	100	1	4	12	$100	10	20	132	132
C	#2	6 Mths.	10	50	1	4	12	$ 60	6	12	74	206
C	#3	12 Mths.	3	15	2	8	24	$ 70	7	14	53	259
C	#4	24 Mths.	1	5	1	4	12	$ 20	2	4	21	280

Figure 8-2 Evaluation of customer mailing list record by recency, frequency, and monetary values of transactions (R/F/M).

as Sears's, Ward's, and Penney's, use this approach in determining who will receive catalogs and how often. This approach relates the cost of promotion to the potential benefits to be derived from each customer.

The exact R/F/M formulation for each direct marketer will, naturally, vary according to the importance given to each of the variables in relation to each other. Under certain conditions, there might be a need for further weighting of the calculations of particular promotions that might have more relevance, for example, to customers who had purchased most recently.

Figure 8-2 illustrates the use of the R/F/M formula in evaluation of customers on a mailing list according to the combined R/F/M values of their transactions over time, with, under certain conditions, further weighting given to recency ($\times$ 5), frequency ($\times$ 3), and monetary ($\times$ 2).

In the example in Figure 8-2 three customers

(identified as A, B, and C) have a purchase history calculated over a 24-month period. Numerical points are assigned to each transaction, according to the derived R/F/M formula. These points are further weighted. The resultant cumulative point calculations, 202 for A, 79 for B, and 280 for C, indicate a potential preference for customer C. Based on C's R/F/M history, a greater amount of promotion dollars (such as mailing a new catalog) could be justified, as it would possibly also be justified for customer A. Customer B might be an unlikely promotion dollar risk.

Match Codes

A serious and often cumbersome problem faced by direct marketers in compiling and maintaining lists is the potential for duplicating the same individual or organization, not only *within* house lists but also *within* and *between* response and compiled lists and even *between* these lists and house lists. If lists are computerized, using a merge/purge process, it is possible to extract from a name/address record abbreviated information about this record. This abbreviation is called a match code and it is constructed so that each individual record can be matched, pairwise, with each other record. Since such matching requires a tremendous amount of computer memory, the match code is abbreviated to minimize the need for such storage. The abbreviation is based on the probability of error occurrences within key parts of a record, such as transposition within a street address number as shown in the two examples below:

Melinda Barton
5410 Salisbury Drive
Falls Church, VA 22042

Melinda Barton
4510 Salisbury Drive
Falls Church, VA 22042

An example of a simple 18-digit match code derived from the name/address above is shown in Figure 8-3. Quite often, direct marketers will add other data to the match code such as a unique identification number or an expiration date for a magazine subscription. Mailing labels for periodicals often demonstrate match codes of this type.

Merge/Purge

The process of merge/purge, using the abbreviated match codes described earlier, is appropriate for identifying or deleting duplicate names/addresses within house lists. It is also used to eliminate names on house lists from outside response and/or compiled lists being used for new customer solicitation. Thus, the organization's own house list will not be duplicated within that promotion effort to prospects. Additionally, the merge/purge process can be used for eliminating duplication between these outside response and compiled lists as well as with the house list.

POSITION	ITEM	DESCRIPTION
1	State	A unique alpha-numeric code assigned to each state
2– 5	ZIP Code	Last 4 numbers of 5-digit ZIP Code
6– 8	Surname	1st, 3rd and 4th alpha characters of surname or business name
9–12	Address	House or business number
13–15	Address	1st, 3rd and 4th alpha characters of street name
16	Surname	Alpha-numeric count of characters in surname
17	Given Name	Alpha initial of first name
18	Given Name	Alpha-numeric count of characters in first name

EXAMPLE ADDRESS

Melinda Barton
5410 Salisbury Drive
Falls Church, VA 22042

DERIVED MATCH CODE

92042BRT5410SLI6M7

Figure 8-3   Mailing list match code.

Although an oversimplification of a highly sophisticated and complex process, a match code is generated for each name/address on each list and these match codes, potentially many million of them at a time, are matched, pairwise, with every other name on the list in sequence. Duplications are identified for special handling.

It is doubtful that a "perfect" match code could be developed, one that would compensate for *all* the idiosyncrasies and potential errors inherent in a name/address record. However, the one shown in Figure 8-3 has a pretty good track record. As is demonstrated in Figure 8-4, even a 5 percent "hit" rate, obviating the need to mail 5 percent duplications, can result in substantial savings. This is especially true when several million name/address records are merged and purged. With reference to Figure 8-4, identification of a potential duplication of 15 percent, when one million names on various lists are merged and purged, would result in a reduction of 150,000

% DUPLICATION (OR MULTI–BUYERS)	TOTAL NUMBER OF NAMES/ADDRESSES MERGED					
	100,000	500,000	1,000,000	2,500,000	5,000,000	10,000,000
5%	$1,000	$ 5,000	$10,000	$ 25,000	$ 50,000	$100,000
10%	$2,000	$10,000	$20,000	$ 50,000	$100,000	$200,000
15%	$3,000	$15,000	$30,000	$ 75,000	$150,000	$300,000
20%	$4,000	$20,000	$40,000	$100,000	$200,000	$400,000
25%	$5,000	$25,000	$50,000	$125,000	$250,000	$500,000
30%	$6,000	$30,000	$60,000	$150,000	$300,000	$600,000

Assumption: Mailing cost is $200 per thousand names mailed (or not mailed).

Figure 8-4 Economic value of merge/purge of mailing lists utilizing match codes to identify duplication as well as multibuyers.

pieces of mail. At an assumed cost of $200 per thousand names mailed, this results in a savings of $30,000. Against this savings, of course, would be the cost of the merge/purge itself, possibly as much as $10 per thousand names examined or $10,000 for a one million name/address input.

✓Multibuyers Whereas the elimination of duplicate names/addresses, together with the savings and minimization of irritation of those receiving such duplicates, is an obvious advantage of the merge/purge process, there is yet another advantage, possibly even greater. If the same name/address is found on two or more response lists simultaneously, it is conceivable that individual is a better prospect for a direct marketed offer since that person is a *multibuyer*.

Experimentation has shown, in fact, that the expectation of a higher rate of response from those names appearing on three lists is greater than the expectation from those names on two lists. Likewise, names appearing on four lists are potentially even more responsive.

Figure 8-5 visualizes results of an actual merge/purge in which, from a gross input of 473,376 name/address records appearing on a total of 35 response lists, the net output was 330,724 records or 69.86 percent of the input. Of the 30.14 percent eliminated, 12.64 percent received the offer within a prior 3-month period. Approximately ½ percent was identified

as intraduplications or duplications within each of the 35 lists. Nearly 15 percent already appeared on the house list of the direct marketer involved. And, 2.15 percent were multibuyers, that is, they appeared on more than one of the 35 lists.

The merge/purge process can also be used to effectively remove names of individuals who have expressed a desire not to receive solicitation as well as those who have been poor credit risks or are otherwise undesirable customers.

Figure 8-6, adapted from an actual merge/purge procedure, displays the manner of showing multiappearances of duplicate names/addresses on two or more lists. Shown are both name and address variations.

MAINTENANCE OF HOUSE LISTS

As noted earlier in this chapter, lists are a perishable commodity. They need constant control and maintenance. This is a day-to-day job, but, whatever the schedule, direct marketers setting such schedules adhere to them rigorously.

An initial requirement for proper list maintenance is that the list be compiled and developed in a *uniform* manner. Only when such uniformity exists within a computerized list is it possible to use match codes with any assurance of control. An alternative to match codes is a unique identification number, such as a

| LIST # | GROSS INPUT | NET OUTPUT | % NET OUTPUT | NAMES DUPLICATED BY REASON | | | | | | | |
| | | | | PRIOR MAIL | | INTRA-DUPS | | HOUSE LIST DUPS | | MULTI-BUYERS | |
				#	%	#	%	#	%	#	%
1	5127	3520	68.65	826	16.11	—	—	697	13.59	84	1.63
2	5256	4179	79.50	586	11.14	—	—	394	7.50	97	1.84
3	63192	39174	61.99	14789	23.40	34	.05	7704	12.19	1491	2.35
4	7195	4412	61.32	727	10.10	5	.06	1955	27.17	96	1.33
5	11997	8400	70.01	1897	15.81	5	.04	1205	10.04	490	4.08
6	8080	5575	68.99	1316	16.28	15	.18	838	10.37	336	4.15
7	12345	7219	58.47	2717	22.00	11	—	1576	12.36	882	7.14
8	6011	4567	75.97	607	10.09	92	1.53	639	10.63	106	1.76
9	12011	8207	68.32	2010	16.73	—	—	1331	11.08	463	3.85
10	10790	9346	86.61	476	4.41	27	.25	851	7.89	90	.83
11	11988	8262	68.91	1816	15.14	—	—	1562	13.03	348	2.90
12	12004	8821	73.48	1568	13.06	151	1.25	1191	9.92	273	2.27
13	25068	21025	83.87	1474	5.88	26	.10	2299	9.17	244	.97
14	15982	10235	64.04	3444	21.54	3	.01	2097	13.12	203	1.27
15	15003	11639	77.57	1588	10.58	42	.27	1480	9.86	254	1.69
16	18607	13485	72.47	2151	11.56	14	.07	2585	13.89	372	1.99
17	27871	22473	80.63	2289	8.21	20	.07	2526	9.06	563	2.02
18	12150	9951	81.90	757	6.23	—	—	1321	10.87	121	.99
19	11925	7750	64.98	1585	13.29	799	6.70	1572	13.18	219	1.83
20	12993	9233	71.06	1734	13.34	140	1.07	1445	11.12	441	3.39
21	8054	4375	54.32	879	10.91	7	.08	2530	31.41	263	3.26
22	7732	5214	67.43	1329	17.18	3	.03	967	12.51	219	2.83
23	11995	9	.07	3	.02	—	—	11982	99.89	1	—
24	6000	3936	65.60	651	10.85	65	1.08	1250	20.83	98	1.63
25	5998	3842	64.05	690	11.50	146	2.43	1232	20.54	88	1.46
26	11693	8275	70.76	1434	12.26	—	—	1775	15.18	209	1.78
27	11993	9802	81.73	828	6.90	3	.02	1185	9.88	175	1.45
28	7625	6136	80.47	619	8.11	10	.13	699	9.17	161	2.11
29	11997	9506	79.23	1045	8.71	20	.16	1205	10.04	221	1.84
30	11978	9665	80.68	516	4.30	11	.09	1695	14.15	91	.75
31	11986	9370	78.17	737	6.14	115	.95	1690	14.10	74	.61
32	11748	8639	73.53	1324	11.27	—	—	1497	12.74	288	2.45
33	24995	18585	74.35	3235	12.94	3	.01	2395	9.56	777	3.10
34	12000	7146	59.55	794	6.61	1	—	3951	32.93	108	.90
35	11987	8751	73.00	1378	11.49	202	1.68	1408	11.75	248	2.06
TOTALS	473376	336734	69.86	57819	12.64	1960	.41	70679	14.93	10194	2.15

Figure 8-5 Results tabulation of actual merge/purge performance to identify duplicates and multi-buyers within and between 35 response lists plus house list.

Social Security number, which identifies only one individual, but this number must be known before access to it within the file can be accomplished.

List maintenance falls into three categories, and we will look at each of these in turn:

1 Nixie removal
2 Change of address
3 Record status

Nixie Removal

The term "nixie" usually refers to mail that has been returned by the Postal Service because it is undeliverable as addressed. This might result from a simple error in the street address or possibly in the ZIP Code. If such an error can be identified, the address can be corrected.

Other possible reasons for undelivered mail

are the person to whom the piece is addressed is deceased or has moved and left no forwarding address. In such cases the name should be removed from the mailing list and, unless updated information is subsequently obtained, it cannot be reinstated.

For house lists that are accessed by telephone, changes in telephone numbers should be made periodically. Customers who have changed to unlisted numbers should be contacted by mail to obtain these numbers.

The Postal Service, for a nominal handling fee, will provide direct marketers with correct address information, if available. Often, however, mail addressed to a deceased person will go to the surviving spouse. Or, mail to an individual who has changed positions or even left an organization will be received by the replacement in that position. Although the Postal Service will not send notifications in such instances, some direct marketers correct their lists in other ways. Special notices might periodically be sent with mailings requesting list correction. Or, if a salesperson from the firm calls on the customer, mailing list change

information could be included in regular communications with the company. In some cases the mail recipient sends such notice directly. Other ways in which lists can be updated include references to news items, periodic updates from telephone and other directories, and references to public records such as birth and death notices and marriage and divorce proceedings.

Change of Address

Whenever possible, address corrections should be requested through the Postal Service. Mail prepaid with first class postage is automatically returned if undeliverable or else it is forwarded without charge, if the new address is known. In the latter instance, for a fee, the change-of-address notification can be sent back to the direct marketer. In the case of third class advertising mail, use of the ''address correction requested'' legend on the mailing envelope guarantees prepayment of any return postage and service fees. There are many variations of this particular list correction service relative

NAME	ADDRESS	CITY	STATE	ZIP
Debra Simpson	948 S Orange Ave	Sober	NJ	08106
Debra Simpson	948 S Orange Ave	Sober	NJ	08106
Safiyya Sobell	107 Alexander St	Sober	NJ	08106
S Sobell	107 Alexander St	Sober	NJ	08106
E Stevens	64 Cedar Ave	Sober	NJ	08106
E Stevens	64 Ceder Ave	Sober	NJ	08106
John Ziebart	44 Marsac Pl	Sober	NJ	08106
Walter Ziebart	44 Marsac Pl	Sober	NJ	08106
Anthony Garcia	360 N 10th St	Sober	NJ	08107
Margaret Garcia	360 N 10th St	Sober	NJ	08107
Clara Stein	215 N 9th St	Sober	NJ	08107
Clara Stein	215 N 9th St	Sober	NJ	08107
W Gallagher	206 12th Ave	Sober	NJ	08107
Winfred Gallagher	206 12th Ave	Sober	NJ	08107
Horacio Roberts	253 N Sixth St	Sober	NJ	08107
Horacio Roberts	253 N 6th Apt 2	Sober	NJ	08107
Brenda Smith	209 No 4th St	Sober	NJ	08107
Clara M Smith	209 N 4th St	Sober	NJ	08107
R Peters	Apt 902 797 N 6th St	Sober	NJ	08107
R Peters	789 N 6th St 63	Sober	NJ	08107
Susie Martin	49 Hawthorne L	Sober	NJ	08107
Susie Martin	49 Hawthorne Lane	Sober	NJ	08107
Susie Martin	49 Hawthorne Ln S	Sober	NJ	08107
Susie Martin	49 Hawthorne Ln S	Sober	NJ	08107

Figure 8-6 Merge/purge duplication listing.

to either individual mail or catalog mail, concerning forwarding and/or return postage guarantees.

Additionally, direct marketers can encourage the recipient of mail to inform them of any change of address or telephone number. If a unique account code is provided to the customer, he or she can be encouraged to reference this code when requesting changes. If the account number is not provided, it is important to have both the old and new address: the former for entering into the system and removing the old record, and the latter for future addressing.

If incorrect addresses or telephone numbers result in misdirected advertising promotions, it should be apparent that the cost is twofold: (1) the cost of the wasted contact and (2) the sacrifice of potential response. Both of these costs emphasize the necessity for constantly keeping mailing lists updated, with new information as well as with removal of old data.

It is not necessary to use the "address correction requested" service on every mailing, once or twice a year should suffice to clean the list. Using the legend more frequently, because of lags in handling times, could result in duplication of returned mail and unnecessary duplication of costs.

Record Status

It is important to maintain lists not only from the perspective of nixie and otherwise undeliverable mail but also to keep the record status of customers up to date.

New orders from customers should be entered into the list promptly as they have major impact on the R/F/M formulation described earlier. Such prompt record keeping also avoids unnecessary duplication of mailings or phone calls to customers who already have what the direct marketer is offering. Keeping mailing lists up to date at all times is a *must* for direct marketers!

Security of Lists

Mailing lists are assets, just as are buildings, equipment, and inventories. Because their value is intangible, however, they are not easily insurable (except for replacement or duplication costs) even if their future value can be determined. Unlike other assets, they're somewhat more portable, especially when several hundred thousand names can be packed on a single reel of computer tape or on a single disk.

For these reasons, special precautions must be taken to prevent theft, loss, or unauthorized use. A list security checklist is provided in Figure 8-7.

Proper Storage   The logical first step in list security is the provision of adequate storage. Usually, such storage protects against natural hazards of fire and water damage, as well as theft or unauthorized use. To discourage theft, access to list files should be limited and controlled at all times. Should a list be lost, possibly, inadvertently, through improper handling, adequate backup should be available in the form of duplicate lists at a remote location.

List Marking   Direct marketers have developed a variety of marking techniques for "seeding" or "salting" lists. In the event a list is misappropriated or misused, such decoys, which are either incorrect spellings or fictitious names that are known and appear nowhere else, can identify the misuse. These may not, however, lead to the guilty person.

The identification programs should be constructed so that they will not be removed through match coding. It is apparent, too, that control of such list markings should be confidential and access to them should be limited.

Discouraging Theft   Steps that have been taken relative to storage and list marking should be communicated to all involved in the

who is responsible

what are legal rami. Acsnds.

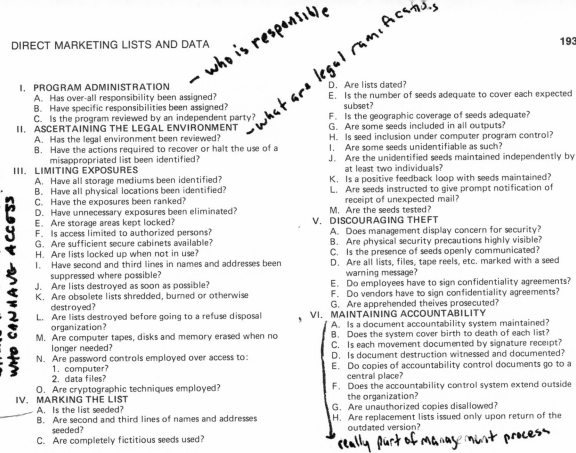

WHERE IS LIST GOING TO BE
WHO CAN HAVE ACCESS

fictitious names

I. **PROGRAM ADMINISTRATION**
  A. Has over-all responsibility been assigned?
  B. Have specific responsibilities been assigned?
  C. Is the program reviewed by an independent party?
II. **ASCERTAINING THE LEGAL ENVIRONMENT**
  A. Has the legal environment been reviewed?
  B. Have the actions required to recover or halt the use of a misappropriated list been identified?
III. **LIMITING EXPOSURES**
  A. Have all storage mediums been identified?
  B. Have all physical locations been identified?
  C. Have the exposures been ranked?
  D. Have unnecessary exposures been eliminated?
  E. Are storage areas kept locked?
  F. Is access limited to authorized persons?
  G. Are sufficient secure cabinets available?
  H. Are lists locked up when not in use?
  I. Have second and third lines in names and addresses been suppressed where possible?
  J. Are lists destroyed as soon as possible?
  K. Are obsolete lists shredded, burned or otherwise destroyed?
  L. Are lists destroyed before going to a refuse disposal organization?
  M. Are computer tapes, disks and memory erased when no longer needed?
  N. Are password controls employed over access to:
    1. computer?
    2. data files?
  O. Are cryptographic techniques employed?
IV. **MARKING THE LIST**
  A. Is the list seeded?
  B. Are second and third lines of names and addresses seeded?
  C. Are completely fictitious seeds used?

  D. Are lists dated?
  E. Is the number of seeds adequate to cover each expected subset?
  F. Is the geographic coverage of seeds adequate?
  G. Are some seeds included in all outputs?
  H. Is seed inclusion under computer program control?
  I. Are some seeds unidentifiable as such?
  J. Are the unidentified seeds maintained independently by at least two individuals?
  K. Is a positive feedback loop with seeds maintained?
  L. Are seeds instructed to give prompt notification of receipt of unexpected mail?
  M. Are the seeds tested?
V. **DISCOURAGING THEFT**
  A. Does management display concern for security?
  B. Are physical security precautions highly visible?
  C. Is the presence of seeds openly communicated?
  D. Are all lists, files, tape reels, etc. marked with a seed warning message?
  E. Do employees have to sign confidentiality agreements?
  F. Do vendors have to sign confidentiality agreements?
  G. Are apprehended thieves prosecuted?
VI. **MAINTAINING ACCOUNTABILITY**
  A. Is a document accountability system maintained?
  B. Does the system cover birth to death of each list?
  C. Is each movement documented by signature receipt?
  D. Is document destruction witnessed and documented?
  E. Do copies of accountability control documents go to a central place?
  F. Does the accountability control system extend outside the organization?
  G. Are unauthorized copies disallowed?
  H. Are replacement lists issued only upon return of the outdated version?

really part of management process

Figure 8-7 List Security Checklist. (*Kenneth L. Emmens, "How to Institute an Efficient Mailing List Security Program,"* Direct Marketing Manual, *Release No. 5310, November 1978.*)

handling of these lists so that each person will be aware of these precautions.

Certain mechanical precautions can be taken, too, to discourage theft, such as leaders on one tape reel that make it impossible to print that tape without first processing a trailer marking on the next preceding tape in a series. A single tape reel in and of itself would thus be inaccessible.

✓ SOURCES OF LISTS

Next to an organization's own house list—active and inactive customers as well as inquiries and referrals—the same categories of lists acquired by other direct marketing organizations are usually the most productive.

Although such response lists developed by others are a key source of prospective customers for a direct marketer, they are not the only source of lists. In fact, as Figure 8-8 demonstrates, there are at least 76 basic mailing list sources, including the organization's own internal records as well as a variety of response lists and compiled lists available from others.

Owners and users of lists are usually brought together by list brokers, list managers, or the compilers of lists themselves. Typically, response lists are rented under an arrangement providing for a specific use. Compiled lists are sometimes sold outright with no limit as to the number of times these names can be mailed. Rented response lists are usually maintained through the owner's use of them and thus often

INTERNAL
1. Sales Records
2. Credit Records
3. Shipping Records
4. General Correspondence
5. Telephone Inquiries
6. Specific Requests
7. Salesmen's Call Reports
8. Sales Force Recommendations
9. Technical & Service Force Recommendations
10. Employee & Stockholder Recommendations
11. Guest Books
12. Dealer & Distributor Lists
13. Warranty Registrations
14. "White Mail"

SOLICITATIONS
15. Mail Order Buyers
16. Expires
17. Inquiry Lists
18. Lead-Producing Publicity
19. Bingo Cards
20. Postcard Mailers
21. Trade Show Registrants
22. Customer Recommendations
23. Contest Entries
24. Sweepstakes Entries
25. Negative Responses to Yes/No Offers
26. Premium Offers
27. Sample Offers
28. Personal Contact
29. WU Survey Service
30. Special Direct Mail
31. Office Managers
32. Merchandise Stuffers
33. Package Inserts

DIRECTORIES
34. Telephone Directories
35. "Yellow Pages"
36. Criss-Cross Directories
37. Community Directories
38. Business Directories
39. Industrial Directories

40. Chamber of Commerce Directories
41. Horizontal Directories
42. Million Dollar Directory
43. Credit Rating Books
44. Thomas Register
45. MacRae's Blue Book
46. Standard Advertising Register
47. Poor's Register
48. Who's Who
49. Social Registers
50. Association Membership Rosters
51. Special Directories

COMPILED LISTS
52. Labor Organizations
53. Religious Organizations
54. School Lists
55. Convention Registration Lists
56. Cultural Interests
57. Birth Lists
58. Alumni Lists
59. Voter Registration Lists
60. Contributors
61. Building Permits
62. "Welcome Wagon"
63. Visitors Lists
64. News Items
65. Automobile Lists
66. Home Owner Lists
67. Other Registration Lists

OTHER
68. Subscription Lists
69. Federal Government Sources
70. Other Government Sources
71. Clipping Services
72. Local Post Offices
73. Business Services and Construction Reports
74. List Exchanges
75. List Compilers
76. List Brokers

Figure 8-8 76 Basic List Sources. (*Richard S. Hodgson, How to Work with Mailing Lists, DMA "Studies in Depth" Series, Direct Marketing Association, 1976, p. 18.*)

have better deliverability than do compiled lists that have not been updated regularly.

List Users

Acquisition of lists begins with the list user who must first understand and then describe what is needed. There are literally thousands of response and compiled lists available from which to choose, but the starting point is usually the direct marketer's own list.

A direct marketer using lists must obviously know one's own customer profile so that it can be matched against available lists. Quite often, too, only segments of these lists will be used, selecting according to geographic, demographic, or psychographic characteristics. Matching one's house list against potential response and compiled lists is in itself a stimulating exercise. In a research sense it often provides the direct marketer with basic knowledge of the marketplace which can be used in product development as well as determination of proper promotional strategies.

List Owners

A key attribute of direct marketing, aside from its measurability and accountability, is the acquisition of lists and data about the individuals or organizations on these lists. Every direct marketer is a list owner. The lists that he or she compiles during new business acquisition activities are described as house lists.

Although the primary purpose for acquisition of house lists is to build and perpetuate an organization through its customers, many direct marketers view their house lists as a profit center in their own right. They rent use of these lists to other direct marketers, under specified conditions, and this activity then becomes an important source of added revenue.

Such transactions are usually conducted as list rentals rather than outright sales of the list. It is an accepted practice, however, that all respondents to a renter's offer become an addition to the renter's own house list. Under a usual rental arrangement, the rented list may be mailed (or telephoned) only one time, and the offer must be approved, in advance, by the list owner. Directly competitive offers may not be approved except in an "exchange" that occurs when two competitive list owners provide each other with comparable numbers of their respective house lists, active or inactive buyers.

An obvious advantage of list rental, rather

```
┌─────────────────────────────────────────────┐
│  ┌────────────────────────────────────────┐  │        Date: February, 1983
│  │                                        │  │
│  │     THE NATIONAL INSURANCE COMPANY     │  │        Sex: 51% Male;
│  │                                        │  │             49% Female
│  │         ACTIVE POLICY HOLDERS          │  │
│  │                                        │  │        Source: Direct Mail
│  │  Active Policy Holders  274,000  $40.00/M │ │
│  │                                        │  │        Selections:
│  │  All of these The National active policy  │ │        State:       $2.50M
│  │  holders handle their                   │ │        Age:         $2.50M
│  │  insurance needs through the mail. They │  │        Sex:         $2.50M
│  │  continually send                       │ │        Keycoding:   $1.00M
│  │  premium payments via direct mail and all │ │
│  │  have current policies,                 │ │        Addressing: 4 or 5-up
│  │  no introduction offers are included. A │  │        9 trk. 1600 Mag. Tape
│  │  mature, middle income                  │ │        Pres. Sens. $4.00M
│  │  audience with the time and money to buy │ │
│  │  the products and                       │ │
│  │  services they desire. A list built     │  │
│  │  around the idea of buying              │ │
│  │  through the mail.                      │  │
│  │                                        │  │
│  │  Minimum Test 5,000   Sample Mail Piece Req. │ │
│  └────────────────────────────────────────┘  │
└─────────────────────────────────────────────┘
```

Figure 8-9 Mailing list data format.

than outright purchase, as is sometimes the case with compiled lists, is that the list owner maintains the list, and, thus, when used by another organization, there is a higher potential for contact by the list user. Another obvious advantage is that the names on such lists have a history of direct marketing activity; thus they are termed "response" lists. A history of prior response, whether by mail or by telephone, is an important advantage to direct marketers.

Owners of response lists or compiled lists provide descriptions of them in a standard format such as the example shown in Figure 8-9. These are often called mailing list "cards" and include key information such as quantities, pricing, and general descriptions of the lists, including available selections, as well as mechanical considerations. The costs of mailing lists can range from less than $10 per thousand names for large quantities of broad-based compiled lists to more than $100 per thousand for highly selected lists of up-scale mail-order buyers. The average list rental charge of approximately $40–$50 per thousand for one-time use usually includes provision of these names on either labels or magnetic tapes for computer processing.

Not all direct marketers make their house lists available for use by others. Often this is for proprietary reasons or to safeguard a very

valuable asset from improper use. Some list owners feel, too, that there is a tendency for a list to wear itself out. Even offers that do not directly compete can vie with each other for discretionary spending, these list owners contend.

The counterargument to this is that it is virtually impossible for individuals and organizations to remain off response and/or compiled lists. Thus, although a list owner has a proprietary interest in a house list, individuals and organizations on the list will inevitably appear on lists owned by others. Another counterargument contends that the more opportunities individuals and organizations are provided, the more likely they are to respond.

Direct Mail List Rates and Data A convenient working tool for direct marketers seeking mailing lists is a compendium, *Direct Mail List Rates and Data*.[2] An example listing from *Direct Mail List Rates and Data* is shown in Figure 8-10. The volume also contains a detailed subject/market classification index as well as a complete title/owner index. Also

[2] This reference is published semiannually by Standard Rate and Data Service, Inc., 5201 Old Orchard Road, Skokie, Ill. 66077.

included are list brokers, list managers, and list compilers. Standard Rate and Data Service, the publisher of *Direct Mail List Rates and Data,* also publishes other volumes relative to other print media of interest to direct response advertisers.

List Brokers

Like real estate brokers or stock brokers, list brokers serve as intermediaries. They do not actually own lists, but, rather, they bring list users and list owners together. In so doing, they perform these functions:[3]

> Find new lists
> Verify information
> Report on performance
> Check instructions
> Clear offer
> Check mechanics
> Clear mailing date
> Work out timing
> Assure delivery date

List brokers are, thus, specialists in the process of bringing list owners and list users together. In so doing, they should have a very clear picture of the products of the list owner as well as the needs of the list user. List brokers usually work on a commission fee basis, which is paid by the list owner.

List Managers

Since the rental of house lists by direct marketers, although generally an attractive profit center, is usually a by-product of their basic business, they often try to maximize returns from this activity through list managers. List managers represent the interests of list owners, especially those who are not staffed or inclined to develop markets for their list properties.

In effect, list managers assume responsibility, on behalf of list owners, in contacts with

[3] Richard S. Hodgson, *How to Work with Mailing Lists,* DMA Studies in Depth Series, Direct Marketing Association, 1976, p. 19.

Buyers Of Advertising

Media Code 3 083 3418 2.00
Member: D.M.M.A
Standard Rate & Data Service, Inc., 5201 Old Orchard Rd., Skokie, Ill. 60077. Phone 312-470-3426.

1. PERSONNEL
List Manager—F. Paulo.
Broker and/or Authorized Agent
All recognized brokers.

2. DESCRIPTION
Agency and advertiser company media decision makers. Agency: pres., VP, Media Dir., Buyers, Planners, Account Exec. Advertiser: Sales Mgr., Ad. Dir., Brand Mgr. Selections available by title and region.
ZIP Coded in numerical sequence 100%.
List is computerized.

3. LIST SOURCE
SRDS inquiries, latest advertising directories, company communications, trade press items, conference attendees.

4. QUANTITY AND RENTAL RATES
Rec'd October, 1981.

	Total Number	Price per/M
Agency list	17,000	45.00
Advertiser list	20,000	"

Selections: SCF, state, key code, no charge; title, billing, Nth name, etc., 5.00/M extra for each selection.
Minimum billing 150.00.

5. COMMISSION, CREDIT POLICY
20% to all recognized brokers; 15% to all advertising agencies.

6. METHOD OF ADDRESSING
4 or 5-up Cheshire labels. 1-up North-South labels, pressure sensitive labels at additional charge.
Magnetic tape available.

7. DELIVERY SCHEDULE
2 weeks.

8. RESTRICTIONS
Sample required for prior approval.

9. TEST ARRANGEMENT
Subject to minimum billing charge.

10. LETTER SHOP SERVICES
Available.

11. MAINTENANCE
Updated January and June.

(D-B, D-C 2)

Figure 8-10 Example listing from *Direct Mail List Rates and Data.*

list brokers as well as list users. They perform the advertising and sales functions and, additionally, often assume maintenance of the lists they manage in their own facility. Like list brokers, list managers receive a commission from the list owner.

List Compilers

Organizations that develop lists and data about them, often serving as their own list managers and list brokers, are called list compilers. This form of list compilation should be distinguished from that which direct marketers do in developing their own house lists through generation of responses and/or transactions.

List compilers usually develop their lists

from public records (such as driver's licenses or motor vehicle registrations), newspaper clippings, directories, warranty cards, and trade show registrations. In fact, the compiler owns such lists and then resells them, rather than renting them for one-time use. Instead of regularly maintaining such lists, compilers usually recompile periodically. Names and addresses in telephone directories, for example, are compiled regularly, at least annually, on issuance of newly published volumes.

EVALUATION OF LISTS

Record keeping is essential to properly evaluate the profitability of response as well as compiled lists. This is necessary, also, to predict future response from lists or segments of lists. An example of a form for ongoing recording of lists/segments is shown in Figure 8-11.

Measurement of Results

Evaluating a list begins with a key code, a unique identifier placed on the response device prior to mailing a promotion piece. Key codes can be simple preprinted numbers identifying the source of the mailing list, or they can be so complex as to incorporate not just the source but the category of list, type of product offered by the list owner, or even the degree of prior direct marketing activity (R/F/M).

Key codes can be structured, too, so that information can be accumulated, across several individual lists, by several category factors. Thus, the direct marketer can tabulate response not only by individual lists, as shown in Figure 8-11, but also by sources of list, product lines, geographical location (ZIP Code), and a variety of other broad qualifiers. Individual lists can then be grouped in such categories and presumptions made as to the overall efficiency of certain list sources, certain ZIP Codes, or certain product lines.

An important consideration is that records

of lists be ongoing and that these be monitored even if it has been determined that they can be contacted frequently. This is because the character and nature of lists change just as the character and nature of the list owner's business may change. In terms of recency, many direct marketers have achieved the highest response rate when they have used so-called "hotline" names. This term refers to the most recent names acquired by specific list owners, but there is no uniformity as to what chronological period "recent" describes.

As was presented in detail in Chapter 3, testing of lists is subject to the usual rigors of research and experimentation, including sampling methods, determination of sample size, and statistical measurement of differences.

Response Differences by Month

An important consideration in evaluating list results is that response differences can occur as a result of timing alone. Certain exogenous factors over which the direct marketer can exert no control, such as economic conditions or climate variations, can have a pronounced effect when lists are developed over a period of time. Other uncontrollable factors include major events or even catastrophes that divert public attention.

Certain mail-order offers, such as a catalog of Christmas gifts, are timely and reflect seasonal differences. Some offers can be affected by the income tax season or by the vacation season. Some direct marketers try to time their mailing releases and telephone marketing efforts so as to avoid arrival during any type of holiday event, especially those that take people out of doors.

Even for nonseasonal offers, however, there is seemingly a month-to-month cycle that affects direct response advertising. All other factors being equal, direct marketers have noted ebbs and flows on a month-to-month basis. Although each direct marketer should develop an index of monthly responses, a fairly

CLASS NUMBER---________ LIST OWNER---________________ PRODUCT---________________

QUANTITY AVAILABLE				YEAR	COST	USED
..........M	☐ Buy.	☐ F. Buy.	☐ Inq.	....	$............/M	....
..........M	☐ Buy.	☐ F. Buy.	☐ Inq.	....	$............/M	....

B.N.	ADDRESS	SOURCE	ARRANGED	LABELS EXTRA	SELECT EXTRA
	☐ Form ☐ Label	☐ D.M. ☐ Pub. ☐ Comp. ☐ Misc.	☐ Geo. ☐ Chron. ☐ None	$............/M	$............/M

SALES

		Date →																											
			1 Week		2 Weeks		3 Weeks		4 Weeks		5 Weeks		6 Weeks		7 Weeks		8 Weeks		9 Weeks		10 Weeks		11 Weeks		12 Weeks		13 Weeks		COST PER SALE
Date Mailed	Key	No. Mailed	No.	P/M	No.	P/M	No.	P/M	No.	P/M	No.	P/M	No.	P/M	No.	P/M	No.	P/M	No.	P/M	No.	P/M	No.	P/M	No.	P/M	No.	P/M	

CONVERSIONS

At End of →		1st Mo.		2nd Mo.		3rd Mo.		4th Mo.		5th Mo.		6th Mo.				Final		PAR RATIO
Date Mailed	No. Mailed	No.	%	No.	%	No.	%	No.	%	No.	%	No.	%	No.	%	%	Comments	

Figure 8-11 Mailing list evaluation form.

typical pattern was developed by Raymond A. Snyder, then sales manager at *World Book.* As reported by Bob Stone, the pattern resulted from a 3-year test program for a nonseasonal product. The mailing list used was divided into 12 parts so that an equal quantity of similar names was released each month of the year. January was determined to be the month with the highest relative response. Rating January as 100 percent, the following months were indexed to it:[4]

Month	Index (%)
January	100.0
February	96.3
March	71.0
April	71.5
May	71.5
June	67.9
July	73.3
August	87.0
September	79.0
October	89.9
November	81.0
December	79.0

Development of such an index can be very useful to the direct marketer who is testing lists on an ongoing basis. It makes it possible to consider the variable of timing in comparing one list with another when these are released during different months of the year.

The direct marketer should be cautious of differences relative to seasonal offers as well as exogenous occurrences that are beyond control. And, of course, one should develop one's own historical pattern, which may or may not look like the example above.

Shared Use of Mailing Lists

To achieve maximum distribution of direct mail at minimal cost, a variety of alternative ways has been developed that enable direct marketers to share use of mailing lists by having two or more advertisers put their literature in the same mailing envelope. Such shared use inevitably divides the attention of the recipient among several alternative offers and thus results in choice of one offer over another or even procrastination so that no response results. The response to any particular offer in such shared mailings is usually less than would be expected if that offer were mailed individually, but at relatively higher cost.

Shared mailings are most often used by those direct marketers who want to obtain market saturation with maximum attention at minimum cost. Packaged goods manufacturers, for example, often use this technique for coupon distribution for redemption at local retail outlets. Typically, such coupon distribution is designed to motivate consumer purchases of an existing product or to introduce new products. In either instance, the use of direct mail, as opposed to newspaper distribution, provides better control over market segmentation as well as the valuable coupons themselves.

Shared mailings include cooperative mailings, joint mailings, and mail or package inserts. In each instance, the objective is to share such cost items as mailing list rental and postage (subject to maximum weight restrictions) among two or more direct marketers.

Cooperative Mailing Consisting of a variety of diverse offerings, perhaps as many as 25 in a single envelope, large-scale cooperative mailings are typically sent to compiled lists, such as names gathered from telephone directories or automobile registrations. Under these circumstances, the cost to a participant in a cooperative mailing can be substantially lower than would be individual mailing to a particular list. Although most participants in cooperative mailings are couponers, these usually include a smaller number of direct response advertisements.

---

[4] Bob Stone, *Successful Direct Marketing Methods,* 2d ed., Crain Books, Chicago, 1979, p. 92.

In addition to these mass cooperatives, some cooperative mailings are put together to reach specific market segments, such as high school students, new mothers, or senior citizens. Other cooperative mailings might be directed to an even more specific market such as the subscribers to a particular magazine.

Typically, the more complex the offer, the less likely it is to succeed in a cooperative mailing because of the simultaneous competition from other offers in the same carrier envelope. This impact is usually greater on direct response advertisements than it is on coupon redemption.

Joint Mailing A variation of the cooperative mailing is the joint mailing. In this instance, usually two direct marketers combine their direct mail packages (each complete and each contained within its own carrier envelope) into a common mailing envelope, thus sharing the cost of the list as well as the cost of postage, although creating additional cost for the common mailing envelope and the inserting into such. These combined offers become separate mailings when removed from the common mailing envelope.

The trick here, of course, is to find offers that have so much in common, yet are not directly competitive, that it is profitable to mail both offers to the same list at the same time.

Mail/Package Inserts Direct response advertisements are often included as enclosures with billing statements or invoices, as well as within package shipments. In effect, these pieces are going to a mailing list under particularly favorable opening and interest conditions. Many bank credit cards, some utilities, department stores, and oil companies enclose one or more such inserts with their periodic billings. Besides the cost of printing, additional cost for this distribution is minimal if the piece remains within postage weight limits. The

advertising thus arrives in a package that is likely to get attention and be opened.

Similarly, exposure of a product or service offer with a package shipment from a firm with a customer mailing list compatible with the direct marketer's own objective arrives at an ideal time, just as the recipient is consummating another purchase. In the case of both billing inserts and package inserts, there is subtle and implied endorsement of the company transmitting the direct marketer's offer to its own customers.

PRIVACY ISSUES

With intimations that "1984" was just around the corner, under a front-page headline of "Lists Help Build Dossiers on You," James Kindall, a member of the staff of the *Kansas City Star,* stated:[5]

> They know about you.
> They know how old you are. They know if you have children. They know about your job.
> They know how much money you make, what kind of car you drive, what sort of house you live in and whether you are likely to prefer pâté de foie gras and champagne or hot dogs and a cold beer.
> They know all this and much, much more. And you know how?
> They know your name.
> What they have done with it is very simple: They have added it to a mailing list.

Albeit an exaggeration, the foregoing is evidence of a widely held concern that a list is a conduit through which personal information is transferred from one mailer to another. To the contrary, as should be apparent from the material contained earlier in this chapter, the purpose is to achieve greater selectivity. The use of records about individuals, coupled with new technological capabilities, is intended to

[5] James Kindall, "Lists Help Build Dossier on You," *Kansas City Star,* September 5, 1978, p. 1.

make direct response advertising more relevant to the recipient.

Even critics of privacy issues relative to mailing lists have been willing to admit that unsolicited direct mail could be a nuisance, an annoyance, or even an abomination, but not a trespass on personal privacy. Direct mail, just as any other form of advertising, can be an unwanted intrusion. Increasing selection and careful segmentation of lists works to minimize this.

Privacy Protection Study Commission

The concern of the American consumer and Congress over the broad issue of privacy, including the subject of mailing lists, culminated in the Privacy Act of 1974. This act established a Privacy Protection Study Commission to determine whether the various restrictions on what the federal government could do with personal information, as provided in the Privacy Act, should also be applied to the private sector. Significantly for mailing list owners and users, Section V (c), (B) (i) of the act directed the commission to report to the President and Congress on whether an organization engaged in interstate commerce should be required to remove from its mailing list the name of an individual who does not want to be on it.[6]

After months of hearing testimony and studying the issues, the 618-page *Report from the Privacy Protection Study Commission* was issued July 1977. Chapter 4 of this report was devoted entirely to the subject of mailing lists.

Observing that the appearance of an individual's name on a mailing list, so long as that individual has the prerogative to remove it from that list, was not in and of itself an invasion of privacy, the commission recommended:[7]

---

[6] *Privacy Act of 1974,* Public Law No. 93-579, codified as a note to 5 USC 522a.
[7] *Report from the Privacy Protection Study Commission,* July 1977, p. 147.

That a person engaged in interstate commerce who maintains a mailing list should *not* be required by law to remove an individual's name and address from such a list upon request of that individual, except as already provided by law.

In reaching this conclusion, the commission observed "that the balance that must be struck between the interests of individuals and the interests of mailers is an especially delicate one." The commission also noted the economic importance of direct mail "to nonprofit organizations, to the champions of unpopular causes, and to many of the organizations that create diversity in American society."

Agreeing that the *receipt* of direct mail is not really the issue but rather how the mailing list record of an individual is used, the commission further recommended:

That a private sector organization which rents, sells, exchanges or otherwise makes the addresses or names and addresses, of its customers, members, or donors available to any other person for use in direct mail marketing or solicitation, should adopt a procedure whereby each customer, member or donor is informed of the organization's practice in that respect . . . [and] is given an opportunity to indicate to the organization that he does not wish to have his address or name and address made available for such purposes.

A recommendation similar to that above required "that each state review the direct mail marketing . . . uses that are made of state agency records about individuals . . . [and to] devise a procedure whereby an individual can inform the agency that he does not want a record pertaining to himself to be used for such purposes." Examples of voluntary mailing list notifications being used to comply with the report of the Privacy Protection Study Commission are shown in Figure 8-12.

Mail Preference Service

Since 1971, the Direct Marketing Association (DMA), through its Mail Preference Service, which was lauded in the Privacy Protection

ABOUT MAILING LISTS...

an important notice to our subscribers.

In recent years we have made the list of subscribers to McGraw-Hill publications (names and mailing addresses only) available to carefully screened companies whose products or services might be of interest to you.

These companies enter into an agreement that permits them to mail information to you without placing you under any obligation.

We have always considered such direct marketing activities to be legitimate and important in the American system of free trade—and we're confident that the majority of subscribers share this position.

However, we respect the interests of those who for some reason may wish to have their names restricted from such use by companies either affiliated or not affiliated with McGraw-Hill, Inc.

If you wish to delete your name from lists we make available to other firms, please fill in the information requested below exactly as it appears on your mailing label on the cover of this issue. Or, if you prefer, attach the label itself to the coupon and return.

McGraw-Hill, Inc.
P.O. Box 555
Hightstown, N.J. 08520
Attn: Mailing List Dept.

☐ Please remove my name from your mailing lists.

Title of this publication _____

Name _____

Address _____
　　　　　(exactly as shown as mailing label, please)

City State Zip _____

IN OUR CONTINUING EFFORTS TO SERVE YOU....

Because of the many fine products and services available by mail, Old American from time to time makes its mailing lists available to certain other carefully selected organizations. The list is provided on a limited use basis and only to those who, in our judgment, offer products and services of recognized quality and value.

In order to protect your privacy we extend this privilege only on a strictly controlled basis. For example, no personal information other than name and address is ever divulged, although names may be selected according to segments to which the particular offer would appeal, on the basis of age groups, sex, geographical location and recency of activity.

More and more organizations are mailing literature about products and services directly to consumers. And more and more people are taking advantage of these opportunities to shop by mail. In 1977, 12% of all consumer purchases were made through the mail ... amounting to some 75 billion dollars.

Most people look forward to receiving information in the mail about a wide variety of items, including many not readily available in local stores. They find such to be interesting, informative, and useful. And they find shopping by mail is a convenient and comfortable way to shop.

However, should you not wish to receive such offers as a result of being on one of our lists, we will certainly respect your wishes and remove your name from the list when it goes to other organizations. If you wish us to do so, simply complete and return the coupon, and we'll identify your record accordingly.

☐ I do not wish my name and address to be made available to others.

IMPORTANT:
Please print your name and address clearly in the space provided below exactly as it appears on this mailing. Be sure to include any code numbers that appear within the address label area. That way we can be certain we are removing your name and not that of another individual with a similar name. The surest way of identifying you personally as a policyholder is to include your policy number(s) as well, if known.

_____

_____

_____

_____

Mail to:
Old American Insurance Company
Name Removal Service: Dept. EDP
4900 Oak Street
Kansas City, Missouri 64141

NOTE:
If you wish to continue to receive mailings of the sort described, it is not necessary to take any action.

Mailing Lists We occasionally make our customer list of names and addresses available to carefully screened companies and organizations whose products and activities might be of interest to you. If you prefer not to receive such mailings, please copy your mailing label exactly and mail it to:

L. L. Bean, Inc.
Mail Preference Service
Freeport, ME 04033

Figure 8-12 Examples of voluntary mailing list notifications to comply with the report of the Privacy Protection Study Commission, July 1977.

Study Commission report, has provided consumers with an opportunity to be removed from (or added to) large numbers of mailing lists. By sending the Direct Marketing Association, Inc., 6 East 43rd Street, New York, NY 10017 a request for either deletion or addition a record will be placed into a computer tape that is circulated on a regular basis to approximately 1,500 members of the DMA who participate in this service. It is interesting to note that more people have asked to have their names *added* than have asked to have their names *deleted* from lists. (In recent years the ratio has been three additions to one deletion.)

United States Postal Service

Two federal statutes, one directed at pandering advertisements (39 U.S.C. 3008) and the other at sexually oriented advertising (39 U.S.C. 3010), provide ways for individuals to stop the flow of unsolicited mail from particular types of sources. Since the definition of "obscene" is left to the individual, recipients have often used the statute to stop the flow of *any* kind of unsolicited mail from any source, even the Internal Revenue Service on occasion. Inasmuch as the individual alone makes the decision about what to receive, there is apparently no constitutional barrier to having the United States Postal Service carry out the wishes of an individual who does not want to receive a particular type of mail.

Privacy vs. Confidentiality

Contrary to commonly held beliefs, lists (even if the data were available to them, which most often is not the case) do not disclose the income of the individuals on them or how much money they have on deposit in the bank or how deeply in debt they are or what their personal habits and attitudes might be. To reveal such information, even if known, would be more of a breach of confidentiality than it

would be an invasion of privacy. Even when utilizing the R/F/M formula for list segmentation, users of a list do not know whether a particular customer spent $10 or $100. Neither is there a way of knowing what particular sections of a magazine a particular subscriber on a subscriber list prefers.

To direct marketers, a list represents a market segment. Direct marketers have no more interest in knowing personal facts about individuals on lists than they have in knowing personal facts about individual subscribers to a magazine (other than the fact that the individual is a reader of that magazine). This preference could be related to preference for certain products or services. An example would be a travel agency's mailing to *National Geographic* subscribers.

The Privacy Protection Study Commission concluded that "the receipt of unauthorized advertising . . . does not transgress generally regarded rights of privacy." The Direct Marketing Association, Inc., has suggested guidelines for personal information protection. These are contained in Figure 8-13.

Henry David Thoreau, who once contended that nothing worthwhile ever arrived in the mail, continues to live on, thanks to the Thoreau Lyceum. This learning center in Concord, Massachusetts, appears as a subscriber to many magazines, some of which rent or exchange their subscriber lists. The following computer-processed letter, from a local Buick dealer, is evidence:

Dear Mr. Thoreau:
As you read through this brochure, you will sense the enthusiasm we have for the all-new 1980 Buick Skylark. Come in and test drive one soon. It might just be the perfect car for you.[8]

Although this cannot be regarded as an invasion of privacy as much as it can be a

[8] William Labens, "Henry Thoreau Behind a Buick Skylark?" *Computer World,* September 7, 1981.

gross error in list compilation and maintenance, it would be of little solace to the
philosopher who spent 2 full years experimenting with a totally natural life-style alongside Walden Pond.

SUMMARY

Lists and the data about the names on them
comprise market segments and are at the very
core of direct marketing. The names on lists,
broadly defined, are of the recipients of mailed,
telephoned, broadcast, and print messages.
Such lists are perishable and require constant
updating and maintenance.

There are three basic types of lists: house
lists, response lists, and compiled lists. House
lists are composed of active and inactive customers as well as inquirers and referrals. Response lists can be categorized in the same
way, the difference being that they are used
by a direct marketer other than the one who
owns such lists. Compiled lists from a variety
of sources such as directories and rosters also
describe market segments, but have not been
generated through response to a direct marketing offer.

The development and maintenance of a house
list calls for meticulous record keeping. Collection and recording of data relevant to the
character or status of the individual names on
these lists are equally important. Response
activity is categorized in terms of recency/
frequency/monetary (R/F/M) experience.

Match codes enable direct marketers to use
merge/purge procedures that not only eliminate duplication within and between computerized lists but also identify multibuyers. List
maintenance calls for removal of nondeliver-
able names as well as changing addresses and
recording the latest transactions.

Since a list is an asset, even though not
usually shown on an organization's balance
sheet as such, it should be treated with adequate security procedures. Such procedures
include proper storage of the list, marking of
the list to identify potential misuse, and internal procedures designed to discourage theft or
misappropriation.

Lists for use by direct marketers are available from a variety of sources, notably other
direct marketers and especially those with
comparable customer profiles. List owners
(including compilers) and list users are brought
together through list brokers and list managers.

The effective testing and continuation use
of specific lists calls for adequate record-keep-
ing procedures through which individual lists
can be evaluated and the results from their
use measured.

Shared usages of mailing lists include cooperative mailings, joint mailings, and inserts
with other mail or packages.

Privacy issues relative to mailing lists have
received considerable attention. Direct marketers need to be mindful of these issues
through respecting the confidential nature of
records as well as providing those on lists the
opportunity to be removed from them. The
Privacy Protection Study Commission, created
as a result of the Privacy Act of 1974, concluded that the appearance of a name on a list
in and of itself did not constitute an invasion
of privacy and that it would not be wise to
place legislative restriction on such use.

CASE: VIEWING LISTS AS MARKET SEGMENTS

Learning Objective

This case study considers lists as market segments and stimulates thinking about the three
basic types of lists: house lists, response lists,
and compiled lists. It is important to recognize,
too, that lists generate lists; that is, prospects
(on lists) become customers (on lists) and these
customers generate more orders and even

For purposes of these Guidelines, the following definitions apply:

Individual: A natural person identified in a file by name and address or other identifier.

Personal Data: Information which is linked to an individual on a file and which is not publicly available or observable.

Direct Marketing Purposes: The purposes of direct marketing are to promote, sell and deliver goods and services; to foster such efforts through the sale, rental, compilation or exchange of lists in accordance with the principles of these Guidelines; to delete and add individuals to lists; to provide all necessary customer services including the extension of credit where appropriate; to raise funds; to perform market research and to encourage recipients to respond by taking direct action.

Article 1. Personal data should be collected by fair and lawful means for a direct marketing purpose.

Article 2. Direct marketers should limit the collection of personal data to only those data which are deemed pertinent and necessary for a direct marketing purpose and should only be used accordingly.

Article 3. Personal data which are used for direct marketing purposes should be accurate, complete and should be kept up to date to the extent practicable by the direct marketer. Personal data should be retained no longer than is required for the purpose for which they are stored.

Article 4. An individual shall have the right to request whether personal data about him/her appear on a direct marketer's file and to receive a summary of the information within a reasonable time after the request is made. An individual has the right to challenge the accuracy of personal data relating to him/her. Personal data which are shown to be incorrect should be corrected.

Article 5. Personal data should be transferred between direct marketers only for direct marketing purposes. Every list owner who sells, exchanges or rents lists containing personal data should see to it that each individual on the list is informed of those practices (Self Disclosure), and should offer an option to have the individual's name deleted. The list owner should remove names from his/her lists when requested directly in a signed writing by the individual, or by use of the DMA Mail Preference Service name removal list.

List brokers and compilers should take reasonable steps to have the list owner follow these list practices.

Personal data should not be put at the disposal of any third party except as set forth in these Guidelines, or with the express consent of the individual, unless required by law.

Article 6. All list owners, brokers and compilers should be protective of the individual's right to privacy and sensitive to the information collected on lists and subsequently considered for transfer.

Personal information supplied by individuals such as, but not limited to, medical, financial, insurance or court data should not be included on lists that are rented or exchanged when there is a reasonable expectation by the individual that the information would be kept confidential.

Article 7. Each direct marketer should be responsible for the security of personal data. Strict measures should be taken to assure against unauthorized access, alteration or dissemination of personal data. Employees who have access to personal data should agree in advance to use those data only in an authorized manner.

Article 8. Visitors to areas where personal data are processed and stored should be specifically authorized by express permission of the direct marketer and should be accompanied by at least one authorized employee of the direct marketer.

Article 9. If personal data are transferred from one direct marketer to another for a direct marketing purpose, measures should be taken by the transferor to arrange strict security measures to assure that unauthorized access to the data is not likely during transfer procedures. It is the responsibility of the direct marketer to whom the list is transferred to arrange strict security measures to insure no unauthorized access to the list during its return to the original owner.

Article 10. The Committee on Ethical Business Practices of DMA is charged with reviewing any complaints by individuals of violation of these Guidelines and shall take appropriate action.

Figure 8-13 The Direct Marketing Association's suggested guidelines for personal information protection.

additional customers through referral and recommendation.

Overview

As organizations evolve, they develop products to fulfill expressed customer needs. Typically, these organizations find their niche in the marketplace, a particular product line positioned to a particular market segment, and, with this niche in mind, they develop distribution systems and promotional strategies. As the organization develops, product lines are expanded to appeal to additional market segments, each with its own positioning and its own promotional strategy. At the core of this total process, which the direct marketer trained in measurability and accountability recognizes, are lists and data about those lists. It helps to view lists as market segments and vice versa.

Procedure

Read the learning objective, the overview, and the case that follows. Identify the market segments and speculate as to why these were appropriate for consideration. Suggest what lists reach each of the selected market segments. Demonstrate how the evolution from prospect to customer is reflected through lists and data.

Case[9]

L'eggs Brand, Inc., Winston-Salem, North Carolina, a subsidiary of the Hanes Corporation, is the mass marketer of L'eggs hosiery through supermarkets. L'eggs entry into mail-order began after 1974 when the L'eggs program was first introduced into high-traffic retail locations. Initially, there were two basic styles of hosiery displayed at these locations: one was pantyhose and the other was a product that was a forerunner of pantyhose, the conventional stocking. When the conventional stocking was substantially removed from the familiar L'eggs self-service display, there was a tremendous amount of mail received by the manufacturer, some 100,000 pieces in all, asking where the conventional L'eggs stockings went.

The L'eggs people created a prospect mailing list out of these 100,000 letter writers and mailed them a small brochure that offered conventional stockings in six pair increments. That was in 1976. Almost immediately after

that, letters started arriving from nurses saying, "We love your product. Can you make it available to us in white?" There was, it developed, a well-defined market segment for a differentiated product, nurses wearing white conventional stockings, which was too widely dispersed for efficient retail store distribution, but was a natural for mail order. The segment was reachable, too, through mailing lists as well as space advertising in nursing publications.

Thus, the direct marketing division of L'eggs was begun and almost instantly expanded. Of approximately 1.5 million nurses, some 200,000 became wearers of L'eggs "Nurse White" hosiery. The L'eggs hosiery product, differentiated for use by nurses, an identifiable and reachable market segment, is ideal for mail order. It has high repeat potential and is a product that is easily merchandised, inexpensively packaged, and conveniently shipped.

During 1981, L'eggs mail-order sales totaled approximately $23.5 million, some 9 percent of L'eggs total sales. Mail-order customer lists consisted of 45,000 buyers of regular stockings in addition to the 200,000 buyers of Nurse White hosiery.

There was also another category of customers: buyers of "slightly imperfect" hosiery. A line of "seconds" (approximately 2 to 3 percent of L'eggs total production considered to be less than top grade) has proven to be L'eggs most successful mail-order venture. Customers for "seconds" totaled more than one million. Further, in the process of identifying these buyers of irregulars through the mail-order channel, L'eggs has been able to emphasize the top quality of its product as distributed through its usual retail store outlets.

The mail-order line of L'eggs hosiery is aimed at the 45–70 age group whereas the white hosiery line is aimed at an occupation, nurses. L'eggs describes the "seconds" buyers as "bargain hunters." The loyalty of these

---

[9] Adapted from Charles W. Chambers, "L'eggs MO Program Segments Mass Merchandise Market," *Direct Marketing,* November 1980, pp. 66–70. Additional data from *NSM Report,* January 11, 1982, Maxwell Sroge Publishing, Inc., Chicago.

customers is felt to be more dependent on price than on brand name.

Orders average $15, with substantial discounts for larger quantity purchases. Lists of women, especially working women, have been continually tested as have further extensions of the product line. The mail-order operation dovetails nicely with the well-known retail store boutiques.

DISCUSSION QUESTIONS

1 What is the basis for viewing lists as market segments?
2 Distinguish between prospect lists and customer lists, and describe how the former relate to the latter.
3 Are all lists *mailing* lists?
4 Discuss individually the three basic types of lists, including the characteristics and potential as well as examples of each:

a House lists
b Response lists
c Compiled lists

5 How is a mailing list developed and maintained? How is duplication within and between lists controlled?
6 What data should be collected with regard to the individuals on specific mailing lists?
7 Why is it important to provide security safeguards for mailing lists? Should these be similar to or different from those provided for other assets of an organization?
8 Define these terms:

a List user
b List owner
c List broker
d List manager
e List compiler

9 Why is it essential to keep complete records of lists used in direct marketing?
10 Discuss the issue of privacy relative to mailing lists.

PART THREE

PRODUCT AND PRICE: OFFER PLANNING

PRODUCT RESEARCH AND DEVELOPMENT FOR DIRECT MARKETING

Products (and services) are the lifeblood of direct marketing. Without products, there can be no justification for direct marketing. One need not look as far back as when buggy whips became obsolete to recognize that old products are continually being replaced by new ones. And, since most new products are failures, it is important to think of product research and development as an ongoing and systematic process.

WHY DO NEW PRODUCTS FAIL?

Most new products are failures. The Edsel automobile, of course, is a classic example of a new product failure about which volumes have been written. Less well known are the ketchup with a nontomato flavor and the clear colored bourbon in a frosted bottle that was supposed to capitalize on the acceptance of bottled gin with those properties. Then there were the breakfast cereals with freeze-dried fruits that looked oh-so-much like impurities before they were hydrated.

The experience of the Du Pont Co., with its leather-substitute called Corfam, presents an interesting case of new product failure, too. First introduced to the United States market in 1964, Du Pont estimated that it had invested up to $100 million in the venture before abandoning the product in early 1971.[1] The basic characteristics of Corfam that made it superior to leather—durability, water repellency, ease of care, and competitive price—lacked appeal in a market seemingly indifferent to these features.

Conference Board Study

When the Conference Board queried more than 100 firms that were looked on as relatively innovative in the area of products,[2] seven

[1] "Du Pont's Corfam Leather Substitute Has Been Given Its Final Walking Papers," *Wall Street Journal,* March 17, 1971.
[2] Earl F. Bailey and David S. Hopkins, "New Product Pressures," *Conference Board Record,* June 1971, p. 16 ff.

major reasons emerged as causes of new product failures. Listed in order of frequency of mention, the reasons given were:

1 Inadequate market analysis
2 Product deficiencies
3 Lack of effective marketing effort
4 Higher costs than anticipated
5 Competitive strength or reaction
6 Poor timing of introduction
7 Technical or production problems

It is significant to note that five of these seven causes of failure can be considered marketing shortcomings. Mindful of this and looking to the future, those executives surveyed suggested three major corrective actions:

1 Changes within organizations to put more emphasis on new product planning and to view this as a marketing function
2 Better analysis and evaluation of preferences and product features through marketing research
3 Careful screening and evaluation of product ideas before introduction

INNOVATION: INVENTION VS. AUTOMATION

Innovation, broadly defined, encompasses two major areas of technology. One of these can be described with the word "invention." This category includes the devices, the machines, and the products that increase productive capacity and/or create demand. Such technological innovations as these include major inventions such as the wheel, the lever, the alloying of metals, electricity, or chemical synthesis. Many of these inventions, in turn, led to the development of machines, railroads, automobiles. Others led to such consumer products as radios, television, and synthetic fabrics for clothing.

Invention by itself, however, is not enough. The economist Joseph Schumpeter argued that finding economic applications for inventions, which he termed as innovations, was a critical need.[3] And, beyond that, in a process that he termed imitation, was the diffusion of innovation throughout the economy. Technological change, thus, is not just a matter of invention or of scientific capability. Rather, it is a combination of both, practically applied through the processes of innovation and imitation.

The second category of innovation is automation. As a term, automation has blossomed in modern times although the word is newer than the fact. In the precise sense, engineers apply the word only to that aspect of technology that promises easier and better means to get certain parts of work done: the substitution of control devices for human observation and decision. Recently, however, a new glitter has been attached to the definition due largely to the vast improvements in control devices and techniques during recent years. As a result, the average person's conception of automation goes beyond the engineer's definition of it.

The essence of automation involves either the continuance or periodic scanning of results (with correlation, if needed, following automatically) or the sequential accomplishment of a series of operations according to prearranged programs. Although there are many repetitive functions that are capable of being automated, automation cannot substitute for human intelligence. The process can accomplish only what human ingenuity devises it to do. In this respect, automation places even greater importance on mental skills, rather than, as some fear, threatening the replacement of these skills by machines. But obviously there are many things, products as well as processes, that are not economically feasible or practical to automate. Certainly a machine could not equal the accomplishments of a concert pianist, a dress designer, an interior decorator, an expert chef, or a capable waiter.

A classic example of automation as an innovation is the dial telephone. It has been postulated that, if the Bell System (AT&T) had not automated when it did, with dial telephones, automatic switching, and area codes, there would not now be enough people in the labor force to serve as telephone operators!

Peter Drucker emphasized the importance of innovation in the context of marketing when he wrote: "Because it is its purpose to create a customer, any business enterprise has two—and only these two—basic functions: marketing and innovation."[4] The essence of marketing *is* innovation. Product innovation alone cannot create a profit, but proper marketing of a product can. On the other hand, marketing alone cannot make a poor product successful in the long run. Product strategy thus needs to be geared to the profit curve and not to the sales curve.

"PRODUCT" DEFINED

The foregoing discussion of innovation, invention as well as automation, leads us to the need for a definition of "product." Just what *is* a "product" or "service," and what special implications does this have for direct marketers?

A product in its purest form can be viewed in terms of its physical properties. Furthermore, as with a bicycle, a product can be associated with its use and even its benefits. Put a brand name such as "Schwinn" on that bicycle and we might conjure up an image of reputation and reliability. Also, the Schwinn dealer from whom that bicycle was purchased has his own reputation associated with, possibly, his reliability and his service facilities. Bicycles come in many sizes and colors, too, and are subject to individual needs and pref-

[3] Joseph Schumpeter, *Capitalism, Socialism and Democracy,* Harper & Brothers, New York, 1942.

[4] Peter Drucker, *The Practice of Management,* Harper & Row, New York, 1954, p. 37.

Figure 9-1 A product is not just a tangible "thing." (*William J. Stanton,* Fundamentals of Marketing, *6th ed., McGraw-Hill Book Company, New York, 1981, p. 161. Reproduced with permission.*)

erences. Such diversity causes even further impressions about the total product.

All of these characteristics of a product or service and more are implied in this definition of "product" presented by William J. Stanton and visualized in Figure 9-1:

> A product is a set of tangible and intangible attributes, including packaging, color, price, manufacturer's prestige, retailer's prestige, and manufacturer's and retailer's services, which the buyer may accept as offering satisfaction of wants or needs.[5]

"Products" Viewed as "Benefits"

Successful direct marketers promote the *benefits* of a product, not the product alone. Charles B. Mills, when asked why he was so adept at writing direct mail copy for O. M. Scott's grass seed, replied "Because I like to talk about your lawn and not about my grass seed." Airlines sell a vacation in some exotic place, not just the air trip getting there. Designers sell fashions, not just the practicality of clothing. Insurance firms sell security and peace of mind, not just a paper contract. Elmer Wheeler, a sales motivator and writer, summed

[5] William J. Stanton, *Fundamentals of Marketing,* 6th ed., McGraw-Hill Book Company, New York, 1981, p. 162.

it up when he said, "Sell the sizzle and not the steak." There is nothing particularly glamorous about a ³⁄₁₆th-inch drill bit, but there is considerable benefit in using such a product to make a ³⁄₁₆th-inch hole when one is needed!

Breadth and Depth of Products

A product has physical properties. It also has functional properties. And, as Thorstein Veblen and others have noted with expressions such as "conspicuous consumption" or "keeping up with the Joneses," a product can also have a psychological perspective.

Breadth refers to the variety of products in a line. The Chevrolet automobile, for example, can be a Citation or a Cavalier, a Chevette or a Corvette, a Camaro or a Caprice, a Chevelle or a Monza, a Malibu or a Nova, a Monte Carlo or a Vega. Viewed as part of the total product line of General Motors, Chevrolets are augmented by Buicks and Cadillacs, Pontiacs and Oldsmobiles. General Motors' line of automobiles, in turn, is expanded by Ford, Chrysler, Toyota, and Volkswagen products.

Depth of a product, on the other hand, refers to the assortment of sizes and colors within a product. These, in turn, constitute an entire array of a product line. Products can be *innovative* (videocassettes, self-developing photos); they can be *adaptive* (freeze-dried coffee, radial tires); or they can be *imitative* (a half-dozen variations of Rubik's cube).

Reasons for Adding New Products

Many reasons can be given for researching, developing, and ultimately adding new products. These include:

Completion of a Product Line There may be shortages in the existing product line in terms of size, color, and packaging. Or, products may have become obsolete and replacement or rejuvenation is needed. A particular price break may be required to be competitive. Any one or all of these could be considerations for enlarging a firm's existing product line.

Diversification of a Product Line Related to the above is the desire to diversify existing products to sell more to present customers or even to reach new markets. Fashion designers such as Bill Blass, Halston, and Anne Klein, whose names originally identified only wearing apparel, add their names (and reputations) to such diversified products as bed sheets, shaving lotion, and perfumes. A retailer of "half-size" dresses for short and stout women, Lane Bryant, augments its line with maternity clothing and further diversifies into other body types through an affiliate, Tall Girl.

Why do organizations diversify? Sometimes firms have a particular entry to a market, such as Gerber did when the company began direct marketing insurance to families with young children with the slogan, "Ask your baby about us." Sometimes marketers have certain production talent for diversified markets, such as does the Columbia Broadcasting System, which markets records and cassettes as well as a variety of publications through both the mail-order channel and at the retail store.

Utilization of an Existing Market or Channel of Distribution Given the choice of controlling the "market" or the "mill"; that is, being known and respected in an established marketplace as opposed to controlling a manufacturing facility, marketing-oriented firms are most often inclined to choose the former. Avon, the world's largest manufacturer and distributor of cosmetics, when it ventured into mail order through a wholly owned subsidiary originally identified as "Family Fashions" (and subsequently named "Family Fashions by Avon") recognized initially the importance of its identity in the marketplace. It recognizes the fact even more now that the subsidiary is called "Avon Fashions." Products offered by Avon Fashions are a complete diversification, wearing apparel, rather than cosmetics, as is the distribution channel, mail order, rather than personal selling. Even within its basic distribution channel, through personal representatives, its product line has been diversified to include costume jewelry along with cosmetics.

Combating Seasonal Peaks and Valleys Firms that offer seasonal products such as Christmas gift items or seasonal services such as tax preparation recognize the need for leveling the work flow in terms of manufacturing as well as marketing. A purveyor of Christmas gift packs of steaks, for example, can extend its efforts into summer cookouts or year-round incentive gifts. The same is true of seasonal wearing apparel catalogs.

Absorbing Excess Production Capacity To enjoy the economies of scale, it is sometimes desirable to add new products that can be produced with existing manufacturing facilities. A greeting card manufacturer, for example, originally concentrated on Christmas cards, then extended into less celebrated holidays (St. Patrick's Day, for instance), and now creates special occasions (Kid's Day, for example). In the long run such absorption of existing capacity lowers manufacturing costs overall.

Approaching Product Innovation

Product innovation is a top management responsibility. It calls for a constructive attitude, one favorable to innovation, throughout the organization hierarchy. Although product research and development is properly a marketing function, as few as 10 percent of all companies view it as such, preferring to leave such decisions to the production people.

Alternative approaches that have been used within organizations to meld the expertise of production people and marketing people include product planning committees, new-product departments, product managers, outside specialists, and venture teams. Such structures are concerned with basic principles of market segmentation and product differentiation as well as product positioning and price discrimination.[6]

Market segmentation involves a division of the total heterogeneous market into smaller and more homogeneous units. Such segments comprise a unique market, large enough to be profitable yet small enough to be distinctive and homogeneous. Thus, the total market is viewed as a series of demand curves rather than as a single demand curve. Segmentation can be performed on the basis of geographic, demographic, and/or psychographic characteristics of the marketplace.

Product differentiation can be either a real or simply an advertised difference between a firm's product and that of its competition in terms of a specific appeal or use. When a detergent is promoted as providing "whiter whites," that claim must be factual. On the other hand, Lucky Strike cigarettes decades ago were advertised with the slogan "It's toasted," but so was the tobacco in *any* cigarette. Put simply, product differentiation involves some distinctive way of treating a product for specific appeal or use.

[6] For a more comprehensive discussion of these principles, refer to Chapter 7.

Price discrimination is one way of creating product differentiation. An example of price discrimination involves identical products sold at different prices: one in a discount department store (where there is minimal personal service) and one in a traditional department store (where there is usually the assistance of a salesperson).

Product positioning is the use of product differences to attract a particular market segment. Thus, the principles of both product differentiation and market segmentation are combined. The Mustang is an automobile manufactured by Ford as is the Granada; yet they are different and each has a specific positioning to a particular market segment. The so-called up-scale catalogs, Neiman-Marcus, Horchow, Sakowitz, have their own product array and each appeals to specific market segments. So do the "outdoor" catalogs of L. L. Bean, Orvis, Eddie Bauer, and Early Winters.

PRODUCT CLASSIFICATIONS

Some firms are concerned with both consumer markets and industrial markets. Thus, they need to understand the distinctions between consumer goods and industrial goods and how these are respectively categorized. Such distinctions cannot always be made on the basis of product alone. A typewriter, for example, is categorized as consumer goods if it is used by a student for a term paper or by an individual writing a personal letter. The same typewriter is categorized as industrial goods if it is used within an organization for billing a shipment or writing a business letter. Likewise, a paper clip is consumer goods if it is used to attach the pages of the student's term paper and it is industrial goods if it is used to attach the pages of the billing for a shipment.

The ultimate uses to which products are put, as well as the manner in which they are purchased, determine whether these are classified as consumer goods or industrial goods.

Industrial goods are further characterized by their *derived* demand; that is, being ultimately dependent on the purchases of consumer goods.

Consumer Goods

Whereas industrial goods (and services) are those that become a part of the process of producing other goods, consumer goods (and services) are those used by the ultimate customer. These are generally categorized as convenience goods, shopping goods, and specialty goods.

Convenience goods are those that consumers tend to buy with minimal shopping effort. Included in this category are such products as toothpaste and deodorant, shaving cream and soap, as well as most drugs and groceries. The customer, generally through exposure to advertising or other promotion, knows the particular product (or a substitute) to buy before going out to make the purchase.

Shopping goods, as the name implies, are those that customers "shop" for and, in the process, compare price and quality of alternatives. Often they visit several stores and read a variety of advertisements as they make comparisons. Product examples in this categorization include clothing, appliances, furniture, and automobiles. The principle of shopping goods comparison explains why car dealers are often congregated. Trial is important in the evaluation of shopping goods whereas price is often secondary.

Specialty goods are those with brand identification and/or recognizable characteristics. Examples include women's and men's fashions, specialty cosmetics, and selected gift items. The unique offerings of many direct marketers fall into the category of specialty goods, not readily available elsewhere. The shopping process for specialty goods does not usually involve comparison or potential substitutes. Buyers of specialty goods are willing and able to make a special purchasing effort.

Industrial Goods

In the case of most consumer goods, the buyer usually visits the seller. The opposite is generally true of industrial goods: usually, the seller comes to the buyer. Direct marketing techniques are often used in lead generation among potential buyers of industrial goods. An IBM word-processing system, for example, is usually not shopped for in a retail store, but a well-designed direct mail letter can often entice an industrial prospect to invite an IBM representative to make a presentation.

A further characteristic of industrial goods is that their purchase usually involves group decision making, and, because a particular component represents only a part of the whole, industrial demand is usually fairly *inelastic*. Producers need a certain quantity of components of their total product, almost regardless of price. The demand for industrial goods *fluctuates* more widely than that for consumer goods.

Industrial products are usually classified as installations, accessory equipment, raw materials, fabricating materials and parts, and operating supplies and services.

Installations include not just buildings and facilities but also major equipment such as generators and diesel engines.

Accessory equipment is that which is used to aid and implement production such as machines, hand tools, and office equipment.

Raw materials are those destined to become part of another physical product but that have received substantially no processing up to the point of purchase by the industrial user.

Fabricating materials and parts, contrasted with raw materials, have already undergone some processing. For example, flour has been processed from wheat or pig iron has been processed from ore.

Operating supplies and services are similar to convenience goods in the consumer market. These include pencils and paper as well as floor wax and lubricating oil. This category

Figure 9-2 Product classifications.

includes maintenance contracts as well as janitorial services and supplies.

PICKING PRODUCTS FOR DIRECT MARKETING

In recent years the scope of products and services offered by direct marketers has expanded substantially. The axiom that "anything that can be sold, can be sold by mail" has become more and more important. The trend has been most pronounced among department stores and major catalog retailers as well as a host of specialty general merchandise firms including clothing, home furnishings, housewares, and gift items.

Another burgeoning category has been insurance and other financial products. Other major categories include magazines, books, sporting goods, crafts, and foods. Among industrial direct marketers, major product categories include office supplies and equipment as well as trade, professional, and educational services.

A pioneer in the sale of specialty products by mail order, notably through syndication to selected customer lists, is Aaron Adler, the former president of Stone & Adler, Inc. When Adler was queried by his colleague and business partner, Bob Stone, as to his own personal guidelines for picking mail-order merchandise suitable for sale outside of a catalog, Adler urged that you "keep your own feelings out of it." He went on to list these three basic criteria for product selection:[7]

Universality: Pick items that have widespread appeal to broad market segments or else specific lists that can be reached cost efficiently. Examples of such products include home movie outfits, small appliances, stereo equipment, watches, and kitchen utensils. Other examples include paint sprayers and power tools for homeowners as well as calculators for scientists and engineers.

Unusuality: A classic example of mail-order success was the offering of a Bell & Howell home movie outfit that included not only a camera, projector, and screen combined into a "package" but also film, processing, and special instructions. Although the components were generally available in retail stores, the unusual feature was the combination of a "home movie outfit" rather than just a "camera" or a "projector" or a "screen." Continuity book clubs with a theme, such as the many series offered by Time-Life Books, are another example of unusuality as are the kitchen knives made with chrome molybdenum.

Uniqueness: Aaron Adler cites as an example a commonplace item, such as an average radio, available in virtually thousands of retail stores, made distinctive by the addition of a high-intensity lamp, a radio log, or a special cabinet.

As a backup to these three basic requirements, Adler further suggests the asking of four critical questions:

1 Does the item offer utility and/or beauty to your prospect?
2 Does the item have the design or style your prospect relates to?
3 Is it priced right for your prospect's economic level?
4 Is it an item for which your prospect is

---

[7] Bob Stone, "Ways to Pick Direct Mail Merchandise," *Advertising Age,* December 30, 1974.

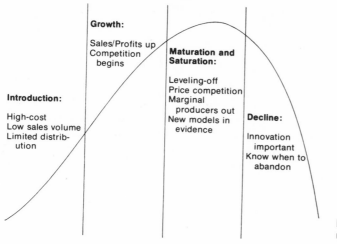

Growth:

Sales/Profits up
Competition
begins

**Maturation and
Saturation:**

Leveling-off
Price competition
Marginal
producers out
New models in
evidence

Introduction:

High-cost
Low sales volume
Limited distrib-
ution

Decline:

Innovation
important
Know when to
abandon

Figure 9-3 Concept of the product life cycle.

likely to feel a need or desire and derive benefits?

As Bob Stone sums it up, "Look at all your options. You have a great many."[8]

PRODUCT LIFE CYCLE

As visualized in Figure 9-3, all products go through a life cycle. Understanding this concept is quite important in direct marketing. Direct marketers should always know at what stage of the life cycle (and competitive environment) a product is to be able to plan and control new product development and to time new product introduction and growth. In reality, product life cycles overlap as products become obsolete and new alternatives emerge.

The stages of a product's life cycle are these:

Introduction: During this stage, customers' needs are analyzed, product concepts are tested, and the marketing plan is developed. Since the product is new, the sales volume is characteristically low and distribution is limited. Because of this, as well as developmental

expenses, the introduction stage involves high cost. Profit is yet to come. The product is being "pulled" (usually through promotional strategies) and distribution is "pushed."

Growth: As demand accelerates, sales increase and profits rise. "Me-too" competition, characterized by Schumpeter's model of the innovator and imitator, enters the market, usually with product variations. Sales and profits rise, and prices begin to decline as competition emerges.

Maturation and Saturation: There is a leveling off. Marginal producers are forced out by price competition. New models are in evidence; stabilization is marked by declining market growth.

Decline and Abandonment: At this stage, innovation once again becomes very important, prior to the next batch of imitators. The product in its existing form loses its appeal and is replaced by either differentiated or substitute products or it is discontinued altogether. Knowing how and when to abandon a product often is as important as innovating a new one.

To be able to pinpoint the exact length of a product life cycle is virtually impossible. Even the stages are most difficult to determine. For this reason, the concept of the product life

[8] Bob Stone, *Successful Direct Marketing Methods*, 2d ed., Crain Books, Chicago, 1979, p. 74.

cycle is most useful when viewed from a purely conceptual, rather than a chronological perspective. Short-lived fad products, such as the hula hoop, are relatively easy to monitor. Certain products, such as the hunting boots of L. L. Bean, might never go beyond the maturity and saturation stage. Still other products, such as electronic calculators, may experience gradual decline as they are replaced by alternatives.

A MODEL OF PRODUCT RESEARCH AND DEVELOPMENT

Product research and development takes time, an average of more than 2 years from generation of an idea to market penetration of a typical product.

The ill-fated Edsel automobile was brought to market in spite of a formal market research and development process, conducted in a textbook manner, which went unheeded. As the research had anticipated, the Edsel was a failure. The Xerox machine, the idea of a single inventor, but augmented by at least 15 years of product research, was an instant success with virtually no market research involved. The Xerox timing was right; the Edsel timing was wrong.

The gestation period for new products has varied widely from the 2-year average. Bird's Eye frozen foods, for example, were 15 years in development. Ban Roll-On deodorant took 6 years; Crest toothpaste took 10 years; Maxim concentrated coffee took 10 years. Minute Rice was 18 years in development and Whisk liquid detergent was just 1 year. The Polaroid camera was developed in 2 years whereas the Polaroid colorpack took 15 years. Color television was 55 years in development.

This time lag is inevitable because there are many steps in the process of product research and development, as shown in Figure 9-4. This illustrates one way of looking at the process. As presented here, five phases are involved:

planning and objectives, idea generation, feasibility studies, product development, and the implementation process.

Planning and Objectives

As a direct marketing organization evolves, it seeks optimum penetration of its potential markets with its existing product lines. Beyond that, it studies its facilities and human resources as it assesses its own capabilities of extending or augmenting existing product lines. Or, having control of a particular market segment, it may choose to diversify itself completely and offer an entirely different product line to its captive market.

During the first phase of product research and development, the organization must assess itself, determine its overall objectives, and conduct its planning for the short run as well as the long run, in accordance with its stated objectives.

At this stage, an organization's management might ask "What business are we in?" Is the firm in the *magazine* business, for example, or is it actually in the *information* business? If it is the latter, the area of product interest can be extended beyond magazines to books, newsletters, and even movies and television. When undergoing such a thought process, however, an organization must be mindful of its own qualifications and the relevance of the product it is considering. Not the least of its considerations are its production and marketing capabilities as well as an awareness of product differentiation and market segmentation.

Idea Generation

Those who adopt the marketing concept know that product ideas begin with establishing consumer needs and wants. Often such needs and wants can be determined through surveys, particularly those that probe future expectations.

Most organizations closely monitor activi-

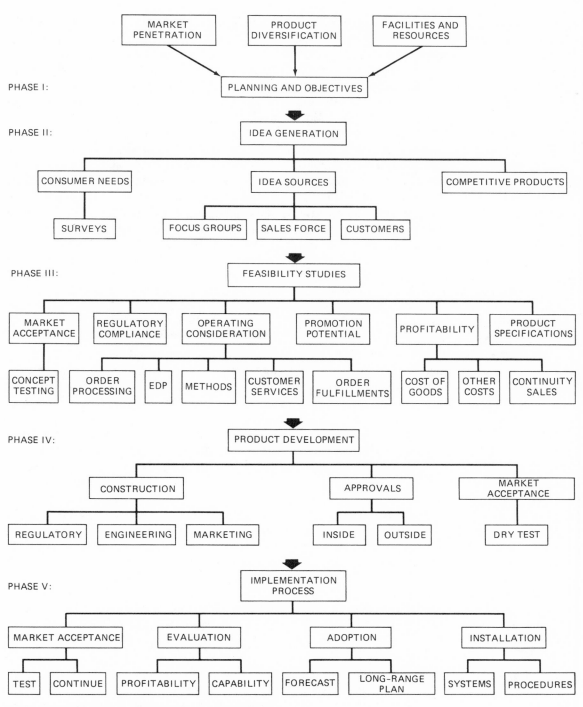

Figure 9-4   Model of product research and development.

ties of competitors to generate new product ideas. Using this source obviously minimizes research and development costs, but a competitor's activity might be declining, a fact not immediately discernible to the casual observer. Or, a competitor might employ a different strategy in calculating customer acquisition costs over an extended period of time. There might also be a relationship between a firm and the marketplace that is not transferable to a newcomer, even with an identical product.

There are many other sources of ideas for new products. Focus groups, for example, are often used to generate new product ideas and concepts. The engineering for power steering for automobiles evolved from a small group discussion of the difficulty encountered in parking parallel to the curb in limited space. Skilled personnel of the firm in day-to-day contact with the marketplace can also be used to generate product ideas. Procter & Gamble and other packaged goods manufacturers closely monitor their incoming correspondence for evidence of product shortcomings as well as potential product needs.

Feasibility Studies

During this phase of product research and development, reality takes over. Is the product practical? Is it operational? Is it feasible?

This is the time of reckoning. Concepts are generated, positioned, and tested. Will the proposed product be accepted in the marketplace? Does it coincide with the image of the firm? How should it be positioned; that is, how should it be *differentiated* for specific market segments? A key concern during the feasibility phase, too, is compliance with all applicable rules and regulations such as those relative to product safety.

Product specifications are a key consideration in this phase as are fulfillment and other operating considerations. Are methods in place for order processing, order fulfillment, and subsequent customer servicing?

During the feasibility phase, potential for promotion must be considered. Just how will the product be merchandised? Will it be "pulled" through advertising or "pushed" through selling? Especially important is the product's susceptibility to visualization and explanation through the written word.

Phase three is the time to think about the mathematical calculations and projections, relative to both short-range and long-run profitability for the new product. Will it be used for new customer acquisition, and, if so, is its markup adequate? Or, will its primary market be among existing customers? What will be the cost of goods sold? What will be the cost of promotion and how will general overhead costs be allocated? Does it offer a potential for continuity; that is, repeat or renewal sales?

Product Development

Phase four is concerned with actual product development: the product must be physically obtained or constructed. This calls for engineering knowledge and an awareness of regulatory considerations. Obviously, marketing needs to be kept in mind when we are concerned with matters such as packaging, display, and shipping. Often a variety of consultants are involved during product development, both inside and outside the organization, and their expertise should be considered. Many direct marketers set up a task force to coordinate all the phases of product research and development.

During this phase, market acceptance remains a continuing concern, as it has been throughout the process up to this point. Dry testing is a device frequently used to determine market acceptance of a product as it has evolved. The structure and content of a new magazine, for example, can be offered through direct marketing promotion even before the product exists. If market acceptance (as measured by money in hand from orders generated) is proven under these conditions, production can begin.

Implementation Process

During phase five, the concern for market acceptance continues, first, through test marketing; then, through "roll-out" or continuation. The direct marketer has the capability, at each stage of the implementation process, to evaluate what has happened to that point. Profitability should be monitored as well as the capacity for production and delivery.

Having obtained positive readings from the evaluation process, the new product (or product line) is adopted and included in both short-range forecasts as well as long-run plans. The product is installed within the organization, with appropriate and ongoing systems and procedures.

The cycle starts all over again or, as is the case with most progressive direct marketers, cycles for new product research and development overlap each other in the manner of the product life cycle described earlier in this chapter.

SUMMARY

Because products and services are the lifeblood of direct marketing and because old products are continually being replaced by new ones, the process of product research and development is an ongoing one in direct marketing. Most new products are failures for reasons that are primarily marketing-oriented; therefore an innovative approach is essential for both invention and automation.

A "product" has been defined as a set of both tangible and intangible attributes; these include a variety of factors such as packaging, color, and price as well as the prestige and services offered by both manufacturers and retailers. Products can come in all shapes and sizes, described as their breadth and depth, but ultimately they must provide *benefits* to

users. The reasons direct marketers add new products are these: to complete a product line, diversify a product line, use an existing market or channel of distribution, combat seasonal peaks and valleys, absorb excess production capacity.

To achieve product innovation, the direct marketer should think in terms of *market segmentation* (dividing the total heterogeneous market into smaller and more homogeneous units); *product differentiation* (real or advertised differences between the firm's products and that of its competition, especially relative to particular market segments); *price discrimination* (one form of product differentiation); and *product positioning* (relating product differences to a particular use or a particular market segment).

Broad classifications of products include consumer goods and industrial goods. The former category is broken down into convenience goods, shopping goods, and specialty goods. Industrial goods, in turn, are subdivided into installations, accessory equipment, raw materials, fabricating materials and parts, and operating supplies and services.

Products especially appropriate for direct marketing are characterized by their universality, unusuality, and uniqueness. Product life cycle is a useful concept in conveying that all products go through a period of introduction, growth, maturation, and decline.

A model for product research and development includes these five phases: planning and objectives, idea generation, feasibility studies, product development, and the implementation process.

CASE: RESEARCHING AND DEVELOPING A NEW PRODUCT

Learning Objective

This case study views product research and development in a systematic way in terms of the model presented in this chapter: planning and objectives, idea generation, feasibility studies, product development, and the implementation process.

Overview

Products are the lifeblood of direct marketing. But, since all products evolve through a life cycle wherein old products become obsolete, the need for an ongoing system for new product research and development becomes apparent. Central to consideration of new product research and development is determination of need.

Procedure

Read the learning objective, the overview, and the case that follows. Identify the product need and elaborate on the alternative fulfillments of this need. Demonstrate how this particular product development can lead to new customer acquisition and show how the long-range value of such a customer can be determined.

Case

Old American Insurance Company of Kansas City, Missouri, had been for 25 years a direct marketer of insurance, primarily to senior citizens, when Medicare was introduced in 1966. The Medicare program, an adjunct to Social Security, was designed by the federal government to provide for the health care needs of those persons age 65-plus as well as those younger persons suffering from a disability entitling them to receive Social Security benefits.

Old American was already a provider of personal insurance coverages (life, accident, hospital) to senior citizens and had a firsthand knowledge of this market segment as well as large mailing lists of older persons. The introduction of the Medicare program held both negative and positive implications for the future course of its business. But, because Old American's direct marketed products had his-

torically been viewed as *supplements* to basic coverages, the firm was as interested in researching what Medicare could not provide for as well as what it could.

Product Need   Some 18 million older Americans found Medicare to be a welcome solution to their health care needs when it was introduced with the stroke of a pen in 1966. And yet, as those covered under it soon learned, Medicare went only so far.

Medicare was designed as a partnership. Should a covered person become sick or injured, the government would pay the major share of covered hospital and medical expenses. To complete the partnership, the beneficiary paid the rest.

But, here was the rub. With health care costs rising faster than any other single item in an American's budget, the share of Medicare-covered expenses that the individual had to pay often added up to many hundreds or even thousands of dollars. Further, it became apparent, not all health care needs were "covered." Many Americans, even with Medicare, found themselves with enormous bills to pay. Furthermore, the inadequacy of Medicare coverage continued to increase so that, after a decade of its existence, the Senate Committee on Aging estimated that only 38 percent of the health care needs of senior citizens were being provided for by Medicare insurance.

At this point, and as the years progressed, the increasing inadequacy of Medicare coverage became apparent to the product researchers at Old American. Furthermore, since the company had traditionally direct marketed products to augment existing basic coverages, it recognized the need for an insurance product to complement Medicare.

The shortfalls of the Medicare hospital expense program were categorized as these: (1) deductibles, (2) coinsurance, (3) covered services, (4) reasonable charges. These shortfalls were summarized as follows:

Deductibles The first charges applicable when a covered person enters a hospital. In 1983 this was $304 plus the cost of the first three pints of blood. This amount was paid, in any event, by the hospitalized person under Medicare.

Medicare also provided for payment of covered doctor and other medical expenses beyond hospitalization. The deductible on this portion of the coverage, during 1983, was $75.

Coinsurance When hospitalized for more than 60 days during 1983, the covered person was responsible for the first $76 of covered services through the 90th day of hospitalization. When hospitalized for more than 90 days but less than 151 days, the covered person paid $152 of expenses for each day until a so-called lifetime reserve was used up. After the 151st day, or whenever the "lifetime reserve" had been used up prior to that, all expenses had to be paid by the patient.

Coinsurance also applied to the doctor part of Medicare. The covered person paid 20 percent of what the government considered to be "reasonable charges" for "covered expenses."

Covered Services Both hospital and doctor expenses are specifically defined by Medicare and are not all-inclusive. For example, the difference in cost between a semi-private and a private hospital room is not covered nor is special nursing care. Psychiatric care is not always covered. Nursing home care is limited to that within defined skilled nursing facilities and only through 100 days (and only following a period of hospital confinement) with a coinsurance amount of $38 applicable during 1983 for the 21st through the 100th day.

Reasonable Charges As part of the doctor and medical expense of Medicare, 80 percent of what the government considers "reasonable, prevailing or customary" charges for

"covered services" is paid. Such charges are determined by the administrators of Medicare and are not always the same as the amount actually billed with the Medicare recipient being responsible for the difference, if any.

The Model

Phase I. Planning and Objectives Early in its history, Old American Insurance Company had established as an objective the provision of supplemental personal insurance coverages to older Americans. Its facilities and resources, including product design and servicing, were attuned to products of the type to fulfill expressed needs. For 25 years prior to Medicare, the firm had done a reasonably effective job of penetrating this market to the extent that it had several hundred thousand older age active policyholders and, additionally, had substantial prospect mailing lists of older Americans. A product line to complement the government's Medicare program would fit into the company's overall planning and objectives.

Phase II. Idea Generation A consumer need, a product to provide for the deductible and coinsurance provisions of Medicare, was readily apparent from a study of the marketplace together with input from existing policyholders. Whereas deductibles and coinsurance served a purpose in the structure of insurance products; that is, they rightfully involved the recipient in part of the cost, these amounts had become more burdensome as they increased, without exception, each year after 1966. Furthermore, the Medicare program provided no hospitalization coverage at all after 5 months or after 3 months for those who had used up their "lifetime reserve." And, although such a length of stay is rare, the insurance company recognized that a primary need for its product was provision for a catastrophic length of hospitalization.

Although competitive products were not immediately apparent with the advent of Medicare, they began to proliferate in the years after 1966, especially among those carriers concentrating in the senior citizen market. These competitors, along with consumer surveys and the company's own creative group brainstorming, generated ideas for specific new insurance products.

Phase III. Feasibility Studies   Various steps detailed in Figure 9-4 were considered as the feasibility of the new product line was studied. Since insurance companies are licensed and regulated (including approval of their products) in each of the states in which they operate, this is a major feasibility consideration.

Operating considerations included the need for increased staffing for servicing policyholders relative to an admittedly complex product line. Increased staffing was needed, too, within the benefit department to anticipate a large influx of claim processing complicated by the intricacies of what Medicare did and did not cover as well as the issue of "reasonable charges."

"Costs of goods sold" to an insurance company is, basically, the amount it pays out in claims, and, for this product line, the calculations had to take into account the higher-than-normal incidences of such costs, due to the nature of the product as well as the nature of the marketplace. Ultimate profitability was to accrue, it was determined, on continuity sales, the sale of additional coverages to those making an initial purchase.

Product specifications, promotion potential, and market acceptance, the last involving testing of a variety of concepts over time, all intertwined during creative group discussions of feasibility. In fact, this intertwining became and continues to be an ongoing process.

Phase IV. Product Development   In addition to constructing insurance products that satisfy consumer wants and needs, the design must also meet a variety of statutory requirements in the various states as well as an abundance of regulations applicable to promotional strategy. And, of course, the structure of the product must be such that it can be advertised effectively and understood by an older person. This involves proper packaging and a minimum of choices.

A variety of creative input is required during product development. For an insurance product such as this, input comes from legal, actuarial, and accounting people, as well as marketing people who are concerned with *both* the sale and service of the new line.

It was agreed that the product line would be called "Medicare-Plus." The initial coverages would be for only the deductible and coinsurance portions of the hospital part of Medicare. Subsequently, those who purchased the basic policy would be offered, at their option, "riders" to provide for the coinsurance portion of stays in a skilled nursing facility, graduate registered nurse care, and miscellaneous hospital expenses not paid by Medicare. The product line would later be augmented to include coverage for the coinsurance portion not paid by Medicare for covered doctor and other medical expenses. No provision was made for payments on other than "covered services" nor was there any provision for payments beyond the Medicare definition of "reasonable charges." There was, however, provision for catastrophic hospital expenses beyond those paid by Medicare, up to a total of $50,000 in lifetime benefits.

The basic product containing hospital benefits featured five guarantees:

Guaranteed Benefit No. 1: Medicare-Plus paid the deductible and coinsurance amounts during hospital confinement beginning after the policy effective date.

Guaranteed Benefit No. 2: Medicare-Plus paid hospital costs, up to $304 a day during

1983, even when Medicare benefits ran out during lengthy or frequent hospital stays, up to a limit of $50,000 over and above what Medicare paid for hospitalization.

Guaranteed Benefit No. 3: Medicare-Plus automatically adjusted to pay the increase in the deductible and coinsurance amounts, which had become an annual reality.

Guaranteed Benefit No. 4: Medicare-Plus guaranteed the policyholder an opportunity to add *additional* benefits, such as those for skilled nursing facilities, graduate registered nurse care, and medical expenses, regardless of the state of health of the policyholder at the time these coverages were offered.

Guaranteed Benefit No. 5: Medicare-Plus guaranteed to issue and renew the policy, regardless of preexisting conditions, unless and until a total of $50,000 in lifetime benefits had been paid. Rates could be increased only if they were increased for all policyholders in the state of the insured's residence.

Phase V. Implementation Process Because the senior citizen market and especially that portion age 65-plus is a well-defined market segment[9] and because Old American Insurance Company owned an extensive mailing list of active policyholders, former policyholders, and prospective policyholders within this market segment, direct marketing techniques were used in experimentation tests to measure market acceptance. Certain media, notably, specifically directed magazines and newspapers read by older persons, were also tested.

Market segmentation had to go beyond simple age differentiation as Old American employed its Life-Style Market Segmentation model[10] to increase the effectiveness of its reach. Use of the model demonstrated conclusively that not all persons 65-plus behaved the

[9] For an extensive discussion of the senior citizen market segment, see pp. 169–175, in Chapter 7.

[10] For a description of Life-Style Market Segmentation, see pp. 93–105, in Chapter 4.

same way as buyers. The rural and urban buyer, for example, were different. Those who moved to high-rise apartment buildings in central cities behaved differently from those who moved to sunbelt communities, and these, in turn, behaved differently from those who remained in their old neighborhoods. Market segmentation, even beyond the simplicity of age, is an important consideration for direct marketing effectiveness.

The promotion medium, direct mail, is reproduced in part in Figure 9-5 and Figure 9-6, the former demonstrating the offering of the Medicare-Plus hospital expense policy and the latter the offering of the Medicare-Plus doctor expense policy. A variety of formats and copy have been tested over the product's life cycle and those shown are simply representative.

The product line has been expanded, during the implementation process, from basic hospital expense coverage to augmented hospital expense coverage (skilled nursing facility, graduate registered nurse care, doctor, and other medical expenses). These alternatives have been provided through an upgrading process in a manner determined by the type of product that the policyholder initially acquired.

The product itself has been differentiated from its competitors in that acceptance of an application is guaranteed. Preexisting health conditions are not excluded from coverage. Thus, the policy is immediately effective when issued for any hospitalization for treatment of sickness or injury beginning after the effective date. Operating procedures and systems have been continually updated to expedite both policy issue and benefit processing. The adoption of the product line has brought about major shifts in both short-range forecasting and long-run planning. Profitability has been and remains a major concern as medical costs continue to soar and those costs not covered by Medicare continue to increase at an average

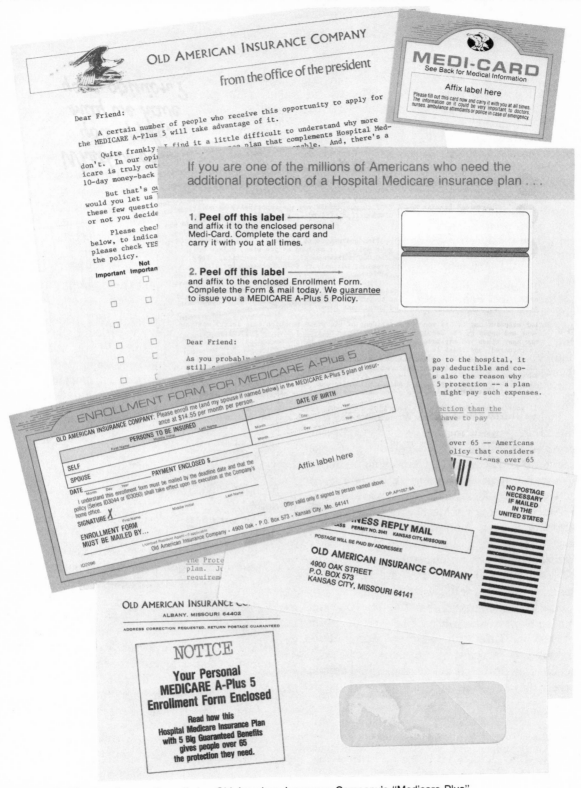

Figure 9-5 Direct mail promotion offering Old American Insurance Company's "Medicare-Plus" hospital expense policy.

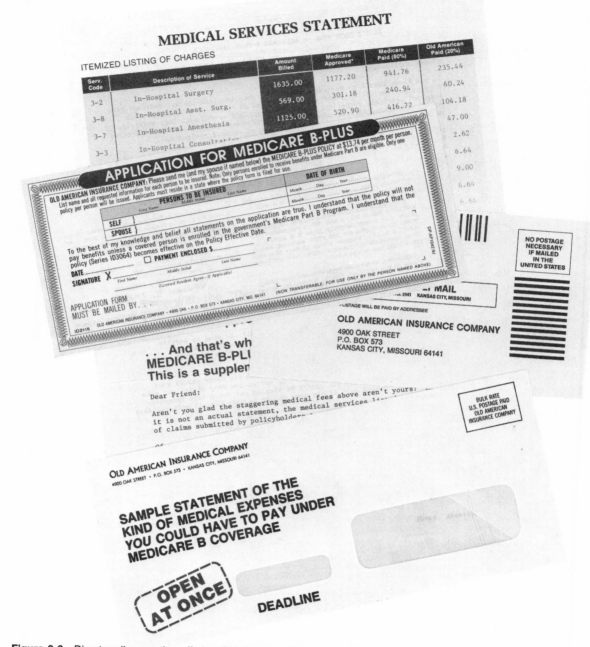

Figure 9-6 Direct mail promotion offering Old American Insurance Company's "Medicare-Plus" doctor expense policy.

annual rate of approximately 13 percent. In fact, during a "catch-up" process, the deductible and coinsurance portions of the hospital expense part of Medicare increased 27 percent at the beginning of 1982.

No way has yet been found to effectively and profitably extend coverage beyond those services specifically covered and enumerated by Medicare nor has a way been found to pay benefits beyond the Medicare-defined "reasonable charges." Additionally, federal legislation, called the Baucus Amendment, has placed severe restrictions on both the coverage and advertising of private insurance products designed to supplement Medicare. Restrictions have increased discretionary costs to the consumer and, in many cases, have curtailed product availability. Curtailment has resulted from both the rebellion against higher prices in the marketplace as well as the profit squeeze on suppliers.

DISCUSSION QUESTIONS

1 Both invention and automation play a significant role in product or service innovation. Distinguish between the two.
2 Define the word "product." How is your definition related to the word "benefit"?
3 Why must product research and development be an ongoing process? How do organizations implement the process?
4 What is price discrimination and how is it related to product differentiation?
5 According to Aaron Adler, what are the three basic criteria for selection of mail-order products?
6 Describe the concept of the product life cycle.
7 What is the average length of time between the generation of a new product idea and penetration of a market with it? Why does it take this long or longer?
8 What categories of consumer goods are most commonly sold through mail order?

PRODUCT POLICY AND STRATEGY FOR DIRECT MARKETERS

In direct marketing it is imperative that one understand the concepts of product line and product mix. An array of products intended for essentially similar uses is a *product line*. *Product mix* comprises the variety of lines and/or individual products offered by a firm.

A direct marketer's catalog might feature a product line of wearing apparel for women or it might contain product lines for both women and men. The product mix within a direct marketer's catalog might also include a variety of household accessory or specialty gift items in addition to wearing apparel.

The contraction of product lines or mix is often as important as the expansion of the product line itself. It is important, too, to look at product line renovation. This would include a redesigning of current products, new packaging, new materials, additives, or product differentiations. Direct marketers are often able to present new uses for old products, by having recipes accompany specialty foods, for example. Sometimes the image projected by a marketer suggests extension of product line or product mix. The brand name General Electric is applied to a broad spectrum of electric products from vacuum cleaners to light bulbs to smoke alarms.

Because customer lists and data about these customers are such a vital part of the total process, direct marketers have become particularly adept at upgrading and downgrading within product lines. Not only is the initial purchase by a customer increased and built on over a period of time but direct marketers also have the capability of offering less costly substitutes to those of their customers who demonstrate a preference for such. Thus, the up-scale merchandise contained in the Horchow Collection is augmented with lower-priced product lines contained within the firm's Trifles catalog, and its Grand Finale catalog offers close-out merchandise at discount prices.

ROLE OF PRODUCT POLICY

Every direct marketer needs to define a product policy.

A product policy is simply a management guide as to what products will be made or sold, product lines as well as product mixes, and what attributes these will have. Such a formal statement provides guidelines for management decisions about product line and product mix including additions, deletions, or alterations. It forces management to evaluate the firm's assets (and its liabilities) and it provides impetus for change and innovation.

The major responsibility for product policy lies with top management. Its establishment involves an evaluation of:

- Strengths and weaknesses of the firm
- Marketing strategy
- Technological base
- Financial strength
- Workforce resources and specializations
- Marketing strengths and weaknesses

Implementation of a formal product policy should be in the form of a statement and should be related to these types of decisions:

- Evaluation of new product ideas
- Determination to "make" or "buy"
- Scrapping of old products

PLANNED OBSOLESCENCE

"As a society becomes increasingly affluent," postulated John Kenneth Galbraith in *The Affluent Society,* "wants are increasingly created by the process by which they are satisfied." Galbraith continued: "Increases in consumption, the counterpart of increases in production, act by suggestion or emulation to create wants . . . wants thus come to depend on output." This phenomenon was called the "dependence effect" by Galbraith and it was an inevitable characteristic of our affluent society.[1]

Although planned obsolescence has often been viewed as a purposeful process in which limited durability is built into products to maintain sales and jobs, the process can also be viewed as a result of innovation. Some consumers would willingly sacrifice durability in favor of frequently changing styles.

Obsolescence, whether planned or not, occurs in one of four ways: *technological, postponed, physical,* or *style.* Many direct marketers are in the forefront with innovative product positioning, thus an understanding of the nature of obsolescence is important to them.

Technological Obsolescence Technical improvements in a product will often make earlier models obsolete. The introduction of automatic transmissions in automobiles, at least for a time, made stick gearshifts obsolete. Technically, features such as power steering and power brakes represented functional product improvements that were optional to the buyer. Heat pumps, too, represent a technological improvement but have certainly not yet replaced traditional heating systems.

Postponed Obsolescence Sometimes, even though improvements in technology have been made, these are purposely withheld until there is a need for demand stimulation. There are those who even contend that some technology, such as an alternative energy source, might be postponed indefinitely in deference to investments in existing technology.

[1] John Kenneth Galbraith, *The Affluent Society*, college ed., Houghton Mifflin Company, Boston, 1960, p. 158.

Physical Obsolescence At the other extreme from postponed technology are those products that are designed to last only a limited time, such as light bulbs or batteries.

Style Obsolescence This form of obsolescence, which is generally quite obvious in the clothing and automobile industries, is the type most often criticized. The product appears out of date even though it still has a useful life.

STYLE, FASHION, FAD

Planned obsolescence and its accompaniments of style, fashion, and fad are controversial. The question frequently arises as to whether or not demand created by obsolescence can be economically justified. Are marketing efforts most efficiently implemented insofar as public policy and economic utilization are concerned?

To approach such questions, the direct marketer needs to know something about the phenomena of style and fashion. The two words are *not* synonymous.

Style has a long-range perspective to it. It denotes a distinctiveness of design or construction or even expression. Thus, there are styles in housing, in clothing, in automobiles, as well as in art and literature. Style is ever present although particular styling may ebb and flow over time.

Fashion denotes the prevailing, the currently accepted, or the popular style. Fashion is thus the style of the moment that has gained popular acceptance.

Fads are short-lived fashions that peak in popularity quickly and disappear almost as quickly. A fad usually has a novelty feature and a relatively short life-span. The hula hoop was a fad as were pet rocks. The fad may die and later be resurrected as has been the case with the Yo-Yo.

Fashion is a tremendous stimulus to innovation. The trend toward nonconformity is itself a trend toward conformity, and the fashion cycle begins again. Witnesses to the fact are men's wide neckties and pinstripe and double-breasted suits.

Direct marketers must have a keen awareness of fashion as well as the stage in the life cycle of a fashion so that they can merchandise accordingly. The trend toward management science and computerization cannot replace the judgment of the buyer on the scene who is face to face with the reality of fashion change.

BRAND NAMES AND TRADEMARKS

The American Marketing Association's definition of *brand* is: "A name, term, symbol or design or a combination of them, which is intended to identify the goods or services of the seller or groups of sellers and to differentiate them from those of competitors."[2] A brand name consists of words in a special formation. Such words might be generic in a particular combination or they might be nondictionary words.

When such words are placed in a particularly distinctive arrangement or illustrated in some way symbolically they are a *trademark*. A trademark, when registered with the Copyright Office, is a legal term; that is, a brand name given legal protection. Coca Cola is a *brand name*. The manner in which it is lettered and illustrated is a *trademark*. Green Giant is a brand name. In combination with an illustration of the Green Giant, it becomes a trademark. The little girl under the umbrella on a package of Morton's salt and the arm and hammer in connection with the distinctive lettering on a package of Arm & Hammer

baking soda translate a brand name into a trademark.

Brand Names as Product Differentiation

Brand names, along with distinctive product design and advertising, are a form of product differentiation. Combining these with the characteristics of the product itself serves to develop an image of the product for customers. The buyer's choice is made dependent on whether or not the image projected is a favorable one.

Brand names also serve to establish reputability. In recent years in the Soviet Union, where historically products in the marketplace had not been associated with their makers, the practice of using brand names has scored a pragmatic victory over earlier Communist economics and practices. The reason given is that, through brand names, consumers are able to check the output of Soviet plants with good reputations and avoid those with poor quality.

Thus, consumer discontent was shifted from the Communist party to the plant with the poor reputation. A form of consumer sovereignty was created, too, a means to identify errant plants and punish shoddy production and to reward quality.[3] Brand names, thus, become measures of quality and integrity.

Brand names enhance advertising and sales promotion programs, help increase control and share of the market, reduce price comparisons, and facilitate the expansion of the product mix of a firm.

"Battle of the Brands"

One of the more significant marketing developments of recent years has been the so-called battle of the brands. Although brand names traditionally had been assigned by manufacturers, there has been an increasing tendency for retailers, as well as wholesalers, to estab-

---

[2] Committee on Definitions, *Marketing Definitions: A Glossary of Marketing Terms*, American Marketing Association, 1960, p. 8.

[3] Theodore Levitt, "Branding on Trial," *Harvard Business Review*, March–April 1966.

lish their own brand names. Some of these retailers, Sears, Wards, J. C. Penney, Safeway, L. L. Bean, Radio Shack, have been extremely successful in superseding manufacturer brand names. The Sears Kenmore washer carries its own image, just as does a comparable RCA Whirlpool washer, even though both are made by the same manufacturer.

A variety of familiar direct marketing brand names are shown in Figure 10-1. Note the preponderance of these associated with retailing rather than manufacturing.

Brand Name Selection

Some brand names have become common household words and they are now generic. This emphasizes the importance of protecting brand names during their usage. Such former brand names as nylon, linoleum, deep freeze, cellophane, aspirin, celluloid, and kerosene are now generic.

A brand name that is to be heavily promoted not only should be legally protectable—it *must* be protected or the brand's owner may lose title to it. When the word "Coke" became a common substitute in the minds of consumers for the brand name "Coca Cola," it was recognized and protected by the manufacturer. When Kodak, in an effort to protect its own trademark, advertises "If it isn't an Eastman, it isn't a Kodak," it is reiterating its right to its brand name. Xerox and Crock-Pot have taken even further precautions, as demonstrated in Figures 10-2 and 10-3.

Some trademarks have become so popular that they are recognizable through illustrations alone without words. Can you identify the trademarks in Figure 10-4?

A brand name may convey something about the characteristics of a product, too. Here are some examples of brand names that do that: Ditto, Thermopane, Spic and Span, Mustang, Beautyrest, Whirlpool, Duz, Close-Up, Trac-II, Frigidaire.

Ideally, brand names should be easy to say

and they should be short and crisp. Here are some examples: Crest, Tide, Ban, Time, Gleem, Saks, Gumps, Figi's, Swiss Colony.

Brand names, too, should be versatile enough to permit expansion of the product line. Don't fall into the trap that Heinz did, with its original Heinz "57" Varieties, when variety number "58" came along. And, although Frigidaire was a good name for a refrigerator, the name had a negative connotation when the line was expanded to ovens and ranges, just as the brand name Hotpoint proved ineffective for a television receiver.

PACKAGING AND LABELING

Packaging has become a characteristic of a product and, as a result, it is an integral part of product planning. So has labeling, not only for identity but also for instruction and image creation. In this context both packaging and labeling are closely allied to brand name as well as overall promotional strategy.

Reasons for Packaging

A basic and fundamental reason for packaging is to provide utility in handling. This is especially true for direct marketers who must ultimately make shipments of individual items as well as combinations of many different and nonuniform items. Packages also identify size and content in addition to serving as protection. And, they keep products from wear and contamination, thus providing a fresh look on arrival and opening.

Another very important aspect of packaging is its promotional value. Especially on retailer shelves, the package serves as a point-of-purchase advertisement. It can do the same thing for direct marketers when it is in the customer's possession. Products are thus further differentiated through packaging. Changing the design of a package, as is frequently done with consumer convenience goods, is sometimes used to convey a modernization or

Figure 10-1 Direct marketing brand names.

Figure 10-2 Protection of its trademark by Xerox.

contemporary styling, even though the product inside the package has not been changed.

Other promotional possibilities involve package designs with particular features such as the potential for reuse or as a container or storage device. The advertising copy on the package thus has an extended life. Packaging may even increase sales by those who actually purchase the package, sometimes as a collector's item. A large trader's market has evolved in Avon cosmetics containers, for example, and Jim Beam bourbon special bottles are collectors' items.

Reasons for Labeling

Labels on products serve not only to identify the product and/or the seller but also to provide descriptive and instructional information about the product.

For brand identification, virtually every Sunkist orange contains a label stamped on it. An oxford cloth shirt from the L. L. Bean catalog identifies the source of this direct marketed product through a label on the collar. Other brand labels might identify wool or cotton or a particular grade of fabric.

Labels can also carry descriptions of the product such as size or contents. They can contain instructive information such as that for laundering.

Some labeling is mandatory. The Food and Drug Administration establishes labeling requirements for products over which it has jurisdiction. The Federal Trade Commission is concerned with false and misleading labeling. Certain products, such as those containing wool or fur, have standard forms of labeling. And, of course, there are a host of labeling requirements relative to safety.

IMAGE BUILDING THROUGH PRODUCTS

Although brand names, packages, and labels along with advertising and other promotional strategies create product and supplier preferences, it is the product itself which must ultimately lead to repurchasing. In the process a desirable image must be established for the product line, the product mix, and the supplier. Product characteristics that do this include, first and foremost, the quality of the product itself. This does not necessarily mean either high quality or low quality but, rather, quality that is consistent with expectation. Related to this important matter of quality is the accompanying warranty and servicing that every reliable direct marketer provides to enhance image and reputation for reliability.

Certain direct marketed products are characterized by their design, size, or color. These characteristics, in turn, create expectations and reorders with those characteristics in mind. Certain colors, for example, have a psychological association with the outdoors and are expected by those who purchase outdoor products. Large packages offer economy whereas small ones offer convenience, and thus certain products become associated with certain uses. Unlike traditional retailers, however, mail-order firms do not generally offer a great range of sizes but, rather, establish and become known for particular sizes.

When all of these image-building characteristics are taken into account it becomes quite clear that product positioning or differentiating products for market segments is a highly relevant aspect of direct marketing.

CONTINUITY SELLING AND CROSS-SELLING

Direct marketers are concerned with creating, caring for, and keeping customers. The objective of profitable direct marketing is not a single sale but, rather, the acquisition of a customer who will remain active for an extended period of time.

Continuity selling is a hallmark of direct marketers. From the inception of the Book-of-the-Month Club a half century ago to its present stature, with a host of imitators, the

Figure 10-3 Protection of its trademark by Crock-Pot.

Gerber	Arm & Hammer	Yellow Pages
Bon-Ami	Mercedes-Benz	Hallmark
Anheuser–Busch	Polo by Ralph Lauren	Merrill Lynch
Cadillac	Bell System	Wool Institute
Shell Oil	Harry & David	American Heart Association

Figure 10-4 Whose trademarks are these?

principle of continuity selling has become well established. The principle applies not only to book clubs but to record clubs as well as magazine subscriptions and insurance policies. It even applies to periodic shipments of fruit, cheese, or other food items. For a long time, a continuity mail-order marketer called Around-the-World-Shoppers Club shipped a variety of unusual gift items monthly to subscribers, each month from a different foreign country.

Often, such continuity programs involve a sometimes controversial marketing technique known as the "negative option." That is, a book will be shipped to a club member monthly unless the member, on receiving advance notification, elects to cancel that shipment. Of course, an undesired shipment can be returned at anytime for credit. Automatic renewals of insurance policies are a variation of this technique, as are automatic renewals of magazine subscriptions.

Cross-selling, like continuity selling, is another important characteristic of direct marketing. With this technique, new and related products or even unrelated ones are offered to existing customers. For example, a purchaser of books and records might be offered other books and records or possibly an insurance policy or a home power tool. The most important attribute of cross-selling is the manner in which the customer views the direct marketer in terms of reputation, reliability, and overall image.

Both continuity selling and cross-selling have become an important part of the product policy and strategy of direct marketing.

FULFILLMENT OPERATIONS

A vital adjunct to any product or service (and this is especially true in direct marketing) is the fulfillment of an order after it has been received. Adequate fulfillment, by minimizing or shortening the time between ordering and receiving, can alleviate two distinct handicaps inherent in mail order: (1) a time lag between placing an order and receiving it; (2) a lack of familiarity with the actual product, which has been purchased remotely by mail or telephone from a visualization or description contained in a direct response advertisement.

A product, we have already seen, comprises a great many tangible and intangible attributes. One of these intangible attributes is delivery of the product in the manner promised and presumed. Ultimate success in direct marketing depends on adequate fulfillment.

Nature of Fulfillment

The fulfillment process actually begins with the offering and initial promotional materials. In sequence, the complete fulfillment process consists of the following:

Offer The product/service offer and the attendant promotion material should be properly addressed and directed and be relevant to the needs of the addressee. The description should be adequate and fair. Copywriters and designers should comprehend the offer as well as its relevance to the needs of the prospect. All disclosures should be made initially and all options, such as sizes and colors, should be clearly stated. Credit terms should be specified. Nothing should be left to the imagination during this initial stage.

A relevant product offering is a timely one and a clear one. Since an order form is a contractual document, it should be legally correct as well as distinct, clear, and easy to follow.

Response Direct marketers generally receive responses (inquiries) or transactions (orders) through the mail or by telephone. If the latter, operators need to be especially diligent in collecting order information. How an organization handles the receipt of a mail or telephone order is a critical juncture in the fulfillment process insofar as total product satisfaction is concerned.

Processing After orders have been received by mail or recorded by telephone, there begins a process that involves editing and coding as well as credit checking and capturing of vital data for mailing list update. It includes, too, preparation of a series of documents such as shipping labels, billing notifications, and inventory instructions.

At this stage, particular attention is given to the possibility that there might be a delay in shipping an order. In that event, acknowledgements are expedited and nonreceipt complaints are anticipated.

Shipping An alert inventory control system is often the key to proper and timely shipment. Out-of-stock and back orders, involving separate shipments later, are costly to the direct marketer and frustrating to the customer and may even result in corrective action by governmental agencies. Order filling and shipping involves attention to inventory availability and to picking, packing, weighing, and shipping the order, in the most economical and expeditious way.

Billing Once an order is on its way, the organization should receive payment as expeditiously as possible. Possibly payment arrangement was made in advance through a credit card. If not and if payment did not accompany the order, then clear billing instructions, with appropriate follow-up, are vital not only to assure payment but also to assure customer goodwill.

This need for clarity also extends to proper receipt and posting of the payment, especially when extended-pay options are offered. We often hear accusations of computer "errors," such as incorrect billings and incorrect postings, but more than likely these are human instruction errors.

Complaint Since 100 percent quality control is often impractical, shipping and billing errors inevitably occur and only prompt handling and adjustment can overcome these. A customer might receive an incorrect shipment or be erroneously billed for a product that has been paid for or be billed incessantly for a product that was returned. Many times such occurrences become extremely complicated but all should be meticulously adjusted.

Inquiry Not all communications from customers relevant to fulfillment are complaints. Many are inquiries. Many seek further information and some request additional orders. These, too, are a proper concern of the fulfillment operation and properly fall under the heading of "customer service."

Fulfillment Standards

Stanley J. Fenvessy, president of Fenvessy Associates, Inc., of New York and author of the Dow Jones–Irwin publication *Keep Your Customers and Keep Them Happy,* has put forth this series of fulfillment standards for direct marketers:[4]

Turnaround time on orders: Customers should receive their orders not more than 20 calendar days from the time they mailed them, less if they phone.

Response time on written inquiries or complaints: Customers should receive a response during the calendar week following the week the letter was mailed.

In stock condition: If back orders constitute more than 3 percent of total shipments, there is a problem. An exception could be a fashion line, in which case a goal of 10 percent back order should be set.

Ratio between orders and customer contacts: Well-run general merchandise mail-order businesses receive four customer communications for each 100 orders processed. In the low-price gift business, the ratio is smaller; in fashion or high-ticket merchandise organizations, the rate can be as high as 10 percent.

Unit cost for total fulfillment service: This depends to some degree on the dollar size of the order. By far, most mail-order businesses fulfill for less than $1.50 excluding packing supplies, shipment charges, and credit costs.

Customer service promotion: In well-run customer service functions the ratio of clerks (mail readers, adjusters, typists, filers, etc.) to customer contacts is one clerk to six to eight contacts per hour.

Package delivery: A survey by the Direct Marketing Association showed that 97 percent of those catalog companies responding used United Parcel Service to ship 90 percent of their packages. The United States Postal Service was principally used for parcels too large or those consigned to destinations not handled by UPS.

Returns: These will vary by the type and price of the product offered. A 10 percent or higher rate of returns is not at all unusual if the direct marketer sells fashions or offers

[4] Stanley J. Fenvessy, "Introduction to Fulfillment," *Direct Marketing Manual,* New York, Direct Marketing Association, October 1979, p. 500:1.

books or other products with a 10-day inspection privilege. Such should be handled, usually, without question.

Credit cards: The revenues per order charged to bank and other credit cards are, on the average, 35 to 50 percent larger than in cash orders. Further, returns and adjustment ratios are lower. Many firms receive 40 percent of their volume from credit cards. Cost of the credit card services ranges from 3 to 6 percent of gross sales.

Avoiding Fulfillment Problems

Fenvessy also offers these 10 suggestions for keeping customers happy and avoiding fulfillment problems:

1 Clarify your promotions and offerings.

2 Don't promise service you can't deliver.

3 Date and control all incoming customer orders and correspondence.

4 Exercise care in billing and collection.

5 Do not abuse the back order privilege.

6 Instruct your customers on how to complain and on how to return merchandise.

7 Use the telephone.

8 Follow the maxim "the customer is always right."

9 Test your own service (as well as that of your competitors).

10 Accumulate data concerning the nature of customer calls and correspondence.

Quality Control

Fulfillment for direct marketers is a highly complex system. The nature of mail-order marketing, which involves remote ordering by customers as well as time lags in receipt of merchandise, underscores the need for meticulous quality control in the fulfillment operation.

Constant monitoring of the process is desirable. Operations research techniques are often used to develop optimum work flow and turnaround time as well as ideal inventory levels. Standards can be set for turnaround times, backlogs, mail answering, and accounts receivable.

Inquiries and complaints, when watched meticulously, not only reveal problems and errors but also point out inadequacies in the initial offering and promotional strategy. Reading of customer mail can be a real inspiration to the direct marketer.

DELIVERY SYSTEMS

Since the delivery of products to customers is such a vital part of the fulfillment operations of direct marketers, we should look at the alternative delivery systems that are available, especially those systems that provide individual delivery to households and businesses rather than those that handle bulk shipments. Direct marketers are concerned with product delivery, but they are also concerned with the delivery of advertising and other promotion materials. The final section of this chapter is about both product and promotion aspects of direct marketing in viewing alternative delivery systems.

United States Postal Service[5]

The volume and the scope of operations of the United States Postal Service is mind-boggling. An average of 360 million pieces were handled each workday during 1981 for a total of 110 billion pieces during the year. The growth in mail volume is visualized in Figure 10-5. Much of this growth is attributable in recent years to the burgeoning use of direct marketing.

Mail volume is divided into four major classes, first through fourth, with each of these having subdivisions and with each receiving different levels of priority and service. This priority and service, together with consideration of the amount of presorting performed by mailers, influence the complex rate applicable to each class and subclass.

---

[5] Much of the material in this section, including statistics, is from the *1981 Fiscal Year Annual Report of the Postmaster General,* United States Postal Service, 475 L'Enfant Plaza West, S.W., Washington, D.C. 20060–0010.

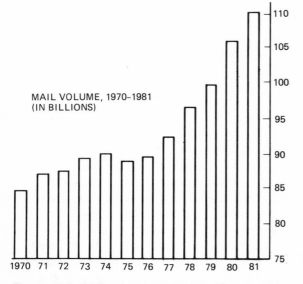

Figure 10-5 Mail volume, 1970–1981. (*Source:* 1981 Annual Report of the Postmaster General, *United States Postal Service.*)

Figure 10-6 visualizes the composition of mail by major class. These mail classes are summarized with their applicability to direct marketers.

First Class Mail   Accounting for nearly 59 percent of all mailed pieces during fiscal year 1981, approximately 20 percent of that total is attributable to direct marketing, including 5 percent of all first class mail consisting of business reply envelopes and cards. The postage rate is higher than that for the other classes but so is the cost of priority handling and individual sorting.

Second Class Mail   Basically, this class consists of publications. It includes magazines, newspapers, and miscellaneous periodicals, such as classroom publications. It accounts for approximately 9 percent of all mailed pieces.

Third Class Mail   As noted in Figure 10-6, this class of mail increased in volume more

than 10 percent between fiscal year 1980 and fiscal year 1981. This is the class of mail mainly used for distribution of direct response advertising. Although postage rates are lower per piece, mailers of this class must ZIP Code their mail, sort, bundle, tie, bag, and personally deliver the sacks of mail to the post office. Thus, the direct mailer performs up to one-half of the basic tasks normally performed by the postal service for first class mail. Additionally, delivery is deferred. This class accounts for more than 30 percent of mailed pieces.

Figure 10-6   Composition of mail, fiscal year 1981. (*Source:* 1981 Annual Report of the Postmaster General, *United Sates Postal Service.*)

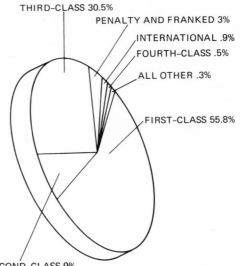

PIECES OF MAIL

MAIL CLASSIFICATION (IN BILLIONS)	1981	1980	Percentage Change
FIRST-CLASS	61.41	60.28	1.9
SECOND-CLASS	9.96	10.22	−2.5
THIRD-CLASS	33.61	30.38	10.6
FOURTH-CLASS	0.59	0.63	−6.3
PENALTY AND FRANKED	3.30	3.50	−5.9
INTERNATIONAL	0.89	0.96	−7.3
ALL OTHER	0.37	0.34	8.8
TOTAL MAIL	110.13	106.31	3.6

Fourth Class Mail This class of mail consists of parcels, with special rates applicable to books and records. It is frequently used by mail-order firms for individual shipment of products, but its use has been declining, for a variety of reasons, including noncompetitive costing, as it tries, by congressional mandate, to serve every nook and cranny of the United States.

Special Mail Services There are certain alternatives for expedited mail service of special interest to direct marketers. These include:

Express Mail Overnight service to designated destination facilities for items mailed prior to 5:00 p.m. is guaranteed. Express Mail service is also available to certain international offices, but without the expedited service guarantee.

Mailgram This is another form of next day service. Mailgram is a joint offering of Western Union and the United States Postal Service. The message goes through the Western Union computer system between post offices and is delivered by postal carrier.

Electronic Computer Originated Mail Service Begun experimentally in January 1982, the Electronic Computer Originated Mail Service (E-COM) permits volume mailers to transmit computer-generated messages via certain telecommunications carriers to 25 serving post offices throughout the continental United States for further postal delivery to businesses and households.

Alternative Delivery Systems

Although the Private Express Statutes grant the United States Postal Service a form of monopoly for first class mail delivery, these have been in transition and, during the process of modernization, have made possible private delivery services under certain conditions.

Alternatives to first class mail, permitted under the Private Express Statutes provided they meet certain criteria, include Federal Express, Purolator Courier, and major airlines. Another alternative to first class mail is the telephone as well as other emerging forms of electronic message transmission.

Certain publications, including *Better Homes and Gardens* and *Wall Street Journal*, have been experimenting with delivery alternatives to second class mail. These alternatives have been increasing as have the number of private firms distributing third class mail advertising, including samples, in selected markets.

Fourth class mail (commonly known as parcel post), is the classification in which major inroads have been made by private parcel delivery systems. It is estimated that as much as 80 percent of all parcel shipments currently are carried by private parcel deliverers, leaving the remaining 20 percent to the United States Postal Service. (In fact, this 80:20 percent ratio has reversed itself in the past 20 years.) The best known of the private parcel services is United Parcel Service. Others include most airlines, Emery Airfreight, and selected bus lines and trucking firms.

SUMMARY

This chapter, as an adjunct to the one preceding devoted to product research and development for direct marketing, describes the implementation of product policy and strategy. The substance of it is the need, within organizations, for a product policy statement. Such a statement should be concerned with the nature of the organization's business as well as the attributes of its products.

Planned obsolescence, which has both positive and negative connotations, takes one of four forms: technological, postponed, physical, or style. This last form, style obsolescence, is possibly the most controversial and the one with which direct marketers are mainly concerned. Style is ever present whereas fashion is the style of the moment and fad usually is a short-lived phenomenon.

Brand names are a form of product differentiation. Although brand names traditionally were the prerogative of manufacturers, more and more brand names are established at the retail and wholesale levels. Direct marketers are often associated with their brands as well as the names of their organizations. Brand name characteristics and the criteria for selection of brand names are important considerations.

Adjuncts to brand names, along with advertising and other forms of promotion, include packaging and labeling. Packaging serves a utilitarian purpose but it also can be viewed as an intangible part of a product and as a promotional strategy. To direct marketers, the protection packaging provides is important. So is the identification, information, and instruction provided on the label.

All of these properties, many intangible, contribute to the image created by a product in relation to a particular firm. Other image-building features of products include design, color, size, and assortment.

Since direct marketers typically are in business for the long run a good deal of the image they build through products is concerned with the long-range aspect of both continuity selling or repeat purchasing, such as through a book or record club, and cross-selling or offering both related and nonrelated products to existing customers.

Since a sale is not completed until a product is delivered and the customer is satisfied, fulfillment operations are of vital concern to the direct marketer. Fulfillment is concerned with the offer, the response, the processing, the shipping, and the billing as well as the handling of complaints and inquiries relative to the products of the firm. Standards for fulfillment need to be established and quality must be controlled.

Although the primary delivery system for mail-order marketers has been the United States Postal Service (and this continues to be the case for distribution of correspondence and advertising, but not package delivery), alternative delivery systems are emerging for all classes of mail.

CASE: PROPER FULFILLMENT IS A PRODUCT STRATEGY

Learning Objective

This case study emphasizes the importance of proper fulfillment operations in direct marketing. These are critical to customer satisfaction and customer retention.

Overview

The very nature of mail order, which involves remote ordering as well as time lags in delivery, underscores the need for absolute quality control in a meticulously maintained fulfillment process. Fulfillment *begins* with the offer as this is contained in the initial promotional materials as well as all of the following: receipt of response/transaction, processing, shipping, billing, complaint handling, inquiry follow-up. Constant monitoring of the fulfillment process is essential. Standards must be set for turnaround times, backlogs, mail answering, and accounts receivable as well as for product quality.

Procedure

Read the learning objective, the overview, and the case that follows. Identify the essential aspects of the fulfillment process. Show how these lead to customer satisfaction and develop customer loyalty. For what reasons is an adequate fulfillment process particularly essential in mail-order operations?

Case[6]

L. L. Bean, Inc., Freeport, Maine, had its beginning in 1912 when Leon Leonwood Bean obtained a mailing list of Maine hunting license holders and sent them a three-page brochure that proclaimed: "You cannot expect success hunting deer or moose if your feet are not properly dressed. The Maine Hunting Shoe is designed by a hunter who has tramped the Maine woods for the past 18 years. We guarantee them to give perfect satisfaction in every way." When the rubber bottoms separated from the leather tops on 90 of the first 100 pairs of boots sold, "L. L." kept his word and refunded the purchase price. Later he said: "Sell good merchandise at a reasonable profit, treat your customers like human beings, and they will come back for more."

Starting with a borrowed $400 in 1912, by the time of his death 52 years later (at age 94), sales had grown to $3 million. Fourteen years later, in 1981, sales had risen to more than $146 million from the mail-order business and $26 million from the one retail store in Freeport, Maine. In the epitome of convenience, customers of today's L. L. Bean, Inc., can purchase from either the catalog or the retail store at any hour of the day or night or on any day of the year (including Christmas).

Geared to processing and shipping some 35,000 parcels a day, the fulfillment operations of L. L. Bean, Inc., include the ability to receive more than 12,000 telephone orders in a single day. The company takes great pride in being able to repair any item that it sells and to custom make or special order many items that it doesn't stock. During 1980, the company processed nearly 16,000 repairs and special orders, including one pair of size 17EEE Maine hunting shoes.

A computerized inventory management system achieves the highest in stock service levels possible: 90 percent of the products ordered will be in stock with an additional 6 percent of the orders requiring only brief back ordering. The error rate is maintained at 1.5 errors for every 1,000 parcels picked and packed.

A highly automated distribution center was expanded in 1979 to 310,000 square feet and includes more than a mile of conveyors. The formal Quality Assurance Department is staffed by more than 30 people, who have a full range of testing facilities and systematically inspect every shipment that enters the distribution center. Product managers regularly visit vendors' facilities to discuss new product developments and new technologies. The Data Processing Department performs a variety of functions related to fulfillment, including selection of the size of the shipping box and determination of which shipping service will be used, at what cost.

The Customer Service Department, also enhanced by computer systems, processed 215,000 customers' questions in 1980 by getting individual replies out within 2 days. Customer service does not end once the package is sent. A recent customer communication said, "Here is a shirt I bought in 1951. Never worn. Please send refund." A refund was sent. F. William Henry, Director of Advertising and Direct Marketing at L. L. Bean, Inc., thinks that efficient customer service is the number one thing that has made L. L. Bean a strong company. The second thing that has contributed to growth, he maintains, "is fast and accurate order fulfillment." Third in importance, he says, "is a high percentage of orders filled when requested." Price/quality relation-

---

[6] Material for this case study was excerpted from a presentation by Leon A. Gorman, President, L. L. Bean, Inc., Freeport, Maine, at the Newcomen Society in North America on July 17, 1981; also, from an article by William Henry, Director of Advertising and Direct Marketing for L. L. Bean, Inc., which appeared in *Direct Marketing*, July 1982, p. 142.

ship is important, he contends, as is the consistency between offering the product and delivering it.

With regard to the fulfillment process at L. L. Bean, Inc., Leon Gorman, its president, said recently:

> We had recognized early on that customer service and favorable word-of-mouth advertising were still the critical elements in any success we were to achieve with our activation and acquisition programs.
>
> This meant a lot of attention to timely order fulfillment, to personal responses to customer requests and problems, and to consistently high levels of product quality. We had observed, too, many others in the mail-order industry who had failed to achieve satisfactory growth because of an over concentration on sales and merchandising. They neglected the less glamorous, but essential, operational areas of the business which meant satisfaction to the customer and, ultimately, success.

As a result of this philosophy, one customer wrote recently:

> You are dependable, efficient and incredible. I think, with the approval of Congress, you should run the country.

Interestingly, L. L. Bean, Inc., does not provide toll-free in-WATS telephone ordering service, but it does prepay all shipping charges.

DISCUSSION QUESTIONS

1 Distinguish between a firm's product line and its product mix. Show specific examples utilizing direct marketing.
2 What should the direct marketer consider in establishing a product policy? Why should there be such a policy?
3 Define obsolescence. How does it come about?
4 Distinguish between a brand name and a trademark. What are important considerations in developing these?
5 How do mail-order product packaging and labeling needs differ from those of the same product sold in stores?
6 Define continuity selling. Define cross-selling.
7 How does a mail-order firm's fulfillment of the orders it receives relate to the definition of a product presented in the preceding chapter? Why is it essential to establish fulfillment standards?
8 Name and describe four alternative delivery systems currently in use by direct marketers.

PRICE DECISIONS IN DIRECT MARKETING

Price is part of the *offer*. It is an adjunct to the product itself. It is a major decision factor. Price should be studied continuously, especially in a competitive environment.

THE NATURE OF PRICE

Much economic theory centers around the price system and the equilibrating force it exerts. Much legislative regulation, as a result, is price-oriented, designed to preserve what is considered by many to be desirable: a perfectly competitive situation in a free enterprise system.

Just how is price a mechanism of equilibrium? Is it, in fact, so simple a truth that "the higher the price, the lower the quantity demanded; the lower the price, the higher the quantity demanded?"

Utility and Value vs. Price

Utility is the satisfaction a consumer derives from the exchange of one product for another. *Value* is some form of quantitative measurement of that satisfaction; that is, the ability of one commodity to command another in exchange. The commodity most frequently exchanged is money, but it could be another commodity.

Price is the value (the measurement of utility) expressed in monetary terms such as dollars and cents or in another currency such as francs or pounds or lire.

Marginal Utility, Total Utility, and Indifference Curves

Marginal utility is defined as the addition to total utility brought about by an exchange. Often, of course, such an exchange results from an increase in purchasing power, which, in turn, commands greater total utility.

Economists sometimes use an alternative approach to putting a value on utility (want satisfaction) through so-called indifference

curves.[1] This form of economic analysis considers that the utility of a particular product may be a function not only of its own quantity but also the nature and quantity of alternative products. To avoid the notion that utility is somehow measurable, indifference curves establish a value for one product in terms of another. Thus, the price for three apples, in exchange, might be 50¢, or it might be two oranges. Hence the buyer, in paying the price of 50¢ for three apples, would derive equal satisfaction from two oranges.

Price is the amount of money (or other commodity) required to exchange for a product (or other commodity) so that the satisfaction derived is at least equal to that given up. The purchaser is, in a sense, "indifferent" as to the two alternatives in the exchange.

THE NATURE OF DEMAND

The theory of demand, although it has been greatly refined since its introduction, was first expressed in 1890 by Alfred Marshall.[2] Marshall's basis for a downward sloping demand curve, as shown in Figure 11-1, was diminishing marginal utility. We now know, from a marketing perspective, that many other dimensions are involved, such as the product life cycle, brand preference, advertising, and the intricacies of consumer behavior. More recently, too, indifference curve analysis has been used to augment the Marshallian theory of demand.

In Figure 11-1 price level is shown on the vertical axis (P) and quantity demanded at each level of price is measured on the horizontal axis (Q). The straight-line demand curve

---

[1] The reader desiring a graphic description of indifference curve analysis should see Al H. Liebhafsky, *The Nature of Price Theory*, The Dorsey Press, Inc., Homewood, Ill., 1966, pp. 83–115.

[2] Alfred Marshall, *Principles of Economics*, 8th ed., Macmillan & Co., Ltd., London, 1938.

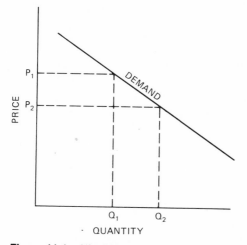

Figure 11-1 Alfred Marshall's theory of demand.

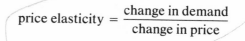

The horizontal demand curve in Figure 11-2 illustrates a case of a perfectly elastic demand curve in which circumstance the buyer will take any amount of the product offered at the current price but will not purchase at a higher price than this. As demonstrated by the totally vertical inelastic demand curve in Figure 11-2, the buyer would purchase the same quantity of the product at all possible prices, presumably limited only by personal resources.

The direct marketer, in initially estimating the demand for products, would first determine if there is a price that the market expects and then would develop an estimate of the sales volume which can be expected at different price levels. A product with an *elastic* market demand should usually be priced lower than an item with an *inelastic* market demand, as demonstrated in Figure 11-2.

Ideally, too, the direct marketer would pre-

shows the quantities of a given product that a consumer will buy at all possible prices at a given moment in time.

The term "quantity demanded" refers to the product amount that will be purchased at any point along the demand curve. At the higher price level, P_1, a lesser quantity, Q_1, will be demanded. Lowering price to the lower level of P_2 will result in movement along the demand curve to the higher quantity of demand, Q_2.

The term "change in demand" refers to the movement of the *entire* demand curve, right or left, depending on whether there has been an increase or decrease in total demand. Advertising, for example, could increase demand at all price levels, and thus the curve would shift to the right.

Price Elasticity of Demand

Price elasticity of demand is the relative change in demand for a given change in price. This measure was developed by Marshall to record the responsiveness of buyers to price changes. The general formula for measuring price elasticity is:

Figure 11-2 Elasticity of demand.

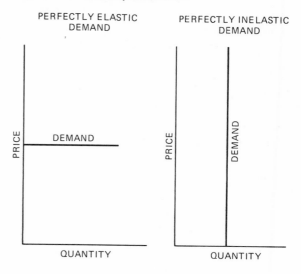

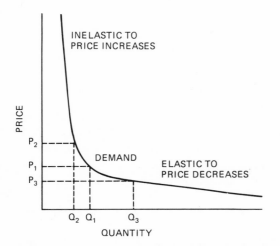

Figure 11-3 Ideal demand is inelastic to price increases and elastic to price decreases. Raising price from P_1 to P_2 lowers quantity demanded from Q_1 to Q_2 but increases total revenue. Lowering price from P_1 to P_3 raises quantity demanded from Q_1 to Q_3 and also increases total revenue.

fer to face a demand curve such as that shown in Figure 11-3, parabolic-shaped, so that changes in demand would be *inelastic* to price *increases* and *elastic* to price *decreases*. A variety of factors can create such a favorable situation for the direct marketer, including quality products, adequate promotion, and other image-building practices.

With reference to Figure 11-3, if the demand is elastic, the total amount spent on the product increases when price declines and decreases when price rises. In such a situation, sales maximization might be preferable to profit maximization, since absolute profit would rise even though unit profit declines.

Estimation of Demand

Direct marketers have at their disposal three ways of estimating demand for their products and services: judgment, surveys, and experiments.[3]

[3] Chapter 3 deals with surveys and experiments in depth.

Judgment   Demand can sometimes be estimated through personal experience as well as drawing on the experience of others. Those within the firm as well as those outside the firm, including consultants and even competitors, are often used as resources. Extremes of opinion, optimistic or pessimistic, can be averaged and further weighted in terms of other elements of the marketing mix such as promotional strategy, extent of distribution, and competitive activity.

Surveys   These, like judgments, can often be biased, especially when expectations are measured through mail, phone, or personal questionnaires. In a survey what a potential buyer says he will do is often quite different from what he actually does when faced with the reality of the marketplace. At best, surveys (like judgments) are estimates.

Experiments   Direct marketers have available and often use this singularly effective tool in that they can test price levels and respective market demands through controlled experiments. Rather than asking what buyers would do under particular sets of circumstances, such as price changes, their marketplace reactions can be scientifically tested under the controlled conditions of an experiment.

PRICE DETERMINATION

The establishment of a specific price level for a particular product can be accomplished in one of two ways:

1 The price can be built up from total cost of goods sold with the addition of a calculated overhead cost and selling cost plus a desired profit margin.

2 The price may be based on competitive market conditions and customer expectations.

Prices can be determined at the extreme of either alternative or at any balance in between cost-plus and market demand. Or, under conditions of nonprice competition through market segmentation, product differentiation, and promotion, prices might be established ultimately by customer preferences.

"Cost-Plus" Pricing

"Cost-plus" price determination should relate to a variety of production costs, as well as overhead cost, selling cost, and profit, but we will confine our discussion here only to those costs of goods sold.[4] The various types of costs react differently to the quantity of product. These are described individually below.

Total Fixed Cost The magnitude of this cost does not vary with quantity of products, at least within a range. Fixed cost occurs initially in a lump sum once an operation begins. As there is expansion in quantity of production, there is little difference in the magnitude. Cost depreciation of a facility, for example, together with the attendant cost of maintaining and operating it, may be the same regardless of level of output.

Total Variable Cost This is the cost directly associated with the quantity of product. It includes such factors as raw materials and related labor costs.

Total Cost The distinction between fixed cost and variable cost, especially certain costs that are not always easily allocable, is not always clear-cut. Combining these costs results in total cost, thus:

total cost = total fixed cost
+ total variable cost

Average Fixed Cost The larger the quantity of product, the smaller will be the average fixed cost. That is because this figure is deter-

[4] An extended discussion of break-even analysis, which is concerned with promotion as well as production costs, appears in Chapter 2. See, specifically, Figure 2-4 on page 38 and attendant description.

mined by dividing total fixed cost by quantity of product. It should be noted, however, that this cost never reaches zero. Further, when necessary facility expansion is undertaken, average fixed cost will increase greatly.

Average Variable Cost This figure is determined through dividing total variable cost at any level of output by the quantity of product at that level. Typically, total variable cost rises relatively rapidly initially and levels off as the economies of scale are realized in production. As existing facilities become inefficient, this cost rises more rapidly.

Average Total Cost From the definition of total cost, it follows that:

average total cost = average fixed cost
+ average variable cost

Marginal Cost This is the cost of producing one more unit. However, since marginal fixed cost is always zero, except for the zeroth unit, then:

marginal cost = marginal variable cost

The important relationship of total fixed cost, total variable cost, and total cost is visualized in Figure 11-4, so that:

$$\frac{\text{total cost}}{\text{quantity}} = \frac{\text{total fixed cost}}{\text{quantity}} + \frac{\text{total variable cost}}{\text{quantity}}$$

Accounting information for direct marketing is almost always in the form of average or total cost rather than marginal cost. Decisions, therefore, are usually on the basis of average cost or revenue or profit largely because of the difficulty of identifying marginal cost. Marginal cost is, however, essential for adequate

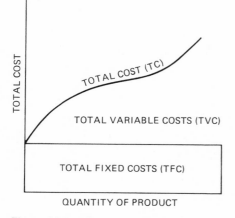

Figure 11-4 "Cost-plus" pricing.

decision making. Promotion cost of direct response advertising, to use an illustration, can (in a sense) be viewed as a fixed cost. Once this has been absorbed at some level of response, marginal sales become even more profitable, as was demonstrated in Chapter 2.

PRICING UNDER MARKET CONDITIONS

An alternative to "cost-plus" is the setting of prices according to market conditions. We will consider these models of competitive marketplace behavior: (1) perfect competition, (2) monopoly, (3) monopolistic competiton, and (4) oligopoly. As we shall see, the first two models are special cases whereas the last two have special relevance for direct marketers.

Perfect Competition

Consider, first, the case of *perfect competition* in which the market, rather than the individual firm, establishes the price. This model is illustrated in Figure 11-5. It prevails mainly in commodity markets and in the case of most agricultural products.

Perfect competition is characterized by these conditions in the marketplace:

1 There are a large number of sellers, any one of whom is incapable of controlling the market.

2 There are a large number of buyers, each feeling that there is no way to influence the price of a product through individual actions.

3 Products are perfectly homogeneous and even interchangeable.

4 Buyers and sellers both have full knowledge of what's going on in the marketplace, including the competition.

5 Buyers and sellers alike behave in a rational manner to maximize their own self-interest, as originally postulated by Adam Smith.

6 There is complete freedom of entry to the market and there is a perfect mobility of inputs to the market.

Monopoly

Next, consider the case of *monopoly,* in which the market *is* the firm; that is, "the only electric utility in town."

As visualized in Figure 11-6, a monopoly firm tends to maximize profit at the price (P_{my}) at which marginal cost (MC) equals marginal revenue (MR) but quantity produced is held to Q_{my}. Excess profit is the difference between monopoly price (P_{my}) and market price (P_{mt}). Under conditions of perfect competition in

Figure 11-5 Pricing under perfect competition. The firm can sell at a price (P_f) no higher than the market price (P_m) regardless of quantity (Q_f) it offers for sale.

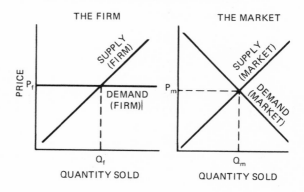

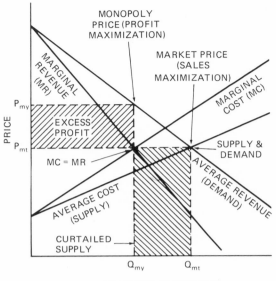

Figure 11-6 Pricing under monopoly. Monopoly price (P_{my}) and quantity produced (Q_{my}) intersect at point where marginal cost (*MC*) equals marginal revenue (*MR*) rather than at the lower market demand price (P_{mt}), which would prevail if market demand quantity (Q_{mt}) were produced. (*Adapted from William Baumol,* Economic Theory and Operations Analysis, *2d ed., Prentice-Hall, Inc., Englewood Cliffs, New Jersey, 1965, p. 319.*)

which supply equals demand (average cost equals average revenue), the market price (P_{mt}) would prevail and the market quantity (Q_{mt}) would be produced.

The difference in quantity actually produced, between Q_{mt} and Q_{my}, is supply purposely curtailed by the monopoly to maximize profits. Although it is generally felt that monopolies do indeed intend to restrict output, this is not necessarily the case in the real world in which monopolies take over competitive industries. In the marketplace today public utilities probably come closest to being true monopolies.

In the situation of monopoly, price is controlled by technology. There is a maximization of profit and there is a complete lack of freedom of entry to the market.

Monopolistic Competition

The market condition of *monopolistic competition,* which occurs as a result of product differentiation as well as market segmentation, is the most prevailing condition for direct marketers. Convenience stores that are open at all hours of the day or night or meat markets that feature high-grade products are examples of monopolistic competition.

As visualized in Figure 11-7, pricing under monopolistic competition recognizes the traditional downward sloping demand curve. However, the supply curve is "U" shaped. This postulates that both very small and very large outputs are difficult and expensive to produce. As a result, the point of tangency between the average cost (supply) and average revenue (demand) curves represents the point of output (Q_{mc}) of the firm, with the price level set at P_{mc}. This means that the firm in monopolistic competition, because it produces less

Figure 11-7 Pricing under monopolistic competition. Product differentiation and market segmentation tend to curtail output (Q_{mc}) of the firm under conditions of monopolistic competition so that price (P_{mc}) is higher than it would be (P_{mt}) under conditions of perfect competition. (*Adapted from William Baumol,* Economic Theory and Operations Analysis, *2d ed., Prentice-Hall, Inc., Englewood Cliffs, New Jersey, 1965, p. 321.*)

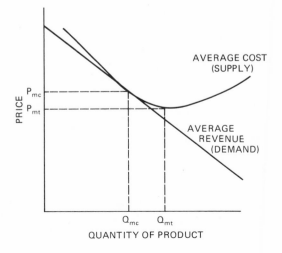

output, has a unit cost that is higher and a resultant price that is higher, than would be the case under perfect competition. Without this restraint, the firm would produce at the point of lowest average cost (Q_{mt}) and would price at the lower level of P_{mt}.

Monopolistic competition is characterized by a large number of sellers, a large number of buyers, elevated price differentials, a high degree of knowledge about competition, and a relative ease of entry. Interdependence among firms in monopolistic competition is ignored; otherwise, the market condition would be considered oligopoly.

Oligopoly

Oligopoly is quite prevalent in the United States today. It is characterized by few sellers, many buyers, restricted entry, relatively good knowledge about competition, product homogeneity, and high barriers to entry. The automobile industry is an example of oligopoly. Oligopoly may prevail among certain categories of products, such as specialty foods, and among certain catalog merchandisers.

The illustration of market conditions under oligopoly shown in Figure 11-8 is characterized by the so-called "kinked" demand curve. If a firm operating under oligopolistic market conditions figures its price above P_o, its competitors will welcome this move since customers will switch over to them. As is visualized, price is elastic above the market-established level. Price moves go unmatched as there is no motivation to match price rises.

On the other hand, if a firm under oligopolistic conditions lowers the price, competitors will quickly match this price cut. Below P_o, therefore, price is viewed as inelastic since price moves will inevitably be matched.

Note that there is a gap in the marginal revenue curve at the market level of output (Q_m). It can be demonstrated that if the individual firm's marginal cost curve happens to

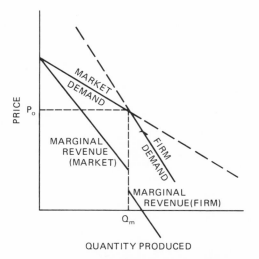

Figure 11-8 Pricing under oligopoly. The "kinked" demand curve indicates that above the oligopoly-established price (P_o) price is elastic in that a little change in P results in a big change in Q since price moves are unmatched. Below P_o, price is inelastic. Big changes in P result in little changes in Q, since price moves are matched. (*Adapted from William Baumol*, Economic Theory and Operations Analysis, *2d ed., Prentice-Hall, Inc., Englewood Cliffs, New Jersey, 1965, p. 331.*)

pass through this gap in the marginal revenue curve, the profit-maximizing firm will not be motivated to leave the current price (P_o). On the other hand, should it drop its price too far, under these conditions, its marginal revenue could in fact be negative as it drops below the zero-point on the price axis.

PERFECT VS. IMPERFECT (NONPRICE) COMPETITION

Although there is still a considerable amount of price competition, marketplace demand today is more often determined by a variety of factors other than price. These are grouped under the general heading of *nonprice competition*. As we have seen, price competition results simply in movements along a demand curve, but the objective of nonprice competition is to shift the entire demand curve to the right to reflect an increase in total demand, at all levels of price.

In perfect competition, price is theoretically the equilibrating force. In monopoly, price is determined by the monopolist. Under conditions of monopolistic competition or oligopoly, however, there is differentiation based on things *other* than price: product differentiation, service, brand preference, promotional activities. There is an increasing use of such form of competition in marketing, especially in direct marketing.

Shopping convenience coupled with clear-cut product descriptions often rivaling those presented by personal salespeople are among the reasons why nonprice competition is particularly prevalent in direct marketing. When purchasing from home or office, price comparison is not so readily available. Furthermore, price becomes less important than the other factors presented through well-conceived promotion. The intangible attributes of a product, including the seller's prestige along with guarantees and service, often influence customer choices more than price alone.

Figure 11-9 shows how nonprice competition can increase total demand, through shifting the demand curve to the right, so that either a higher quantity of the product can be sold at the same price (P_1Q_2) or the same quantity can be sold at a higher price (P_2Q_1).

A further objective of nonprice competition is to change the shape of the demand curve from a straight line (D_1) to a parabola (D_2), demonstrating that it becomes inelastic to price increases and elastic to price decreases. Increases in price result in relatively small decreases in demand whereas decreases in price result in relatively large increases in demand.

Superior Goods, Inferior Goods, and Substitutes

It is possible but contrary to the economic theory of demand for more of certain goods to be purchased, rather than less, when the price goes up. This is true in the case of certain products, the purchase of which is a way of impressing others. Thorstein Veblen, in his description of conspicuous consumption, referred mainly to "wasteful" and "superfluous" goods. Sometimes such behavior by

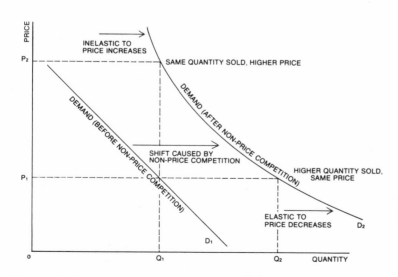

Figure 11-9 Perfect vs. imperfect (nonprice) competition. The objective of nonprice competition (market segmentation, product differentiation, promotion) is to shift the demand curve in its entirety whereas price competition results simply in movements along a curve.

consumers, purchasing more of particular goods at a higher price than at a lower price, is described as a "snob effect."

It is likewise true that sometimes a decrease in the price of particular goods leads to a decrease in demand. Such goods are termed "inferior." In contrast, "superior" goods are those with higher prices that result in higher demand. Potatoes have been presented as an example of this phenomenon: the quantity purchased is thought to decline as price declines. A nineteenth-century economist, after whom the so-called Giffen Paradox is named, observed a substitution effect, of bread for potatoes, whenever the price of potatoes decreased. Consumers, through such substitutions, demonstrate their superior or inferior reputability in associating with goods that themselves are perceived to be superior or inferior.

SUMMARY

Price is part of the *offer* and is an adjunct to the product itself. Price is a monetary expression of value. Value is a measurement of utility.

The theoretical basis for a downward sloping demand curve, demonstrating that the quantity demanded lowers as the price increases, is diminishing marginal utility; that is, the notion that value is created by scarcity. From the perspective of the direct marketer, however, other dimensions are involved: the stage of the product life cycle, prevailing brand preferences, the extent of promotion, and the intricacies of consumer behavior.

Price elasticity of demand is the relative change in demand for a given change in price. As an analytical tool, it is used to record the responsiveness of buyers to price changes. Preferably, the demand curve should be shaped so as to be inelastic (resistant) to price increases and elastic (receptive) to price decreases. Under such circumstances, the total

amount spent on the product increases when price declines and decreases when price rises.

Demand can be estimated through judgment, surveys, or experiments. This last alternative is especially relevant for direct marketers who have at their disposal a scientific mechanism for controlled testing.

The two basic methods for price determination are (1) "cost-plus" pricing and (2) pricing in response to market conditions. Under conditions of nonprice competition, characterized by market segmentation, product differentiation, and promotion, prices might be established ultimately by customer preferences. When pricing in response to market conditions, direct marketers could be faced with conditions of either perfect competition or monopoly, but, more realistically, they are faced with conditions of monopolistic competition or oligopoly.

Although there is still a considerable amount of price competition, resulting in movements along a demand curve, subject to price changes, there is an increasing amount of nonprice competition in today's marketplace. Under these conditions, the direct marketer is concerned with things, *other than* price, that create customer preferences. These include a variety of promotional strategies as well as such factors as product differentiation and shopping convenience. In using such strategies, the objective is to *shift* the entire demand curve to the right to reflect an increase in *total* demand, at *all* levels of price. A further objective of nonprice competition is to create demand that is *inelastic* to price increases and *elastic* to price decreases.

CASE: PRICING OF SUPERIOR GOODS

Learning Objective

This case demonstrates that selling price is not the sole determinant of market demand. Certain products, sometimes described by economic theorists as "superior" goods, actually have higher demand at a higher price than they do at a lower price.

Overview

Mail-order marketing of collectibles—initially stamps and old coins but, more recently, reproducible coins and porcelain as well as nonreproducible art and antiques—accounted for an estimated $980 million of sales during 1982. Often, these products are priced "blind." That is, there is no established marketplace at which prices can be determined based on demand. Often, too, such products are direct marketed on a continuity basis. That is, a series of silver coins or porcelain plates, usually produced in limited editions, is shipped periodically until the series ends or the order is canceled. As a result of the intended scarcity of limited editions, sometimes such products are perceived as investments by the buyer, and at other times they are perceived as conspicuous consumption.

Procedure

Read the learning objective, the overview, and the case that follows. Be prepared to discuss those aspects of the case that demonstrate market demand based on investment contrasted with that based on conspicuous consumption. Which buyer motivation is more valid?

Case[5]

The business of the Franklin Mint is the conceptualizing, creating, manufacturing, and marketing of products designed to be collected:

[5] Material facts for this case study were excerpted from a talk given by Charles Wickard, Executive Vice President of Franklin Mint, International, at the 8th Annual Direct Marketing Symposium held April 28–30, 1976, at Montreux, Switzerland. Additional data appeared in *Direct Marketing*, December 1976 and May 1974.

coins, metals, books, crystal, porcelain, lithographs. Franklin Mint sells these items exclusively by mail order, and, more often than not, these collectibles are sold to people who have never collected before.

Thus, coins that Franklin Mint produces and markets in many of the world's nations are sold to millions of people who have never before collected coins. Franklin Mint is in the business of creating markets as well as creating products.

In 1965 the company was founded in the United States and did less than $1 million of sales. In 1969 it conducted its first international mail-order operations in France and the United Kingdom. By 1982 U.S. sales alone were estimated to be $241 million.

At the close of 1973, the Franklin Mint Corporation announced plans for diversification into yet another area of strong collector interest: fine book publishing. Whereas publishing is a highly competitive market, Franklin Mint officials believed they would be able to capture an important and generally overlooked portion of the book market.

The plan called for the newest division, the Franklin Library, to offer works of proven literary significance whose popularity had withstood the test of time. The books would be designed as works of artistic importance as well as literary merit. Bound in genuine leather, decorated with pure gold and crafted to the highest standard of quality, the books were to be worthy of inclusion in the ultimate library, books many families would pass down from generation to generation as true literary heirlooms.

The first mail-order experiment by the Franklin Library involved direct mail sent to 800,000 active collectors of the Franklin Mint plus the entire American Express credit card list. Thus, a total of approximately three million prospects were allowed 6 weeks in which to place an order for 100 classic books to be delivered over the next 8 years at $28 each. The offer generated $90 million in commitments for the books. Some 32,000 customers responded affirmatively.

DISCUSSION QUESTIONS

1 Define these terms: utility, value, price.
2 Discuss the economic truism: "The higher the price, the lower the quantity demanded; the lower the price, the higher the quantity demanded."
3 Identify reasons why demand for a product might be inelastic to price increases and elastic to price decreases.
4 Under what market conditions would a direct marketer be more likely to use "cost-plus" pricing?
5 Which of these models of competitive marketplace behavior has special relevance for direct marketers and why: (1) perfect competition; (2) monopoly; (3) monopolistic competition; (4) oligopoly?
6 What is "nonprice" competition?
7 Explain the pricing phenomenon of superior goods.

CHAPTER 12

PRICE POLICIES AND STRATEGIES FOR DIRECT MARKETERS

The actual determination of price is only a part of the total pricing procedure. Direct marketers must consider the pricing philosophy relative to costs, competition, and market demand. They must also consider price as part of the promotional strategy as well as a mechanism for appealing to specific market segments.

In terms of the product life cycle, prices might be high at product innovation, while demand is inelastic. Later, as price competition appears, demand becomes elastic, and prices might have to be lowered. If products are differentiated or if so-called superior goods are involved, price may not be the major determinant of buyer behavior. Market acceptance may be dependent more on factors other than price.

Although price is a determining factor in many buying decisions, it is not the only factor. Direct marketers need to understand this and they need to develop pricing policies and strategies that are aimed at achieving their overall objectives.

PRICING OBJECTIVES

As a policy, direct marketers may seek either profit maximization or sales maximization. They may "skim-the-cream," or the objective might be to penetrate the market deeply. Distribution may be intensive, selective, or exclusive.

Once a direct marketer has established a pricing policy, adherence to it may be good strategy not only to preclude price wars but also to maintain image. The Horchow Collection, for example, avoids price cutting in its basic catalog through use of a supplemental catalog, Grand Finale, to offer close-out merchandise. Major retailers, including Sears, Wards, and Penneys, often provide outlets for their close-out merchandise, at large discounts, within special stores intended for this purpose.

Traditionally, retail merchants have used two ways to convey the image of being a "price" store. One employed by the discount merchandiser involves routinely pricing goods at less than the usual markup. Thus, the discounter accepts lower markups but must necessarily deal in large volume. Another way to convey the same image is to run many sales, even during key selling seasons. Oftentimes, retailers offer leader merchandise, that which is popular and appealing enough to bring customers into the store, at heavily discounted prices. Although a low markup may be used for such leader merchandise, other items in the store may have higher markups.

Other merchants consistently price above the market to appeal to those who prefer to buy exclusive types of goods and who are willing to pay higher prices. Because these goods typically are of higher quality and because they are often unusual, even exclusive, the marketer can justify the prices and higher markups.

In one study of 200 manufacturers the relative importance of pricing was investigated. More than one-half of the respondents *did not* select pricing as one of the five most important policy decision areas.[1]

Profit Maximization

The direct marketer who establishes profit maximization as a pricing objective holds sales to the point at which marginal revenue (MR) equals marginal cost (MC). At this point the revenue from one additional sale is exactly equal to the cost of that sale. This quantity of sales is visualized as Q_2 on the horizontal axis of Figure 12-1. The corresponding price level is P_2 on the vertical axis. The shaded area CDFE represents the total profit area. The quantity sold at intersect P_2Q_2 is not as much

---

[1] Jon G. Udell, "How Important Is Pricing in Competitive Strategy?" *Journal of Marketing*, January 1964, pp. 44–48.

as it could be under existing market conditions, but profits are maximized and price is at a somewhat higher level than would be the case if sales were maximized. The sales maximization point in Figure 12-1 is at intersect P_3Q_3.

Although it is technically correct that the point of profit maximization is at the intersect of $MR = MC$ (point F), note that there are actually two such intersects in Figure 12-1, the second occurring at point C. This is a point of minimum profit even though MR equals MC at this point, too. To the left of this point, the area bounded by ABC, there is a loss. Profit, defined as the difference between total revenue and total cost, is represented by the area bounded by CDFE *less* the area bounded by ABC.

If the direct marketer chooses to confine sales to that point at which marginal cost is at its lowest level, point D, the quantity sold would be at Q_1 in Figure 12-1 with the price level at P_1. Although this procedure would maximize profits per unit of sales, it would not result in the highest possible *total* profit. The profit in this instance would be the shaded area bounded by CDE.

If a firm views its investment in customers as a capitalized cost, in the manner presented in Chapter 2, the point at which MR = MC may not necessarily be the best point for the firm's future growth. With this viewpoint, the marginal cost curve would be lowered, as a result of the capitalization process, and thus the point of intersect would shift to the right on the marginal revenue curve.

Sales Maximization

The sales maximizing direct marketer is more concerned with market penetration, rather than maximum profits through a cream-skimming pricing policy. This firm will concentrate on intensive, rather than selective or exclusive, distribution. Sales volume would then be at point Q_3 on the horizontal axis of Figure 12-1,

with price level established at point P_3 on the vertical axis.

In the process of sales maximization, acquiring and activating new customers with an eye toward future sales will incur a loss bounded by the shaded area FGH on Figure 12-1. This loss occurs because marginal costs exceed marginal revenue on sales volume between Q_2 and Q_3. In calculating profit the area bounded by FGH would have to be deducted from the area bounded by CDFE, along with the area bounded by ABC. A pricing policy aimed toward sales maximization, especially if the value of a customer is considered, can be a proper policy if growth, coupled with *future* profit, is an objective. Sales maximization refers to the maximization of unit volume or sales revenue, either of which, to the direct marketer, can be the measure of what has been sold.

Appropriate promotional strategy will depend on the direct marketer's objective, whether

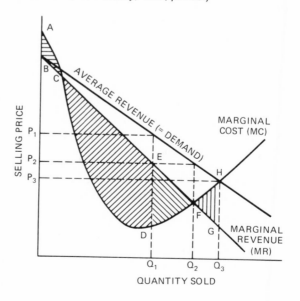

Figure 12-1 Profit maximization vs. sales maximization. (*Adapted from William Baumol,* Economic Theory and Operations Analysis, *2d ed., Prentice-Hall, Inc., Englewood Cliffs, New Jersey, 1965, p. 298.*)

it be profit maximization or sales maximization. Since rational planning requires that marginal revenue attributable to promotion be positive, promotion should be used to increase sales only up to the point at which it continues to contribute to gross margins.

Full Service vs. Limited Service

An important criterion for establishing pricing policy is the range of customer services to be provided. Full service typically results in higher prices, and limited service usually results in lower prices.

Full-service retailers, for example, might include delivery and credit charges in the basic price as well as such niceties as gift wrapping, alterations, and a liberal exchange policy. Each of these services has a cost attached to it that somehow must be borne by the customer. A limited-service retailer, in an effort to keep prices low, may not provide these services except at an additional charge.

Even certain promotional strategies, such as sweepstakes, gifts, premiums, and introductory offers, must somehow find their way into the price level established by policy, just as does the level of service need to fit into this policy. Obviously, the direct marketer cannot afford to ignore such costs when establishing pricing policy.

PRICING CONSIDERATIONS

The direct marketer must consider a variety of factors during the early stages of establishing a pricing policy. Answers to such questions as these must be sought:

1 What are current preferences in the marketplace and what is the current behavior pattern of consumers?

2 What price preference levels exist and can consumers be educated to accept different pricing under certain conditions?

3 What are expected price/quality relationships?

4 What is estimated product demand and what will be the acceptability of it at specific time intervals?

5 What is the estimated time of entry of competition?

6 What is the target market segment? What share of it is desired and at what speed?

7 Can a promotional strategy be developed that assures flexible marketing effort?

8 Is the objective to skim profits or to penetrate markets?

Additionally, the direct marketer must consider that distribution costs in direct marketing are most often relatively fixed. Unlike a sales commission, which occurs only when a sale is made, the costs of direct mail or broadcast or print advertising are expended *in advance* and are the same whether a great many or a very few sales result. Under such conditions, pricing must be established in advance, often through experimentation, so as to either maximize sales or maximize profits.

GROSS MARGINS, MARKUPS, AND MARKDOWNS

The difference between selling price and the cost of goods sold is termed *gross margin* and is sometimes called *gross profit*. Selling as well as general operating expenses are deducted from gross margin to determine *net profit*. Gross margin may also be viewed as *markup*.

Markups

The difference between the price the customer pays and the price paid by the retailer to either the wholesaler or the manufacturer or, in the case of the manufacturer, the cost of production, is called a *markup*. Markup may be expressed as a fixed percentage of selling price above cost, or it may be calculated as a percentage of selling price. Figure 12-2 gives the equivalency of selected markup percentages based on cost to markup percentages based on selling price.

The formula for determining the markup percentage if it is based on cost is:

$$\frac{\text{markup}}{\text{cost}} = \text{markup \% (based on cost)}$$

The formula for determining the markup percentage when it is based on the selling price is:

$$\frac{\text{markup}}{\text{price}} = \text{markup \% (based on price)}$$

For example, if the selling price of a product is $50 and the cost to the middleman is $30, the markup of $20, based on cost, is calculated as follows:

$$\frac{\$20}{\$30} = 66.7\%$$

Or, if this same markup is based on selling price, the calculation yields the following result:

$$\frac{\$20}{\$50} = 40.0\%$$

In the first example, based on cost, the markup is 66.7 percent. In the second example, based on price, the markup is 40 percent.

The practice of determining markup based on cost is sometimes called the *percentage-determined method* since the markup is the cause of the selling price rather than the result.

If price is established in the market, either through a manufacturer's suggested price or because of competitive pricing, the markup is determined as a result of that price and this is called the *price-determined method*.

Markups occur at each level of a distribution channel to provide compensation for the mar-

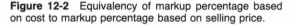

A MARKUP PERCENTAGE BASED ON COST OF	IS EQUIVALENT TO	THIS MARKUP PERCENTAGE BASED ON SELLING PRICE
25%		20.0%
30%		23.1%
35%		25.9%
40%		28.6%
45%		31.0%
50%		33.3%
60%		37.5%
70%		41.2%
80%		44.4%
90%		47.4%
100%		50.0%
150%		60.0%
200%		67.7%
250%		71.4%
300%		75.0%

Figure 12-2 Equivalency of markup percentage based on cost to markup percentage based on selling price.

keting functions performed by middlemen. This process is demonstrated in Figure 12-3. Note that the price at one level is the same as the next level's cost. Note, too, that markups generally increase as a product moves through a channel, again, because of the marketing functions performed, allocable to progressively smaller units of sales.

In Figure 12-3 the markup percentage from

Figure 12-3 Prices, costs, and markups at different levels of a distribution channel.

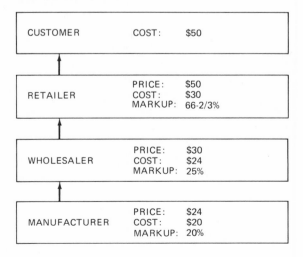

manufacturer to wholesaler is 20 percent (calculated on a cost of $20, a selling price of $24, and a resultant markup of $4); the markup percentage from wholesaler to retailer is 25 percent (calculated on a price of $24, a selling price of $30, and a markup of $6); the markup percentage from retailer to customer is $66\frac{2}{3}$ percent (calculated on a price of $30, a selling price of $50, and a markup of $20). If, in this example, the retailer and the wholesaler were removed from the distribution channel, the markup ($30) on a manufacturer's cost of $20 at a selling price of $50 would be 150 percent. In this event, the manufacturer would be performing the marketing functions traditionally assumed by wholesalers and retailers. Such a shortened channel is many times the case in mail-order distribution.

Not only do markups vary at different levels of a channel of distribution but they also vary across types within a level as well as by types of products. As already noted, retailers establishing a "discount" image (and usually offering less personal service) operate on smaller percentage markups. Typically, too, convenience goods, such as bread and milk, carry smaller percentage markups than specialty goods such as designer clothes.

Markup percentages usually vary inversely with unit costs. The higher the unit cost, the lower the percentage markup. Markup percentages also usually vary inversely with turnover; the faster the turnover, the lower the percentage markup.

Beyond the basic markup philosophy, the direct marketer may also establish an even higher price, in the form of *additional markup,* to make a product more attractive to buyers, as is the case with so-called superior goods. Additional markups may be the rule, too, if products become scarce or operating costs (including the cost of maintaining inventory) rise. Alternatively, markups may be reduced, or even canceled, in the event of sales or inventory clearances.

Markdowns

A reduction in an established selling price is termed a *markdown*. Markdowns are calculated in the following manner:

$$\frac{\text{markdown}}{\text{price}} = \text{markdown}\,\%$$

For example, a reduction of $10 in the aforementioned selling price of $50 would result in a markdown of 20 percent, calculated in this way:

$$\frac{\$10}{\$50} = 20\%$$

Markdowns occur to meet competition, to clear out inventory, or to effect special sales. A markdown can be canceled if any of these three special situations no longer exists.

Markdowns are usually expressed as a percentage of the customary selling price. They are not rightfully calculated from a higher selling price, such as the manufacturer's suggested selling price if, in fact, the product was never priced at that level in the particular firm effecting the markdown.

Discounts and Allowances

Discounts and allowances at any level within a channel of distribution are, ultimately, reductions from established selling prices. They may be thought of as compensation for a marketing function performed by a middleman or as an incentive to purchase. They take these forms:

Trade discounts: These discounts are allowed to compensate for certain marketing functions performed by middlemen or, alternatively, for functions foregone by buyers.
Quantity discounts: These reductions from price are allowed in recognition of the "economies of scale," in that larger purchases can usually be processed more efficiently than smaller orders.

Cash discounts: Cash discounts are, in effect, a return for an investment that did not have to be made by the seller in long-term or short-term financing of customers and thus must take into consideration a time period as well as a percentage markdown.

Seasonal discounts: Seasonal discounts, applicable to Christmas items or snow tires, for example, help level out a manufacturer's production and thus lower costs.

Promotional allowances: As a form of discount, these are used to encourage advertising and sales activity by middlemen.

Brokerage allowances: These are a form of discount allowed if no physical transfer of goods actually takes place insofar as the agent is concerned; that is, a mailing list broker does not actually take possession of a list as it transfers from list owner to list user.

In connection with discounts and allowances, it should be noted that the Robinson-Patman Act is concerned with controlling price discrimination under certain conditions. This legislation and other regulatory considerations relative to pricing policy will be dealt with later in this chapter.

PRICING STRATEGIES

There are a variety of pricing strategies with which direct marketers should be familiar if they are to achieve their objective, whether that objective be profit maximization or sales maximization. In this section we will discuss these strategies.

Geographic Pricing

The costs of shipments to various geographic locations are a vital consideration to the direct marketer. These costs inevitably occur because of the very nature of direct marketing. Prices that are quoted free on board (f.o.b.) direct marketer's plant assure the seller a constant price level. Delivered prices, on the other hand, assure the buyer a constant price

level, regardless of distance from the direct marketer's plant.

Under a zone price policy, the seller's market is divided into a limited number of broad geographic areas (zones) and a uniform delivered price is set within each area. Basing-point pricing adds established shipping costs to the quoted selling price, regardless of the actual point of shipment. Sometimes, sellers absorb shipping costs to meet competition, even though they have established an f.o.b. shipping-point price policy.

The direct marketer, in establishing geographic price policy, has these options: (1) quote prices f.o.b. shipping point and add actual delivery costs to the billing; (2) quote prices f.o.b. shipping point and add a predetermined "average" amount, possibly according to weight and zone; (3) quote prices delivered to the buyer, having included shipping costs as an overhead item. Several examples of geographic price policy alternatives are illustrated in Figure 12-4.

One Price vs. Variable Price

The nature of mail-order marketing is such that most practitioners adhere to a one-price policy. This is because direct marketers preprint their prices in catalogs and other direct mail pieces or otherwise visualize them in print and broadcast media. The price quoted is typically not negotiable.

In contrast to such a one-price policy, a variable-price policy results in price haggling. This is an expected procedure in some forms of transaction as, for example, a purchase from a street merchant in Hong Kong or from a used car dealer in Chicago. Whereas a one-price policy builds customer confidence, a variable-price policy does not.

It is difficult to administer a variable-price policy, especially in mail-order marketing. Obviously, too, a one-price policy is the best way to maintain ongoing customer goodwill. Under

How to Order

Delivery
Shipments are made postpaid by United Parcel Service, Parcel Post, or Priority Mail.

Air Freight Shipments
For faster delivery, air freight shipments will be made upon request. We'll bill you the difference between air costs and the usual rates. (This extra charge is usually $15.00 or more.)

Shipments to International Addresses
Please call or write us for details.

Other Offers
Your name, as a part of our customer family, is made available to carefully screened organizations with an offer or appeal that might interest you. If you would rather not receive such offers, please let us know.

New! Shipments to Hawaii and Alaska
Popular packages of Omaha Steaks products are now available for delivery in Hawaii and Alaska at regular prices — with no extra shipping charge. Call Free 800/228-9055 for details.

And Canada, too!
We can now deliver certain packages of Omaha Steaks to Canada — at very reasonable prices. Call free to find out more.

Shipping
We normally ship via <u>United Parcel Service</u> or <u>Parcel Post</u>. (**Within** the S.F. Bay Area United Parcel zone, add only $3 for handling/delivery for each "SHIP TO" address for a purchase of $50 or less.)

To delivery points **beyond** the S.F. BAY AREA UNITED PARCEL ZONE, add the charge shown in parenthesis [   ] for each unit ordered.

<u>If you want Air Delivery</u> please check the box on the Order Form; that charge will be billed to your Gump's Charge Account or Credit Card (on prepaid mail orders, please call our Toll-Free number: in California 800-652-1662, from other states call 800-227-4512 for the extra air charges).

It's Easy to Order by Phone
Just call us—toll free—at

800/228-9055 And now, you can call Free from Puerto Rico and the Virgin Islands, too!

anytime, 24 hours a day,
7 days a week with credit card orders.

You may find it helpful to fill out an Omaha Steaks order form to use as a reference when calling.

For customer service, call (800) 228-9872 toll free—anytime.

Nebraska residents, call (402) 391-3660 collect.

When you call, ask about our

Special of the Day!

It may be just what you're hungry for — a box of juicy steaks, a heat-and-serve entree, or one of the other luscious foods shown in this catalog. While it's on special, you can have it delivered with your order at a special low price! Just ask our operator about our "Special of the Day" any time you call in an order.

*Postage handling and insurance of $8.50 on each Heart & Soul Pendant (plus any applicable state and/or local taxes) will be added to the first payment of the Installment Plan or to the Single Payment Plan.

ADD FOR SHIPPING / HANDLING
ORDER VALUE TO $19.95   ADD $2.00
ORDER VALUE TO $29.95   ADD $3.00
ORDER VALUE TO $49.95   ADD $4.00
ORDER VALUE TO $99.95   ADD $6.00
ORDER VALUE OVER $100   ADD 6%

SHIPPING AND HANDLING CHART

lbs.	Charge*	lbs.	Charge*
1	1.30	26	4.34
2	1.43	27	4.46
3	1.54	28	4.59
4	1.67	29	4.70
5	1.79	30	4.82
6	1.91	31	4.95
7	2.03	32	5.07
8	2.15	33	5.20
9	2.27	34	5.31
10	2.39	35	5.43
11	2.52	36	5.57
12	2.64	37	5.68
13	2.76	38	5.80
14	2.89	39	5.92
15	3.00	40	6.05
16	3.13	41	6.16
17	3.24	42	6.29
18	3.36	43	6.41
19	3.50	44	6.52
20	3.61	45	6.66
21	3.73	46	6.77
22	3.85	47	6.89
23	3.98	48	7.01
24	4.10	49	7.14
25	4.22	50	7.26

Postpaid We prepay regular U. S. Postage on all orders delivered in the U. S. and its possessions, unless otherwise stated in this catalog.

☐ One for only $5.99 + 70¢ postage and handling.
☐ SAVE! Two for only $10.99 + $1.00 P&H.
☐ SAVE MORE! Three for only $15.99 + $1.40 P&H.

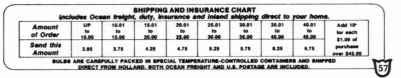

	SHIPPING AND INSURANCE CHART								
	Includes Ocean freight, duty, insurance and inland shipping direct to your home.								
Amount of Order	UP to 10.00	10.01 to 15.00	15.01 to 20.00	20.01 to 25.00	25.01 to 30.00	30.01 to 35.00	35.01 to 40.00	40.01 to 45.00	Add 10¢ for each $1.00 of purchase over $45.00
Send this Amount	2.95	3.75	4.25	4.75	5.25	5.75	6.25	6.75	

BULBS ARE CAREFULLY PACKED IN SPECIAL TEMPERATURE-CONTROLLED CONTAINERS AND SHIPPED DIRECT FROM HOLLAND. BOTH OCEAN FREIGHT AND U.S. POSTAGE ARE INCLUDED.   57

Figure 12-4   Examples of geographic price policies used by direct marketers.

such a condition, there is less chance that a customer will feel resentful because he or she paid a higher price for the same purchase than did a neighbor. If trade-ins are involved, as is often the case with automobiles or appliances, differential treatment (if any) of one customer over another is not as easily recognizable.

To price multiple products (product lines or mixes) the strategy followed under a one-price policy is generally the same as that for pricing single products. Quantity discounts are, of course, recognizable, as is differential pricing for deluxe or superior goods.

Price Lining

The practice of price lining consists of selecting a limited number of prices or ranges of price at which direct marketers sell their products. Examples of this form of price strategy are "Dime Stores" and "Dollar Stores." Other examples are those retailers that typically sell their product lines at $19.95, $29.95, or $39.95.

Certain products, such as shoes, naturally fall into one of these price lines according to quality. Sometimes price lines, rather than being specific amounts, are ranges. A specific pair of shoes, for example, might fall into a $10 to $25 range, the second range might go up to $50, and a third range might extend to $75 or even $100. Ranges are apparent in the Sears' "good/better/best" offer strategy. Such strategy can provide the direct marketer with the advantages of price lining, notably, developing images within certain price ranges, but still gives the customer a depth of product assortment. Typically, higher quality commands a higher price as does a product innovation or new fashion.

An important objective of price lining is to establish a balance between freedom of choice and the complexity of choice. A customer faced with two dozen toothpaste brand names, sizes, and product differentiations on a retailer's shelf can well appreciate the value of price lining. Is the "freedom of choice" worth the trouble? Mail-order marketers often limit choice and resort to price lining to avoid such potential confusion.

A serious impediment to price lining is rising cost of products as well as overhead. As such costs go up, the direct marketer might have to either lower gross margin or else increase the price line from, say, $29.95 to $34.95. Change in price lines often can destroy an established image. Direct marketers who operate within price line ranges, rather than specific prices, are not as susceptible to this ongoing problem of cost increases.

Leader Pricing

Leader pricing involves markdowns, sometimes temporary and often substantial, of a few items, usually those with broad-based demand to provide an incentive for a customer to place an order. Hopefully, once resistance to ordering has been overcome, the customer will order *additional* items providing normal gross margins. To realize full potential from leader pricing, the item should be well known, have a well-established usual selling price, and have the potential for purchase by many customers. The item should not be so low priced that savings appear insignificant or be so high priced that it could be purchased only by a limited number of customers. Convenience goods, such as coffee and razor blades, are often used to build store traffic in traditional retailing. A direct marketer might use an entire product line for leader pricing, for example, fruit trees in a mail-order nursery catalog.

The concept of impulse buying plays an important part in calculating the success of leader pricing. Once that impulse buying is motivated for a particular product, customers ordering by mail or telephone may very well purchase other items at regular prices, even ones that they had originally not intended to buy. This is the rationale for leader pricing.

Psychological Pricing

There are those who feel that a buyer can be psychologically influenced by the way prices are quoted. Price lining is, in effect, one form of psychological pricing.

Prestige pricing, even above the competitive market, is often used by direct marketers. Especially when products are fashionable or dramatically displayed, some customers decide that a product is "superior" or "inferior" solely on the basis of the price charged. These buyers are often suspicious of low prices and presume that high prices automatically denote high quality. Sometimes such prices are thought to be "blind" and beyond comparison. A specific item of jewelry containing precious gems, for example, is not easily compared with another.

At the other extreme from prestige pricing would be a low-level price to which buyers might not respond because it denotes something less than their expectations. Offering a pair of shoes at 99¢, for example, might cause buyers to become suspicious of its quality and, in fact, of its origin.

Odd amount pricing has been viewed by some merchandisers as having psychological appeal, although there is little empirical evidence to support this feeling. Interestingly enough, odd amount pricing was originally devised to keep clerks honest, to force them to make change and thus ring up a sale at a cash register. That was before the advent of sales taxes, which now make virtually all prices odd amounts!

A price of $6.98 is viewed as an odd amount price, whereas $7.00 is not. The issue here is whether the buyer views the former as "six-something" and the latter as "seven dollars." If the purpose of odd amount pricing is to cause the customer to feel that it is a lower price, the psychological value of odd amount pricing can be justified.

Mail-order marketers today shy away from odd amount prices if only to simplify the addition of figures on an order form as well as to simplify check writing and record keeping. Higher priced items, too, are less likely to have more appeal at $69.98 than they would at $70. More likely, prices will be quoted in even dollars, half dollars, or quarter dollars.

Multiunit pricing can also offer a psychological appeal. The price of three for $10.50 offers no real savings but implies a quantity discount. The individual product priced at $3.50, on the other hand, when combined into a price of three for $10, provides a demonstrated savings. A classic example of such psychological impact (as ridiculous as it may appear) would be a quoted price of "10¢ each or 2 for 25¢!" There is an illusion of lower price when the multiple unit is offered.

Price Discrimination

Price discrimination is a form of differentiating products, through price, to establish appeal to specific market segments. The operations of a traditional department store, when compared with those of a discount store, demonstrate the willingness of customers to pay different prices for identical merchandise.

Oftentimes, it is desirable to engage in price discrimination without affecting the one-price policy, or the price image, of a particular direct marketer. One way of doing this is through the use of private brands and private labels. An example of this technique is the Sears' Kenmore brand of washers and dryers. The Whirlpool Corporation makes the Kenmore line for Sears, and a very similar line sold under the Whirlpool brand name. Private brand tires, manufactured by well-known tire companies, abound, as do a variety of private label food and drug products. (A more recent variation in food distribution has been the introduction of generic labels: no brand, just identification of the product category, that is, "canned peas.") Certain intangible features of a product, such as customer service and warranties, may not be present if the product is sold under a private label at a lower price.

Another way of engaging in price discrimination to differentiate products for different market segments is to offer irregular or slightly blemished merchandise ("seconds") at lower prices. Such a price strategy dictates that the direct marketer establish an image and become known for such a policy. Some direct marketers might even reserve a special section of their catalogs for merchandising discounted products.

CREDIT AND COLLECTIONS

The advent of credit, open-account billing as well as credit cards, provided a tremendous impetus to the growth of direct marketing. This innovation occurred primarily in the 1950s when mail-order merchandisers began offering high-priced specialty products, many of which required installment financing. Prior to that time, most mail-order transactions were either cash with order (CWO) or collect on delivery (COD). The former (CWO) required that the buyer send cash in advance, most often without actually seeing or feeling the product, a distinct disadvantage when compared with in store shopping. The latter (COD) is cumbersome, costly, inconvenient, and sometimes results in refusal of merchandise at the time of delivery.

During the 1950s, credit checking became somewhat more sophisticated and this process was hastened by computer capabilities for storing, processing, and retrieving payment information. The real breakthrough for direct marketers, however, was the introduction of the plastic credit card.

Credit Cards

Credit cards and their variations in the form of charge cards, debit cards, and transaction cards burgeoned in popular usage during the 1950s. Their use was quickly adopted by direct marketers anxious to overcome the CWO/COD disadvantages and experiencing severe problems with their own open-account credit checking. These have become so popular that a 1981 survey[2] revealed that at least 87 percent of direct marketers selling to consumers offered one or more credit card options. The

same survey determined that 57 percent of those direct marketing to business/industrial firms offered one or more credit card options. (Business/industrial direct marketers usually sell to firms that have been credit-rated through Dun & Bradstreet or another credit rating service and are less likely to *need* the credit card alternative, relying more on open-account billing to approved credit accounts.)

Although credit cards had been in limited use prior to the 1950s by some large retailers as well as prestige hotels and restaurants, popular usage was largely confined to oil company cards.[3] Today, there are two major forms of credit card in general usage: bank cards and travel and entertainment (T&E) cards. Although many large banks issue their own cards, the two major ones in use currently are VISA and MasterCard. The Direct Marketing Association estimates that there were 64,586,000 VISA cards and 55,655,534 MasterCards in circulation in 1980.[4]

Although active use of T&E cards in direct marketing began in 1958 when Diners Club launched its Executive Shopping Service, American Express is the major T&E card in use today with an estimated 8,500,000 cards in circulation during 1980.

The *Nilson Report* has estimated that, as of June 1980, there were 88 million credit cardholders in the United States, many of whom, obviously, had a variety of cards, out of a market potential of 106 million (or 83 percent market saturation). It was further estimated that the average credit cardholder has 6.2 cards.

Possibly as much as 20 percent of all direct marketing transactions are charged on a credit card. And, some direct marketers report that a catalog sale charged to a credit card is

---

[2] Direct Marketing Association, *Fact Book on Direct Marketing*, 1983, p. 148.

[3] Although credit cards extended the horizons of direct marketers, they also put oil companies into the merchandise business via direct marketing.

[4] Direct Marketing Association, *Fact Book on Direct Marketing*, 1983, p. 147.

generally 25–50 percent larger than a cash sale. The use of credit cards is especially popular if orders are placed by telephone.

Open-Account Billing

Many direct marketers, notably book publishers, record clubs, and insurance companies, still use open-account billing, with or without advance credit checking. Some offer the option of credit card charging. Some continue to remain CWO.

The United States Postal Service's Inspection Service, which recognizes more than 60 major categories of mail fraud, identifies one of the fastest growing of these categories to be that of consumers attempting to bilk direct marketers by ordering merchandise with no intention of paying for it. Known as "deadbeats" to direct marketers, the estimated number of these ranges as high as 10 million. This contingency emphasizes the need for direct marketers to use some form of credit screening.

A 1980 survey by the Direct Marketing Association revealed an average annual bad debt percentage among consumer direct marketers of 7.2 percent and that among business direct marketers of 4.2 percent. In an effort to keep bad debt percentages low, outside collection agencies were used by 42 percent of consumer direct marketers and 72 percent of the business group.

Most direct marketers using open-account billing send as many as three billing-collection efforts, with usually 3 to 4 weeks elapsing between efforts.

In summarizing results of its survey, the Direct Marketing Association offered the following advice for those who would minimize their billing-collection problems:

1 Select mailing lists properly.
2 Screen incoming orders carefully.
3 Use order form psychology; that is, require a signature or a down payment.

4 Pay attention to the billing-collection effort, following up regularly.
5 Consider a collection agency, when all else fails.

Credit Regulations

There are several major credit regulations that are enforced by the Federal Trade Commission (FTC) and are of special interest to direct marketers. These include: Truth in Lending Act, Regulation Z (its amendments concerning credit cards); Fair Credit Billing Act; Equal Credit Opportunity Act, Regulation B; Fair Credit Reporting Act; and Fair Debt Collection Practice Act. Full text of these regulations may be obtained from the FTC or the *Code of Federal Regulations*.

REGULATORY CONSTRAINTS IN PRICING

Federal and state legislation has evolved over the years that regulates pricing and, ultimately, regulates trade. A major objective of such regulation is to prevent pricing tactics that could prove injurious to retailers as well as their suppliers and customers. Much legislation concerned with pricing, in fact, has received heavy support from retailer groups, especially during the 1930s when a proliferation of chain stores began.

Although such legislative regulation is concerned with price-fixing between competitive retailers or manufacturers, there is also concern with both predatory pricing and discriminatory pricing. The regulatory intent is to prevent unfair or deceptive pricing practices.

Sherman Antitrust Act

The roots for prohibition of horizontal price-fixing as a potential restraint of trade are contained in the Sherman Antitrust Act, passed by the United States Congress in 1890. The act was intended to prevent monopoly and collusion, and makes price-fixing illegal regardless of how reasonable the prices resulting from collusion might be. The provisions of the act continue to be actively enforced.

To cope with the inadequacies of the original act, the Congress in 1914 passed two additional laws: the Clayton Antitrust Act, which generally outlawed price discrimination, and the Federal Trade Commission Act, which generally prohibited unfair competition.

Miller-Tydings Act

There was strong support from retailers, especially the National Association of Retail Druggists, when the Miller-Tydings Act was passed by the Congress in 1937 and the McGuire Act was passed in 1953. Enacted as amendments to the Sherman Antitrust Act and the Federal Trade Commission Act, respectively, these laws were enabling legislation for the states to pass laws allowing manufacturers to specify a resale price. Although "fair trade" has ultimately proven to be a misnomer, 36 states passed "fair trade" laws as specified by the federal legislation. These exempted vertical price-fixing from the law that prevented restraint of trade and thus encouraged resale price maintenance. The 1975 Consumer Goods Pricing Act effectively ended the use of "fair trade" resale price maintenance in interstate commerce. The demise of "fair trade" actually began in 1957, when the U.S. Supreme Court upheld the right of an out-of-state direct marketing company to sell products in "fair trade" states at less than "fair trade" minimum prices.[5]

Robinson-Patman Act

Price discrimination, the practice of charging different prices to different customers, is illegal under certain conditions of the Robinson-Patman Act of 1936. This federal legislation was subsequently augmented by laws enacted by several states. An interesting feature of the act is that a buyer who knowingly induces or receives an unlawful price discrimination is as guilty as the seller.

Although trade and quantity discounts are permitted forms of price discrimination under the Robinson-Patman Act, this is true only if such discounts represent differences in costs in performing marketing functions at different levels of the distribution channel and do not cause injury to direct competitors. Promotional and advertising allowances are permissible under the Robinson-Patman Act only if they are offered to competitors on *proportionally equal terms*. Interpretation of the legalities of trade discounts and promotional allowances are, however, still fuzzy, and it is best to seek experienced legal counsel before implementing any promotional plan involving different prices to different customers.

SUMMARY

The direct marketing organization, before establishing price policies and strategies, must first determine whether its objective is profit maximization or sales maximization. The resultant pricing philosophy considers not only cost, competition, and market demand but also promotional strategy and appeal to specific market segments. The objective determines whether distribution will be intensive, selective, or exclusive. The resultant image in the marketplace is most important.

The difference between a direct marketer's selling price and cost of goods sold is termed *gross margin* or *gross profit*. If selling as well as general operating expenses are deducted from gross margin, the result is *net profit*. Gross margin may also be viewed as markup, the calculation of which can be on either cost or selling price. The markup percentage based on cost is determined by dividing the amount of markup by cost. The markup percentage based on selling price is determined by dividing the markup by selling price. Markups occur throughout a channel of distribution and should

---

[5] *General Electric Co.* v. *Masters Mail Order Company of Washington, D.C., Inc.,* 244 Federal (2D) 681, *cert. denied,* U.S. Supreme Court 355, U.S. 824 (1957).

be thought of as a return for marketing functions performed in the distribution process. The buyer's cost can be viewed as the seller's price. Markup percentages usually vary inversely with turnover and they also vary inversely with cost. Sometimes additional markups are taken, as is the case with so-called superior goods.

Markdowns are used to meet competition, to clear out inventory, or to effect special sales. Markdowns are usually expressed as a percentage of the customary selling price and are determined by dividing the markdown by the selling price.

Discounts and allowances are ultimately reductions from established selling prices and may occur at any level within a channel of distribution, serving either as compensation for a marketing function performed by a middleman or as an incentive to purchase. They take these forms: trade discounts (compensation for marketing functions performed by middlemen or functions foregone by buyers); quantity discounts (recognition of the "economies of scale"); cash discounts (return for an investment which a supplier did not have to make to finance accounts receivable); seasonal discounts (incentive used to help level out a manufacturer's production and thus lower cost); promotional allowances (used to encourage advertising and sales activity to be performed by middlemen); brokerage allowances (if the middleman does not actually take title to the goods).

A variety of pricing strategies was discussed in this chapter. Geographic pricing is concerned with whether or not the shipping cost is separately identified to the buyer. A one-price rather than a variable-price strategy is most often used by direct marketers since this precludes personal negotiation. Other price strategies include: *price lining* (establishing recognizable price points or price ranges); *leader pricing* (taking smaller than usual markups with products of high market demand to stimulate ordering); *psychological pricing* (including prestige as well as odd amount pricing); and *price discrimination* (selling to different market segments at different prices for the same product, but not always with the same service features).

The advent of credit cards in the 1950s provided direct marketers with a tremendous impetus. Alternative credit terms include open-account billing, cash with order (CWO), and collect on delivery (COD).

Major regulatory constraints to be considered in pricing relate to price fixing, price discrimination, and predatory pricing.

CASE: PRICE COMPARISON IN DIRECT MARKETING

Learning Objective

This case study demonstrates that there can be price comparison in direct marketing just as there is in traditional shopping. Typically, too, the selling prices that are printed in promotional materials used in direct marketing can be compared with competitive offers.

Overview

Price determination is never a simple matter. Consideration must be given by a direct marketer to cost, competition, and market demand. The product and its selling price make up the offer and are typically part of the direct marketer's promotional strategy. The objective, always, is to price for profit, with total profitability ultimately dependent on both profit per unit *and* total number of units sold.

Procedure

Read the learning objective, the overview, and the case that follows. Be prepared to suggest ways in which buyers can compare prices between direct marketed offers as well as similar offers in local stores. How important are convenience and availability in price comparison?

Case[6]

Comp-U-Card Marketing is a membership/buying service in the beginning stages of developing an electronic home shopping service. The service is two-way interactive, initially by telephone and ultimately by computer or two-way interactive television. Comp-U-Card members are able to shop, order, or simply compare prices via electronic media. Although Comp-U-Card receives a small selling commission from the suppliers it represents, it also charges an annual membership fee. For that fee, members receive access to an "800" toll-free number that provides them unlimited access to Comp-U-Card's shopping consultants. Members are able to price merchandise Monday through Friday, from 9:00 A.M. until 9:00 P.M. and on Saturday from 9:00 A.M. until 5:00 P.M. They can use the service as often as desired for price comparison or purchasing. Customer service problems are also handled through this toll-free number.

More than two million members use the Comp-U-Card service to shop and obtain price and product information on more than 60,000 brand-name products; everything from home appliances to watches. The Comp-U-Card shopping consultants are specially trained and usually have had retail store experience. Included are specialists in such products as china, crystal, silver, and furniture. Although telephone calls are received randomly, these can be referred to a product specialist if need be.

Approximately 60 percent of the calls received by Comp-U-Card are pure price comparisons. These comparisons are often used in the buyer's own local marketplace. The balance of the calls result in orders being placed through Comp-U-Card.

Unlike catalog showroom dealers, Comp-U-Card views itself as a shopping service assisting the buyer in making an intelligent purchase and wants to make sure the buyer is ultimately satisfied and remains a Compu-U-Card member.

Comp-U-Card has recently announced an interactive electronic catalog that enables the member to "shop" through a computer terminal at home. Although still embryonic, this is the direction in which Comp-U-Card is moving.

---

[6] This case study was adapted from an interview with John Fullmer, President, Comp-U-Card Marketing, Stamford, Conn., which appeared in *Direct Marketing*, July 1982, pp. 127–128.

DISCUSSION QUESTIONS

1 Differentiate between a pricing policy that seeks to maximize profits and one that seeks to maximize sales.
2 Define gross profit and net profit.
3 Is markup based on cost or selling price or either? How is it calculated?
4 When markups occur at various levels of a distribution channel, how are these justified?
5 Name and describe various discounts and allowances and the rationale for each.
6 Why is a variable-price policy usually not practical for direct marketers?
7 Give an example of leader pricing used by a direct marketer.
8 How did the proliferation of credit cards accelerate the growth of mail order?

PART FOUR

PROMOTION:
ALTERNATIVES AND
STRATEGIES

THE NATURE OF PROMOTION IN DIRECT MARKETING

Promotion is an important and necessary part of any marketing system. It is vital in direct marketing since, with buyer and seller physically removed from each other, promotion becomes the means of communicating information about products and services through a variety of media.

OVERVIEW OF PROMOTION

Promotion is a part of the total marketing mix: product, price, place, and promotion. Its relevance in the overall perspective is visualized in Figure 13-1.[1] Although promotion is a vital part of the marketing mix, it should be viewed as a *means* and not an *end*. The objective of promotion is to complete the direct marketing process. It is not the process itself. Direct marketing is mistakenly viewed by some as being the promotion process, that is, "direct mail" or "direct response advertising," when in fact it encompasses much more than that as an aspect of total marketing. The distinctive features of direct marketing, measurability and accountability, are especially important when promotion is viewed as part of the total marketing mix. Thus, direct marketers always relate promotion costs to results.

Promotion is, to a large extent, a function of imperfect competition. In a perfectly competitive situation, price is theoretically the equilibrating force. In monopoly, aside from its institutional value, there is theoretically no need for promotion. In imperfect competition and in monopolistic competition, however, differentiation is based on things other than price and such differentiation must be communicated, preferably by market segment.

Such communication is subject to criticism because often, by its very nature, it is an intrusion. One should not, however, confuse the tool with its uses. Legitimate direct mar-

[1] James U. McNeal, editor, *Readings in Promotion Management*, Appleton-Century-Crofts, New York, 1966.

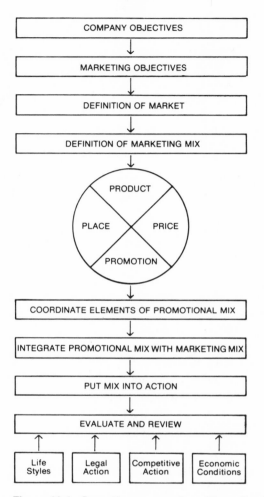

Figure 13-1 Promotion: an overview. (*From:* Readings in Promotion Management, *James U. McNeal, ed., Appleton-Century-Crofts, New York, 1966.*)

keting *uses* promotion; it does not *abuse* it. Although good promotion must be noticed to create response, the ultimate objective of direct marketing, it must do this by presenting benefits and creating desire rather than through gimmickry, deception, and exaggeration.

The use of promotion as a part of the direct marketing mix is not confined to business organizations. It has relevance also for nonprofit organizations as well as governments, including those politically inclined who aspire to or hold public office. Whereas the objective response for a business might be sales or interest; that for a nonprofit organization might be fund raising or participation; that for government might be political action or support.

FORMS OF PROMOTION

Promotion has four basic forms: selling, advertising, publicity, or support. (See Figure 13-2.) Bearing in mind that they are used by both private and public sector organizations, each of these four forms will be considered in a direct marketing context.

Selling

When measured in terms of expenditure, the "one-on-one" contact of a salesperson with a prospect or a buyer usually accounts for the largest share. Although personal selling has traditionally been viewed as "eyeball-to-eyeball" contact, direct marketing recognizes the use of personal selling through the telephone and other emerging electronic media, such as interactive television. Further, direct marketing techniques are often used to pave the way for personal selling. A variety of media are used for "prospecting" and for the development of inquiries for sales follow-up. Direct marketing often combines selling with advertising in a total process.

Advertising

As a promotional strategy in direct marketing, advertising is most often combined with selling with the objective of developing a measurable response or transaction. Although advertising has often been viewed, in contrast to the "one-on-one" format of personal selling, as mass communication, present-day direct marketers have capabilities for individualizing and personalizing their direct mail and other advertising media. Even when not individually personalized, furthermore, direct marketers most often think in terms of another form of promotion personalization, that is, market segmentation, when directing their advertising/selling message, whether the medium is newspaper, television, magazine, radio, or outdoor advertising,

Publicity

Contrasted with advertising, publicity (a tool of public relations) reaches readers, viewers, and listeners in the context of "news" rather than "advertising." Such space or time is not generally paid for, as in advertising, but that is not to imply that publicity has no cost associated with it. Obviously, the communication of the newsworthy happening and, indeed, the happening itself have a price tag. Thus, publicity is not "free" while advertising has a "cost."

Promotion includes:

(1) Selling — "one-on-one" contact by an individual.

(2) Advertising — mass, although often individualized, conveyance of sales messages in various media: newspapers, television, direct mail, magazines, radio, billboards, etc.

(3) Publicity — a tool of public relations. Contrasted to advertising, such space or time is not paid for, but that should not imply that it costs nothing.

(4) Support — incentives such as sweepstakes, contests, premiums or giveaways; point-of-purchase activities, exhibits, displays and other forms of advertising.

Figure 13-2 Forms of promotion.

Support

This category of promotion, which is often used by direct marketers to gain attention as well as an incentive to action, includes such devices as sweepstakes, contests, premiums, or other giveaways. It also includes point-of-purchase activities, exhibits, displays, and other forms of merchandising.

Push-Pull Strategies

Promotional strategies are often distinguished between those that *push* (sell) and those that *pull* (advertise) goods and services as they move from producer to user. The distinction is usually made in terms of the selling or advertising influence that is used in the process. Direct marketing, by its very nature, often combines both push and pull strategies.

Push strategies, those involving selling in person or with electronic intervention, are most often used if the product is a technical one that needs demonstration or if the potential buyer needs a high degree of persuasion. A push strategy is very often used, for obvious reasons, with high-quality products that are high-priced. Advertising often plays a lesser role if push strategies are used because the emphasis is on selling and even demonstration. Mail-order marketers through printed or broadcast promotion could include such strategies, as could direct marketers using personal sales follow-up.

Pull strategy relies heavily on mass communication and is the opposite of push strategy. The major objective of pull strategy is to create buyer demand at the end of a distribution channel. With convenience packaged goods, such as typical food and drug items, pull strategies are often used to create demand in the sense that consumers *ask for* the product at their retail outlets.

Products promoted through pull strategies usually have a short shelf life and high turnover

with consequent low profit margins to middlemen. This is partially because the producer has paid a high percentage of the allowable promotion budget on advertising so as to create demand at the point of purchase.

Certain personal products and services, life insurance, for example, can employ pull strategies up to a point. After that, because of product complexity and the consequent need for explanation, push strategy is also used. These direct marketers are more concerned with push strategies and use lengthy, explanatory promotional presentations for this reason.

Promotion as Information

Promotion should be viewed as a technique for information dissemination and not just as a tool for persuasion and influence. Promotion is, in the context of direct marketing, a procedure for disseminating information so as to effect responses and/or transactions. Such information can be directed to either the ultimate buyer or intermediaries in a distribution channel.

Contrary to dogma, advertising is not confined to capitalistic societies. Information dissemination through advertising, a process Karl Marx branded as "unproductive exploitation," appeared in the Soviet Union as early as 1958. A Soviet distribution expert, S. V. Serebrikov, wrote in 1956 that "the gradual widening of knowledge of buyers about goods by means of advertising works a positive influence on the simplification of merchandising."[2] In 1973 it was reported that domestic advertising in Russia was conducted through 72 regional advertising agencies with more than 7,000 employees. All major media were being employed, with *Veneshtorgreklam* (the All Union Foreign Trade Advertising Agency)

---

[2] S. V. Serebrikov, *Organizatsiia i Tekhnika Sovietskoi Torgolvi,* Gostorgiadat, Moscow, 1956, p. 76.

Figure 13-3 The communication process.

claiming to have mailing lists, arranged by type of industry or profession, to reach decision makers important to foreign advertisers.[3]

COMMUNICATION PROCESS[4]

Communication, derived from the Latin word *communis,* meaning common, is the process of establishing *commonness.* The process of communication has three essential elements: a *source,* a *message,* and a *destination.* Transmittal of the message requires a *channel.* The communication process is visualized in Figure 13-3.

The source of a direct marketing communication may be an individual or an organization, with either "encoding" a message in such a way as to make it easy for the destination to establish a commonness with it. Such an encoded message may be one that is read, heard, or seen. To complete the act of communication, the message must be "decoded" at its destination. The message decoded by the receiver, however, might be quite different from that intended when it was encoded by the sender. Because of this possibility, an understanding of the communication process is particularly important in direct marketing. This is especially true in that direct marketing promotion must not only state the offer clearly

[3] Lyman E. Ostlund, "Russian Advertising: A New Concept," *Journal of Marketing Research,* February 1973, pp. 11–19.
[4] Much of the discussion in this section is based on Wilbur Schramm (ed.), "How Communication Works" in *The Process and Effects of Mass Communication,* University of Illinois Press, Urbana, Ill., 1955, pp. 3–26.

and precisely, but also anticipate and overcome potential objections.

Both senders and receivers of messages, in their respective acts of encoding and decoding, tend to view messages in terms of their own fields of experience. A message encoded in Chinese, for example, cannot be decoded by a receiver who does not understand the language. Likewise, the direct marketer wanting to communicate the benefits of an electronic calculator must be clearly understood when the message is decoded by the prospect on a mailing list to whom this message is sent. Whereas the word "soap" might conjure a fairly common image in the minds of most recipients of messages about soap, the interpretation of the word "calculator" may not be so common. That is the challenge faced by creators of direct response promotion.

Communication and the Learning Curve

The purpose of communication is to influence buyer behavior. In terms of the learning curve, promotion plays a role in extensive problem solving, limited problem solving, or automatic response behavior.

Extensive Problem Solving Promotion provides actual information. It also helps to create interest and product awareness. It makes the potential purchaser aware of a relative deprivation.

Limited Problem Solving If the potential purchaser already has some experience with a product or service, promotion serves to stimulate the sale directly. The problems and the goals of the customer are better known. Promotion helps to rationalize decisions and gives "reasons why." It keeps the buyer aware and interested, reminding him or her of product benefits.

Automatic Response Behavior In this instance, promotion results in automatic purchase. This involves the principle of generalization. That is, if a specific product is desired and it is not readily available, an alternative is selected. For example, if a particular toothpaste containing fluoride, one that has been heavily advertised, is not on the retailer's shelf, an alternative might be chosen without benefit to the original advertiser.

With regard to such a learning process, these conditions must all be met for a direct response communication to be successful:

1 The message must gain the attention of the intended destination.
2 It must be so encoded and decoded that it draws on experience common to both source and destination.
3 The message must arouse, as a result of a statement of benefits, perceived needs at the destination and at the same time suggest ways of meeting those needs at the source.
4 The message must suggest a way to meet those needs at the destination that is appropriate to the group (market segment) at the time a response is desired.

Steps in the Buying Decision

As presented in Figure 13-4, the steps in a typical buying decision are these: awareness, interest, evaluation, trial, purchase, postpurchase evaluation, and repurchase.

Usually, in terms of mass communication, advertising is relied on to create awareness and interest in a potential purchase of a product or service. The steps that follow, from evaluation through repurchase, call for a selling,

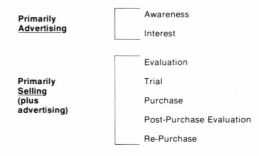

Figure 13-4 Steps in the buying decision.

as well as an advertising, strategy. In direct marketing, selling is typically a part of the total promotional strategy. There may, of course, be personal intervention through the telephone or even a personal visit as a follow-up.

The effectiveness of a promotion can be measured by the buyer's awareness as well as attitude toward it. The objective, of course, is the purchase of the product or service offered in the promotion. It is here that direct marketers can be particularly adept in their ability to experiment and to measure actions (responses/transactions) rather than simply replies (opinions/attitudes).

The process of postpurchase evaluation has a greater impact on future behavior than does, even, the initial promotion. This is the acid test. The direct marketer cannot long survive with a poor product and/or service. This is why the real value of a direct marketing operation lies in its lists of customers and data about those customers.

Campaign Concept

As defined by William J. Stanton, "A *campaign* is a coordinated series of promotional efforts built around a single theme or idea and designed to reach a pre-determined goal."[5]

---

[5] William J. Stanton, *Fundamentals of Marketing,* 6th ed., McGraw-Hill Book Company, New York, 1981, p. 391.

Successful direct marketers view campaigns as an integral part of total promotional strategy and not simply as a series of advertisements. One well-known campaign theme is that of Hallmark Cards, Inc.: "When You Care Enough to Send the Very Best." Although this theme has been used for many years in the promotion of Hallmark greeting cards, its connotation is also implicit in the more recent direct marketing activities of Hallmark Cards, including the Halls' catalog of up-scale merchandise as well as the distinctive products featured in the Little Gallery series of collectibles.

A campaign falls on deaf ears, of course, if the product is not there to back it up. That is why it is so very important for promotion to be coordinated with distribution efforts. That is why, too, the benefits delivered by the products and services sold by direct marketers must be at least equal to the promotional claims made for them.

Direct marketers view the initial promotion effort to obtain a new customer as only the first step of a total campaign integrated with that initial effort. Subsequent promotions take the form of follow-up efforts, seeking additional sales of the same product, as well as additional corollary sales, cross-selling, and continuity selling. The campaign concept extends, too, to referral of *new* customers by *existing* customers as well as reactivation of *lost* customers. A characteristic of a campaign is continuity. Continuity is a characteristic of direct marketing.

Design of a Communication Strategy[6]

Development of a proper communication strategy involves a thought process as well as an implementation procedure. From a direct marketing perspective, the following steps outline a design of a communication strategy, working backward from the ultimate objective:

[6] Adapted from J. Taylor Sims, J. Robert Foster, and Arch G. Woodside, *Marketing Channels,* Harper & Row, New York, 1977, p. 257.

Objective setting: To define goals and determine desired responses and/or transactions.

Market definition: To determine one or more market segments; that is, message destinations.

Experimentation: Through testing, to gather data on how alternative messages will be decoded and responded to.

Message creation: To develop offers and other elements of the message that are likely to achieve the desired response.

Media selection: To search and define those media that can most efficiently and effectively deliver the intended messages to the target market segments.

Image building: To create a reputation or favorable attitude toward the organization as a source of communication on products and services.

Feedback: To measure and evaluate response to communication as an aid to designing subsequent strategies.

THE OFFER AS A PROMOTIONAL STRATEGY

The manner of presentation by a direct marketer, coupled with the all-important request for a response, encompasses what is termed an *offer.* The offer (see Figure 13-5) is concerned with not only the product and its pricing including its positioning (differentiating products for market segments) but also payment

Figure 13-5 Some elements of the direct marketing offer.

PRICING

PAYMENT AND TERMS

TRIAL OR EXAMINATION

GUARANTEE

SWEEPSTAKES/CONTESTS

GIFTS/PREMIUMS

TIME LIMIT

CONTINUITY

methods and terms, guarantees, and a host of other devices to incite action and overcome human inertia. Next to the product itself and its special relevance for a market segment, the offer is a key determinant of success (or failure) in direct marketing. Since so much of a direct marketer's promotional strategy hinges on the offer, it would be well to review key elements of an offer.

Pricing

It is not just whether a price is high or low that is important. Equally important is the manner in which a price is stated. Is it a discounted offering? Is it a sale? Does it represent a savings from the established price as would, for example, a prepublication offering of a new magazine? Can there be substantial savings through quantity purchasing?

Payment and Terms

The way payment can be made is a vital part of the offer. The payment methods that have been offered by direct marketers in the past, cash with order (CWO) and collect on delivery (COD), basically lacked convenience and often were a deterrent to ordering. On the other hand, an offer to absorb shipping costs if cash payment is sent with the order can be a distinct incentive.

A bill me later (BML) payment offer that includes credit card options, either the direct marketer's own, a bank card, or a T&E card, not only offers convenience but also avoids procrastination when placing an order. In certain cases, such as a free trial offer with full return privileges, the BML offer is a necessity.

Delayed payment, as an offer, is sometimes extended to provide installment terms. This option is usually confined to higher priced products, with or without an interest charge. Payment in installments is an attractive incentive to many consumers and such an offer can be a strong one. However, the advantages of this incentive must be weighed against the cost of financing the resultant accounts receivable, the potential for bad debts, and the ultimate return on the direct marketer's investment.

Trial Offers

The concept of providing a "free trial" or "free examination" is an important form of offer because of the very nature of direct marketing in which, typically, the buyer does not have the opportunity to see or feel the product before ordering. The free trial or free examination offer helps overcome this distinct disadvantage of ordering by mail or telephone from a printed or broadcast presentation.

The trial offer might even be an introductory one involving remittance of a nominal amount (such as 25¢ for the first 30 days of coverage under an insurance policy or $1.97 for the first 3 months' subscription to a magazine). If the buyer's examination reveals that the insurance policy or magazine does not meet expectations, even the small introductory payment might be refunded.

Full return privileges are, of course, a vital part of any offer. Trial offers, whether or not they involve a nominal prepayment, have long been among the most effective ways used by direct marketers for many products and continuity programs.

Guarantees

The 1744 catalog of colonial America's first important printer, Benjamin Franklin, guaranteed customer satisfaction with the following statement printed on its front cover:

> Those persons who live remote, by sending their orders and money to said B. Franklin, may depend on the same justice as if present.

On the inside front cover of the 1875 Montgomery Ward catalog appeared this pledge of guarantee:

> We guarantee all our goods. If any of them are not satisfactory after due inspection, we will take

them back, pay all expenses and refund the money paid for them.

The 1,786-page catalog of Sears Roebuck, Inc., published in 1897, contained the following statement under the heading "About Our Reliability" on page 2:

> We give you this privilege: if you have any doubt as to our reliability you can send your order and money to the National Bank of the Republic or any express company in Chicago, with instructions not to turn it over to us unless they know us to be thoroughly reliable and a concern that will do exactly as we agree.

A guarantee of "complete satisfaction or your money back" is an inherent necessity of direct marketing. This assurance, and the manner in which it is presented, is a vital part of the offer. L. L. Bean, Inc., offered this "100 percent guarantee" in a recent catalog:

> All our products are guaranteed to be 100 percent satisfactory. Return anything purchased from us that proves otherwise. We will replace it, refund your money, or credit your charge card.

Although guarantees are a necessity in virtually any offering, they are especially instrumental in overcoming a potential buyer's reluctance to purchase an unseen product from a remote location. Certain direct marketers of collectible items even guarantee to buy back some products at a later time and certain direct marketers of insurance guarantee to accept all applicants for some types of policies. Guarantees have been developed for extended time periods. Some even offer "double your money back" if the buyer is less than completely satisfied.

Sweepstakes and Contests

Sweepstakes and contests have been widely used by direct marketers as an ordering stimulus. To avoid being considered a lottery, however, a winner must be guaranteed. Further, actual purchase cannot be a determinant for entering the sweepstakes or contest. This results in a "yes/no" form of option: the "yes" option for those who also accept the product offer and the "no" option for those who desire only to enter the contest. (It should be apparent that attractive prize offerings necessitate large volumes of "yes" responses.)

Winners are selected by random drawing sometimes made in advance of the mailing so that the contest will not be construed as a lottery. A key to the success of sweepstakes and other forms of contests is involvement by the respondent in some way. Often perforated tear-offs, die-cuts, tokens, and stamps, as well as answers to questions, problems, or puzzles, are used.

Gifts and Premiums

An effective device for stimulating response to a direct marketed promotion is the offer of a free gift or premium, either for purchasing or for simply examining the product. Although such incentives, as do sweepstakes and contests, increase response, they may also attract less qualified respondents in terms of credit worthiness and/or final product acceptance.

Some gifts are termed "keepers," meaning that the premium can be retained whether or not the product is kept. In some cases the gift must be returned if the product itself is returned. Ideally, to be most effective, the premium used should be related to the product being sold or to the specific audience being sought.

A gift can be offered for buying, for trying, or for simply inquiring. Sometimes, multiple gifts are provided or there can be a choice. A gift may even be "a mystery" until it is received. It can have tangible and apparent value or the value can be intrinsic, such as a booklet containing advice. Sometimes the free gift offer can be as nominal as providing information or a price estimate.

Time Limits

This type of offer often involves limited quantity as well as specified time period. The offer can even quote "while they last." A limited time offer typically specifies a deadline, an enrollment period, a charter membership, a limited edition, or a prepublication offer.

Continuity Offers

Continuity or club offers are often used by book and record direct marketers. These include *positive* option (the customer must specifically request shipment for each offer in a series) or *negative* option (the shipment is sent automatically unless the customer specifically requests that it not be).

With a 'til-forbid offer, an insurance policy or a magazine subscription, as examples, would be renewed automatically until the customer instructs otherwise. Some clubs (senior citizens groups or automobile clubs) include specific services with an annual membership fee.

PROMOTIONAL MIX: SELLING VS. ADVERTISING

Both advertising and selling have roles in the total promotional mix of an organization. Inherently, personal selling can provide person-to-person, two-way communication, and this is its fundamental strength. The ability of a salesperson to tailor promotional messages to individual buyers, the ability to compensate for variety or complexity of behavioral competence of individual buyers, and the ability to provide feedback are also important advantages of personal selling.

In contrast, advertising is generally seen as a one-way communication system that is necessarily generalized to fit the needs of many, diverse prospects. Especially if the unit value of a sale is small, advertising can be more economical than personal selling. In fact, there can be a tremendous monetary difference between the cost of an advertising impression and the cost of a personal sales call.

If the prospective buyer has been qualified (often through advertising), is serious, and has a sincere interest, a personal sales call can be definitely worthwhile. McGraw-Hill, which has for many years measured the escalating costs of an individual sales call, summarizes the corollary value of advertising in a classic advertisement. Their ad presents a large photograph of a stern-looking purchasing agent viewing the reader of the ad (presumably a salesperson) over his desk and saying:

> I don't know who you are.
> I don't know your company.
> I don't know your company's product.
> I don't know what your company stands for.
> I don't know about your company's customers.
> I don't know your company's records.
> I don't know your company's reputation.
> Now . . . what was it you wanted to sell me?
> *Moral:* Sales start before your salesman calls—with business publication advertising.

In direct marketing the objective response is a sales transaction (mail order), and the elements of *both* advertising and selling are necessarily present. The selling attributes of promotion are often contained within the printed or broadcast advertising message, or they might include the interactive intervention of a salesperson in a one-on-one mode through an electronic medium such as the telephone. In another instance, not mail order, direct marketing techniques could be employed to generate a response in the form of an inquiry requesting a salesperson to call on a (hopefully) qualified prospect. Similarly, a mailed catalog (from a retail store, for example) might cause the recipient to personally visit the store where a salesperson would complete the transaction.

Characteristics of Selling

Of the available promotional alternatives, personal selling is the major one. Escalating costs of personal (eyeball-to-eyeball) sales contacts, however, have resulted in more use of mail and telephone. Even face-to-face contacts are often prequalified to assure that the prospect is in a buying mood.

Much has been written about personal selling. Major businesses have been built around the care and feeding of salespeople: their recruiting, selection, training, motivation. The play entitled *The Death of a Salesman,* by Arthur Miller, presented the character Willie Loman, the model of a "typical" (circa 1940) salesman. Another production entitled *The Music Man,* by Meredith Wilson, presented Harold Hill, whose counterpart probably no longer exists today. Gone is the day, too, when a silver-tongued and glib salesperson, in the style of P. T. Barnum, could "sell" the Brooklyn Bridge to an innocent buyer. Today's buyer is much too educated, informed, and sophisticated for that. Today's salesperson must be knowledgeable about the product as well as about the market.

If personal selling has a major limitation today, it is high cost. If such cost can be justified, however, personal selling offers the advantages of flexibility, specific action, and performance of corollary functions such as credit inspection and trouble shooting right on the scene. The average salesperson's prime responsibility today is no longer selling as much as it is consummating a sale that has already been set in motion. Today's "super salesperson" must relate the product to the prospect to satisfy a need, rather than simply sell a product. His or her knowledge might have to range from equipment amortization to inventory control.[7]

Recruiting, Selecting, Training, Motivating Salespeople

The process of developing salespeople involves recruiting, selecting, training, and motivating.

Recruiting is the process of attracting sales applicants through advertising, employment

[7] "The New Supersalesman: Wired for Success," *Business Week,* January 3, 1973.

agencies, personal contact, or word of mouth. The recruiting system involves continuity as well as exhaustive search of all potential sources.

Selection begins with a determination as well as an exact definition of needs: number, qualifications, territories, job descriptions. Frequently, a variety of testing procedures are used for professional as well as personal evaluation. Assimilation into a sales organization is also an important factor to be considered in selection of a salesperson.

Training comprises a most important part of the personal selling process. It needs to be carefully planned, scheduled, coordinated, and directed by a responsible person. Training encompasses company orientation as well as product and market knowledge. For those who have not yet mastered the basic techniques of selling or getting along with people, training includes these skills as well as outfitting the salesperson for the job.

Motivation involves compensation as well as a host of other incentives. Compensation may be financial (salaries, commissions, paid vacations, pensions, insurance plans) or nonfinancial (opportunity, recognition, prestige, fulfillment). Supervision on the job is a key method of motivation as is ongoing training.

Selling in Direct Marketing

Personal selling can be an important adjunct of direct marketing. Personal selling may be conducted at the buyer's location, as would be the case if a salesperson for an equipment manufacturer responds to an inquiry. It may be conducted at the seller's location, as would be the case if the recipient of a mailed catalog chooses to personally visit a retail store. The personal selling experience need not necessarily be face to face. Oftentimes it involves communication by telephone.

The strength of personal selling in direct marketing is centered around the ability of the salesperson to develop, modify, and maintain a flexible intercommunicating relationship with customers. The face-to-face situation can be both complex and variable. As a result, sales-people can be most difficult to manage. A key objective of the direct marketer, under such diverse conditions, is to strike a happy medium between the desirability of flexibility and the need for organizational control. Through careful planning of scheduling, measuring results, and accounting for time, the salesperson can benefit from the rigors of direct marketing.

Characteristics of Advertising

Advertising is not a separate and distinct force within our socioeconomic structure. It is not an entity by itself, with the key attribute of persuasive power. Like selling, it is a tool of promotion. Promotion in turn is part of a total marketing process. Possibly the most vital function that advertising performs is dissemination of information, letting the buyer know that a particular product or service is available. Advertising endeavors to tell buyers about the performance characteristics of a product (with which they might be totally unfamiliar), in a manner that will benefit them. In this sense advertising is intended more to stimulate and increase total demand than to shift demand from one product to an alternative. Sometimes the effect of advertising is institutional or indirect. At other times, as is most frequently the case with direct marketing, advertising calls for a direct response.

Media of Advertising

The major media for advertising, virtually all of which are used in some way for direct response, in the manner shown in Figure 13-6, are these, rank ordered according to dollar expenditure:

Newspapers
Television
Direct mail
Telephone
Radio

Magazines
Outdoor
Car cards

Although expenditures for advertising have been increasing at a rate greater than 5 percent annually, the total expenditure has averaged only approximately 2 percent of the Gross National Product for the past 40 years. Overall, advertising expenditures when related to expenditures for personal selling are somewhat lower. An exception, of course, is direct response advertising, which incorporates selling strategy and is a vital part of the direct marketing process. An exception, too, is that advertising for certain consumer products in which salespeople are not involved to any great degree: drugs, toiletries, tobacco, beverages. Ultimately, of course, any advertising expenditure, whether for institutional purposes or to create response, has a common objective: *to sell something!*

Advertising in Direct Marketing

Advertising is a *means* to an end, *not the end itself!*

Advertising is thus only a part, albeit an important part, of a total direct marketing system. It complements direct marketing research, market planning, offer planning, product/price planning, and the other vital element of promotional planning, personal selling, as well as marketing workforce development and administration.

Advertising, viewed as a promotional strategy in direct marketing, is a means of communication and information dissemination. The key difference between general advertising and direct response advertising, as used by direct marketers, is that the latter must be measurable and accountable in terms of responses and transactions as well as in the generation of customer lists and data. General advertising, on the other hand, is most often concerned

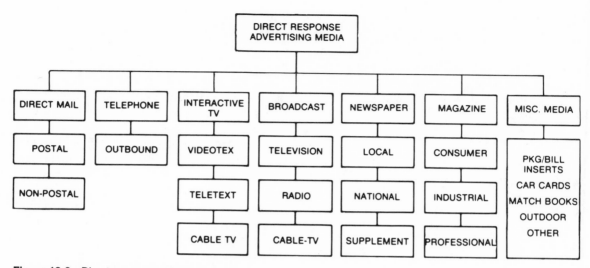

Figure 13-6 Direct response advertising media.

with the development of an awareness, creation of interest, and building of an image.

Because direct response advertising is so vital to direct marketers, it often incorporates selling strategies to be fully effective.

EVALUATION OF EFFECTIVENESS

The real measure of direct response advertising incorporating, as appropriate, personal selling, is contained in the evaluation of its costs in comparison to results, short run or long range.[8]

Whereas general advertising is often difficult to quantify, to isolate, to compare, direct response advertising is always structured so as to make measurability and accountability possible. Further, it is important to know not only *which* direct response advertisement is best but also *why.*

Direct response advertising, and especially direct mail, because of its very nature, is most susceptible to controlled testing and consequent measurement. These attributes, together

with pinpoint selection capability, form the basis of this observation by Levitt:[9]

No communication process today is growing more rapidly in the United States than direct mail. The computer, working with Census tracts, ZIP Codes, and a vast variety of specialized mailing lists, is having an increasingly more important impact on sales communications.

Direct mail makes possible selected communications for selected readers, addressing itself to their distinctive needs and styles of life. This principle of communication is now rapidly catching on even for mass media.

Direct mail, of course, has the greatest potential of becoming increasingly more discriminating. The result could conceivably be that we will get more third class mail, but less of it will be quickly disposed of as "junk mail." It will be mail geared to our interests and needs, rather than merely to "occupant." The old law of nature will be reversed: as the mail gets more abundant, it will also get more discriminating and relevant.

Although general advertisers conduct a great

---

[8] Refer to the discussion of "The Value of a Customer" in Chapter 2.

[9] Theodore Levitt, "Advertising: The Sphinx That Thinks," in *The Marketing Mode,* McGraw-Hill Book Company, New York, 1969.

deal of research into "readership," "recognition," and "recall," direct marketers are more concerned with "response." Direct response advertisers are not so much interested in the impact of advertisements, but rather the effect they have on sales transactions.

REGULATION AND INTERVENTION

By their very nature, direct marketing promotional activities, as they inform and persuade, often in very large numbers, are highly visible. The volume of direct mail accelerated rapidly in the 1950s, 1960s, and 1970s. As it did, some was branded as "junk mail" by those receiving it who did not find it relevant, by those resenting its intrusion, and even by those representing competing advertising media. During this period of proliferation of direct marketing, abuses by individual organizations ultimately resulted in intervention by regulatory authorities.

The Federal Trade Commission (FTC) has issued several very important trade regulation rules and guides that affect direct marketing. The FTC has also issued several guides and advisory opinions relative to unfair competition in the form of misleading or deceptive acts or advertising. State and local governments also intervene in advertising and selling practices as do the United States Postal Service, Better Business Bureaus, trade associations, the advertising media, and, ultimately, consumers themselves.

Federal Trade Commission[10]

The major federal legislation regulating the promotional activities of direct marketing is the Federal Trade Commission Act together with its Wheeler-Lea Amendment. (Addition-

---

[10] Full text of the specific FTC trade regulation rules, guides, and advisory opinions referenced in this section may be requested from the Federal Trade Commission, Office of Public Information, 6th & Pennsylvania Ave., N.W., Washington, D.C. 20580.

ally, the Robinson-Patman Act, discussed in Chapter 12, prohibits price discrimination in the form of inequitable promotional allowances.)

The FTC is charged with regulating content of promotional messages used in interstate commerce. In Section 5 (A), intended to prevent unfair competition, the Wheeler-Lea Amendment to the FTC Act strengthened this provision by making it a violation of the law whenever such competition injured the public regardless of its effect on a competitor. The amendment also prohibited false, misleading, or deceptive advertising by enumerating four types of products in which advertising abuses existed and in which the public health could be directly involved: foods, drugs, cosmetics, and therapeutic devices.

Although in some cases FTC actions have been controversial, the FTC recently has become much more aggressive in its enforcement, especially when false or deceptive advertising is involved. Enforcement is through issuance of cease and desist orders that become effective in 60 days unless the defendant appeals to the federal courts. The FTC can compel companies to provide documentation to substantiate advertising claims. And, in certain cases that came to be known as "scarlet letter" rulings, the FTC stipulated that firms must run "corrective" notices in future advertising if, in its own judgment, it felt that advertising claims were erroneous.

Certain FTC trade regulation rules, guides, and opinions have particular relevance in direct marketing and are referenced here.

Delayed Delivery Rule   Possibly the most important regulation affecting mail-order firms was that promulgated by the FTC on February 2, 1976, and popularly referred to as the "30-Day Delayed Delivery Rule." The rule provides that, if it is believed that goods will not be shipped within 30 days of receiving a properly completed order, an advertisement must include a clear and conspicuous notice of the time in which delivery is expected to be made. If no such statement is made, shipment *must* be made within 30 days. The 30-day delayed delivery rule applies to all direct marketing media but specifically exempts photofinishers, garden centers offering seeds and growing plants, and publication subscriptions *after* the first issue. Also exempt are COD orders, negative option plans, or credit transactions in which the seller does not charge the buyer's account prior to shipment.

Negative Option Rule   This trade regulation rule, effective June 7, 1974, governs prenotification negative option sales plans. Under negative option plans, sellers notify buyers of the periodic selection of merchandise to be shipped. Unless the buyer requests that the merchandise not be shipped, the seller ships and bills the buyer for the merchandise. Negative option plans are frequently used by those merchandising book and record clubs. The rules set forth the requirements for disclosure in promotional material. They also provide that the seller cannot refuse, under certain conditions, to give the buyer full credit for a returned selection.

Guides against Deceptive Guarantees   The FTC promulgated seven guides on April 26, 1960, for the purpose of self-regulatory adoption by marketers in their advertising of guarantees. These guides are intended to ensure that the buyer is fully apprised of the conditions governing any guarantee. The seven guides describe the general nature of guarantees, prorated adjustments, "satisfaction or your money back," lifetime guarantees, savings guarantees, nonperformance guarantees, and misrepresentations in guarantees.

Guides to Use of Endorsements and Testimonials   These FTC guides, which became effective May 21, 1975, relate to the use of expert and organizational endorsements and testimonials in advertising. Not only must endorsements reflect the experience of "actual consumers" but there must be disclosure of any material connections between the endorser and the seller that might affect the weight or credibility of the endorsement.

Advisory Opinion on Dry Testing   Dry testing is a term used by marketers to describe the practice of promoting a product, such as a book or a magazine, that has not yet been manufactured. Whether the product is actually made available will depend on the size of the response to the dry test solicitation. An advisory opinion issued by the FTC on March 27, 1975, allows such dry testing under very strict guidelines to ensure that the potential customer is in no way misled about the terms of the offer.

Mailing of Unordered Merchandise   Coming under the category of fraud and deception, the FTC considers the mailing of unordered merchandise, that sent without the prior expressed request or consent of the recipient, an unfair method of competition and an unfair trade practice in violation of the FTC Act. Any such merchandise may be treated as a gift by the recipient without any obligation whatsoever to the sender. It is a separate violation for a shipper of unordered merchandise to mail to any recipient of such merchandise a bill or any dunning communication.

Guides against Deceptive Pricing   Effective January 8, 1964, these guides are concerned with offers stating reductions from a "former," "regular," "comparable," "list price," or "manufacturer's suggested retail price." One guide is specifically concerned with bargain offers based on the purchase of other merchandise, such as "Buy One—Get One Free" or "Two-for-One Sale."

Guides against Bait and Switch Advertising
The four guides against bait and switch advertising that were issued by the FTC on December 4, 1959, define this type of advertising as that which is "alluring but insincere in offering to sell a product or service which the advertiser in truth does not intend or want to sell." Its purpose is to switch consumers from buying the advertised merchandise in order to sell something else, usually at a higher price or on a basis more advantageous to the advertiser. The mere presence of the advertised merchandise does not preclude the existence of a bait and switch scheme.

Guide Concerning Use of the Word "Free"
This guide issued by the FTC on December 16, 1971, is intended to prevent deceptive or misleading offers of "free" merchandise or services if, in fact, such is available only with the purchase of some other merchandise or service. If the purchaser is told that an article is "free" if another article is purchased, the word "free" indicates that the purchaser is paying nothing for that article and no more than the regular price for the other. The term "gift" is to be used so that the article so described is actually a donation or a present, not dependent on the purchase of something else.

Advisory Opinion on Use of the Word "New"
This advisory opinion, issued January 4, 1969, is concerned with merchandise that has been used by purchasers on a trial basis, returned to the seller, refurbished, and resold as new. The FTC has pointed out that the word "new" may be properly used only if the product so described is either entirely new or has been changed in a functionally significant and substantial respect.

Advisory Opinion on Disclosure of Foreign Origin Merchandise   Direct marketers when advertising or promoting goods of foreign origin must clearly inform prospective purchasers that such goods are not made in the United States if, in fact, the goods originated elsewhere. According to the FTC, "the underlying reason for the disclosure requirement is that mail order purchasers do not have the opportunity to inspect the merchandise prior to the purchase thereof and be apprised of the material facts bearing upon this selection," such as would appear on a label or a sticker.

Warranties   The FTC is empowered by the Magnuson-Moss Warranty Act, effective July 4, 1975, with enforcement. Although no organization is required to give a written warranty and state a minimum duration for a warranty, the National Retail Merchants Association, in summarizing the act and the FTC rules relative to it, describes the following responsibility of direct marketers under the act:

> Catalog or mail order solicitations must disclose for each warranty product either the full text of the warranty or notice that it may be obtained free upon written request. This information must be located on the same page or the facing page as a description of the warranted product or in a clearly referenced information section of the catalog. In addition, the retailer must promptly fill the requests it receives for copies of written warranties.

State and Local Regulation

Certain organizations using direct marketing strategy, including insurance companies, small lenders, banks, and pharmaceutical firms, are closely regulated by state legislation, especially relative to promotion and pricing tactics. State legislators have become increasingly active in consumer issues and in privacy matters such as those that affect mailing lists and promotional use of the telephone. The matters of state sales and use taxes, as they relate to taxation of advertising and promotional services, are also of vital concern to direct marketers.

"Truth in Advertising" Legislation Mainly fashioned after a model statute first proposed in 1911, most states have so-called truth in advertising legislation relative to the conduct of promotional activities in intrastate commerce.

"Green River" Ordinances This type of local legislation regulating personal selling was named after the town of Green River, Wyoming, where it was first enacted. Such ordinances, which require prior licensing for any door-to-door selling, solicitation, or even marketing research interviews, have been challenged in courts with mixed results.

United States Postal Service

Through its Inspection Service and in compliance with the Private Express Statutes, the United States Postal Service has established rules and regulations that bear impact on the promotional activities of direct marketers. The Inspection Service is constantly on the lookout for fraud and deception through the mails and the Private Express Statutes, by granting the United States Postal Service a form of delivery monopoly, determine classification and cost of promotional matter that can be circulated outside the postal monopoly.

Private Organizations

Better Business Bureaus, the history and influence of which go back more than half a century, are located in most major cities and are sponsored by private businesses and organizations to prevent promotional abuses through common sense regulation.

Likewise, trade groups, such as the Direct Marketing Association, have promulgated ethical guidelines for use by their members and others desiring to adhere to them. These are codes of conduct with particular emphasis on the avoidance of deception and outright fraud. The National Association of Broadcasters and other organizations of media have adopted guidelines for the acceptance of advertisements, refusing to accept those that they feel to be false, misleading, or in bad taste.

Ultimately, of course, the public itself becomes the prime regulator through refusal to patronize those organizations that use deceptive tactics in their promotion. This, possibly, is the best policing action of all. Stating that "it is easy to confuse two quite separate things, the legitimate purpose of advertising and the abuses to which it may be put," Theodore Levitt went on to say that "it is difficult, as a practical matter, to draw the line between legitimate distortion and essential falsehood."[11]

SUMMARY

Promotion, along with product, price, and place, is an important and necessary part of the total marketing mix. It takes four basic forms: selling, advertising, publicity, and support. Each of these four forms has special meaning in the context of direct marketing.

Certain promotional strategies *push* (sell) and others *pull* (advertise) goods and services as they move from producer to user. Direct marketing, by its very nature, often combines both push and pull strategies.

In the context of direct marketing, promotion is a procedure for disseminating information so as to effect responses and/or transactions. It is not simply a tool for persuasion and influence, as is much general advertising.

[11] Theodore Levitt, "The Morality of Advertising," *Harvard Business Review,* July–August 1970, p. 85.

In any communication there are three essential elements: a source, a message, and a destination. Direct marketing communication, whether from an individual or an organization, can be encoded in such a way that the message will be decoded at its destination in the same context as intended at the source. This calls for clarity and precision as well as anticipation of potential objections and is a challenge often faced by the creators of direct marketing promotion.

The steps in a typical buying decision are these: (1) awareness, (2) interest, (3) evaluation, (4) trial, (5) purchase, (6) postpurchase evaluation, and (7) repurchase. Although, in terms of mass communication, advertising is usually relied on mainly to create awareness and interest, direct marketers often incorporate selling in their printed or broadcast messages. Direct marketers, too, sometimes augment such messages through the use of the telephone or even a personal visit by a salesperson.

Direct marketers view the initial promotional presentation effort as only the first step of a total promotion campaign designed to create, care for, and keep customers. Subsequent promotions to these customers often seek additional sales of the same product or corollary sales of additional products. This campaign concept extends, too, to referral of new customers by existing customers as well as reactivation of lost customers. Such continuity is a key characteristic of direct marketing, which thrives on customer lists and data.

The offer is a vital part of the overall promotional strategy of a direct marketer. Key elements of an offer include these: pricing, payment and terms, trial and examination, guarantees, sweepstakes and contests, gifts and premiums, time limits, and continuity offers.

Advertising and selling both play key roles in the promotional mix of direct marketers. Personal selling is characterized by face-to-face contact but there is a trend toward electronic intervention, such as the telephone. The key elements in the development of salespeople include recruiting, selection, training, and motivation. Advertising, on the other hand, takes the form of mass communication in its dissemination of information intended to stimulate and to increase total demand. Major media of advertising, virtually all of which are employed in some way for direct response, include these: newspaper, television, direct mail, telephone, radio, magazine, outdoor, and car card.

It is important to view promotion as a *means* to an end, not as an *end*. Advertising and selling, combined as promotion, are a part of the total direct marketing system, offering a means of communication and information dissemination. The key difference between general advertising and direct response advertising, as used by direct marketers, is that the latter must be measurable and accountable and result in the generation of lists and data. Response advertising is always structured so as to make measurability and accountability possible.

Prior abuses of advertising, coupled with legitimate concerns of consumers, have brought on an abundance of regulation of promotion activities. This regulation, at the federal level, is mainly a concern of the Federal Trade Commission. Other regulation and intervention occurs at state and local levels as well as within the United States Postal Service and private organizations such as Better Business Bureaus, trade associations, and the various media used by direct marketers.

CASE: UTILIZING THE PROMOTIONAL MIX

Learning Objective

This case discussion demonstrates the use of all four forms of promotion: selling, advertising, publicity, and support, in the context of direct marketing. The interaction of these elements of the promotional mix is seen to be an integral part of dissemination of information about, and persuasion of attendance at, Missouri Repertory Theatre, a nonprofit organization.

Overview

It has been established that direct marketing, an aspect of the total marketing concept, is as applicable to public organizations, culture and the arts as well as political groups and government entities, as it is to business organizations. Direct marketing strategies are used not just for fund raising to support civic and charitable causes but also for participation in and attendance at such activities. It is important to recognize that direct marketing is *not* unique to the private sector.

Procedure

Read the learning objective, the overview, and the case that follows. Be prepared to observe and discuss these specific elements of the promotional mix in the context of direct marketing: (1) selling; (2) advertising; (3) publicity; and (4) support. How does support of and attendance at the Missouri Repertory Theatre differ from simply a contribution to a worthy cause? Does the use of direct marketing promotion strategies differ for public or private organizations?

Case

Recognized as one of the country's leading professional regional theatres, Missouri Repertory Theatre was founded in 1964 at the University of Missouri–Kansas City by its current artistic director, Dr. Patricia McIlrath. Her belief in the blending of top quality professional theatre with a practical training ground for theatre students was a pioneering one. In terms of product, time has proved her concept remarkably successful.

Much of the growth of the Missouri Rep-

ertory Theatre and its establishment in the forefront of the area's artistic community is due to Dr. McIlrath's success in attracting outstanding actors and directors to work with the Rep's talented professional company. Some of the guest directors who have come to Kansas City from all parts of the world are Alan Schneider, Cyril Ritchard, John Houseman, Ellis Rabb, Adrian Hall, Vincent Dowling, and Cedric Messina.

Missouri Repertory Theatre, Inc., through a Board of Trustees made up of concerned community leaders, keeps a watchful eye on the production, financial, and marketing courses of this not-for-profit organization. Grants from the arts and public and private foundations, together with individual and organization donors, make it possible to tour Missouri Repertory Theatre productions to outlying towns in midwestern states. As an addition to the experience of professional theatre, students in these smaller communities are offered drama workshops and assembly programs by the Rep's professional actors.

No seat is farther than 23 rows from the stage in the intimate Helen F. Spencer Theatre, home for the Rep. The location is convenient, in the multimillion dollar Center for the Performing Arts on the University of Missouri–Kansas City campus. Performances are enhanced by the most modern technical facilities. There are two hydraulic elevators for thrust staging, computerized lighting, a state-of-the-art sound system, and two-storied side stages. Backstage shops feature the newest equipment for scenery, property, and costume design and construction.

An informed and sophisticated audience from throughout the midwest has come to expect the finest from the Missouri Repertory Theatre. Each season they look forward to masterful classical drama. At the same time, they welcome the work of new playwrights and the theatre's dedication to the nurturing of young artistic talent. These objectives guide the trustees and management of Missouri Repertory Theatre, Inc.:

1 To present, as a resident professional repertory theatre, high quality productions of a wide range of works selected from the full spectrum of dramatic literature, to enrich the lives of theatregoers in metropolitan Kansas City and in other communities served by touring productions

2 To interact in a mutually beneficial way with the University of Missouri–Kansas City professional theatre training program by offering to students of demonstrated ability the opportunity to work with professional directors, actors, designers, and theatre technicians

3 To contribute to the development, improvement, and appreciation of theatre on a local, regional, and national basis by the quality of productions and through impact on professional theatre people and students

4 To manage all of its responsibilities well, with special concern for the continued financial success and enhanced artistic reputation of Missouri Repertory Theatre, Inc.

In a 1981 survey of 147 nonprofit professional theatres with annual operating budgets ranging from $100,000 to $6.5 million, Theatre Communication Group, Inc., of New York, found that the 1980 income of the total group was $113.6 million. Total attendance at home and on tour was almost 14.2 million theatregoers. More than 42,000 performances were given of 2,400 productions. The theatres surveyed provided paid employment to a total of 14,566 individuals. Professional actor workweeks totaled 71,754 with related salaries of $19.1 million.

A 1982 survey of theatregoers in the Kansas City area, conducted by the Theatre League, Inc., revealed that two-thirds of the local subscribers to theatre were female, two-thirds were married, and 95 percent had some college education. The median age reported was 44. The ZIP Code areas having the greatest penetration of theatre subscribers contained

households with these characteristics as well as above average median household income.

Of those season subscribers surveyed, more than 90 percent read the daily newspaper regularly and 30 percent read the *Wall Street Journal* regularly. More than 75 percent watched the late evening news on television regularly and more than 50 percent watched the early evening news. Radio listeners favored popular and classical music as well as easy listening.

The primary reasons given for purchasing season subscriptions were these: to obtain priority seating, an interest in professional theatre, an assurance of seeing all the shows. The availability of discounts to season subscribers, preference for the shows presented, and socializing with friends were other reasons given by at least 15 percent of the respondents. Important performance characteristics listed were good sound, comfortable seating, parking convenience, usher assistance, prompt show starting time, and low ticket prices.

During the 10-year span 1972–1981, the number of Missouri Repertory Theatre season subscribers and the number of individual ticket purchasers had both more than doubled. In the same period the number of performances had increased from 90 to 148. Most importantly, earned income or that accruing from ticket sales, rather than from grants and contributions, approached nearly 70 percent of the total operating budget. This achievement, coupled with near capacity audiences, was considered significant among cultural and arts groups.

A major factor in the increase in both season subscriptions and individual tickets was increasing support by businesses and other groups. These organizations were called on personally by staff salespeople as well as volunteers and assistance was rendered in making tickets available to individual members of groups as well as employees of organizations. Direct mail was used extensively in contacting groups and businesses both to solicit direct orders

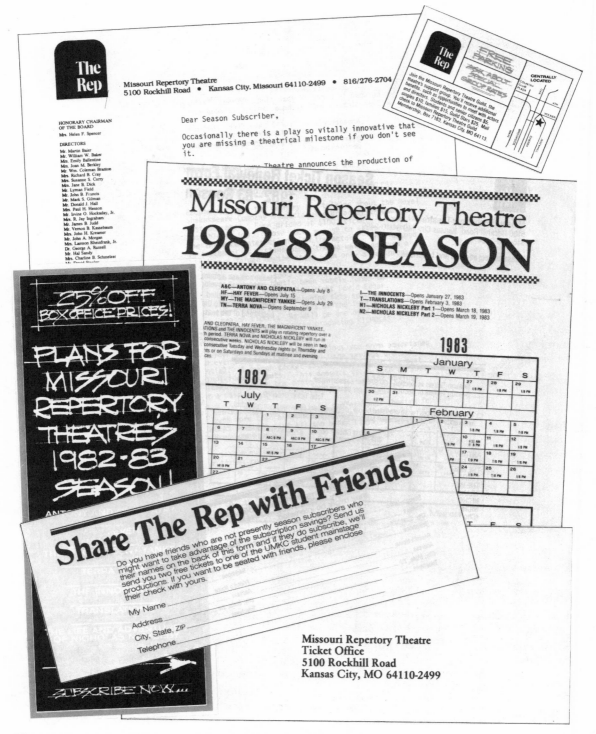

Figure 13-7 A typical direct mail package for the Missouri Repertory Theatre.

and to obtain inquiries for personal sales follow-up.

Promotional planning for the 1982–1983 Missouri Repertory Theatre season was built around the Rep's innovative production of *The Life and Adventures of Nicholas Nickleby,* one of the first offerings outside of London and New York of the Royal Shakespeare Company's Tony Award–winning spectacular 8½ hours of Charles Dickens' theatre. Tickets for the limited run of *Nicholas Nickleby* on Broadway were priced at $100, with tickets becoming virtually impossible to buy. The 1982–1983 Missouri Repertory Theatre season included this 8½-hours, together with six other productions, at a season price of $76 for best seating.

Promotional strategy for 1982–1983 relied heavily on direct mail, as it had for the prior several years. A typical mailing package is visualized in Figure 13-7. A variety of direct mail is sent to subscribers of the prior season, inactive former subscribers, and single-ticket buyers. Other selected prospects are often segmented by lists and/or ZIP Code areas. Multiple follow-ups go to selected categories. Direct mail is also sent to groups and business organizations, with subsequent follow-up by a personal sales call. Personal telephone calls are used as a follow-up, and, of course, box office personnel are trained in the nuances of personal selling.

Direct mail advertising is augmented by newspaper advertising, soliciting a direct response by mail or by telephone, as visualized in Figure 13-8. Thirty-second spots are used on television with longer spots on radio. Often, these are public service announcements and a telephone number is featured for response.

A representative radio spot is this one:

Occasionally there's a new play so innovative you'll miss a theatrical milestone if you don't see it. Charles Dickens' epic story, THE LIFE AND ADVENTURES OF NICHOLAS NICKLEBY, is just such a play. Theatregoers in New York

Tonight at The Rep

Peter Umbras is Scrooge

A Christmas Carol

**Now through Dec. 27
Tues.-Sun. 8 p.m.
Sat. and Sun. 2 p.m.**

Missouri Repertory Theatre, 4949 Cherry on UMKC campus. Free parking. Call 276-2704 Ext. 103. Tickets also at Computicket outlets.

Figure 13-8   A typical newspaper advertisement for the Missouri Repertory Theatre.

clamored to see it at $100 a ticket. Now, this trend-setting play . . . plus six other exciting Missouri Repertory Theatre productions . . . are yours for as little as $60. Your Rep season ticket is the best entertainment buy in town. Ask about it. Call Missouri Repertory Theatre, 276-2704.

A special performance of Charles Dickens' *Christmas Carol* was presented during the 1982 holiday season. Radio announcements urged the respondent to dial ''Dic-kens,'' a special telephone number that spelled out the author's last name. Outdoor advertising also featured such an easy-to-remember telephone number.

Figure 13-9 Publicity for the Missouri Repertory Theatre.

Figure 13-10 Support promotion for the Missouri Repertory Theatre.

Publicity prior to opening and all during the season is extensive in 125 metropolitan, suburban, and rural publications of the six-state area. Television and radio are also used for publicity. Programming features stories about the productions, human interest features, and interviews with the cast and directors. A typical newspaper story is shown in Figure 13-9.

Support promotion includes a slidefilm presentation for showing to groups as well as posters, bumper stickers, two-for-one offers for special performances, discounts to senior citizens, and incentives to convert single-ticket buyers to season subscribers. Several support pieces are shown in Figure 13-10.

DISCUSSION QUESTIONS

1 Explain why promotion should be viewed as a "means" and not as an "end" in direct marketing.
2 What are the four basic forms of promotion? Briefly describe each.
3 Distinguish between "push" and "pull" promotion strategies. When is each type used?
4 Name and describe the steps in a typical purchase decision.
5 What is an "offer" in direct marketing? Of what might it consist?
6 Describe a continuity offer.
7 Why are guarantees important in direct marketing?
8 Direct marketing is sometimes viewed as a process that is intended to eliminate personal selling. Is that a correct view? Does your answer also fit the parameters of mail order?
9 As a promotional strategy in direct marketing, what is the major purpose of advertising?
10 How do the key characteristics of direct marketing, measurability and accountability, apply specifically to advertising?
11 Discuss the major rules and regulations of the Federal Trade Commission of which the direct marketer should be aware.
12 How does the United States Postal Service regulate direct marketing?

DIRECT MARKETING'S PROMOTION FORMATS

The promotion formats of direct marketing are virtually unlimited. They can be basically categorized, however, according to the media in which they are used: direct mail, print (magazines and newspapers), broadcast (television and radio), interactive media (telephone and television), and other media. Such a grouping of formats is shown in Figure 14-1. In reviewing these formats, it should be noted that the promotional strategies of personal selling, publicity, and support are often incorporated into direct response advertising. This distinguishes such advertising from most general advertising, whether the intended response and/or transaction is to be by mail, by telephone, or by a personal visit to either the buyer's or seller's location.

This chapter is devoted to the promotion formats used in the media categorized in Figure 14-1, including their creation and their production. First, however, we will look at the creative process as it relates to the development of copy, design, and graphics for direct marketing.

GETTING ATTENTION: BENEFITS VS. PERSUASION

Thirty-six years separate the dates on the two direct mail solicitation letters that open with the lead paragraphs shown in Figure 14-2. These examples aptly illustrate the evolution of direct response copy that has occurred during that time. Direct marketing promotion

Figure 14-1 Formats of direct response advertising/selling/support.

DIRECT MAIL	PRINT	BROADCAST	INTERACTIVE MEDIA	OTHER MEDIA
Letters/Letterheads	Newspaper	Television Scripts	Telephone Scripts	Poster Displays
Personalized	Display Ads	Spot Announcements	Outbound	Billboards
"Lift" Letters	Inserts	Demonstrations	Inbound	Car Cards
Memorandums	Supplements	Radio Scripts	Interactive TV Scripts	Exhibits
Cards	Magazine	Spot Announcements	Videotex	
Self-mailers	Display Ads	Narrative	Teletext	
Circulars	Inserts	Cable Television	Sales Persons	
Folders	Supplements	Selective Markets	Retail Locations	
Broadsides				
Brochures				
Booklets				
Catalogs				
Publications				
Bulletins				
Price Lists				
Inserts/Reprints				
Phonograph Records				
Invitations				
Survey Research				
Coupons/Tickets				
Specialty Items				
Calendars				
Novelties				
Action Devices				
Order Forms				
Applications				
Reply Envelopes				
Reply Cards				
Reply Labels				
Mailing Envelopes				
Package Inserts				
Statement/Invoice Inserts				
Co-ops				
Syndications				
Couponing				

experts today rely more on the selling value of *benefits* than on the hard sell of *persuasion*. Copy, design, and graphics are combined with arousing headlines and compelling offers to create an enticing first impression.

The creative process used in developing direct marketing promotion, whatever the format, necessarily begins with research that leads to idea generation before writing. This creative process includes familiarization with both product and market and draws heavily on promotion that has already been created by the direct marketing organization as well as by its competitors. Such research and idea generation ultimately lead to development of a *concept* and then an *offer*. After organization comes copywriting.

WRITING THE COPY

Copywriting is an art, especially when it is intended for direct marketing. Good direct response copywriters are very much in demand. They have the ability to translate product features into benefits and benefits into words, design, and graphics.

Formula Writing

Successful copywriters often follow a writing formula to keep copy flowing in a logical sequence. Several of these are presented in this section.

Bob Stone's Seven-Step Formula[1]

1 Promise a benefit in your headline or first paragraph, your most important benefit.
2 Immediately enlarge on your most important benefit.
3 Tell the reader specifically what he or she is going to get.
4 Back up your statements with proofs and endorsements.
5 Tell the reader what will be lost by not acting.

6 Rephrase your prominent benefits in the closing offer.
7 Incite action now.

A-I-D-A   Of unknown origin, this formula has been used extensively by copywriters for many years:

Attract *Attention*
Arouse *Interest*
Stimulate *Desire*
Call for *Action*

P-P-P-P   Created by Henry Hoke, Sr., and popularized by Edward N. Mayer, Jr., is this formula for direct marketing copywriting:

Picture—get attention early in the copy to create desire.
Promise—tell what the product or service will do, describe its benefits to the reader.
Prove—show value, backed up with personal testimonials or endorsements.
Push—ask for the order.

Star-Chain-Hook[2]   Invented by Frank Dignan, L. E. "Cy" Frailey described the "Star, the Chain, and the Hook" as follows:

First, get the reader's favorable *attention*. Do it deliberately with an opening paragraph which is bright and brisk—the *Star*.

Second, follow quickly with a flow of facts, reasons, benefits, all selected and placed in the best order to transform attention to real *interest* and finally to *desire*—that's the *Chain*.

Third, suggest *action* and make it as easy as possible—the *Hook*.

Frank Egner's Nine Points[3]

1 Write a lead to create desire as well as get attention.
2 Add an inspirational beginning.

[1] Bob Stone, *Successful Direct Marketing Methods*, 2d ed., Crain Books, Chicago, 1979, pp. 210–211.

[2] L. E. "Cy" Frailey, *Handbook of Business Letters*, Prentice-Hall, Inc., Englewood Cliffs, New Jersey, 1948, p. 110.
[3] Maxwell C. Ross, *How to Write Successful Direct Mail Letter Copy*, Direct Marketing Association, Inc., New York, 1976, p. 11.

KIRKLAND 7-9800

EDWARD C. BURSK
SOLDIERS FIELD
BOSTON, MASSACHUSETTS 02163

Please reply to me in care of:
Transpolar Expedition
Admiral Richard E. Byrd Polar Center
18 Tremont Street
Boston, Massachusetts 02108
September 3, 1968

EDITOR
HARVARD BUSINESS REVIEW

Mr. Richard N. Archer
121 Corlies Ave.
Pelham, N.Y. 10803

Dear Mr. Archer:

As Chairman of the Admiral Richard E. Byrd Polar Center, it is my privilege to invite you to become a member of an expedition which is destined to make both news and history.

It will cost you $10,000 and about 26 days of your time. Frankly, you will endure some dist... ...may even face some danger.

On the other h... ...of taking part in a mission of great ...world.
A mission, incident...

You will pers...
knowledge about tw...

I am invitin...
fly around the wo...
will commemorate...

Among the h...
flight ever to c...
stopovers at th...
McMurdo Sound,...

Because t...
World, you and...
even celebrit...
You will have...
portant natio...
of Japan, Ge...
history.

By agre...
yourself in...
Admiral Ric...

Your...
future his...
will be p...
with thos...

BRYAN KING
LEASES ·· ROYALTIES
FORT WORTH, TEXAS

February 6th, 1932

Dear Associate:-

YOU MUST ACT THE VERY MINUTE YOU FINISH READING THIS LETTER -- or else! -- IF YOU FAIL, -- IF YOU LET A SINGLE THING ON EARTH KEEP YOU OUT NOW ------- YOU MAY BE TURNING DOWN THE GREATEST CHANCE OF YOUR WHOLE LIFE TO BECOME INDEPENDENTLY RICH -- TO KNOW THE BLOOD SURGING THRILL OF THE BIGGEST! -- RICHEST! -- FATTEST! -- FORTUNE IN CASH PROFITS YOU HAVE EVER HAD A CHANCE AT IN YOUR WHOLE LIFE!!

Shell Turns Rusk Lease to J. Cloud

HENDERSON, Texas, Jan. 30.— Shell Petroleum Corporation has turned its 109-acre W. F. Neal lease in the J. Lindley survey, Rusk County, to Jim Cloud, Inc., who agrees to drill three tests, the first of which has already been started.

If you paid one bit of attention to my last two letters to you -- you have instantly recognized that I am "ON THE TRAIL" of the very biggest thing we have ever had a chance at!!

Now you HAVE GOT TO ACT!!

YOU HAVE GOT TO ACT QUICK! BY RETURN MAIL -- IF YOU ARE GOING TO GRASP THIS CHANCE TO PARTICIPATE IN ABSOLUTELY THE BIGGEST AND MOST ASTOUNDING -- RECORD BREAKING, -- PROFIT CLEAN UP WE HAVE EVER KNOWN!!

In my last letter I gave you an "inkling" of what I saw coming. I gave you a bare "thimble full" of the utterly amazing -- brain staggering -- mountainous mass of sensational advance information that has come to me!!

You know what I am telling you IS RIGHT -- absolutely RIGHT! You KNOW the information I put in your hands in my last letter is CORRECT because the things I told you are IRREFUTABLE FACTS ----- FACTS .... I say! -- that you can PUT YOUR FINGER ON ---- THAT YOU CAN EASILY...N-O-W... VERIFY!! -- SITTING RIGHT IN YOUR OWN HOME!!

You know the difference in Exchange between the countries remaining on the Gold Standard, and those who are now off of it. And you can instantly recognize what this one thing alone means to the oil industry -- to those big major oil moguls who have been looking to European markets for the output of their refined products.

I told you in my letter of February 2nd, -- in the first paragraph at the top of page Two -- that for the first time in

---

Figure 14-2 Contrasting examples of getting attention, persuasion vs. benefits.

3 Give a clear definition of the product.

4 Tell a success story about the use of the product.

5 Include testimonials and endorsements from satisfied customers.

6 List the special features of the product.

7 Make a statement of the value to the purchaser.

8 Devise an action close that will make the reader want to buy immediately.

9 Conclude with a P.S. rephrasing the headline.

William Steinhardt's A-B-C Checklist

*A*ttain attention.
*B*ang out benefits.
*C*reate verbal pictures.
*D*escribe success incidents.
*E*ndorse with testimonials.
*F*eature special details.
*G*ild with values.
*H*onor claims with guarantees.
*I*nject action in reader.
*J*ell with postscript.

Copywriting Rules

Whether one writes direct marketing copy to formula or to feel, there are guidelines and rules that seasoned copywriters follow, knowingly or not. One experienced direct response copywriter and counsel, Pat Farley, has developed a series of such rules, which, she admonishes, "should be broken only with great care and good reason." Including a few additions to her basic list, Pat Farley's writing tips follow:[4]

1 Keep words, sentences, and grammar at an easy reading level. Use short, "Hemingway-like" sentences as much as possible.

2 Avoid semicolons—they slow the reader down. Dashes and ellipses can separate complex or long thoughts . . . yet carry the reader onward.

[4] Pat Farley, "Direct Mail Copy—The Marketing and Creative Process," in *DMA Manual*, Release No. 3103, Direct Marketing Association, Inc., New York, May 1979.

3 Keep copy in the active tense—complex sentence structures make copy boring and hard to follow.

4 Generally avoid humor or being too cute. Both can backfire.

5 Avoid too much involvement such as puzzles or riddles. They can occupy the reader to the detriment of the copywriter's offer.

6 Start with a strong opening headline and lead paragraph, immediately stressing benefits to the reader.

7 Appeal to the emotions and self-interest.

8 Describe products or services adequately. Take nothing for granted. Repeat key features.

9 State the price and offer on all interior package elements unless they are being tested.

10 If available, include testimonials. They are unbeatable assurance. Names are better than initials; specific comments on specific aspects of the product are better than general praise; results are more powerful than opinions.

11 Specifics are always more effective than generalities. Concentrate on examples, titles, names, even quotes. Position product benefits as reader benefits—tell the reader what's in it for him or her.

12 Follow the "rule of three"—a series of three has more rhythm and balance than two or four examples or adjectives.

13 Odd numbers ("seven reasons why," "21 basic rules") are more effective than even numbers.

14 Always seek a rhythm in copy—it should "sing." Read your copy out loud or have someone read it to you to be sure it reads the way you hear it in your mind.

15 Whenever someone has to reread a sentence or ask for clarification, change the copy—it will bother a substantial portion of the audience as well.

16 Suit imagery and vocabulary to the market and the product. If you are selling a magazine, for instance, the copy should reflect the style of the magazine.

17 The headlines, subheads, boxes, photograph captions, and sunbursts in a brochure should be a full sales presentation for nonreaders.

18 Underlines, indents, and a second color

in the letter should be used for pacing (to break up the copy) and to make all the key sales points stand out clearly to the prospect who only skims.

19 Never ask a reader a question in a key headline or on the outer envelope that can be answered, "No, I don't want this" or "I don't care."

20 The letters in a package should be personal and look like letters, with typewriter type, a salutation, and signature. Use "I" and "you," with more of the latter.

21 The first paragraph of a letter should be no more than one or two lines, three at most, to make it easy to begin reading.

22 At least the first page of the letter should "break" to the next page in midsentence, preferably at a point that pulls the reader onward. For example, "The small child ran directly in front of the speeding car and . . .".

23 Mention the product on page one of the letter; include price and offer if either is a key selling point. If the letter has a "story" opening, consider a "preface" above the salutation to state the offer.

24 Present an ironclad and absolute guarantee of satisfaction.

25 In concluding the letter, return to the theme that began it.

26 Ask for the order.

27 A postscript is one of the most read portions of a letter. Use it to reinforce the sales pitch and stress the incentive for immediate response.

28 Components of a direct mail package do not all have to be "themed" together, but there should be a sense of continuity throughout.

A tongue-in-cheek example of direct marketing copy written according to many of these rules is reprinted in Figure 14-3.

DESIGN AND GRAPHICS

Hand in hand with copy, the words, the expressions, the ideas, the meanings, go the related subjects of design and graphics: the art, the layout, the symbols, the effects. Here are included the impact of photographs, illustra-tions, type styles, paper, inks, size, and a variety of attention-getting devices. Through the discriminate use of design and graphics, the designer, like the copywriter, creates mood and feeling while getting and holding attention. In direct marketing the ultimate goal of the designer, like that of the copywriter, is to stimulate action, to generate measurable response. Thus, design (like copy) becomes a means and not an end, another element of the total promotion process.

Elements of Design

The designer of direct marketing promotion has available a great many graphic techniques for use in a variety of media: direct mail, print, television, and other printed display such as posters and billboards. These include:

Layouts These involve positioning copy and illustrations to not only gain attention but also direct the reader through the message in the sequence intended by the copywriter. Compelling layouts make optimum use of type as well as "white space," photographs along with illustrations, and a host of other graphic techniques: shapes, sizes, folds, die-cuts, and even "pop-ups."

Illustrations and Photographs A compelling illustration can create attention and photographs of products in use, especially those involving people, can dramatize benefits. Graphic illustrations can even extend to designed borders, highlighting of certain copy elements for prominence, tint blocks, and emphasis of elements such as product features and response forms.

Involvement Devices There are many devices used in direct response advertising that have been demonstrated to spur action through involving the reader in some way. These include tokens, stamps, punch-outs, puzzles, premiums, and gadgets. Using these so that they receive attention and encourage involvement is an important factor in design.

ROLLED IN RARE BOHEMIAN ONYX, THEN VULCANIZED BY HAND

DEAR EMINENT PATRON OF THE MAIL ORDER ARTS,
    Imagine a collector's item so exquisitely detailed that each is actually *invisible* to the naked eye.

Think of an heirloom so limited in availability that when you order it, the mint specially constructed to craft it will be *demolished*.

Ponder an item so precious that its value has actually *tripled* since you began reading this.

Kiln-Fired in Edible 24-Calorie Silver

Never before in human history has the Polk McKinley Harding Coolidge Mint (not a U.S. Government body) commissioned such a rarity.

Consider: miniature pewterine reproductions, authenticated by the World Court at The Hague and sent to you in moisture-resistant Styrofoam chests, of the front-door letter slots of Hollywood's 36 most beloved character actors and actresses.

A special blue-ribbon Advisory Panel will insure that the Foundation Council's certificated and inscribed insignia is approved by Her Majesty's Master of Heralds before the application deadline.

Meanwhile, they are yours to inspect in the privacy of your home, office, shop, or den for *twenty years* by express permission, already withdrawn, by the Polk McKinley Harding Coolidge Mint—the only mint authorized to stamp your application with its own seal.

The equivalent of three centuries of painstaking historical research, supervised by the U.S. Bureau of Mines, has preceded this issue of *The Ornamental Handles of the Walking Canes of the Hohenzollern Princelings*.

Our miniature craftsmen have designed, cast, struck, etched, forged, and finished these authentic reproductions—not available in any store, even before they were commissioned—literally *without regard* for quality.

Certified by the American Kennel Club

But now, through a special arrangement with the Postmaster General of the Republic of San Marino, this 72-piece commemorative plinth, honoring *The Footprints of the Great Jewel Thieves of the French Riviera*—each encased in its own watered-silk caddy that revolves 360 degrees on genuine Swedish steel ball bearings—has been cancelled.

A unique way, you will agree, of introducing you and your loved ones to *The Great Cookie Jars of the Restoration*, just as Congreve the boy must have pilfered from.

They are so authentic that you can actually smell them with your nose.

And don't forget: every set of hand-fired porcelain reproductions of *The Padlocks of the Free World's Great Customs Houses* comes sealed in an airtight cask, fashioned after the shoe locker of a Mogul emperor so famous that we are prohibited from disclosing his name.

12 Men Died to Make the Ingots Perfect

But why, as a prudent investor, should you spend thousands of dollars, every month for a lifetime, to acquire this 88-piece set of *Official Diplomatic License Plates of the World's Great Governments-in-Exile*?

One Minnesota collector comments, "I never expected to buy an item so desirable that it has already kept its haunting fascination forever."

But even this merely hints at the extraordinary investment potential of the Connoisseur's Choice selection of *Great Elevator Inspection Certificates of the World's Tallest Buildings*.

Molded in unobtainable molybdenum, each is precision-ejected from a flying aircraft to check a zinc content that must measure .000000003 per cent or the entire batch will be melted down, discarded, and forgotten.

But "keepsake" is an inadequate term. Your Jubilee Edition of the 566 *Tunic Buttons of the World's Legendary Hotel Porters* will take you from New York City to San Francisco to Hong Kong to Bombay . . . and then actually *pay your way* back home.

There is one more aspect for you to consider before refusing this offer.

If you wish, you can have *The Lavaliere Mikes of TV's Greatest Talk Show Celebrity Guests*, custom-mounted on driftwood plaques that serve as 175 dainty TV snack tables—free.

There is, of course, a surcharge and a handling fee, as well as the 25 per cent duplication cost. But so amazing is this offer that you need only pay this levy once—and never again be bothered by it in your mortal life.

If for whatever reason you elect not to purchase the complimentary *Tokens of the World's Great Subway Systems*, you still profit:

The solid-gold *Venetian Gondolier's Boat Pole Toothpick* and velvet-lined presentation case are yours to treasure for as long as this incredible offer lasts.

Our *Distinctive Axe Marks of the Immortal Brazilian Rubber Planters* are in such short supply that an advance application in your name is already reserved for you. To protect your investment, *none* will be made.

Registered with the Department of Motor Vehicles

A dazzling proposition, you will agree. If you do not, your 560-piece set of *Belgium's Most Cherished Waffle Patterns*, together with your check or money order, will be buried at sea on or before midnight, April 15, 1982—the 70th anniversary, college-trained historians tell us, of the sinking of R.M.S. Titanic, one of the 66 *Great Marine Disasters* commemorated in this never-offered series, each individually bronzed, annealed, Martinized, and hickory-cured by skilled artisans working under the supervision of the Tulane University Board of Regents.

Please note that each comes wrapped in authentic North Atlantic seaweed, its salt content confirmed by affidavit.

Best of all, you need not order. Simply steal a new Rolls-Royce, fence it, and turn the bills into small denominations of used money (U.S. currency only, please). No salesman will call. The Polk McKinley Harding Coolidge Mint is not a U.S. Government body. This is not an offering.
    THE POLK MCKINLEY HARDING COOLIDGE MINT
P.S. If you have already begun your *Napkin Rings of the State Supreme Court Dining Rooms* collection, please disregard.   —BRUCE MCCALL

Figure 14-3 A "tongue-in-cheek" example of direct marketing copywriting, exaggerated, but written according to the "rules." (Bruce McCall, "Rolled in Rare Bohemian Onyx, Then Vulcanized by Hand," © 1982. Originally in *The New Yorker*.)

Type Typefaces can have meaning: boldness or dignity, Old English or Oriental, antiquity or space age, masculinity or femininity, movement or emphasis. When used in direct reponse advertising, typefaces need to be relevant to the message but they also need to be easily and instantly readable. Sizes of typefaces used are a factor to consider as are the thickness and complexity of the type's structure. When more than one typeface and/or type size is used, these should blend and the variety should not become complicated. Sometimes typefaces are overprinted on one another and sometimes they are "reversed," that is, white on color. Certain specially designed typefaces become recognizable logotypes for organizations, such as Sears, Swiss Colony, Time, RCA.

Paper Here the designer is concerned with substance, texture, and finish as well as color, weight, size, and shape. A linen or laid finish can denote elegance. A parchment stock can denote permanence. Paper can have a high gloss finish for use in a catalog of up-scale merchandise or it can simulate the look of a newspaper to convey timeliness. Paper can be used to convey the impression of the "Yellow Pages" of a telephone book or the urgency of a Western Union telegram. Paper not only helps set the tone of a direct response advertisement but, because of its texture, weight, and size, its choice can have substantial impact on cost.

Ink Like paper, ink can convey impressions, through color, gloss, intensity, and placement. Ink selection must consider the paper and the printing process as well as design. Some inks are even available with fragrances, such as the smell of old lavender or of pine trees. Some can be embossed to simulate gold and silver coins. Some can be scraped off to reveal a printed message underneath. Some can be printed on unusual paper stock such as cellophane or waxed paper or foil.

Importance of Color Much information has been developed about the physical and psychological effects of color since Sir Isaac Newton first associated basic colors with sunlight. We know that light and heat and color have much in common. The darker the color, the more light and heat are absorbed. Certain colors, notably yellow, can be seen farther than others; black printed on yellow provides maximum readability. Some colors convey associations: purple implies regality, red is associated with danger, green denotes safety. Psychologically, the "warm" colors, yellow, orange, red, stimulate; the "cool" colors, blue, green, violet, sedate. Thus, the former might more likely encourage action if used in a direct response advertisement.

Colors have different meanings to various cultures, to various ages, in various geographic locations, and the designer of direct response advertising needs to be aware of these differences.

Role of the Graphic Designer

The designer of direct response advertising augments knowledge of art direction with knowledge of product positioning within market segments. It is necessary to have an understanding of the production processes to recognize what is and what is not possible as well as practical. Design must be related to effectiveness and costs to results.

When developing a complete direct mail package, the graphic designer must understand the role of each component of the package as well as the abundance of new technology being used, including computer personalization, ink-jet, and laser printing. These technologies should be used for a reason, not simply because they are available. Even with these new technologies and the new techniques available for reproduction, the graphic designer still must coordinate the basic elements of the classic direct mail package: an outside envelope, a letter, a circular, a response device, and a reply envelope.

In urging the graphic designer to view the total picture and not be led astray by the new technologies, Edmund D. Smith (President, Smith Associates, Inc., New York, New York) suggested that all the elements of a direct response mailing package must be designed to work harmoniously. He presents these points to serve as guidelines for evaluating the potential effectiveness of direct mail package design:[5]

1 Will it segregate itself from other mail in the mailbox?

2 Does it have the necessary initial impact to make the recipient want to open it?

3 Does it give away too much up front?

4 Does the letter invite the recipient to read on, as an initial introduction to the product once the package is opened?

5 Are the pieces designed as a whole? Do they relate both physically and graphically to one another?

6 Is the reader involved enough in the response vehicle? Is he or she invited to "do things?"

7 Has the product been "glorified" enough to warrant the reader's buying it?

8 Has the designer found the most cost effective and economical means of producing the package without taking away from the product merits or the graphic philosophy?

9 Is it easy for the reader to respond and/or order without confusion or inconvenience?

10 Does the package deal honestly with the recipient with regard to both the product and his or her wants and needs?

DIRECT MAIL PACKAGES

The primary medium for direct response advertising is direct mail. This medium offers a choice of formats that is quite extensive. Com-

[5] Edmund A. Smith, "The Graphics of the Direct Mail Package," in *DMA Manual,* Release No. 3302, Direct Marketing Association, Inc., New York, May 1979.

pared with other media (print, broadcast, interactive electronics, personal selling), it provides considerably more space and opportunity to tell a complete story. It can gain attention and develop an orderly and logical flow of information leading to action by the reader.

Direct mail, too, has a unique capability to involve the recipient and, compared with other forms of advertising, faces less competition for attention at the time it is received. It is certainly the most testable of all media, with control of experimentation being an inherent advantage.

Direct mail affords the opportunity for positioning products to specific market segments and can, through computer and printing technology, individualize each piece to each recipient, thus being extremely personal in its character. The inherent advantages of direct mail also cause it to have the highest cost per reader, resulting in a need for the highest response rate, when compared with other media.

The Classic Format

Although the possible formats for direct mail packages are extensively varied, from simple postcards to self-mailers to elaborate catalogs and complex showmanship pieces, the "classic" format consists of a mailing envelope, a letter, a circular, a return device, and a reply envelope. If there is lack of experience and uncertainty about the promotion format to be used, this is usually the starting point. An example of a classic direct mail format appears in Figure 14-4.

The Mailing Envelope Many consider this element most vital to the success of a direct mail package, for unless the carrier envelope receives attention and is opened the contents will never be revealed. For this reason, teaser copy is often used to lead the recipient inside the mailing envelope: to entice but not reveal. Size and shape, along with paper and illustra-

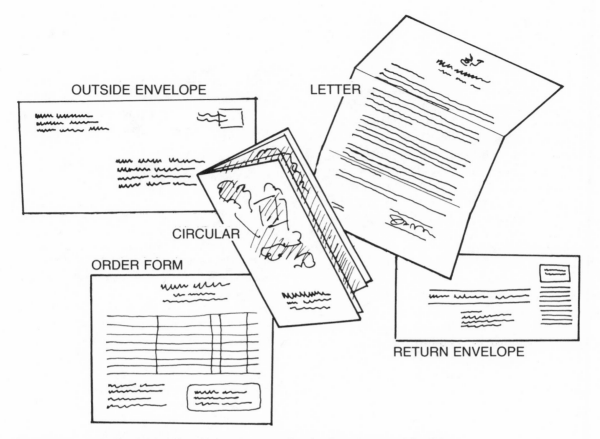

Figure 14-4 A classic direct mail package, primary medium for direct response advertising.

tion, can provide a look and a feel of importance, urgency, prestige, bargain.

The Letter This is possibly the principal element of the package since it provides the primary means for communication and personalization. A frequently asked question about letters is "How long should a letter be?" The answer is obvious: as long as it *needs* to be; or, as Abraham Lincoln responded when he was asked how long a man's legs should be, "Long enough to touch the ground." Letters can be narrative and intriguing (such as those setting the scene for books and magazines) or they can be factual and staccato (such as those used for general merchandise or insurance).

The Admiral Richard E. Byrd Polar Center letter, of which only the lead paragraphs are shown in Figure 14-2, ran seven pages in its entirety to make a $10,000 "sale"!

The "P.S." (postscript) at the end of a letter has high visual value, frequently being read by the recipient right after reading the lead. For that reason, it is often used to restate the offer, highlight benefits, direct the reader to another part of the package.

Mailing lists and data about those on such lists (including occupation, age, education) allow for personalization of letters. Current printing technology, including laser and ink-jet printing, provides a wide variety of formats: vertical or horizontal positioning as well as a mixing of type styles and sizes. An example of such personalization is shown in Figure 14-5.

The Circular   Although not always a requirement, the circular (often called a folder or brochure) is used to augment the letter, to provide product specifications, to cover technical points such as pricing, to provide scene-setting narrative and photographs, to dramatize and illustrate, all with the incorporation of benefits to the reader, in the manner of the letter. A circular is sometimes a physical part of the letter itself, pages two and three of a four-page letter/brochure format, for example. It can be as simple as a single sheet printed on one side only or as complicated as multi-folded brochures, giant broadsides, or multi-page booklets.

Headlines and illustrations are vital parts of circulars, along with subheads and body copy adequate to provide full description and to entice action. An example of a circular with many of these elements is shown in Figure 14-6.

The Response Device   Once the mailing envelope, letter, and circular have performed their particular functions, the response device provides the means for the action requested of the recipient of the direct mail package. This device can be as simple as a postage paid return card with a mere "check off" of instructions, or it can be an order form providing for remittance or credit instructions along with specific product/service selections, or it can be as complex as an application for insurance or a credit card or an investment. In any event it should be a selling piece. It should have a name to identify it, it should be well designed graphically, it should contain compelling and clear-cut copy. It should be easy to complete and handle.

The real challenge in developing response

devices is to provide, in a condensed format, all the necessary elements of the response/ transaction while, at the same time, keeping the form logical, orderly, and simple. Involvement devices (tokens, stamps, yes/no options, sweepstakes, and contest entries) should be constructed so as to lure the reader into action. Obviously, a signature is required in many cases, such as a charged merchandise order, an insurance application, a credit authorization, or an investment instruction.

The Reply Envelope   Unless a card is used as a response device, a separate reply envelope is usually provided both as an incentive and as a convenience, expecially if remittance is requested. Often, depending on the mathematics of the offer and whether or not curiosity seekers are to be discouraged, reply postage is prepaid. Sometimes wallet-flap envelopes incorporate an order form on the seal flap. There are, too, a great variety of specialty envelopes that can provide an order blank combined with a reply envelope. Examples of such order forms can be found bound into many mail-order catalogs. Like the other elements of the classic direct mail package, the reply envelope should be designed and illustrated to encourage action.

Seven Cardinal Rules for Direct Mail Success

Edward N. Mayer, Jr., whose untiring efforts to encourage direct marketing education among college students as well as experienced practitioners earned for him the designation of "dean of direct marketing," many years ago developed what he called "The Seven Cardinal Rules for Direct Mail Success." They have stood the test of time and they warrant presentation here in a slightly condensed form:[6]

[6] Edward N. Mayer, Jr., "The Seven Cardinal Rules for Direct Mail Success," reprinted in *DMA Manual*, Release No. 1206, Direct Marketing Association, Inc., New York, July 1977.

Figure 14-5 Direct mail, through computerized lists and data, can be highly personalized. Laser and ink-jet printing technology make possible a variety of formats and type styles.

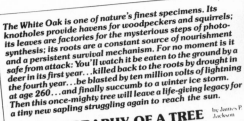

Figure 14-6 A direct mail brochure created by Donna Baier Stein for the Nature Book Club, visualizing good use of layout, headline, subheads. Body copy sets the scene to encourage action.

1 *What is the objective?* This is a vital principle. Objectives stated as "more inquiries" or "more sales" are much too broad. Is your objective to get inquiries that will convert to a higher percentage of sales? Is your objective to get more profitable sales? Is your objective to get back your investment from sales immediately or over a longer period of time? No direct mail program can be successful unless objectives are clearly defined.

2 *Address correctly to the right list.* No principle is more important than reaching the right person on the right list. What is the profile of your prospect or customer list? Is there duplication of names between the lists you are using? Reaching the right person at the right time always has been, and always will be, a prime key to success.

3 *Write your copy to show what the product or service offered does for the reader.* This principle relates to the importance of copy that offers *benefits* to the reader. It emphasizes the *you* attitude. It suggests the use of copy-writing formulas.

4 *Make the layout and copy fit.* What an important principle this is. You use one type of direct mail for high school dropouts and quite another type for educators. The layouts and graphics should be quite different in presenting a big ticket item in comparison to a low cost gadget. Layouts and copy that fit markets and offers can mean the difference between success and failure.

5 *Make it easy for the prospect to take whatever action you want him or her to take.* Direct mail is the action medium. Every mailing should call for an action of some kind: inquiry, purchase, referral, contribution, phone call, visit to a local dealer, an action that the mailer wants the prospect to take. You can incite action through the appeal of the offer or through the device for responding.

6 *Tell your story over again.* Most mailers don't mail often enough. In many lines of business that employ salespeople, it has been found that most sales are completed after the fifth call. And yet scores of people tried direct mail once, didn't get dramatic results, and quit. Tell your story over again and again.

7 *Research your direct mail.* Make your good packages better. Keep testing. Keep trying to beat the best. Test all the time. Never stop. But make sure you test the big things, not the trivia. Test the products or services you provide, the offers you make, the copy you write, the lists you use, and the timing of mailings.

The 49 Ways to Use Direct Mail

Henry Hoke, Sr., was a pioneer in direct mail and a mainstay during the early years of the Direct Mail Advertising Association (now the Direct Marketing Association). He was also the publisher of the *Reporter of Direct Mail Advertising,* which evolved from John Howie Wright's *Postage Stamp* and evolved into today's *Direct Marketing* magazine.

More than half a century ago, Henry Hoke, Sr., felt strongly that "direct mail" was not a synonym for "mail order." He and Lorne Cameron of R. L. Polk Co. were appointed by the Direct Marketing Association to make up a list of "The 49 Ways to Use Direct Mail." This list subsequently became a traveling exhibit used to promote direct mail as an advertising medium, in contrast with the other media of the day: newspapers, magazines, outdoor, and display advertising. These 49 ways are reproduced in Figure 14-7 exactly as they were presented and without editing to emphasize that today's direct marketing, which evolved from direct mail (an advertising medium) and mail order (a selling method), embraces both of these and more.[7]

Although Figure 14-7 emphasizes the variety of ways in which direct mail can be used, reference again to Figure 14-1 will emphasize the variety of formats that direct mail can provide. Neither list should be considered complete, but both are indications of the universality and flexibility of the medium.

[7] Henry Hoke, Sr., *Dogs That Climb Trees,* Graphic Books, Inc., New York, 1946, p. 56.

1. Building Morale of Employees
2. Securing Data from Employees
3. Pushing Salesmen to Greater Efforts
4. Paving the Way for Salesmen
5. Securing Inquiries for Salesmen
6. Teaching Salesmen "How to Sell"
7. Selling Stockholders and Others Interested in your Company
8. Keeping Contact between Sales Calls
9. Further Selling Prospective Customers after a Demonstration Call
10. Acknowledging Orders or Payments
11. Welcoming New Customers
12. Collecting Accounts
13. Securing New Dealers
14. Securing Direct Orders
15. Building Weak Territories
16. Winning Back Inactive Customers
17. Developing Sales in Territories Not Covered by Salesmen
18. Developing Sales among groups
19. Following Inquiries Received from Direct Mail or Other Advertising
20. Driving Home Sales Arguments
21. Selling Other Items in Line
22. Getting Product Specified
23. Selling New Type of Buyer
24. Bringing Buyer to Showroom
25. Helping Present Dealer Sell More
26. Merchandising Your Plans to Dealer
27. Educating Dealers on Superiorities of Your Product or Service
28. Educating Retail Clerks
29. Securing Information from Dealers
30. Referring Inquiries from Consumer Advertising to Local Dealers
31. Creating Need or Demand for Product
32. Increasing Consumption of a Product among Present Users
33. Bringing Customers into a Store
34. Opening New Charge Accounts
35. Capitalizing on Special Events
36. Building Good Will
37. Capitalizing on Other Advertising
38. As a "Leader" in Other Advertising
39. Breaking Down Resistance to Product
40. Stimulating Interest in Coming Events
41. Distribution of Samples
42. Announcing a New Product, New Policy or New Addition
43. Announcing a New Address or Change in Telephone Number
44. Keeping a Concern or Product "In Mind"
45. Research for New Ideas and Suggestions
46. Correcting Present Mailing Lists
47. Securing Names for Permanent Lists
48. Protecting Patents or Processes
49. Raising Funds

Figure 14-7   The 49 Ways to Use Direct Mail.

Catalogs

Certainly one of the most challenging and popular formats for direct marketers is the catalog. The *1980 Great Catalog Guide,* published by the Direct Marketing Association, lists 630 catalogs, which is but a cross section of many times that number currently being distributed. In its introduction, the *Guide* states:[8]

Catalog shopping offers almost every product imaginable. From art supplies to gourmet food and drink. Children's clothing, games and toys. Home furnishings. Perfumes. Gear for camping and sporting. Automotive supplies, gardening tools, jewelry, books. You can also find the latest greatest fashions.

Copy, Design, and Graphics   A notable attribute of catalog copy is succinctness, brevity and conciseness, few words and to the point. Catalog copy goes hand in hand with design, illustration, and graphics. The picture shows it, the words describe it. Words often found in catalog copy include these: quality, you, genuine, fine, full, comfortable, heavy, natural, best. Like all direct marketing promotional copy, the words are arranged to spell out benefits. The words *state* at the same time they *sell*.

Layout, including space allocation, is important. Like the store retailer who allocates shelf space and position according to the potential profitability of products displayed, a catalog retailer allocates space and position in print. The copywriter must anticipate objections and overcome them in advance, at the same time holding the number of words used to a minimum. The catalog copy must be concise, yet it must be complete and clear.

An Illustrative Example   A direct response advertisement offering the mail-order catalog for Lands' End, Direct Merchants, is shown in Figure 14-8. A few paragraphs from this print advertisement point up the benefits of shopping by mail/telephone:[9]

---

[8] *1980 Great Catalog Guide,* published by the Direct Marketing Association, New York.
[9] *Fortune,* June 14, 1982, p. 22.

Why we call ourselves Lands' End, Direct Merchants.

These days, on top of everything else, you don't need the added frustrations you often face when you go shopping.

Threading your way through traffic into parking lots, in distant suburbs. Shouldering your way through crowded malls into stores well-stocked with goods, but staffed too sparingly to serve you well.

Lacking clerks who know the stock, you paw over counters, and shuttle hangers back and forth on racks.

Finally, when you've found what you want, there's that added wait while a cashier communes with her computer, recording everything about the item sold except that you've been standing in line waiting to pay for it.

There has to be a better way. And there is.

Shop with Lands' End, Direct Merchants.

We call ourselves direct merchants because we provide a straight line service, from us to you, with *no middle men* (or *middle-persons,* if you prefer.) Our way lets you shop at leisure in your home. From a colorful catalog. 24 hours a day, 365 days a year. By mail if you like. But, better still, by phone.

You pay no toll. No parking fees. You burn no gas. You lose no patience. And you have direct access to an astonishing array of quality products, about which we give you no-nonsense information, and which we offer at no-nonsense prices.

We didn't originate this method of shopping. But not a day goes by but what we at Lands' End ponder ways to re-invent the system, simplify it, refine it, or add to it when appropriate.

We roam the world in your behalf.

The search for quality is endless at Lands' End. And we go to the four corners of the earth in quest of it. In so doing, we practice a tough philosophy. Simply stated, it goes like this:

First, *quality.* Then, *price.* And always, always *service.*

Once an item seems right for our customers, as direct merchants we seek out the prime quality source; the one not only best suited to manufacture it, but the one that can make it most efficiently as well.

When we're sure we can offer you Lands' End quality at a Lands' End price, we pass the word on to you promptly in our catalogs. If we can't price a quality item so it's to your advantage to buy it from us, we don't offer it. But we continue to search for a new prime source of that item. And occasionally—as with our soft luggage lines—we undertake to make the items ourselves.

Millions use us. Millions more could.

We have served and satisfied millions of customers, but there remain millions more of you who have never experienced our direct service.

If you're among the latter group, why not try us now? Let us prove to you that you can trust us, too.

Ask us to send you a catalog by return mail. Better still, call us right now on our toll-free number (800-356-4444). We have over 100 friendly, well-informed operators waiting to answer your call personally, 24 hours a day. They're trained to serve you, and serve you they do. With answers to questions on sizes, styles, shipments and prices. On colors, on care, on delivery. Should an item be temporarily out of stock, they'll tell you and suggest an alternative. (Including, if need be, referring you to a respected competitor.)

What can you lose?

Understand, we're not all things to all shoppers. We don't initiate or pursue fads. We don't start or ride trends. We deal in clothing and accessories that know no time or season.

And we guarantee every item, in these unconditional terms:

"If you are not completely satisfied with any item you buy from us, at any time during your use of it, return it and we will refund your full purchase price."

Call us right now, and let us begin to serve you. From our brand-new Catalog, featuring pages of solid values, we can ship to you within 24 hours, or we'll know the reason why, and so will you.

Lands' End, Direct Merchants. The exciting new way to shop in today's world.

LANDS' END
DIRECT MERCHANTS

of fine wool and cotton sweaters, Oxford button-down shirts, traditional dress clothing, snow wear, deck wear, original Lands' End soft luggage and a multitude of other quality goods from around the world.

☐ **Please send free catalog.**

Lands' End Dept. J-09
Dodgeville, WI 53533

Name _____

Address _____

City _____

State _____ Zip _____

Or call Toll-free
800-356-4444
(Except Wisconsin, call 608-935-2788)

Figure 14-8 Direct response advertisement offering mail-order catalog.

These days, on top of everything else, you don't need the added frustrations you often face when you go shopping.

Threading your way through traffic into parking lots, in distant suburbs. Shouldering your way through crowded malls into stores well-stocked with goods, but staffed too sparingly to serve you well.

Lacking clerks who know the stock, you paw over counters, and shuttle hangers back and forth on racks.

Finally, when you've found what you want, there's that added wait while a cashier communes with [the] computer, recording everything about the item sold except that you've been standing in line waiting to pay for it.

There has to be a better way. And there is.

Shop with Lands' End, Direct Merchants.

The inquirer is sent a Lands' End catalog containing copy such as the boxed material, accompanied by product photographs in color and illustrations of special features such as "double-track collar stitching," "box pleat with loop," and "buttoned-sleeve placket". See box in next column.

PRINT ADVERTISING (NEWSPAPERS AND MAGAZINES)

A key consideration in the development of direct response advertisements for use in print media, newspapers and magazines, is space limitation, when compared to direct mail packages. And, since print advertisements must compete with other advertisements as well as the editorial content of the print media, the headline is a most important element. Like catalog copy, the headlines of print ads must gain attention quickly and the body copy must tell the story completely yet concisely. The copy must be benefit-oriented and the graphic design should lead the reader through the advertisement's elements in the sequence intended. Illustrations augment copy.

THE HYDE-PARK OXFORD

A Detailed Dress Shirt Of 100% Imported Cotton

The cloth in our Hyde-Park is sturdier, and woven more densely, than that of our standard Oxfords. So it launders better. Wears longer. And has the unmistakable classic drape of an "expensive" shirt.

Our Hyde-Park has standard touches—softly-rolled button-down collar, seven-button front, long tails—plus the unusual ones we picture for you. It is single-needle stitched. The cut is civilized, shaped just enough to avoid sloppiness. This, and the natural "breathing" ability of the cotton, makes the Hyde-Park one of the most comfortable dress shirts you'll ever wear. And one of our best Lands' End values. Pink, ecru, blue, maize, white. For sizes see chart on page 52. $22.00. (Priced $1.00 under '81.)

Elements of Print Ads

The direct response advertisement selling the product from the Halls Collection shown in Figure 14-9 visualizes many of the elements that are necessary. The headline complex shown consists of an overline, a main headline, and a main subhead. The body copy, which, if it is lengthy, can include additional subheads, in this instance describes the product and the crystal from which it is fashioned. Sometimes testimonials or endorsements can lend credence to product claims or report satisfied users. Photographs are often used to convey visually what the words describe. Price and

PHOTO OR
ILLUSTRATION

OVER-LINE

HEAD-LINE

SUB-HEAD

COPY

GIFT

PRICE/
TERMS

RESPONSE
COUPON

Figure 14-9 Direct response advertisement selling product.

terms are presented along with a gift incentive for ordering. The response coupon provides for ease of ordering and the toll-free "800" number makes ordering even more convenient. Additional graphic design could include a signal box (to call attention of special groups to whom the ad is aimed) or a contents box (to feature product claims).

Headlines Possibly the most important element of a direct response print advertisement is the headline, and possibly the most famous

direct response headline of all times is this one created by John Caples for the U.S. School of Music:

> *They Laughed When I Sat Down*
> *at the Piano*
> *But When I Started to Play!—*

Many years after the first appearance of this precedent-setting headline, the following appeared in a business magazine advertisement sponsored by the Southwestern Bell Telephone Company:

> *They Laughed When I Sat Down*
> *at the Telephone*
> *But When I Started to Dial!—*

More recently, this headline appeared in a trade publication advertisement for Applied Automation, Inc., an advertisement that won an "Effie" Award for its creator:

> *They laughed when*
> *You sat down at the*
> *Computer . . .*
> *But then you*
> *Started to play!*

Productive headline ideas are repeated, as the examples above demonstrate. Here are some other headlines from recent direct response advertisements:

> How to Subscribe to the *Wall Street Journal.* (*Wall Street Journal*)
> Suddenly I Lost My Memory! (Career Institute)
> The Lazy Man's Way to Riches. (Joe Karbo)
> Instant Heat Wherever You Want It. (Better Ideas)
> How to Save Your Life. (Henniker)
> Now . . . $25,000 Term Life Insurance for Only $1.00 a Month. (Allstate Insurance)
> What Everyone Ought to Know . . .

About This Stock and Bond Business. (Merrill Lynch, Pierce, Fenner, and Smith)

Attention-getting words often found in headlines include these: How . . . New . . . Why . . . You . . . Free . . . Today . . . Save . . . At Last . . . Limited Offer.

Body Copy   Direct response copy starts with benefits and ends with a request for action. Typical sentences are short and active, including phrases such as these:

Today more than ever . . .
Fortunately for you . . .
There's a new way . . .
Authorities have proved . . .
Try it for 10 days . . .
Judge for yourself . . .

Response Devices   When all is said and done, the time comes to "ask for the order." A good way to determine whether or not the advertisement can be categorized as "direct response" is if it *asks* for action and how effectively it does so. Remember that a key characteristic of direct marketing is that it is measurable and accountable. Such measurement is of responses and/or transactions; that is, orders, inquiries, contributions, votes cast. A direct response can be *any* of these. Such response can involve the mailing of a coupon or order form or the telephoning of an inquiry or an order or it can be a visit to the seller's location or a request for the seller to come to the buyer's location. Many otherwise good advertisements with effective headlines and compelling body copy fall down when they do not specifically ask the reader to order the product, fill out the coupon, call the "800" telephone number.

If a coupon is involved in the direct response print advertisement, the designer must be careful that enough room is provided for the requested fill-in and that the paper used is designed to take handwriting with ink. This may sound overly basic, but a good designer will, as a test, fill out the coupon. Inadequate space allocation might necessitate cramped writing that becomes illegible.

The terms of the offer, including price, need to be clearly stated. But, above all, the response mechanism must provide a sense of *action now*. Although not always easy to control, it is desirable to have right-hand coupons on advertisements that run on right-hand pages of print media (especially magazines) and vice versa for left-hand pages. The reason is obvious: it's easier to clip such a coupon if it adjoins an outside edge of the page.

Inserts   A popular form of print advertisement in a magazine is an *insert*. Printing technology has made possible a great many variations for such inserts, including folding, gumming, consecutive numbering, die-cutting, and even personalization on a printing press. The insert might be a multipage piece or it can be a simple reply card bound next to a full-page advertisement and serving as the response device.

Newspaper inserts abound and appear in a variety of formats, especially on Sundays and midweek, on Wednesdays and Thursdays, which are typically "grocery shopping days" for many newspaper advertisers. Coupons are a major response format used in such inserts. Direct response advertisers using newspaper inserts include insurance companies, record clubs, land developers, trade schools, retail stores, book clubs, magazine publishers, and film processors. A metropolitan newspaper, such as the *New York Times,* can provide circulation of inserts to as many as 1.5 million readers in a single edition.

A key advantage of newspaper inserts is controlled timing. In many markets, demographic selection, often by ZIP Code definition, makes possible pinpointing messages to specific market segments.

Copy and format are important considerations for inserts, whether in newspapers or magazines. Single-page or multipage formats are available along with special features, such as perforated coupons and gummed reply envelopes, incorporated right into the format. Inserts offer a chance for unbounded creativity for the writer and designer of direct response print advertisements.

Advertising with Television Support Although support with spot television comercials has been used effectively with direct mail and magazine inserts where timing of delivery can be controlled, such support has been particularly effective with newspaper inserts. Some direct response newspaper advertisers report as much as a 40 percent increase in response from newspaper inserts if these are supported by spot television. Typically, such support might begin in midweek to call attention to an insert appearing in the following Sunday's newspaper.

Obviously, television support is most efficient in markets in which the newspaper has saturation coverage in an area that coincides with the coverage of the television station. Typically the television support commercials are of short duration, 10 to 30 seconds, and are repeated frequently during the several days preceding the newspaper's appearance. Such commercials usually visualize the newspaper insert, which should be readily recognizable.

BROADCAST ADVERTISING (TELEVISION AND RADIO)

The use of broadcast media—television and radio—by direct marketers is still relatively recent. Television accounted for approximately 1 percent and radio for approximately one-tenth of 1 percent of all direct response advertising expenditures during 1980.[10]

[10] *DMA Fact Book,* 1983 ed., published by the Direct Marketing Association, Inc., New York, p. 1.

Television's limitations for direct response advertisers are its high cost and the short duration of an individual commercial in which to present a message. Television has, however, been gaining momentum as a *support* medium. The advent of cable television, including interactive features, has made possible more specifically directed messages and even market segmentation, thus increasing the effectiveness (results vs. costs) of the medium.

Radio has practical limitations, too. Much of radio comes to listeners while they are driving an automobile or are otherwise occupied, when telephones or pencil and paper are out of reach. Further, radio does not provide the opportunity to visualize; thus, it is most effective with known products or those which do not require visualization.

Creating Television Commercials

In addition to its use as *support* by calling attention to direct response advertising in other media, television is especially suited to demonstration or visualization of action. Appropriate products include phonograph records, houseware items, and a variety of services. In this last category AT&T has been especially successful in promoting its Long Lines services and related equipment, with response through an "800" telephone number directed to the Bell System Sales Center in Kansas City, Missouri.

One major limitation in the creation of direct response television commercials is *time*. Commercial time is usually available in multiples of 10 or 30 seconds; that is, 10, 20, 30, 60, 90, up to a usual maximum of 120 seconds. Whereas television support of direct response advertising in other media can be effectively presented in 10 or 30 seconds, a maximum air time of 2 minutes allows for approximately 200 words. Of course, since audio and visual can be used simultaneously in television, the old adage that "one picture is worth a thousand words" applies *if* the product is one that can be demonstrated, such as a "handy, dandy, utterly amazing kitchen slicer-dicer."

In allocating time for a typical 120-second spot announcement, it is suggested that 20 seconds are needed for attention getting, up to 75 seconds are required for demonstration, and the remaining 25 seconds are used for action through providing a mailing address or a toll-free telephone number.[11] Because 120 seconds on prime time television is prohibitively expensive for direct marketers, most direct response commercials appear during low cost fringe time (early morning, late night, and weekend hours). Often, too, markets can be segmented through specific programs usually aired at such times.

Concept   The logical starting point in creating direct response television commercials is the determination of just what the advertising is about and what it is to do. Possibly it is to be used as support, to call attention to a newspaper insert. Or, its intent might be to get leads for sales follow-up. Or, it might be used to actually generate orders. Unlike direct mail or print media, there is no written record to refer to at a later time. Thus, the television viewer can't be asked or expected to do or remember too much. Logic and clarity are most important.

Storyboards   The visual portion of a television commercial is usually presented through a series of storyboards to demonstrate the continuity and the video action. Storyboards demonstrate the art and graphics as well as the action and photography. Video (the picture) is combined with audio (spoken word) and graphics (written word) in outline form through storyboards. These are used as a presentation of the initial concept.

[11] *Grey Matter*, vol. 53, no. 1, 1982, p. 4, published by Grey Advertising, Inc., 777 Third Avenue, New York, New York 10017.

Script   Although a script for a television commercial containing no more than 200 words cannot verbally "explain" a product as thoroughly as a direct mail package or even a print advertisement, the combination of words with pictures and graphics, audio with video, can exert considerable impact. That is why one of the most effective uses of direct response television is to support other direct response advertising media through copy such as "Watch your mailbox for" or "Watch for this offer in next Sunday's *Chicago Tribune*." This copy is often accompanied by an actual visualization of the insert to which attention is being drawn.

An effective television script needs to be tightly woven and fully coordinated with the visual and graphic elements involved. As with good letter copy or well-written print ads, the television script needs to first get attention, through audio coupled with video and graphics, and then do its job in presenting product features as it gets the viewer involved and geared to action. In fact, in a limited time frame, easily grasped action is a key requirement of direct response television.

Graphics   Direct response television graphics begin with the words or script coordinated with the other elements that bring the message to life in both audio and video: images, actions, effects, and direction. Actors who deliver the words must be credible, professional, and appropriate to the product. Filming and editing are important so that spoken words are synchronized with pictures and illustrations as well as written words, often superimposed to present response addresses or telephone numbers. Television graphics are concerned with the interaction of audio and video and the ultimate effect of the message on the viewer in much the same way that the design of direct mail packages or print advertising have an effect on the reader.

Production   After storyboards and scripts have been used to express concepts, the actual production team for a direct response television commercial involves a variety of highly specialized technicians, coordinated by a producer. Typical concerns at this juncture are whether to use motion-picture film or videotape, live actors or animation or still illustrations. Directors and actors and graphic designers become involved as do camerapeople and film editors.

The cost of producing a quality television commercial in 1982 began at around $14,000 and went up to approximately $40,000 with these costs estimated to be rising approximately 10 percent annually.[12] Spectacular commercials involving a large number of actors, star personalities, and special effects cost as much as $250,000 (or more) to produce. Proper advance planning is one way to keep costs down.

Creating Radio Commercials

The process of developing radio commercials is somewhat less complex than that for television. Radio, too, offers the additional advantage of flexibility in that live commercials, often read by a station announcer or known local personality, can be scheduled quickly. If need be, these can be revised right up to air time. Radio commercials are far less expensive than television, too, in air time costs as well as production costs. Through use of particular radio station formats, "easy listening" or "rock and roll" or "news/talk shows," the direct response advertiser can develop a substantial degree of market segmentation. Positioning adjacent to particular programs, such as early morning farm programs or a particular disc jockey, can further segment markets. Positioning during so-called morning and evening

[12] John Witek, "Response Television," *DMA Fact Book,* 1983 ed., published by the Direct Marketing Association, Inc., New York, pp. 124–127.

drive time, when office or factory workers are driving to and from their jobs, is another means of market segmentation.

As with the other media used for direct response advertising, radio advertising must first get attention. Sometimes a radio personality reading a script, even in an ad-lib manner, can attract attention. If the product being sold involves music or a musical instrument, a few bars of a popular song can make an effective "headline" for a radio commercial. Or, a few headline words such as the following can get attention:

> An important message for persons over age 65.
> Are you tired of the back-breaking work caring for your lawn?
> At last a simple, effective way to rid your house of bugs.
> Do you need a room added to your house or a new roof?
> Here's a message of special interest to taxpayers.

The close and request for action are of special concern in using radio for direct response. Many times, radio listeners are performing another activity simultaneously such as driving an automobile, reading a book, or doing household chores. Pencil and paper for writing down addresses and telephone numbers are not readily available nor is it feasible for a listener to "stop everything" and get them. As a result, the most effective response instruction is one that is easy to remember such as use of a telephone number that spells out a word: "Dial 'Dic-kens' for your tickets to see *Christmas Carol.*" Or, the use of a post office box with a significant number can be more easily recalled ("Write P.O. Box 1776, Philadelphia, Pennsylvania, to subscribe to *Colonial America.*"). Repeating the address or number helps, too: "Call 1-800-832-3300, that number again is 1-800-832-3300."

TELEPHONE PROMOTION

The telephone, as an alternative to the mail, is becoming an increasingly important vehicle for *response* in direct marketing, either for ordering or for inquiring. Other emerging electronic communication such as interactive television, for example, Teletext or Viewdata, may soon perform the same function. In addition, however, the telephone is extensively used by direct marketers as a promotional medium: outbound as well as inbound. Here, the promotion is actually presented via telephone by a sales representative, a fund raiser, a politician.

Outbound Calls (WATS)

Outbound telephone calls, often employing Wide Area Telephone Service (WATS) for economical long-distance calling, are used by direct marketers for a variety of purposes.

Although well-prepared scripts and well-structured offers can cause telephone promotion to be highly effective, the medium is usually most efficient if calls are directed to persons who have been prequalified in some way. The reason for this is that the cost of an individual telephone call can be as much as four times the cost of an individual direct mail letter and thus it must be four times as productive to be comparable costwise.

Prequalified outbound calls might include these: response to an inquiry, up-grading of a just received order, a new product offer to an existing customer, reactivation of a dormant account, or generation of responses/transactions from a carefully selected list. "Cold calls," when there is no existing relationship with, or recognition of, the direct marketer, must be carefully structured in content since, by its very nature, a telephone call usually interrupts some other activity of the person being called. Such interruption, in itself, can make the called person angry.

Scripts   Development of scripts for out-bound telephone calls offer the dual challenge of maximizing the words to gain a favorable response and, at the same time, minimizing the length and the cost of a call. In some cases a live operator might introduce a call and request permission to play a taped message, often from a celebrity or a personality. At the conclusion of the taped message, the live operator comes back on for close and action.

Although entirely automated telephone calls have been used in the past, utilizing automatic dialing together with taped messages and recorded responses, these generally have not been effective and they have met with considerable criticism. Properly used, however, outbound telephone promotion can be particularly effective and even well received if the offer is about a specific product, an event, a sale, a theatrical performance, or an election.

In creating persuasive telephone scripts, Aldyn McKean (a telephone consultant) has suggested that a good script is composed of at least 11 parts.[13]

1 *Opening:* Greet person being called; identify caller.

2 *Empathy/involvement stage:* Establish rapport, emphasize common concerns, and create involvement.

3 *Product information:* Describe the product/service and its benefits.

4 *Offer:* Explain and clarify terms.

5 *Close:* Request action.

6 *Reconfirmation:* Repeat the terms agreed to.

7 *Probe:* Inject a query designed to prompt negative or undecided prospects into offering questions or objections.

8 *Answers to questions:* These answers should lead back to the close.

9 *Responses to objections:* Commonly raised objections should have prescripted responses, also leading back to the close.

[13] Aldyn McKean, "Promotional Techniques in Telephone Advertising," *DMA Fact Book*, 1983 ed., published by the Direct Marketing Association, Inc., New York, pp. 127–131.

10 *Second effort:* An additional short presentation should be made whenever a prospect is undecided or is negative without offering specific objections.

11 *Farewell:* No matter what, the telephone call should always end on a reassuring, friendly, and polite note.

Inbound Calls ("800" Service)

The use of the telephone for placing orders has increased dramatically in recent years with catalog direct marketers reporting as much as one-half of their orders reaching them through this medium, especially during holiday seasons. The telephone is also being used increasingly to inquire or to otherwise respond to a solicitation through another medium. Prepared scripts covering individual situations are often important. In some instances, word-for-word scripts are desirable, whereas, in others, trained telephone sales representatives refer to a call guide that outlines points for easy reference.

The Bell System Sales Center in Kansas City, demonstrating its use of the telephone in direct marketing of its own facilities, Long Lines service, and related equipment, provides a call guide through a cathode ray tube (CRT) display unit at each telephone communicator's work station, with instant access to relevant information available about the caller.

The toll-free "800" telephone service has itself been a tremendous incentive to the use of inbound telephone calls to respond/transact. Much of the incentive for using this service must be contained in the direct reponse advertising used by the direct marketer in other media. Such promotional copy might appeal to the emotions (as does the Jerry Lewis muscular dystrophy telethon on Labor Day). Or, it might point up the advantages of personal service and convenience of having a telephone order-taker on-hand 24 hours a day to answer questions and assure faster deliveries or services.

PRODUCTION: SUPPLIES AND SERVICES

The creation and physical production of the direct marketing promotion formats described in this chapter call for a variety of specialized services and supplies. The direct marketer seeking such production sources can often find them listed in the Yellow Pages of the telephone book. Specific firms and organizations can also be found listed or advertised in the trade press such as *Direct Marketing* (224 Seventh Street, Garden City, L.I., NY 11530) or from the Direct Marketing Association (6 East 43rd Street, New York, NY 10017). A handy reference, updated annually, is the *Direct Marketing Market Place* published by Hilary House Publishers, Inc. (1033 Channel Drive, Hewlett Harbor, NY 11557).

Service Firms and Suppliers

The types of service firms and suppliers often used by direct marketers include these:

Computer services, data processing firms, service bureaus
Envelope manufacturers and suppliers
Equipment manufacturers and suppliers
Lettershops and mailing services
Product and subscription fulfillment services
Mailing list brokers and compilers
Printers, lithographers, and related services
Media: newspapers, magazines, television, radio, outdoor
Telephone services: inbound and outbound
Delivery systems: United States Postal Service or other private carriers

Creative and Consulting Services

The types of creative and consulting services often used by direct marketers include these:

Agencies: advertising, direct mail, direct response, direct marketing
Direct marketing consultants
Artists, art studios, and graphic designers
Copywriters

Production Controls

The variety of details involved in the production of direct marketing's promotion formats points up the importance of controls: keeping track of estimates and quotations, purchase orders, job tickets, printing specifications, mailing schedules, media orders, etc.

All of this calls, too, for an organized approach to production planning. Figure 14-10 presents an example of a typical direct marketing production flow chart, created for a specific complex mailing situation. However, the logistics contained in this chart could be applicable to any campaign or medium and may be adjusted to individual requirements.[14]

SUMMARY

The promotion formats of direct marketing appear in a variety of advertising media: direct mail, print (magazines and newspapers), broadcast (television and radio), and interactive electronic media (telephone and television). An important consideration in developing formats for these media, however, is that the promotional strategies of personal selling, publicity, and support are often incorporated within direct response advertising.

Combining copy and design with graphics, direct marketing promotion relies more on the selling value of benefits than the hard sell of persuasion often found in general advertising. The basis for such promotion is research, that is, product and market familiarization, and the objective is measurable and accountable results.

Copywriters often rely on writing formulas and discipline themselves with rules to assure that their promotions achieve their objectives. Design and graphics (art, layout, symbols, effects) go hand in hand with copy (words,

expressions, ideas, meanings). The objective is to stimulate action, measurable and accountable responses.

Although it is no longer the *only* advertising medium for direct marketers, direct mail is still the medium most often used. It offers a broad choice of formats and if compared with the other media, print, broadcast, interactive electronics, personal selling, it provides considerably more space and opportunity to tell a complete story. Of all the media, direct mail affords maximum opportunity for positioning products to specific market segments. The classic format for direct mail includes these elements: mailing envelope, letter, circular, response device, and reply envelope. But, it can vary in format from a simple postcard to a complex merchandise catalog.

Direct response print advertisements in newspapers and magazines must necessarily be more condensed than direct mail packages. These rely heavily on headlines to generate attention and interest, body copy to describe, and action copy in the form of a coupon or telephone number. Inserts, often bound into magazines or placed loose into newspapers, provide room for much more copy and offer the direct marketer a variety of formats. Whereas inserts provide the format advantages of a direct mail piece, they compete with other contents of the publication in which they are carried and thus they do not usually receive the same attention as does mail.

Broadcast advertising (television and radio), after development of a concept, is visualized in storyboards and relies on distinct scripting to fully utilize the limited time, measured in seconds, available for it. The graphic interaction of audio and video (for television), however, can provide a great deal of impact, even in a short time.

The telephone can be used as a promotion medium for outbound calls as well as for inbound calls. Outbound calls are most effective if there is a prequalification of the person

---

[14] Shirley Stevens, "Direct Marketing Production Flow Chart," in *DMA Manual,* Release No. 4007, Direct Marketing Association, Inc., New York, April 1978.

Figure 14-10 Direct marketing production flow chart.

Times will vary depending on the complexity of the marketing effort, the availability of decision making people and the promptness of decisions.

329

called. Inbound calls are often used for placing orders as well as inquiring.

The great variety of promotion formats used in direct marketing calls for an awareness of production processes and the supplies and services utilized. A reverse timetable or production flow chart is often useful for keeping track of the many details of a typical direct marketing promotion.

CASE: EVALUATING BENEFITS VS. PERSUASION IN COPY

Learning Objective

This case study presents a variety of different copy approaches featured on several mailing envelopes, with each control-tested against the others. Certain of these copy approaches describe benefits whereas others use persuasion. All are designed to get attention. Discussion should develop the rationale for each copy approach and why it was featured before considering the relative response results.

Overview

Particularly in the sale of intangible services and especially in fund raising, the direct marketer needs a keen awareness of what motivates response. Donors to worthy causes often contribute for reasons of their own and these reasons may have nothing whatever to do with the cause itself. The potential benefits received by such donors are not always readily apparent, which poses a particular challenge to the direct marketer engaged in fund raising.

Procedure

Read the learning objective, the overview, and the case that follows. See if you can determine which of the copy approaches might suggest benefits to the respondent and which rely more on persuasion. Evaluating the results reported in the case history, suggest why the "best" package provided the highest response. Why were the others "good" or "poor"?

Case[15]

The American Heart Association needed to raise more funds for its health improvement activities at a lower cost. Direct mail had historically been the most important medium for the organization's fund raising and an effort was to be made to improve on current response.

Several new copy approaches were developed. Through scientific experimentation involving test mailings in excess of 200,000 pieces and confirmation with another 200,000 pieces, these copy approaches were tested against each other and against the "control" currently being used. With experimentation, of course, it is necessary to have all aspects of the mailing remain the same except for one variable within each test segment. In this way the change in response can be attributed to the change in that variable.

The decision was made to test six copy approaches in the form of "teasers" displayed on the outside of the mailing envelope. Six such envelope "teasers" would be tested against each other and also against the control, the envelope that the fund raiser had been using successfully in the past, but which did not have any "teaser" at all.

These seven envelope panels, six tests and one control, are visualized in Figure 14-11. A letter, contribution form, and reply envelope, also shown, were enclosed in each mailing envelope. These forms contained within a mailing envelope were essentially the same for all seven packages except for the beginning of the letter. This emphasized the particular copy approach that was featured on the outside mailing envelope.

The American Heart Association sent these solicitation mailings to their current donors as well as "cold" prospects; that is, those who

---

[15] This case was originally developed by Freeman F. Gosden, Jr., President, Smith-Hemmings-Gosden, Direct Response Advertising, El Monte, California, who conducted the test from which it was derived.

Figure 14-11 Copy approaches tested by the American Heart Association.

had not given a contribution before. The response from each group and for each copy approach was tabulated separately through key coding appearing on the contribution form.

The following copy approaches were tested, as shown in Figure 14-11:

Effort   Copy Approach
1   "Use the enclosed FREE GIFT."
2   "Emergency Heart Attack Card Enclosed."
3   "4 years ago Billy Thompson's dad would have died . . ."
4   "If you have ever worried about having a heart attack—"
5   "You hold lives in your hands . . . TODAY . . . AND THAT'S IMPORTANT!"
6   "We'd like to show you how you can help save a life. YOURS."
7   (Control). No teaser copy.

The response results were these:

The best package: 6 "We'd like to show you how you can help save a life. YOURS."

Good packages: 4 "If you have ever worried about having a heart attack—"
                  3 "4 years ago Billy Thompson's dad would have died . . ."

Poor packages: 1 "Use the enclosed FREE GIFT."

5 "You hold lives in your hands . . . TODAY . . . AND THAT'S IMPORTANT!"
7 No teaser copy.
2 "Emergency Heart Attack Card Enclosed."

DISCUSSION QUESTIONS

1 Distinguish between print and broadcast advertising media. Give examples of each.
2 What, specifically, is direct response advertising?
3 Show examples of benefits expressed in recent direct mail advertising of which you are aware.
4 What is meant by "writing by formula"? Give an example.
5 Why are design and graphics important in the creation of direct response advertising? What are the elements of design?
6 Why is direct mail considered the primary medium for use by direct response advertisers?
7 Of what elements does a "classic" direct mail package consist?
8 What is a catalog?
9 What distinguishes direct response advertising in newspapers and magazines? What is the most important element in such advertising?
10 Name and describe four forms of response to direct response advertising.
11 In what ways is television used by direct marketers? Radio?
12 How does the telephone differ from other media used by direct response advertisers?

CHAPTER

MEDIA OF DIRECT MARKETING

The promotion *formats* of direct marketing are discussed in Chapter 14. These formats, categorized by media, are displayed in Figure 14-1 on page 305. Chapter 15 is concerned with the *media*, the attributes of each medium, and the potential for multimedia mix. The location of a promotion format within a medium will be explored as will timing. Discussed, too, is the potential for market segmentation through reading, hearing, or viewing a particular medium at a particular time.

Direct mail is the basic promotion format for direct marketers. As a medium, it relies on mailing lists and data about the individuals or organizations on such lists to most effectively reach market segments. Chapter 7 is devoted to the subject of market segmentation and Chapter 8 is concerned with lists and data. Certain specialized direct mail, such as coupons, cooperative mailings, package inserts, and syndications, is discussed in this chapter.

The other media of direct marketing, in addition to direct mail, are presented in this chapter. These are print media (magazines and newspapers); broadcast media (television and radio); and interactive media (telephone, television, and salespeople).

DIRECT MAIL AS A MEDIUM

Although direct marketers use virtually all major advertising media to generate measurable responses, direct mail still accounts for approximately one-half of the total expenditure on direct response advertising, estimated at $25.0 billion (not including creative costs) for 1982.[1] The number of pieces of mail carried by the United States Postal Service in 1982 that were attributable to direct mail was 41.1 billion, 36 percent of the total number of 114.1 billion pieces of mail for that year.[2] Not all direct mail is carried by the United States

Postal Service, however; some goes by private carrier such as door-to-door distributors. Sometimes, too, direct mail offers are combined into a single mailing (such as coupon or other cooperative distribution) and some offers are enclosed with other mail or parcels (such as statement stuffers or package inserts).

Of all the media available for direct response advertising, direct mail is the most selective and offers the most potential for personalization. It is also the most flexible and the most suitable for testing. Because of the pinpoint attributes of its distribution, it has the potential for the highest rate of response.

Its inherent advantages, however, cause it to be the most expensive medium per prospect reached. Even in large volume, it is difficult to distribute direct mail for less than $250 per thousand (M) pieces. As shown in Figure 15-1, 1982 costs for a typical direct mail package were estimated by the Direct Marketing Association to be $289.93/M in a quantity of 250,000 and $355.99/M in a quantity of 50,000.[3] (This compares to a cost of approximately $10/M viewer households for a 120-second television commercial; a cost of approximately $9.00/M reader households for a full-page newspaper advertisement; and a cost of approximately $5.00/M circulation for a full-page advertisement in a mass circulation national magazine.)

In connection with the costs shown in Figure 15-1, it should be noted that preferential postage rates apply to nonprofit organizations and also to those large volume mailers who presort their direct mail by ZIP Code or by carrier route. Volume mailers can benefit, too, from lower average printing and production costs.

Market Segmentation   The mailing list is the medium for direct mail. Highly sophisticated techniques for compiling and maintaining mailing lists, coupled with computer technol-

---

[1] *DMA Fact Book*, 1983 ed., Direct Marketing Association, Inc., New York, p. 1.
[2] *DMA Fact Book*, 1983 ed., p. 86.

[3] *DMA Fact Book*, 1983 ed., p. 88.

COMPONENTS	50M (Per M)	250M (Per M)
1. Letter — 4 pages/2 colors 8½ x 11 (11 x 17) (60 lb. white)	$ 36.10	$ 25.88
2. Brochure — 4 pages/4 colors 8½ x 11 (11 x 17) (70 lb. text)	83.90	51.80
3. Order Card — 2 colors 5 x 7 (65 lb. cover index)	20.80	14.00
4. Reply Envelope — 1 color 5½ x 7¼ (24 lb. white)	21.20	15.56
5. Outside Envelope — 1 color 9 x 6 (24 lb. white)	27.93	20.44
6. Lettershop Charges — per M	23.54	19.73
7. House List — 50% of mailing per M (Running Costs)	2.21	2.24
8. List Rental — 50% of mailing per M	25.20	25.38
9. Merge/Purge — per M	6.11	5.90
10. Postage — (Fixed)	109.00	109.00
11. TOTAL PER M	$355.99	$289.93

Figure 15-1 Average cost of a typical direct mail package sent at third class regular bulk mail postage rates.

ogy for most effectively using demographic and other data inherent to them, can pinpoint prospects and identify market segments in a highly efficient manner.[4] With such data, the direct marketer can efficiently segment house lists (active and inactive customers as well as inquirers) and also the response and compiled lists of others.

Computer match coding and merge/purge techniques can eliminate duplicate mailings within and between lists, and data about buying patterns and psychographics can further determine customer potential. Mailing lists are at the heart of direct mail as a medium.

Syndication Mailings

Syndication direct mail, usually arranged by an intermediary between the producer and the seller, involves the offering of a product to an established (and usually credit-approved) customer list. The most common users of syndi-

[4] Chapter 7 covers in detail the subject of market segmentation in direct marketing; Chapter 8 is devoted to mailing lists and data.

cation are book companies, oil companies, bank cards, department stores, and mail-order merchandisers, organizations that have an existing customer relationship within their credit-approved mailing lists. These direct marketers supply the lists, provide the goodwill inherent within their customer relationships, and assume the accounts receivable after the sale. The producer benefits from an efficient and effective distribution system for products. The syndicator or intermediary bears all promotion costs, supplies and ships merchandise, handles customer service, and pays the direct marketer a sales commission for the use of the list.

Syndication mailing had its roots in the 1950s when large lists of mail-order buyers and direct mail respondents began to proliferate, notably among publishers of encyclopedias and other books as well as certain mail-order merchants. Most of these early syndications involved relatively high unit sales, a home movie outfit at $150, for example, or a power tool at $100, and the cost of individual credit checking, coupled with high bad debt ratios, called for some refinement. Solution to the credit problem came, during the 1960s, with the appearance of the syndicator (who assumed all risks) and large-scale syndication by major oil companies (with customer lists, although not inherently mail responsive, that were credit worthy). Subsequently, syndication was picked up by the travel and entertainment cards (Diners Club, Carte Blanche, American Express) and by the bank credit cards (BankAmericard and Master Charge; now VISA and Master-Card, respectively).

Whereas the early users of syndication mailings were as much interested in activating their credit cards as they were in earning a profit from the merchandise sale itself, today's direct marketers look on syndication as a profit center in itself and another indication of the inherent value of a customer. Syndication can provide an unusually high rate of return for a nominal investment by the mailing list owner.

Direct mail formats used in syndication include individual mailing packages, catalogs, package and statement inserts, and remittance reply envelopes on which the offer has been printed. Direct marketing through syndication is used today not just by oil companies and credit card organizations, but by airlines, finance companies, encyclopedia publishers, book clubs, department stores, and a host of others. These list owners earn profits, their customers are served through convenience in ordering and paying, and producers have a new direct marketing distribution alternative.

On the negative side is the fact that, as syndication has increased, response has decreased and the costs of syndication have risen. Not all products are suitable for syndication and a key requirement is to define those that are, as well as those that can be supplied with some degree of assurance.

Couponing

Although only 3.3 percent of the 102.4 billion coupons distributed during 1981 were sent by direct mail, they are discussed here as an important promotional medium. Most coupons, 78.5 percent, were distributed through newspapers in 1981 with another 11.8 percent distributed through magazines and 6.4 percent appearing in or on packages.[5]

As a promotional medium, a coupon is an offer made by a manufacturer or retailer that includes an incentive for purchase of a product or service in the form of a specified price reduction. A major objective of couponing is to modify buyer behavior by offering an incentive to try a new product or to convert occasional users to regular customers. A further objective is to increase sales volume enough to warrant greater display of the product by the retailer.

Coupons distributed by direct mail can be for a single brand sent as a self-mailer or they can be enclosed in an envelope with descriptive literature; or, there may be several brands cooperating in a single distribution sponsored by either the manufacturer or a mailing organization. An example of the latter is the periodic Carol Wright direct mail cooperative packages distributed by Donnelley Marketing. Often, too, cooperative coupon mailings are directed to specific market segments such as teenagers or senior citizens, professionals, or business organizations. Although the cost of direct mail distribution of coupons is somewhat higher than that of newspapers or magazines, redemption rates can run 10 percent or more in the former compared with 5 percent or less in the latter. Redemption rates increase, of course, as distribution is increasingly pinpointed to specific market segments.

Approximately one-third of the coupons distributed during 1981 had a face value of less than 15¢ and the average face value was 19.8¢.[6] Improper redemption is a major problem confronting couponers. Direct mail coupon distribution, because the coupon is enclosed in a sealed envelope addressed to a particular person and thus is generally unavailable in volume for fraudulent use, has the lowest rate of misredemption.

According to a 1977 survey by the U.S. Department of Agriculture, of 1,433 consumer households, 80 percent were using coupons, up from 76 percent a year earlier. Further, the survey revealed, one-third of the coupon users said they were using *more* coupons.

Those providing coupons do so to improve their penetration in a market or to stimulate product demand by accelerating the introduction of a new product or obtaining new users for an old product. These advantages have been presented for using direct mail to distribute coupons:[7]

---

[5] *DMA Fact Book*, 1983 ed., p. 101.

[6] *DMA Fact Book*, 1983 ed., p. 103.

[7] John C. Holt, "Direct Mail Couponing," in *DMA Manual*, Release No. 230.2, April 1979.

1 Direct mail can be a highly efficient medium for coupon distribution when considering cost per valid redemption.

2 Mail distribution pinpointed to market segments can achieve the highest redemption rates.

3 Direct mail is the most flexible medium in combining coverage with selectivity.

4 Direct mail distribution of coupons can be better controlled and thus local merchandising can be better coordinated.

5 Direct mail can be researched and tested most effectively.

Cooperative Mailings

Cooperative direct mailings provide participants, usually a group of noncompetitive direct response advertisers, the opportunity to reduce mailing cost in reaching common prospects. Because the attention of the recipient of cooperative mailings is divided among the several advertisers, response expectation is also lower.

The distribution of cooperative mailings ranges from consumer distribution, such as the Donnelley Marketing/Carol Wright cooperative reaching as many as one-half of all U.S. households periodically, to those reaching highly pinpointed market segments, such as Doctor's Marketplace. Another form of coop is called a "ride-along," in which a direct marketer might include one or more noncompeting offers with a catalog or individual mailing.

Mass cooperatives frequently combine couponing with other direct response offers. Some mass distribution can provide opportunities for market segments such as apartment dwellers, Hispanic-speaking households, or lifestyles of particular ZIP Code clusters. Although cost of participation in a cooperative mailing can be $10 or less per thousand (plus cost of printing the enclosure), this cost rises according to degree of selectivity achieved. As many as 100 offers might be contained in a mailed cooperative to a specific market

segment. Mass cooperatives are sometimes distributed through other print media, newspapers and magazines.

Miscellaneous Distribution

Several other alternative distribution methods for the direct mail medium are worthy of mention:

Statement/Invoice Stuffers Periodic bills and reminder statements mailed to customers of department stores, banks, utilities, oil companies, magazines, and credit cards provide an opportunity for merchandising appropriate, but not competitive, offers of products and services. Quantity potential for such distribution is relatively high, and cost is relatively low, ranging from $15 to $40 per thousand, plus printing. Deliverability is assured, since most bills travel via first class mail, and opening of such matter is virtually certain. Thus, readability is high. There is, too, an implied endorsement of the offer by the billing company. In some cases, credit is offered by the billing company. Market segmentation is possible, too, through selection of the particular organization sending out the bills.

Package Inserts This form of distribution of direct mail is related to the one above but offers the additional advantage of arriving at a time when the recipient has just consummated a purchase. Certain direct marketers offer the opportunity for one or more direct response advertisers to include inserts with customer shipments and some even offer specific selection by product line or geographic location. Inserts might be loose or contained within a separate folder in the package. Cost is about the same as that for billing inserts. Large volume is potentially available.

Mailed Circulars "Shoppers," or mailed circulars, such as those distributed by variety or food stores, sometimes provide an opportunity for direct marketers to include inserts. Distribution costs range under $25/M. Although coverage is spotty, readership is high. A variation of the mailed circular is door-to-door distribution, including delivery with certain mass circulation magazines.

Take-One Racks   Another alternative method of distribution is the use of take-one display racks in supermarkets, drug stores, restaurants, transportation terminals, vehicles, or other high-traffic locations. An advantage of such distribution is that those who voluntarily take a promotion piece from the rack are usually more than casually interested. Thus, the redemption rate from take-one rack inserts is relatively high. Even though distribution within a single rack might be quite low, less than 100 per month, the number of potential outlets for racks is quite large and distribution could total into the millions.

PRINT MEDIA

There are two fundamental means of conveying mass communication: printing presses and electronic transmitters. In this section we look at the print media. Later in this chapter, we will look at electronic transmissions: broadcast (television and radio) as well as interactive (telephone and television).

Direct mail, in its various forms, is itself a print medium. Printed publications, magazines and newspapers, represent another form of distribution of printed communication. In contrast with direct mail, which is usually delivered individually, magazines and newspapers convey direct response advertising to measurable groups of readers in a "package" along with other advertisements as well as editorial matter. The total content of these print media largely preselects the individual publication's types of readers. In most cases, too, the reader subscribes to and pays for the publication content.

Magazines

In the 1970s there was major restructuring of magazines, and this had great impact on the use of direct response advertising by direct marketers. The demise of three mass circulation magazines, *Life, Look,* and *Saturday Evening Post,* during the early part of the decade was followed by a proliferation of smaller circulation, special interest magazines.

Market Segmentation   Special interest magazines, through definition of content and readership of specific publications, serve to describe market segments and even psychographic life-styles for direct response advertisers. Categories of special interest magazines are virtually unlimited: class (*New Yorker, Smithsonian, Museum*); literary (*Atlantic, Harpers, New York Times Book Review*); sports (*Sports Illustrated, Ski, Golf*); how to (*Popular Mechanics, Popular Science, Mechanix Illustrated*); news (*Time, Newsweek, U.S. News/World Report*); religious (*Christian Herald, Catholic Digest*); and others (*Psychology Today, Ms., Playboy*).

Certain magazines are available in demographic editions describing market segments. Representative demographic editions of some magazines are shown in Figure 15-2.[8] Note that many of these editions are described by ZIP Code areas.

Categories of Magazines   Magazines generally can be grouped into five major categories:

General mass: Characterized by high circulation and relatively low cost per thousand readers, such magazines include *Readers Digest, TV Guide, National Geographic.*
Women's service: Like the category above, these are characterized by heavy circulation and reasonably low cost per thousand readers.

[8] "Burnett on Demographic Editions," *Magazine Age,* October 1981, p. 42.

DEMOGRAPHIC EDITION	YEAR INTRODUCED	ISSUES PER YEAR	TARGET SUBSCRIBER	DERIVATION
Newsweek Woman	1980	12	Female subscribers of *Newsweek*	Subscriber of national edition identified by female first names or by Miss, Ms., or Mrs. prefix
Newsweek Executive	1974	26	Professional or managerial job title with individual income of $20,000 or more	Those that fulfill $20,000 minimum personal income and have professional or managerial status are chosen from subscriber questionnaire
Sports Illustrated Select	1976	26	ZIP code areas where household income exceeds $40,000	Subscriber's address
Sports Illustrated Homeowners	1978	7	3,750 ZIP code areas that have the highest proportion of private homeowners	Subscriber's address
Time Z	1976	26	Subscriber households geographically located in the top income ZIP codes	Subscriber's address
Time B (Business edition)	1970	26	Job title of household head is professional or managerial	Ongoing subscriber census
Time A +	1978	26	Professional or managerial households with ultra-high incomes	Subscriber's address
Time T (Top Management portion of *Time* B)	1976	26	Job title is company president, owner, partner, or director	Ongoing subscriber census
U. S. News & World Report Blue Chip	1979	26	Household heads with a professional or managerial title	Selection formula by R. H. Donnelly based on household-characteristic data provided by U.S. Census Bureau
Better Homes and Gardens Super Spot	1969	12	Subscriber households with median incomes of $27,000	Subscriber households from 1,995 upper-income ZIP codes defined by U.S. Census Bureau
Ladies' Home Journal Prime Showcase	1972	12	Subscriber households with median incomes of $25,000	Subscriber households from upper-income ZIP codes defined by U.S. Census Bureau
McCall's V.I.P. ZIP	1972	12	Subscriber households with median incomes of $26,000	Subscriber households from upper-income ZIP codes defined by U.S. Census Bureau
Redbook Gold	1979	12	Subscriber households with median incomes of $23,000	Subscriber households from upper-income ZIP codes defined by U.S. Census Bureau

Source: Leo Burnett U.S.A.

Figure 15-2 Representative demographic editions of magazines.

Included are magazines such as *McCall's, Good Housekeeping, Redbook, Family Circle, Ladies Home Journal.*

Shelter: With selected demographics and increased cost per thousand circulation, shelter publications include *Architectural Digest, Better Homes & Gardens, House & Garden, House Beautiful.*

Business: This category includes publications such as *Forbes, American Banker, Business Week, Nation's Business.*

Special interest: With highly selected demographics and even life-style definition, this category would include magazines such as *Travel & Leisure, Cosmopolitan, Gourmet, Boys Life.*

Advantages and Disadvantages As seen from the above, magazines can be selected to reach mass or class audiences. Modern printing technology permits excellent reproduction at a relatively low cost per thousand circulation relative to other forms of printed media. Because magazines usually come out periodically, weekly, monthly, or quarterly, they enjoy relatively long life and often experience many readers per copy. Through split-run techniques in which alternative advertisements are placed in every other issue, they can be tested relatively inexpensively for techniques of maximizing direct response.

On the negative side, however, magazines offer direct marketers less space in which to tell their story when contrasted with direct mail. Additionally, closing dates for magazines are most often considerably in advance of the issue dates and, because of staggered distribution, response is usually slower than that from direct mail.

Relative Cost   Although there are literally thousands of magazines published, only approximately 400 are circulation audited by the Audit Bureau of Circulations. These 400 have a combined circulation of more than 300 million and the cost of one black-and-white advertising page is generally in the range of $3 to $10 per thousand for large circulation publications; and approximately $35 per thousand for trade or business publications. This is considerably less than the cost of direct mail at $250 or $300 per thousand pieces, especially when a degree of market segmentation can be obtained through specific magazines.

These factors influence costs of magazine advertising: the amount of space purchased in the magazine; the use of color vs. black and white, and whether or not ink "bleeds" off the page; the use of regional, demographic, or test market selections. Certain magazines offer discounted rates for direct response advertisers as well as special rates for categories such as publishers or schools. Sometimes, standby or remnant space is available at substantial discounts.

Position and Timing   Although the front and back covers usually get maximum readership in a magazine, many publications do not permit direct response coupons in these preferred positions. Alternatively, the front portion of the magazine, assuming a full page, is preferable. A right-hand page is usually better for direct response than a left-hand page, but there are exceptions, such as the last left-hand page in the book. Whether right-hand or left-hand page is provided, the response coupon, if there is one, should always appear on the outside margin and never in the gutter (center fold) of the magazine. Inserts and bind-in response devices, reply cards or envelopes, serve to call attention to the advertisement since the book naturally falls open to these inserts.

Aside from seasonal offers, response from magazine advertisements usually follows the normal direct marketing cycle. Strongest response occurs in January-February and September-October, with poorest response during June-July. These are *circulation* dates and not the dates appearing on the cover of the magazine.

Newspapers

Along with magazines, newspapers represent a major medium for distribution of printed direct response advertising. An estimated 1,730 daily newspapers with a total circulation of 62 million per day were being published in 1983.[9] A sizable number of weekly and farm newspapers are also available for use by direct marketers.

Market Segmentation   Like magazines, markets can be segmented for direct response advertising in newspapers, although not as finely. National newspapers, such as the *Wall Street Journal, Christian Science Monitor, Capper's Weekly,* and *National Enquirer,* are directed to well-defined market segments. Additional opportunities for market segmentation through newspapers include: urban vs. rural; dailies vs. weeklies; commuter editions vs. those intended for home delivery; morning vs.

[9] *DMA Fact Book*, 1983 ed., p. 93.

evening editions; tabloids; comic sections; Sunday supplements. Location of direct response advertisements within the newspaper, such as in the sports, television, comic, or business sections, can also serve to select specific types of readers.

Categories of Newspaper Advertising Aside from type and location of a newspaper's circulation, there are three distinct ways to reach a newspaper's readers: (1) run-of-paper (ROP), (2) preprinted inserts, or (3) syndicated Sunday supplements.

Run-of-Paper Advertisements Although position in a newspaper can sometimes be specified and paid for, ROP advertisements do not normally have the visual impact or dominance required for direct response advertisers. Most ROP direct response advertisements are small or appear in specific mail-order sections of newspapers. (Full-page direct response advertising in newspapers will, of course, increase dominance wherever placed.) The cost of 1,000 lines, black and white, ROP, is approximately $8 to $9/M circulation.

Preprinted Inserts These run typically in Sunday editions or on Wednesday or Thursday mornings. Inserts are preprinted by the direct response advertiser and provided to the newspaper according to the publication's specifications. An average cost for a six-page newspaper insert is $40 to $50/M, approximately one-half being the cost of preprinting the insert. Costs saved, compared with direct mail, are postage and mailing list rental.

Sunday Supplements Mass circulation Sunday supplements, such as *Parade* and *Family Weekly*, are edited nationally but appear locally in the Sunday editions of many newspapers. They offer large circulation (21 million for *Parade* and 12 million for *Family Weekly*) and a great deal of flexibility at relatively low

cost ($5 to $6/M for a four-color page). One variation of the Sunday supplement is the comic section, the two major syndicated comic groups being *Puck* and *Metro*. As many as 50 million households can be reached through comic sections with a four-color page costing approximately $7/M circulation. Sunday supplements, both magazine and comic sections, have proven successful for many direct response advertisers.

Advantages and Disadvantages Key advantages of newspapers for direct response advertisers include short closing dates and relatively fast response. A wide variety of formats is available, as well as broad coverage of geographic or demographic areas.

Although not necessarily true of preprinted inserts, the print quality of newspapers is generally not as good as that of the other print media, direct mail and magazines, and there is limited color availability. At times, too, the timeliness of the "news" in newspapers and their abundant advertising content detract from the readership of direct response advertising in them.

BROADCAST MEDIA

Broadcast is the most universal of all communications media. Unlike print media, broadcast reaches virtually everyone and every location. It has been estimated that there are more than two radios for every individual in the United States with 80 percent of all individuals over age 12 listening to radio during some part of each day. Approximately 98 percent of American households have television sets, 78 million in all, with more than one-half of these having more than one set. The average television set is in use more than 6 hours per day, and this medium long ago replaced the newspaper as the primary source of news.[10]

[10] *DMA Fact Book*, 1983 ed., p. 94.

In spite of their universality, however, the broadcast media, television and radio, account for less than 2 percent of the total expenditures for direct response advertising. The universality of broadcast implies a complete range of geographic, demographic, and psychographic market segments, which are not always readily identifiable. Relatively high costs associated with relatively low response rates result from reaching (and paying for) nonqualified prospects. Measurability and accountability, the hallmarks of direct marketing, are often difficult, if not impossible, with the broadcast media. Still, the potential is there, if it can be harnessed.

Television

Television has been a minor medium for direct response advertising, but its importance has been increasing as direct marketers learn how to use it for this purpose. The medium should become even more important as cable television refines the potential for market segmentation and as interactive modes of television provide the measurability and accountability on which direct marketers thrive. Viewers of television have one of two objectives: entertainment or information. Direct response advertisers on television use it in three ways:

1 To sell products or services: a record album, for example, or a political candidate
2 To get inquiries: expressions of interest or sales leads
3 To give support to other media: newspaper inserts or heavy penetration direct mail.

Market Segmentation   When a farmer "broadcasts" seed, much of that seed lodges in moist, fertile ground and, under ideal growing conditions, it is nurtured into a living plant. Another portion of the broadcast seed is borne by the wind or, for other reasons, fails to realize the proper conditions for germination. Television broadcasting is like the farmer sowing seed. Although television has the potential for reaching virtually everyone, it can achieve the objectives of the direct response advertiser only if it is in the right place at the right time under the right conditions. Market segmentation, in television as in other media, is one way to maximize direct response.

Television programming can play an important role in defining specific audience segments. Television programs, such as situation comedies, western lore, variety shows, documentaries, wrestling matches, and Shakespearean drama, can describe market segments of viewers and thus provide a showcase for a particular direct response offer. Other factors, in addition to programming, that can help segment markets include time of day or even day of the week. Viewers of one of television's greatest audience events each year, the football Super Bowl, are large in numbers and broad in characteristics. On the other hand, viewers of an old Alfred Hitchcock movie can be more clearly defined, and whether that viewing is late at night or midafternoon can make a difference, too, in *demographic* and *psychographic* terms. The "reach" of a local station can itself describe *geographic* markets.

Emerging rapidly and offering direct response advertisers even greater opportunities for market segmentation is cable television, with approximately one-third of all television homes in America now cable-equipped. Highly specialized programming, news, sporting events, and a variety of movie fare, helps define cable television audiences.

Characteristics of Television Time   Like playing a movie to empty seats in a theatre, television time is perishable. Furthermore, once 24 hours per day have been used within a market, coverage cannot be extended. Only circulation or actual television viewing within that coverage can be increased. It is this actual penetration of potential coverage that determines the price of commercial television time.

This price usually peaks during "prime time," the early evening hours, and drops to a minimum during the wee hours of the morning.

Buying Television Time The cost of television time is highest when the viewing audience is the largest. This may not necessarily be the best time for direct response advertising, however, unless an offer has universal appeal to a broad audience. Although a 120-second selling commercial on television can be purchased for less than $10/M television households reached, this figure alone may not be an adequate indication unless it is related to benefits received by the direct response advertiser. The key lies in market segmentation: just who are these viewers at a particular time and how receptive are they to the direct marketed offer?

Because of wide variation in television costs and equally wide variation in television audience segments, the most valid measurement for the direct marketer is *cost per response,* not cost per viewer. Nielsen audience ratings, gross rating points (GRPs), and areas of dominant influence (ADIs), the glossary of television time buying for the general advertiser, have little or no relevance for the direct marketer who wants somewhat more from direct response advertising than simply "total recall." The acronym that counts is CPR (cost per response)!

Direct Marketing Uses of Television There are three basic ways in which television is used by direct marketers. The first of these ways is to *sell something*: a record album, a magazine subscription, a kitchen utensil. To achieve such a direct sale, usually a 2-minute (120-second) commercial is necessary. Response can be by mail to a convenient address or, more likely, it can be by telephone to an "800" number. Rarely can items priced at more than $40 be sold in this manner, however.

The second way television is used by direct marketers is to *generate leads* for products or services, for organizations raising funds, or for political candidates seeking votes. Such direct responses involve a two-step process with the original inquiry generated by the television commercial and subsequent follow-up by mail, by telephone, or by a personal visit. A 60-second television commercial is usually adequate for the purpose of generating leads.

The third direct marketing use of television, probably the one that has been most successful to date, is as *support* of direct response advertising in another medium, such as a newspaper. Support has been used successfully by *Readers Digest*, Publishers Clearing House, *Time-Life* Books, and others. Usually 10- or 30-second commercials are adequate as reminders, with extensive repetition over a period of several days being the key to success. Support television creates interest in the offer and directs the viewer to the printed medium, which, in turn, provides detailed explanations as well as the means for response.

Although support television can be delivered through a network, to an average of approximately 200 affiliated stations, it most often is purchased as spot, or local television, which is available in more than 200 markets.

Advantages and Disadvantages Television, when used for direct response advertising, can provide a wide choice of cost alternatives and achieve quick responses. The combination of video and audio simultaneously providing a sales message along with a product demonstration can deliver a lot of impact in a short time. The limited time, however, is one of the medium's disadvantages when product descriptions are complex or are not subject to simple visualization. A major drawback, too, is the lack of a permanent response device, one that can be referenced by the viewer at some later time.

Radio

When radio broadcasting was still in its infancy in the 1920s, it became a major medium for direct response advertising. It was productive for books and records, as it is today, but also in that early period for proprietary medicines and health cures. A powerful radio station in Del Rio, Texas, with the call letters XERA, built its transmitter across the border in Mexico to circumvent regulation of its direct response advertisements, which were, at best, exaggerations of the truth. This radio station (and others) solicited orders for "genuine synthetic diamonds" as well as inquiries for Dr. Brinkley's "goat gland transplants," the answer for those seeking perpetual youth. Mail-order nurseries, pioneers in direct marketing, offered their plants and trees through the medium of radio and religious groups raised funds for their evangelists with the same medium. Radio is still probably as strong a direct response medium as it was then, although it is minimally used today.

Market Segmentation   More so than television stations, individual radio stations tend to develop strong images of programming, attracting particular types of listeners. Such program formats can segment markets into an array of specific subgroups that is virtually unlimited: all-music, all-news, all-talk shows. Program format doesn't stop with just music: music can be "rock" or "classical" or "easy-listening" or "country/western" or "show tunes" or even nostalgic "music-of-your-life" programming.

There appears to be a loyalty to certain stations by their listeners so that direct response advertising, presented within an established program format by a well-known personality, derives an air of credibility or even an implied endorsement from the station announcer. Unlike television, in which viewers are constantly "dial-switching" among a dozen or more channel alternatives, the Radio Ad-

vertising Bureau reports that the average radio listener "tunes in regularly to less than three stations—no matter how many he can receive." In 1979 there were 8,537 radio stations on the air (4,544 AM stations and 3,993 FM stations).[11] That's a lot of choices but there appears to be relatively little switching!

In addition to program format and station loyalty, another means of market segmentation, through radio, is its use during particular times of the day or even days of the week. Unlike the television viewer, the radio listener can be involved in another activity while listening to the radio. As a result, the listener can be reached in an automobile, on arising, or even in front of a mirror while shaving. Of course, the listener's attention is not always "undivided" at these times, and the real challenge to the direct marketer is delivery of a direct response instruction that can be delayed, but remembered and recalled.

Rate Structure   A major boost for the use of radio for direct response advertising is its relatively low cost. Whereas the economics of television dictate a maximum commercial length of 2 minutes, radio advertising is different in that commercial messages can be melded with disc jockey chatter. An entire 15-minute information radio program has been built around the content of a magazine, such as *Changing Times*, for which subscriptions are being simultaneously solicited. The same format has also been applied to advice for household repairs at the same time as orders are being solicited for a *Home Handyman's Guide*.

Some radio stations accept "per inquiry" arrangements under which the station runs commercial messages, at its own discretion, in return for remuneration from a direct response advertiser for each sale or inquiry produced in this manner.

[11] Shan Ellentuck and James R. Springer, "Techniques of Radio Direct Response Time Buying," in *DMA Manual*, Release No. 260.2, April 1979.

Advantages and Disadvantages   Radio is possibly the most flexible of all direct response media in that it requires relatively little in the way of preparation, and it can be scheduled or the copy can be changed right up to the time the message is aired. In contrast with the cost of printing for direct mail or print media and the high preparatory cost of television video, radio has minimal production costs, virtually none, if the message can be typed for reading by a local station announcer. The various program formats of radio are conducive to testing, and direct response advertising in connection with these formats can be accomplished at relatively low cost.

A major disadvantage of radio, like that of television, is the absence of a permanent response device, one that can be referenced at some later time. Radio, too, lacks the visual impact afforded by direct mail and the other print media as well as by television.

INTERACTIVE MEDIA

The interactive media of direct marketing encompass the electronic capabilities of the telephone (outbound *and* inbound) as well as the emerging technology of interactive television (videotex, teletext, and cable television). Under certain conditions, too, direct marketing also embraces the interaction of a salesperson. This may occur if direct response advertising results in a personal visit, as the result of an inquiry, to a buyer's location; or, it can involve a buyer's visit to a retail location, as a result of a mailed catalog. At either location, there can be interaction with a salesperson.

Telemarketing

As an interactive direct response medium, the telephone occupies a dual position in direct marketing. Like print or broadcast media, it is a conduit for direct response advertising. Additionally, it can be used, as an alternative to mail, for the response itself. Thus, *tele-*

marketing (the use of the telephone in direct marketing) can be viewed as *outbound* (solicitation of responses by a local or a WATS telephone call) or *inbound* (processing of the responses themselves). The rapid growth of telemarketing between the years 1976 and 1980 is demonstrated in the statistics shown in Figure 15-3.[12] It has been estimated by the Bell System that as much as two-thirds of future telephone usage could be telemarketing applications.

Like the individual salesperson involved in face-to-face contact, the telephone is an interactive medium, which provides the flexibility and immediate response of a personal conversation. It conserves personal time and cost. The telephone can be especially effective when used in concert with other direct response media.

Applications   The telephone can be used for a great variety of *outbound* call applications, including these:

- Generating new sales, including reorders and new product introductions
- Generating leads and qualifying inquiries for personal sales follow-up
- Serving present accounts
- Reactivating old customers
- Upgrading and increasing incoming orders
- Validating the legitimacy of orders before shipping
- Responding to customer service needs, including customer complaints
- Surveying customers, members, donors, voters
- Substituting for a personal sales call
- Expressing thanks to a customer or a donor or a voter
- Credit screening and checking as well as collection
- Performing research and gathering or disseminating information

[12] *DMA Fact Book*, 1982 ed., p. 92.

	1980	1976
Residential Originated Local Calls	$ 569	$ 232
Residential Originated Toll Calls	689	269
Business Originated Local Calls	4,144	3,045
Business Originated Toll, WATS, 800* Calls	4,443	2,502
Total	$9,845	$6,048

These figures include a pro-rata share of equipment costs but do not include labor costs. These equipment costs are included in Local Revenues.

*800 is composed of all calls paid by businesses, therefore, residential (consumer) placed 800 calls are included in this value.

TELEMARKETING—CONSUMER

	1980	1976
Total U.S. households	79,870,000	72,194,000
Total main phone numbers	78,273,000	68,585,000
Estimated phone-reachable customers/prospects at a given time*	67,393,000	59,052,000
Total phones (including ext.)	134,248,000	114,673,000
Estimated total annual calls made	148,561,000,000	122,008,000,000
Average number of annual calls made per main phone	1,898	1,779
Average number of daily calls made per main phone	5.20	4.87

TELEMARKETING — BUSINESS

	1980	1976
Total establishments	7,100,000+	6,100,000+
Total main phone numbers	14,511,000	12,161,000
Total phones	47,907,000	40,500,000
Estimated total annual calls made	134,679,000,000	113,052,000,000
Average number of annual calls made per main phone	9,281	9,296
Average number of annual calls made per phone	2,811	2,791
Average number of business-day calls made per main phone**	35.7	35.7

*13.9% of main phone numbers are not listed
**Based upon 260 business days per year

Figure 15-3 Estimated telephone expenditures for telemarketing applications. (Dollars in millions.)

The interactive nature of telemarketing is most especially relevant to these examples of *inbound* uses of the telephone:

- Ordering or inquiring
- Clarifying or requesting assistance
- Responding immediately to an advertisement
- Expediting processing
- Locating a dealer or a product servicing location
- Making reservations for travel accommodations, hotel rooms, conferences
- Obtaining financial data, stock prices, yields, etc.
- Making pledges and contributions
- Obtaining warranty information

Economics Experienced telemarketers report that, used correctly and usually in tandem with other media, the telephone can generate 2½ to 7 times the response achieved by mail alone.[13] At an average cost of $20 per hour, depending on the length of an individual contact, the cost of a telemarketing call could average as little as $1.00. Compared with the cost of an average mailing piece of approximately 25¢, however, a telemarketing call would have to be at least four times as effective as a mailing piece.

When calculating telemarketing costs, the direct marketer needs to consider not only the line and hardware of the installation, but also the program design, creative development, and labor costs. The latter should include supervisory as well as clerical support costs. If the telephone is used as an alternative to a personal visit by a salesperson, as is often the case, the telephone can be tremendously more efficient.

[13] Ernan Roman, "Telephone Marketing: The Most Direct Direct Response Medium," in *DMA Manual,* Release No. 250.1, April 1979.

Wide Area Telephone Service Wide Area Telephone Service (WATS) lines are bulk purchases of beyond-local telephone service. WATS charges are based on usage measured to the nearest $\frac{1}{10}$th hour with the average call billed at a minimal length of 1 minute, calculated to the coverage area (distance) from the telephone center.

There are two types of WATS service:

1 Out-WATS used to place calls *from* the telephone center
2 In-WATS (now known as "800" service) used to bring calls *to* a telephone center

During the decade or so that "800" in-WATS service has been available, area toll-free service has revolutionized direct marketing. With an estimated 30,000 businesses using the "800" system, catalog direct marketers have reported that as much as 35 to 50 percent of their incoming orders are received by telephone and the size of the orders average 20 percent greater than those received by mail.[14]

Future Telemarketing is being woven into the planning of most direct marketers. To those who know how and properly use it, the interactive features of the telephone are, in many cases, replacing the face-to-face contact of a salesperson's visit to a prospect or a buyer's visit to a retail location. The telephone makes it possible to talk *with* and not just *to* customers and prospects.

Especially if used in conjunction with the other media of direct response, the possibilities of the telephone in direct marketing appear virtually limitless.

Interactive Television

Even as the use of the telephone is burgeoning as an interactive electronic medium for direct marketers, another form of interactive tele-communications is emerging that combines the capabilities of television, radio, telephone, and computer networks. Under the broad heading of "interactive television" the system culminates in a home installation that looks like a standard television set merged with a standard telephone and connected with a microprocessor. With the addition of a small television camera and microphone, the video-audio receiving unit can become a sending unit as well. If the user wants hard copy, the system provides that along with display on the video screen.

"Broadcasting" becomes "narrow casting" and the ultimate individual selectivity sought by direct marketers is instantly at hand. In *The Third Wave* Alvin Toffler writes, "thus begins a truly new era—the age of the demassified media. A new info-sphere is emerging alongside the new techno-sphere . . . instead of masses of people all receiving the same messages, smaller de-massified groups receive and send large amounts of their imagery to one another."[15]

Implications for Direct Marketers Although two-way interactive television is practical and even more advanced in some European countries than it is in the United States at this writing, it is still highly experimental and the experimentation is expensive.

Forward-looking direct marketers, however, view the experimentation with emerging technology as symptomatic of the inevitability of Alvin Toffler's "electronic cottage" and the reality of shopping by computer as little as a decade away.

Some of the technology is already in place. Interactive video games have invaded home television sets. The nation's largest retailer, Sears Roebuck & Company, has experimentally converted certain specialized catalogs to

---

[14] Tom Wolf, "Direct Marketing Pushes '800' Buy-Now Bid in '80," *Kansas City Star*, February 24, 1980.

[15] Alvin Toffler, *The Third Wave*, William Morrow & Co., Bantam Book ed., New York, 1981, p. 165.

a television program to find out if customers will shop electronically. After decades of pouring dollars into giant retail stores in shopping centers, many retailers are confronting the possibility that these stores may someday be obsolete. Although no one has yet predicted the disappearance of shopping malls altogether, certain economic facts have led to innovations in retailing, many of which use direct marketing. In a Florida test market, consumers ordered merchandise from Sears and J. C. Penney by punching buttons on a key pad attached to their television sets and telephones.

Noting that technology has already altered retail business and that even greater changes are expected in the future, Touche Ross, a national accounting firm that specializes in retail clients, views the following economic factors as conducive to the future of electronic shopping and direct marketing:[16]

Inflation: Growth cycles and economic uncertainty are testing the ability of retailers to manage growth and profits.

Energy costs: With higher gasoline costs changing American driving patterns, retailers are beginning to wonder if they built too many stores and whether these stores are located too far away.

Technological development: The price of equipment necessary for electronic shopping is approaching the price range of the middle-class American family.

Retail automation: The need for greater productivity has resulted in automated systems for inventory control and customer billing.

Women in the work force: The increasing number of women working outside the home has changed life-styles as well as shopping habits.

General aging of the American population:

A more affluent class of older consumers is spending more time in leisure activities.

As the new technology and shifting economic and social patterns lead toward the acceleration of direct marketing through electronic shopping, we should look at the forms that this technology is taking.

Cable Television   According to the A. C. Nielsen Company, as of May 1982, cable television subscription penetration in the United States was estimated at 27.4 million homes, representing 33.4 percent of all U.S. television-viewing homes. There were 4,700 cable systems, serving 13,000 communities with channel capacities approaching 54 and upward. Cable television subscribers have been described as discriminating up-scale viewers, particularly regarding the programming they choose to watch and *pay for*.

QUBE, a cable television experiment in Columbus, Ohio, was launched by Warner Communications on December 1, 1977. It was the first in the U.S. to provide subscribers with a two-way interactive system. The interaction, however, is limited to a "yes/no" type of active participation by viewers. The viewer is able to respond to questions presented on the television screen with up to five answers. Although choices are limited and there can be no random access to information, such as from a catalog, activation of one of the five buttons could generate an order from a QUBE television household for a book or other demonstrated product.

Other cable television experiments have included "home shopping shows," 30 minutes long, including specific catalog offer product demonstrations with responses via telephone. One cable television experiment for direct response advertisers has been offered by a "super station" in Atlanta, Georgia. This system transmits its total news programming via

---

[16] Robert L. Bartlett, "The Future of Electronic Shopping," in *Retailing,* Winter 1980–1981, published by Touche Ross & Co., 1633 Broadway, New York, NY 10019.

satellite to local cable stations, thus offering broad circulation for direct marketers. Response is geared to a unique "800" in-WATS number.[17]

Videotex Adopted in 1981, the generic term videotex (also known as viewdata) is used to describe a database connected by telephone to a television set or to a terminal. Videotex is fully two-way interactive with the viewer having unlimited ability to explore the database. The viewer can also be equipped with a keyboard used in transactional routines such as sending messages or activating orders. A printer can be attached so that what appears on the television set screen can be, if desired, printed out in hard copy. Examples of videotex transmission are shown in Figure 15-4.

The first videotex system, called Prestel, was started in England in 1979. Beginning service with approximately 1,500 viewers, mostly businesses, there were approximately 12,000 viewers by 1982, with these still heavily weighted to business users. Products and information being provided by Prestel are extensive: timetables, shopping guides, classified advertisements, news, touring guides, financial data, and an encyclopedia. The amount of data on the screen at any one time (that is, per frame) is a maximum of 960 characters, equivalent to approximately two or three paragraphs of newsprint. Simple graphics can be reproduced using small blocks of color. Still photos or moving pictures are not yet in use, although the technology to transmit such is being developed.[18] The Prestel system is described in Figure 15-5 and an information retrieval example is shown in Figure 15-6.

[17] Donna M. Inzinga, "Success for Direct Marketers Using the Cable Medium," *Information Central,* Direct Marketing Association, New York, March 1982.
[18] Patricia K. McCarthy, "Interactive Television: A Direct Marketing Tool," *Direct Marketing,* February 1980, p. 30ff.

An Antiope system, similar to Prestel, but with better resolution and graphics, was developed originally in France and is now called Teletel. The complete Teletel videotex network is charted in Figure 15-7. In early 1982, 2,500 French households in the Velizy suburb of Paris were participating in an imaginative experiment of the Teletel system under the auspices of the French government. At that time the French government was predicting extension to 100,000 households by 1983 and an extension to all households in France, 22 million, by the year 1990. Direct marketers experimenting with the Teletel system in France included three giant catalog firms: *Les Trois Suisses, La Redoute,* and *Camif.* Teletel users can also book railway tickets, consult bank accounts, dispatch and receive written messages, play video games, and consult classified advertising. They can also send orders to mail-order firms or to local shopkeepers. The French government believes, too, that it can save money in providing a terminal permitting citizens to access telephone numbers nationwide and thus replace the cost of the printed telephone directory.

Canada has developed its own high-resolution system called Telidon, whereas in the United States Knight-Ridder and AT&T have completed the second phase of a market trial experiment in Coral Gables, Florida, using a system called Viewtron. AT&T has also begun a joint venture with CBS for an experiment in New Jersey, and a videotex system called *Bildschirmtext* has been developed in Germany.

Teletext Teletext is a generic term for broadcasting text information. A loop of potentially up to 9,900 frames is broadcast continually; a page or a frame at a time at high speed. The viewer, using a numeric key pad, can key a frame number and obtain the desired page as it passes in the broadcast loop. A form

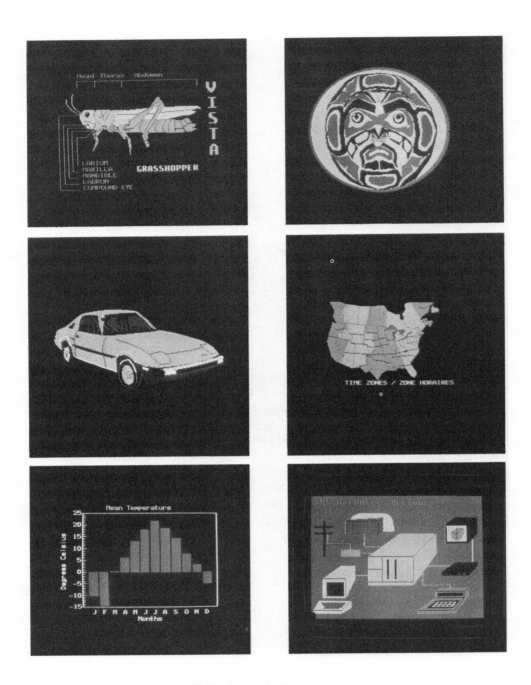

Figure 15-4 Examples of videotex (Telidon) transmissions.

of interactive system, but not connected to a telephone, it is useful for transmitting news, weather, stock tables, and other standard information.

Digital Broadcasting Telecomputing Corporation of America, McLean, Virginia, unveiled The Source in June of 1979. Now a subsidiary of *Readers Digest,* The Source was the first nationwide information and service network to be offered to personal computer owners in the United States. As a result, these personal computer owners can make airline reservations, buy and sell real estate, get instant news, sports, and weather reports from UPI or access *The New York Times* Information Bank. An interactive system, The Source provides either video display screen or hard copy print.

The Source also provides the ability to send electronic mail anywhere in the United States. Electronic Computer Originated Mail (E-COM) has also been instituted by the United States Postal Service and offers similar transmission capability. Another form of digital transmissions is that provided by QWIP.

Videodisc The application of videodiscs to direct marketing was pioneered by Sears Roebuck & Company with its 236-page Summer 1981 catalog. The basic experiment was conducted in nine stores and 1,000 households. It has since been extended. Videodiscs provide the opportunity for graphics that include color photographs and motion pictures, which are not yet available in either the videotex or teletext systems. Obviously, the recipient of a videodisc catalog would need a videodisc player to display it. For those so equipped, the advantage of adding a videodisc to videotex is an obvious one for direct marketers.

Salespeople

Our discussion of interactive media will conclude with reference to the place of personal selling in direct marketing. Salespeople are involved in telemarketing. They are also involved in face-to-face contact if a direct marketing offer brings a buyer into a retail location to be served by a salesperson. Or, conversely, an inquiry resulting from a direct response advertisement could cause a salesperson to call on the buyer at his or her location. In either instance direct marketing has involved the interactive salesperson in closing the sale.

There are other opportunities for the intervention of salespeople, such as at displays, exhibits, or fairs. In any event the salesperson becomes an important adjunct of the direct marketing process, often used as an interactive medium as the occasion warrants.

SUMMARY

Of all the media used by direct marketers, direct mail remains the primary one, relying on mailing lists and data about the individuals or organizations on such lists to most effectively reach market segments. Direct mail still accounts for approximately 50 percent of the total expenditures on direct response advertising. It is the most selective, the most flexible medium, and it offers the greatest potential for the highest rate of response although it is the most expensive medium per prospect mailed. Variations of direct mail include syndication, couponing, cooperative mailings, and miscellaneous distribution such as statement/invoice stuffers, package inserts, mailed circulars, and take-one racks.

Printed media, other than direct mail, include magazines and newspapers. Magazines, as they have trended away from mass circulation to special interest circulation, offer increased opportunities for market segmentation through definition of content and readership. Magazines generally can be categorized as being general mass, women's service, shelter, business, and special interest. Thus, magazine readership can help describe markets. Although they offer high-quality printing repro-

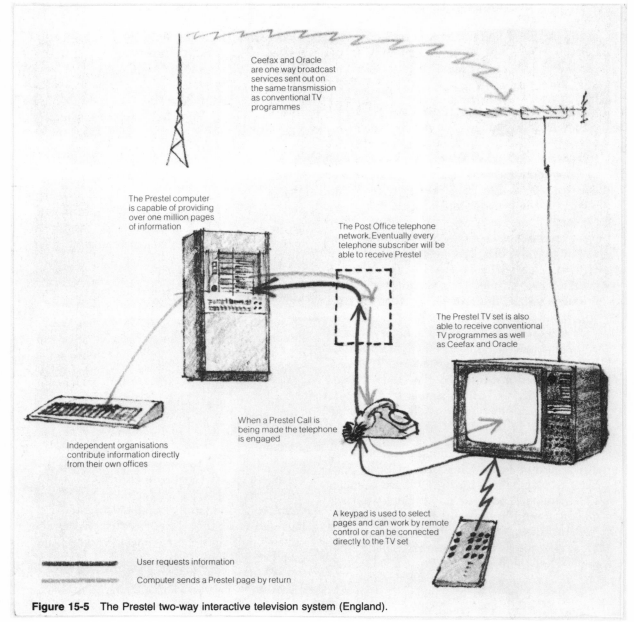

Figure 15-5   The Prestel two-way interactive television system (England).

duction, magazines give direct marketers less space than direct mail in which to tell their story.

The cost of circulation of magazines is substantially lower than that of direct mail, but response rates to individual advertisements are also much lower.

There are approximately 1,730 daily news-papers in the United States with a total daily circulation of more than 62 million. This circulation does not include weekly and farm newspapers, which are also used extensively by certain direct marketers. Like magazines, newspapers can be segmented for direct response advertisers by geographic location, by special positioning within the paper, and by

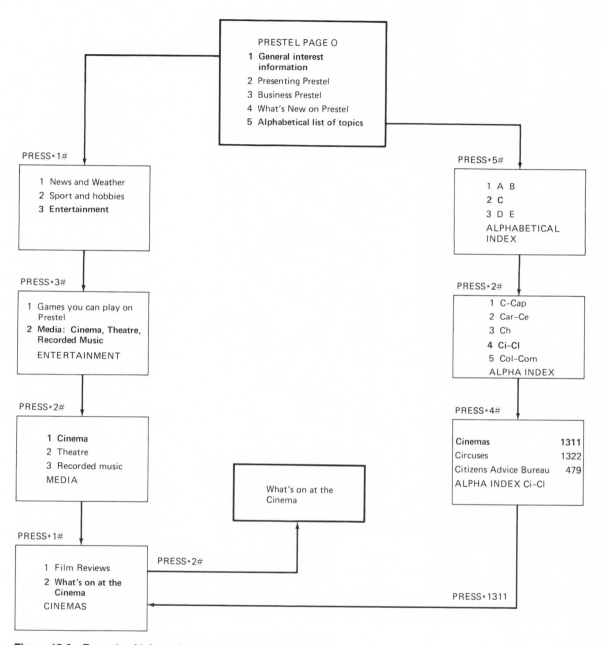

Figure 15-6 Example of information retrieval via Prestel system.

other factors such as morning or evening editions and commuter or home delivery circulation. Response advertisers can use ROP (run-of-paper), preprinted inserts, or Sunday supplements.

Direct response advertising in broadcast media involves electronic transmission through television or radio. Both of these media are virtually universal insofar as their reach is concerned. Specific programming of individual

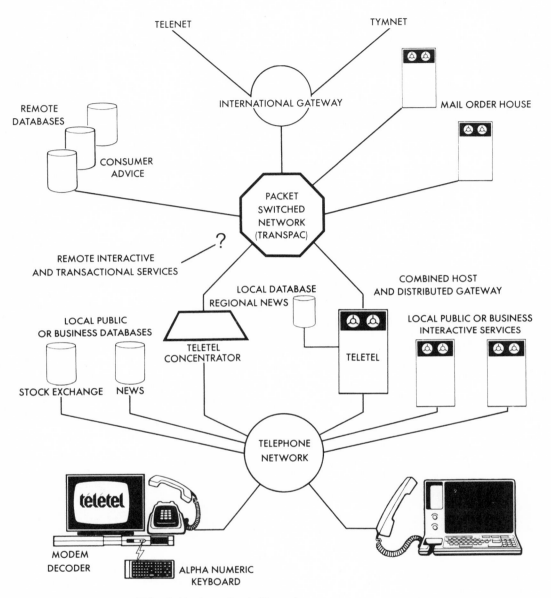

Figure 15-7   Complete Teletel videotex network (France).

radio stations make these more susceptible to market segmentation than television. Additionally, the cost of television, without such segmentation, is typically too high for direct response advertisers. Implementation in television involves specific programming, timing, and positioning as well as geographic location by market.

Among interactive electronic media, the telephone has become increasingly important not only as direct response advertising (outbound), but also as a response device (inbound), an alternative to mail. Telemarketing encompasses both outbound (WATS) and inbound (800) services. Properly used, especially in concert with other media, the telephone is a vital medium for direct marketers, a one-on-one contact that is as close as possible to a personal visit.

The emerging technology of interactive television, coupled with the telephone to provide interactive two-way communication, is of special interest to direct marketers. Although still largely experimental, more direct response advertisers are realizing the future potential of cable television, videotex, and teletext systems as well as videodisc and digital broadcasting.

Another vital interactive medium in direct marketing, of course, is the salesperson. Not only is personal selling involved in telemarketing, but salespeople often respond to inquiries or serve customers visiting a retail location as a result of direct response advertising.

CASE: ESTABLISHING THE TELEPHONE AS A MEDIUM

Learning Objective

The purpose of this case study is to view the telephone (and, potentially, other interactive electronic systems) as an advertising medium and further as an integral part of the response mechanism of direct marketing.

Overview

Telemarketing, as it has been called by the Bell System, marries telecommunications and information processing technologies to market strategies. As a strategic marketing tool, telemarketing can be used as a response system. Responses and transactions from direct marketing programs, utilizing any medium, can be consummated through a telemarketing center.

Procedure

Read the learning objective, the overview, and the case that follows. Be prepared to distinguish between outbound and inbound telemarketing. Show how marketing communications components, like media, interact with the telemarketing center. Evaluate the impor-

tance of data, record keeping, and follow-up. Why does the Bell System Sales Center use other media for its initial direct response?

Case

Practicing what it preaches, AT&T Long Lines has established its Bell System Sales Center (BSSC) in Kansas City, Missouri, with seemingly two purposes: (1) to engage in direct marketing to retain market share, to increase sales volume, and to control sales expense; (2) to serve as a model for those other organizations that can benefit from telemarketing. As presented by John Wyman, Vice President–Marketing for AT&T Long Lines, these are the specific objectives of their direct marketing program:[19]

- To contact the greatest possible number of medium and small accounts in the most economical fashion
- To provide the best possible customer service
- To increase the Bell System's sales and revenues
- To improve the Bell System's public image in the business community
- To enhance management efficiency in a telemarketing center supported with a sophisticated database and providing the necessary information to revise, as needed, direct response promotion in other media.

Established in 1976, the BSSC is a proven direct marketing success, a model for others who would use telemarketing in their own direct marketing operations. In 1982 the Center produced more than $101.9 million in sales of telephone equipment and Long Lines service, with 95 percent of customers' needs handled *entirely* by telephone. The remainder was referred for personal sales follow-up.

---

[19] Bob Stone, "Ma Bell Joins the Ranks of Direct Marketers," *Advertising Age,* September 22, 1980, p. 64. Excerpted with permission. Copyright 1980 by Crain Communications, Inc.

Bell can show you how to do more with less.

A single, toll-free 800 number can take the place of the two or more you have now. Your advertising can become less complicated. More effective. You can increase sales while reducing costs.

You do it by choosing Expanded 800, an innovation of the Bell network, the world's largest and most advanced information management system. It's one of the latest developments in the mix of technology and management systems called Telemarketing, and it can give you better control and greater flexibility in running your business.

With Expanded 800, your customers call the same toll-free number whether they're calling from out of state or within. Since a single number is easier to remember, you're likely to get more calls, write more orders, make more sales.

The network can also route customer calls the way you want them handled. When it's quitting time for your East Coast office, calls can shift to your offices still open further west. You pick up added sales and provide nonstop customer service while saving on overtime expenses.

Expanded 800 can also help your telephone sales become a mirror of your field sales operation. If you know that certain areas demand special attention, calls from those areas can go to your people best equipped to handle them.

Bell can demonstrate to you right now the effectiveness of Telemarketing with Expanded 800. We use it ourselves.

All you have to do is call 1 800 821-2121. **1 800 821-2121**

Put our knowledge to work for your business. **Bell System.**

The knowledge business

Figure 15-8   Bell System direct response magazine advertisement utilizing telemarketing to sell telemarketing.

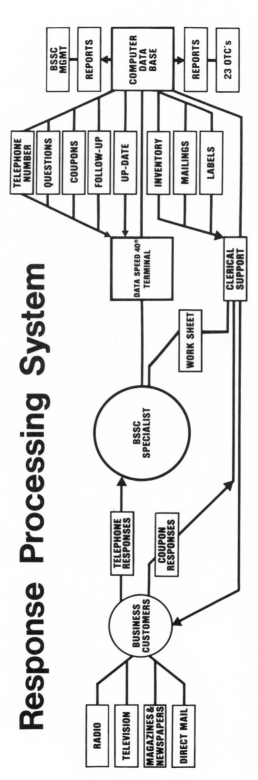

Bell System Sales Center

Response Processing System

Figure 15-9 Bell System Sales Center response processing system.

Figure 15-10   Bell System Sales Center telemarketing operation.

Direct Response Media Advertising   Using a variety of response media (direct mail, print, broadcast, and telephone), the Bell System creates interest in and generates inquiries about a variety of telecommunication products and services with response specifically directed to an in-WATS "800" number: 1-800-821-2121. An example of a typical direct response magazine advertisement, one suggesting consideration of "expanded 800" service, is shown in Figure 15-8. Although advertisements such as this one cover a wide range of products and services with some being very high priced items, John Wyman reports that approximately two-thirds of the revenue generated from direct marketing activities comes from the sale of WATS lines, "800" service, and telemarketing programs (as featured in the Figure 15-8 advertisement), with the remainder of the reve-nue coming from remote call forwarding and other telephone usages. Typically, direct response advertisements feature applications (benefits) rather than particular products.

Whereas the Bell System's direct response print and broadcast advertisements feature an in-WATS "800" response mechanism, their direct mail encourages response by either telephone or mail. As a result of extensive testing, John Wyman reports, the Bell System has determined that 60 percent of responses arrive by mail and 40 percent by telephone. However, the closure rate from telephone-originated inquiries is four times that from mail inquiries.

Response Processing System   Whether the response is a telephone call or a mailed coupon, the business customer inquiry, generated by print media, broadcast media, or direct mail,

Bell System Sales Center

Worksheet / Rev. 5-80 / No Ret. Req'd.

COUPON QUEUE
RESPONSE RECORD

Response No. ___ ___ ___ ___ ___ ___

Called By ___ ___ ___

How Received ☐ Wats ☐ Mail ☐ Initiated

Date Called ___ ___/___ ___/___ ___

Time Called ___ ___ ___ ___

RESPOND TO

Name ____________ Title ____________

Company ____________ Street ____________

City ____________ ☐ State ____________ Zip ____________

Bus. Phone ___ ___ ___ - ___ ___ ___ - ___ ___ ___ ___

Decision Maker ☐ Yes ☐ No Sex ☐ Male ☐ Female

2nd Name ____________ 2nd Phone ___ ___ ___ - ___ ___ ___ - ___ ___ ___ ___

Program ____________

Media ____________

SIC Code ___ ___ ___ ___ MMC Code ___ ___ ___

BOC ____________

Scope

☐ 1) International
☐ 2) National
☐ 3) Regional
☐ 4) Statewide
☐ 5) Metro (Message Units)
☐ 6) Local
☐ 7) Residence
☐ 9) Not Applicable

Callers Interest

☐ 19) 800 Service
☐ 20) WATS
☐ 21) Telemarketing
☐ 22) CRMG
☐ 23) SEC
☐ 24) ONA
☐ 25) Bus Lcl Serv Repair
☐ 29) HI
☐ 34) RCF
☐ 40) INTERNATL
☐ 41) PRODUCTS
☐
☐ 26) PRIVATE LINE
☐ 99) All Other

Qualifying Questions

1) ____________ ☐
2) ____________ ☐
3) ____________ ☐
4) ____________ ☐
5) ____________ ☐
6) ____________ ☐
7) ____________ ☐
8) ____________ ☐
9) ____________ ☐
10) ____________ ☐
11) ____________ ☐
12) ____________ ☐
13) ____________ ☐
14) ____________ ☐
15) ____________ ☐

POTENTIAL

___ [H]igh ___ [M]edium ___ [L]ow ☐

___ [N]ot Applicable ___ [I]ndep

ACTION ☐

___ [A] Referred To BOC For Sales Contact

___ [B] Referred To BOC At Customer Request

___ [C] For BSSC Sales Contact FU Date ___ ___/___ ___/___ ___

___ [D] Closed By BSSC

Fulfillment:

Type	Quan.		
___ ___ ___ ___	___ ___	___ ___ ___ ___	___ ___
___ ___ ___ ___	___ ___	☐ No Mailing Required	

Remarks: ____________

Rev. 8-81 MEW

Figure 15-11 Bell System Sales Center customer response record.

is routed to a sales specialist at the BSSC, whose objective is to close the sale on the first contact. The response processing system at the BSSC is shown in Figure 15-9. Using a CRT at a telephone work station, the BSSC specialist simultaneously draws information from a computer database while collecting further information from the inquirer. The telephone communication is subsequently confirmed by a direct mail follow-up containing information relevant to the inquirer's specific needs. A view of the BSSC's telemarketing operations is shown in Figure 15-10.

The BSSC telemarketing operation is a cooperative venture between AT&T Long Lines and most of the individual Bell Telephone operating companies. If direct response comes from large telecommunication users, it is referred to appropriate field sales staff. Although the BSSC closes sales, it obviously does not implement service. Information for this is electronically relayed to individual Bell Telephone operating companies.

Information and Follow-Up   When the telephone sales specialist has completed the call and direct mail follow-up has been triggered (in response to some 272,000 inquiries in 1982 on behalf of 23 Bell Telephone operating companies), relevant information is stored in the computer database for follow-up. The form on which this information is collected by the BSSC sales specialist is shown in Figure 15-11.

This customer response record is coded into the database by a clerical support team. Should the original inquirer, on receipt of mail follow-up, have further questions or desire to implement service, he or she can call back to 1-800-821-2121. No matter which BSSC sales specialist answers, the telephone number of the inquirer provides the communicator with instant access, through a desk top CRT, to the computer database containing information about prior contact. If, after the lapse of a suitable

period of time, the inquirer has not responded, the system reminds a BSSC sales specialist of this and automatically triggers a telemarketing follow-up.

In 1982 John Wyman was looking to expansion of telemarketing at AT&T Long Lines in a variety of ways. He saw an extension of the "800" WATS and network services that can be sold through direct marketing. It is conceivable, too, that the BSSC could do more implementation of sales with the Bell Telephone operating companies, through offering services such as remote call forwarding. He saw telemarketing, too, as a means of maintaining an ongoing relationship with the Bell System's customers. Thus, a telemarketing medium itself has become a telemarketer.

DISCUSSION QUESTIONS

1 What is the major advantage of direct mail over other media for direct response advertising?
2 What is meant by syndication of direct mail?
3 Why is a coupon considered to be direct response advertising?
4 Suggest ways for market segmentation through print media: magazines and newspapers.
5 How can positioning of an advertisement in a magazine or newspaper influence response?
6 Evaluation of media for direct response advertising must relate costs to results. How might this be done?
7 What is a major disadvantage of broadcast media (television and radio) for direct response advertising?
8 In what ways do direct marketers use television as a medium?
9 Distinguish between videotex, teletext, and cable television.
10 Discuss the variety of uses of the telephone in direct marketing. Under what circumstances is the telephone more cost efficient than direct mail?
11 Explain the technology of interactive television. What are the implications of this medium for direct marketers?

DIRECT MARKETING IN THE DISTRIBUTION SYSTEM

The systematic process of moving an offer (product or service at a price) from a producer to a customer in a market (consumer or industrial) is called *distribution*. Figure 1-4 on page 8, presents the positioning of distribution within a marketing system.

We now look at the distribution process, of which promotion (selling, advertising, publicity, and support) is a part. Direct marketing, more accurately, *mail order,* is sometimes viewed as an alternative distribution system. Although that is technically correct, our definition of direct marketing goes considerably beyond that. We view direct marketing as an aspect of the total marketing concept which is *measurable* and *accountable* and which relies on *lists* and *data*. Direct marketing operates in a variety of alternative distribution channels.

DIMENSIONS OF DISTRIBUTION CHANNELS

The linkages between producers and users are termed *channels of distribution*. Such channels involve intermediate markets and include interacting *institutions* as well as *agencies* in the distribution process. As goods and services flow through a channel, there is a series of movements from one organization to another, with still other organizations aiding and abetting the flow.

Distribution channels can be short or long. They can include many or no intermediaries in the form of middlemen, which may or may not take physical possession (or title) to the products involved. Other organizations, such as banks, advertising agencies, transportation companies, also play a part in the distribution channel, performing specific functions, such as financing, advertising, or physical movement of goods. Still other intermediary middlemen, retailers, wholesalers, and brokers, also perform specific marketing functions within the channel: buying, transporting, storing, selling, financing, risk taking, promoting, processing payments, etc.

Each of these intermediaries, whether institution or agency, embraces some part of the total marketing effort and there are a series of relationships among them that culminate in a flow or movement through a distribution channel.

Evolution of Mail Order to Direct Marketing

Whereas mail order is a selling method, it is not *in and of itself* necessarily a distribution channel. Many mail-order transactions, for example, insurance, books, nursery stock, involve a *direct* channel from producer to user. Others, such as clothing, gift, and specialty items, may occur at intermediate points *within* a channel. A kitchen appliance, for example, might be sold by a manufacturer to a mail-order catalog firm in much the same way it would be sold to a retail store or to a wholesale distributor. Thus, mail order is not really an alternative distribution channel. It is, rather, a means of transaction within a channel, which is characterized usually by the *absence* of a "store" or a "salesperson."

Many of today's leading direct marketing organizations, book clubs and record clubs, as examples, are categorized as mail-order distributors in the sense that they do not employ salespeople or operate retail stores. These same book and record manufacturers might also distribute certain products through book stores and record stores, in addition to their mail-order clubs, and might use salespeople to accomplish distribution to these retail stores. The retail stores might employ salespeople of their own. Thus, mail order is an alternative selling method, but it is not necessarily a distribution channel.

Out of mail order (a selling method) and direct mail (an advertising medium) has evolved direct marketing as an aspect of the total marketing concept. Some view direct marketing, in a limited and narrow sense, as a distribution system. Retailers, having noticed the success of their mailed catalogs, not only in terms of mail and telephone orders but also in terms of increased store traffic, might rightfully call themselves direct marketers. Firms that have used direct mail (or other advertising media) to generate leads for their salespeople might also view themselves as direct marketers. As long as their promotion activities are *measurable* and *accountable* and result in the capturing of *lists* and *data,* their definitions of themselves are valid. They are using direct marketing techniques as a part of their total marketing system.

Thus, direct marketing has evolved from mail order, as all or part of a distribution channel, and needs to be viewed in the distribution system, even with the intervention of retail stores, salespeople, or other intermediaries. Impetus for this thinking has come from major corporations such as those listed in Figure 16-1. These are but a sampling of firms who have started or acquired direct marketing operations.[1]

Use of Direct Marketing in Distribution

Richard A. Hamilton, associate professor of marketing at the University of Missouri–Kansas City, has reported the following variety of products being distributed using direct marketing techniques:[2]

- The General Services Administration sold 923,000 historic silver dollar coins in 10 days, which netted the United States Treasury $50 million. Requests for more than 4 million coins were unfilled because of a lack of supply.
- IBM received 20 percent response from a multiple mailing to 3,500 customers; the mailings promoted IBM software with monthly licensing fees ranging from $40 to $1,000.
- Don Stewart Evangelistic Association's telegram mailing pulled a 16 percent response and raised almost $99,000 in emergency funds for The Philippine Project.
- John Deere increased its snowmobile sales

29 percent, while industry sales slumped 30 percent during the month of October, through a cooperative mailing with its dealers.
- Dayton Speedometer, which repairs speedometers, tachometers, cruise controls, automobile clocks, and windshield wiper motors for dealers, accounts for 10 to 15 percent of its sales through use of direct marketing techniques.
- Neal Manufacturing, which sells asphalt-sealing machinery and related items primarily to contractors but also to municipal agencies, universities and colleges, shopping center developers, airports, and others, relies heavily on direct mail and the telephone.
- JS&A Group, Inc., sold a 1978 Aerostar 601P aircraft in 1 day for $225,000.
- Rockwell International sold 15 Rockwell Jetprop Commander business airplanes, worth $1 million each, during an 8-week direct mail program.
- A Sakowitz catalog shopper purchased and charged a $35,000 necklace.
- Chris-Craft sold two luxury yachts as a result of initial contacts made through direct mail.
- Through the use of a direct response television campaign that offered memorial windows, steel pillars, $1,500 pews, and 11,000 ceiling stars, Robert Schuller, Jr.'s Crystal Cathedral became a debt-free reality in less than 4 years.

IBM Canada, Ltd., has reported a direct marketing distribution experiment that uses automated product displays in waiting areas and high-traffic pedestrian corridors in shopping malls. Passersby can walk up to display booths and operate computer products placed there. Through an interactive keyboard, the viewer activates the machine to give a demonstration of its capabilities. Telephone receivers on the front of the booths provide prerecorded messages about the products. Literature is available for viewers to take with them and a postage paid reply card on the literature puts interested prospects into direct contact with an IBM ordering center. At other displays, viewers use an IBM personal com-

---

[1] *Mail Order Industry Estimates, 1982,* Maxwell Sroge Company, Inc., Chicago.

[2] Richard A. Hamilton, "Direct Marketing—The Practitioner's Side," unpublished research, August 1981.

CORPORATION	SUBSIDIARY
Aluminum Co. of America:	Wear-Ever Aluminum, Inc.
American Can Company:	Fingerhut; Figi's
Amfac:	Gurney Seed; Henry Field
Armstrong Cork Company:	The Decorator's Guild
Bear Creek Corporation:	Harry & David; Jackson & Perkins; Shopping International
Beatrice Foods:	Day-Timers, Inc.
Beneficial Corp.:	Beneficial Finance Co.
Bliss & Laughlin Industries:	Jensen Tool & Alloys Co.; Markson Science, Inc.
Bradford Exchange:	Hammacher Schlemmer
Cadence Industries:	Hudson Pharmaceutical; U.S. Pencil & Stationery; Cadence Mail Order of Canada, Ltd.
Campbell Soup:	Pepperidge Farm Mail Order Co.
Carlson Companies, Inc.:	Hennikers; K-Promotions; Ambassador of Canada; E.F. McDonald
Chartcom, Inc.:	Hamilton Mint; Sportswares
CBS, Inc.:	CBS/Columbia Group; Columbia House
Combined International:	Union Fidelity
Consolidated Foods:	Electrolux; The Fuller Brush Co.; Hanes Corp. — L'eggs Direct
Darby Drug:	Barth-Spencer
Dart Industries, Inc.:	Coppercraft Guild; The West Bend Co.; Tupperware Home Parties; Vanda Beauty Counselor
Drew National Corp.:	American Furniture — Jewelry Corp.; Carsons of Atlanta, Inc.; M. Kovens Co.; Reliable of Portsmouth, Inc.; Standard Distributors, Inc.
The Dreyfus Corporation:	Dreyfus Management, Inc.
Fox-Stanley Photo Products, Inc.:	Ball Photo; Owl Photo; Fox Professional Color Labs; 35 Unlimited
G.R.I. Corp.:	The Butterfly Group; Homeward House; World of Beauty Club
General Mills:	Eddie Bauer, Inc.; H. E. Harris & Co.; Lee Wards Creative Crafts, Inc.; The Talbots, Inc.; Bowers and Ruddy Galleries Frostline; Jafra Cosmetics, Inc.
Gillette Co.:	
W. R. Grace:	Berman Buckskin Co.; Herman's World of Sporting Goods; Sheplers, Inc.; Home Improvement Centers
Greyhound Corp.:	Armour Food Co.: Pfaelzer Bros.
Grolier, Inc.:	Grolier Enterprises, Inc.
Gulf Oil Co.:	Gulf Consumer Services
Horn & Hardart:	Hanover House Industries, Inc.: First Editions; Hanover House; Lakeland Nurseries; Lana Lobell; New Hampton General Store; Old Village Shop; Pennsylvania Station; Unique Products
IBM Corp.:	Science Research Associates
IT&T:	Howard W. Sams & Co., Inc.; W. Atlee Burpee Co.; Educational Services, Inc.; Palm Coast Real Estate; Speedwriting Home Study

CORPORATION	SUBSIDIARY
Intex, Inc.:	International Correspondence Schools
S.C.J. Investment Co.:	Downs & Co.
S.C. Johnson:	Elsa Williams; Holubar; H. L. Leonard Rod
MCA Inc.:	Spencer Gifts
Macmillan, Inc.:	Gump's; LaSalle Extension University; Macmillan Arts & Crafts, Inc.; Macmillan Book Clubs, Inc.; Macmillan Educational Corp.
Mattel, Inc.:	Western Publishing Co., Inc.
McGraw-Hill:	National Radio Institute
Meredith Corp.:	Better Homes & Gardens: Family Book Service; Crafts Clubs; Family Shopping Service
Mobil Corp.:	Marcor, Inc.: Montgomery Ward & Co.; Montgomery Ward Life Insurance Co.; Montgomery Ward Auto Club, Inc.; Montgomery Ward Enterprises, Inc.; Signature Financial/Marketing, Inc.; Signature Agency, Inc.; SignatureCard, Inc.
Modern Merchandising, Inc.:	Anchor Distributors, Inc.; Dolgin's, Inc.; Great Western Distributing Co.; LaBelle's Distributing of Arizona, Inc.; Phil Miller, Inc.; Rogers Distributing Co.; Standard Sales Co. of Florida, Inc.
Oshman's Sporting Goods, Inc.:	Abercrombie & Fitch
Pitney Bowes:	The Drawing Board; Monarch Marking Systems; Dictaphone: Grayarc
Purex Corp.:	Ferry-Morse Seed Co.
Quaker Oats Co.:	Herrschners Inc.; Brookstone; Joseph Bank Clothiers
RCA Corp.:	RCA Music Service
Scott & Fetzer Co.:	Kirby Co.; World Book-Childcraft
Standex International Corp.:	Club Products; Yield House; Crest Fruit
Tandycrafts, Inc.:	American Handicrafts/Meribee
Tenneco Inc.:	Tenneco West; House of Almonds
Time Inc.:	Book-Of-The-Month Club; Time/Life Books, Inc.
Times Mirror Corp.:	Fuller & Dees
Torstar (Toronto Star):	Harlequin: Miles Kimball
Otto Versand:	Spiegel
Warner Communications:	Franklin Mint; Eastern Mountain Sports
Xerox Corp.:	Xerox Publishing Division: Xerox Educational Publications
Zenith Radio Corp.:	Heath Co.

Figure 16-1 Major corporations with direct marketing operations. (*Source:* Mail Order Industry Estimates, 1982. *Maxwell Sroge Company, Inc., Chicago, Illinois.*)

puter keyboard that is hooked up to a laser-operated videodisc to select audio-visual presentations on how computers work and to solve games and puzzles that demonstrate computer concepts. They can even view applications of other IBM products. The computer terminal itself accepts a direct response inquiry.[3]

Mannington Mills, Inc., manufacturer of vinyl covering, has reported a similar experiment using a computer as an alternative to a salesperson to demonstrate its Compu-Floor to potential customers at its displays in several hundred retail locations. The *Wall Street Journal* reports other experiments by Helene Rubinstein cosmetics and by the computer maker Atari. The latter has provided a retail location alternative to a salesperson, which is nicknamed ''Eric,'' for ''Electronic Retail Information Center.''[4]

ESTABLISHING CHANNELS OF DISTRIBUTION

Selection of one or more distribution channels is frequently among the marketing executive's most difficult tasks. A channel cannot be established and forgotten. It needs to be lived with and looked into periodically, even though there is no specific problem. The concept of ''innovate or die'' applies to distribution channels.

Typically, a distribution channel comprises various types of marketing middlemen, wholesalers, retailers, and brokers, each performing a marketing function and each involved in the process of moving goods from producers to users. Ultimate selection of a channel depends on the nature of the product or service, the purchasing habits and preferences of users, and the overall economic structure of the organizations. When establishing distribution channels, the marketing executive is concerned with (1) selecting the channel to be used; (2) selecting the type and number of middlemen (if any) to be employed; (3) selecting the specific middlemen.

Direct marketers, in establishing channels, might be producers or middlemen in the channel. They might be distributing to ultimate consumers, or the customer might be an industrial user, purchasing for resale or for fabrication into a manufactured product. Channel(s) ultimately selected, of course, should be appropriate to the basic objectives of the firm's marketing program, including adequate service if that is required. The channel should provide the direct marketer with access to a predetermined share of the market, including a predetermined level of market penetration. If middlemen are involved, these will survive only so long as they are economically and socially justifiable in the distribution process.

Possibly the most basic decision to be made in selection of a distribution channel involves a determination of which of the functions of marketing will be performed by each of the channel intermediaries or middlemen. This decision is especially important in viewing direct marketing in the distribution system. The ultimate objective of the system should be delivery of the *right product* to the *right place* at the *right time,* with adequate provision for servicing and follow-up, if and as required.

Alternative Channels: Consumer Products/Markets

Figure 16-2 illustrates the four most common alternative distribution channels available to producers of consumer products for reaching the users of such products. Direct marketing can be employed at any level of any channel, and mail order is not confined to the direct producer-consumer channel. Figure 16-2 does not provide *all* of the alternatives. A producer might employ sales offices or branches or might serve as its own wholesaler. In complex dis-

[3] Douglas J. Garnett, ''New Directions in Marketing Computers,'' presentation at the Canadian Direct Marketing Association, 18th Annual Conference, June 2, 1982.

[4] ''Firms Start Using Computers to Take the Place of Salesmen,'' *Wall Street Journal,* July 15, 1982, p. 29.

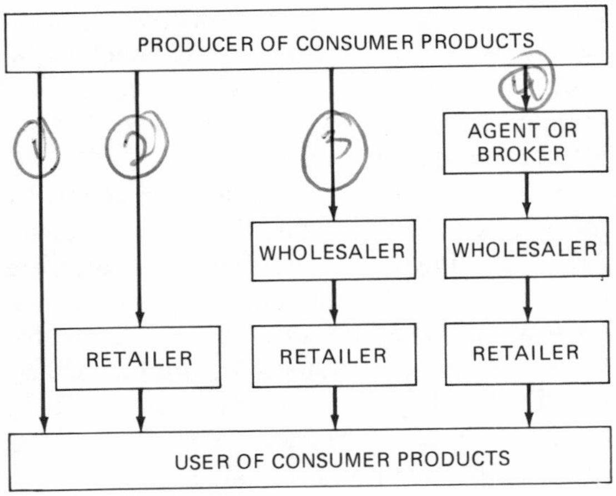

Figure 16-2 Alternative distribution channels: consumer products/markets.

tribution systems, there might even be more than one level of wholesaling middleman.

Producer-Consumer This, the shortest channel, often involves mail order, door-to-door distribution, or direct salespeople. Examples of organizations using this form of distribution include Avon and Amway, magazines such as *Better Homes & Gardens,* household products of Fuller Brush, or insurance companies with direct salespeople.

Producer-Retailer-Consumer Many retailers of clothing, including direct marketers through catalogs, employ this channel, purchasing directly from manufacturers. Automobile dealers are another example as are "fast food" retailers. Certain producers, such as paint manufacturers, sometimes own their retail outlets.

Producer-Wholesaler-Retailer-Consumer This distribution channel is so common as to be called "traditional." Note again that direct marketing could be employed between producer and wholesaler, between wholesaler and retailer, or between retailer and consumer.

The first could include a mail-order seller of stationery products, such as ball-point pens sold by office supply stores, whereas the latter could be a catalog merchant of handicraft products purchased from a wholesaler.

Producer-Agent or Broker-Wholesaler-Retailer-Consumer An agent or broker is usually employed when trying to distribute through small retailers or when the producer is otherwise unable to economically justify a sales force. Commonly, too, direct marketing techniques can substitute for an agent or broker.

Alternative Channels: Industrial Products/Markets

Figure 16-3 illustrates the most popular alternative distribution channels used by producers to reach industrial markets. Although these are the most widely used channels, they are not necessarily exhaustive. Direct marketing may be used throughout the channel or else between any of the channel levels.

Producer–Industrial User This is the most widely used channel for industrial products especially if there are large costly installations, such as power plants involving complex selling and engineering.

Figure 16-3 Alternative distribution channels: industrial products/markets.

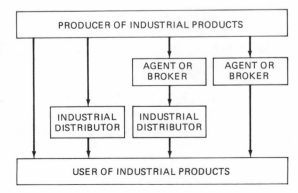

Producer–Industrial Distributor–Industrial User Direct marketing by catalog is often used in this channel alternative when distributing operating supplies and accessory equipment, both to and through industrial distributors. Examples of products distributed in this way include air conditioning equipment as well as building materials and other construction supplies.

Producer-Agent or Broker–Industrial Distributor–Industrial User Intervention of an agent or broker, as is the case with consumer products, is relevant for industrial products with small unit sales or, possibly, specialty products requiring decentralized inventories in the hands of many industrial distributors. In such instances, direct marketing catalogs may replace the agent or broker.

Producer-Agent or Broker–Industrial User As with consumer products, producers finding it economically unfeasible to develop their own sales organizations employ agents or brokers as intermediaries. Direct marketing is an alternative.

DEVELOPMENT OF MARKETS

The objective of a distribution system is, ultimately, customer satisfaction. For customer satisfaction to occur, products and services must be distributed in the right *form*, at the right *time*, in the right *place*, in a manner that will provide for *possession* when demanded. Distribution is thus concerned with four kinds of utility: *form, time, place,* and *possession.*

The dynamic nature of distribution systems tends to evolve a structure for economy and efficiency in exchange to create these four kinds of utility. Such economy and efficiency imply an optimum use of resources through a systematic structure of routinized transactions rather than an individual negotiation of each sale.

Discrepancy of Quantity, Assortment, and Timing

Producers, to realize and benefit from the economies of scale, need to produce large quantities of relatively few items. Users, on the other hand, need relatively small quantities of many different items. This diversity creates a basic *discrepancy* in quantity and assortment between the needs of producers and those of users. Furthermore, use is not always as uniform a process as is production. Since users, more often than not, consume at a rate different from that at which producers produce, there is also a discrepancy of timing.

Such discrepancies demonstrate two major processes of a distribution system: *accumulation* and *allocation*. Accumulation, which often includes sorting or grading, involves the bringing together of goods from a number of sources to a larger homogeneous supply. Allocation, which includes assorting, involves breaking down this homogeneous supply into smaller units.

A manufacturer of nylon tents, for example, might also manufacture sleeping bags or collapsible cot beds, with each product line being produced in volume to benefit from economies of scale. A wholesaler might acquire these nylon products from the manufacturer in carload lots and resell them to retailers in case lots. The individual camper, however, might purchase just one of each of these three items: tents, sleeping bags, collapsible cots.

But, that camper might also require a pair of hunting boots, a rifle case, and a kerosene stove, each of which has been produced in volume by a different manufacturer. A properly designed distribution channel brings producers and users of outdoor products together in a store location or a mail-order catalog appealing to a specific market segment, which in this case is campers. If the objective market segment is small and geographically dispersed, a mail-order catalog can often accomplish distribution more efficiently and can also often reach these potential markets more effectively. A total process is visualized in Figure 16-4.

The Need for Specialists Originally, households operated as self-sufficient systems. As these households developed special skills, however, surpluses developed and the individual households began to trade with each other. The exchange process was simplified through development of centralized markets. Still, each transaction was an individual one and consumed time. In the search for efficiency, the need for transactions specialists, or middlemen, became apparent. Middlemen, wholesalers, retailers, agents and brokers, charged

Figure 16-4 Visualization of the processes of accumulation and allocation in a distribution system to overcome the discrepancies of quantity, assortment, and timing.

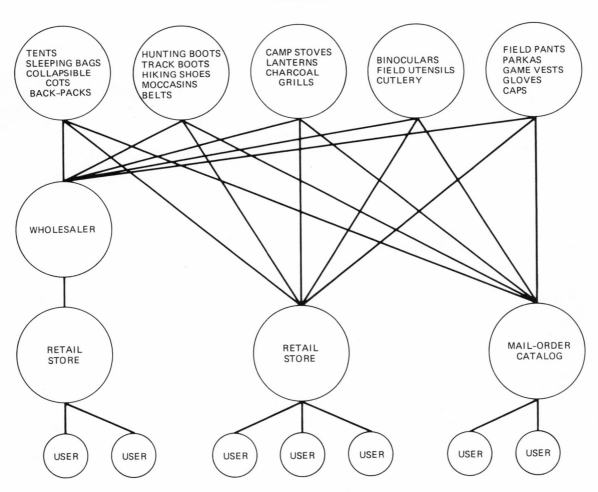

for their services, but the savings in time and physical movement provided for their compensation.

More recently, the distance between producers and users and the intervening markets has increased; clearly defined market segments have proliferated and become geographically dispersed; products and product lines have become much more complex. All of these factors have emphasized the need for specialists in distribution and they have also provided an environment for the growth of direct marketing in the distribution system.

Extent of Consumer Distribution

The extent of consumer distribution, whether *intensive, selective,* or *exclusive,* can be roughly equated to three kinds of goods with which shoppers are concerned as consumers: *convenience goods, shopping goods,* and *specialty goods.*[5] Although the categorization is not always clear-cut, an implication of intensive distribution is the availability of convenience goods in a great many outlets. Selective distribution of shopping goods implies a limited number of outlets. Exclusive distribution of specialty goods implies one or very few outlets. These categorizations apply primarily to consumer markets and consumer goods. In these markets direct marketing techniques have been used chiefly for shopping and specialty goods rather than convenience goods, which are generally more readily available on short notice.

Intensive Distribution To achieve market saturation and thus benefit from the promotion efforts of manufacturers, many middlemen, wholesalers as well as retailers, are required. Typically, the purchase of convenience goods is for immediate satisfaction. Such purchases are usually consummated with a minimum of effort and virtually no salesperson involvement.

Selective Distribution Relying on outlets, suppliers of shopping goods, such as automobiles, home appliances, furniture, clothing, invite comparison. Selective distribution, too, can be less costly than intensive distribution through the elimination of less efficient middlemen and through the screening of customers in such areas as average order size and credit risk. For these reasons, selective distribution often calls for the use of direct marketing techniques.

Exclusive Distribution Many distinctive products, specialty goods such as designer fashions, brand name cosmetics, and patented nursery stock, are geared to exclusive distribution, often through specialized mail-order catalogs intended to reach specific consumer market segments. Specialty goods usually call for a distinct purchasing effort with a significant number of buyers willing to go out of their way to acquire them. Distribution of such goods implies an aura of exclusivity which benefits the user as well as the producer and retailer. Harry & David at Bear Creek Orchards in Medford, Oregon, promotes the exclusivity of its Royal Riviera pears, whereas its mail-order affiliate, Jackson & Perkins, promotes the exclusivity of its patented rose bushes. Direct marketing is employed heavily by both of these firms.

Extent of Industrial Distribution

Industrial distribution differs from consumer distribution, first of all, in its extent.[6] In terms of buying units, there are approximately 10 times as many purchasing households as there are industrial organizations and approximately

---

[5] A discussion of convenience, shopping, and specialty goods is contained in Chapter 9.

[6] See Chapter 6 for a more comprehensive discussion of characteristics of industrial markets, types of industrial goods, and special characteristics of industrial demand.

30 times as many individual consumers. It follows from this numerical disparity that industrial users will be much more spread out geographically. Whereas consumers with like interests tend to cluster, often geographically, there is no such common geographic clustering of industrial organizations.

Industrial goods producers normally call on industrial users, rather than the other way around, as when customers shop for consumer goods. Calls by salespeople on industrial buyers take more time and are more costly than calls on individual consumers, even though industrial purchases usually cost more. Industrial buyers are also usually much better informed, have more specialized interests, and are involved in a process of joint decision making with others within their respective organizations. Repeat purchases are made more frequently in industrial markets.

Direct Marketing to Industrial Users A feature of industrial distribution that causes it to be especially susceptible to the techniques of direct marketing bears repeating. Producers and their middlemen are more likely to call on industrial users, whereas the users of consumer goods are more likely to call on the producers and middlemen for such goods.

Distributors of consumer goods using direct marketing techniques, in effect, bring their products and services to users, just as do distributors of industrial goods. Similarly, direct marketing has been used effectively in industrial distribution to augment personal selling to industrial organizations. An industrial distribution system can be intensive, selective, or exclusive, just as in consumer markets.

Forces Affecting Distribution Channels

A variety of social and economic forces have contributed to the ongoing evolution of distribution channels and the development of both consumer and industrial markets. Many of these forces have been conducive to the growth of direct marketing. These forces can be categorized as *demographic, economic, legal/political,* and *technological.*

Demographic   Recent years have witnessed the relocation of population away from rural communities and into suburban areas. We are witnessing a trend back to central cities to minimize transportation costs. As sprawling shopping malls appeared on the outer fringes of metropolitan areas, large discount stores and supermarkets proliferated in those same remote regions. More recently, as the result of the ongoing population relocations and high energy costs, these suburban sprawls might be giving way to multilevel urban malls and strip shopping areas in urban neighborhoods.

Along with the waning impact of suburban living, too, there has been a redistribution of the population by age, with new emphasis on the *older* ages. As fewer marry and average family size decreases, more women have entered the work force, with more than one-half of women now gainfully employed. Simultaneously, there are more one-parent, childless, and single-person households.

All of these factors have contributed to changes in taste, changes in preference, changes in value systems. These are coupled with new life-styles, new shopping patterns, and new attitudes toward leisure time.

Economic   Along with income redistribution have come rises in disposable personal income, changing land and home values, a proliferation of new product needs for these homes, multiple automobiles, and leisure-time activities.

The need for distribution efficiency has emphasized the importance of economies of scale as evidenced by discount houses and large supermarkets with tremendous varieties of products under one roof.

Legal/Political   Regulation and compliance have become, increasingly, a way of life as have a vast array of legal and public policy constraints. Product liability legislation, for example, has emphasized the need for convenient servicing and/or exchange.

Technological Just as the automobile was a major factor in changing life-styles and modes of living and shopping patterns, the reversal to urban living might also be attributed to the high cost of obtaining and maintaining automobiles. There's little doubt, too, that computers are having a distinct impact on the way we live and work as well as the way we shop. Interactive electronic media, now the telephone and soon interactive television, have served as an impetus to direct marketing in the distribution system. So have printing technology, credit systems, and new concepts in market segmentation.

SELECTING AND ORGANIZING MIDDLEMEN

The linkage between seller and buyer in a marketing system is the distribution channel. A proper objective of the seller in channel selection and organization is maximization of marketing effectiveness and thus the maximization of potential profit within each market segment. It is entirely possible that a different channel might be required for one or more market segments of interest.

Regardless of the number of channels and irrespective of their form, the seller should observe two basic goals in selecting and organizing channels:

1 The achievement of a sufficiently broad product availability to assure ready exposure to potential buyers
2 The creation of uninterrupted trading relationships between sellers and buyers composing the channel.[7]

[7] Alfred R. Oxenfeldt, *Executive Action in Marketing*, Wadsworth Publishing, Belmont, Calif., 1966, p. 392.

Middlemen in the Channel

The essence of distribution is buying and selling. As goods move from producer to user, one or more middlemen may perform one or more marketing functions in the exchange process. If a middleman takes title to the merchandise during the exchange process, he or she is called a *merchant middleman*. Merchant middlemen buy their goods from the previous owner, the seller. At least for a period of time, they own them. In the performance of their own functions in the distribution system, they become sellers, either to other middlemen in the channel or to the ultimate user. The functions they perform include accumulating (collecting and concentrating the output of a variety of producers); allocating (subdividing and dispersing assortments in units desired by users); creation of utility (*time, place,* and *possession* but not necessarily *form*).

In contrast with merchant middlemen, *agent middlemen* do not take title to the goods but they do actively assist in the transfer of title. Examples of agents are those who independently represent manufacturers or those who independently represent insurance companies in the movement of their products or services. Examples of brokers are food brokers, stock brokers, and real estate brokers.

Channel competition today is keenest between different systems of distribution, rather than between the component units of a system. Mail order, for example, might be an alternative form of distribution directly from producer to consumer or it might be just one stage in the channel from producer to retailer. In either event this distribution form can compete with the traditional wholesaler or the traditional retailer. Or, it can augment either as an alternative to personal selling, using a variety of media for promotion and either mail or telephone for response/transaction. In direct marketing the salesperson often remains in the channel but is made more efficient with augmented techniques.

In a very real sense the buyer helps structure the channel through expressing preferences for negotiating with the seller. Selecting and organizing a proper channel and ultimately controlling that channel are assets to the seller as well as a preference of the buyer.

Wholesalers as Middlemen

Wholesalers are middlemen who buy from producers and sell to: (1) those who resell to ultimate users or (2) industrial firms who are themselves the ultimate users. In the process of *buying* (acting as purchasing agents for their customers) and *selling* (performing certain marketing functions for producers), wholesaling middlemen not only *divide* or *bulk-break,* they also *transport, warehouse, finance, riskbear,* and often provide *management service* and *advice.* Such full-service functions as these occur between any two stages of the distribution process. Performance justifies the existence of the wholesaling middleman, who is sometimes called a distributor, mail supply house, industrial distributor, or jobber.

A specialized form of wholesaling is that of *rack jobbers,* who provide and maintain displays and inventories of hardware and houseware items, books and magazines, ready-to-wear, etc. Another form of wholesaling includes *commission men* who are used primarily in the distribution of agriculture products, fresh fruits and vegetables, livestock, and grains. Limited function wholesalers include *truck (wagon) jobbers, drop shippers, cash-and-carry wholesalers, retailer cooperative warehouses.* Wholesaling services, often performed by nonmiddlemen, are also provided through fairs, trade shows, exhibits, merchandise marts, and even public warehouses and freight forwarders.

Although wholesaling middlemen have been bound by traditions in the past, not easily subject to change, their importance and number have been increasing in recent years as the array of goods and distribution systems themselves become more complex. Wholesalers, thus, are certainly not anachronisms so long as they perform the specified marketing functions for which they exist.

Catalog Sales   Wholesalers frequently use catalogs, either mailed or carried by salespeople, to provide potential buyers with information and visualization of items warehoused. Or they may be used to display certain types of products, furniture, for example, which is not always in warehouse stock. Or, catalogs can also visualize food service equipment that might have to be custom made to individual specifications. The wholesaler thus uses direct marketing techniques, even with the intervention of salespeople, either for sale to those who themselves resell or else for sale to industrial users.

Retailers as Middlemen

A retailer, whether doing business in a store or through a catalog, is a middleman who buys from producers or wholesalers and sells primarily to ultimate consumers for nonindustrial use.

Many new concepts in retailing have been presented during the last half-century: chain stores, department stores, mail-order houses, supermarkets, boutiques, discount houses, giant shopping malls, and neighborhood strips of stores. Interestingly enough, none of these nontraditional forms of retailing crowded out established retailers as expected. Rather they augmented them and strengthened them as the passage of time provided for change and new ways of doing things. Although the number of retail stores has remained relatively constant for many decades, retail sales volume has increased tremendously.

Mortality among retailers is typically higher than among any other classifications of business and industry, primarily because of ease of entry into retailing. In spite of relatively high turnover, however, retailers have persisted, mainly because of their ability to serve the needs of individual consumers and, secondarily, because of the marketing functions they perform in the distribution system.

Classification of Retailers Retailers may be classified according to size (with most of them being relatively small) or according to geographic location (central city or neighborhood, suburban or rural). They can be classified, also, by the extent of the product lines they handle. This ranges from full-service department stores to single-line stores (drugs, hardware, sporting goods) to specialty stores (bakeries, furriers, gift boutiques).

Another way of classification is by form of ownership: chain store systems, voluntary associations of independently owned stores, franchising systems. Franchises can be either an association of independent retailers (IGA stores, Thriftway stores) or they can be manufacturer-sponsored systems (McDonalds, Holiday Inns). Franchising is an important new concept in the structure of distribution and its real strength lies not so much in combined buying power as in superior management provided by specialized personnel and techniques.

Yet another way of classifying retailers, especially important in the perspective of direct marketing, is according to method of operation. This includes in store retailing (full-service department stores, supermarkets, and discount houses) and nonstore retailing (mail order, direct selling, and automatic vending).

Recent Trends Changes in the structure of distribution channels have accelerated recently. Such changes have been brought about by changing consumer markets and life-styles; the search for more effective and profitable methods; and the pressing needs for mass marketing techniques to keep pace with mass production techniques.

From large-scale retailing institutions down through the smallest of boutiques, direct marketing alternatives have been in the forefront of the changing nature of distribution. Although the objective reflected by these recent trends has been marketing effectiveness, coupled with efficiency, the key to success has been in the provision of more service, not less.

LOGISTICS OF DISTRIBUTION

There is an aspect of distribution that is purely physical, concerned with materials handling, inventory management, and transportation. Physical distribution of goods is essentially concerned with problems of logistics. These evolve from the need for moving the right product in the right amount to the right place at the right time.

A strategic approach to physical distribution has, as its initial objective, improvement of customer service as well as, if possible, reduced costs. It goes further, however, if it considers such things as the loss of sales volume when the goods are not where they are wanted and needed. Proper storage creates *time* utility and appropriate transportation creates *place* utility.

Materials Handling

The key logistical consideration to materials handling is inventory management: size, location, moving, and transporting. Certain operations research techniques can provide simulation of alternative forms of inventory management. Distribution centers, obviously, should be planned around markets rather than around transportation facilities. Public warehouses can sometimes augment a firm's own branches or private warehouses as distribution centers.

The selection of proper materials handling equipment is an important logistical consideration as is appropriateness of palletization and containerization. The relative advantages of one floor vs. multistoried warehousing should be considered.

Inventory control and management are essential. Inventory optimization is attainable through use of operations research techniques and computer technology. The objective is to balance market demand and two major cost factors: (1) cost of *acquiring* product and (2) cost of *holding* product. To be considered, too, is the degree of customer satisfaction desirable or affordable. The logistical result of such calculation is called the "economic order quantity."

Transportation Modes

A major decision in the logistics of physical distribution is selection of the proper transportation mode. Six such modes are generally available:

Railroads: Particularly suited for long hauls of bulk quantities that have low value in relation to their weight (coal, lumber, etc.)

Truck lines: Advantages include speed, flexibility, less handling, and less expensive packaging

Waterways: For bulk shipments, like the railroads, provide the cheapest mode of transportation and also generally the slowest

Pipelines: Largely limited to transport of petroleum products

Airlines: When speed is of the essence, the most customer-oriented carrier, especially for fashions, fresh foods, flowers, etc. (transportation costs must be related to cost of inventory)

Bus lines: An alternative to airlines, when speed is not so important, for small shipments

The above listing, it should be noted, refers to transportation modes and not to individual carriers. Carriers would include, as examples, Union Pacific Railroad, Trans World Airlines, Yellow Freight Lines, Greyhound Package Express, Emery Air Freight, Federal Express, United Parcel Service, and the United States Postal Service.

Strategy of Location

The general classification of products based on consumer purchasing patterns, convenience, shopping, and specialty goods, has played an important part in the strategy of retail locations. Convenience goods, for example, are generally sold in stores that are not only conveniently located but also display a large variety of such goods. Because of the convenience of location, specialty goods are sometimes sold through convenience stores. Hours of opening, in addition to strategic location, also play an important part, as with 7–11 and other so-called convenience stores.

For shopping goods, outlets are sometimes physically clustered to make search-shopping easier. This helps explain the variety of shoe stores within a large shopping center as well as the adjacent location of several competitive automobile dealers. One study, conducted several years ago, suggested consumers were shopping less, visiting only one store and rarely more than two.[8] Undoubtedly, demographic shifts and life-style changes have played a part in this lessening of shopping activities, and those factors have contributed also to the growth of nonstore retailing.

Trading Areas   These have been traditionally viewed as the area from which a retailer expects to draw customers. Determination of a trading area is a complex process since it involves a variety of factors including geography and population distribution as well as character and mode of operation of the individual retailer. High fashion specialty goods stores, for instance, might view their trading area as considerably beyond that of a super-

[8] William P. Dommermuth and Edward W. Cundiff, "Shopping Goods, Shopping Centers and Selling Strategies," *Journal of Marketing*, October 1961, p. 33.

market offering convenience goods. When such stores become catalog-oriented, as has been the case with Nieman-Marcus, Sakowitz, and Saks Fifth Avenue, trading areas can be extended virtually without limit.[9]

CHANNEL CONFLICTS AND CONTROL

The root of the struggle between and within traditional channels of distribution is the shifting nature of market demand as well as the economic growth and competitive activities among the organizations comprising channels. Just as manufacturers tried to usurp the prerogatives of wholesalers 50 years ago, retailers are challenging manufacturers today. Strong retailers now mean more to the public than do many of the manufacturers' brand names they sell. The question as to who actually controls channels today and who should still remains largely unanswered.

Competitive Conflicts

Competitive conflicts among the middlemen within a channel of distribution and even between alternative channels grow out of tensions created by real or perceived inequities. This conflict takes one of three forms:[10]

1 Horizontal competition or that occurring between competitors of the same line or type, for example, chains of supermarkets
2 Intertype competition or that occurring between different methods of distribution; that is, mail order and department stores or chain and independent service stations
3 Vertical competition or that occurring between different stages in the channel; that is, manufacturers vs. wholesalers vs. retailers

It is the third type of conflict, vertical competition between manufacturers and retailers, especially, which has had major impact on channels of distribution in recent years. Causes of such conflict have been described as rivalry over channel duties, divergences in channel goals, and differences of opinion as to resource allocation.

Manufacturers and retailers often do not think about goods and distribution of these goods in the same way. Manufacturers tend to be dynamic whereas retailers, especially the smaller ones, tend to be static. Large retailers, on the other hand, tend to want to dominate the channel through promotion of their own brand names and products. It is this form of competition between different stages in the distribution channel that has, in effect, promoted alternative distribution, including direct marketing through mail order.

Control Strategies

The short-run objectives for channel control have been presented as these: control over product resale, especially price and/or selling effort; improvement of channel profitability; expansion of market share; implementation of marketing policy; anticipation of conflict situations; and emphasis on nonprice competition.[11]

The major control strategies available to a marketer occupying a leadership position in a distribution channel include these: franchising or control of the entire operation; control of prices; restrictions on handling competitive merchandise; control of selling territory; and control of promotion.[12]

---

[9] Rita Reit, "Mail Order: Old Road to New Sales," *New York Times,* Section 3, August 24, 1978, p. 1.
[10] J. Taylor Sims, J. Robert Foster, and Arch G. Woodside, *Marketing Channels Systems and Strategies,* Harper & Row, New York, 1977, pp. 205–208.

[11] David Revzan, *Wholesaling in Marketing Organizations,* John Wiley & Sons, New York, 1961, p. 144.
[12] Stanley C. Hollander, "Restraints upon Retail Competition," Bureau of Business and Economic Research, Graduate School of Business Administration, Michigan State University, Marketing and Transportation, East Lansing, Mich., paper no. 14, 1965.

Franchising Franchising or control of the entire operation of a middleman is not as new as the proliferation of fast food chains might suggest. Early franchisers included Singer Sewing Machines, Rexall Drug Stores, and General Motors Corporation. Subsequently, franchising has occurred in petroleum, soft drink bottling, auto accessories, and variety stores. Currently, it is seen in the sale of automobiles, appliances, hearing aids, televisions, and wallpaper plus services such as dance instruction, motels and hotels, eating and drinking establishments, and real estate brokerages.

Franchising comprises a continuing relationship and a standardized structure between producer and user. Products are usually distinctive and readily identifiable. Since franchising typically involves investment by the franchisee, there is usually a high degree of personal motivation in franchise operation.

Control of Resale Prices Subject to adherence to applicable laws, producers can influence resale prices through suggesting those prices, through consignment selling, or even through refusal to sell to certain middlemen. (Court decisions have viewed this last practice as coercion and have restricted its use.)

Restrictions on Handling Competitive Merchandise Two commonly used methods of encouraging loyalty by middlemen to a producer include granting of exclusive distributorship and the use of so-called tying contracts, whereby rights to offering a certain product are "tied" to one or more other products or even an entire product line.

Control of Selling Territories A producer might grant exclusive rights to a specific territory, possibly defined in terms of ZIP Code areas, in return for assurance by the middle-man that he or she will actively solicit business in that territory or else give it up.

Control over Promotion In a manner similar to granting exclusive sales territories, a manufacturer might exert influence over promotional activities of middlemen through cooperative advertising programs, rebate plans, or even through establishing a minimum advertising requirement to be expended by the dealer.

Such control strategies as these are used to assure adequate promotion effort within the distribution channel and also to assure adequate feedback of market information. They are used, too, to establish a favorable image and assure proper servicing as well as low distribution costs.[13]

TRENDS IN RETAILING

In recent years we have witnessed in consumer retailing a synthesis of disparate types; that is, the collection of different types of retail stores under one roof. These so-called superstores take the form of giant supermarkets, discount houses, and sprawling shopping malls. At the same time, there has been a growth of highly specialized stores: small gift boutiques, as well as meat markets, bakeries, and craft stores.

We have seen, too, mixed methods of selling even in a single store. The store might be self-service for the most part but offer demonstration of vacuum cleaners and personal service at the candy counter. There has been an increasing use, too, of selected promotional devices: contests, sweepstakes, credit, special price offers, trading stamps. To realize economies of scale and the benefits of specialized management, there has been an increasing

[13] Much of this discussion is based on material contained in Sims et al., *Marketing Channels Systems and Strategies*, pp. 186–224.

number of contractual obligations, voluntary and cooperative chains as well as franchises. There has been a growth of company-owned stores: tire shops, dairies, automobile dealers.

Coupled with all of the above there has been a rapid increase of nonstore retailing and commensurate growth of direct marketing. Not only has there been a proliferation of general as well as specialized mail-order catalogs, but these together with individualized direct mail offers have been used to promote store traffic plus the use of interactive electronic media, notably the telephone. Promotional media other than direct mail have been used, also, to accomplish the same objectives.

Such direct marketing strategies as these, with or without retail store locations and with or without salespeople, are designed to be *measurable* and *accountable*. A further objective is the acquisition and development of *lists* of customers together with *data* about these customers, so that direct marketing can make retailing even more effective and efficient than it has been.

SUMMARY

Distribution is the systematic process of moving an offer from a producer to a user. Although mail order is sometimes viewed as an alternative distribution system, direct marketing should be viewed as an aspect of the total marketing concept, operating in alternative channels of distribution.

The distribution channel between producer and user includes a variety of interacting middlemen, wholesalers, retailers, agents, and brokers, as well as agencies: transportation companies, advertising firms, banks. Each of these intermediaries performs one or more specific marketing functions and thereby justifies its existence in moving goods from producers to users.

Direct marketers, in establishing a channel

of distribution, might be the producer or one of the middlemen. They might be distributing to ultimate consumers or to industrial users, who purchase either for resale or for fabrication into a manufactured product. The ultimate objective of the distribution system, whether consumer or industrial, should be delivery of the right product to the right place at the right time in the right form.

The four most common alternative distribution channels for consumer goods are these: producer-consumer; producer-retailer-consumer; producer-wholesaler-retailer-consumer; producer-agent or broker-wholesaler-retailer-consumer. The four most popular channels for industrial goods are these: producer–industrial user; producer–industrial distributor–industrial user; producer-agent or broker–industrial distributor–industrial user; producer-agent or broker–industrial user.

The four kinds of utility with which distribution is concerned are: time, place, possession, and form. Basic discrepancies of quantity and assortment, as well as timing, often explain why, between producer and user, there must be a system for first accumulating and then allocating goods. As households evolved from being self-sufficient systems and began to exchange with each other through centralized markets, the need for specialists in the form of middlemen became apparent.

Consumer distribution can be intensive, selective, or exclusive, roughly equated to the three kinds of goods with which consumers are concerned: convenience goods, shopping goods, and specialty goods. Industrial distribution differs from consumer distribution not only in there being a fewer number of buying units but also in that each of these units purchases in larger volume, more frequently, and with much greater skill and knowledge. A distinctive feature of industrial distribution, too, is that producers usually call on users, which is also a characteristic of direct marketing in consumer as well as in industrial markets.

Distribution channels are affected by demographic, economic, legal/political, and technological forces. All of these forces bear ultimately on the selection and organization of middlemen: wholesalers, retailers, agents, and brokers.

Physical distribution is largely a matter of logistics. Of concern are inventory management, materials handling, transportation, and the strategy of location. In the case of this last factor, as retailers become more specialized and as market segments become more geographically dispersed, direct marketing promotional techniques and nonstore retailing become even more prevalent.

Conflicts within channels of distribution can occur between middlemen at the same level of a particular channel; that is, between wholesalers. They can occur between channels, also; that is, mail-order selling vs. department store selling. And, they can occur between various levels of the channel, primarily between manufacturers and retailers. Among strategies used to control channels are franchising, resale price maintenance, restrictions on handling competitive merchandise, control of selling territories, and control over promotion.

Recent trends in retailing have been highly conducive to the growth of direct marketing. These have been accelerated by demographic shifts and life-style changes. Direct marketing is characterized by *measurability* and *accountability* and by the acquisition of *lists* and *data*. Direct marketing is, thus, an aspect of the total marketing concept.

CASE: DIRECT MARKETING TO OPTIMIZE DISTRIBUTION

Learning Objective

This case study is intended to generate discussion of the premise that the concept of direct marketing is applicable not only to mail

order . . . but also to personal selling at either the buyer's or seller's location.

Overview

Traditional distribution channels have included seller's location (such as department stores or industrial sales offices) staffed by salespeople. Other transactions have been consummated by salespeople at the buyer's location (a business or a household). When the transaction is consummated by mail (or telephone) as a result of advertising in a variety of media, it has been called mail order. Certainly, however, the elements of what we now term direct marketing have gone beyond direct mail (an advertising medium) and mail order (a transaction method). These elements have been effectively applied to total distribution systems involving salespeople at either the seller's or buyer's location. As with any direct marketing, however, such applications are always measurable and accountable, and they rely heavily on lists and data.

Procedure

Read the learning objective, the overview, and the case that follows. Identify the elements of direct marketing and the specific instances in which these are used. How are they measurable? Can you determine and describe the use of lists and data?

Case[14]

The International Business Machines Corporation (IBM) no longer sells only very large computers to a relatively small number of data processing professionals for very select and specialized applications. They also sell very small computers to be used in an incredibly wide range of ways to an extremely large and

---

[14] This case study has been adapted from a presentation by Douglas J. Garnett, Direct Marketing Advertising Manager, IBM Canada, Ltd., Don Mills, Ont., Canada, at the Canadian Direct Marketing Association, 18th Annual Conference, June 2, 1982.

diverse audience. Accompanying this widening market has been a reduction in the cost of computers along with escalating costs of selling.

With that combination of factors, it became obvious to IBM that new and different ways to sell low cost computers to increasing numbers of market segments had to be found. Expensive personal selling had to be replaced by less expensive methods of reaching the increasing numbers of potential computer users. At the same time, computers had to be made more accessible, more understandable, more friendly, less threatening, and less imposing to these new audiences of nontechnical buyers.

IBM Canada, Ltd., in facing these realities has not abandoned personal selling. It has, however, adopted alternative direct marketing strategies: mail-order catalog selling, telephone marketing, direct response advertising, IBM retail stores, and even automated demonstration booths located in high-traffic pedestrian areas.

IBM began first, in the mid-1970s, by introducing mail and telephone ordering for its line of office supplies. These products (typewriter ribbons, removable type fonts for Selectric®[15] typewriters, typing correction tape, photocopier paper, diskettes, etc.) are essentially low cost consumables that lend themselves to repetitive and routine purchasing. Customers look primarily for price competitiveness, fast delivery, and ordering convenience. These supplies as well as IBM typewriters are contained in direct mail catalogs from which customers can order by mail or telephone. Orders are shipped by special courier or parcel post. Other IBM catalogs offer a wide range of other IBM products including computer supplies, computer terminals, and even IBM software.

As another distribution alternative, IBM

Product Centers, which are actually retail stores, have been designed to encourage customers to come to the seller's location. This has proven less costly than having an IBM salesperson visit the buyer. Traditional retail promotion techniques used in these stores include point-of-purchase displays, price tags, cash-and-carry discounts, retail newspaper and radio response advertising, in store promotions, and direct mailings to build store traffic.

As a natural extension of the retail Product Centers, IBM Canada, Ltd., has installed automatic product displays in airport waiting areas and high-traffic pedestrian corridors in shopping areas. With an interactive keyboard, passersby can activate a computer to give a demonstration of its capabilities. Telephone receivers on the front of the display provide a prerecorded message about the products. Descriptive literature is available for viewers to take with them if they are interested in the product. A postage paid reply card on the literature puts interested prospects into direct contact with an information and ordering center.

At other displays, viewers can use an IBM Personal Computer keyboard, hooked up to a laser-operated videodisc to select audio-visual presentations on how computers work, solve games and puzzles, and to demonstrate computer concepts. In the future videodiscs and teletext will also be used to display IBM product messages at these locations. Thus, the interactive computer display becomes its own direct marketing promotion medium. The medium itself *is* the message!

Further use of direct marketing techniques by IBM includes telephone marketing, coupled with direct mail, to generate qualified sales leads for its sales force. Such qualified leads obviously reduce the amount of unproductive prospecting by sales representatives. The heart of the telemarketing and direct mail activity is a computer-based prospect masterfile: a list and database. The masterfile has also been

---

[15] Selectric® is a registered trademark of International Business Machines Corporation.

matched to a sales territory grid so that it can be used for territory analysis and marketing research. Additional data gathered through telephone and direct mail contact are incorporated into the masterfile. Once in the masterfile, customers as well as prospects are contacted regularly. And, using information stored in the database, IBM is able to analyze the number of sales leads generated, the number sent for follow-up to each salesperson, the resultant sales activities, and the cost per sale. Other advertising media are used to augment the telephone and direct mail solicitation.

IBM's direct marketing embraces mail-order catalogs, retail stores, automated displays, as well as direct response advertising for qualified lead production. Salespeople, thus, are made much more productive. Direct marketing makes possible such a total approach to media, markets, and methods of selling.

DISCUSSION QUESTIONS

1 What is a channel of distribution? How are the middlemen in a channel justified?
2 In terms of distribution, how is mail order distinguished from direct marketing?
3 List and describe possible distribution channels for consumer goods. Do the same thing for industrial goods.
4 What are the discrepancies of quantity, assortment, and timing relative to the delivery of goods from producer to user?
5 Define these degrees of distribution: intensive, selective, exclusive. For what types of goods would each apply: shopping, convenience, or specialty?
6 Discuss the various exogenous forces affecting distribution channels.
7 What functions do middlemen in a channel perform?
8 With what are the logistics of distribution concerned?
9 Describe these three forms of competitive conflicts relative to distribution channels: horizontal, intertype, vertical.
10 Discuss recent trends in distribution and prognosticate the future.

INDEX

INDEX